THE MARTIN MARPRELATE TRACTS

The Martin Marprelate tracts are the most famous pamphlets of the English Renaissance; to their contemporaries, they were the most notorious. Printed in 1588 and 1589 on a secret press carted across the English countryside from one sympathetic household to another, the seven tracts attack the Church of England, particularly its bishops (hence the pseudonym, "Mar-prelate"), and advocate a Presbyterian system of church government. Scandalously witty, racy, and irreverent, the Marprelate tracts are the finest prose satires of their era. Their colloquial style and playfully self-dramatizing manner influenced the fiction and theatre of the Elizabethan Golden Age. As historical and social texts, they provide an important link in a tradition of oppositional writing in England from the early Reformation through to the civil wars of the 1640s, and their appeal to a popular audience contributed to the development in England of a public sphere of debate. This is the first fully annotated edition of the tracts to appear in almost a century. A lightly modernized text makes Martin Marprelate's famous voice easily accessible, and a full introduction details the background, sources, production, authorship, and seventeenth-century afterlife of the tracts.

JOSEPH L. BLACK is Assistant Professor in the Department of English at the University of Massachusetts Amherst. He is co-editor of *The Broadview Anthology of British Literature,* Volume II: *The Renaissance and Early Seventeenth Century* (2006), and *The Broadview Anthology of Seventeenth-Century English Verse and Prose* (2000). He has published articles on Renaissance English literature and book history, and wrote the entry on "Martin Marprelate" for the *Oxford Dictionary of National Biography* and for the *Dictionary of Literary Biography.*

THE MARTIN MARPRELATE TRACTS

A Modernized and Annotated Edition

EDITED BY

JOSEPH L. BLACK

CAMBRIDGE
UNIVERSITY PRESS

CAMBRIDGE UNIVERSITY PRESS

Cambridge, New York, Melbourne, Madrid, Cape Town, Singapore, São Paulo, Delhi

Cambridge University Press
The Edinburgh Building, Cambridge CB2 8RU, UK

Published in the United States of America by Cambridge University Press, New York

www.cambridge.org
Information on this title: www.cambridge.org/9780521875790

First published 2008

Printed in the United Kingdom at the University Press, Cambridge

A catalogue record for this publication is available from the British Library

ISBN 978-0-521-87579-0 hardback

Contents

Illustrations

Acknowledgments

The Martin Marprelate tracts were written, printed on a hand press that had to be carted slowly on bad roads in long journeys from one sympathetic household to another, and then distributed by foot and horseback across an entire country, all in far less time than it took me to edit them. This book's journey began at the University of Toronto, where Hugo de Quehen, Germaine Warkentin, and the interdisciplinary community of scholars at the Centre for Reformation and Renaissance Studies offered advice, inspiration, and support. Jonquil Bevan and the Centre for the History of the Book at the University of Edinburgh were generous hosts for a summer in Scotland. The Department of English at the University of Tennessee provided support for research and for an assistantship that allowed Rich Bryant to type original-spelling versions of all the tracts, an unenviable job that he performed with remarkable accuracy. New colleagues at the University of Massachusetts and the Massachusetts Center for Renaissance Studies have helped in the final stages. Funding was provided by grants from the National Endowment for the Humanities and the Bibliographical Society of America. Knowledgeable librarians at many institutions have helped over the years, and I am particularly grateful to staff at the Lambeth Palace Library, the Huntington Library, the National Library of Wales, the Surrey History Centre, the Warwickshire County Record Office, and the Union Theological Library for their generous replies to questions. In addition, the Lambeth Palace Library, the Houghton Library, the Beinecke Library, the Huntington Library, the Surrey History Centre, and the Canterbury Cathedral Archives have kindly given permission to reproduce images of their books or to quote from manuscripts in their collections. Allen Carroll, Arthur Kinney, Eugene Hill, Urmila Seshagiri, and Jane Degenhardt read parts of the manuscript and made many useful suggestions. Reports by Alastair Bellany and two anonymous readers for Cambridge University Press also prompted much-needed changes. Working with Cambridge University Press has been a pleasure. Sarah Stanton, Rebecca Jones, and Elizabeth Davey were unfailingly helpful throughout the process, and Jacque French provided meticulous copyediting. Finally, my greatest obligation is to Lisa Celovsky, who with patience and good humor saw this book through every stage of its journey, and who read the manuscript with expertise.

Notes on conventions

THE EDITION

This edition offers lightly modernized texts of the seven Martin Marprelate tracts. For a full discussion of the editorial procedures employed, see the Textual Introduction (cxiii–cxvi). Annotations are printed as endnotes at the back of the volume; marginal notes in the original editions are reproduced as footnotes, signaled in the text with superscript letters. Each of the seven tracts opens with a short introduction that sketches that tract's main features and concerns. The general introduction provides more detailed information about their collective content, style, printing history, and authorship.

QUOTATIONS AND CITATIONS

References to and quotations from the Marprelate tracts are to this edition. Unless otherwise noted, classical texts are cited from the Loeb editions. Biblical quotations are from *The Geneva Bible: A Facsimile of the 1560 Edition* (Madison, WI: University of Wisconsin Press, 1969). Statutes are quoted from *The Whole Volume of Statutes at Large* (1587), the most complete edition available prior to the publication of the Marprelate tracts. References to Shakespeare's plays are to David Bevington, ed., *The Complete Works of Shakespeare*, updated fourth edition (New York: Longman, 1997). Annotations drawn from the *Oxford English Dictionary* provide the full *OED* reference only if needed to clarify the particular meaning cited within a long entry. Quotations from early printed books and manuscript documents retain their original spelling and punctuation, except that contractions are silently expanded and u/v and i/j regularized. For early books, place of publication is London unless otherwise indicated.

QUOTATIONS FROM MANUSCRIPTS CONNECTED
WITH THE MARPRELATE CONTROVERSY

Many (but not all) of the manuscript documents connected with the
Marprelate tracts are printed in either Edward Arber's *Introductory Sketch
to the Martin Marprelate Controversy* (1879) or William Pierce's *An
Historical Introduction to the Marprelate Tracts* (1908). These manuscripts
are cited here from the versions printed in Arber and Pierce. While their
editions do not offer perfect transcriptions (the original manuscripts were
all consulted), they have become the standard sources used in almost all
work on the Marprelate tracts, and are easily accessible to readers who want
to examine the full textual context of any given citation.

Abbreviations

Admonition	Thomas Cooper, *An Admonition to the People of England* (1589), first issue, *STC* 5683a
Arber, *Introductory Sketch*	Edward Arber, *An Introductory Sketch to the Martin Marprelate Controversy, 1588–1590* (1879; repr. Westminster: Archibald Constable, 1895)
Arber, *Transcript*	Edward Arber, ed., *A Transcript of the Registers of the Company of Stationers*, 5 vols. 1875–94; repr. Gloucester, MA: Peter Smith, 1967
BCP	Book of Common Prayer (1559)
Bancroft, *Sermon*	Richard Bancroft, *A Sermon Preached at Paules Crosse* (1589)
BL	British Library
Bridges, *Defence*	John Bridges, *A Defence of the Government Established in the Church of Englande for Ecclesiasticall Matters* (1587)
Carlson, *Martin Marprelate*	Leland H. Carlson, *Martin Marprelate, Gentleman: Master Job Throkmorton Laid Open in His Colors* (San Marino, CA: Huntington Library, 1981)
Collinson, *Movement*	Patrick Collinson, *The Elizabethan Puritan Movement* (London: Jonathan Cape, 1967)
DNB	*Dictionary of National Biography*, ed. Leslie Stephen *et al.*, 63 vols. (London: Smith, Elder, 1885–1900)
DSL	*The Dictionary of the Scots Language*, Victor Skretkowicz (project director), Susan Rennie (project editor), University of Dundee, 2004. Online text: www.dsl.ac.uk/dsl
Hartley, *Proceedings*	T. E. Hartley, ed., *Proceedings in the Parliaments of Elizabeth I*, 3 vols. (Leicester and London: Leicester University Press, 1981–95)
HL	Huntington Library

HMC	Historical Manuscripts Commission
Hooker, *Works*	*The Folger Library Edition of the Works of Richard Hooker*, gen. ed. W. Speed Hill, 7 vols. in 8 (Cambridge, MA: Harvard University Press, 1977–98)
Lyly, *Works*	*The Complete Works of John Lyly*, ed. R. Warwick Bond, 3 vols. (Oxford: Clarendon Press, 1902)
Nashe, *Works*	*The Works of Thomas Nashe*, ed. Ronald B. McKerrow, 5 vols. (London: A. H. Bullen, 1904–10)
ODNB	*Oxford Dictionary of National Biography* (Oxford: Oxford University Press, 2004). Online edition: www.oxforddnb.com
ODCC	*Oxford Dictionary of the Christian Church*, 2nd edn, rev. F. L. Cross and E. A. Livingston (Oxford: Oxford University Press, 1983)
OED	*Oxford English Dictionary*, 3rd edn (Oxford: Oxford University Press). Online edition: www.oed.com
Pierce, *Historical Introduction*	William Pierce, *An Historical Introduction to the Marprelate Tracts* (London: Archibald Constable, 1908)
Pierce, *Marprelate Tracts*	*The Marprelate Tracts 1588, 1589*, ed. William Pierce (London: James Clark, 1911)
PRO	Public Record Office
SP Dom.	State Papers Domestic
SPR	*The Seconde Parte of a Register: Being a Calendar of Manuscripts under that Title intended for Publication by the Puritans about 1593, and now in Dr Williams's Library, London*, ed. Albert Peel, 2 vols. (Cambridge: Cambridge University Press, 1915)
STC	*A Short-Title Catalogue of Books Printed in England, Scotland, & Ireland … 1475–1640*, comp. A. W. Pollard and G. R. Redgrave, 2nd edn rev. W. A. Jackson, F. S. Ferguson, and Katharine F. Pantzer, 3 vols. (London: Bibliographical Society, 1976–91)
State Trials	Thomas Bayley Howell, ed., *Cobbett's Complete Collection of State Trials*, 34 vols. (London, 1809–28)
Sutcliffe, *Answere*	Matthew Sutcliffe, *An Answere unto a Certaine Calumnious Letter Published by M. J Throkmorton* (1595)

Tilley   Morris Palmer Tilley, *A Dictionary of the Proverbs in England in the Sixteenth and Seventeenth Centuries* (Ann Arbor: University of Michigan Press, 1950)

Wing   *Short-Title Catalogue of Books Printed in England, Scotland, Ireland, Wales, and British America* ... *1641–1700*, comp. Donald Wing, 2nd edn rev. Timothy J. Crist (vol. I), John J. Morrison and Carolyn W. Nelson (vols. II–III), 3 vols. (New York: MLA, 1982–94)

Introduction

"I think the like was never committed to presse or paper . . ."
Thomas Cooper, *An Admonition to the People of England* (1589)

"SCURRILOUS PAMPHLETTS"

In June 1637, Nicholas Darton, the vicar of Kilsby, Northamptonshire, petitioned Archbishop William Laud for help in bringing his unruly and disaffected parishioners to order: they were refusing to pay tithes, openly mocking the church hierarchy, and seditiously withholding the unpopular tax of ship money. The cause of these "tumultuous outrages," Darton suggested, was the availability in Kilsby of dangerous books. For years, Darton had reproved the "haveing and reading (amongst some of his parishioners) of certaine scurrilous pamphletts, suprest by authoritie, utter enemies to the present State." These pamphlets, he reported, were read aloud to public approval, the audience "geering and sporting themselves, when ever any thing was read which inveighed against the Jurisdiction Episcopall." Darton's factious flock had even attempted to use these readings to "pervert the minde of your most humble petitioner, from the discipline of our Church of England."[1] Could the archbishop help? The archbishop was a busy man, but notes and confessions attached to the original petition testify to a thorough official response, a response encouraged by other recent reminders that oppositional texts were circulating among the population at large. As Laud noted in his personal diary, that same June the polemicists John Bastwick, William Prynne, and Henry Burton were punished with the loss of their ears for publishing "Libells against the Hierarchy of the Church"; soon afterward, manuscript verses were posted around London celebrating the martyrdom of this puritan triumvirate and attacking Laud as the bloody-handed archwolf of Canterbury.[2] Suspicious reading matter demanded investigation: the wrong books could infect entire communities with subversive ideas, and the pamphlets causing the troubles in Kilsby were not ones

Laud wanted in circulation, particularly at a time of public agitation against political and religious authorities. The writer who confronted the archbishop in the pages of the vicar's petition was not one of his recently punished opponents. He was in fact an old enemy of the established church, an adversary who almost fifty years earlier had prophesied that the oppositional force he represented would see the end of archiepiscopal power. His name was Martin Marprelate.

The pseudonymous Martin Marprelate tracts are the most famous pamphlets of the English Renaissance; to contemporaries, they were the most notorious. There are seven tracts altogether, a broadsheet and six short books ranging from thirty pages of text in octavo format to fifty-six in quarto, all printed on a secret and peripatetic press between October 1588 and September 1589. They attack the Elizabethan church, particularly church government by bishops (hence the pseudonym, Mar-prelate), and advocate instead an alternative, Presbyterian polity. Even in an age accustomed to aggressively partisan pamphlet warfare, the writings of Martin Marprelate provoked immediate and widespread scandal. "I think the like was never committed to presse or paper, no not against the vilest sort of men, that have lived upon the earth," exclaimed Thomas Cooper, the bishop of Winchester and one of Martin's targets.[3] But the novelty of the Marprelate tracts did not lie in the substance of their arguments: the reform agenda they proposed had been honed over decades of Presbyterian opposition to the established church. Instead, what seemed shockingly new was Martin's method of presentation. With his wittily irreverent and conversational prose, ironic modes of argument, fluid shifts among narrative voices, swashbuckling persona, playful experiments with the conventions of print controversy, and willingness to name names and to tell unflattering stories about his opponents, Martin shattered conventions of decorum that had governed debates about the church since the Elizabethan Settlement. Some elements of Martinist style would have seemed familiar to readers whose memories stretched back before Elizabeth to the vehement exchanges of the earlier Reformation. But even with these possible models in mind, nobody in England had ever read anything quite like these publications. The appearance of the first tract sparked a nation-wide manhunt, accompanied by a multimedia campaign in which church and state joined forces to counter the influence of what Martin and his opponents both termed "Martinism" – the public jeering of authority that Nicholas Darton heard decades later among his pamphlet-reading parishioners.

The Marprelate tracts continued to be denounced as base, scurrilous invective for centuries after the underground press was discovered and silenced.[4] Beginning in the later nineteenth century, however, pioneering research by Edward Arber, William Pierce, J. Dover Wilson, Ronald B. McKerrow, and Georges Bonnard won the tracts a new reputation not only as some of the finest Elizabethan prose satires, worthy of their own chapter in the literary history of the sixteenth century, but also as significant texts in the religious, political, legal, and social history of the English Renaissance.[5] By uncovering the operations of the Marprelate project and recuperating its aims, context, and consequences, these scholars provided the foundation for an extensive and rapidly growing body of subsequent research, and their work remains indispensable for any study of the tracts.

Accounts of the Marprelate controversy published over the past few decades address a broad range of interconnected literary, historical, and social issues.[6] Martinist style remains the focus of many articles and shorter treatments, particularly the influence of Martin's comic prose on the literature of the Elizabethan Golden Age of the 1590s. But the tracts are also increasingly recognized as playing a key role in the broader history of Renaissance English pamphlet warfare. They initiated influential debates concerning libel and decorum, provoked responses that crystallized contemporary anxieties over the uses of print, and probably contributed to the development in England of a proto-public sphere of debate.[7] More generally, the tracts helped create a tradition of oppositional writing that extended from the earliest stages of the English Reformation through to the civil wars, and spurred counterarguments that would become standard weapons in future campaigns against religious and political opposition. In addition, the anti-Martinist campaign generated evidence unmatched for this period for many aspects of the history of books and reading. Depositions and trial records provide extraordinarily detailed information about how the tracts were printed on the run, distributed across the country, sold under the counter in London shops or out of back doors by sympathetic local officials, and discussed in underground reading groups. Furthermore, references to the tracts at the time of their appearance and throughout their seventeenth-century afterlife illuminate contemporary perspectives on complex issues of authorship and collaboration, and document the intersections of popular and learned readerships, popular and elite kinds of texts, and print, manuscript, and oral cultures. From the 1590s through the 1640s and well into the Restoration, Martin retained his reputation as a dangerous writer whose violations of acceptable discourse threatened all forms of authority. As Darton's outrage and his parishioners' disobedient sporting both suggest, this reputation informs all later engagements with Martin Marprelate: for almost a century, uses of the Marprelate tracts open windows onto the social uses of texts in early modern England.

The primary aim of the Marprelate project was to publicize a Presbyterian system of church government. To the Elizabethan reform movement, the state church established in 1559 at the accession of Elizabeth was an unsatisfactory compromise that retained a fundamentally Catholic structure and liturgy as well as a fundamentally Catholic attitude toward ecclesiastical polity. Presbyterian reformers believed that the New Testament established a single, unambiguous, and immutable apostolic model for church organization. This model sanctioned four church offices, each with a role at the parish level: pastors (to exhort, preach, and administer the sacraments), doctors (to teach and expound scripture), elders (to govern, and oversee discipline), and deacons (to administer finances and poor relief). All other offices – archbishops, bishops, deans, archdeacons, chancellors, vicars general, canons, prebendaries, the entire traditional apparatus that Martin dismisses, with glib exaggeration, as the "24 orders of bishops" (*Schoolpoints*, 92) – were unnecessary human inventions, parasitical accretions on the body of the true church. Ministers were to be equal in standing: scripture offered no warrant for clerical hierarchy, for ecclesiastical "lords" who ruled over inferiors and did not themselves minister in a parish. Clergy furthermore were not to hold civil office or fulfill other functions properly belonging to the magistrate, a prohibition that challenged church courts as well as more obvious targets, such as the presence of clerics on the privy council. On the other side of these debates, defenders of the church questioned the reformers' reading of scripture and noted that the early church contained episcopal as well as Presbyterian elements. In the clear absence of a binding divine blueprint, they argued, the church in these matters was a human institution: forms of worship and church organization were subject to human authority, to be changed, or not, as those authorities saw fit. Such ideas were anathema to Martin Marprelate, who defends the Presbyterian discipline throughout the tracts as the divinely sanctioned but suppressed ideal.

These four arguments – immutability of scripture, the fourfold ministry, ministerial equality, and separation of ministry and magistracy – were the foundational principles of Presbyterianism. But reformers with uncompromisingly sticky consciences also objected to many specific elements of church ceremony. They challenged the Book of Common Prayer, particularly its use of texts from the Apocrypha, which they considered a collection of corrupt human writings, not divinely inspired ones. They denounced the reading of homilies as a substitute for genuine preaching, which they saw as the ordinary means of salvation. They resisted clerical vestments, because distinctive clothing functioned as a sign of hierarchy and spiritual set-apartness. Finally, they opposed kneeling at communion, the use of "priest" for minister, organ music and counterpoint choral singing in church services, the ring in the wedding service, the sign of the cross and "interrogation of infants" in baptism, and the ceremony of "churching" women after childbirth: all these and other such practices, Presbyterians argued, were sacramental leftovers, dangerous remnants of Catholic ritual. More broadly, many Presbyterians also allied themselves with older traditions of reform agitation by buttressing anti-episcopal arguments with the perennially popular tropes of anticlerical complaint, denouncing such abuses as non-residency, pluralism, and simony, and accusing the "higher" clergy of pride, ambition, greed, lordliness, and various misuses of spiritual and secular power. All of these arguments, objections, and accusations appear throughout the Marprelate tracts.

Despite their overarching focus on issues connected with the church, however, the Marprelate tracts are not in essence works of doctrinal controversy: to a greater or lesser degree, Calvinism was the shared theological standard of conformist and reformer alike throughout this period. The primary subject of Elizabethan debates between the established church and its Protestant critics was not religion per se but polity. How should the church be structured and governed? What was its proper relationship to the state? What elements of worship and ceremony accorded best with scripture? On these questions, Martin Marprelate makes no original contributions. The tracts faithfully lay out the Presbyterian platform as presented in England by Thomas Cartwright in his 1570 Cambridge lectures, unveiled to the English public by John Field and Thomas Wilcox in the *Admonition to the Parliament* (1572), defended at length by Cartwright in polemical battle with John Whitgift throughout the 1570s, and fine-tuned over almost two decades in numerous publications, in Latin and in English, in learned scholarship and in heated manifestos, in sermons, petitions, and popularizing dialogues, not to mention in countless manuscript documents, unprinted sermons, and other communications within a highly organized community.[8] Martin's originality lay in his polemical aggressiveness, not his ecclesiology. Like any broad social movement, Presbyterianism itself was not unified and immutable: it encompassed a range of attitudes toward reform, accommodation, and acceptable ways to

advocate change, attitudes that furthermore shifted over time, in many
cases in the direction of more moderate positions.[9] The Marprelate tracts
were the radical culmination of Elizabethan Presbyterian lobbying, and
their aggressiveness reflected a discontent verging on desperation within
the movement's radicalized core as it witnessed the ongoing inefficacy of
more moderate approaches.

A final note concerning terminology and the Presbyterian platform. The
word "Presbyterian" does not appear in the tracts, nor does it appear in the
published accounts that preceded Martin of the "discipline" (a word
reformers themselves used to describe their model). As terms for a specific
ecclesiology, "Presbyterian" and its analogues were not yet in common use
in England.[10] Drawing on vocabulary available at the time, Martin identifies the Presbyterian cause as that advocated by his "puritan" brethren. As
commentators from the seventeenth century to the present have pointed out,
"puritan" is a term of abuse, a hostile label applied imprecisely to a range of
social, devotional, and ecclesiological stances.[11] Nevertheless, as Peter Lake
observes, "all presbyterians were puritans," even if "not all puritans were
presbyterians."[12] Presbyterians sought changes that would push the church
well beyond the Elizabethan Settlement: they are by definition to be
included among the "godly," "advanced," "forward," "zealous," or "hotter
sort of" Protestant reformers commonly labeled puritans. Some accounts
treat the labels as nearly synonymous ("Puritan-Presbyterians"); others distinguish Presbyterians as "radical puritans." One potential source of confusion is Separatism ("Brownism" at the time, Congregationalism or
Independency later), the main form of non-Presbyterian puritanism. In
theory at least, Presbyterians espoused a state church, like that established
in Scotland: Martin himself distinguishes his "puritans" from the disdained
Separatist "sectaries" who had abandoned the ideal of national uniformity.[13]
In practice, however, the lines that separated the two groups blurred,
primarily because of English Presbyterianism's congregationalist emphasis.[14]
While some Presbyterian reformers dutifully explained the national structures of their ideal church, most – like Martin – focused their passions on the
fate of devotional life at the parish level.

The religio-political frustrations that would culminate in the Marprelate
campaign began in 1583, when John Whitgift, an old opponent of reform,
was named archbishop of Canterbury. In his polemical battles with
Thomas Cartwright in the 1570s, Whitgift had formulated the basic
elements of the Elizabethan conformist position, an approach to polity
he now had the opportunity not just to argue but to implement.[15] In

reaction to the perceived leniency of his predecessor, Edmund Grindal, Whitgift initiated sweeping efforts to clamp down on dissent and impose uniformity within the church.[16] Whitgift's inaugural sermon stressed the necessity of obedience to all higher powers, a theme he soon repeated in the more concrete form of a demand that all ministers subscribe to three articles of belief. Agreeing to royal supremacy and the church's articles of religion raised few objections. The trouble was the second article: agreeing that the Book of Common Prayer contained nothing contrary to scripture. This requirement targeted the scruples of a broad range of moderate puritan incumbents, who objected to the prayer book's use of apocryphal texts and its prescriptions concerning vestments and other elements of ceremony and worship. The ensuing subscription crisis pitted an archbishop confident that most ministers would return to the fold when faced with deprivation against a reform movement determined to use the occasion to generate an anti-episcopal revolt.[17] Whitgift's seeming intransigence aroused widespread discontent, even within the privy council, and Presbyterian polemic of the time eagerly encouraged readers to identify the general cause of the "Godly disaffected" with their platform.[18]

Whitgift's tactics were a gamble: between three and four hundred ministers refused to subscribe immediately, numbers that might easily have formed the core of a genuinely popular opposition movement. In the end, however, the archbishop wisely distinguished between moderate and radical elements among the non-subscribers. With adroit offers of concession and conditional subscription, he convinced most of these ministers to sign and thereby undermined the possibility of a united front in the puritan camp. Martin would continue to fight the battle over subscription five years later, repeatedly demanding the return of the deprived ministers and insisting that "uncle Canterbury's drift in urging subscription is not the unity of the church (as he would pretend) but the maintenance of his own pride and corruption" (*Epistle*, 39). But for English Presbyterianism the subscription crisis was an opportunity lost. The movement regrouped sufficiently two years later to campaign on behalf of bills introduced in the 1586 Parliament, and the ambitious "Survey of the Ministry" compiled at the time to document the pressing need for reform reveals the continued effectiveness of Presbyterian grass-roots organization.[19] But while the threat of underground support remained potent, Whitgift made it increasingly difficult for the movement to gain access to other channels of influence. He tightened restrictions on printing, with the Star Chamber decree of 1586 enacting his suggestion to require licensing of many books by the archbishop of Canterbury, the bishop of London, or other church authorities.[20] He helped block parliamentary discussion of the Presbyterian agenda. Finally, he gave church officers and a reconstituted court of high commission investigatory powers that even Lord Burghley, the Queen's chief minister, described as too "much savouring of the Romish Inquisition." Burghley was referring in particular to the notorious oath *ex officio*, which enabled courts to convict without the testimony of witnesses by demanding that the accused answer self-implicating questions; Burghley termed the policy "a device to seek for offenders then to reform any."[21]

The Marprelate tracts dwell on Whitgift's initiatives of the 1580s, denouncing the *ex officio* oath and the suppression of godly books through-out the tracts: to Presbyterians, these constraints proved that the church sought to prevent any discussion of reform for fear of exposing the fragile foundations on which its authority rested. Unrestricted public debate had been a key Presbyterian demand ever since the movement's 1572 manifesto, the *Admonition to the Parliament*, had asked for "free conference in these matters."[22] Reformers believed that open discussion would inevitably validate their reading of scripture. Furthermore, an anti-hierarchical polity required individuals to take some responsibility for their own understand-ing of religious practice: interpretation was not something handed down from above, but a process to which all contributed. The traditional figure of the scripture-literate ploughman was the ideal toward which the move-ment aimed. In a tract printed on the Marprelate press, John Udall announced that Presbyterian writings were designed to "manage" their cause so "that many ploughmen, artificers, and children do see it, and know it, & are able by the worde of God to justifie it."[23] With the options available to Presbyterian lobbying becoming increasingly limited, Martin Marprelate set out to force the public discussion on reform he believed John Whitgift was using all possible means to suppress.

The chain of published attack and counterattack that preceded the first Marprelate tract recapitulated these concerns and helped shape "Martinist" polemical strategies. The exchange began with two contributions to the subscription crisis: William Fulke's *Briefe and Plaine Declaration* (1584), usually known as *The Learned Discourse*, and Theodore Beza's *The Judgement of a Most Reverend and Learned Man ... Concerning a Threefold Order of Bishops* (c. 1585). Both were printed by Robert Waldegrave, who would print the first four Marprelate tracts, and both were seen into print by John Field, who translated Beza's work and probably wrote the polemical preface to Fulke's. Originally written in the early 1570s, the *Briefe and Plaine Declaration* accorded greater decision-making power to the "whole multi-tude" of each congregation than had been the norm in Presbyterian thought,

---

and Fulke's innovative insistence on collective governance was perhaps why the book had been withheld initially from publication.[24] With subscription now threatening the unity of the church, Fulke's idea of the interpretative community was now offered to the public as the best means to settle the issue of reform. According to the preface, the "best learned, most Godly & moderate men" on both sides should meet in debate modeled on the deliberations of Presbyterian assemblies, in which

> there bee much searching of the trueth by sufficient reasoning without all by matters, quarrels, evasions and colours whatsoever, that there be much order, when the spirite of everye prophet shall be subject unto the spirits of the other prophets, & the judgement of al shalbe sufficiently heard, without stopping of free & sufficient answere, without Lordly carrying away of the matter. (A3r)

Summarizing Fulke, Field here prescribes a distinctly Presbyterian scheme of conflict resolution, one which legitimated individual contributions and presented truth as a product of consensus among equals, not a magisterial prerogative.

The French Calvinist Beza offered a similar program, and from a position of authority within the Continental Reform tradition: he, not Calvin, was the first to argue that Presbyterianism "was the only legitimate form" of church government, and his name appears repeatedly throughout Elizabethan debates concerning the church.[25] Beza's *Judgement* began with the problem of episcopacy. The "threefold order" of his title comprised the bishop ordained by God, that is, a regular pastor; the bishop created by man, that is, a pastor set above his fellow ministers; and finally the bishop of the devil, the corrupt version of the bishop of man, who took upon himself civil roles and who lived in lordly luxury. But if "bishop" were simply the scriptural name for a parish pastor, how was the church to be administered? In answer, Beza outlined the Presbyterian system of progressively representative elected bodies and emphasized that representatives at all levels were chosen "by common voyces," not appointed permanently, and in no way "superior in authoritie" to their fellows who had elected them (B5r–v). Enthusiasm for lay participation and lay education was not universal among Presbyterians, and many who advocated such programs in the 1570s and 1580s – including Fulke himself – later hedged their support.[26] But the model Fulke, Field, and Beza collectively presented for discussion of controverted issues in a non-hierarchical context underlies Martin Marprelate's experiments in the use of print to encourage public debate.

These Presbyterian requests for plain style and unadorned reasoning, Fulke's means for non-magisterial deliberations, elicited a 1,400-page rebuttal from John Bridges, dean of Salisbury, entitled *A Defence of the Government Established in the Church of Englande for Ecclesiasticall Matters* (1587). The title page of the *Defence* advertised Fulke's *Briefe and Plaine Declaration* and Beza's *Judgement* as its two primary targets. On the subject of popular debate, Bridges insisted that the Presbyterian program was politically dangerous, as it encouraged widespread questioning of church authority: "in all degrees of men and women, noble, worshipfull, and of the vulgar sort, many begin to doubt of our established government" (¶4r). Developing objections Whitgift had made in his exchanges with Cartwright and anticipating the position advanced subsequently by Richard Hooker, Bridges argued that Presbyterian demands on this issue were simply self-serving attempts to popularize their ideas of reform. Why should the church debate those who so obdurately refused to acknowledge the validity of the status quo? The central issue was the question of interpretative authority, as Hooker suggested when he wondered if reformers would ever be content "to referre your cause to any other higher judgement then your owne."[27] In response to the reform attack on the very idea of hierarchy, Bridges raised the stakes by advocating divine right episcopacy, a position other theologians would continue to push in the wake of the Marprelate controversy.[28]

Bridges' *Defence* generated conventionally polemical responses by Presbyterian stalwarts Dudley Fenner and Walter Travers.[29] Both accused Bridges of relying on logically faulty arguments and both condemned his polemical manner, pointing angrily to the dean's casual colloquialisms, impertinent "jestes and scoffes," and insulting habit of "trifling" with his opponents' language by interspersing brief quotations from their texts into lengthy, often playful sentences. "No wordes," Fenner complained, "no sentences, never so clearelie and manifestlie set downe of us, can escape at his handes most violent and forced interpretations, most ridiculous and slanderous gloses." Not only was the church determined to turn its back on the model divinely provided for its organization, they argued, but it appeared also to be thumbing its nose at reformers as it did so. As Travers complained, to see Bridges "thus discourse upon everie seconde or thirde worde, and to playe and sport him selfe, as if he were at great leysure, and had as little to doe as one that should playe with a feather: may shewe how easilie men of his coate, beare the burden of the Church."[30]

Martin Marprelate would add his voice to this chorus of complaint some months after the appearance of Travers' *Defence of the Ecclesiastical Discipline*. Like his predecessors, Martin demands open discussion of controverted issues, advocates a syllogistic manner of disputation, and rebukes the church for refusing to take seriously the debate over reform.

But Martin also suspected that the public the reform movement was so eager to engage had, after decades of pamphlet warfare, ceased paying attention to the arguments presented on either side. A new strategy was clearly required. The difficulty lay in crafting an appeal to popular taste while still honoring the call for scholarly discussion "without all by matters, quarrels, evasions and colours whatsoever." The resulting tension between means and ends informs the entire Marprelate project: Martin advocates an embattled disputational ideal in a polemic that defiantly and innovatively flouts that ideal. These counterpoised discourses of tradition and innovation form a creative ambivalence that lies at the heart of Martinist style, a productive tension that arises out of Martin's experiment in the social uses of print. The same ambivalence would be replicated in texts produced by the anti-Martinist campaign, where it would in turn provoke debates throughout the 1590s on issues of appropriate style, the relationship of writer to textual personae, and the social responsibilities of authorship at a time when texts were increasingly coming to be regarded as commodities.

MARTINIST STYLE

The first two Marprelate tracts mount sustained critiques of John Bridges' brick-sized *Defence*, "a portable book, if your horse be not too weak," as Martin remarks (*Epitome*, 56). Like Fenner and Travers, Martin condemns the *Defence* as unconscionably verbose, filled with solecisms, and characterized by such sins of intellectual dishonesty as plagiarism and misrepresentation of sources. While attacks on an opponent's syntax and grammar might seem pedantic or frivolous, Martin argues that form reflects substance. While "honest and godly causes" could be defended by "good proofs and a clear style," Bridges had "defended our church government which is full of corruptions, and therefore the style and the proofs must be of the same nature that the cause is" (*Epitome*, 57). That is, a defense of the indefensible could be founded only on specious logic and slippery language. Similar arguments had long abounded on all sides of Elizabethan ecclesiological debate. What was unusual for this period was Martin's addition of the weapons of satire and parody to the polemical arsenal of Presbyterian reform. Fenner and Travers had accused Bridges of playing rather than arguing; Martin asserts that a senseless book deserved a foolish response, and so adopts the voices of the episcopal dunce, stage clown, and rustic simpleton to represent the opponents such jesting deserved. He had no choice, Martin claims with an air of naive scrupulousness, "otherwise dealing with Master Doctor's book, I cannot keep *decorum personæ.*" Should anything in Martin's text consequently prove "too absurd," the reader could put the book down and go confront the person responsible: "ride to Sarum [Salisbury], and thank his Deanship for it" (*Epistle*, 7). With characteristic irony, Martin on his opening page simultaneously distances himself from outrages of polemical manner by blaming them on his opponent, and establishes a sly, sophisticated narrative voice that gleefully exploits in every way imaginable his own refusal to play by the polemical rules.[31]

Doubleness and fluidity characterize the Martinist voice throughout the tracts. "Martin Marprelate" is both an opponent of the bishops and a fellow "primate and metropolitan" as foolish as his episcopal brethren: he reveals the faults of his opponents, even as he exemplifies those faults in himself. Repeatedly shifting perspective, he is both person and stance, Martin and *a* Martin. The name itself is multivalent. "Martin" might glance at Martin Luther, though English reformers were more likely to identify with the originary figure of John Calvin, founder of the Reformed tradition of Protestantism. More immediately, the name plays ironically with contemporary valences of "Martin" as monkey, bird, ass, gullible dupe, or rustic clown. As anti-Martinist writers would frequently note, "Martin" was a name associated in general with foolery or madness.[32] Confident, witty, and direct, the voice models spoken discourse and soon becomes an almost physical presence at the reader's side. We hear Martin's laughter ("py hy hy hy. I cannot but laugh, py hy hy hy"); we see him struggling to read one of John Bridges' lengthy sentences ("Do you not see how I pant?"); we watch with complicit amusement as he conjures up and confronts opponents, then responds to onlookers butting into the conversation from their seats in the margins.[33] Speakers and addressees walk in and out of Martin's pages, like actors making their entrances and exits. Opponents deliver their own set-piece speeches, instructing the anti-Martinist troops; Martin's two sons, Martin Junior and Martin Senior, exchange texts that, in the process of being read, become reported conversations between the two. Indirect address slides mid-sentence into direct address; text and dialogue, conventions of print and conventions of orality, repeatedly blur. The Marprelate tracts are fundamentally performative.

Contemporaries denounced all of Martin's popularizing gestures, primarily by associating the tracts with other disreputable cultural sites that targeted popular taste with colloquial language and irreverent scurrility. Anti-Martinist commentary often commented on the inappropriate theatricality of the Marprelate tracts, for example. Francis Bacon would speak for many when he condemned the cultural turn Martin had apparently initiated: "matters of religion," he complained, were now being "handled in the style of the stage."[34] Others were more specific in the theatrical analogues they invoked. One official announced that Martin's approach to controversy was "fit for a vice in a play," and several contributors to the anti-Martinist campaign compared the Martinist persona with the comic actor Richard Tarleton.[35] The performances of both figures were associated with direct audience address, racy insinuations, taunting personal attacks, and extensive wordplay, including the use of such Martinist ploys as deliberate misinterpretation, verbal distortion, and nonsense or hybrid words.[36] The Vice was a particularly appropriate analogue, being known for a defiant quarrelsomeness that Martin echoes in his verbal fencing and swaggering self-confidence in his ability to out-insult and out-reason any-one who dared try. Clowns like Tarleton were famous for their abilities to improvise, and the comparison reflects uneasiness with Martin's fluidly extemporizing discursive mode. Clowns were furthermore associated with the jig, a form of stand-up routine comprising jokes and bawdy stories accompanied by side drum or pipe. With their narrative economy in scene-setting and characterization and frequent use of rustic dialect and personae, the jig and its print counterpart the jestbook offer clear formal and tonal analogues for Martin's offhand one-liners and pointed *ad hominem* anecdotes.[37]

To contemporary readers, Martin's irreverent, even libelous personal attacks on church officials were his most immediately striking innovation. While reform polemicists had inveighed against episcopacy for years, they had on the whole denounced the office rather than the individuals who occupied it. Restraint had been the convention on this issue, at least since the accession of Elizabeth. As Francis Bacon asserted with characteristic certainty in his response to the Marprelate controversy, "indirect or direct glances or levels at men's persons" were "ever in these cases disallowed."[38] But Martin, as Thomas Cooper complained, was "not contented to lay downe great crimes generally, as some other have done, but with very undecent tearmes, charge[d] some particular Bishops with particular faultes" (*Admonition*, 36–37). These "faultes" ranged from stupidity to bigamy, closet Catholicism to contented cuckoldry, swearing, gambling, and Sabbath-day bowling to theft, corruption, and public brawling, all in addition to the more usual reform complaints that bishops were traitors to her Majesty, tools of Antichrist, and active hinderers of salvation, com-plaints the tracts instantiate with respect to particular bishops on specific occasions. In many cases, Martin cites his sources and supplies corroborat-ing details, giving readers the information they needed to check the facts for themselves. "My book shall come with a witness before the high commission," he remarks, after providing the names and addresses of several men victimized by John Aylmer, bishop of London (*Epistle*, 13). The point of Martin's *ad hominem* stories was to make the Marprelate tracts a trial of the Elizabethan episcopate in the court of public opinion, and Martin justifies his course by contrasting his "open" examinations supported by witnesses with the procedures the bishops themselves employed against reformers. What was "the seat of justice they commonly use in these cases, but only some close chamber at Lambeth, or some obscure gallery in London palace? Where, according to the true nature of an evil conscience, that flyeth and feareth the light, they may juggle and foist in what they list without controlment" (*Protestation*, 203). Denied trial by debate, Martin shifted the venue to print, with the entire reading or listening public his jury.

Jig and jestbook provided one set of analogues for Martin's *ad hominem* tales; manuscript satire, ballad, and other vehicles of popular and coterie culture provided another. Thomas Bulkeley's manuscript "Libel of Oxford" (*c.* 1564), for example, circulated the rumor current in Oxford circles that Amy Cooper, Thomas Cooper's wife, and Dr John Day, fellow and librarian of Magdalen College, were lovers. Martin either heard the rumor or saw a copy of the well-known poem, a rollicking account of the sexual peccadillos of local personages that survives in several versions. Martin repeats all the details Bulkeley had provided of the indiscretion, and echoes Bulkeley's use of stage dialect, rustic persona, and even specific wordplay: Bulkeley had opened his stanza on Cooper with the lines "he that all our tubbes coould trimme / can never keepe his vessell staunch," and Martin calls Cooper "Tom Tubtrimmer of Winchester" throughout *Hay any Work for Cooper*, the title of which plays on Cooper's name.[39] What was new, at least to Elizabethan ecclesiological debate, was Martin's readiness to publicize such stories for polemical purposes. His apparent suggestion of homoerotic intimacy between John Whitgift and Andrew Perne, the dean of Ely and master of Peterhouse, for example, might have made its way into manuscript libel or orally circulated ballad; only Martin Marprelate would dare put it in print.[40]

While drawing polemical strategies and even content from the theatre, prose fiction, coterie verse, and popular ballad, the Marprelate tracts also experiment with the conventions governing print publication. Martin's critique of episcopacy extends into all available textual space: his mockingly discursive titles, facetious imprints, self-reflexive and conversational marginal notes, inventive running heads, coy, hint-dropping subscriptions, and even irreverent errata all become sites for polemical point-scoring.[41] The tracts also play with expectations of genre. Five of the seven experiment with the fictive possibilities of the personal letter. The *Epistle* gestures ironically at the conventional rhetoric of petitions, contrasting the colloquial confidence of Martin's charges with the self-abasing feebleness of the language of supplication. Several of the tracts similarly undermine the quotation-response form of the animadversion, the traditional mode in which much ecclesiological debate was conducted, by juxtaposing Martin's conversational responses with his opponents' formal language. The *Just Censure* rewrites to Presbyterian ends John Whitgift's own articles of examination, concluding with the mock-legalistic vow "I . . . do here protest, affirm, propound, and defend, that if John Canterbury will needs have a fool in his house, wearing a wooden dagger and a cockscomb, that none is so fit for that place as his brother John a Bridges, dean of Sarum" (181). The broadsheet *Schoolpoints* likewise packages scandalous charges against named bishops in the formal wording of theological disputation. The ironic contrast between the genre and the at times ludicrous resolutions he asks the church to defend – that a bishop may have two wives at once, for example – makes refutation unnecessary.

Of course, Martin Marprelate was not the first English polemicist to employ such popularizing means as colloquial prose, irreverent abuse, dialogue, ironic personae, or linguistic, textual, and typographical play. Pamphlet wars and propaganda campaigns throughout the earlier stages of the Reformation had produced numerous analogues for all these devices, and the Marprelate tracts draw repeated attention to their own polemical genealogy. Most obviously, Martin positions himself as the latest champion of two decades of aggressive Presbyterian protest, citing such predecessors as Thomas Cartwright, Anthony Gilby, John Field, Walter Travers, Dudley Fenner, John Udall, and John Penry. But Martin also anchors Presbyterian writings in a tradition of reformist challenge by writers of the previous generation such as William Tyndale, John Frith, Robert Barnes, John Hooper, James Pilkington, and John Foxe. Other publications associated with the Marprelate project extend this family tree. A 1592 Presbyterian petition attributed to Job Throkmorton defends Martin Marprelate by allying him with an oppositional culture that reached back through Tyndale, Barnes, Hooper, and Hugh Latimer to John Wyclif, *Piers Ploughman*, and the pseudo-Chaucerian *Ploughman's Tale*.[42] A mysterious book printed around the time the first Marprelate tracts appeared likewise associates Martin Marprelate with a native tradition of plainspeaking denunciation of ecclesiastical abuses. *O Read me, for I am of*

great antiquitie. I Plaine Piers which can not flatter (London? 1588?) is an
incomplete reprint of *I Playne Piers which can not flatter* (1550?), a "ploughman" text first published in the campaign to legitimize Edwardian reforms
by popularizing the idea that they fulfilled a legacy of proto-Protestantism
that reached back to the Lollards.[43] The prospective reprint might have
been meant to play a role in the Marprelate project: Piers Ploughman, the
title page announces, was "Gransier of *Martin mare-prelitte*," and the title
page and new preface both borrow (or anticipate?) words and phrases
employed in Martin's *Epistle*. The preface furthermore threatens that
similar material would be forthcoming. "These," Piers writes, are "my
first labours, which I pray you accept, but in time when I shall bee more
able, you shall then here oftner from mee."[44] Because anticlerical and anti-
Catholic arguments were easily repackaged for anti-episcopal purposes, an
alliance with the heroes of the English Reformation and with proto-
Protestant complaint helped legitimate the cause of Presbyterian reform
and rebut the charge of introducing innovations.

Writings of the earlier Reformation also offered Martin Marprelate
models of style, language, and polemical approach. The colloquial direct-
ness and linguistically inventive abuse employed by William Tyndale, for
example, clearly influenced Martinist style, as attested by the extensive
citations from Tyndale's work in *Theses Martinianae*. In addition to the
writers actually cited in the tracts, other possible influences include John
Bale, William Turner, Luke Shepherd, Simon Fish, John Skelton, Robert
Crowley, and Thomas Becon: all exploit, to varying degrees, the resources
of colloquial prose, wordplay such as puns and alliteration, personal attack,
anecdotes, satire, fictive framing strategies, shifts of narrative voice, and
typographical and textual play.[45] Similar strategies also appear in the
pamphlet warfare in France and the Netherlands in the two decades before
the Marprelate tracts appeared, much of which was far more free in
approach than English polemic of the 1580s and 1590s.[46] Proselytizing
English Catholic performances of the early 1580s, textual and otherwise,
also popularize their cause in ways analogous to Martin's efforts.[47] But
while these sources and analogues all share elements of Martinist style, few
offer anything like Martin's narrative sophistication, virtuoso prose, and
ironic, self-reflexive play with textuality, qualities reminiscent of two
writers often invoked in discussions of Martinist style, Desiderius
Erasmus (particularly the Erasmus of *Encomium Moriae* and *Colloquia*)
and François Rabelais.[48]

Martin's innovative means of enlisting public support made fellow
reformers deeply uneasy. "The puritans are angry with me, I mean the

puritan preachers," he admits in the second tract. "And why? Because I am too open. Because I jest" (*Epitome*, 53). Many puritan leaders did indeed dissociate themselves from the Marprelate project. Thomas Cartwright, writing Burghley in 1590, insisted, "that from the first beginning of Martin unto this day, I have continually, upon any occasion, testified both my mislike and sorrow for such kind of disordered proceeding." When Robert Waldegrave left the project after printing the fourth tract, he claimed to be doing so because the preachers he consulted disapproved of Martin's course. At his trial in 1590, John Udall testified that "But for *Martin* and the rest of those Bookes ... they were never approved by the godly learned." Even John Penry, manager of the Marprelate press, wrote shortly before his execution in 1593 that he "disliked manie thinges in Mart. both for his maner and matter of wryting."[49] As Martin ruefully notes, "Those whom foolishly men call puritans, like of the matter I have handled, but the form they cannot brook" (*Theses Martinianae*, 147).

Opposition from his own side eventually prompted Martin to defend his use of satire in the fourth tract, *Hay any Work*. "I am not disposed to jest in this serious matter," he claims. But he was confronted with a situation in which "the cause of Christ's government" and "the bishops' antichristian dealing" were both kept hidden from the public by a church he believed was determined to suppress discussion of reform. Furthermore, Martin also recognized that, however worthy the cause, conventional religious polemic had limited marketplace appeal:

The most part of men could not be gotten to read anything written in the defence of the one and against the other. I bethought me therefore of a way whereby men might be drawn to do both, perceiving the humors of men in these times (especially of those that are in any place) to be given to mirth. I took that course. I might lawfully do it. Aye, for jesting is lawful by circumstances, even in the greatest matters. The circumstances of time, place and persons urged me there-unto. I never profaned the word in any jest. Other mirth I used as a covert, wherein I would bring the truth into light. The Lord being the author both of mirth and gravity, is it not lawful in itself for the truth to use either of these ways, when the circumstances do make it lawful? (115)

Martin rests his case primarily on a contrast between his responsible play-fulness (no profanation, mirth as a means to a good end) and the irrespon-sible and damaging foolery exhibited by opponents like Bridges, whose jesting made light of all the "antichristian dealing" the tracts were exposing to public gaze. But Martin also asserts the lawfulness of his approach by invoking the "circumstances of time, place, and persons," the traditional terms that governed decorum. The argument here allies the tracts with a

classically inspired tradition of learned satire, as exemplified by such
continental writers such as Theodore Beza, Philips van Marnix van Sant
Aldegonde, and Caelius Curio.[50]

But most contemporary readers would recognize that the Marprelate
tracts were operating in a discursive mode far removed from such culturally
acceptable traditions. Martin Marprelate assumed what book historians
have only recently begun to acknowledge, that books, particularly pamphlets, were not static objects of attention for one reader but were passed
around, read aloud to others, and discussed at home, in the tavern, or in the
market. The style of the tracts encouraged public dissemination of their
content by rewriting traditional ecclesiological polemic for the popular
culture of ballad, jig, and libel, the weapons of the politically weak. Stories,
for example, are above all transportable, easily assimilated into oral culture:
with every retelling, Martin would secure broader attention to his scrutiny
of episcopal claims to spiritual and secular authority. The tracts are a kind
of spectacle – a "display," to use Martin's own repeated term – staged to
demonstrate to the community at large the invalidity of an office and the
unworthiness of the men who occupied it.[51] Every reader of the tracts,
Martin implies, could be *a* Martin: the role required only a willingness to
abandon traditions of deference and see that in neither its actions nor
language could the church withstand close examination. As Martin warns
his opponents, finding and punishing the author of the tracts would not
keep them secure, because with the attitude he modeled in circulation, "the
day that you hang Martin, assure yourselves, there will twenty Martins
spring in my place" (*Hay any Work*, 119). The main goal, in Martin's view,
was to get talked about, because in the marketplace of ideas God's
(Presbyterian) truth would eventually emerge the winner.

Was the Marprelate project successful in reaching a public audience?
Contemporaries thought so: almost all references to the controversy
remark on Martin's popularity among "the common people." An anonymous memorandum on the project explained that Martin's "seditious
libelles" made easy way into "the hartes of the vulgar," because such people
were always "apt to entertaine matter of Noveltie especiallie if it have a
shew of restraining the authoritie of their Superiours."[52] The church
historian Thomas Fuller, writing in the seventeenth century, talked with
ministers who were active when the tracts appeared and summarized in
similar terms their collective memory of these "bastardly *Libels*": "it is
strange how secretly they were printed, how speedily dispers'd, how generally bought, how greedily read, yea and how firmly beleeved, especially of
the common sort, to whom no better musick then to hear their betters

upbraided."[53] Hostile claims that the tracts were being read by the common sort does not prove that they actually were: anti-Martinist texts relentlessly warn readers of the destabilizing potential of a popularizing polemic in a hierarchical society (see below, lviiff.), so the charge itself sufficed as a damning accusation. Documenting reading history is always a challenge in this period, even for books that were not treasonous to own. But a few examples of popular reading emerge from contemporary records. At the trial of Sir Richard Knightley, in whose manor the second tract was printed (see below, li–lii), one witness testified that "Fox his schoolmaster, and Wastal his man, would commonly read the books in sir Richard's house, and scoff and scorn at John of Canterbury."[54] In late 1588, Robert Cawdrey, an uncompromising puritan minister with a long history as a trouble-maker, was brought before high commission for a variety of offenses, including holding private meetings at which the Marprelate tracts were read aloud.[55] Cawdrey's underground study group, moving from house to house, suggests one way the tracts might have circulated. Nicholas Darton's 1637 petition from Kilsby – about ten miles north of Knightley's Fawsley manor – reveals a similar mode of communal reading fifty years later. In each of these examples, audiences listened to the Martinist voice and then, in Kilsby and Fawsley at least, appropriated and imitated it, scoffing and scorning, jeering and sporting at church authorities. In other words, becoming Martins themselves.

The anti-Martinist pamphlet *Martins Months Minde* (1589) depicts such "Martinizing" in action, imagining a scene probably far more appealing in its overall effect than intended. Marphoreus, the book's anonymous author, grudgingly admits that Martin "had some wit (though knavish)" and that his books "woulde make some foolish women, and pot companions to laugh, when sitting on their Alebenches, they would tipple, and reade it, serving them in steede of a blinde Minstrell, when they could get none, to fiddle them foorth a fitte of mirth" (Div). Hostile contemporaries read the tracts as an attempt to package the reform agenda as popular entertain-ment, and in response painted this attempt to address a popular constitu-ency as both novel and dangerous. But were readers entertained by Martin's irreverence for authority convinced thereby of the Presbyterian platform? The tracts undoubtedly had the power to push traditional anticlerical sentiments into a specifically anti-episcopal direction. But the specifics of reform polity were probably a hard sell to the tavern crowd. As the many passages of straight ecclesiology in the Marprelate tracts indicate, Presbyterianism is at heart a learned piety, an elite and in many respects austere form of worship and belief. Presbyterians shared their opposition to hierarchy and high-handed authorities with the Separatists but did not offer Separatism's essential autonomy; on the other hand, their ecclesiological ideal also lacked the potential openness and flexibility of the established church, notwithstanding John Whitgift's drive to greater uniformity. A few years after the collapse of the Elizabethan reform movement in the early 1590s, a collapse to which the Marprelate controversy likely contributed (see below, lxxiv), Richard Hooker's *Of the Lawes of Ecclesiasticall Politie* (1593) would justify the social functions of church ceremony, functions for which Presbyterianism largely failed to account in its insistence on an unchanging, scripturally based template. An argument could be made that Martin's appeal to a popular audience would always be compromised by the exclusionary rigor of his platform, one that contained little room for many forms of popular devotional practice.

AUTHORSHIP: JOB THROKMORTON, WITH JOHN PENRY

The search for Martin Marprelate was one of the great manhunts of the English Renaissance. Within weeks of the appearance of the first tract in October 1588, local officials were taking depositions and working to build cases against reform-minded troublemakers such as Giles Wigginton and John Udall. Before the end of the year, church and state were coordinating their investigations at the highest levels and setting in motion an orchestrated anti-Martinist campaign. When the Marprelate press was finally discovered in August 1589, the captured printers provided information that enabled authorities to round up almost everyone involved in the production of the tracts. The state eventually gathered enough evidence to reconstruct in detail the workings of the project, and over the following eighteen months almost all the "Martinists" were indicted, tried, and fined or imprisoned. These proceedings generated a great deal of legal documentation, much though not all of it extant. But no one ever confessed to being the writer of the tracts, and, despite the strong suspicions of those close to the investigation, authorship could not be established with legal certainty. While his project had been uncovered, Martin Marprelate himself remained masked.

The contrast between the wealth of contemporary evidence about the Marprelate project and the mystery of pseudonymity at its center continues to tantalize investigators centuries later: the hunt for Martin continues, though the trial has moved to the venue of the attribution study. More than twenty candidates have been proposed over the years, as sole authors or as writers working in variously configured cabals, and names continue to be added to the list.[56] Clerical suspects have included the puritan (mostly Presbyterian) clergymen John Penry, John Udall, John Field, Eusebius Paget, Henry Barrow, Giles Wigginton, Walter Travers, Francis Marbury, William Fludd, Thomas Cartwright, and Philip Martin.[57] Non-clerical candidates have included the puritan gentlemen Job Throkmorton and George Carleton; the soldier Sir Roger Williams; the writer Gabriel Harvey; government officials such as Michael Hickes (a secretary to William Cecil, Lord Burghley) and Laurence Tomson (one of Sir Francis Walsingham's agents); lawyers and members of parliament such as Sir Francis Knollys, Robert Beale, and James Morice; and the aristocrats Sir Robert Cecil, later 1st earl of Salisbury, Robert Devereux, 2nd earl of Essex, and Edward De Vere, 17th earl of Oxford.[58] For most of these potential Martins there is no evidence whatsoever for involvement in the Marprelate project, a fact that Elizabethan authorities tended to acknowledge more readily than their author-hunting successors. On the whole, the state's suspicions were well founded and its investigations thorough. Subsequent research has recovered much of the information gathered at the time but has not yet added anything on which to base conclusions different from those reached in the 1590s. Elizabethan investigators examined and cleared potential Martins such as Giles Wigginton; they rightly judged others, such as John Udall and John Field, to have played supporting roles. They do not appear to have taken seriously the rumors about Cecil, Essex, or other courtly or governmental sources. By the time Elizabethan officials had completed their investigations, they had built cases against two men: Job Throkmorton and John Penry. Was there also a great unknown, a third man standing in the shadows behind these two, planning, writing, and ultimately escaping without leaving any trace in the records? Possibly, and the project does appear to have attracted conspiracies of silent support. But the fact remains that of all the proposed candidates for Martin Marprelate, Throkmorton and Penry are the only two for whom there was ever any evidence for the attribution. Both, it appears, contributed to the tracts. Of the two, though, the one responsible for Martin Marprelate's characteristic style – the major source of the tracts' contemporary notoriety and the primary reason why they continue to be read – is almost certainly Job Throkmorton.

While the evidence gathered at the time points to Throkmorton as the voice of Martin and consequently as the creator of "Martinism," the same evidence also demonstrates that more than one person is required to run a successful pamphlet campaign. The following discussion introduces the project's two central figures, Throkmorton and Penry, and surveys their

respective claims for being Martin Marprelate. Shorter profiles follow of
other prominent members of the project, and a final section introduces
the remainder of the Martinist community through a narrative of the
tracts' production. While most writing about the Marprelate tracts has
focused on identifying their author, it should not be forgotten that the
investigative work by contemporary officials and later scholars has provided us with a richly detailed account of the day-to-day, communal
operation of a secret press in early modern England.

Early suspicions focused on John Penry (1563–93), at the time a high-
profile Presbyterian polemicist and a figure long afterward celebrated as a
pioneer of Welsh nonconformity.[59] Penry left his native Wales in 1580 to
matriculate at Peterhouse, Cambridge, where Martinist target Andrew
Perne was College master. After graduating BA in early 1584, Penry
disappears from the College records for a year. He probably spent some
of this period in Northampton, a major center of puritan activity: over the
next few years, Northampton was where Penry would join a Presbyterian
classis, meet his future wife Eleanor Godley, and become acquainted with
many people subsequently involved in the production of the Marprelate
tracts. He returned to Cambridge in late 1585, then transferred to Oxford in
1586 to complete the requirements for his MA, which he was awarded in
July. Penry decided against ordination, probably indicating that he already
disagreed with established ecclesiology, and returned to Wales, where his
travels convinced him of the need to publicize the cause of church reform.
His earliest publications, the pamphlets *A Treatise Containing the Aequity
of an Humble Supplication* (Oxford, 1587) and *An Exhortation unto the
Governours and People of Wales* (1588), deplored the "spirituall miserie" of
his native country (*Treatise*, 14), a deprivation he believed was largely the
fault of the bishops, "the butchers and stranglers of the soules of my deare
countrymen" (*Exhortation*, 29).

Penry's *Treatise* was presented to parliament in late February 1587 as part
of the political maneuvering to support the introduction of Anthony
Cope's "Bill and Book," an audacious attempt to have parliament abolish
episcopacy and replace it with a Presbyterian system of church government.
The presentation sparked a debate on church reform that ended with the
imprisonment of Cope, Peter Wentworth, and three other members.[60]
Whitgift subsequently issued a warrant for Penry's arrest and ordered the
Stationers' Company to confiscate all copies of his *Treatise*.[61] Penry soon
found himself before the court of high commission and was sentenced to
twelve days in prison (he would remain there a month); Martin dramatizes
his examination in the *Epistle* (28). One consequence of this brush with

episcopal authority is that the *Treatise* would be the only one of Penry's many publications to be printed openly in England: the rest were published either on secret presses or in such centers of puritan printing as La Rochelle, Middelburg, Edinburgh, and Amsterdam.

Penry spent the eighteen months from spring 1588 to autumn 1589 as a leading agent in the clandestine operation that published the Marprelate tracts. A more detailed chronology of this operation follows later in this section. In October 1589, with the investigative net closing in, Penry fled to Scotland; the privy council declared him an enemy to the state and issued a warrant for his arrest. Despite months of diplomatic efforts by English officials to have him banished, Penry remained hiding in Scotland until the summer of 1591, when he risked a trip to London to see if the Coppinger–Hacket conspiracy was truly the beginning of the final reformation of England.[62] It proved instead a mad fiasco, and on the day Hacket was executed Penry once more left hastily for Scotland. After a year in hiding, in September 1592 Penry once again tempted fate by returning to England. He had by this point converted from Presbyterianism to Separatism, and in London he joined the Separatists Francis Johnson and John Greenwood. Along with many other members of their congregation, Penry was captured in March 1593. After a brief escape and recapture, Penry was for two months repeatedly examined about his activities over the previous five years. He was finally indicted on May 21, on charges based on manuscript notes that had been discovered in a raid on his rooms in Scotland. Four days later, however, a new indictment was drawn up that added evidence based on passages in one of his printed books, *A Treatise Wherein is Manifestlie Proved* (Edinburgh, 1590), a book usually known, from its running head, as *Reformation No Enemie*. Penry had voiced the unwillingness of a personified "England" to enact reform (A2v–A3r); the passage was read as an attack on the Queen, and Penry was charged with publishing seditious and scandalous words, apparently under the Act of Uniformity (1 Eliz. c. 2), though possibly under "An act against seditious words and rumors" (23 Eliz. c. 2), a bill aimed originally against Catholic recusants and under which the Separatists Henry Barrow and John Greenwood had been hanged in April.[63] Found guilty on the same day on which he was indicted, Penry was hanged four days later, on May 29, 1593. No warning was sent to the court or the prison that might have allowed friends and family to attend him, and he was forbidden from making any speech from the gallows. He was thirty years old.

John Penry was not executed for being Martin Marprelate: the tracts were not mentioned in his indictment, and no evidence respecting them was introduced at his trial. But many contemporaries assumed that Penry's involvement with the project had played an unofficial role in the sentence against him, an assumption shared by most subsequent commentators. Burghley himself informed Penry that church officials accused him of being Martin: if that report were true, wrote the imprisoned Penry in return, "I desire to be called to my tryall in this point."[64] The lengthy summary of evidence against Penry compiled in 1593 for attorney-general Sir Thomas Egerton represents a sustained attempt to read the "seditious" texts Penry produced in Scotland as proceeding naturally out of his association with the Marprelate publications.[65] While this evidence seems ultimately to have been considered too circumstantial to use in court, other contemporaries freely linked Penry's punishment to his role in the production of the tracts. Philip Gawdy of Clifford's Inn wrote to his brother Bassingborne, high sheriff of Norfolk, that "Mr. Pendry is executed for writing of Martin Marprelate. I do not muche rejoyce therein."[66] A newsletter drafted by Thomas Phelippes, coordinator of English agents abroad, was happier with the court's judgment, though more scrupulous in its choice of epithet: "Penry the sonne of Martin Marprelate was hanged latelye as two of the principall Brownists Barrow and Grenewood were before so as that sect is in effect extinguished."[67] The hanging of Penry, sometimes remembered as the hanging of Martin Marprelate, would be mentioned in official and other correspondence for decades to come, often invoked as an effective response to the more radical forms of godly challenge.[68]

There was, and remains, no doubt that Penry played an important role in the collaborative Marprelate project. Witnesses deposed that he was present while the tracts were printed; that he knew when and how manuscripts of new tracts were to arrive, and that he personally handed some of these manuscripts over to the printers; that parts of at least two of these manuscripts were in his handwriting; and that he paid the printers and made arrangements for accommodating and moving the press. Henry Sharpe, a leading figure in the Northampton puritan community who joined the Marprelate project as a "binder" (that is, stitcher), provided the usefully summarizing statement with which authorities ended one collection of evidence: "he never saw, nor knew any other Man to busye himself so much about the Books as Penry did."[69] But was Penry also their primary author? In September 1589, one month after the discovery of the Marprelate press, a two-page summary was prepared for Burghley of the results produced by ten months of investigation.[70] This document names Penry as a likely candidate for being Martin, citing in particular the presence of his handwriting (along with that of another person, later identified as Throkmorton) in the seized manuscript of *More Work for Cooper*. These "Briefe instructions" do not mention Throkmorton, who had so far avoided being associated with the project. A more detailed compilation of evidence, undated but probably produced a few months later, also concludes with a list of "Praesumptions that Penry is the Author of theis libelles." This document also offers the first glimpse of Throkmorton, now recorded as one of those who had visited the press.[71] But a new summary was compiled by the queen's serjeant John Puckering in early 1590 that drew on depositions from nineteen witnesses and was substantially longer than previous compilations.[72] Throkmorton had by this time been fully implicated, and this summary, known as the "Puckering brief," marshals evidence against him; perhaps because there were now two candidates, the brief draws no conclusions about authorship. While documents compiled for Penry's trial fill in the details of his participation, they avoid making the charge that he *was* Martin, and at the trial itself the state cautiously put this evidence aside and focused on a text demonstrably written by Penry.

Donald J. McGinn, Penry's most ardent twentieth-century champion, believed that the Elizabethan state had been overcautious. In "The Real Martin Marprelate," a 1943 article subsequently expanded into a book-length attribution study, *John Penry and the Marprelate Controversy* (1966), McGinn cast aside the hesitancy of contemporary officials and defended the claim that Martin Marprelate was to be identified as Penry, and, furthermore, as Penry alone. His case for Penry, however, is a sustained exercise in special pleading. Scholars have sketched the many weaknesses of McGinn's argument, particularly his problematic use of sources and his decision not to look at any manuscripts not already printed; these manuscripts undermine many of McGinn's assumptions.[73] External evidence aside, Penry's candidacy for sole author of the tracts has received little support primarily because of questions of style. While often passionate in his denunciations of episcopacy, Penry displays few signs of the polemical strategies or performative stylishness that characterize the Marprelate tracts in any of his dozen or so acknowledged writings.[74] William Pierce, who wrote a biography of Penry and edited the Marprelate tracts, thought the stylistic differences sufficiently apparent as to be scarcely worth arguing: "that Penry was not Marprelate is obvious enough to those who are familiar with their respective writings."[75] McGinn disagrees with these observations, but his assertions of a stylistic continuity between the Marprelate tracts and Penry's acknowledged writings are founded on continuities of polemical concern, on common matter rather than manner. McGinn seems to be the only commentator ever to see style as offering evidence in Penry's favor. Even contemporary officials certain of Penry's involvement in the project acknowledged the difference between Martin and Penry in his known writings. The style of the Marprelate tracts, one early compiler of evidence concludes, "doth alltogether resemble" Penry's own writings – when, he adds, Marprelate was "out of his scoffinge veyne."[76] That is, Marprelate sounded like Penry, but only when he did not sound like Martin. While arguments for and against authorship based on style will always be open to dispute, it should be safe to say that McGinn's case for Penry as the "great prose satirist of the Elizabethan period" (200) is substantially weakened by the complete absence of satiric strategies in all of the many books Penry is known to have written.

Unsurprisingly, Penry denied that he was Martin once he was captured. But he did so not only to state officials but also in private letters to friends within the reform community.[77] Furthermore, Penry drew attention in these denials to the key difference between Martin's approach to controversy and his own. In the draft of a letter to Burghley, Penry claimed that he disliked Martin's "manner" of writing: "Unseemely jestes uncomly rayling I allow not, and judge them more beseeming the Prel[ates] and theyr Parrasites then anie modest Christian."[78] Admittedly, this letter is self-exculpatory, and much of its discussion of the Marprelate tracts has the distinct sound of equivocation. After all, Burghley knew that Penry had believed sufficiently in the project to be its manager. But in his own published work Penry had avoided the polemical use of ridicule and the *ad hominem* attack, two of Martin's most characteristic strategies. In his *Exhortation* (1588), he deplored "the humors of busibodies, who increasing themselves still unto more ungodlinesse, thinke nothing so well spoken or written, as that which is satyrical and bitingly done against L. Bishops and the rest of that stamp" (29). The "only scope of my writing," he argued in *A Viewe* (Coventry, 1589), was to convince those in authority that episcopacy was a barrier to the spread of preaching; he denounced "the discrediting or galling of our Lorde Bb." (44). To speak of men's persons, he explained in a confession of faith written shortly before his trial, was to assume an authority available only to the divine: it "touch[es] the Lords election."[79] While Penry did not hesitate to denounce bishops in general as cormorants and soul-murderers, he distinguished between this impersonal invective and Martin's targeting of individuals. Besides, as he pointed out to Burghley, why should he attack the bishops pseudonymously when he had been daring enough to challenge them repeatedly in books to which he attached his name?[80] It bears remembering that Penry continued to write and publish his own attacks on episcopacy throughout the period in which he managed the Marprelate press: Penry's involvement with the project was not solely in the service of the Marprelate texts. Henry Sharpe reported that Waldegrave had printed Martin's *Epistle* against Penry's will, because Penry had wanted a book of *his* printed first; the complaint makes little sense if Penry had written both.[81]

All that said, Penry does appear to have written parts of some of the Marprelate tracts. One-third or more of the seized manuscript of *More Work for Cooper* was written in his hand, and Humphrey Newman, the distributor of the tracts, deposed that Penry was "part authour" of *Hay any Work*.[82] This evidence indicates that the writing of the tracts was to some extent collaborative. While Penry's style in his own writings makes it unlikely that he was responsible for the tracts' "Martinist" elements, he likely contributed to their expositions of the Presbyterian platform. It would have been natural enough for him to do so: Penry was a skilled, published polemicist on these issues. But the reputation of the Marprelate tracts is not founded on the passages in which they sound like other reform polemic of the period: they won notoriety in their day, and continue to be read, primarily because of the voice of Martin Marprelate. Furthermore, this voice remains consistent over the entire series of seven extant Marprelate tracts, despite the different names it playfully adopts (Martin Junior and Martin Senior, as well as Martin Marprelate himself). And the writer almost certainly responsible for that voice is Job Throkmorton.

Throkmorton (1545–1601) – unlike other Throckmortons, even in his own family, he spelled his name without the "c" – was a well-connected Warwickshire gentleman from a prominent family.[83] The adjacent counties of Warwickshire and Northamptonshire, in which much of the Martinist activity took place, had a strong tradition of gentry puritanism,[84] and Throkmorton was a leading local figure in these networks. He graduated from Oxford in 1566 and made his first appearance on the national stage in 1572, when Edward Manners, third earl of Rutland (1549–87), arranged for his election to parliament as a member for East Retford, Nottinghamshire. Throkmorton was related to the earl through his mother, and Rutland would have been a powerful patron: devoted to Elizabeth, he held many offices and was lord chancellor designate at his death. Throkmorton appears to have kept a low profile in the 1572 parliament: he is scarcely mentioned in any of the extant records. Leland Carlson, however, has argued that Throkmorton was already playing an important, if behind-the-scenes, role in the reform movement, attributing to him a half dozen manuscript and printed contributions to the campaign that followed the 1572 publication of the Presbyterian *Admonition to the Parliament*.[85] While Carlson's attributions are plausible, they are based entirely on stylistic parallels and remain, in the absence of other evidence, unproven.

The death of his father in 1573 left Throkmorton the lord of the family manor in Haseley, Warwickshire, and he seems to have spent the next decade leading the quiet existence of a country squire. He next appears in the extant records with a report he made in 1584 to Ralph Warcuppe, a Warwickshire justice of the peace, who had asked him to question some local Catholics about their support of Mary Queen of Scots; the nine depositions attached to the report testify to Throkmorton's enthusiastic compliance.[86] But this primarily local life ended with the calling of the 1586 parliament. Throkmorton's election as a burgess for Warwick has attracted the attention of historians, because it is an unusually well-documented example of the political maneuvering that took place in some parts of the country to elect MPs sympathetic to the cause of church reform. After a controversial campaign, and with the support of neighboring gentry such as Sir John Harington and Fulke Greville, Throkmorton was elected over the opposition of prominent local officials.[87] As it happens, Throkmorton's parliamentary career lasted only a few months, though this proved time enough for him to cause an international diplomatic incident and to deliver three speeches that provide evidence for his authorship of the Marprelate tracts. Throkmorton delivered his first speech in early November, the first week of the parliament. Addressing the succession question about which he had examined local suspects two years earlier, Throkmorton called for the execution of Mary Queen of Scots, whom he denounced with eloquent vituperation:

> Yf I should tearme her the daughter of sedition, the mother of rebellion, the nurce of impietie, the handmaide of iniquitie, the sister of unshamefastenesse; or yf I should tell you that which you know allreaddye, that she is Scottishe of nation, French of education, papist of profession, a Guysian of bloude, a Spaniarde in practize, a lybertyne in life: as all this were not to flatter her, so yet this were nothinge neere to dyscrybe her.[88]

This is the performative, rhetorically fluent voice that would within a couple of years outrage Martin Marprelate's enemies, the men he termed the "proud, popish, presumptuous, profane, paltry, pestilent and pernicious prelates" (*Epistle*, 10). Throkmorton's second speech, delivered on February 23, 1587, was an equally impassioned appeal for English support for the Low Countries in its fight against Spain. His criticism of James VI prompted an admonishment from Christopher Hatton, the lord chancellor, and complaints from the Scots led Burghley to promise that Throkmorton would be imprisoned in the Tower where he would, "for the rashness of his tongue, feel smart in his whole body." Throkmorton eventually offered an apology of sorts, explaining in a letter to Burghley that "The privilege of the place [was] apt enough to bring a young head into a distemperature."[89]

Throkmorton would avoid the Tower by fleeing the city, but he managed one parting shot before he left the House. His final speech, delivered February 27, 1587, was offered in support of Cope's "Bill and Book" during the debate initiated by the presentation of Penry's *Treatise*. Throkmorton began with a defense of parliamentary privilege, complaining that the "shew of freedome" offered members on entering the House was a sham, for the liberty to speak held only if the speaker "medle neyther with the reformation of religion nor the establishment of succession, the verie pillers and grounde workes of all our blisse and happines." Throkmorton then revealed his religio-political sympathies, as well as his gift for expression, in a protest against attacks on the Bill that dismissed it and similarly motivated efforts as "puritan":

To bewayle the distresses of God's children, it is puritanisme. To finde faulte with corruptions of our Church, it is puritanisme. To reprove a man for swearing, it is puritanisme. To banishe an adulterer out of the house, it is puritanisme. To make humble sute to her Majestie and the High Courte of Parleament for a learned ministery, it is puritanisme. Yea, and I feare me we shall come shortly to this, that to doe God and her Majestie good service shalbe coumpted puritanisme, and thease are of the cunning sleightes of Sathan and his instrumentes in this age.[90]

The concern Throkmorton displays here for the polemical uses of calumny and the "rewriting" of reformist language by their opponents would become a central feature of the Marprelate tracts.[91]

The February 1587 debate on the state of the church was the high-water mark of Elizabethan Presbyterianism as a movement with a political voice on the national scene. For both Penry and Throkmorton, it also marked the end of their efforts to use official channels, such as legitimate printing or parliamentary debate, to publicize the cause of reform. Over the next year they joined forces to continue the reform campaign by other means (the narrative below of the movements of the Marprelate press sketches their activities during this collaboration). After the discovery of the press and Penry's flight to Scotland, Throkmorton managed for a few months to avoid being implicated in the project. But by early 1590 his name starts to appear in official records as a suspect, and in October of that year he was indicted in Warwick for being Martin Marprelate; he was eventually released, possibly due to a legal technicality (see below). A year later, Throkmorton, like Penry, became tangentially involved with the Coppinger–Hacket conspiracy and would defend himself from this association in the print exchange with Matthew Sutcliffe, dean of Exeter, discussed below. Apart from this last skirmish, however, Job Throkmorton lived out his last decade as a prosperous country squire, enlarging and improving his estate at Haseley to pass on to his children. He makes his last appearance in contemporary records in early December 1600, shortly before his death in February 1601: the puritan diarist Lady Margaret Hoby lists Throkmorton among the social and political elite she met during a stay in London.[92]

We owe much of our knowledge of the contemporary case that identified Throkmorton as Marprelate to the efforts of Matthew Sutcliffe (1549/50–1629). A prolific polemicist, Sutcliffe was drawn into the later stages of the Marprelate controversy when he responded to *A Petition Directed to Her Most Excellent Majestie* (Middelburg, 1592) and, in passing, mentioned Throkmorton as the author of "Libels, and scoffes published under the name of *Martin*."[93] Sutcliffe's accusation prompted Throkmorton to write *The Defence of Job Throkmorton against the Slaunders of Maister Sutcliffe* (1594), the only work he published under his own name. Sutcliffe in turn responded with *An Answere unto a Certaine Calumnious Letter Published by M. J. Throkmorton* (1595), in which he spends twenty-five folio pages detailing the case against Throkmorton, summarizing for the reading public the evidence generated by the investigation of the Marprelate tracts. Throkmorton responded in a preliminary epistle to his edition of *A Brief Apologie of Thomas Cartwright* (Middelburg, 1596), but in this pamphlet war it was Sutcliffe who would have the final word, in *The Examination of T. Cartwrights Late Apologie* (1596).

Sutcliffe did his homework before writing his 1595 *Answere*: he read all the relevant texts, and examined all the reports and depositions generated by the investigation. Some of the evidence he cites is no longer extant, but most of it survives and confirms his reliability: by the standards of the time, Sutcliffe is unusually scrupulous. He begins his case against Throkmorton with the later Marprelate productions. The captured printers John Hodgkins, Valentine Simmes, and Arthur Thomlin deposed that the manuscripts of *Theses Martinianae* and *Just Censure*, and at least half of the manuscript of *More Work for Cooper*, were written in one hand, and that they believed Throkmorton the author; Sutcliffe, with access to samples from seized letters, confirmed the hand as Throkmorton's. In addition, Throkmorton made all the printing arrangements for *Theses*

Martinianae and *Just Censure*, provided the manuscripts, and visited the house where they were being produced.[94] Acknowledging that Throkmorton had been more cautious in the earlier stages of the project, Sutcliffe offers two major arguments for his authorship of the other tracts. The first is style. Citing passages from writings known or deposed by witnesses to be Throkmorton's – *Theses Martinianae*, *Just Censure*, the para-Martinist *M. Some Laid Open in His Coulers* (La Rochelle, 1589),[95] the parts of *More Work for Cooper* in his hand, his parliamentary speeches, seized letters and other manuscripts – Sutcliffe points to the stylistic and verbal continuities between these works and the remaining Marprelate tracts. The passages he cites from Throkmorton's letters are particularly striking, with their Martinist irony, conversational mode, imagined dialogues, and voicings of opponents. The style of *Hay any Work*, and by extension the other tracts, Sutcliffe concludes, "is so like to *Job Throkmortons* talking and writing, that as children do declare whose they are by the lineaments of their visage and proportion of parts, so these libels doe bewray their natural father, by the frame of the words and sentences, and such draughtes as can proceed from no other authour."[96]

Sutcliffe's second general argument is the indictment. Unlike Penry, Throkmorton was officially accused of writing the Marprelate tracts. According to Sutcliffe, in early October 1590, one year after the discovery of the Martinist press, a grand jury at Warwick indicted Throkmorton for "disgracing her majesties government, & making certaine scorneful and Satyricall libels under the name of *Martin*." The records of these proceedings are not extant. But local magistrates had convened jurors, heard witnesses, debated a bill of indictment, and swore it was true. The judges of Assize, Edward Fenner and Francis Gawdy, agreed that the charges deserved further inquiry and bound Throkmorton in recognizance to appear before judges in Westminster in April 1591. The Westminster arraignment was deferred, and then eventually suspended, apparently because of a legal technicality: Sutcliffe remarks that "an enditement may be overthrowen for want of forme, and due circumstance; yet may the matter therein conteined be true, and the partie againe bee called upon a new enditement." That is, after being indicted Throkmorton was neither acquitted nor pardoned, but in effect remained on probation for the remainder of his life. Since problems with form and process did not necessarily hinder the completion of legal proceedings in this period, Sutcliffe speculates about the refusal to prosecute Throkmorton. Perhaps he benefited from the intervention of Lord Chancellor Hatton, to whom Throkmorton wrote a petition of apology and submission in mid-October

1590. Perhaps it was the power of his supporters: any favor Hatton might have shown Throkmorton, Sutcliffe insists, was "extorted from him by the importunitie of some friends, which are to be named." Perhaps he enjoyed protection at an even higher level: Sutcliffe at one point accuses Throkmorton of ingratitude to the Queen, for striving to overthrow her ecclesiastical supremacy even after Elizabeth had "winked at so many lewd pranks of his, & shewed him so many favours."[97] The source of Throkmorton's protection remains the primary historical mystery connected with the Marprelate project. One possibility is that his apologies and submissions sufficed, and no particularly strong intervention was required: church and state appear in general to have been more concerned to punish nonconforming ministers and preachers than they were to punish the reform movement's supporters among the gentry.

Writing six years after the discovery of the Marprelate press and drawing on evidence gathered over years of investigations, Sutcliffe concluded that Job Throkmorton was the "principall agent" in all the Martinist productions and "the man that principally deserveth the name of *Martin*."[98] The most recent attribution study of the Marprelate tracts comprises an extended endorsement of Sutcliffe's argument. In *Martin Marprelate, Gentleman: Master Job Throkmorton Laid Open in His Colors* (1981), Leland H. Carlson uses several manuscripts he had rediscovered to confirm the details of Sutcliffe's case for Throkmorton and weaken McGinn's for Penry. Carlson, however, organized his study in such a way as to leave room for continued speculation: he buries good arguments among a confusing welter of weaker ones, and repeatedly overvalues the evidence of stylistic parallels drawn from numerous anonymous texts he himself has attributed to Throkmorton.[99] But once these often circular exercises in attribution are set aside, the remaining historical, legal, and stylistic evidence points convincingly to Job Throkmorton as the writer most responsible for Martin Marprelate's distinctive voice.

THE MARTINIST COMMUNITY AND THE MARPRELATE PRESS

As a genre of scholarly investigation, the attribution study focuses on authorship. More often than not, the psychology of attribution work, along with our post-Romantic celebration of the solitary creative artist, leads to the discovery of single authors and the subordination of other kinds of contribution to a text.[100] Carlson, for example, dismisses in a footnote "any theory of composite authorship," even when the very same depositions on which he relies for his case for Throkmorton clearly state that Penry wrote parts of at least two tracts.[101] But if the hunt for the elusive Martin proved one thing, it is the extent to which the Marprelate project was a collaborative effort. While Job Throkmorton "is" Martin Marprelate in that he appears to be the writer principally responsible for the Martinist voice, John Penry does appear to have contributed some writing. Furthermore, Throkmorton and Penry together are but two of the almost two dozen people known to have been involved in the production and dissemination of the tracts. A royal proclamation responded to the tracts by distributing agency among all those responsible for their existence and their circulation, comprehensively forbidding anybody "to write, contrive, print, or cause to be published or distributed, or to keep" such works, or even to "give any instruction, direction, favor, or assistance to the contriving, writing, printing, publishing, or dispersing of the same."[102] To contemporary officials, the tracts were products not just of an author but of a community, bonded in opposition by a program collectively and defiantly promoted through print. To be involved in any way, even by reading a copy, was to be treasonously complicit.

But the Marprelate tracts were also collaborative texts in other, more general ways. They present a platform built over decades of Presbyterian opposition: their authority therefore rests not on individual inspiration but on this time-tested, communally sanctioned vision of the divine truth. The scurrilous stories that play such an important role in Martinist style were drawn from sources compiled over the years with contributions from the "godly" across the country, as contemporaries realized. Do not "thinke there was no more heades in it then his owne," warns the anti-Martinist pamphlet *An Almond for a Parrat* (1590): "For I can assure you on the contrary, that moste of the Puritane preachers in Northampton shire, Warwick shire, Sufolke and Northffolke, have eyther brought stone, strawe, or morter to the building of this *Martin*."[103] Finally, as discussed earlier, those involved in the project sought to position the Martinist voice within a vigorous native tradition of plain-speaking complaint. Few polemicists in the sixteenth century wanted to be innovators in religious or political issues, and Martin was not among their number. He writes explicitly on behalf of a constituency, and it was his claim to be representative that defenders of the church found most threatening. To reduce Martin to an individual author is in many ways to deprive the tracts of the textual and concomitant moral authority he sought to invoke.

Matthew Sutcliffe draws attention to the broader kinds of collaboration that underlay the Marprelate project: while he insists that Throkmorton was the principal author, he adds that "John Penry ... John Udall,

John Fielde, all Johns, and Job Throkmorton, all concurred in making Martin."[104] John Udall and John Field, both prominent figures in the Presbyterian movement, had indeed played roles in the project. The minister Udall (1560?–1592/93) graduated MA from Trinity College, Cambridge, in 1584 and was presented to the living of Kingston-upon-Thames. He quickly proved a popular preacher and successful writer, publishing five collections of sermons between 1584 and 1588. In 1586, Udall appeared before the court of high commission to answer for his efforts on behalf of Presbyterian reform. On this occasion, he was restored to the ministry through the influence of the countess and earl of Warwick. Despite aristocratic protection, however, Udall was again summoned to Lambeth in July 1588 and was this time deprived of his living; Martin discusses the local politics of the actions against Udall in the *Epistle* (31–32). During the investigation of the tracts, the vicar who replaced Udall in Kingston deposed that Udall had in a conversation with him "uttered these words, That if they put him to silence, he would give the Bishops such a blow as they never had."[105] The Marprelate project offered Udall his opportunity: a contemporary of Penry's at Cambridge, Udall admitted that Penry was often at his Kingston house, and he had likely known of the project from its inception. His Presbyterian manifesto *A Demonstration of the Trueth of that Discipline* (East Molesey, 1588) was printed on the Marprelate press while it was in hiding, with Udall present during the printing.[106] But Udall's involvement with the Marprelate project ended soon after the publication of the second tract, the *Epitome*: near the end of 1588, Henry Hastings, earl of Huntingdon, invited him to resume his ministry, this time in Newcastle upon Tyne. Udall remained a suspect, however, and in December 1589 he was summoned to London to be examined by the privy council. He denied authorship of the Marprelate tracts but was eventually sentenced to death for writing the *Demonstration*. Pressure from many influential people, including James VI, Walter Ralegh, and the earl of Essex, eventually won Udall a pardon, but he died in prison before he could take advantage of the reprieve.[107]

The last of Sutcliffe's four collaborators was John Field (1545–88), the administrative heart of the Elizabethan puritan movement and a propagandist convinced of the power of print.[108] Field began his involvement with printing as a researcher for the 1570 edition of John Foxe's *Actes and Monumentes*. In the early 1570s he co-authored the *Admonition to the Parliament* and managed the press on which it and several subsequent manifestos were produced. While Field would continue occasionally to publish titles of his own, he saw his major role as providing a "helping hande, in the furtheraunce of any profitable worke, that may bee for thy building up in Jesus Christ."[109] One way to further the cause was to use the press, and Field edited or translated and arranged the publication of numerous important works by British and continental reformers. Another was to record the experiences of those involved in the movement. With help from sympathizers throughout the country, Field spent years gathering grievances, transcripts of trials and interrogations, stories of clerical scandals, and other information related to the repression of reform.[110] Patrick Collinson suggests that Field learned the propaganda value of such material while working with Foxe; in essence, this register imitated Foxe's attempt to present the history of a movement through the lives of those persecuted on its behalf.[111] Hostile contemporaries interpreted these efforts to document communal experience in this light. At the trial of John Udall, for example, one of the examiners asked Udall why he kept notes of his conferences with the bishops and their officers. Recognizing the use Field and others made of this kind of information, John Young, bishop of Rochester, supplied an answer: "Because he and such like might apishly imitate the Martirs of former times, and accompt themselves persecuted by us as those were by the Popish Bishops."[112] Field died seven months before the first Marprelate tract appeared. But Sutcliffe included him among the writers who "concurred" in the making of Martin because he knew that Penry had been in communication with Field in 1587, and because he assumed that the Marprelate tracts had drawn on material supplied by Field through his register.[113] Martin implicitly refers to Field's compilation midway through the *Epistle*, when he warns the bishops that they should note "what a perilous fellow M. Marprelate is: he understands of all your knavery, and it may be he keeps a register of them: unless you amend, they shall all come into the light one day" (33). Martin's threat to make "known unto the world" (33) the less flattering actions of the church and its officers invokes the idea of scrutiny that underlay Field's carefully compiled community memory, and the public display of this record would characterize the polemical strategy that Martin and other contemporaries would call "Martinism."

   The one major participant in the project not mentioned by Sutcliffe was the printer of the first four tracts, Robert Waldegrave (d. 1604). Born near Fawsley in Northampton, where Sir Richard Knightley would house the Marprelate press for the printing of the second tract, Waldegrave was one of the great puritan printers of the period. In 1584, the court of high commission directed the Stationers' Company to seize Waldegrave and any unlicensed books they found in his shop, an action likely prompted by his publication of two aggressively Presbyterian works, *A Briefe and Plaine Declaration* (1584), by William Fulke, and *A Dialogue, Concerning the Strife of our Churche* (1584). Waldegrave was subsequently committed to prison for six weeks; he claimed to have been imprisoned again the next year, this time for twenty weeks, for printing another series of manifestos.[114] Waldegrave's legitimate printing career in England ended in April 1588, when his shop was raided after he had printed *The State of the Church of Englande* (1588) and the court of the Stationers' Company ordered that his press, type, "and printinge stuffe [be] defaced and made unserviceable."[115] When the first Marprelate tract appeared later that year, it was therefore not only illegal in itself, as an unauthorized publication, but it was also printed by a man who had been barred from practicing the trade. Martin discusses the predicament of the fugitive Waldegrave, "utterly deprived for ever printing again," as part of his general attempt to particularize and make human the consequences of repression. In this case, he presents the plight of Waldegrave's "poor wife and six orphans, without anything to relieve them" as a further example of Whitgift's "unnatural tyranny" (*Epistle*, 23–24). As it happened, Martin was wrong about his friend's future career: after a brief period in La Rochelle, Waldegrave eventually fled north to Scotland, where James VI named him King's Printer. He continued to print books that irked English officials and English stationers (his publications included, e.g., a pirated edition of Sir Philip Sidney's *Arcadia*).[116] But Waldegrave also became an important figure in the development of Scottish printing: over one hundred books bear his Edinburgh imprint, including first editions of several titles by King James himself. Despite James's attempts to win Waldegrave a pardon, his exile lasted until the death of Elizabeth.

The story that investigators eventually pieced together of the production and distribution of the Marprelate tracts exemplifies the collaboration the project required. Waldegrave printed the first tract on a press hidden in the manor of Elizabeth Crane in East Molesey, Surrey, about thirteen miles southwest of London, across the Thames from the royal palace of Hampton Court. Crane (d. in or before 1606) and her first husband, Anthony Crane (d. 1583), had been active in the reform movement since at least the early 1570s; in 1589, she would marry George Carleton (1529–90), a prominent figure among the puritan gentry in the midland counties.[117] The press is regularly described in depositions as being Penry's, who apparently bought it from an unnamed Dutchman.[118] Penry and Waldegrave brought the press to East Molesey in the summer of 1588, and over the next few months Waldegrave printed John

Udall's *A Demonstration of the Trueth of that Discipline*, Penry's *A Defence of That Which Hath Bin Written*, an expanded edition of Penry's *Exhortation*, and, by about the middle of October, Martin's *Epistle*.[119] One of Crane's servants, Nicholas Tomkins, deposed that the retail price of the *Epistle* was ninepence, but that he had been able to buy copies from Waldegrave for sixpence; rather wistfully, he concluded that if he had been more enterprising he might "have had all the Martin Mareprelates, and so have gained 20 marks by them."[120] Tomkins based his calculations on a print run of slightly more than one thousand copies, a figure supported by evidence that print runs for other Martinist productions ranged from at least five hundred to fifteen hundred copies.[121] With the *Epistle* completed, Crane "grew fearfull" about having the press in her house and asked the Martinists to remove it.[122] When she was eventually arrested, Crane refused to answer any questions, telling authorities "she would not be her own Hangman," nor would she "in her Conscience, be an Accuser of others."[123] In May 1590 Star Chamber fined her 1000 marks (£666) for being in contempt of court for her refusal to answer *ex officio* questions and a further £500 for harboring the press, and committed her to the Fleet prison. Extant records do not indicate how long she remained there, nor if her fines were eventually remitted, as they were for others charged with assisting the Martinist project.

Elizabeth Crane's was the first of several households to accommodate the Marprelate press. In early November, the operation moved to Fawsley Hall, Sir Richard Knightley's mansion in Northamptonshire, about twelve miles southwest of Northampton. Knightley (1533–1615), high sheriff and deputy lieutenant for Northampton, had long been a leading patron of the Presbyterian movement, using his lieutenancy to promote a puritan ministry in the county.[124] The press had been dismantled and hidden in a cart for the almost hundred-mile journey, which took about two weeks and was made by R. Jeffs of Upton, a tenant-farmer under Knightley's son Valentine. Jeffs, who had to ask Penry what the "small things of lead or Iron" in his cargo were, earned the substantial sum of fifty shillings for the dangerous work. Penry gave him the first thirty shillings at a meeting on Hounslow Heath, and the remainder at the house of Penry's in-laws, the Godleys, in Northampton.[125] The press was set up in a locked room, and Waldegrave installed under an assumed name with the cover story that he was there to examine Knightley's title-deeds.[126] By late November he had printed the second Marprelate tract, the *Epitome*. Humphrey Newman, who would become the main distributor of the tracts,[127] brought 400 copies to London, borrowing Penry's mare to do so; Mary Waldegrave, Robert's wife, also took 200 copies for distribution. One of Knightley's servants told an acquaintance that paper and other printing supplies for the operation were "allwayes sent down from a Spurrier dwellinge aboute Pie Corner neere West Smithfield, who sent thither and receyved thinges from thence."[128] This is one of the few references in the extant documents to what must have been a well-developed network of suppliers and importers in the London area, all working to provide the project with the large quantities of materials it required to print all these books. Knightley testified at his trial that he had not been present while the *Epitome* was being printed, and that he had only granted Penry permission to print books on the religious condition of Wales. With some justification, the court found the second of these claims unconvincing. Knightley had in fact sent copies of the tracts to his brother-in-law, Sir Edward Seymour, earl of Hertford, and had let Humphrey Newman wear the livery of his household staff to render his travels around the country less suspicious.[129] Knightley was fined £2,000 and sentenced to "Imprisonment at her majesty's plea-sure," but the fine and sentence were remitted at the request of John Whitgift, who appears to have focused his rigor against reformist clerics rather than their lay supporters.[130]

Local rumors that a press was being operated at Fawsley spurred the Martinists to move the operation in early January 1589. At first the press was hidden in an unoccupied farmhouse Knightley owned in Norton, in Northamptonshire near Daventry. But in mid-January it was moved to White Friars, the house of John Hales in Coventry.[131] Hales was Knightley's nephew by his first marriage. At his trial he "disclaimed the books" and implied that he had agreed to house the operation only because of his obligations to Knightley; the court nonetheless fined him 1,000 marks (eventually remitted).[132] Steven Gyfford, a servant whom Knightley "used secretly in these matters," was employed to move the press. Henry Sharpe deposed that as he and Gyfford were riding together one day, Gyfford pointed to a gutter in the road and commented that "he was never so affraid as he was least his Carte should have stuck fast" at that place as he was driving the press to Coventry.[133] Waldegrave printed three texts at White Friars. He started with the third Marprelate tract, the broadsheet *Certain Mineral and Metaphysical Schoolpoints*, and completed the run of about 1,000 copies in late January or early February.[134] These were stored in Henry Sharpe's house in Northampton until the distributor Newman could be summoned; Newman paid one pence each for 700 copies, 500 of which he proceeded to carry back to London.[135] With *Schoolpoints* finished, Penry finally got his wish and Waldegrave printed his *A Viewe of Some Part of Such Publike Wants* in February.[136] After that, by the second half of March, Waldegrave completed the fourth Marprelate tract, *Hay any Work*.[137] At fifty-eight quarto pages, *Hay any Work* is a relatively long text; Henry Sharpe stated that the printing took about three weeks. The total print run was at least 1,000 copies. Waldegrave kept "200 and more" and sent them to his contacts in London; Sharpe received 700 copies for stitching, and tried to keep back 100 of these once he had finished – but was thwarted by Newman, who "did fetch the most of them again" and whom Sharpe accused of being "loth to have any to gayne but himself."[138] The wholesale price was sixpence. During the period that *Hay any Work* was in preparation, Penry moved into Throkmorton's manor in Haseley, about twelve miles from Coventry: from this point on, Throkmorton appears to have become more closely involved in the project's day-to-day operations.[139]

Shortly after *Hay any Work* was completed, Sharpe and Waldegrave met for dinner at Sharpe's in-laws and afterward "walked into the fields" while they discussed work at the "mill" (their code word for the press). According to Sharpe, Waldegrave complained about the conditions under which he had been working the previous two months. John Hales, justifiably nervous, wanted the press out of White Friars as soon as possible, and Waldegrave consequently had been kept "so closely at worke, that for that tyme, he had lyved as in a Prison, and could not have oftentymes warme meate." Waldegrave told Sharpe that he was quitting the project, partly because (he claimed) the preachers he consulted "misliked" the Martinist approach to religious controversy. Soon afterward Waldegrave left for La Rochelle, taking with him the "Dutch letters" with which the first four Marprelate tracts had been printed.[140] With the departure of Waldegrave, the Marprelate press remained silent until John Hodgkins joined the project in mid-July, apparently recruited in London by Humphrey Newman.[141] Hodgkins does not appear in the records of the Stationers' Company, and might have gained his printing experience on the Continent. He was apparently trained as a "saltpeterman," leading Matthew Sutcliffe to comment that he was "a good printer for such saltpeter and gunnepowder workes."[142] But his two assistants, Valentine Simmes and Arthur Thomlin, were both licensed printers.[143] The work was dangerous and illegal, so Hodgkins swore the two to secrecy and promised Simmes twenty pounds a year and Thomlin eight pounds; Hodgkins in addition would provide both with their meat and drink.[144]

Hodgkins met Penry and Throkmorton at Throkmorton's Haseley manor, and learned that the press had been moved to The Priory in Wolston, about six miles southeast of Coventry. The Priory was the residence of Roger Wigston, who later confessed that he had harbored the operation at his wife's request. She admitted that "zeal of reformation in the Church, caused her to give them entertainment," and asked that her husband not be punished. The court was not impressed: one judge thought Wigston "worthy of the greater punishment for giving such a foolish answer, as that he did it at his wife's desire." Wigston "for obeying his wife" was fined 500 marks, and his wife £1,000; both fines were eventually remitted.[145] The morning after the meeting with Throkmorton, Penry and Hodgkins left together and, walking toward Warwick to meet Simmes, found some rolled up sheets of paper lying in the path within "a boult [crossbow] shoote of the house"; these sheets were the first part of the manuscript of the fifth tract, *Theses Martinianae*.[146] The ploy indicates that Throkmorton was still being circumspect, though he did drop by The Priory a few days after the men had started printing, apparently to bring the remainder of the manuscript. While there he deciphered some of the copy for Simmes' benefit, and "asked Hodgkins softly in his eare, whether these examinants [Simmes and Thomlin] were good workmen and able to serve the turn."[147] The printers were installed in The Priory under the guise of embroiderers, and by the end of July 1589 they had finished both *Theses Martinianae* (often known as "Martin Junior") and the sixth tract, *The Just Censure and Reproof of Martin Junior* (often known as "Martin Senior"). Each print run took about a week to complete, and for *Theses Martinianae* at least consisted of 1,500 copies, sold to the distributor Newman for threepence each. When the work was finished, Penry paid Hodgkins five pounds.[148]

While Hodgkins was printing *Just Censure*, he received word that the next Marprelate tract, *More Work for Cooper*, was ready for the press. Soon after, the manuscript was dropped into a room where Hodgkins would find it. "An unhappy drop for poor Hodgkins," Matthew Sutcliffe later wrote, "who if her Majesty had not been gracious to him, had dropped off the gibbet for it."[149] According to Henry Sharpe, Penry and Mrs Wigston entreated Hodgkins to remain at Wolston and print *More Work* there, but Hodgkins had refused, "partly because that presse was nought; and partly for that he had promised his wife to have been in Lancashire three weekes before that time." Hodgkins told his assistants a different story: "for feare of being taken" at Wolston, their employers had decided that "they should depart to another place." In either case, the press was taken apart and hidden at Wolston; Hodgkins already had his own press waiting for him in Lancashire. The printers packed up three pairs of type cases with three "sorts" of letters, ink, and twelve reams of paper, and left that night on the hundred-mile journey to Hodgkins' home in Warrington, Lancashire, midway between Liverpool and Manchester.[150]

Their cart took only about six days to make the trip, arriving on August 4, 1589. As the men were unloading their equipment, one of them dropped a case, spilling some type. Like Jeffs, the farmer who had carted the press to Fawsley, the villagers in Warrington did not recognize the small objects: "Diverse standing by and marvayling what they shold be Hodgkins answered they were shott." For the moment at least, he was believed. But word of the incident, or perhaps even a sample, soon reached someone who knew the difference between lead shot and type. Ten days later, on August 14, agents employed by Henry Stanley, earl of Derby, tracked the men to a rented house in Newton Lane, just outside Manchester, where they seized press, paper, and printed sheets of the book in progress.[151] After questioning by local officials, the three captured printers were brought to London by August 23, and the information they provided, possibly as a result of being put to the rack, marked the beginning of the end of the most famous pamphlet war in Elizabethan England.[152]

The final tract, *The Protestation of Martin Marprelate*, was defiantly published in late September just as the net was closing in on the whole operation. The *Protestation* was printed at Wolston on the original Marprelate press Hodgkins had left behind. Penry wrote to Humphrey Newman with instructions to acquire ink, paper, type, and an "iron frame to print in"; the materials duly arrived, with the help of the reliable Newman and other Northampton friends.[153] The first gathering was set by amateurs, possibly Throkmorton and Penry themselves. The justification is hopelessly crooked, and many words are misspelled and letters reversed because the setters had difficulty creating the mirror image of their text that typesetting requires (see illustration no. 4). The quality of the printing improves markedly with the second gathering: Robert Waldegrave, traveling on his way back from La Rochelle with copies of the books he had printed there, stopped on his way to Scotland to lend a much needed hand.[154] While there is some evidence that Throkmorton wrote additional tracts that employed the Marprelate persona ("Martin's Interim" and "The Crops and Flowers of Bridges Garden"), these texts either were not printed or do not appear to have circulated: *The Protestation* was Martin's final curtain call.[155]

The Marprelate project was a communal operation. Job Throkmorton and John Penry wrote the tracts and Penry managed the press, but many others contributed. Throkmorton and Penry drew heavily on material gathered over the years by John Field from reform-minded contributors from across the country. John Udall was present in the early stages. Producing and circulating the books required several printers and two presses, a stitcher, suppliers of ink and paper, the sympathetic members of four large households, and several wholesale and probably scores of local distributors. Some Martinists, such as Waldegrave, the stitcher Henry Sharpe, and the distributor Humphrey Newman, played well-documented roles. Other names flit more tantalizingly through the extant records. John Bowman and Augustine Maicocke worked for Throkmorton, who addressed them under the *noms de guerre* "Archer" and "May" respectively.[156] Mary Waldegrave, Robert Waldegrave's wife, managed some large-scale distribution. "Master Pigot" of Coventry hosted various Martinists to dinner while the project was in operation. "Mr Grimston" and Richard Holmes, both of Northampton, brought supplies to Wolston after the press was seized in Manchester and hid the materials in the house of "Mistress More." One "Gardiner of Northampton" brought news to Haseley that the house of Penry's in-laws had been searched, and then used Penry's mare to transport 1,600 books (comprising three different titles) to the house of "widow Adams" in Banbury. The completed bundles of *Just Censure* were sent to Lawrence Wood, a tailor "dwelling at the end of Fish Street" in London who was to deliver them to Newman.[157] The community that produced and distributed the Marprelate tracts was a broadly constituted one: it included women as well as men, and its members ranged from prominent local gentry with aristocratic support, to local magistrates, merchants, and clergy, to respectable widows, journeyman workers, and servants. All risked being charged with treason.

THE ANTI-MARTINIST CAMPAIGN, 1588–1590

By early November 1588, Martin's *Epistle* was being sold in communities around London; by the middle of the month, church and state were coordinating efforts to find the press, identify the author, and prevent copies of the tract from circulating. But Martin struck again in late November, and the appearance of the *Epitome* meant that two tracts were now spreading the Martinist message across the country. As the legal investigation dragged on without success into the new year, Elizabethan authorities decided that they needed to engage Martin publicly. In mid-January 1589, Thomas Cooper's *An Admonition to the People of England* launched what would become a protracted anti-Martinist campaign. In its opening stages, the campaign deployed traditional means to disseminate official response and condemnation: the point-by-point rebuttal (Cooper's *Admonition*), the sermon (delivered to one audience and then printed for wider distribution), and the royal proclamation. But the church eventually decided to fight Martin on his own terms and took the unusual step of sponsoring a parallel pamphlet campaign in which hired pens deployed Martin's full stylistic repertoire on behalf of the embattled bishops. Martin in turn taunted his opponents for the undignified depths to which they were willing to descend in their self-defense, particularly once the controversy made its way into the public theatre in the form of stage burlesques.

Over time, the independently outraged added their voices to the fray on behalf of the church. But some contemporaries deplored the polemical tactics of both sides, and these "neutral" commentators articulate some of the broader issues at work in the pamphlet warfare generated by the Marprelate tracts. Martin courted a notoriety that would ensure wide-spread circulation of Presbyterian challenge; implicitly or explicitly, anti-Martinist texts warn readers of the destabilizing, and thereby treasonous, potential of a popularizing polemic in a hierarchical society. This battle between Martin and the anti-Martinists reveals a political world still negotiating the uses and implications of print culture. While the anti-Martinist campaign condemned Martin's attempts to open up the public sphere by fostering popular debate, it did so by appropriating Martin's own polemical mode and pamphlet medium to address the same audience Martin himself had targeted. The disjunction between means and ends worried some contemporaries, who argued that the pamphlets commissioned to defend the church helped legitimize rather than suppress Martinist discursive freedom. Despite these accusations that major components of the campaign were self-contradictory, the polemical tactics and tropes Elizabethan authorities employed to combat the Martinist threat would remain standard weapons against religious and political opposition for much of the following century. On the other side of these debates, however, the Marprelate project would provide several generations of religious and political reformers with an influential model for popularizing oppositional ideas.

Burghley set the official investigation of the Marprelate press in motion with a letter to Whitgift on November 14, 1588. The Queen, Burghley wrote, had been informed of "a lewd and seditious book lately prynted as it should seme in secret manner, and as secretly dispersed by persons of unquiet spyrrites." Martin's *Epistle*, this language implies, was a challenge to good order and social "quietness," the Elizabethan ideal of a political realm free of divisive controversies. Instead, the book aimed to "move a mislyke" of church government by bishops and offered slanderous reports of church officers. Even more fundamentally, the *Epistle* was seditious, setting a "daungerous example" that encouraged others to work in a similarly covert manner to "subvert all other kyndes of Government under hir Majesties charg, both in the church and commen weale." Similar anxieties would reappear in the proclamation the Queen issued a few months later and repeatedly in subsequent anti-Martinist texts: in a culture that conceived all authority as interdependent, a threat to one form of authority threatened the entire network. Whitgift was therefore instructed to initiate a search for the authors and their accomplices, using "all privy meanes, by force of your Commission ecclesiasticall or otherwise" to ensure that all those involved in the project were speedily apprehended and committed.[158]

Whitgift instituted a nationwide hunt for the Martinist press, and the narrative of the remaining Marprelate tracts was played out against a backdrop of informers, raids, disguises, codenames, manuscripts left surreptitiously under hedges, conversations in the middle of fields, and ever closer pursuit as the secret press was carted from one house to another. A letter sent by high commission to chapter officials of Canterbury Cathedral in mid-December provides a glimpse of the investigation as it was conducted at the local level.[159] Condemning the tracts as seditious and "dangerous to the present state of this realme," the high commissioners authorized officials to search persons, houses, shops, or cellars for the pamphlets, and to bring in for questioning anyone suspected of involvement in their production or distribution. If copies of the book were found, they were to be forwarded to Lambeth Palace. Anyone brought in for questioning should be administered the oath *ex officio* and required to answer all questions deemed "most convenient and effectuall for the openyng and boltinge owte of the truthe." Anyone refusing to answer questions was to be imprisoned until the high commissioners sent further instructions. If anyone denied the official searchers (pursuivants) access to their house, the searcher was authorized to take a constable along to compel compliance. Finally, church officials were given authority, in the Queen's name, to require cooperation from all civil officials (mayors, bailiffs, sheriffs, constables): those who refused to help would "answer the contrary at theyr perilles." Similar letters would have been sent to every cathedral chapter in the country.

While local officials were searching cellars and questioning suspects, Thomas Cooper, bishop of Winchester, was preparing the first printed response to the tracts. While largely Cooper's own work, *An Admonition to the People of England* includes responses from five other bishops, including John Whitgift, all attempting to clear their names from Martin's "untruethes, slaunders, reproches, raylinges, revilings, scoffings, and other untemperate speeches" (35). But in addition to these engagements with specific accusations, the *Admonition* reframes Martin's own foundational narrative of patriotic piety as one of treasonous railing against all forms of order. Cooper himself reminds readers of the recently averted threat of the Spanish Armada, and contrasts the pious gratitude of those loyal to the crown with Martin's "slaunderous Pamphlets fresh from the Presse, against the best of the Church of England ... not giving prayse to God, but scoffing, mocking, rayling, and depraving the lives and doings of Bishoppes" (34). He concludes with the warning that, "if this outragious spirit of boldenesse be not stopped speedily, I feare he wil prove himselfe to bee, not onely *Mar-prelate*, but *Mar-prince, Mar-state, Mar-lawe, Mar-magistrate*, and all together, until he bring it to an Anabaptisticall equalitie and communitie" (36). Cooper's reading of Martinist style as a threat not only to the dignity of libelled bishops, but ultimately also to the country's fundamental religious, political, legal, and social structures, would become the core message of the anti-Martinist campaign.

That the highest church officials in the land felt compelled to respond publicly to Martin's charges reveals how seriously both the work and the medium of the attack were taken: Elizabethan print culture remained sufficiently small-scale to lend some authority to any printed text. A dignified silence appears not to have been an option once accusations against the bishops had been circulated in print. John Aylmer, for one, might have been better advised to restrict himself to a general condemnation of Martin's text rather than offering detailed, magisterial, and usually self-implicating justifications of his behavior in Martin's unflattering stories. While Aylmer in particular struggled to distinguish banter from serious charges, his heavy-handed literalism signals a general difficulty the church had in learning to *read* Martin's text. These officials, perfectly comfortable with the weapons of scripture, tradition, and authority, were less prepared for the sharper edge of satire and the *ad hominem* thrust. In fact, the *Admonition* played right into Martin's hand by providing him with a great deal of new fodder for polemical anecdote as well as an irresistible new target: Cooper himself would become "the Tubtrimmer of Winchester" throughout the tracts that followed. The object of Martin's attack had been to push discussion of controverted issues into the public realm, and his episcopal opponents appeared only too eager to oblige him.

In mid-February 1589, a few weeks after the publication of Cooper's *Admonition*, the Queen issued *A Proclamation against Certaine Seditious and Schismatical Bookes and Libels*. While the proclamation does not name

Marprelate, the tracts are clearly its target: an official document in the Canterbury city archives lists a payment to a pursuivant for delivering copies of the proclamation "for Martin Marprelate."[160] The Queen describes the consequences of the three Marprelate tracts that had appeared so far in language that exposes the concerns fueling the archbishop's search for the press. These "schismatical and seditious books, defamatory libels, and other fantastical writings" tended ultimately to the "abridging, or rather to the overthrow, of her highness' lawful prerogative allowed by God's law and established by the laws of the realm."[161] In other words, to push for innovation in church government was to call into question the legal foundations of monarchical sovereignty, a version of the slippery slope argument that James I, drawing on his experience in Presbyterian Scotland, would later summarize as "No Bishop, no King."[162] To Elizabeth, as to James and Charles after her, episcopacy was the natural corollary of monarchy, whereas the more republican polity of Presbyterianism was by nature antipathetic to rule by a queen or king. Elizabeth warned James about the political dangers of Presbyterianism in a private letter in July 1590, advising her fellow monarch to "stop the mouths or make shorter the tongues of such ministers" lest they "stuff your realm with venom."[163] The proclamation furthermore associates the liberties of language in the tracts with the political liberties they threaten. In "railing sort and beyond the bounds of all good humanity," Martin presents "matters notoriously untrue, and slanderous" against "the persons of the bishops and others placed in authority ecclesiastical under her highness by her authority."[164] Elizabeth and her courtiers were experts in constructing images of authority, and by calling attention to what is most characteristic of Martin's approach – his attack on the bishops' "persons" as well as on their office – the proclamation reveals their awareness of how vulnerable these images were to deflation. Other readers of the tracts drew similarly worrying conclusions. When Sir Richard Knightley (in whose house the *Epitome* was printed) sent copies of the first three pamphlets to Sir Edward Seymour, earl of Hertford, he received a message in return that spoke to the concerns of the aristocracy with the same analogical argument that James would invoke at Hampton Court: "as they shoote at Bishopps now," the earl warned his brother-in-law, "so will they doe at the Nobilitie also, if they be suffred."[165]

In early March, Richard Bancroft published *A Sermon Preached at Paules Crosse*, an expanded version of an anti-Martinist sermon he had delivered on February 9, the first Sunday of the 1589 parliament. Located in the churchyard of St. Paul's Cathedral, Paul's Cross was the traditional site for the dissemination of the official line on political and religious issues: Bancroft was delivering a warning message to the newly assembled MPs as well as to the broader London public. Later bishop of London and archbishop of Canterbury, Bancroft was at the time personal chaplain to Sir Christopher Hatton and a canon at Westminster with a rising reputation for assertive response to those who challenged church authority. Beginning with the injunction from 1 John 4:1, "beleeve not every spirit, but trie the spirits whether they be of God," Bancroft reduces Martin's platform to a desire that men should be able "to do as they list." But since "It falleth not within the compas of everie mans understanding to determine and judge in matters of religion," Bancroft urges the necessity of obedience to tradition and the established order.[166] Similarly conventional arguments would appear in anti-Martinist sermons delivered at Paul's Cross and elsewhere over the next two years.[167] But, more influentially, Bancroft follows the lead of John Whitgift and John Bridges by defending the scriptural basis of episcopacy against his Presbyterian opponents by tracing the office back to apostolic times, defending episcopacy *jure divino*. Along with other conformist writers, such as Hadrian Saravia and Matthew Sutcliffe, Bancroft would extend this line of argument in the early 1590s, giving Marprelate an ironic role in the expanded claims of episcopal authority that marked the late Elizabethan and Jacobean church.[168]

Bancroft was quicker than his older colleagues in the church to see that the rules of engagement were changing. He had been preparing for the appearance of something like the Marprelate attack since the early 1580s, when he compiled *Certen Slaunderous Speeches against the Present Estate of the Church of England Published to the People by the Precisians*, a manuscript brief that refuted reformist texts and had probably won the attention of the then newly appointed Whitgift.[169] Developing the arguments he would later employ against Martin, Bancroft links the Separatist platform with various ancient heresies, and then tars Presbyterians ("Precisians") with the same brush. Separatists and Presbyterians alike, he asserts, advocated platforms that were at heart seditious; most worryingly, as his title notes, their books were "published to the people." Bancroft recognized that ecclesiological debate was beginning to enter the public realm, and he believed that official responses needed to reach the same audience. When the Marprelate tracts appeared a few years later, Bancroft consequently acted on this insight and suggested that Martin be fought with his own weapons. A testimonial Whitgift wrote in 1597 when Bancroft was being considered for the bishopric of London outlines his role in the anti-Martinist campaign. According to Whitgift, Bancroft was "the first detecter of Martin Mar-Prelates presse and books: where and by whom they were printed," and by "his advise that course was taken which did principally stoppe Martin and his fellowes mouthes: viz to have them aunswered after theyr owne vayne in writing."[170] Whitgift had appointed Bancroft his personal chaplain in 1592 and consequently, as Patrick Collinson points out, had "a motive for exaggerating the services of his candidate." But other evidence links Bancroft with the prosecution of the Martinists, and the efforts to suppress Martin reflect the aggressiveness with which Bancroft would conduct his life-long pursuit of uniformity in the church.[171]

While no evidence is extant concerning Bancroft's involvement with any given anti-Martinist text, there seems little doubt that major elements of the campaign were officially organized and sanctioned. More than twenty explicitly anti-Martinist works survive from the period during which the tracts were being published, or shortly afterward.[172] Not all were part of the official response: independent productions probably include works such as A. L., *Antimartinus* (1589), the only anti-Martinist work not in English; a set of printed Cambridge Act verses *c.* 1589;[173] three pamphlets by Leonard Wright, *A Summons for Sleepers* (1589), *The Hunting of Antichrist* (1589), and *A Friendly Admonition to Martine Marprelate, and his Mates* (1590); Tobias Bland, *A Baite for Momus* (1589); Anthony Marten, *A Reconciliation of all the Pastors and Cleargy of this Church of England* (1590); and *Asinus Onustus: The Asse Overladen* (1642), a text (its title page claims) presented in manuscript to the Queen in July 1589. But Whitgift's testimonial on Bancroft's behalf implies that many of the remaining anti-Martinist texts, those that deploy a recognizably Martinist style, were published with some measure of official encouragement.

Anonymous rhymesters were first off the mark, with two pamphlets featuring anti-Martinist verse appearing in early summer 1589: *Mar-Martine*, a collection attributed to a collaboration between John Lyly and Thomas Nashe; and *A Whip for an Ape: or Martin Displaied*, also published as *Rythmes against Martin Marre-prelate*, attributed to Lyly working alone.[174] A couplet in the opening poem of *Mar-Martine* borrows a key line from Cooper's *Admonition* to summarize the collection's polemical drift: "*Martine* the merry, who now is *Mar-prelate*, / Will prove madde *Martine*, and *Martine* mar-the-state." *Mar-Martine* justifies its literary crudity by invoking Martin's own strategy of mockingly appropriate decorum: "My rithme shall be as dogrell, as unlearned is thy prose." The collection supplements its downmarket style with its use of such "popular" literary vehicles as the ballad stanza and the fourteener line, and with its imitation of Martin's aggressively colloquial voices: one poem is composed in an unevenly sustained Scots dialect (perhaps as a dig at Martin's

Presbyterian genealogy), and others employ a pastiche of phrases used by Martin's rustic persona. On the whole, the text's power of satirical invention lags well before it reaches the end of its allotted single sheet of four quarto leaves. As if to shift responsibility for the poor quality of verse on offer, *Mar-Martine* blames the Marprelate tracts for lowering the bar and introducing theatrical license, here associated with the comic actor Richard Tarleton, into serious debate: "These tinkers termes, and barbers jestes first *Tarleton* on the stage, / Then *Martin* in his bookes of lies, hath put in every page."[175] *A Whip for an Ape* takes this argument a step further, foregrounding the theatricality of Martin's self-presentation with an extended metaphor in which Martin plays the role of performing ape, for whom "Martin" had been a traditional name.[176] The poem draws attention to Martin's pseudonymity – "A Dizard late skipt out upon our Stage; / But in a sacke, that no man might him see" – then offers a series of similarities between Martin and his animal namesake. The emphasis, to be repeated throughout the anti-Martinist campaign, is on the gap between the matter under discussion and the style in which Martin has handled it: "But *Martin*, why in matters of such waight / Doest thou thus play the Dawe and dancing foole?"[177] Martin presented himself as participating in an honorable tradition of popular complaint; *A Whip for an Ape* responds by giving him an alternative genealogy as stage clown, the successor not of Piers Ploughman but of the recently deceased Tarleton or of the famous fool John Scoggin, thought in the period to have been a friend of Chaucer's.[178] The repeated identification of Martin with Tarleton, who was famous for his extemporized comic routines, responds to the improvised quality of Martin's style and reveals the concern generated by his deliberate appeal to popular taste through theatrical techniques.

Six anti-Martinist prose satires were published in 1589–90: Marphoreus, *Martins Months Minde* (1589), *Pappe with an Hatchet* (1589), Cutbert Curry-Knave, *An Almond for a Parrat* (1590), and three tracts by Pasquill, *A Countercuffe Given to Martin Junior* (1589), *The Returne of the Renowned Cavaliero Pasquill of England* (1589), and *The First Parte of Pasquils Apologie* (1590). Their authorship remains unclear. *Pappe with an Hatchet* is probably by John Lyly and *Almond for a Parrat* is probably by Thomas Nashe; Nashe, Robert Greene, and Anthony Munday have been speculatively associated with the other four.[179] The prevailing ethos of these works tends toward literary one-upmanship, as if their authors were competing not only with Martin but also with one another to devise the most imaginative insults, scatological metaphors, or witty comparisons. *An Almond for a Parrat* is probably the most successful in literary terms, as an appropriation of Martin's style and voice. But the most polemically effective is probably the one least discussed by literary critics: *Martins Months Minde* makes good use of a fictive frame built around the conventions of the deathbed, providing the reader with the narrative of Martin's last days, his speeches of repentance, the results of the autopsy, his funeral, last will, and epitaphs. As a group, these texts are stylistically and linguistically interesting, even virtuoso on occasion, though rather opaque in their allusiveness and learned in their wit. But the general problem with much of the "Martinizing" anti-Martinist prose is that style is often an end in itself, and the forced relentlessness of the abuse gets tiresome – even, at times, to the writers themselves. In *Pappe with an Hatchet*, for example, John Lyly appears frustrated with the conventions of scurrility the attack required: after slips into serious response, he pulls himself back into polemical character with lines such as "Hollow there, give me the beard I wore yesterday," or "A fine period; but I cannot continue this stile." Lyly also recognized that his borrowed manner might make readers uneasy and asked them to blame Martin for any "bad tearmes" they might find in his text.[180] Other anti-Martinist writers had fewer qualms: given official sanction to publish in a language that matched Martin's, these polemical mercenaries clearly relished the opportunity. Nashe, for example, warns the readers of *An Almond for a Parrat* to "catch not the hicket with laughing" and appropriates for himself the theatrical and jest-book genealogy his colleagues had accorded Martin by dedicating his own contribution to the comic actor William Kemp, "Jestmonger and Vice-gerent generall to the Ghost of Dicke Tarlton."[181]

As Whitgift's glowing testimonial for Bancroft indicates, by the later 1590s the anti-Martinist strategy appears to have been thought a success in official circles.[182] Lyly, however, was not the only contemporary to sense a problem with the campaign. In a 1592 sermon at Paul's Cross, Robert Temple deplored Martin's "spirite rather of scorne and slaunder, then learninge and love." But, he continued, "shall I saye my conscience, and speake indifferentlye? Fie for shame both *Martin* and *Antemartin*."[183] While writers such as Francis Bacon and Gabriel Harvey saw political dangers in the decision to answer Martin in his own manner (see below, lxxi–lxxiii), Lyly and Temple register a more generalized uneasiness about a campaign that claimed the moral high ground on issues of decorum in texts that deployed rhetorical strategies identical to those they denounced. The slippage consequent to Bancroft's approach to Martinist challenge is best exemplified by the appearance of anti-Martinist burlesques on the public stage. Throughout the summer of 1589, notes *Martins Months Minde*, "everie stage Plaier made a jest of him, and put him cleane out of countenance" (E4r). Anti-Martinist theatre was indeed ubiquitous over these months: the Queen's Men, the Lord Strange's Men, the Lord Admiral's Men, and Paul's Boys all appear to have contributed to the campaign.[184] Descriptions of these performances are all that remain.[185] While some elements in these contemporary accounts are themselves polemical or metaphoric, and probably do not record what actually happened on stage, on the whole these performances appear to have drawn on the conventions of such traditional genres as the beast fable and the morality play. Furthermore, they assume widespread awareness of the Martinist challenge: an audience first needs to know about the polemical Martin before it can make sense of a character in an ape mask scratching Dame Divinity in the face.[186] Apprehension eventually spread over the bawdiness of these performances, however, and in November 1589 they were banned, in their own right, for treating matters "unfytt and undecent to be handled in playes, both for Divinite and State."[187] Those involved in the Marprelate project assumed that anti-Martinist theatre was officially initiated and supported, despite the state's own policies that forbade matters of religion from the stage; many subsequent commentators share this assumption.[188] But the evidence for the connection is tenuous. Whitgift praises Bancroft only for having the Martinists "aunswered after theyr owne vayne in writinge," a formulation that could be read as omitting theatrical performance, and the documents connected with the November ban voice strong disapproval. Anti-Martinist theater seems just as likely to have been independent of the official campaign, a product more of theatrical enterprise than episcopal propaganda – though the Elizabethan government was not above officially condemning what it unofficially supported. John Lyly, who wrote for Paul's Boys, regretted the government's decision and implied that more substantial theatrical texts were under preparation: "Would those Comedies might be allowed to be plaid that are pend, and then I am sure he [Martin] would be decyphered, and so perhaps discouraged."[189]

Whether verse, prose, or performance, official or unofficial, anti-Martinist texts all work with the political and social arguments established by Cooper's *Admonition*, the Queen's proclamation, and Bancroft's sermon. Most of these lines of response were in some degree traditional, in that they had been used in England against reformers long before Martin Marprelate appeared on the scene. But to meet the challenge of what contemporaries recognized as the radical culmination of Presbyterian rhetoric, these countering measures were given unusually strong formulations,

formulations that would dominate defenses of the church through to the 1640s and survive in one form or another to the end of the seventeenth century.[190] At the root of all these anti-Martinist tropes was the argument that any challenge to the authority of the church was fundamentally treasonous. From the earliest official responses to Martin to the documents compiled for the 1591 trials of the Presbyterian leadership, the government used the Marprelate tracts to construct an image of Presbyterianism as a sect given to violence and revolution. At the trial of those accused of harboring the press, officials charged that the tracts "tended to the ruin of the whole state, next to the abolishing of all ecclesiastical government, to the removing of all manner of service, the overthrow of laws."[191] The court of high commission asked the distributor Humphrey Newman to confess that Martin aimed "not only against her majestie, her lawes, parlamentes and godly government: But also against sundrie in authoritie, as well spirituall as temporall under her majestie tendinge to the erecting of [a] new forme of government contrarie to her majesties supremacie, crowen, regallitie, lawes and statutes."[192] One of the Star Chamber briefs for the 1591 trials cites "Martin" for the charge that "One of our late libellers braggeth of an hundreth thousand handes: & wisheth the Parlement to bring in this Refourmation, though it bee by with-standinge her Queenes majestie."[193] If the forms of church government were not divinely ordained but subject to the discretion of the magistrate, ran this argument, then ecclesiological challenges were simultaneously challenges to the monarch's prerogative powers. According to *An Almond for a Parrat*, Martin was celebrated on the continent for attempting what "neither the Pope by his Seminaries, Philip by his power, nor all the holy League by their underhand practises and policies could at any time effect": to draw the English away from their allegiance to their sovereign. Lyly rhymes the charge concisely in *A Whip for an Ape*: "Yes, he that now saith, Why should Bishops bee? / Will next crie out, Why Kings? The Saincts are free."[194] Anti-Martinist writers consistently paint the Presbyterian challenge to episcopacy as the first step in a selfish elevation of the individual over all external forms of authority, including the monarch from whom that authority ultimately derived.

The standard Presbyterian response to this argument was that if the forms of church government prescribed by scripture were immutable and binding, as they believed, then efforts to restore the church to its divinely ordained model in no way impinged on the legitimate powers of the state. Martin consequently argues throughout the tracts that the bishops, not the reformers, were the real usurpers of royal power. Those involved in the Martinist project were not the only ones to view the anti-Martinist campaign as a self-serving effort to use the threat of treason as a pretext for an aggressive assertion of episcopal authority. Sir Francis Knollys, the Queen's cousin, drew the same conclusion by reading the work of John Bridges and Richard Bancroft.[195] Knollys prepared several warning reports on the subject for Burghley, and in September 1589 he solicited expert opinion on Bancroft's Paul's Cross sermon from the scholar John Rainolds. He also asked Rainolds for his thoughts on Martin, and Rainolds' response likely reflected the feelings of other contemporaries about the fine line that divided argument for reform from treason: "Touching Martin; if any man behave him selfe otherwise then in discretion and charitie he ought: lett the blame fall, where the fawte is; I defend him not. But if by the way he utter a truth mingled with whatsoever else: it is no reason that that, which is of God, should be condemned for that, which is of man."[196] Rainolds' letter would become an important text for seventeenth-century critics of divine right episcopacy.[197]

Presbyterian arguments on this issue, however, were seriously compromised by the juxtaposition of the Marprelate attack with the attempted invasion by the Spanish Armada. In his opening oration at the 1589 parliament, Christopher Hatton surveyed the enemies of England, beginning with the pope and the Spanish king. But in an implicit reference to the Marprelate tracts, he introduced the specter of native Protestants "of latter daies risen up," men "of a verie intemperate humour" who "do greatlie deprave the present estate and reformacion of religion." While the Queen expected such railing from the Catholic opposition, he reported, she grieved to find her own subjects joining them in slandering the church. Hatton consequently warned the assembled members that their sovereign had commanded them not to "so much as once meddle with anie such matters or causes of religion, except it be to bridle all those, whether papists or puritanes, which are therewithall discontented."[198] Anti-Martinist writers exploited this officially sanctioned connection, and the representation of puritan agitation and Catholic machination as equally dangerous to the state continued as a polemical commonplace throughout the following century.

Some Catholic controversialists attempted to turn the threat of puritanism to their advantage. In October 1591, the Queen established commissions against seminary priests and Jesuits.[199] The antiquary Richard Verstegan argued in response that the "cause of the troubles" the Queen hoped to remedy was not the loyal and peaceful Catholics: the "Martinistes or Puritans," he writes, were "much more dangerous for domistical broyles, then the Spaniardes for open warres," citing both Martinist and anti-Martinist

works to illustrate the point.[200] But to English officials, the justice of
Hatton's comparison was confirmed by evidence of Catholic approval of
Martin supplied by English agents on the continent. In April 1591, Sir
Thomas Heneage received news of a Catholic plot to burn the naval
shipping moored at Chatham; among the "publicke matters" the inform-
ant discussed with his Catholic contact, a man named Howson, was the
"sucsese the new seckt of martinists had in England, which sayd Howson
was a thinge raysed by god to win manye to the catholicke faythe."[201]
During an examination in 1592, the Jesuit George Dingley (alias Thomas
Christopher, alias James Young) claimed that English Catholics abroad
knew of the tracts, and that "the muttering of the martinists they gretlye
rejoysed translating that boke into spanishe & presenting it unto the king
[Philip II] judging by the hote woordes viz of an C [hundred] thousand
fystes about ther eares that were uttryd in the boke, that shortlye some
uprore wold be movyd by the factyon." A marginal note in a different hand
summarized the danger: "hope of contencion by [i.e. as a result of] the
marttynistes."[202] Some officials were exploiting for their own ends the
possibility of Catholic approval of Martin even before the Marprelate press
had been discovered. In June 1589, Thomas Phelippes, the co-ordinator of
English agents abroad, supplied one of his spies with suggestions for a
credential-establishing letter to a Catholic contact. Among the tidbits of
intelligence he provides was that "the division betwene the protestants &
puritanes is no other than [it] hath bene a long time ... that which latelye
hath bene bruted [concerned] the boke which came forth in the name of
martine marprelate." A similar letter to the same agent for use with a
different contact notes that Marprelate is "in every mans mouth" and that
"a boke in rime called marmartin published then sold in every booke
shoppe was it seemeth to be *cum privilegio.*"[203] These letters confidently
invoke "Martin Marprelate" as if there were no doubt that English
Catholics in France would have heard of him. Phelippes in fact appears
to be using the Martinist attack as a tool with which to gain the confidence
of Catholic conspirators: England, the letters imply, *is* weak and self-
divided. One question is the extent to which Phelippes and others in the
government actually thought this. Do they inform their contacts of genuine official anxieties in order to hear about Catholic plots initiated in
consequence of the encouraging news, or were they using the controversy
as a ploy to spread disinformation – or something in between? In any case,
the Marprelate tracts offered a tidy synecdoche for the "puritan" cause. In
the wake of the anti-Martinist campaign, Martin became widely identified,
even on the continent, as the epitome of domestic opposition, the

summarizing statement of all who, as Phelippes suggests in the first letter cited above, "finde fault with the church."

Anti-reform polemic associated Catholics and Presbyterians as types of the bad subject. Both, it was argued, owed primary allegiance to a power other than the monarch: the pope on the one hand, a self-serving individual conscience on the other. But Presbyterians were also linked with enemies on the other end of the religious spectrum: accusations of Anabaptism provided the reform movement with an appropriately frightening myth of origin. Thomas Cooper's warning in the *Admonition* concerning the Anabaptists and their leveling principles was frequently repeated in subsequent anti-Martinist writing. Popularly represented as advocating a radical overthrow of all custom, the Anabaptists served as reminders that even in times of rapid social and political change, certain boundaries of behavior should remain inviolate.[204] In the context of English reform, fearmongering over Anabaptist tendencies crystallized anxieties about the egalitarian implications of Presbyterian ecclesiology. Matthew Sutcliffe, for example, conjures up the ghosts of Münster to counter any sympathetic feelings a reader may have about the reformers' willingness to solicit popular participation in decisions concerning the church: "the precedents of the Anabaptists, doe teach us what an unbrideled thing the people is, where they take the sword to worke reformation with."[205] Other writers invoke the comparison in such a way as to make explicit the appeal to economic self-interest that underlay the trope. In his Paul's Cross sermon, Richard Bancroft linked Anabaptist claims for equality with the accusation that English reformers wanted to challenge lay impropriations, asking his audience, "especially to you of the richest . . . how you like this doctrine."[206] Where the link with Catholicism worked to make suspect Presbyterian professions of loyalty, the link with Anabaptism provided a suitably threatening image of the inevitable conclusion to any call for reform.

Through allusion and association, the anti-Martinist campaign sought to reveal Martin in his true colors: far from being a politically benign purification of the church, Presbyterianism was a treasonous attack on both the foundations of the country and the economic rights of the (monied) individual. Recurrent attacks on the scholarship of Presbyterian polemic clinched the argument by revealing that at the root of reform lay ignorance. Learning "hath lost almost all reputation, while these unlearned and unwise consistorians declame against learning, and seeke no further divinitic, then *Calvins* and *Bezaes* and Junius his glosses and commentarics," Sutcliffe complained. According to *Martins Months Minde*, reformers lacked Latin and "would correct *Magnificat*, not knowing *Quid significat*."

An Almond for a Parrat mocked "Profound *Cliffe*, the ecclesiasticall cobler," a man Martin had named as a "godly" witness to episcopal mendacity, and condemned in general the reform movement's indiscriminate call for preaching: "The blinde, the halt, or the lame, or any serves the turn with them, so he hath not on a cloake with sleves, or a cap of the university cut."[207] Of course, reformers had been levelling similar charges against the church for decades, especially against its representatives at the parish level. In the early 1580s, the charge that the church was ordaining ignorant men as part of its effort to oust godly ministers played a central role in the "Abstract" controversy between Richard Cosin and Dudley Fenner.[208] The Presbyterian "Survey of the Ministry" of 1586 was in part an attempt to quantify and draw attention to the numbers of "unlearned" or otherwise unqualified ministers. On both sides, arguments about education recapitulate the more general conflict between the claims of the individual interpreter and the claims of institutional tradition. The concept of the priesthood of all believers challenged hierarchy, not only that of the church but also, by analogy, that of the body politic. Martin Marprelate had set new precedents for the extent to which conventions of discourse could be violated; the anti-Martinist response consequently challenged the authority of all reform utterance. The charge that reformers sought to elevate the uneducated to the ministry functioned as shorthand for their subversive desire to bypass the traditions on which the major institutions of the country were founded.

The Martinists responded to the work of Bancroft's hired pens throughout the last four Marprelate tracts, taking advantage of the opportunity the campaign presented to return the arguments of decorum with which they had been attacked. But they were not alone in their objections to the strategies the anti-Martinists employed: the style of the controversy generated works that objected to the tactics of both Marprelate and the church. *A Myrror for Martinists* (1590), for example, criticized both "the late *Martine* libellers" and their "repliers, who notwithstanding they have chosen the better part, yet handle it not so charitably and modestly as it requireth." *Marre Mar-Martin* (1589?) went further by arguing that the accusations of treason leveled by both sides masked the real danger: "Traitor, no traitor, here's such traitors striving, / That *Romish* traitors now are set a thriving."[209] *Marre Mar-Martin*'s fear for the future of religion indicated that he was not indifferent to established polity. What unites the works of these "neutral" commentators is disapproval not of church government by bishops but of the tactics the hierarchy adopted in its defense: they regret the unexpected direction that discussion of serious issues had taken. Richard Harvey's *Plaine Percevall the Peace-Maker of England* (1590) by no means defends Martin: "Thy foming mealy mouth betokeneth stomacke, and young unbridled fits, for all that fatherly countenance" (4). But he is equally hard on the anti-Martinists, those "Whip Johns, and Whip Jackes: not forgetting the Cavaliero Pasquill, or the Cooke Ruffian, that drest a dish for Martins diet, Marforius and all Cutting Hufsnufs, Roisters, and the residew of light fingred younkers, which make every word a blow, and every booke a bobbe" (A2r). Harvey blamed Martin's audacity of style – "a certaine *Pipe of Pistling*" (13) – for luring his confuters into imitating his manner in their desire for revenge. But Harvey himself soon succumbed to the tracts' colloquial appeal, adopting Martin's rustic persona and homespun metaphors in his own contribution.

In a work written in 1589 but not published until 1593, Gabriel Harvey, Richard's brother, offers a more scholarly version of the neutralist position. Attacking Lyly as the author of *Pappe with an Hatchet*, he argues that it were better to confute levity with gravity, "ridiculous Martin with reverend Cooper," than enlist in the defense of the church this "professed jester, a Hick-scorner, a scoff-maister, a playmunger, an Interluder; once the soile of Oxford, now the stale of London, and ever the Apesclogg of the presse." Harvey denounces Lyly's "alehouse and tinkerly stuffe," pointedly noting the inappropriateness of such "rancke scurrility" in discussion of ecclesiastical causes. But Harvey's argument appeals to more than decorum. In both the *Advertisement* and *Pierces Supererogation* (1593), the attack on Nashe in which the *Advertisement* was published, Harvey sets anti-Martinist prose by Lyly and Nashe against a range of recent English and continental publication, contrasting his opponents' railing wit with their contemporaries' more substantial literary, scholarly, scientific, and devotional achievements. The implied critique is partly the insider's snide refusal to be impressed by the efforts of a fellow stylist: "the finest wittes," he remarks, "preferre the loosest period in M. Ascham, or Sir Philip Sidney, before the tricksiest page in Euphues, or Pap-hatchet." But Harvey also wants to argue that this appropriation of Martin Marprelate's disorderly language threatened to displace not only quality literature but also the fundamentals of civil discourse on which society rested. "If the world should applaude to such roisterdoisterly Vanity," he warns, "what good could grow of it, but to make every man madbrayned, and desperate; but a generall contempt of all good order, in Saying, or Doing; but an Universal Topsy-turvey?" As for Martin, Harvey takes his own advice and offers a moderate and scholarly rebuttal of what he saw as the fundamental weaknesses of the Presbyterian cause. His central argument is that the creation of a "perfect Ecclesiasticall Discipline, or autentique Pollicy of the Church" was not the work of one pamphlet or one man. Arguing along lines later developed by Richard Hooker in his *Lawes of Ecclesiasticall Politie* (1593), Harvey insists that government is a long-term, negotiated process that works within the given social and political structures of a state. Harvey's prevailing vision is corporate rather than individual: given a monarchical framework, he concludes, there could be no further reformation in England without "an Upsy-downe" in political structure.[210]

Attacks on Thomas Nashe by both of the Harvey brothers led to the Harvey–Nashe quarrel, a complex polemical exchange that continued the debate generated by the Marprelate controversy concerning the social uses of print. The Harveys, arguing for the role of print culture in promoting good learning and proper behavior, accused Nashe of taking "uppon him in civill learning, as *Martin* doth in religion, peremptorily censuring his betters at pleasure"[211] But of all the contemporary responses the Marprelate tracts generated, the most sophisticated analysis of the controversy is a government brief written by Francis Bacon, *An Advertisement Touching the Controversies of the Church of England* (c. 1589–90).[212] Reading polemic with an empiricist's eye for constituent causes, Bacon concludes that the central problem was neither theology nor ecclesiology, but the language in which the debate had been conducted. He begins his analysis by denouncing the theatrical turn the controversy had taken: "it is more than time that there were an end and surseance made of this immodest and deformed manner of writing lately entertained, whereby matters of religion are handled in the style of the stage." While he deplores Martin's undignified tendency "to turn religion into a comedy or satire," he finds the strategy of lowering the response to Martin's level equally misguided. Bacon did not accept the official line that the reformers were simply a turbulent faction. He recognized the need for the church to compromise, to assimilate what was good in the reformers – their faith – and to remedy or at least admit its own failings, which he itemizes with some daring: "The wrongs of them which are possessed of the government of the church towards the other, may hardly be dissembled or excused." The sanctioned pamphlets, Bacon consequently argues, deserved suppression just as much as the works they attacked.[213]

Foreshadowing the methodological concerns he would later develop in his philosophical and scientific writings, Bacon analyzes the psychology of controversy to discover the mistakes against reason typically found in "church controversies." While these included the inappropriate use of foreign models, *ad hominem* attacks, and "the undue and inconvenient propounding, publishing, and debating of the controversies," the primary source of difficulty lay in human nature. The accident of personality, not reason, was the prime mover in these debates. Neither side lacked those who sought authority over the opinions of others, nor those who were easily led. Like Harvey, Bacon consequently seems less concerned with the validity of the arguments offered by either side than with stability and social harmony. As Julian Martin points out, Bacon viewed the debate from the essentially secular perspective of the statesman: his "arguments imply that the Church government was legitimate because it was a *part* of the royal machinery of governance."[214] Given these concerns, Bacon was well equipped to see beyond the ecclesiological implications of the Martinist program. His emphasis is on the politics of style, and his message to the state is that the freeing up of polemical language, this "strange abuse of antics and pasquils," represented a danger that the state's own campaign was helping to legitimate rather than suppress. Bacon realized that printed controversy tended to become self-perpetuating, and the stir caused by the Marprelate project had revealed how quickly these controversies could become widely public matters. A colloquial, popular polemic – a polemic that used the language of the stage – could only help speed up this diffusion. The style of both Marprelate and the anti-Martinists reached out to a more broadly constituted audience than had been the norm for ecclesiological debate, and Bacon was no egalitarian: "whatsoever be pretended, the people is no meet judge nor arbitrator, but rather the quiet, moderate, and private assemblies and conferences of the learned."[215]

Martinist and anti-Martinist works participated in a complex dialogue. The Marprelate project probably did not begin with a plan for a grand narrative spread over eight or more publications; the entire campaign might have ended with the second tract, the *Epitome*, if Thomas Cooper had not provided the irresistible fresh fodder of the *Admonition*. Each successive work consequently shaped ensuing publication on the opposing side, both in terms of argument, as they alternated efforts to rebut individual charges and to take advantage of rhetorical slips, and in terms of framing strategies, as they played on and developed the fictive tactics adopted by one another. Martinism and anti-Martinism are collaborative discourses, and not only because both are products of communities acting on shared beliefs. In a real sense, they are also products of one another. What came out of this paper skirmish were not new ideas about the ideal organization of the church but new ways of presenting those ideas to a public increasingly recognized as an entity that could be addressed in print.

The polemical strategies developed by Martinist and anti-Martinist alike while competing for this audience subsequently helped shape pamphlet wars through the next century.

MARTINISM AND ANTI-MARTINISM, 1590–1700

As far as most Elizabethans were concerned, the Marprelate tracts were written on behalf of a losing cause. Over the winter of 1589–90, the investigation of the project broadened into a judicial crackdown on the entire reform movement; nine leading Presbyterian ministers, including Thomas Cartwright, were eventually imprisoned and subjected to lengthy proceedings in high commission and Star Chamber. Officially, their trials ended in legal stalemate. But unofficially, the ministers and the program they represented were, in Patrick Collinson's words, "worn down and all but defeated," and by the middle of the decade organized Presbyterianism had collapsed.[216] Widespread disapproval of Martinism, even among fellow reformers, likely contributed to the movement's decline. Writing in 1602, the puritan divine Josias Nichols cited the publication of the tracts as one of three "most greevous accidents" that did "verie much darken the righteousnes of our cause."[217] The other two were the rise of Separatist polemic and the 1591 Coppinger–Hacket conspiracy, and defenders of conformity had indeed conflated these three challenges to the church throughout the 1590s. Writers such as Richard Cosin, Richard Bancroft, and Matthew Sutcliffe all argued at length that Thomas Cartwright's apparent moderation had masked the reform movement's true agenda of eliminating hierarchy and authority, first in the church and then in the state, and that the call for reform had been shown to culminate in blasphemy, treason, and mad fanaticism.[218] The line linking Martin to a mainstream Reformed ecclesiology had been rerouted to the byways of the lunatic fringe.

But though the Marprelate project failed in its campaign to topple episcopacy, the tracts and the controversy they generated had an immediate influence on late Elizabethan literature and culture. Martin's success in getting himself heard over other voices competing in print caught the attention of an emerging class of professional writers, including those who had been hired to denounce Martin's polemical strategies. Thomas Nashe's post-Martin prose, for example, is frequently discussed as exemplifying the influence of Martinism, particularly with respect to his performative manner and self-reflexive play with ironic personae.[219] Elements of Martinist style have also been observed in the work of Robert Greene,

Thomas Dekker, and Thomas Middleton.[220] The effectiveness of Martin's strategies for reaching a popular audience also probably encouraged the general transition in prose style over the 1590s from rhetorical formality to extemporizing colloquialism, and thereby contributed to the development in this period of English comic fiction.[221] In addition, Martin's *ad hominem* attacks and the equally abusive anti-Martinist response popularized the satiric and ironic modes that would characterize so much literary production in the decade after their publication.[222] Finally, Martin Marprelate and the demonized Martin of the anti-Martinist campaign provided models for various manifestations of the stage puritan in Elizabethan and Jacobean theatre, creating conventions that shaped broader cultural representations of puritanism throughout the following decades.[223] Traces of the Marprelate controversy have been seen in drama produced throughout the 1590s, including Anthony Munday's *John a Kent and John a Cumber* (*c.* 1590), the anonymous *A Knack to Know a Knave* (*c.* 1592), and Shakespeare's *Comedy of Errors, Love's Labour's Lost, Titus Andronicus, As You Like It, Twelfth Night*, and English history plays.[224]

But the afterlife of the Martin Marprelate was not restricted to the literary works of the Elizabethan Golden Age. The tracts would be read, cited, imitated, appropriated, and condemned for years to come, in official as well as unofficial venues, in scholarly writings and in more popular texts, and in oral culture as well as in manuscript and print. These uses invoked multiple and often competing resonances. Martin could signify the political dangers that underlay any call for reform, or plain-speaking opposition to abuses of power. His voice could represent a scurrilous threat to social order, or exemplify cleverness and wit. Like any signifying topical reference, allusions to the tracts decrease in frequency after about a decade of popularity. But Martin Marprelate retained some measure of cultural currency right through to the outbreak of civil war, when a newly revived Martinism and episcopacy once again stood poised to do battle through the agency of print. Civil war Martinism in turn gave the Marprelate controversy a role in Restoration debates concerning dissent and toleration, ultimately extending to almost a century the continued presence of Martin Marprelate in English pamphlet warfare.

Extant sources provide only occasional, representative glimpses of certain kinds of contemporary uses of the Marprelate tracts. Up to a few years after the discovery of the press, for example, reminders of the Martinist threat were still sufficiently potent to play a role in court politicking. In 1591, the judge Francis Wyndham criticized the use of the *ex officio* oath in church courts and accused Lord Hunsdon with maladministration;

Hunsdon retaliated by suggesting to the privy council that the Queen suspected Wyndham of "sympathizing with the Martin Marprelate tracts."[225] Similarly politic accusations appear in local and provincial disputes. In May 1591, a Surrey laborer named William Bowell accused his neighbor John Fenne of owning a book by "martyne marr prelate" which contained "treason to the queen."[226] While the ensuing depositions make it reasonably clear that Bowell was lying, the accusation indicates that an illiterate (as he admitted) laborer knew of Martin Marprelate, and knew furthermore that owning a copy of one of Martin's books meant treason. References to Martin were probably also common in church courts. In 1592, a Northamptonshire yeoman named Robert Welford was brought before a diocesan court for refusing communion, "despising the discipline of the church," and abusing the local minister. The list of charges concludes by denouncing Welford as "a notable Brownist, a Martin, despising government since time he was Hackett's companion."[227] In this case, "Martin" has been detached from the tracts to become a generic label for a religious troublemaker, the name appearing alongside others in a rogue's gallery that indistinguishably grouped Separatist, Presbyterian, and mad Millenarian.

Martin also made his way into oral culture and popular lore, though examples of this kind of discourse are notoriously fugitive and survive only in variously mediated forms. In a digressive diatribe against the Marprelate project in his *Ancient Funerall Monuments* (1631), the antiquary John Weever prints two "Rythmicall numbers" written against Martin. One is a version of a lengthy Latin epitaph included in the anti-Martinist pamphlet *Martins Months Minde* (1589). The second poem, which Weever attributes to a "certaine Northern Rimer," appears to have been written in 1593, the year John Penry was executed:

> The Welchman is hanged,
> Who at our Kirke stanged,
> And at her state banged,
> And brened are his buks.
> And tho he be hanged;
> Yet he is not wranged,
> The de'el has him fanged
> In his kruked kluks.[228]

Verses like these might have arisen out of the world of popular ridicule and rhyming libels in which derided puritans took their knocks along with other unpopular figures.[229] On the other hand, they might very well have originated in a "high" or learned culture appropriation of a popular voice, an exercise in rustic persona such as those created for the anti-Martinist verse collections. The boundary between these cultures was in any case permeable, particularly with verse, which could shift easily among oral, manuscript, and print modes of transmission. This epitaph, for example, was reprinted in Royalist drolleries published during the interregnum,[230] which might suggest transmission in manuscript miscellanies between appearances in print.

Early uses of Marprelate were not all hostile. While positive endorsements of the Martinist agenda are understandably scarce, one contemporary manuscript transcribes the opening thiry-line poem from the anti-Martinist verse collection *Mar-Martine* (1589) and then provides a mirror-image Martinist response: "Martin the mery who now is marreprelate / Will prove mad martyn, & martyn marre the state" (lines 5–6) is answered by "Whitgift the wrangler who now is make of bate / Will proove mad Whitgift & Whitgift marre the state" (lines 5–6).[231] The two poems balance one another, but the Martinist voice here gets the last word. Other Martinist verse probably circulated in manuscript in the period: recent work on verse libels reveals the significant role such texts played in late Elizabethan and Jacobean political life.[232] While popular verse often targeted puritans for their disruptions of the status quo, manuscript libel also functioned at times as a vigorous anti-court, anti-authoritarian – even puritan – genre.[233] But writers did not need to share Martin's oppositional agenda to borrow from him for their own purposes. For the more discursively daring, the Marprelate persona could be appropriated to signify cleverness or satirical bite. One of the earliest references to Martin appears in a letter from the antiquary Francis Thynne to Burghley dated November 15, 1588, only a few weeks after the appearance of the *Epistle*. Lobbying for a position in the College of Arms, Thynne prefaces an account of shortcomings among its current officers with the ironic disclaimer that he "will not Anotomyze every perticular default of everye manne and matter in that office. (Lest I might be counted one of thee foolishe sonnes of Martine Mareprelate)."[234] Thynne had noticed Martin's threat to place his "sons" in every parish to scrutinize the behavior of officials in residence (*Epistle*, 36, 39): to play the Martin, as Thynne proceeds to do with rhetorical flair, is to watch how the world goes and to tell uncomfortable truths about the status quo. Unfortunately for Thynne, his ostentatiously *au courant* appropriation of Martinist "foolishness" in the interests of winning admiration and patronage was poorly timed. Burghley had been hearing about the *Epistle* from other sources, and he would have received this letter only the day after sending the letter to Whitgift that had launched the anti-Martinist investigation. Francis Thynne was probably the first and last government job-seeker ever to invite a comparison of himself with Martin.

The epigrammatist and divine Thomas Bastard made a similar miscalculation when he wrote a verse satire modeled on Thomas Bulkeley's Oxford libel (see above, xxviii). Bastard signals his debt to Marprelate by concluding his "Admonition to the City of Oxford" (*c.* 1591) with the lines "Youres still shall *Martins Bastard* be / And so my Brethren Deare Adiewe"; other sources refer to the poem as "Bastards Libell cal'd Martin marre prelates bastarde" or "Marprelate's Basterdine."²³⁵ As Anthony Wood notes, the poem reflects "upon all Persons of note in *Oxon* that were guilty of amorous exploits, or that mixed themselves with other Mens Wives, or with wanton Huswives in *Oxon*."²³⁶ By affiliating himself with Marprelate, Bastard encouraged readers to associate his satiric strategies with Martin's *ad hominem* approach. The poem names names, and its riddling allusiveness invites readers to play the Martin themselves, which they gleefully proceeded to do: contemporary glosses in some copies identify the people left unnamed in the poem, and even at times provide the scene of the indiscretion. Once the poem started to circulate in manuscript, Oxford authorities promptly deprived Bastard of his fellowship at New College.

A couple of Martinist appropriations appeared in print in the years immediately following the controversy. A John Davies drew on Marprelate's notoriety in *Sir Martin Mar-People, His Coller of Esses* (1590), a sweepingly Juvenalian denunciation of "these dismal daies" (line 3) in alliterative rhyming fourteeners. Like Bastard, Davies looks to Marprelate primarily as a model of satirical address: on the whole, his targets are conventionally moral. *Martine Mar-Sixtus* (1591), by "R. W." – possibly actor and playwright Robert Wilson (d. 1600) –, does invoke the subversive political implications of Martinist language, but to the patriotic end of attacking Pope Sixtus V for his defense of Jacques Clement, the Dominican friar who assassinated Henri III in 1589. Defending the pseudonym he has adopted, Mar-Sixtus explains that he "purposed for once to play the *Martine*" and defines the role with an explicatory etymology. Since the first syllable, Mar, is "headded with a *Tine*, the murdering end of a forke, it must needes be that *Mar-tine* . . . signifieth such a one as galleth and pricketh men to death." Furthermore, he notes, "We live in a printing age" (A3v, A4v): Martinist aggression might be offensive and indecorous, but it certainly helped a text stand out among all those competing for reader attention.

These early references to the Marprelate controversy rely primarily on the images of Martinism painted by the anti-Martinist campaign and, in more local contexts, by sermons that never made their way into print and presumably took their cue from official disapproval. After 1593, however, many references to the tracts would also be mediated though influential books by Richard Bancroft and Richard Hooker, publications that codified the official line on reform challenge. With the Presbyterian movement now in disarray, Bancroft and Hooker both sought to ensure that lessons learned in the pamphlet warfare of the previous two decades would not be lost to future defenders of the church. For Bancroft, the primary lesson was the centrality of print in ecclesiological debate. The Marprelate controversy confirmed his sense that the press was the reformers' most dangerous weapon because it enabled them to disseminate their platform among a popular audience. But Bancroft also recognized that print was a weapon that could cut both ways: what the church needed to do was maintain records of past battles so that defenders of conformity would not be compelled to reinvent the polemical wheel at each new outbreak of dissent. One of Bancroft's solutions to the problem of institutional memory was to publish two detailed accounts of the beliefs and acts of Elizabethan reformers. In effect, he sought to create a public archive that countered the anti-episcopal "register" of documents compiled by the reform movement and deployed so effectively in Martin's publications. Bancroft's *Survey of the Pretended Holy Discipline* (1593) offers a hostile history of Presbyterianism, beginning with its continental roots and then moving to such English advocates as Thomas Cartwright, Walter Travers, John Field, Dudley Fenner, Anthony Gilby, John Greenwood, John Udall, and Martin Marprelate. With the aim of providing readers with a convenient resource with which they themselves could test future challenges to the church, Bancroft outlines the Presbyterian platform and provides the biblical and patristic authorities at issue on each disputed point. While Bancroft's primary target was Cartwright, the doctrinal prime mover of English Presbyterianism, he repeatedly cites the Marprelate tracts as the radical culmination of Cartwright's ecclesiology. "*Cartwright* is the chiefe man, that began this course in *Englande*," he begins, in a passage that leads into quotations from *Hay any Work*, *Theses Martinianae*, and *Just Censure*: "and you shall see howe pretily his schollers follow him" (123).

Where *A Survay* summarizes the issues under debate, Bancroft's *Daungerous Positions and Proceedings* (1593) describes attempts to establish Presbyterianism in Scotland and England. The story, in Bancroft's account, is one of manifest treason and disorderly railing. *Daungerous Positions* distills Bancroft's extensive reading of reform polemic and often resembles a legal brief: he groups excerpts under headings such as "Some of their rayling speaches against the high court of Parliament" (50) or "How they

charge the present government with persecution" (56). Not surprisingly, the
Marprelate tracts figure prominently in these lists.[237] *Daungerous Positions*
would become a standard account of Elizabethan puritanism, especially after
it was reprinted in 1640. When seventeenth-century writers cite alarming
threats from the Marprelate tracts, Bancroft is very often the source. In 1673,
Samuel Parker, self-appointed scourge of Nonconformity, summarized an
eighty-year tradition of reading when he described *Daungerous Positions* as "an
exact Collection of all the Treason in the world."[238]

Bancroft recognized the value of knowing one's enemy, and by publishing selections from a wide variety of oppositional texts he encouraged
engagement with reform polemicists on their own grounds. In addition,
Bancroft sought to establish the institutional resources that would give later
defenders of the church the weapons they needed to continue the fight. By
the time of his death in 1610, Bancroft had put together a remarkable
library of over 6,000 books, including numerous Presbyterian and
Separatist publications, among them a bound-together volume of the
Marprelate tracts.[239] He left the books as the foundation of the archiepiscopal library at Lambeth Palace and emphasized in his will the impor-
tance of keeping the collection intact.[240] On the advice of Francis Bacon a
catalogue was made, and Bancroft's successor, George Abbot, supplied a
preface in which he expressed hope that the library would "descend from
age to age, and from succession to succession, to the service of God, and his
Church, of the Kings, and Common-wealth of this Realme, and particularly of the Archbishops of Canterbury."[241] Except for a fifteen-year
interval beginning in 1647, when a victorious parliament declared the
library public property and transferred it to Cambridge University, the
books remained at Lambeth Palace, where to this day they constitute one of
the finest extant collections of Elizabethan polemic.[242]

Published in the same year as Bancroft's two aggressively partisan
collections, Richard Hooker's *Lawes of Ecclesiastical Politie* (1593) is often
regarded as standing serenely above the clamor of controversy. But the
Lawes is also a polemical text that takes up the argument against
the church's Protestant critics where John Whitgift had left off in the
1570s.[243] Hooker clears the ground for his defense of conformity by developing lines of response that reflect and codify tropes established by the
anti-Martinist campaign. A central concern of the *Lawes*, for example, is
the popular appeal of Presbyterianism: two chapters of the Preface address
the means by which "the people" and "the learneder sort" were persuaded
into approval of the discipline.[244] Hooker's analysis repeats the anti-
Martinist contention that Presbyterianism was a pious fraud, designed to

satisfy the greed and ambition of a few and offering its adherents the seductive power of challenging authority. By recognizing the allure of a polemic that openly criticized the status quo, and a polity and hermeneutics that offered administrative and interpretative power to the lay believer, Hooker builds on lessons learned during the campaign against the Marprelate tracts. When he takes the argument a step further and invokes the treason concomitant with the Presbyterian project, he cites Martin's *Hay any Work*: those urging reform, Hooker claims, sought to impose their discipline by force, "whether hir Majestie and our state will or no" (I, 50).[245] While this is the only explicit reference to the tracts in the Preface, the fears Martin generated inform the remainder of Hooker's opening discussion. If the Presbyterians were successful in their campaign, he warns, the "manifold strange and dangerous innovations" likely to follow would include constraints upon royal prerogative, rebellion among the nobility, the overthrow of all learning, the abolition of civil law, and destruction of the court system. Having advised his readers that all forms of authority were under threat, Hooker clinches the argument by invoking Anabaptist anarchy as the state toward which these beliefs inexorably led.[246]

The tendentiousness in these passages is likely attributable to George Cranmer, who encouraged his former teacher to foreground the social and political implications of the Presbyterian program. Cranmer offered this editorial advice in a letter that constitutes a self-contained treatise concerning the dangers of reform, and it was printed as such in three editions in royalist Oxford in the 1640s.[247] Surveying the history of Presbyterian polemic, Cranmer blames Martin for breaking a tradition of moderation in language: where Thomas Cartwright and others had "set out the discipline as a Queen, and as the daughter of God," Martin "contrariwise to make her more acceptable to the people, brought her forth as a vice upon the stage."[248] Hooker incorporated Cranmer's suggestions in the lengthy eighth chapter of the Preface. Fifty years later, these warning passages were extracted from Hooker's *Lawes* and joined Cranmer's letter in being published for propaganda purposes by Oxford royalists.[249] These editions of Elizabethan polemic, published in the months just prior to the outbreak of civil war, were among the few Oxford productions of the time that were not documents of state such as declarations or proclamations. They reminded readers of the dangers of innovation, especially as threatened by a revived Presbyterianism. After the Restoration, editions of Cranmer's letter continued to provide writers such as Izaak Walton and John Dryden with the raw material from which they could construct warning narratives for their time of the dangers of Martinism.

Once past the Preface, Hooker adopts a more moderate, irenic approach to opposition. In the Dedication to Whitgift of Book Five, he follows Francis Bacon in admitting that official responses to "our Antagonists" have on occasion been immoderate, and in Book Seven he acknowledges the human failings of bishops in a vivid survey that recapitulates complaints made by reformers over the decades.[250] Nonetheless, Hooker argues that deference to authority was the remedy for "passions of the mind," and the *Lawes* is above all concerned to demonstrate the reasonableness of that authority. Even if some efforts to defend the church were ill-advised, they were not nearly as intolerable "as on the contrarie side the scurrilous and more then Satyricall immodestie of Martinisme." Hooker consequently defines his method in opposition to both Martin and the anti-Martinists. Each side sought to sway the "wits of the multitude" by appealing to "partiall and immoderate desire"; he, on the other hand, would anchor his enterprise in the collective authority of "Scriptures, councels, Fathers, Histories, the lawes and practises of all Churches, the mutuall conference of all mens collections and observations" (II, 3–6). Against Martinist individualism and anti-Martinist bravado, Hooker offers the claims of the communal, the ceremonial, and the traditional; against the ephemera of the pamphlet and the broadsheet, he offers the authority of the folio, the repository of established practice to which the individual should defer.

These books by Bancroft and Hooker joined Matthew Sutcliffe's *Answere*, Thomas Cooper's *Admonition*, Richard Bancroft's *Sermon*, and other anti-Martinist texts as standard sources for many seventeenth-century writers or ministers who wanted to address the dangers that puritan challenge posed to political and religious order. Some of these later works offer detailed accounts of the Martinist challenge; others simply drop the name and assume the familiarity of Martin's reputation as an emblematic monster of sedition, the figure Thomas Lodge called one of the "Devils incarnate of this age."[251] Later writers also made use of Elizabethan condemnations of Martinist style. Martin appears repeatedly in seventeenth-century pamphlet warfare as the archetypal bad polemicist, his name a convenient shorthand for somebody who had crossed acceptable polemical boundaries. In 1602, for example, the English Catholic priest William Watson attempted to smear his Jesuit opponents in the "Appellant" controversy by equating their polemical strategies with those employed by Martin.[252] William Covell similarly played the Marprelate card against Josias Nichols' Presbyterian apologia *Plea of the Innocent* (1602), countering Nichols' efforts to distance himself from radical reform with repeated references to the tracts.[253] The royal chaplain Peter Heylyn charged many of his polemical adversaries with Martinist tendencies. He cast aspersions on attempts by John Williams, archbishop of York, to forge a moderate episcopacy by claiming that the style of Williams' *The Holy Table, Name & Thing* (1637) was "composed indifferently of *Martin Marre-Prelate*, and *Tom: Nash*: as scurrillous and full of folly, as the one; as scandalous and full of faction, as the other."[254] Heylyn also accused the Separatist Henry Burton of Martinist sedition and scurrility, and cited Martin to discredit Thomas Fuller's *Church-History of Britain* (1655).[255] Polemical uses of Martin along these lines would continue into the Restoration, with accusations of Martinism retaining sufficient cultural currency to be wielded against John Milton and Andrew Marvell (see below).

Another category of seventeenth-century references involves the use of Martin as a "character" or personal type, an embodiment of various qualities inimical to the smooth workings of social order. To Adam Hill, in a sermon delivered at Paul's Cross in 1592, Martin exemplified the sins of pride and self-love: "as *Augustine* noteth … selfe-love giveth us this counsell, thou art better then all others in eloquence, riches, and honours, and in all giftes both spirituall and corporall, despise therefore all and make thy selfe better then all: so saith Martin, that hee is better then all the Bishops and Ministers of this land."[256] The university drama *The Pilgrimage to Parnassus* (c. 1598/99) borrows a prominent anti-Martinist trope to equate reform with ignorance: the play targets the puritan William Gouge in the character Stupido, who advises his more studious fellows to sell their books "and buye a good Martin" instead.[257] Martin also appears in Thomas Tomkis' *Lingua: or, The Combat of the Tongue* (1607), when Mendacio, Lingua's page, claims to have jogged the elbow of all "lying" writers since antiquity: his list places Martin Marprelate in the company of Homer, Pliny, Lucian, Mandeville, Rabelais, Robin Hood, the chroniclers Stow and Holinshed, and the authors of various popular romances (D1r). In general, these references detach Martin from ecclesiological challenge and use him to figure a wilful self-conceit grounded in ignorance and conducive to mendacity. That the trope was commonplace is implied by its casual appearance in one of Gervase Markham's books on horsemanship, where Markham defends his expertise against critics who, like Martin, had such high opinion of their own under-standing that they scorned those with true knowledge.[258]

As these examples indicate, Cooper, Sutcliffe, Bancroft, and Hooker largely succeeded in redefining Martinism on their own terms: the over-whelming majority of references to the Marprelate tracts before 1640 are hostile, and these representations attached Martin's name to various social, political, religious, or discursive anxieties. Not surprisingly, Martin's attempt to popularize the reform agenda through the means of colloquial satire and *ad hominem* anecdote attracted few imitators before the civil wars. Censorship of printed texts in England certainly discouraged any overt revivals of Martinist oppositional strategies.[259] But many advocates of reform published their work abroad in this period, and, even with their relative freedom from official restraints, they seem largely to have agreed with Josias Nichols that the Martinist approach to controversy rendered their cause more harm than good.[260] A few Jacobean texts are sometimes thought to bear traces of Martinist style. The choleric Hebraist Hugh Broughton occasionally adopted a Martinist acerbity in his disputes with John Whitgift and Richard Bancroft. Samuel Rid's *Martin Mark-All, Beadle of Bridewell* (1610), a treatment of the language of vagabonds and thieves that responded to two pamphlets by Thomas Dekker, implicitly invoked Martin's name and, to some extent, imitated his voice. In the early 1620s, the Norwich minister Thomas Scott attacked the king's Hispanophile policies in pamphlets that employed fictive and theatrical strategies similar to those found in the Marprelate tracts.

But militantly anti-episcopal polemic only began to reappear in the later 1620s, with texts such as Alexander Leighton's vitriolic *An Appeal to the Parliament; or Sions Plea against the Prelacie* (Amsterdam, 1629). In 1630, Star Chamber sentenced Leighton to a substantial fine, mutilation, and imprisonment; he was the first of the decade's martyrs of the (reformist) book, followed by William Prynne and the printer Michael Sparke (tried for sedition in 1633), the puritan "triumvirate" of Prynne, John Bastwick, and Henry Burton (tried in 1637), and John Lilburne (tried in 1638). To contemporaries, these were the most prominent figures among an opposi-tional community that had become increasingly daring in its uses of print over the 1630s, particularly after William Laud was made archbishop of Canterbury in 1633 and began his drive toward uniformity and "Arminian" ceremonialism.[261] The sustained anti-episcopal invective, rampant pun-ning, and mock liturgical form of Bastwick's remarkable four-part *Letany* (Leiden, 1637), for example, make it the most Martinist English publica-tion since the seizure of the Marprelate press. While there is no explicit evidence that the Marprelate tracts influenced these writers, contempora-ries readily made the connection. Dr Samuel Brooke, master of Trinity College, Cambridge, wrote Laud in 1630 to complain that "Puritanisme" was making many thousands of people "Laytons in their hearts," and traced this tradition of "schisme, and sauciness" back to Penry and Wigginton, both of whom were associated primarily with Marprelate.[262] More explic-itly, in Abraham Cowley's comedy *The Guardian* (1650), performed in 1641 before the future Charles II, the ingenue Aurelia jokes that if the "old puritan" widow were made mistress of the house, "The first pious deed will be, to banish *Shakespear* and *Ben. Johnson* out of the parlour, and to bring in their roomes *Mar-prelate*, and *Pryns* works."[263]

Nonetheless, one reason why Nicholas Darton's Northamptonshire parishioners were reading the Marprelate tracts in 1637 (see above, xv–xvi) was because little else had appeared in print that fulfilled the same purpose. Martinist style was designed to encourage precisely the kind of reading that so outraged Darton: aloud, to communal enjoyment, in a collective act of public ridicule that soon led to collective acts of defiance. Within a couple of years of Darton's petition to Laud, however, reform-minded villagers in Kilsby and elsewhere would no longer need to rely on dog-eared copies of fifty-year-old originals. The calling of parliament in November 1640 to deal with the humiliating failure of the second "Bishops' War" against Scotland, accompanied by the triumphant return from exile of Burton, Bastwick, and Prynne, generated a wave of anti-episcopal agitation, including the republication of Elizabethan polemic. As Edward Hyde, later earl of Clarendon, complained, in the early 1640s "all possible license was exercised in printing any old scandalous pamphlets" against episcopal jurisdiction and power.[264] At the heart of the contention between Charles and both his Scottish and English subjects was the mutually leveled charge of introducing innovations, ecclesiological as well as political. Reprints of and allusions to Elizabethan debates concerning church government consequently provided a usable oppositional past, a tradition of challenge rooted in texts against which the growth of episcopal power could be measured. And it was in this context of renewed anti-episcopal attack that Martin Marprelate was resurrected as an exemplary voice of reform-minded opposition.

Between 1640 and 1643, four pamphlets appeared under Martin Marprelate's name, comprising two editions each of two different works, published under four different titles. In 1640, a press in Amsterdam reprinted the para-Martinist *A Dialogue. Wherin is Plainly Layd Open the Tyrannicall Dealing of Lord Bishops against Gods Children*, originally printed by Robert Waldegrave in La Rochelle in 1589.[265] The reprint retains the full title of the original, including its gibe against John Bridges and its lengthy epigraph from Malachi 2:7–9. But the title page also features the imprint from Martin's *Protestation*, announcing that the book was first "Published, by the worthy Gentleman Dr. MARTIN MAR-PRELAT, Doctor in all the Faculties, Primat and Metropolitan." An additional, new imprint draws attention to the book's status as a redeployment of an older text and to the renewed possibilities of reform created by the recently changed political landscape: "Reprinted in the time of *Parliament, Anno Dom.* 1640" (see illustration, no. 6). The reprinted text is otherwise identical to the Elizabethan original, the only changes being the addition of a vigorously anti-Catholic prayer to the beginning and a fifty-line poem, the "description of a *Puritan,* (as they are now termed) by *profane Papists* and *Atheists*" at the end (D2r–v). This concluding poem in turn provided the title for another reprint of the same work, otherwise identical, published as *The Character of a Puritan; and His Gallimaufrey of the Antichristian Clergie; Prepared with D. Bridges Sawce for the Present Time to Feed On* (1643). The appearance of these two reprints under the name of Martin Marprelate, and the references to John Bridges on the title pages, suggest that Martin and his original opponent retained cultural currency as voice and object respectively of reformist challenge.

The second Marprelate production to appear in the 1640s was *Hay any Work*, the only one of the original Marprelate tracts to be reprinted before the nineteenth century. It was published in 1641 under the title *Reformation No Enemie*, the popular name for John Penry's *A Treatise Wherein is Manifestlie Proved* (Edinburgh, 1590); and then published again in 1642, this time under the title of the 1589 original. Other than the new title in the 1641 edition, both editions reproduce the Elizabethan text word for word, even including the list of "Faults Escaped" on the last page, none of which has been corrected. The only instance of deliberate updating appears in the title of the 1642 edition, which now claims that the bishops need to be "barrelled up, for feare of smelling in the nostrills of his Majesty"; the original, of course, had "her Majestie." Copies of other Marprelate tracts do appear to have been in circulation: in addition to the borrowed imprint from *The Protestation*, tracts such as *Queene Elizabeths Bishops* (1642) reprise some of Martin's favorite incidents of episcopal ignorance or misbehavior. But of the original Marprelate tracts, *Hay any Work* was best suited for re-use in its entirety: less relentlessly topical than the others, it offered a more sustained engagement with the fundamental issues of ecclesiological reform.

These four reprints are the only publications either by or credited to Martin to appear in the civil war period. But Martin was not the only Marprelate to resurface in 1640: over the course of 1640–41, five pamphlets invoked "Margery Mar-prelate" in their imprints. Four of these publications can be linked to the "Cloppenburg" press in Amsterdam, the same press that produced the 1640 reprint of the para-Martinist *A Dialogue*: two texts by the Scottish army that justified their successful invasion of England;[266] a sermon by George Walker, a London minister who would become an active member of the Westminster Assembly of Divines;[267] and Richard Overton's *Vox Borealis, or The Northern Discoverie.*[268] The fifth, an anonymous anti-episcopal work "Imprinted LONDON, by Pasquin, Deputy to Margery Mar-prelate," was indeed probably printed in London.[269] The names Margery and Martin were traditionally linked as proverbially rural: in the parade of the seven deadly sins in Marlowe's *Doctor Faustus*, the godparents of Gluttony include Martin Martlemas-beef and Margery March-beer.[270] The name signals the polemical tradition with which a new generation of oppositional writers sought to identify their writings, a usable past that reached back not only to the Elizabethan reform movement but also, with the rustic associations of Margery's name, to the native tradition of plain-speaking opposition associated with Piers Ploughman. With parliament once more in session and the forces of the Presbyterian Scots occupying Newcastle, a Marprelate once again stood facing the bishops: but this time *she* had a Scottish army at her back.

The person responsible for reviving Martin Marprelate and for creating Margery is probably Richard Overton, one of the more formidable polemicists of the period and a leader of the Leveller movement in the late 1640s. Elements from the Martinist reprints re-appear in later pamphlets that are definitely Overton's work, and he was arrested in 1646 for helping operate a secret press.[271] But the strongest argument for Overton's role in these publications is his personal identification with the Marprelate persona in *Vox Borealis* and in the six Martin Marpriest tracts he published in the mid-1640s (discussed below). *Vox Borealis*, probably Overton's earliest publication, is a dialogue between two Scottish intelligence scouts, one just returned from London. In slangy, colloquial prose, the speakers recapitulate the grounds of the contention between the two kingdoms, celebrate the abolishment of episcopacy in Scotland, and recite the latest pro-Scots and anti-English ballads. *Vox Borealis* pulls no punches on the subject of episcopal responsibility for the war between England and Scotland: as one of the speakers notes, "I hope to see some of those bigg bellied Bishops like so many false fellowes . . . shake their shanks upon a Gallowes" (A4v). A prefatory poem expands on the hint in the "Margery Mar-prelat" imprint to invoke the tradition of irreverence that lay behind the pamphlet's approach to current events. It begins:

> MARTIN MAR-PRELAT was a bonny Lad,
> His brave adventures made the Prelats mad:
> Though he be dead, yet he hath left behind
> A Generation of the MARTIN kind.

The message brought by this voice from the north was one of successful anti-episcopal challenge, and Margery, the poem continues, will use the press to harness this force for change by packaging a serious call for united political action as entertaining reading.

Richard Overton was not the only writer to recognize that a popular polemical style was an effective means of gaining attention through print. From late 1640 through to the outbreak of open hostilities in August 1642, numerous anti-episcopal pamphlets appeared that employed such imaginative strategies as dialogues, playlets, mock letters or proclamations, fictive news bulletins, allegorical trials, funerals, fairs, recipes, final testaments, banquets, and dream visions.[272] Their language is consistently conversational, full of scatological humour and comic wordplay. Many make their point by scripting self-implicating speeches for their opponents; others popularize grievances by telling stories of those who had run afoul of the prerogative courts or suffered under a monopoly-dominated economics. Like the Marprelate tracts, these pamphlets anchor their denunciations of the religious and political status quo in the details of their readers' everyday lives, scrupulously providing names, places, and dates that lend their narratives an air of authority. They packaged the oppositional case for an audience that might have been less susceptible to other forms of printed persuasion, such as the learned scholasticism of more traditionally argued controversy, or the nuanced political negotiations between king and parliament. Their aim was both to shape popular opinion and to legitimize it as a political force. Many writers other than Overton named the tradition that lay behind this public appeal.[273] The speaker in an ironic "character" pamphlet, *Roger the Canterburian* (1642), for example, described the readers of these anti-episcopal pamphlets as the "Schismaticall Sectaries of *Martin Mar-Prelate*," and approvingly cited Bancroft's anti-Martinist *Sermon* as the last piece of real theology published in England.[274] In a more genuinely hostile act of naming, royalist poet Anna Ley (née Norman) invoked Martin in her response to the anti-Laudian tract *Mercuries Message, or the Coppy of a Letter Sent to William Laud* (1641) in a manuscript poem written in 1641:

> Whie how now Martin what's the newes from hell,
> . . .
> How fares old Satan there, and all the rest
> Of those Marprelates, now in this Strange time,
> When such as raile at goverment speede best,
> And on the Churches ruines hope to climbe.

Ley associates contemporary anti-episcopal writers with their "predeces-sour Martine and that crew / Of barkeing libellers," whose attempts to "crush religion" were thwarted only "by that bright Star / Whitgift, the glorie of our Church."[275]

On the other side of these debates over episcopacy, conformist and royalist writers experimented with an equally wide range of polemical strategies, deploying colloquial language, fictive devices, satiric verse, and ironic personas in scores of publications. Defenders of Laud and the church also countered the Presbyterian use of the past by resurrecting works by their own champions. Richard Bancroft's *Daungerous Positions* (1593) was reprinted in 1640 to accompany earlier reprints of his 1589 Paul's Cross sermon (1636, 1637). As mentioned earlier, the royalist press at Oxford published pamphlets by George Cranmer and Richard Hooker on the dangers of the "new discipline." John Taylor (the "water poet") published three tracts that used the persona of Thomas Nashe, "the old *Martin* queller," to attack a new crop of "Nonconformists, Schismatiques, Separatists, and scandalous Libellers."[276] Francis Bacon's *Admonition* was also printed, under the title *A Wise and Moderate Discourse, Concerning Church-Affaires* (1641). While originally a neutral text, in its new context the *Admonition* functioned as a pro-episcopacy work because it sought to discourage attempts to enlist public opinion on behalf of reform. In this round, however, Bancroft, Nashe, Hooker, Cranmer, and Bacon were on the losing side: the numbers of pamphlets now appearing created an expectation of public discussion, and would make it impossible for Bacon's "private assemblies and conferences of the learned" to monopolize the debates that preceded the outbreak of war.

In the final Marprelate tract, Martin had defiantly announced that despite his apparent defeat, "Martinism" would outlive "Lambethism" by a full two years (*Protestation*, 198). In a series of pamphlets published in the two years following the execution of William Laud in January 1645, Richard Overton ensured that Martin's prophecy was fulfilled. Ironically, Overton's seven Martin Marpriest pamphlets wielded the Marprelate persona against a newly triumphant Presbyterianism.[277] His primary target was the Westminster Assembly of Divines, established in June 1643 to advise parliament on ecclesiological and religious matters. Many Separatists and religious Independents, however, thought that the Presbyterian-dominated Assembly had begun to act as a policymaking body that sought to usurp parliamentary prerogatives. Numerous anti-Presbyterian pamphlets of the mid-1640s consequently asserted a continuity from the episcopal past to the Presbyterian present, a position Milton pointedly summarized in the last line of "On the New Forcers of Conscience under the Long Parliament" as "New *Presbyter* is but old *Priest* writ large" (line 20).[278] Using the press as an agent of exposure and employing such Martinist polemical devices as fictive frames, colloquial prose, and irony, the Marpriest tracts offer a satiric complement to the critique of Presbyterian intolerance developed in the mid-1640s by writers such as William Walwyn, John Lilburne, John Goodwin, and Roger Williams. The filiation with Marprelate, made explicit throughout the Marpriest tracts, provides the analogical argument that sustains the entire series. Just as "old Martin the Metropolitan" had adopted a certain kind of polemical language to counter the prelates of his day, his son Marpriest, "young Martin," employs the same weapons against their descendants, the Presbyterian divines, who had substituted the tyranny of prelacy with their own.[279] Martinism did indeed outlast Lambethism, only to be deployed against the very polity it had been devised to defend. But while Martin Marprelate's ecclesiologically exculsive certainties were antipathetic to tolerationist Independents such as Overton, Leveller writings of the later 1640s can nonetheless be read as the seventeenth-century culmination of the Martinist polemical tradition.[280] Like the Martinists (and Milton in *Areopagitica*), Leveller writers sought to combat the magisterial mode: they believed that the test of truth was the consensus of an interpretative community, and that the wider public therefore required free access to information that would enable them to form opinions on controverted issues. This confidence that readers/listeners were rational agents, capable of arriving at the truth undeterred by traditions of deference, underlies and unites a wide range of oppositional polemical strategies from Marprelate to Marpriest.

While Richard Overton appears to be the last writer to fashion himself explicitly as a son of Martin, the Marprelate tracts continued to play a role in polemical battles well into the Restoration. They first appear in discussions soon after 1660 concerning the role of pamphleteering in the civil wars. The "Act for the Preservation of the King" (1661) expressed the belief of many contemporaries with its assertion that "the late troubles & disorders did in very great measure proceed from a multitude of seditious Sermons Pamphlets and Speeches dayly preached printed and published with a transcendent boldnes."[281] The Licensing Act (1662) made similar claims for the destabilizing potential of printed polemic as a rationale for renewed controls. Roger L'Estrange, appointed surveyor of the press in 1663, repeatedly blamed unregulated printing for the troubles of the 1640s. To L'Estrange, discursive liberties led to political liberties, and he saw this tradition of dangerous books as one that extended well before the wars: in a tract written soon after the Restoration, he characterizes Presbyterian unwillingness to subordinate individual opinion to the dictates of authority as "but *Martin Junior Revived*," citing *Theses Martinianae*.[282]

This conjunction of nonconformity, rebellion, and Martinist discursive freedom reappeared in the debates surrounding the Declaration of Indulgence (1672), particularly in the exchanges between Andrew Marvell and Samuel Parker, the future bishop of Oxford.[283] One reason why Marvell was tempted out of his "modest retiredness" to write the two parts of *The Rehearsal Transpros'd* (1672, 1673) was Parker's style: "I must needs say I never saw a Divine guilty of so much ribaldry and prophaneness," he complains (169). But Parker felt no need to apologize for the lashing vehemence with which he attacked his Nonconformist adversaries. What were harsh words when lives and the nation were at stake? To support his contention that the inevitable tendency of the unrestrained puritan conscience was to run itself "into all manner of Disloyal outrages against the State," Parker refers the reader to the "writings and practices" conveniently anthologized by Richard Bancroft in *Daungerous Positions*. It was these sixteenth-century radicals, Parker claims, who bore ultimate responsibility for the bloodshed of the 1640s. "The Story is too long, too sad, and too well known to be here repeated," he concludes: "'tis sufficient that it [Elizabethan Presbyterianism] improved it self into the greatest Villainies, and concluded in the blackest Tragedy that was ever acted upon this Island."[284]

With the appearance of Marvell's reponse in *The Rehearsal Transpros'd*, Parker looked to the tradition of sedition he had outlined with Bancroft's help to answer Marvell's use of satiric strategies. If Nonconformist theology were but the "Vomit and Choler of that proud Schismatick" Cartwright,[285] then the only appropriate polemical precursor to the language of Marvell's *The Rehearsal Transpros'd* was Martin Marprelate. Parker invokes the Marprelate tracts throughout his answering *Reproof* (1673). Challenging the use of the word "unhoopable," for example, he notes that "you and your Puritan Coopers, or (as Mar-prelate words it) *Tub-trimmers*, have been pleased to contract their [the Magistrates] Power." To the threat that he will be addressed not as his grace but as "his Morality," Parker responds "I thank you Sir, it is a much more civil and cleanly Title than his *Belzebubship of Kanterbury*, which yet was the softest word your meek-spirited Puritans could in the days of your Predecessor *Martin* afford to that pious and humble man Arch-Bishop *Whitgift*." On the central issue of decorum, he notes that "you humbly crave leave to treat me according to *Decorum*, *i.e.* like a Buffoon; the very same Request word for word that

Martyn-Mar-Prelate has often put up to his Readers to be allowed the same freedom with his *Nuncka John* the Arch-Bishop of *Canterbury*."[286] Unlike most of his contemporaries, Parker appears to have read the Marprelate tracts themselves: the citations and examples he gives are not always in Bancroft, Sutcliffe, and other published sources. Since Parker was appointed chaplain to archbishop of Canterbury Gilbert Sheldon in 1667, he probably did his reading in the Lambeth Palace library, using the pamphlets in Bancroft's collection of "libri puritani" precisely as Bancroft had intended.

The identification with Marprelate was not one Marvell himself would invoke, and he acknowledges the comparison in the second part of *The Rehearsal Transpros'd* only to take a swipe at Parker's eager vehemence of style: "In many places of your Book, and sure you think it a lucky hit, you would fix upon me the old *Martin Mar-Prelate* (in one page you do it four times)."[287] But Parker's use of the tracts helped create a Restoration sense of a Marprelate tradition, one that extended from the 1580s to their present day. By crediting this style of polemic with a leading role in the civil war, Parker continued the effort begun in the anti-Martinist campaign to link irreverent language to political liberties. Contemporaries developed the association. In *The Transproser Rehears'd: Or the Fifth Act of Mr. Bayes's Play* (1673), for example, Richard Leigh picks up on Parker's discussion of the "fustian bumbast" of *Areopagitica* to posit Milton as the tradition's missing link: "Once, perhaps in a Century of years, there may arise a *Martin-Mar-Prelate*, a *Milton*, or such a *Brave* as our present Author [Marvell]. Every day produces not such Wonders ... Time forms and perfects such as slowly, as teeming Elephants their young, and is deliver'd but of one at a Birth."[288]

As mentioned earlier, George Cranmer's anti-Presbyterian letter to Richard Hooker appeared as an appendix to the first edition of Izaak Walton's *Life* of Hooker (1665) and was reprinted in the 1666 edition of Hooker's *Works*. In addition, Walton himself mentioned the Marprelate tracts in the *Life*, praising Thomas Nashe for the "merry Wit" with which "he put a greater stop to these malitious Pamphlets, than a much wiser man had been able."[289] These accounts of Martin by Walton, Hooker, and Cranmer joined Bancroft's *Daungerous Positions* and the politicized reading of a Marprelate tradition formulated by Parker and Leigh to create the image of the Marprelate tracts that found its way into polemic of the 1670s and early 1680s. In 1673, for example, Clarendon defended Edward Stillingfleet against the converted Catholic Hugh Cressy, beginning with a discussion of polemical decorum in which he compares Cressy with Martin: "The spirit of *Martin Marprelate*, which hath for so many years been expired, or extinguished, is revived with greater insolence, and improved, and heightened as well against the State, as the Church," he complains.[290] Thomas Tomkins likewise argued against toleration by citing Bancroft and Hooker on Martin and connecting Martinist ideas with the "Tumults in *Scotland.*"[291] Finally, in what is likely the best-known Restoration use of the tracts, John Dryden asserts in the preface to *Religio Laici* (1682) that "Martin Mar-Prelate (the Marvell of those times) was the first Presbyterian scribbler who sanctified libels and scurrility to the use of the Good Old Cause." Drawing on Cranmer in particular, Dryden links Martin's choice of the low style to a deliberate and subversive bid for popular approval. Whether 1588, 1642, or 1682, Dryden argues, the fundamental strategy of radical reform was to circumvent the legitimate forums of court and parliament and appeal directly to the self-serving passions of the ignorant multitude.[292]

Dryden's warning about the dangers of a popularizing polemic concludes nearly a century of vilification in which Martin Marprelate was held to exemplify an approach to controversy that threatened the foundations of both church and state. Polemicists in the great age of pamphlet warfare to come, the age of Defoe and Swift, would continue to address issues of church and state with such weapons as satire and irony, personas and fictive frames, anecdotes and *ad hominem* attack, and they would experiment with the resources of colloquial prose, banter, and self-reflexive play with the conventions of debate in their appeals to popular as well as to more learned audiences. But by the late seventeenth century, the Marprelate tracts themselves had started to attract scholarly and antiquarian interest, a sure sign that texts once regarded as a danger to society had become books with an interesting and puzzling history. In the late 1690s, the librarian and antiquary Humphrey Wanley discussed some correspondence "about the printing of Martin-mar-prelate" with the book dealer John Bagford.[293] In a similarly impartial and antiquarian vein, a manuscript entitled "Observations of some Bookes writ against the Cleargey but more espesialley Marten Marprelate with the Names of such Bookes pro & con as were writ" (*c.* 1700) establishes a bibliography of the controversy, listing many works from the original anti-Martinist campaign as well as such later Martinist items as Overton's *Vox Borealis* and Marpriest tracts, and the outrageously libellous anti-Anglican pamphlets of Ralph Wallis, the "Cobbler of Gloucester" (d. 1669).[294] The author has also compiled information about John Penry, John Udall, Henry Barrow, Robert Browne, John Greenwood, and other early reformers. These are very much a scholar's notes, the first stages of the bibliographical investigations that would be continued in the mid-eighteenth century by Herbert Ames.[295] A century after the publication of his first tract, Martin Marprelate was no longer a voice to be feared and condemned, but a writer whose works were to be researched, catalogued, and collected.

NOTES

1. PRO SP Dom. 16/362/96, Nicholas Darton to William Laud ([June,] 1637).
2. Laud, *History of the Troubles and Tryal* (1695), 54. For the contemporary association of Prynne with Marprelate, see below, lxxxiv–lxxxv.
3. Cooper, *Admonition* (1589), 35.
4. For representatively vituperative remarks, see Dexter, *Congregationalism* (1880), 188–90. Early accounts of the controversy include Disraeli, *Quarrels of Authors* (1814), III, 203–82; Maskell, *History of the Martin Marprelate Controversy* (1845); and Hunt, *Religious Thought in England* (1870), I, 71–107. For a comprehensive survey of nineteenth-century references, see Greene, "The Martin Marprelate Controversy" (1923).
5. The key works in this reevaluation are Arber, *Introductory Sketch* (1879); Pierce, *Historical Introduction* (1908); Wilson, "The Marprelate Controversy," in *Cambridge History of English Literature*, III (1909), 425–52; McKerrow, "The Marprelate Controversy," in Nashe, *Works*, V (1910), 34–65; *Marprelate Tracts*, ed. Pierce (1911); Bonnard, *La controverse de Martin Marprelate* (1916).
6. Recent accounts of the Marprelate controversy include McGinn, *John Penry* (1966); Anselment, *"Betwixt Jest and Earnest"* (1979), 33–60; Carlson, *Martin Marprelate* (1981); Kendall, *Drama of Dissent* (1986), 173–212; Benger, "The Authority of Writer and Text in Radical Protestant Literature 1540–1593" (1989); Tribble, *Margins and Marginality* (1993), 101–16; Black, "Pamphlet Wars: The Marprelate Tracts and 'Martinism,' 1588–1688" (1996); Clegg, *Press Censorship in Elizabethan England* (1997), 170–97; Lake and Questier, *Antichrist's Lewd Hat* (2002), 505–68; Raymond, *Pamphlets and Pamphleteering* (2003), 27–52; North, *Anonymous Renaissance* (2003), 133–58; Lander, *Inventing Polemic* (2006), 80–109.
7. For Marprelate, print culture, and the public sphere, see the scholarship published from 1996 forward listed in the previous note, and Black, "The Rhetoric of Reaction" (1997); Halasz, *Marketplace of Print* (1997), 84–86; Bruster, "The Structural Transformation of Print" (2000).
8. Milward lists the major works published on both sides in *Religious Controversies of the Elizabethan Age* (1978), 29–33, 77–93.
9. Scholarship on the Protestant reformist challenge to the Elizabethan church is extensive. The standard narrative account remains Collinson, *Movement* (1967); other important studies cited frequently in this introduction include Lake, *Moderate Puritans* (1982), Lake, *Anglicans and Puritans?* (1988), and Brachlow, *Communion of Saints* (1988).
10. According to the *OED*, the earliest uses of "Presbyterianism" and most of its analogues are in the seventeenth century, though "Presbyterial" first appears in the titles of books that followed in the wake of the Marprelate

controversy: Richard Cosin, *Conspiracie, for Pretended Reformation: viz. Presbyteriall Discipline* (1592), and Richard Bancroft, *Daungerous Positions and Proceedings, Published and Practised … for the Presbiteriall Discipline* (1593). A few Scottish uses of "presbytery" are recorded in the 1570s and 1580s.

11. For the term's historiographical problems, see the summary in Lake, "Defining Puritanism – Again?" (1993).

12. Lake, *Anglicans and Puritans?*, 7.

13. See, e.g., *Hay any Work*, 123, and *Protestation*, 204–05.

14. Brachlow surveys the continuities between Presbyterians and Separatists in *Communion of Saints*.

15. For the conformist position, see Lake, *Anglicans and Puritans?*, 13–66. For Whitgift as polemicist, see Kendall, *Drama of Dissent*, 132–74, and Sanders, "John Whitgift: Primate, Privy Councillor and Propagandist" (1987).

16. For Whitgift, see *ODNB*. For Whitgift's initiatives upon becoming archbishop, see Collinson, *Movement*, 243–88, and Guy, "Elizabethan Establishment" (1995).

17. For the subscription crisis, see Collinson, *Movement*, 243–72.

18. See Lake, *Anglicans and Puritans?*, 72–81.

19. The survey (printed in *SPR*, II, 70–174) records the "conversation and unfitnes" of over 2,500 ministers, offering a fascinating record of puritan perceptions of daily parish life. For the parliamentary campaign to which the "Survey" contributed, see below, xxxvi, xliii.

20. For a revisionist discussion of the 1586 decree that diminishes the role traditionally accorded Whitgift in its creation, see Clegg, *Press Censorship in Elizabethan England*, 54–60. Clegg acknowledges Whitgift's appropriation at this time of licensing and censoring authority (60).

21. PRO SP Dom. 12/172/1, William Cecil, Lord Burghley to John Whitgift (July 1, 1584). Other contemporaries invoked the comparison with the Inquisition: see, e.g., Morice, *A Briefe Treatise of Oathes* (Middelburg, 1590), 57. For debates over the *ex officio* oath in the early 1590s, see Guy, "Elizabethan Establishment," 137–49.

22. Field and Wilcox, *Admonition to the Parliament* (Hemel Hempstead? 1572), *2r. For a thorough discussion of Elizabethan debates between reformers and conformists over the role of the laity in the church, see Kaufman, *Thinking of the Laity* (2004).

23. Udall, *A Demonstration of the Trueth of that Discipline* (East Molesey, 1588), A2v.

24. See Fulke, *Briefe and Plaine Declaration*, esp. 77–90, and Kaufman, *Thinking of the Laity*, 155–58. For the delay in publication, see Collinson, *Movement*, 108.

25. Lake, *Anglicans and Puritans?*, 3–4. For Beza's role in the English reform movement, see Collinson, *Movement*; Lake, *Moderate Puritans*; Brachlow, *Communion of Saints*, esp. 30, 36–37.

26. See Kaufman, *Thinking of the Laity*, 6, 118–19, 167–69. Kaufman notes that Beza too thought "broad lay participation" institutionally imprudent (91), a disapproval left undeveloped in the broadly sketched argument of the *Judgement*.

27. Hooker, *Works*, I, 29. For conformist objections to lay participation, see Kaufman, *Thinking of the Laity*, passim.
28. Bridges is sometimes credited with initiating the Elizabethan claim to episcopacy *jure divino*, though John Whitgift appears to have suggested the position in the 1570s: see Guy, "Elizabethan Establishment," 127–28, and Lake, "Presbyterianism" (1987), 208. For developments of the claim in the 1590s, see below, lxi.
29. Fenner, *Defence of the Godlie Ministers* (Middelburg, 1587); Travers, *Defence of the Ecclesiastical Discipline* (Middelburg, 1588).
30. Fenner, *Defence of the Godlie Ministers*, D1v–D2r; Travers, *Defence of the Ecclesiastical Discipline*, 38, 138.
31. For Martinist style and issues of decorum, see Coolidge, "Martin Marprelate, Marvell and *Decorum Personae*" (1959), and Anselment, "*Betwixt Jest and Earnest*," 33–60. For Martin's theatricality, see Kendall, *Drama of Dissent*, 173–212. For the polemical advantages of pseudonymity, see North, *Anonymous Renaissance*, 133–58. For the ambivalence that informs Martin's popularizing approach, see Lake and Questier, *Antichrist's Lewd Hat*, 505–20. The most thorough discussion of Martinist style and its analogues is Benger, "Authority of Writer and Text" (1989), 168–307.
32. See *OED*. Monkeys or apes were traditionally associated with foolish imitation, and martins (birds that returned to England in March) with "March madness." For the rustic associations of the name, cf. Piers Ploughman, *I Plaine Piers* (London? 1588?), which figures Martin Marprelate as the grandson of Piers Ploughman (see below, xxx), and Christopher Marlowe's *Doctor Faustus*, in which Gluttony's rural godparents include "Martin Martlemas-beef and Margery March-beer" (Marlowe, *Doctor Faustus and Other Plays*, ed. Bevington and Rasmussen, 2.3.139–42 (A-text), 2.3.140–42 (B-text); see also below, lxxxvii). For the association with human foolery, see the ballad "Martin said to his man who is the fool now?" (c. 1588), entered in the Stationers' Register the week before the first Marprelate tract appeared (Arber, *Transcript*, II, 506), but either not published at the time or no longer extant as a separate publication. It is printed in Fellowes, ed., *English Madrigal Verse* (1967), 225–26, from a version in a printed seventeenth-century songbook.
33. *Epitome*, 66; *Hay any Work*, 103.
34. Bacon, *Advertisement Touching the Controversies of the Church of England* (c. 1589–90), in *Francis Bacon*, ed. Vickers, 3. For Bacon's *Advertisement*, see below, lxxii–lxxiii.
35. The reference to the Vice was made at the trial of Sir Richard Knightley (*State Trials*, I, 1265). For the comparison with Tarleton, see below, lxiii.
36. For the characteristics of the Vice, see Cushman, *Devil and the Vice* (1900), 70ff., and Mares, "The Origin of the Figure Called 'The Vice' in Tudor Drama" (1958).
37. For the influence of the jig, see Gurr, *The Shakespearean Company* (2004), 71; for the jestbook, see Benger, "Authority of Writer and Text," 261–89. For a contemporary comparison of Martin with the jestbook published under the name of John Scoggin, see below, lxiii.

38. Bacon, *Advertisement*, in *Francis Bacon*, ed. Vickers, 19.
39. In Hughey, ed., *Arundel Harington Manuscript* (1960), II, 277–86 (282); for Bulkeley, see also Benger, "Authority of Writer and Text," 278–80. For Martin's gibes about Amy Cooper, see *Schoolpoints*, 93, and *Hay any Work*, 102, 112. For recent work on the culture of libel in this period, see below, notes 229, 232–33.
40. See *Epistle*, 29, and *Just Censure*, 180.
41. For the running heads, see Appendix, 209–10; for subscriptions, see *Epistle*, 45; for errata, *Epitome*, 85–86, and *Protestation*, 207.
42. *A Petition Directed to Her Most Excellent Majestie* (Middelburg, 1592), esp. 34–38. For the attribution to Throkmorton, see Carlson, *Martin Marprelate*, 117–19.
43. For Piers Ploughman, *I Playne Piers* (1550?), see Wawn, "Chaucer, *The Plowman's Tale* and Reformation Propaganda" (1973), 185–86, and King, *English Reformation Literature* (1982), 323–26.
44. Piers Ploughman, *I Plaine Piers* (London? 1588?), A2v. The *STC* changed the date from 1589? to 1588? in its appendix of "Addenda and Corrigenda" (III, 300). The type used for *I Plaine Piers* is very similar to that Robert Waldegrave used to print the first four Marprelate tracts. The one extant copy is incomplete: its nine leaves comprise about 20 percent of the text in the 1550? version. Two signatures (B and C) are corrected proofs; the failure to correct signature D suggests that printing was interrupted, and that the extant pages are all that were ever set: see Simpson, *Proof-Reading* (1935), 69–71.
45. For a thorough survey of Martin Marprelate's possible indebtedness to earlier traditions of Protestant satire, see Benger, "Authority of Writer and Text."
46. For surveys of these texts, see Harline, *Pamphlets, Printing, and Political Culture* (1989) and Sawyer, *Printed Poison* (1990).
47. See Lake and Questier, *Antichrist's Lewd Hat*, 187–314.
48. For Erasmus, see, e.g., Coolidge, "Martin Marprelate, Marvell and *Decorum Personae*" and Benger, "Authority of Writer and Text," 284–85. For Marprelate and the Rabelesian carnivalesque, see Poole, *Radical Religion* (2000), 16–44, and Navitsky, "'Words with Words Revenged'" (2006), ch. 1.
49. For Cartwright, see Strype, *Life of Whitgift* (1822), III, 231–32, and Cartwright, *A Brief Apologie* (1596), C2v. For Waldegrave, see Arber, *Introductory Sketch*, 99 (Sharpe deposition). For Udall, see his *A New Discovery* (1643), 24, and *State Trials*, I, 1294. For Penry, see *Notebook of John Penry* (1944), 71, and below, xl–xli. For disapproval among Separatists, see Henry Barrow, in *Writings*, ed. Carlson, 439–40, and Bancroft, *A Survay* (1593), 430 (quoting an intercepted letter by John Greenwood).
50. John Penry cited these three writers when defending Martinist style to Henry Sharpe, the project's "stitcher" (Arber, *Introductory Sketch*, 97). For Martin's use of continental traditions of satire, see Coolidge, "Martin Marprelate, Marvell and *Decorum Personae*" and Lecocq, *Satire en Angleterre* (1969), 199–207.
51. For Martinism as "display," see, e.g., *Theses Martinianae*, 161, and *Protestation*, 198, 199.

52. BL Cotton MS Julius F vi, 76r.

53. Fuller, *Church-History of Britain* (1655), IX, 193.

54. *State Trials*, I, 1270.

55. BL Lansdowne MS 57/77, Richard Howland to William Cecil, Lord Burghley (Dec. 19, 1588). For Cawdrey, see *ODNB*, and Guy, "Elizabethan Establishment," 130–35.

56. For a survey of suggested attributions, see Carlson, *Martin Marprelate*, 22–28; for detailed summaries of discussions up to 1923, see Greene, "The Martin Marprelate Controversy," 784–967.

57. For Martin (not mentioned in Carlson), Collinson cites a letter to Whitgift from John Woolton, bishop of Exeter: hearing that "a slaunderous libell" had been "caste abroade in London intituled Martin Mar Prelate," Woolton suggests that the writer was Philip Martin, a recently expelled preacher and schoolmaster suspected of circulating manuscript libels ("Ecclesiastical Vitriol" (1995), 162–63). The same Martin is mentioned in *SPR*, I, 298.

58. Other than Marbury, Fludd, and Martin, all have biographies in the *ODNB* (Marbury is mentioned in the biography of his daughter, Anne Hutchinson). Collinson discusses the careers of Beale, Morrice, Carleton, and Knollys in "Puritans, Men of Business, and Elizabethan Parliaments" (1994). For the implausible suggestion of Oxford (not mentioned in Carlson), see Marprelate, *Martin's Epistle*, ed. Green (1990), i–ii; for Oxford, equally implausibly, as the author instead of the three anti-Martinist "Pasquill" tracts, see Appleton, *Anatomy of the Marprelate Controversy* (2001), 153–62.

59. See *DNB* for Penry's traditional reputation. More recent accounts note that this status is largely a retrospective creation, and that Penry's influence on the church in Wales was likely negligible. The standard biography remains Pierce, *John Penry* (1923), but details have been corrected by subsequent discoveries. See *ODNB*; *Notebook of John Penry*, vii–xxv; Penry, *Three Treatises Concerning Wales*, ed. Williams (1960), ix–xxix; Williams, *Recovery, Reorientation, and Reformation* (1987), esp. 321–22; Jones, *Wales and the Tudor State* (1989), 111–16; Thomas, "John Penry and the Marprelate Controversy" (1993); Jones, *Early Modern Wales* (1994), 159–63.

60. For the debate on the Bill and Book, see Neale, *Elizabeth I and her Parliaments* (1957), 148ff.; Collinson, *Movement*, 303–16; Hartley, *Proceedings*, II, 203–205, 333–54, 390, 393–96.

61. Penry describes these events in *Th'Appellation of John Penri* (La Rochelle, 1589), 3–5, 39–43.

62. For the Coppinger–Hacket conspiracy, see *ODNB* (qq.v. Coppinger, Edmund; Hacket, William), and Walsham, "Frantick Hacket" (1998).

63. Both statutes are cited in texts connected with the trial. For these proceedings, see Coke, *Booke of Entries* (1614), 352v–53v; *The Examinations of Henry Barrowe, John Grenewood and John Penrie* (Dort? 1596?); Burrage, *John Penry* (1913); Pierce, *John Penry*, 393–481; *Notebook of John Penry*, xx–xxi; Carlson, *Martin Marprelate*, 85–88.

64. *Notebook of John Penry*, 70.
65. HL Ellesmere MS 2148. This document offers extracts from several depositions not otherwise extant and is a central piece of evidence for the movements of the Marprelate press. It has not been printed; an edition is in progress.
66. HMC, *Seventh Report* (1879), Appendix, 523.
67. PRO SP Dom. 12/245/30, William Sterrel to Charles Paget, draft suggested by Thomas Phelippes (June 12, 1593).
68. See, e.g., PRO SP Dom. 12/284/4, Thomas Phelippes to Robert Cecil (May 4, 1602); PRO SP Dom. 16/142/47, Leonel Sharpe to Dudley Carleton (May 8, 1629).
69. Arber, *Introductory Sketch*, 128 ("Puckering brief"), information extracted from Sharpe deposition (Arber, *Introductory Sketch*, 103–104). For Sharpe's role among Northampton reformers, see Sheils, "Religion in Provincial Towns" (1977), 170.
70. "Briefe instructions towchinge the Printer and place of Printinge the 3 first bookes of Martin and the Minerall Conclusions" (endorsed Sept. 21, 1589), printed in Arber, *Introductory Sketch*, 114–17, and Arber, *Transcript*, II, 816–17. Arber prints from BL Lansdowne MS 61/22.
71. Lambeth Palace Library MS 3470, 105r–06v, "A breiffe of the depositions allredy taken, touching the printing and publishing of Martins Libelles, and of the supposed Author thereof." This document has not been printed; an edition is in progress.
72. John Puckering, brief against the Martinists ("Puckering brief"), printed in Arber, *Introductory Sketch*, 119–36. Arber prints from BL Harley MS 7042, 6r–11v.
73. See, e.g., Williams, "John Penry: Marprelate and Patriot?" (1966–67), and Carlson, *Martin Marprelate*, 297–307.
74. For Martinist characteristics absent from Penry's acknowledged work, see Carlson, *Martin Marprelate*, 210–20.
75. Pierce, *John Penry*, 222. Williams ("John Penry: Marprelate and Patriot?," 367) and Carlson (*Martin Marprelate*, 154–57) cite similar observations by other scholars.
76. Arber, *Introductory Sketch*, 117 ("Briefe instructions").
77. At his trial in 1591, John Udall cited a letter in which Penry denied authorship of the *Epistle* "with such tearmes as declare him to bee ignorant and cleere in it." See Udall, *A New Discovery* (1643), 3.
78. *Notebook of John Penry*, 71. An earlier draft of the letter, containing a similar passage, is in *Notebook of John Penry*, 63.
79. *I John Penry* (Printed abroad? 1593?), 3.
80. *Notebook of John Penry*, 64–65.
81. Arber, *Introductory Sketch*, 94 (Sharpe deposition).
82. Arber, *Introductory Sketch*, 117 ("Briefe instructions"); Sutcliffe, *Answere* (1595), 70v (citing Newman deposition), 71v (describing the manuscript of *More Work*); HL Ellesmere MS 2148, 87r (extract from Hodgkins deposition). None of the manuscripts of the tracts is extant.

83. The most complete account of Throkmorton's life is Carlson, *Martin Marprelate*, 95–131, though *ODNB* and Hasler, ed., *History of Parliament*, III, 492–94 add some new information.
84. See Collinson, *Movement, passim*; Sheils, *Puritans in the Diocese of Peterborough* (1979); Hughes, *Politics, Society, and Civil War in Warwickshire* (1987), esp. 64–69.
85. See Carlson *Martin Marprelate*, 314–31.
86. PRO SP Dom. 12/167/21, Job Throkmorton to Ralph Warcuppe (January 13, 1584). Throkmorton's report is discussed by Woodall, "Recusant Rowington" (1978), 6–7, and Brown, "Paperchase: The Dissemination of Catholic Texts in Elizabethan England" (1989), 135–37.
87. See Kemp, ed., *Black Book of Warwick* (1898), 385–97; Neale, *Elizabethan House of Commons* (1949), 250–54; Hirst, *Representative of the People?* (1975), 210–12; Hasler, ed., *History of Parliament*, III, 492.
88. Hartley, *Proceedings*, II, 229.
89. The speech is printed in Hartley, *Proceedings*, II, 277–89. For Burghley's letter and Throkmorton's apology, see Neale, *Elizabeth I and her Parliaments*, 174; Hasler, ed., *History of Parliament*, III, 493–94; Carlson, *Martin Marprelate*, 342.
90. Hartley, *Proceedings*, II, 311, 314. The quotation here has been corrected in accordance with its manuscript source, Pierpont Morgan Library MS MA 276: *Proceedings* mistakenly inserts the final phrase ("and thease are . . . this age"), an interlinear addition, between the final "Yea" and "and I feare."
91. See, e.g., the discussion of "Bishops' English" in *Just Censure*, 183–84.
92. Hoby, *Diary*, ed. Moody (1998), 127–28.
93. Sutcliffe, *Answere to a Certaine Libel Supplicatorie* (1592), 202. Carlson attributes the *Petition* to Throkmorton: see *Martin Marprelate*, 117–20. For Sutcliffe, see *ODNB*.
94. Sutcliffe, *Answere* (1595), 71r–v; Pierce, *Historical Introduction*, 333–34 (examination of Hodgkins), 336–37 (examinations of Simmes and Thomlin).
95. *M. Some Laid Open* is a satirical attack on Robert Some (1542–1609), chaplain and later master of Peterhouse, Cambridge; he is mentioned in *Schoolpoints*, 92, 93, *Just Censure*, 181, and *Protestation*, 205–06. The work is characteristically Martinist, though it does not employ the Marprelate persona. For the attribution to Throkmorton, see Carlson, *Martin Marprelate*, 132–57.
96. Sutcliffe, *Answere* (1595), 70v–71r.
97. Sutcliffe, *Answere* (1595), 76r–78v. Throkmorton's submission to Hatton is Lambeth Palace MS 2686, 29r–30v (formerly PRO Manchester Papers 30/15/124).
98. Sutcliffe, *Answere* (1595), 70v, 73v.
99. For a list of these attributions organized by *STC* number, see Carlson, *Martin Marprelate*, 338–39. See also notes 85, 93, and 95 above.
100. For a discussion of these issues in connection with the Marprelate tracts, see North, *The Anonymous Renaissance* (2003), 139–58.
101. Carlson, *Martin Marprelate*, 407n.

102. Hughes and Larkin, eds., *Tudor Royal Proclamations* (1969), III, 35. For this proclamation, see below, lix–lx.
103. In Nashe, *Works*, III, 368.
104. Sutcliffe, *Answere* (1595), 70v, repeating a similar remark in his *Answere* (1592), 78.
105. Udall, *A New Discovery* (1643), 11. This vicar, Stephen Chatfield, is the subject of some unflattering sentences in *Epistle*, 32.
106. Arber, *Introductory Sketch*, 122 ("Puckering brief").
107. *A New Discovery* prints Udall's letters to the Queen and Ralegh, the letter from James VI, and the various submissions Udall was asked to sign. Records of his examination are printed in Arber, *Introductory Sketch*, 88–93. For other material relating to Udall's imprisonment and pardon, see Carlson, *Martin Marprelate*, 83–85.
108. For Field, see *ODNB*; Collinson, "John Field and Elizabethan Puritanism" (1961); Collinson, *Movement*, *passim*; Benger, "Authority of Writer and Text," 28–37.
109. Field, "Epistle," in Viret, *A Faithfull and Familiar Exposition* (1582), ¶2r.
110. A portion of this material was published in *A Parte of a Register* (Middelburg, 1593?). The rest remained in manuscript, and was calendared by Albert Peel in 1915 as *The Seconde Parte of a Register* (*SPR*). For Field's role in the compilation, see *SPR*, I, 14–18; Collinson, "John Field and Elizabethan Puritanism," 145–47.
111. Collinson, "John Field and Elizabethan Puritanism," 146–47.
112. Udall, *A New Discovery*, 3. Young is mentioned in *Epistle*, 9, 15.
113. An extract from the intercepted correspondence with Penry is included in HL Ellesmere MS 2148, 85r. Henry Sharpe deposed that Penry had told him that the *Epistle* printed notes "found in Master Feilds Study." While the attribution to the deceased Field was politic, it was in a general sense accurate. See Arber, *Introductory Sketch*, 94 (Sharpe deposition).
114. *Hay any Work*, 133–35. For Waldegrave, see *ODNB*.
115. Greg and Boswell, eds., *Records* (1930), 28; Arber, *Transcript*, I, 528. Martin mentions the raid in *Epistle*, 23–24.
116. See Van Eerde, "Robert Waldegrave" (1981).
117. For Crane and Carleton, see *ODNB*; McCorkle, "A Note Concerning 'Mistress Crane'" (1931); Carlson, *Martin Marprelate*, 22, 78.
118. According to the compilation of evidence in Lambeth Palace MS 3470, "the Presse was Penryes, which a Dutchman formerly examined confesseth he sold to Penry" (105r).
119. HL Ellesmere MS 2148, 85r (extract from Newman deposition); Arber, *Introductory Sketch*, 86 (Tomkins deposition), 124 ("Puckering brief").
120. Arber, *Introductory Sketch*, 85 (Tomkins deposition). Another deponent claimed that the price was twopence, but, given other evidence for the tracts' prices, this is likely an error: Arber, *Introductory Sketch*, 82 (Kydwell deposition).
121. According to depositions, the project printed 1,000 copies of *Schoolpoints*, at least 1,000 of *Hay any Work*, 1,500 of *Theses Martinianae*, and at least 500 of

Protestation: see HL Ellesmere MS 2148, 86r, 86v, 88r (extracts from depositions by Newman, Sharpe, Hodgkins, Simmes, and Thomlin); Arber,
Introductory Sketch, 99 (Sharpe deposition).

122. HL Ellesmere MS 2148, 85r (extract from Tomkins deposition).

123. Arber, *Introductory Sketch*, 123 ("Puckering brief").

124. For Knightley, see *ODNB*; Hasler, ed., *History of Parliament*, II, 405; Sheils,
Puritans in the Diocese of Peterborough, passim; Collinson, *Movement*, 142–43.

125. HL Ellesmere MS 2148, 85r–v (extracts from depositions by Sharpe and Jeffs);
Arber, *Introductory Sketch*, 95 (Sharpe deposition), 123, 126 ("Puckering brief").

126. Arber, *Introductory Sketch*, 125, 130 ("Puckering brief").

127. HL Ellesmere MS 2148, 85v (extract from Newman deposition). Newman
had been trained as a cobbler. In his *Answere* (1595), Matthew Sutcliffe
referred to Newman's extensive travels while distributing the tracts, writing
sardonically that "good it was for him, that he was a cobler, for if he had not
bin able to mend his shoes himselfe, he had never bene able to beare the
charges" (73r). At his 1591 trial, Newman was found guilty of dispersing
seditious books and sentenced to death; the privy council intervened and he
was allowed to sign a submission for pardon. See *Acts of the Privy Council*, n.s.
XXI, 130. The submission is printed in Carlson, *Martin Marprelate*, 79–80.

128. Arber, *Introductory Sketch*, 115 ("Briefe instructions").

129. *State Trials*, I, 1265–66, 1269; Arber, *Introductory Sketch*, 114 ("Briefe instructions"); HL Ellesmere MS 2148, 85v (extract from Newman deposition).

130. BL Cotton MS Julius F vi, 76r; *State Trials*, I, 1270–71; Paule, *Life of Whitgift*
(1612), 39–40; Camden, *Annales* (1615), 498; Camden, *Annales* (1625), 290–91.
Knightley's case set a legal precedent for a person being tried for "suffering a
seditious booke to be printed in his house": see Crompton, *Star-Chamber
Cases* (1630), 29.

131. HL Ellesmere MS 2148, 85v (extracts from Knightley and Sharpe depositions);
Arber, *Introductory Sketch*, 97 (Sharpe deposition), 130 ("Puckering brief").

132. *State Trials*, I, 1267–68; Arber, *Introductory Sketch*, 132 ("Puckering brief").

133. Arber, *Introductory Sketch*, 97 (Sharpe deposition).

134. Newman deposed that *Schoolpoints* was printed in late January or early
February; Sharpe deposed that it was printed about February 20: see HL
Ellesmere MS 2148, 86r (extract from Newman deposition); Arber,
Introductory Sketch, 98 (Sharpe deposition). Many of the dates Sharpe provides, however, are contradicted by other witnesses, and his errors might have
been deliberate. In the case of the *Schoolpoints*, the date supplied by Newman
accords better with the chronology established by other records.

135. HL Ellesmere MS 2148, 86r (extracts from Newman and Sharpe depositions).

136. HL Ellesmere MS 2148, 86r (extract from Newman deposition); Sharpe
dated the printing, probably incorrectly, to early March (Arber,
Introductory Sketch, 98).

137. Sharpe and Newman agree that *Hay any Work* was finished a week or so
before the end of March: HL Ellesmere MS 2148, 86r (extracts from Newman
and Sharpe depositions); Arber, *Introductory Sketch*, 99 (Sharpe deposition).

138. HL Ellesmere MS 2148, 86r (extracts from Newman and Sharpe depositions); Arber, *Introductory Sketch*, 98–99 (Sharpe deposition). Newman claimed a print run of 1,500 copies. But Sharpe's numbers (200 or more to Waldegrave, 700 to him) imply a run closer to 1,000.

139. HL Ellesmere MS 2148, 86r (extracts from Newman and Sharpe depositions). The deposition dates Penry's move into Haseley as March 2, 1589.

140. Arber, *Introductory Sketch*, 99–100 (Sharpe deposition). According to Newman, Waldegrave left the project because "Penry and Walgrave fell at some litle jarre" (HL Ellesmere MS 2148, 86r).

141. HL Ellesmere MS 2148, 86v (extract from Newman deposition). Hodgkins' name is also spelled "Hodgskin" and "Hoskins"; *STC* and *ODNB* both use "Hodgkins."

142. Sutcliffe, *Answere* (1595), 71r.

143. Thomlin (sometimes "Thomlyn") was admitted a freeman of the Stationers' Company in 1581 and Simmes (sometimes "Symmes" or "Sims") in 1585 (Arber, *Transcript*, II, 685, 694). Beginning in the mid-1590s, Valentine Simmes would become a major literary printer: see Ferguson, *Valentine Simmes* (1968).

144. Pierce, *Historical Introduction*, 335 (examination of Simmes and Thomlin).

145. *State Trials*, I, 1270–72.

146. Pierce, *Historical Introduction*, 333 (examination of Hodgkins). In the second part of this text, Martin Junior claims in a self-reflexive joke that he had found the first part "besides a bush, where it had dropped from somebody passing by that way" (*Theses Martinianae*, 159).

147. Pierce, *Historical Introduction*, 336 (examination of Simmes and Thomlin).

148. Arber, *Introductory Sketch*, 102 (Sharpe deposition); Pierce, *Historical Introduction*, 335–37 (examination of Simmes and Thomlin); HL Ellesmere MS 2148, 86v, 87r (extracts from depositions by Newman, Hodgkins, Simmes, and Thomlin).

149. Sutcliffe, *Answere* (1595), 72r; Arber, *Introductory Sketch*, 127 ("Puckering brief"); HL Ellesmere MS 2148, 87r (extract from Hodgkins deposition).

150. HL Ellesmere MS 2148, 87v (extracts from depositions by Sharpe, Hodgkins, Simmes, and Thomlin); Arber, *Introductory Sketch*, 102–103 (Sharpe deposition).

151. Pierce, *Historical Introduction*, 337–38 (examination of Simmes and Thomlin); HL Ellesmere MS 2148, 87v (extract from depositions by Simmes and Thomlin).

152. Whitgift wrote Burghley a letter describing the seizure of the press (printed in Arber, *Introductory Sketch*, 112–13). The privy council examined the printers on August 24, then handed them over to a committee with instructions to "put them all to the torture" if they continued unforthcoming (*Acts of the Privy Council*, n.s. XVIII, 59, 62). Hodgkins claimed that the confessions by Simmes and Thomlin "had bene violent extorted from them" and that he too had been forced to confess "by rackinge and great torments"; one of the commissioners, however, denied that torture was used, at least in Hodgkins' case. See Pierce, *Historical Introduction*, 334–35 (examination of Hodgkins).

153. HL Ellesmere MS 2148, 88r (extracts from depositions by Newman, Grimston, and Holmes).
154. HL Ellesmere MS 2148, 88r (extract from Newman deposition); Sutcliffe, *Answere* (1595), 72r, 73r. The books Waldegrave had printed in La Rochelle were Penry's *Th' Appellation of John Penri* (1589) and two para-Martinist tracts attributed to Throkmorton, *M. Some Laid Open in his Coulers* (1589) and *A Dialogue. Wherin is Plainly Laide Open* (1589).
155. The opening "Epistle to the Terrible Priests" printed in *Hay any Work* calls itself an "Interim" (106). But this text does not contain the passages Sutcliffe quotes from the manuscript "Martin's Interim," which he says was written in Throkmorton's hand: *Answere* (1595), 56r, 72r–v. This manuscript was apparently seized with Penry's papers but is not extant (HL Ellesmere MS 2148, 87v, 88v). Sutcliffe had not seen "The Crops and Flowers of Bridges Garden," but cites Newman and a letter by Throkmorton for the claim that it had been printed in Middelburg: *Answere* (1595), 72v. If it were indeed printed, no copies survive.
156. Cited in Sutcliffe, *Answere* (1595), 72v–73r. The depositions by Bowman and Maicocke are not otherwise extant.
157. HL Ellesmere MS 2148, 85v (Mary Waldegrave), 86r (Pigot), 88r (Grimston, Holmes, More, Gardiner, Adams); Arber, *Introductory Sketch*, 103, 131 (Wood, Pigot).
158. Arber, *Introductory Sketch*, 107–108.
159. Canterbury Cathedral Archives MS Dcb/PRC 44/3. This manuscript is an official copy, dated January 3, 1589, of a letter dated December 16, 1588.
160. Cited in Hughes and Larkin, eds., *Tudor Royal Proclamations*, III, 34. Clegg discusses this proclamation in *Press Censorship in Elizabethan England*, 73–75.
161. Hughes and Larkin, eds., *Tudor Royal Proclamations*, III, 34.
162. Recorded in Barlow, *The Summe and Substance of the Conference ... at Hampton Court* (1604), 36, 82. Cooper makes this point in *Admonition*, 82–83.
163. Letter 83, Elizabeth to James (July 6, 1590), in *Elizabeth I: Collected Works* (2000), 364–65. Elizabeth also asks James "not to give more harbor room to vagabond traitors and seditious inventors but to return them to me," probably referring to John Penry and Robert Waldegrave.
164. Hughes and Larkin, eds., *Tudor Royal Proclamations*, III, 34.
165. Arber, *Introductory Sketch*, 114 ("Briefe instructions").
166. Bancroft, *Sermon*, 1, 14, 40.
167. See, e.g., James, *A Sermon* (1590), C3r (delivered Nov. 9, 1589); White, *A Sermon* (1589), 45 (delivered Nov. 17, 1589); Rogers, *A Sermon* (1590), 6, 13–14, 21 (printed April 13, 1590); Babington, *A Sermon* (1591), 43 (delivered Oct. 11, 1590).
168. See *ODNB* (Bancroft); Cargill Thompson, "A Reconsideration of Richard Bancroft's Paul's Cross Sermon" (1969); Guy, "Elizabethan Establishment," 127–28; Lake, "Presbyterianism," 208.
169. Printed in *Tracts Ascribed to Richard Bancroft*, ed. Peel (1953), x.
170. Inner Temple Library, Petyt MS 538, vol. 38, no. 68, 155r. A modernized version is printed in Peel, ed., *Tracts Ascribed to Richard Bancroft*, xvii–xviii.

171. Collinson, *Movement,* 404; see also Chadwick, "Richard Bancroft's Submission" (1952).

172. For summaries of these works, see Pierce, *Historical Introduction,* 219–41, Carlson, *Martin Marprelate,* 53–74, and Milward, *Religious Controversies of the Elizabethan Age,* 88–93. For an extended analysis of the anti-Martinist campaign, see Lake and Questier, *Antichrist's Lewd Hat,* 521–58.

173. *Atra bilis est causa potissima diuturnae vitae / Martinomania est reip. perniciosa* (Cambridge, *c.* 1589), *STC* 4474.14. Act verses are "briefly propounded theses ... circulated by those taking part in public disputations as Acts for degrees" (*STC*). For a discussion and translation of this text, see Steggle, "A New Marprelate Allusion" (1997).

174. For these attributions, see Lyly, *Works,* I, 387–88; III, 415–16.

175. *Mar-Martine, I Know Not Why a Trueth in Rime Set Out* (1589), A1v, A4v.

176. *OED* (martin n^2) cites examples through to the late seventeenth century.

177. Lyly, *Works,* III, 418–19 (lines 3–4, 43–44).

178. For the references to Tarleton and Scoggin, see lines 53–56. The historical Scoggin was probably a fool at the court of Edward IV (*ODNB*). The reference is to the jestbook published under Scoggin's name, probably in many editions: see *STC* 21850.3.

179. For Lyly as the author of *Pappe with an Hatchet,* see *Works,* III, 390–92. McKerrow included *An Almond for a Parrat* among Nashe's "doubtful" works (see Nashe, *Works,* V, 59–63), but the argument for the attribution in McGinn, "Nashe's Share in the Marprelate Controversy" (1944) has been generally accepted. For Greene and Munday, see, e.g., Wilson, "Anthony Munday" (1909); Nicholl, *Cup of News* (1984), 69, 72–73; Hutson, *Nashe in Context* (1989), 67; Lake and Quester, *Antichrist's Lewd Hat,* xxviii, 515, 537, 550, 556; Kumaran, "Robert Greene's Martinist Transformation" (2006).

180. Lyly, *Works,* III, 403, 396.

181. Nashe, *Works,* III, 339, 341.

182. This success became conventional wisdom: nearly a century after the controversy, Anthony Wood approvingly claimed that anti-Martinist "Buffooneries and Pasquils" had rendered Martin's message "more ridiculous among the common sort, than any grave or learned Answer could do." See Wood, *Athenae Oxoniensis* (1721), I, 260.

183. Temple, *A Sermon Teaching Discretion in Matters of Religion* (1592), B8v–C1r.

184. See Gurr, *The Shakespearean Stage* (1992), 33, 36, 118.

185. These references are collected in Chambers, *The Elizabethan Stage* (1923), IV, 229–33.

186. Repeated references to this performance suggest that it took place more or less as described: see Pasquill, *The Returne,* in Nashe, *Works,* I, 92; *Pappe with an Hatchet,* in Lyly, *Works,* III, 408; *An Almond for a Parrat,* in Nashe, *Works,* III, 354.

187. *Acts of the Privy Council,* n.s. XXVIII, 215; Chambers, *The Elizabethan Stage,* I, 295. See also Clare, *"Art Made Tongue-Tied by Authority"* (1990), 24–26; Dutton, *Mastering the Revels* (1991), 74–81. But see also Dutton, "The Revels

Office and the Boy Companies" (2002), in which he revises his earlier work and notes the lack of evidence for official action actually being taken against the companies (esp. 327–28).

188. See *Theses Martinianae*, 161–62, *Just Censure*, 171, and *Protestation*, 204.
189. *Pappe with an Hatchet*, in Lyly, *Works*, III, 408.
190. For polemical anti-puritanism before and after the Marprelate controversy, see Holden, *Anti-Puritan Satire* (1954).
191. *State Trials*, I, 1268.
192. Carlson, *Martin Marprelate*, 79–80 (Newman's submission).
193. BL Lansdowne MS 120/3, "Proceedinges of certeyne undutifull [mi]nisters tending to innovation," 75v. In addition, BL Lansdowne MS 119/7, "The doctrines, and some practises of sundry troublesome Ministers in England," cites *Epitome* and *Just Censure* (105v); BL Lansdowne MS 101/51, which comprises twelve leaves of quotations extracted from *Epistle*, *Epitome*, and *Hay any Work*, likely also played a role in the prosecution of the case. A similar set of excerpts is in Bodleian Library, Tanner Papers, vol. 78, 192r–93v. For the 1590–91 Star Chamber proceedings, see Collinson, *Movement*, 403–31. For the source of the claim of the hundred thousand supporters, see *Just Censure*, 183.
194. Nashe, *Works*, III, 342; Lyly, *Works*, III, 420 (lines 83–84).
195. See *ODNB*; Cargill Thompson, "Sir Francis Knollys's Campaign against the *Jure Divino* Theory of Episcopacy" (1980); Collinson, *Movement*, 397; Hooker, *Works*, VI, 25, 32–33.
196. BL Lansdowne MS 61/27, John Rainolds to Francis Knollys (Sept. 19, 1589).
197. The letter was printed on William Jones' secret press in 1608 (*STC* 1084), and reprinted twice in 1641 (Wing R142 A, R142B). It is cited, e.g., in Alexander Leighton's *An Appeal to the Parliament* (Amsterdam, 1629), 8.
198. Hartley, ed., *Proceedings*, II, 419–20.
199. See Hughes and Larkin, eds., *Tudor Royal Proclamations*, III, 86–93.
200. Verstegan, *An Advertisement* (Antwerp? 1592), 19. This work summarizes Andreas Philopatrum (i.e., Robert Parsons), *Elizabethae Angliae Reginae haeresim Calvinianam propugnantis* (Antwerp, 1592). Parsons returned to the argument that the battle between Martin and Mar-Martin proved Protestantism's fundamental divisiveness in *The Warn-Word* (Antwerp, 1602), 51v–52r.
201. PRO SP Dom. 12/238/135, declaration of Roger Walton (April 30, 1591).
202. PRO SP Dom. 12/243/11, examination of George Dingley (Sept. 14, 1592). There is no evidence for the Spanish translation.
203. PRO SP Dom. Addenda 13/31/32, Thomas Phelippes to Thomas Barnes (June 23, 1589); PRO SP Dom. Addenda 13/31/33, Thomas Phelippes to Thomas Barnes (June 1589).
204. For contemporary English accounts of Anabaptism as the logical culmination of reform, see Cosin, *Conspiracie, for Pretended Reformation* (1592), 81–96, and Hooker, *Works*, I, 42–51. Nashe draws on this association of Presbyterianism with Anabaptism in his fictive description of Jack Wilton's visit to Münster in *The Unfortunate Traveller* (1594).

205. Sutcliffe, *Answere* (1592), 72.
206. Bancroft, *Sermon*, 26. For a similar argument, see *An Almond for a Parrat*, in Nashe, *Works*, III, 352.
207. Sutcliffe, *Answere* (1592), A2v; *Martins Months Minde*, B1v–B2r; Nashe, *Works*, III, 344, 370.
208. For the *Abstract* controversy, see Milward, *Religious Controversies of the Elizabethan Age*, 78–79. For a general discussion of debates over clerical education, see Morgan, *Godly Learning* (1986).
209. T. T., *A Myrror for Martinists, and all other Schismatiques* (1590), 1; *Marre Mar-Martin: or Marre-Martins Medling, in a Manner Misliked* (1589?), A3r. This pamphlet was originally published as *Mar-Martin. I Knowe Not Why a Frutelesse Lye in Print* (1589?) but was reprinted with an added title page that reflected its position more accurately.
210. Harvey, *An Advertisement for Pap-hatchet, and Martin Mar-prelate*, published in *Pierces Supererogation* (1593), 72–76, 84, 98, 137. For Harvey's role in the Marprelate controversy, see Stern, *Gabriel Harvey* (1979), 85–89. Stern notes that, despite these public condemnations, in private Harvey appears to have admired Marprelate's wit: annotating his copy of Lodovico Domenichi's *Facetie, Motti, et Burle* (Venice, 1571), Harvey writes that "The Baker of Bononia [i.e., Bologna, a figure from Italian jest books], & owr Martin Martprelate, two good od fellows, made it a pollicie, to jest at reverend Fathers, & all solemn ceremonies as matters of show, not of bonde, or valour – the stratagem of sum greater politicans in flore [i.e., Machiavelli]" (183).
211. Richard Harvey, *A Theologicall Discourse of the Lamb of God* (1590), a2v. This prefatory epistle "To reader" is not in all copies. Nashe responded to the juxtaposition in *Strange News* (1592), in Nashe, *Works*, I, 270. For the Harvey–Nashe quarrel, see Nashe, *Works*, V, 65–110; Hutson, *Nashe in Context*, 197–214; Halasz, *Marketplace of Print*, 84–113.
212. *An Advertisement* remained in manuscript until 1641, when it was published under the title *A Wise and Moderate Discourse, Concerning Church-Affaires*. But it did circulate in manuscript outside government circles, and is cited in works on both sides of the controversy: see, e.g., *A Petition* (Middelburg, 1592), 6; Richard Bancroft, *A Survay* (1593), *2r-v; and the manuscript "An advertisement towching seditious wrytings" (*c.* 1590), which reproduces many phrases from the *Advertisement* (PRO SP Dom. 12/235/81).
213. *Advertisement*, in *Francis Bacon*, ed. Vickers, 3–4, 14.
214. Martin, *Francis Bacon, the State, and the Reform of Natural Philosophy* (1992), 38.
215. *Advertisement*, in *Francis Bacon*, ed. Vickers, 6, 19.
216. Collinson, *Movement*, 431.
217. Nichols, *Plea of the Innocent* (1602), 31–32.
218. In Cosin, *Conspiracie, for Pretended Reformation* (1592), Bancroft, *Daungerous Positions and Proceedings* (1593), and Sutcliffe, *Answere* (1595).
219. These discussions build on McGinn, "Nashe's Share in the Marprelate Controversy," and Summersgill, "The Influence of the Marprelate Controversy" (1951). See, e.g., Hibbard, *Thomas Nashe* (1962), 28, 40–48;

Rhodes, *Elizabethan Grotesque* (1980); Crewe, *Unredeemed Rhetoric* (1982), 34–35; Hilliard, *Singularity of Thomas Nashe* (1986), 34–48.

220. For Dekker, Middleton, and Greene, see, e.g., Jones-Davies, *Thomas Dekker*, I, 107; Rhodes, *Elizabethan Grotesque*, 48; Heinemann, *Puritanism and Theatre* (1980), 57–58, 76; Hutson, *Nashe in Context*, 8–9; Kumaran, "Robert Greene's Martinist Transformation."

221. See, e.g., Lewis, *English Literature in the Sixteenth Century* (1954), 404ff.

222. See Collinson, "Ecclesiastical Vitriol"; Clegg, *Press Censorship in Elizabethan England*, ch. 9; McRae, *Literature, Satire, and the Early Stuart State* (2004), 8.

223. See Collinson, "Ben Jonson's *Bartholomew Fair*: The Theatre Constructs Puritanism" (1995) and Poole, *Radical Religion*, 16–44.

224. See, e.g., Adkins, "The Genesis of Dramatic Satire" (1946); Baldwin, "*Errors* and Marprelate" (1967); Simmons, "A Source for Shakespeare's Malvolio" (1972/73); Rhode, *Elizabethan Grotesque*, 89–101, 129; Honigmann, "*John a Kent* and Marprelate" (1983); Poole, *Radical Religion*, 16–44; Knapp, "Preachers and Players" (1993); Jorgensen, "Alienation in *Twelfth Night* and Anti-Martinist Discourse" (1999); Dusinberre, "Kemp and Mar-text in Arden" (2003); Moschovakis, "*Titus Andronicus* and the Case of William Hacket" (2006).

225. *ODNB* (Wyndham); Hasler, ed., *History of Parliament*, III, 668–70.

226. Surrey History Centre, Loseley Manuscripts, LM/1036/20. The accusation appears to have been pre-emptive: Fenne was planning to charge Bowell for non-payment and assault. Quoted with the kind permission of the Surrey History Centre.

227. Peterborough Diocesan Records, X648/1, 83v, cited in Sheils, *Puritans in the Diocese of Peterborough*, 128.

228. Weever, *Ancient Funeral Monuments* (1631), 56.

229. For this world of popular libel, see Fox, *Oral and Literate Culture* (2000), esp. 299–334.

230. *Recreation for Ingenious Head-Peeces* (1650, 1654), O3v.

231. Oxford, Bodleian MS Rawlinson C. 849, 396r–v. Listed as L776 in Crum, *First-Line Index* (1969), I, 540, and as EV14130–31 in May and Ringler, *Elizabethan Poetry* (2004), II, 983.

232. See, e.g., Cogswell, "Underground Political Verse" (1995); Croft, "Libels, Popular Literacy, and Public Opinion" (1995); McRae, "The Literary Culture of Early Stuart Libeling" (2000); McRae, *Literature, Satire, and the Early Stuart State*.

233. See, e.g., Cust, "News and Politics" (1986); Croft, "The Reputation of Robert Cecil" (1991); Bellany, "Raylinge Rymes" (1994); Bellany, "A Poem on the Archbishop's Hearse" (1995). Croft explicitly cites the Marprelate tracts and lobbying by radical Presbyterianism in the 1580s as influencing the development of "popular political consciousness" in the early seventeenth century (68).

234. PRO SP Dom. 12/218/23, Francis Thynne to William Cecil, Lord Burghley (Nov. 15, 1588).

235. Corpus Christi College, Oxford, MS 327, 21r, as cited by Sanderson, "Thomas Bastard's Disclaimer" (1962), 149; Bodleian Library Rawl. Poet. MS 212, 123v, as printed in Hughey, ed., *Arundel Harington Manuscript*, II, 277.

236. Wood, *Athenae Oxoniensis* (1721), I, 431–32.

237. See, e.g., *Daungerous Positions*, 43, 46, 48–51, 55–60, 125–26, 137–40.

238. Parker, *A Reproof to the Rehearsal Transprosed* (1673), 395.

239. The 1612 catalogue of Bancroft's library includes 117 entries under the heading "Libri Puritanici"; they include "Martini Marpr: varia" and "Penry varia" (Lambeth Palace, Library Record F1, 75r–76v).

240. The will is printed in Babbage, *Puritanism and Richard Bancroft* (1962), 386–89.

241. Lambeth Palace, Library Record F1, 2r.

242. For the library's history, see Cox-Johnson, "Lambeth Palace Library" (1954–58).

243. For Hooker's polemical context, see Cargill Thompson, *Studies in the Reformation* (1980), 131–92, and Lake, *Anglicans and Puritans?*, ch. 4. For the debates over the extent to which Hooker either reasserts or establishes the principles of conformist thought, see Perrott, "Richard Hooker and the Problem of Authority" (1998).

244. Hooker, *Works*, I, 12–26.

245. As the editors of Hooker's *Works* point out, "Puritan writers consistently avoided any such openly seditious language," and Martin was no exception: Hooker misrepresents the passage (*Works*, VI, 40, 470n). See *Hay any Work*, 124.

246. Hooker, *Works*, I, 36–51 (36).

247. See Hooker, *Works*, VI, 44–51, which argues against Izaak Walton's date of 1598 for Cranmer's letter and discusses the role it played in Hooker's Preface. The letter was printed as *Concerning the New Church Discipline* (Oxford, 1642), and reprinted in 1643 and 1645.

248. Hooker, *Works*, VI, 443.

249. Hooker, *The Dangers of New Discipline* (Oxford, 1642).

250. Hooker, *Works*, II, 5; III, 290–312.

251. Lodge, *Wits Miserie, and the Worlds Madnesse* (1596), 68. Representative denunciations of Martin include Ormerod, *Picture of a Puritane* (1605), A4r, O1r, 6, 18, 22, 25, 61; Camden, *Annales* (1615), 497–98; Burton, *A Sermon Preached … in Warwicke* (1620), 17–18; Burges, *Fire of the Sanctuarie* (1625), 82; Sydenham, *The Foolish Prophet. A Sermon Preached … at Taunton in Somerset*, in *Sermons* (1637), 270.

252. Watson, *A Decacordon of Ten Quodlibeticall Questions* (1602), 266.

253. Covell, *A Modest and Reasonable Examination* (1604), 28, 36–37, 44, 52, 90, 118, 121.

254. Heylyn, *Antidotum Lincolniense* (1637), A3r.

255. Heylyn, *A Briefe and Moderate Answer, to … Henry Burton* (1637), B3v, 187–89, 193; Heylyn, *Examen historicum* (1659), 150, 156, 172, 256. Heylyn's *Aerius Redivivus, or, The History of the Presbyterians* (1670) offers an extended account of the Marprelate project (279–86).

256. Hill, *The Crie of England. A Sermon Preached at Paules Crosse in September 1593* (1595), 51–52. *STC* notes that "1593" is probably an error for 1592.

257. *Pilgrimage to Parnassus*, in Leishman, ed., *Three Parnassus Plays* (1949), 113–14. The play also refers to "Newman the cobler" (127), suggesting that other players in the Marprelate project remained familiar ten years after the event.

258. Markham, *The Complete Farriar* (1639), 10.

259. Recent revisionist work on censorship in early modern England has persuasively challenged earlier arguments about pervasive state control of the press. Nevertheless, some controls were in place, some books suppressed, and explicitly oppositional books almost unknown. For the debates about the extent and nature of censorship in the decades before the civil wars, see Clegg, *Press Censorship in Jacobean England* (2001), 1–19, and Towers, *Control of Religious Printing in Early Stuart England* (2003), 1–15, 277–81.

260. For English printing in the Netherlands up to 1640, see Sprunger, *Trumpets from the Tower* (1994).

261. For Leighton, Burton, Bastwick, Prynne, Sparke, and Lilburne in this period, see *ODNB*; Sprunger, *Trumpets from the Tower*; Foster, *Notes from the Caroline Underground* (1978).

262. PRO SP Dom. 16/177/8, Samuel Brooke to William Laud (Dec. 15, 1630).

263. Cowley, *The Guardian* (1650), act 4, scene 7 (E1v). When Cowley revised the play as *Cutter of Coleman-Street* (1663), he substituted Fletcher for Shakespeare, cut Prynne, but kept Marprelate (act 3, scene 1).

264. Clarendon, *History of the Rebellion* (1888), III, 56.

265. This reprint has been associated with the "Cloppenburg" press: see Johnson, "The 'Cloppenburg' Press" (1958), 280–82; Sprunger, *Trumpets from the Tower*, 104–105, 210–11.

266. *Our Demands of the English Lords Manifested, Being at Rippon Octob. 8 1640* (Amsterdam, 1640), and *The Lawfulnesse of our Expedition into England Manifested* (Amsterdam, 1640).

267. *A Sermon Preached in London by a Faithfull Minister of Christ* (Amsterdam, 1641); for Walker, see *ODNB*.

268. For attribution, date, and place of publication, see Wolfe, "Unsigned Pamphlets of Richard Overton: 1641–1649" (1958), Gimelfarb-Brack, *Richard Overton* (1979), 124–26, 432–33, and note 265 above.

269. *Questions to be Disputed in Counsell of the Lords Spirituall after their Return from their Visitation* (1641).

270. Marlowe, *Doctor Faustus and Other Plays*, ed. Bevington and Rasmussen, 2.3.139–42 (A-text), 2.3.140–42 (B-text).

271. The Latin device "Anglia Martinis disce savere tuis" and the mocking formula for John Whitgift, "the John of all Sir Johns," are in both *Reformation No Enemie* and Overton's *The Araignement of Mr. Persecution* (1645). For the press with which Overton was involved, see Plomer, "Secret Printing During the Civil War" (1904). For Overton as (probably amateur) printer, see *ODNB*; the examination of stationer Nicholas Tew (Feb. 10, 1645) in HMC, *Sixth*

Report (1877), Appendix, 46; and the petition by stationer Robert Eeles (Aug. 13, 1646) in HMC, *Sixth Report* (1877), Appendix, 130–31.

272. For detailed descriptions of scores of these satirical pamphlets, see Gimelfarb-Brack, *Richard Overton*; the attributions to Overton, however, need to be treated with caution. For arguments that link Marprelate with other polemical texts of the 1640s, see Egan, "Milton and the Marprelate Tradition" (1975) and "Nathaniel Ward and the Marprelate Tradition" (1980).

273. For a number of additional references to Martin from the 1640s, see Raymond, *Pamphlets and Pamphleteering*, 204–205.

274. G. T., *Roger the Canterburian ... or The Character of a Prelaticall Man Affecting Great Heights* (1642), 2–4.

275. Ley, "An answer to Mercuries message anno 1641," in *Early Modern Women's Manuscript Poetry*, ed. Millman and Wright (2005), 83–86 (lines 1, 5–8, 45–49).

276. John Taylor, *Differing Worships ... Or Tom Nash His Ghost (the Old Martin Queller) Newly Rous'd* (1640), title page. The other two pamphlets are *Tom Nash His Ghost* (1642) and *Crop-Eare Curried, or, Tom Nash His Ghost* (1644).

277. For the Marpriest tracts, see Smith, "Richard Overton's Marpriest Tracts" (1986); Smith, *Literature and Revolution* (1994), 297–304; Gimelfarb-Brack, *Richard Overton*, 119–80.

278. Milton, *Complete Shorter Poems*, ed. Carey (1997), 300.

279. Marpriest describes himself as the son and heir of "Old Martin the Metropolitan" on the title pages of *The Araignement of Mr. Persecution* (1645), *The Ordinance for Tythes Dismounted* (1646), and *Divine Observations* (1646); and as "young Martin" on the title pages of *A Sacred Decretall* (1645) and *Martin's Eccho* (1645).

280. This is the implicit argument of Hill, "Radical Prose in Seventeenth-Century England" (1982).

281. *Statutes of the Realm*, V, 304–305.

282. L'Estrange, *Interest Mistaken, or, The Holy Cheat* (1661), 30.

283. For the uses of Marprelate in this debate, see Coolidge, "Martin Marprelate, Marvell, and *Decorum Personae*"; Anselment, *"Betwixt Jest and Earnest"*, 94–125; Egan, "Andrew Marvell Refashions the Marprelate Tradition" (1995). Quotations are from Marvell, *The Rehearsal Transpros'd and The Rehearsal Transpros'd: The Second Part*, ed. Smith (1971).

284. Parker, *A Discourse of Ecclesiastical Politie* (1670), 60–62.

285. Parker, *A Defence and Continuation of the Ecclesiastical Politie* (1671), 446.

286. Parker, *A Reproof to the Rehearsal Transprosed* (1673), 11, 49–50, 105. For additional references to the Marprelate tracts, see 113, 124, 135, 191–92.

287. Marvell, *The Rehearsal Transpros'd*, 294.

288. Parker, *Reproof*, 191; Leigh, *Transproser Rehears'd*, 55, and, for other references, 30, 32, 41–43, 72, 110, 126–27, 133, 135, 146–47.

289. Walton, *The Life of Mr. Rich. Hooker* (1665), 88–89.

290. Clarendon, *Animadversions* (1673), 2.
291. Tomkins, *Inconveniences of Toleration* (1667; repr. 1683), 24–25.
292. In Dryden, *Poems*, ed. Hammond and Hopkins (1995–2005), II, 102.
293. Wanley to Bagford (Sept. 21, 1697), in Wanley, *Letters*, ed. Heyworth (1989), 76. Wanley's initial correspondent was Robert Beake, mayor of Coventry.
294. BL Sloane MS 885, 102r–05v. For Wallis and his writings, see *ODNB*.
295. Ames, *Typographical Antiquities* (1749), 482–83, 556–61.

Textual Introduction

The Martin Marprelate tracts are frequently mentioned but infrequently read. To encourage more direct familiarity with one of the most remarkable voices of early modern English prose, this edition offers a modern-spelling text. The decision to modernize was made easier by the ready availability of the tracts in their original form: readers who prefer to see the tracts as they first appeared may do so in print in the facsimiles published in *The Marprelate Tracts [1588–1589]* (Leeds: Scolar Press, 1967), on microfilm in the Early English Books microfilm series, and as digitized images through the Early English Books Online (EEBO) project published by ProQuest and Chadwyck-Healey. To facilitate reference to these facsimiles, this edition provides the original page breaks within the text.

SOURCES OF THE TEXTS

The Marprelate tracts are not textually complex: no manuscripts are extant, only one edition was printed of each tract, and there appears to be only one stop-press correction within the entire series (see *Hay any work*, 121 and 258 n.77). The text of this edition is based on the facsimiles published by Scolar Press mentioned above. For six of the seven tracts, each facsimile copytext was collated with at least five copies of the original edition; the one exception is the broadsheet *Certain Mineral and Metaphysical Schoolpoints*, which was collated with the only two extant copies.

EDITORIAL PROCEDURES

This edition uses the following editorial procedures:
- Spelling is modernized, though obsolete, archaic, colloquial, dialectical, and nonce forms are retained, with their spelling regularized. Consistency has not been imposed on variant spellings (e.g., -our/-or endings). Personal and place names are regularized. Abbreviations are expanded,

unless there is a possibility of wordplay (e.g., "John of Cant."), or if the abbreviated word cannot be identified with certainty (e.g., "D." for either "Dean" or "Doctor," or "M." for either "Martin" or "Master").

- Formatting is regularized: titles of books italicized, periods removed after numbers, and apostrophes added to possessives. But quotation marks have not been introduced: the tracts use differences in font to set off many direct quotations as well as to emphasize certain words, and this edition follows that convention, using italic. Passages of dialogue are reproduced as they are in the original, without quotation marks or the use of a different font: the consequent blurring of voices is one of the defining stylistic features of the Marprelate tracts.

- The occasional new paragraph break has been introduced to help clarify a shift in argument or subject. Almost all sentence breaks are those of the original edition. Some new sentence breaks reflect typographical idiosyncrasies: for example, the tracts often omit a period and initial capital after a closing parenthesis, even when what follows is clearly a new sentence. The first four tracts, printed by Robert Waldegrave, rely heavily on colons to mark the end of syntactic periods. Very occasionally, these colons have been replaced with periods when doing so clarifies meaning. Colons appear with less than half this frequency in the two tracts printed by John Hodgkins (two for every five used in the first four tracts, on average), and so their usage seems to reflect the habits of the printers more than the writer(s).

- Capitalization in the original editions is inconsistent within each tract individually, and broadly different between the tracts printed by Robert Waldegrave and those printed by John Hodgkins. In general, capitalization has been regularized according to current convention: most offices and titles, e.g., are in lower case, but revert to upper case when used as a title of address ("the bishop of London," but "Bishop Aylmer"). In most cases, the Marprelate tracts mirror recent convention by employing lower case (in the majority of their uses) for words such as parliament, privy council, earl, puritan, church (the institution), lord treasurer, etc. Some words remain capitalized when used in headings, when used for rhetorical emphasis, or when consistently capitalized in the original (e.g., "Majesty").

- Punctuation has been lightly regularized, primarily with regard to comma usage. But it has not been modernized: on the whole, this edition retains the tracts' rhetorical, rather than syntactic, punctuation. As with capitalization, punctuation differs between the tracts printed by Robert Waldegrave and those printed by John Hodgkins. Waldegrave, but not Hodgkins, uses the virgule or slash ("/"); these are replaced with commas, according to conventional practice. Hodgkins, on the other hand, uses semicolons and exclamation marks, neither of which appears in the tracts printed by Waldegrave. These differences are all probably a consequence of the different type fonts the printers happened to be using. Waldegrave, for example, uses question marks to conclude sentences that are clearly exclamations, presumably since his black letter font lacked the character called at the time the "note of admiration." Since exclamation marks do appear in the texts printed in roman type, this edition uses exclamation marks in place of Waldegrave's exclamatory interrogatives.

• Other changes: on a few occasions, words are interpolated editorially, in square brackets, to help readers make sense of particularly opaque sentences. Editorial corrections of biblical references or of page references to other books are also included in square brackets. Obvious typographical errors are silently corrected; all emendations that might be considered substantive are discussed in notes keyed to the change in the text. Two changes to the mise en page of the original publications were necessitated by the exigencies of modern printing and publication. The running heads of the *Epitome*, the one tract to feature different running heads on every page, are listed in an appendix (along with the uniform running heads to the other tracts); and the side notes of the original editions have had to be reproduced here as footnotes, signaled in the text with letters.

OTHER EDITIONS

William Pierce edited the only previous scholarly edition of the tracts almost a century ago: *The Marprelate Tracts 1588, 1589* (London: James Clark, 1911). Pierce's text is also modernized, though with a heavier hand than that employed in this edition (he modernizes punctuation as well as spelling), and it features occasional misreadings and mis-modernized words. But Pierce was a fine scholar, and his thorough annotations have been indispensable to generations of readers, as well as to the preparation of this edition. Pierce's commentary, however, is also highly partisan: he freely brought his own anti-episcopal bias to bear on his remarks on the Elizabethan episcopate.

A few reprints of individual tracts preceded Pierce's complete edition. John Petheram published lightly annotated editions of *Epistle* (London, 1842 and 1843), *Epitome* (London, 1843), and *Hay any Work* (London, 1845) in his series "Puritan Discipline Tracts." Edward Arber reprinted the *Epistle*, without annotations, as no. 11 in his series "The English Scholar's

Library of Old and Modern Works," vol. II (London, 1880; Westminster, 1895). Other than the Scolar Press facsimile mentioned earlier, the only printed edition to appear since Pierce is of an individual tract: Maria Giannina Green, ed., *The Marprelate Tracts: Martin's Epistle* (Kelowna, BC: Devere Press, 1990). Green has also published modern-spelling electronic editions of all seven tracts online on "The Oxford Authorship Site" (www.oxford-shakespeare.com), where the Marprelate tracts are claimed for the anti-Stratfordian Oxford canon. Also available online are original-spelling *and* lightly annotated modern-spelling editions of all seven tracts on "The Anglican Library" site (www.anglicanlibrary.org), prepared by John D. Lewis.

TRACT I

The *Epistle*

The *Epistle*
(October 1588)

The first Marprelate tract has always been known as the *Epistle*, a word introduced only in the twentieth line of the title page but featured in the pamphlet's repeated running head ("An Epistle to the terrible Priests of the Confocation house"). Robert Waldegrave printed about 1,000 copies on a press hidden in the manor of Elizabeth Crane in East Molesey, Surrey, employing a black letter type (described in contemporary documents as his "Dutch Letters") and setting the pamphlet in quarto format: at fifty-six pages inclusive, the *Epistle* required seven sheets per copy (collating 4°: *A*⁴ B–G⁴; 28 leaves, pp. [2] 1–54). The wholesale price was sixpence apiece, the retail price about ninepence (see Introduction, l–li).

As its title suggests, the *Epistle* takes the form of a letter addressed to the leading members of the clerical hierarchy. Martin invokes the traditional language of supplication and petition, only to subvert those rhetorical conventions by using them as the vehicle for aggressive, mocking attacks. The *Epistle* opens with an assault on John Bridges, dean of Salisbury, whose *Defence of the Government Established in the Church of Englande* (1587) helped spur the Marprelate project into action (see Introduction, xxiii–xxiv). But Martin soon introduces other figures who would become favorite targets throughout the tracts, particularly John Whitgift, archbishop of Canterbury, John Aylmer, bishop of London, and Andrew Perne, dean of Ely and master of Peterhouse, Cambridge. The *Epistle* eventually addresses more than a dozen clerics whose scholarship, ethics, or personal life, Martin argues, made them unfit to hold ecclesiastical office but fit representatives of a corrupt church.

The *Epistle* displays all the defining features of the Marprelate style: *ad hominem* attacks, conversational prose, swashbuckling self-confidence, self-reflexive play with typographical and polemical conventions, and the use of such devices as direct address, dialogue, and dramatization. The mocking, irreverent voice of Martin Marprelate entered the realm of public discourse fully developed and immediately distinctive. But the *Epistle* also balances these strategies, novel by the standards of the immediate period, with many elements traditional to reform polemic. Martin uses syllogistic argument to challenge the legitimacy of clerical hierarchy in general and episcopacy in particular; advocates instead the four-part Presbyterian system of church government; and deplores non-residency, the lack of a preaching ministry, the use of the *ex officio* oath, the liturgical use of Apocryphal texts, the lack of due process in the proceedings of the church courts, and the misuse of excommunication. He asserts that the church tolerated Catholic practices and winked at the production of Catholic texts while harshly suppressing loyal, reform-minded Protestants. To humanize the cause of reform, Martin sets his stories of autocratic clerics against the stories of those who suffered at their hands, dramatizing the distresses of reformers such as John Penry, Robert Waldegrave, Giles Wigginton, Eusebius Paget, and John Udall. He also attempts to legitimize his cause by calling attention to its polemical and institutional genealogy, citing the works of such Presbyterian stalwarts as Thomas Cartwright, Dudley Fenner, and Walter Travers, and invoking the practices of reformed churches on the continent.

About two-thirds of the way through the *Epistle*, Martin calls attention to the key element of his polemical strategy: the attempt to move ecclesiological controversy out of the study where learned polemic was written and read and into the wider public sphere of popular debate. He warns the bishops "what a perilous fellow M. Marprelate is: he understands of all your knavery, and it may be he keeps a register of them: unless you amend, they shall all come into the light one day" (33). This "register" comprised, at least in part, the collection of records that formed the communal memory of the reform movement, a project initiated by John Field (see Introduction, xlviii–xlix). This willingness to expose his opponents' less flattering actions to public view is a defining feature of the polemical style that would become known as "Martinism."

Oh read over D. John Bridges, for it is a worthy work:[1]

Or an Epitome of the first book of that right worshipful volume
written against the puritans, in the defence of the noble clergy,
by as worshipful a priest, John Bridges, Presbyter, Priest
or Elder, Doctor of Divility, and Dean of Sarum.[2]
Wherein the arguments of the puritans are
wisely prevented,[3] that when they come
to answer Master Doctor, they must
needs say something that hath
been spoken.

Compiled for the behoof and overthrow of the Parsons,
Fyckers, and Currats,[4] that have learnt their catechisms,
and are past grace:[5] by the reverend and worthy
Martin Marprelate gentleman, and dedicated
to the Confocation House.[6]

The Epitome is not yet published, but it shall be
when the bishops are at convenient leisure to
view the same. In the mean time, let them
be content with this learned Epistle.

Printed oversea, in Europe, within two furlongs
of a Bouncing Priest, at the cost and charges
of M. Marprelate, gentleman.[7]

To the right puissant and terrible Priests, my clergy masters of the
Confocation House, whether Fickers General, worshipful
Paltripolitans, or any other of the Holy League of
Subscription,[8] this work I recommend unto
them with all my heart, with a desire to see
them all so provided for one day, as I
would wish, which I promise them
shall not be at all to their hurt.

Right poisoned,[9] persecuting and terrible priests, the theme of mine Epistle unto your venerable masterdoms is of two parts (and the Epitome of our brother Bridges his book, shall come out speedily). First, most pitifully complaining, Martin Marprelate, etc. Secondly, may it please your good worships, etc.

Most pitifully complaining therefore, you are to understand that D. Bridges hath written in your defence a most senseless book, and I cannot very often at one breath come to a full point, when I read the same.

Again, may it please you to give me leave to play the Duns for the nonce as well as he,[10] otherwise dealing with Master Doctor's book, I cannot keep *decorum personæ*. And may it please you, if I be too absurd in any place (either in this Epistle, or that Epitome), to ride to Sarum, and thank his Deanship for it. Because I could not deal with his book commendably according to order, unless I should be sometimes tediously dunstical and absurd. For I have heard some clergymen say, that Master Bridges was a very patch and a duns when he was in Cambridge.[11] And some say, saving your reverence that are bishops, that he is as very a knave, and enemy unto the sincerity of religion, as any popish prelate in Rome. But the patch can do the cause of sincerity no hurt. Nay, he hath in this book wonderfully graced the same by writing against it. For I have heard some say, that whosoever will read his book, shall as evidently see the goodness of the cause of reformation, and the poor, poor, poor nakedness of your govern- [2] ment, as almost in reading all Master Cartwright's works.[12] This was a very great oversight in his grace of Cant. to suffer such a book to come out.[13] For besides that an archbishop is very weakly defended by Mass Dean,[14] he hath also by this means provoked many to write against his gracious fatherhood, who perhaps never meant to take pen in hand. And brother Bridges, mark what Martin tells you, you will shortly I hope have twenty fists about your ears more than your own.[15] Take heed of writing against puritans while you live, yet they say that his grace would not have the book to be published, and if you mark, you shall not find *seen and allowed* in the title of the book.[16] Well fare old mother experience yet, the burnt child dreads the fire: his grace will carry to his grave, I warrant you, the blows which Master Cartwright gave him in this cause: and therefore no marvel though he was loth to have any other so banged as he himself was to his woe. Others say that John Cant. oversaw every proof. If he did, then he oversaw many a foul solecism, many a senseless period, and far more slanders. Slanders my friends? I think so. For what will you say, if our brother Bridges, and our cousin Cosin,[17] with many others, have had their grace of the bishops *ad practicandum* in Flanders?[18] How could their government stand, unless they should slander their brethren, and make her Majesty believe that the church government prescribed in the word would overthrow her regiment, if it were received in our church, and that the seekers of reformation are a sort of malcontents, and enemies unto the state?

Item, may it please your worthy worships to receive this courteously to favour at my hand, without choler or laughing. For my Lord of Winchester is very choleric and peevish, so are his betters at Lambeth,[19] and Doctor Cosin hath a very good grace in jesting, and I would he had a little more grace, and a handful or two more of learning, against he answer the *Abstract* next. Nay believe me, it is enough for him to answer the *Counter-Poyson*.[20] And I am none of the malicious sectaries, whereof John of London spake the last Lent, 1588, in his letters written to the archdeacon of Essex, to forbid public fasts.[21] Ha, ha, Doctor Copcot, are ye there, why do not you answer the confutation of your sermon at Paul's Cross?[22] It is a shame for your grace John of Cant. that Cartwright's books have been now a dozen years almost unanswered: you first provoked him to write, and you first have received the foil.[23] If you can answer those books, why do you suffer the puritans to insult and rejoice at your silence? If you cannot, why are you an archbishop? He hath proved the calling to be unlawful and antichristian. You dare not stand to the defence of it. Now most pitifully complaineth, M. Marprelate desireth you either to answer what hath been written against the gracelessness of your archbishopric, or to give over the same, and to be a means that no bishop in the land be a lord any more. I hope one day her Majesty will either see that the lord bishops prove their calling lawful by the word, or as John of London prophesied saying, come down you bishops from your thousands, and content you with your hundreds, let your diet be priestlike, and not princelike, etc., quoth John Elmar in his *Harborowe of Faithful Subjects*.[24] But I pray you bishop John, dissolve this one question to your brother Martin: if this prophecy of yours come to pass in your days, who shall be bishop of London? And will you not swear as commonly you do, like a lewd swag,[25] and say, by my faith, by my faith my masters, this

[3]

gear goeth hard with us. Now may it please your grace with the rest of your worships, to procure that the puritans may one day have a free disputation with you about the controversies of the church, and if you be not set at a flat *non plus*, and quite overthrown, I'll be a lord bishop myself: look to yourselves, I think you have not long to reign. Amen. And take heed brethren of your reverend and learned brother Martin Marprelate. For he [4] meaneth in these reasons following, I can tell you, to prove that you ought not to be maintained by the authority of the magistrate in any Christian commonwealth: Martin is a shrewd fellow, and reasoneth thus. Those that are petty popes and petty antichrists ought not to be maintained in any Christian commonwealth. But every lord bishop in England, as for ilsample,[26] John of Cant., John of London, John Exeter, John Rochester, Thomas of Winchester, the bishops of Lincoln, of Worcester, of Peterborough, and to be brief, all the bishops in England, Wales, and Ireland, are petty popes and petty antichrists.[27] Therefore no lord bishop (now I pray thee good Martin speak out, if ever thou diddest speak out, that her Majesty and the council may hear thee)[a] is to be tolerated in any Christian commonwealth: and therefore neither John of Cant., John of London, etc., are to be tolerated in any Christian commonwealth. What say you now brother Bridges, is it good writing against puritans? Can you deny any part of your learned brother Martin his syllogism? We deny your minor, M. Marprelate, say the bishops and their associates.[28] Yea my learned masters, are you good at that?[b] What do you brethren? Say me that again? Do you deny my minor?[29] And that be all you can say, to deny lord bishops to be petty popes, turn me loose to the priests in that point, for I am old suresby at the proof of such matters, I'll presently mar the fashion of their lordships.[30]

They are petty popes and petty antichrists, whosoever usurp the authority of pastors over them, who by the ordinance of God are to be under no pastors. For none but antichristian popes and popelings ever claimed this authority unto themselves, especially when it was gainsaid, and accounted antichristian, generally by the most churches in the world. But our lord bishops usurp authority over those, who by the ordinance of God are to be [5] under no pastors, and that in such an age, as wherein this authority is gainsaid, and accounted antichristian, generally by all the churches

[a] [side note:] What malapert knaves are these that cannot be content to stand by and hear, but they must teach a gentleman how to speak.
[b] [side note:] Look the doctor's book, page 107, line 20, and page 113, line 13 [=23].

in the world for the most part. Therefore our lord bishops – what sayest thou man? – our lord bishops (I say), as John of Canterbury, Thomas of Winchester (I will spare John of London for this time, for it may be he is at bowls,[31] and it is pity to trouble my good brother, lest he should swear too bad), my reverend prelate of Lichfield,[32] with the rest of that swinish rabble, are petty antichrists, petty popes, proud prelates, intolerable with-standers of reformation, enemies of the gospel, and most covetous wretched priests.[c] This is a pretty matter, that standers-by must be so busy in other men's games: why sauceboxes must you be prattling? You are as mannerly as bishops, in meddling with that you have nothing to do, as they do in taking upon them civil offices. I think for any manners either they or you have, that you were brought up in Bridewell.[33] But it is well that since you last interrupted me (for now this is the second time) you seem to have learnt your Cato *De moribus* in that you keep yourselves on the margent.[34] Would you be answered? Then you must know, that I have set down nothing but the truth in the conclusion, and the syllogisms are mine own, I may do what I will with them, and thus hold you content. But what say you my horned masters of the Confocation House?[35] You deny my minor again I know. And thus I prove it.

First,

That our prelates usurp their authority.

They usurp their authority, who violently and unlawfully retain those under their government, that both would and ought (if they might) to shake off that yoke wherewith they are kept under. But our lord bishops retain such (namely other pastors) and unlawfully under their yoke, who both would and ought to reject the same. For all the pastors in the land that deserve the [6]   names of pastors are against their will under the bishops' jurisdictions. And they are unlawfully detained by them, because no pastor can be lawfully kept under the pastoral (I mean not the civil) authority of any one man. Therefore our bishops and proud, popish, presumptuous, profane, paltry, pestilent and pernicious prelates, bishop of Hereford and all,[36] are first usurpers to begin the matter withal.

Secondly,

Our prelates claim this authority over those, who by the ordinance of God, are to be under no pastors.

---

[c] [side note:] M. Marprelate you put more than the question in the conclusion of your syllogism.

That is, they claim pastoral authority over other ministers and pastors, who by the ordinance of God are appointed to be pastors and shepherds to feed others, and not sheep, or such as are to have shepherds by whom they are to be fed and overseen: which authority the bishops claim unto themselves. For they say that they are pastors of all the pastors within their diocese. And take this of M. Marprelate's word, that there is no pastor of pastors, but he is a pope. For who but a pope will claim this authority.

Thirdly,

This authority of our lord bishops in England
is accounted antichristian of the most churches in the world.

As of the Helvetian, the Scottish, French, Bohemian, and the churches of the Low Countries, the churches of Polonia, Denmark, within the dominions of the Count Palatine, of the churches in Saxony, and Swevia, etc., which you shall see evidently proved in the *Harmony of the Confessions* of all those churches, section the eleventh.[37] Which *Harmony* was translated and printed by that puritan Cambridge printer, Thomas Thomas.[38] And although the book came out by public authority, yet by your leave the bishops have called them in, as things against their state.[39] And trust me, his grace will owe that puritan printer as good a turn as he paid unto Robert Waldegrave for his sauciness, in printing my friend and dear brother Diotrephes his *Dialogue.*[40] Well friend Thomas, I warn you before hand, look to your self.   [7]

And now brethren bishops, if you will not believe me, I will set down the very words of the French Confession, contained page 359 of the *Harmony.* We believe (saith the Confession, art. 30) that all true pastors, in what place soever they be placed, have the same and equal authority among themselves, given unto them under Jesus Christ the only head, and the chief alone universal bishop: and that therefore it is not lawful for any church to challenge unto itself dominion or sovereignty over any other.[41] What an horrible heresy is this, will some say, why! gentle Martin, is it possible that these words of the French Confession should be true? Is it possible that there ought to be an equality between his grace and the dean of Sarum, or some other hedge priest? Martin saith it ought be so: why then Martin, if it should be so, how will the bishops satisfy the reader in this point? Alas simple fellow, whatsoever thou art, I perceive thou dost not mark the words of the Confession.[d][42] My good brethren have long since taken order for this gear: for the Confession doth not say that all pastors, but that all true

---

[d] [side note:] At a dead lift well fare a good gloss.

pastors, and all pastors that are under Jesus Christ, are of equal authority.
So that all men see that my brethren, which are neither true pastors, nor
I fear me under Jesus Christ, are not to be of equal authority. And because
this doth not touch them, I will end this whole learned discourse with the
words of Pope Gregory unto John, bishop of Constantinople (for I have
read something in my days), which words you shall find in our own English
Confession, written by a bishop, page 361 of the *Harmony*.[43] The pope's
words be these: *He is also the king of pride, he is Lucifer, which preferreth
himself before his brethren, he hath forsaken the faith, and is the forerunner of
Antichrist.*[e] And have not I quitted my self like a man, and dealt very
valiantly, in proving that my learned brethren the lord bishops ought not to
be in any Christian commonwealth, because they are petty popes, and
[8]   petty antichrists? But what do you say, if by this lusty syllogism of mine
own making, I prove them popes once more for recreation's sake.

Whosoever therefore claim unto themselves pastoral authority over
those Christians with whom they cannot possibly at any time altogether
in the same congregation sanctify the Sabbath: they are usurping prelates,
popes and petty antichrists.[f] For did you ever hear of any, but of popes and
dumb ministers,[44] that would challenge the authority of pastors over those
Christians unto whom they could not possibly on the Sabbath discharge
the duty of pastors? But our lord bishops challenge unto themselves pastoral
authority over them unto whom they cannot possibly on the Sabbath
discharge the duty of pastors, vz. over people inhabiting divers shires distant
asunder, with whom, gathered together on the Sabbath, they cannot by
order of nature perform any duty of pastors. Therefore all the lord bishops
in England, Ireland and Wales (and for the good will I bear to the reverend
brethren, I will speak as loud as ever I can), all our lord bishops I say, are
petty popes, and petty usurping antichrists, and I think if they will still
continue to be so, that they will breed young popes, and antichrists: *per
consequens*, neither they nor their brood are to be tolerated in any Christian
commonwealth, quoth Martin Marprelate. There is my judgment of you,
brethren, make the most of it, I hope it will never be worth a bishopric unto
you: reply when you dare, you shall have as good as you bring. And if you
durst but dispute with my worship in these points, I doubt not but you
should be sent home by Weeping Cross.[45] I would wish you, my venerable

[e] [side note:] Put the case that my Lord of Canterbury is such a one.
[f] [side note:] Why Martin, what meanest thou? Certainly an thou takest that course but a
   while, thou wilt set thy good brethren at their wits' end.

masters, for all that to answer my reasons, or out of doubt you will prove
petty antichrists, your corner caps and tippets will do nothing in this point.[46]

Most pitifully complaineth Martin Marprelate unto your honorable
masterships, that certain thieves, having stolen from dyers in Thames street
as much cloth as came to £30, did hide the said cloth in Fulham, which is a   [9]
place within the territories of the Lord dumb John, who by occupation is
lord bish. of London. The thieves were apprehended, the cloth came within
your clutches Don John of London, and all is fish that comes to the net
with your good honor.[47] The thieves being taken, the dyers came to
challenge their cloth: John London the bishop said it was his own, because
it was taken within his own lordship. But, saith he, if the cloth be yours, let
the law go upon the thieves, and then I'll talk farther with you: well, one or
two of the thieves were executed, and at their deaths confessed that to be the
cloth which the bishop had, but the dyers could not get their cloth, nor
cannot unto this day, no though one of their honors wrote unto him to
restore the cloth unto the poor men.[48] What reason were it he should give
them their own, as though he could not tell how to put it unto good uses as
well as the right owners? It is very good blue, and so would serve well for the
liveries of his men, and it was good green, fit to make cushions and
coverings for tables. Brother London, you were best to make restitution,
it is plain theft and horrible oppression: Bonner would have blushed, to
have been taken with the like fact.[49] The popish sort your brethren will
commend this unto posterity by writing, assure yourself. The dyers' names
are Baughin, Swan and Price. They dwell at the Old Swan in Thames
street,[50] I warrant you Martin will be found no liar, he bringeth in nothing
without testimony.[g] And therefore I have set down the men's names and
the places of their abode, that you of this Conspiration House may find out
this slander of truth against the Lord of good London. It was not therefore
for nothing (John of London I perceive) that Mistress Lawson, the shrew at
Paul's Gate and enemy to all dumb dogs and tyrannical prelates in the land,
had you throw down yourself at her Majesty's feet, acknowledging yourself
to be unsavory salt, and to crave pardon of her highness, because you had so   [10]
long deceived her and her people.[51] You might well enough crave pardon
for your theft, for Martin will stand to it, that the detaining of the men's
cloth is plain theft.

Riddle me a riddle, what is that, his grace threatened to send Mistress
Lawson to Bridewell,[52] because she showed the good father Doctor Perne a
way how to get his name out of the *Book of Martyrs*, where the turncoat is

[g] [side note:] My book shall come with a witness before the high commission.

canonized for burning Bucer's bones.[53] Dame Lawson answered, that she
was an honest citizen's wife, a man well known, and therefore bade his grace,
an he would, send his Uncle Shorie thither.[54] Ha ha ha: now, good your
grace, you shall have small gains in meddling with Margaret Lawson, I can
tell you. For if she be cited before *Tarquinius Superbus* Doctor Stanhope,
she will desire him to deal as favorably with her in that cause, as he would
with Mistress Blackwell, tse tse tse, will it never be better with you, Mistress
Lawson.[55]

Sohow, brother Bridges, when will you answer the book entitled an
Answer to Bridges his Slanders?[56] Nay I think you had more need to gather a
benevolence among the clergy to pay Chard toward the printing of your
book, or else labour to his grace to get him another protection, for men will
give no money for your book, unless it be to stop mustard pots, as your
brother Cosin's *Answer to the Abstract* did.[57] You have been a worthy writer
as they say of a long time, your first book was a proper interlude, called
Gammer Gurton's Needle.[58] But I think that this trifle, which showeth the
author to have had some wit and invention in him, was none of your doing:
because your books seem to proceed from the brains of a woodcock, as
having neither wit nor learning. Secondly, you have to your mediocrity
written against the papists: and since that time, you have written a sheet in
rhyme of all the names attributed unto the Lord in the Bible, a worthy
[11]   monument.[59] What, hath the hedge priest my brother written any more? O
is, I cry him mercy, he hath written this great volume which now I have in
hand against his brethren.[60] The qualities of this book are many, Master D.
showeth himself to be very skillful in the learning of *ob* and *sol.*[61] If ever you
read old Father Bricot upon Aristotle: Master Dean's manner of writing
and his, are not much unlike, Doctor Terence of Oxford and this Doctor
may be near of kindred for their learning.[62] There be periods in this learned
book of great reason, though altogether without sense. I will give you a
proof or two, page 441: *And although* (saith the Doctor) *Paul afterward, 1
Cor. 1:14, mentioning this Crispus, term him not there, the archgovernor of the
Jews' Synagogue, yet as it farther appeareth, Acts 18:17, by Sosthenes, who was
long before a faithful Christian, and as some allege out of Eusebius, lib. I, cap. 13,
he was also one of the 72 Disciples chosen by Christ.*[h]

Fleering, jeering, leering: there is at all no sense in this period. For the
words (*yet afterward*) unto the end, Master D.'s mind was so set upon a
bishopric, that he brought nothing concerning Crispus to answer the word
(*yet*).[63] Therefore I will help my reverend brother to make the sentence in

[h] [side note:] Sosthenes, and not Crispus, was one of the 72 disciples.

this sort: And although, etc., yet afterward my learned brother, Doctor Young, bish. of Rochester, having the presentation of a benefice in his hand, presented himself thereunto, even of mere goodwill. I, John of Rochester, present John Young, quoth the bishop.[64] Now judge you, good readers, whether Martin saith not true, that there is too much cozenage nowadays among the clergy men.

This sentence following of Master Dean's hath as good sense as the former, page 655. The D. citeth these words out of the *Learned Discourse*: *God grant that instead of ordinary forms of prayers, we have preaching in all places.*[65] And instead of Amen, God forbid say I, quoth the Doctor, with another prayer to the contrary (now mark my masters, whether you can find any sense in this contrary prayer, for I assure you reverend Martin can find none),[i] *if it be his good will not so much (good Lord) to punish us, that this our brethren's prayer should be granted.*[66] If this be a senseless kind of writing, I would there were never a lord bishop in England.

And learned brother Bridges, a man might almost run himself out of breath before he could come to a full point in many places in your book, page 69, line 3, speaking of the extraordinary gifts in the apostles' time, you have this sweet learning. *Yea some of them have for a great part of the time, continued even till our times, and yet continue, as the operation of great works, or if they mean miracles, which were not ordinary no not in that extraordinary time, and as the hypocrites had them, so might and had divers of the papists, and yet their cause never the better, and the like may we say of the gift of speaking with tongues which have not been with study before learned,[j] as Anthony, etc., and divers also among the ancient fathers, and some among the papists, and some among us, have not been destitute of the gifts of prophesying, and much more may I say this of the gift of healing, for none of those gifts or graces given then or since, or yet to men, infer the grace of God's election to be of necessity to salvation.*[67]

Here is a good matter delivered in as good grammatical words. But what say you if Master Doctor can prove that Peter was prince of the apostles? That is popery (quoth Martin) to begin withal. Nay, but what say you if he proveth that one priest among the residue may have a lawful superior authority over the universal body of the church,[k] is not this plain treason?[68] Is forsooth, if a puritan had written it. But Mas. Dean of Sarum that wrote these things is a man that favoreth bishops, a nonresident, one that will not

[12]

---

[i] [side note:] These be the D.'s own words.
[j] [side note:] Whoa whoa, Dean, take thy breath and then to it again.
[k] [side note:] Both these points are set down page 443, line 3.

[13] stick to play a game at cards, and swear by his troth: and therefore he may write against the puritans what he will, his grace of Canterbury will give a very Catholic exposition thereof. This gear maintaineth the crown of Canterbury, and what matter is it though he write, for the maintenance thereof, all the treason in the world? It will never come unto her Majesty's ear, as my friend Tertullus in the poor *Dialogue* that the bishops lately burned hath set down.[69] His grace is able to salve the matter well enough: yea my brother Bridges himself can answer the point. For he hath written otherwise, page 288, line 26, in these words: *Neither is all government taken away from all, though a moderate superior government be given of all to some, and not yet of all in all the church to one, but to one over some in several and particular churches.* The Dean will say, that concerning the superiority of bishops this is the meaning. As concerning the treason written page 448, it may be the fox Doctor Perne, who helped him as they say to make this worthy volume, was the author of it.[70]

Now brethren, if any of you that are of the Confocation House would know how I can prove Master Dean to have written flat treason, page 448 as I have before set down: draw near, and with your patience I will prove it so, that Master Dean will stand to his own words, which I care not if they be set down: page 448, line 3. Thus you shall read, *Doth S. Peter then forbid that any one elder should have and exercise any superior government over the clergy, understanding the clergy in this sense, if he doth not but alloweth it, and his self practised it:*[l] *then howsoever both the name, both of governing and clergy, may be abused, the matter is clear,*[m] *that one priest or elder among the residue may have a superior authority over the clergy, that is, over all the universal body of the church, in every particular or several congregation, and so not only over the people, but also over the whole order of ministers.*

[14] Would your worships know how I can show and convince my brother Bridges to have set down flat treason in the former words? Then have at you Dean. 1. It is treason to affirm her Majesty to be an infidel, or not to be contained in the body of the church.[n][71] 2. It is treason to say that one priest or elder may have a lawful superior authority over her Majesty. Take your spectacles then, and spell your own words, and you shall find that you have affirmed either of these two points. For you affirm that a priest may have a lawful superior authority over the universal body of the church. And you dare not deny her Majesty to be contained within the universal body of the

---

[l] [side note:] I commend thee yet good D. for thy good English tongue.
[m] [side note:] Clear quoth he, yea who will make any question thereof.
[n] [side note:] Look stat. 13 Elizabeth.

church. Therefore, to help you to spell your conclusion, you have written treason, if you will be as good as your writing: your learned friend Martin (for no brother, Master Dean, if you be a traitor) would not mistake you, and therefore say what you can for yourself: you mean not that this priest shall be over all the church: do you? But how shall we know that? Forsooth because you say that this superiority must be in every particular or several congregation. Is this your answer, brother John? Why, what sense is there in these words? One priest may have a superior authority over the universal body of the church, in every particular or several congregation? The universal body of the church is now become a particular or several congregation with you? And in good earnest Dean John, tell me how many orders of ministers be there in a particular congregation? For there must be orders of ministers in the congregation, where you mean this bouncing priest should have his superiority, and because this cannot be in several and particular congregations, therefore you cannot mean by these words, *over the universal body of the church*, any other thing than the whole church militant. But you would mend your answer? And say that this superior priest must be an English priest and no foreigner: as, for ilsample, his grace of Canterbury is an English priest?[o] Do you mean then, that his grace should be this superior priest, who by Sir Peter's allowance may have a lawful superior authority over the universal body of the church?[p] [72] Truly I [15]
do not mean so. And good now, do not abuse his grace's worship in this sort, by making him a pope. Be it you mean this high priest should be no stranger, yet your treason is as great or greater. For you will have her Majesty to be subject unto her own subject and servant. And if it be treason to say that the pope, who hath princes and cardinals for his servants, being far better than were John with his Canterburiness, may have a lawful superior authority over her Majesty, as one being contained within the universal body of the church: is it not much more traitorous to say, that an English vassal may have this authority over his sovereign? And brother John, did Sir Peter his self indeed practise this authority?[q] Why, what a priest was he! Did he allow others to have this authority? Truly this is more than ever I knew till now. Yet notwithstanding, I think he never wore corner cap and tippet in all his life, nor yet ever subscribed to my Lord of Canterbury his articles.[73] Now the question is, whom Sir Peter his self now alloweth to be this bouncing priest? The pope of Rome, yea or no? No in no case, for that is against the statute.[74] For will my brother Bridges say that the pope may

[o] [side note:] A good ilsample. [p] [side note:] Sir Peter never allowed this.
[q] [side note:] Here be those that can be barbarous as well as Mass Dean.

have a lawful superior authority over his grace of Canterbury? I'll never believe him though he say so. Neither will I say that his grace is an infidel (nor yet swear that he is much better),[r] and therefore Master Dean meaneth not that the pope should be this high priest.

No brother Martin (quoth Master Dean) you say true, I mean not that the pope is this priest of Sir Peter. And I have many reasons why I should deny him this authority. First, he is a massmonger, that is, a professed idolater. 2. He weareth a triple crown,[75] so doth not my Lord of Canterbury. 3. He hath his seat in Romish Babylon in Rome within Italy: you know the number 666 in the Revelation signifieth *Lateinos*, that is, the man of Rome, or *Ecclesia* [16] *Italic*, the Italian church.[76] Lastly, he must have men to kiss his toes, and must be carried upon men's shoulders, and must have princes and kings to attend upon him, which showeth his horrible pride. Sir Peter's universal priest and mine shall be no such priest I trow, ka Mas. Doctor.[77] No shall not Doctor John, I con thee thank.[78] Then thy universal priest, 1. must be no idolater, 2. must be no proud priest, and have never a triple crown (and yet I hope he may wear as brave a satin gown as my Lord of Winchester weareth, and be as choleric as he), 3. he must have his seat out of Italy, as for fashion sake, at Lambeth, Hippo, etc., but at Rome in no case.[79] If I should examine these properties, I think some of them, if not all, have been accidents unto English priests.[80] For how many bishops are there in England which have not either said Mass, or helped the priest to say Mass, or been present at it? As for the triple crown, Pope Joan the English harlot hath woon it: so did Urban the 5 an English man.[81] And concerning pride, I hope that our bishops now living have to their mediocrity taken order that some popes may be inferior unto them, as for ilsample, his Canterburiness, etc. And I cannot see how the planting of the chair in Rome any more than Canterbury can make a pope. Seeing that Clement the 5, John 22, Benedict 12, and all other popes from the year 1306 unto 1375 sat not in Rome, but for the most part at Avignon in France.[82] But notwithstanding all this, out of your meaning Mass D. such a simple ingram man as I am,[83] in these points of universal superior priests, I find three differences between my Lord of Peterborough, or any other our high priests in England, and the pope's holiness: and three impediments to hinder the pope from being Sir Peter's high priest and yours, vz. 1. his idolatry, 2. his triple crown, 3. his seat at Rome. But if Hildebrand pope of Rome had been a professor of the truth (as his grace Doctor Turncoat's – Perne, I should [17] say – scholar is),[84] had worn no triple crown, had been archbishop of Canterbury (and I think we have had Hildebrands there ere now), then he

---

[r] [side note:] His grace shall never get me to swear against my conscience.

might by the judgement of the learned Bridges, and the allowance of that Peter which his self practised that authority, have a lawful superior authority over the universal body of the church.[85] And what a worthy Canterbury Pope had this been, to be called my lord's grease![86] Thus you see brother Bridges, M. Marprelate, an please him, is able to make a younger brother of you: he hath before proved, that if ever you be archbishop of Canterbury (for you wrote this foul heap against the holy Discipline of Christ – as Whitgift did the like – in hope to be the next pope of Lambeth), that then you shall be a petty pope, and a petty Antichrist. Nay he hath proved you to have deserved a caudle of hempseed, and a plaster of neckweed, as well as some of your brethren the papists.[87]

And now brother Bridges once again, is it good writing against the puritans? Take me at my word, unless you answer the former point of antichristianism, and this of treason, I will never write again to my brethren bishops but as to usurpers and antichrists, and I shall take you for no better than an enemy to her Majesty's supremacy. And because you have taken upon you to defend lord bishops, though you be as very a sot as ever lived (outcept dumb John of London again), yet you shall answer my reasons, or else I will so course you,[88] as you were never coursed since you were a simoniacal dean, you shall not deal with my worship, as John with his Canterburiness did with Thomas Cartwright, which John left the cause you defend in the plain field, and for shame threw down his weapons with a desperate purpose to run away, and leave the cause, as he like a coward hath done. For this dozen years we never saw anything of his in print for the defence of his cause, and poor Master Cartwright doth content himself with the victory, which the other will not (though indeed he hath by his silence seem to) grant.[89] But I will not be this used at your hands, for unless [18] you answer me, or confess (and that in print) that all lord bishops in England, Wales, Ireland, yea and Scotland too, are petty popes, and plain usurpers, and petty antichrists.[s] I'll kindle such a fire in the holes of these foxes, as shall never be quenched as long as there is a lord bishop in England. And who but the worthy Martin can do so valiantly? Page 560: Master Dean bringeth in Aretius to prove that kneeling at the communion is not offensive. And how is the argument concluded think you? Forsooth even thus. Aretius saith, that in Berne they receive the communion sitting or standing: therefore, saith my brother Bridges, kneeling at the communion is not unlawful.[90] I marvel whether he was not hatched in a goose nest, that would thus conclude.

---

[s] [side note:] Ha, priests, I'll bang you, or else never trust me.

In another place, page 226 or thereabouts, he proveth that one man may have two spiritual livings,[t] because the puritans themselves say that one charge may have two ministers, to wit, a pastor and a doctor.[91] And these be some of the good proofs whereby our established government is upheld.

It would make a man laugh, to see how many tricks the Doctor hath to cozen the silly puritans in his book, he can now and then without any noise allege an author clean against himself, and, I warrant you, wipe his mouth cleanly, and look another way, as though it had not been he.[u] I have laughed as though I had been tickled, to see with what sleight he can throw in a popish reason, and who saw him? And with what art he can convey himself from the question, and go to another matter! It is wonderful to think. But what would not a dean do to get a bishopric? In this one point, for sparing labor he is to be admired, that he hath set down under his own name those things which (to speak as I think) he never wrote himself. So let the puritans answer when they will, he hath so much of other men's helps, and such [19] contrarieties in this book, that when they bring one thing against him out of his own writings, he will bring another place out of the said book, flat contrary to that, and say that the latter is his, and not the former. For the former, it may be, was some other friend's, not so fully seen in the cause, as Presbyter John Bridges was. The reason of these contrarieties was very expedient: because many had a hand in the work, every man wrote his own mind, and Mass Doctor joined the whole together.

Now forasmuch as he hath played the worthy workman, I will bestow an Epitaph upon his grave when he dieth, which is thus:

Here lies John Bridges, a worthy Presbyter he was.

But what if he be a bishop before he die? What, brethren? Do you not think that I have two strings to my bow, is us have I, and thus I sing, if he chance to be a bishop.[92]

Here lies John Bridges late bishop, friend to the Papa.[93]

I care not an I now leave Mass Dean's worship, and be eloquent once in my days: yet brother Bridges, a word or two more with you, ere we depart. I pray you where may a man buy such another gelding, and borrow such another hundred pounds, as you bestowed upon your good patron Sir Edward Horsey for his good word in helping you to your deanery:[94] go to, go to, I perceive you will prove a goose. Deal closelier for shame the next

[t] [side note:] My brother Bridges now reasoneth in good earnest for nonresidents.
[u] [side note:] What a crafty knave is Mass Dean.

time: must I needs come to the knowledge of these things? What if I should report abroad, that clergymen come unto their promotions by simony? Have not you given me just cause? I think Simony be the bishops' lackey. Tarleton took him not long since, in Don John of London's cellar.[95]

Well now to mine eloquence, for I can do it I tell you. Who made the porter of his gate a dumb minister?[96] Dumb John of London. Who abuseth her Majesty's subjects, in urging them to subscribe contrary to law? John of London. Who abuseth the high commission, as much as any? John London (and Doctor Stanhope too).[97] Who bound an Essex minister in £200 to wear the surplice on Easter day last? John London. Who hath cut down the elms at Fulham?[98] John London. Who is a carnal defender of the breach of the Sabbath in all the places of his abode? John London. Who forbiddeth men to humble themselves in fasting and prayer before the Lord, and then can say unto the preachers, now you were best to tell the people that we forbid fasts?[99] John London. Who goeth to bowls upon the Sabbath?[100] Dumb dunstical John of good London hath done all this.[v] I will for this time leave this figure, and tell your venerable masterdoms a tale worth the hearing.[101] I had it at the second hand: if he that told it me added anything, I do not commend him, but I forgive him. The matter is this. A man dying in Fulham made one of the bishop of London's men his executor. The man had bequeathed certain legacies unto a poor shepherd in the town. The shepherd could get nothing of the bishop's man, and therefore made his moan unto a gentleman of Fulham that belongeth to the court of requests.[102] The gentleman's name is Master Madox. The poor man's case came to be tried in the court of requests. The bishop's man desired his master's help: Dumb John wrote to the masters of requests to this effect, and I think these were his words.

My masters of the requests, the bearer hereof, being my man, hath a cause before you: inasmuch as I understand how the matter standeth, I pray you let my man be discharged the court, and I will see an agreement made. Fare you well. The letter came to Master Doctor Dale, he answered it in this sort.[103] *My Lord of London, this man delivered your letter, I pray you give him his dinner on Christmas day for his labour, and fare you well.*

Dumb John not succeeding this way, sent for the said Master Madox: he came, some rough words passed on both sides, Presbyter John said Master Madox was very saucy, especially seeing he knew before whom he spake: namely, the Lord of Fulham. Whereunto the gentleman answered, that he had been a poor freeholder in Fulham before Don John came to be lord

[20]

[21]

---

[v] [side note:] I'll make you weary of it dumb John, except you leave persecuting.

there, hoping also to be so when he and all his brood (my lady his daughter and all) should be gone. At the hearing of this speech, the wasp got my brother by the nose,[104] which made him in his rage to affirm that he would be Lord of Fulham as long as he lived, in despite of all England. Nay soft there, quoth Master Madox, except her Majesty I pray you. That is my meaning, ka dumb John, and I tell thee Madox, that thou art but a Jack to use me so. Master Madox replying said that indeed his name was John, and if every John were a Jack, he was content to be a Jack (there he hit my lord over the thumbs).[105] The bishop growing in choler, said that Master Madox his name did show what he was, for, saith he, thy name is Mad-ox, which declareth thee to be an unruly and mad beast. Master Madox answered again, that the bishop's name, if it were descanted upon, did most significantly show his qualities. For, said he, you are called Elmar, but you may be better called Mar-elm, for you have marred all the elms in Fulham: having cut them all down. This far is my worthy story, as worthy to be printed as any part of Dean John's book, I am sure.[106]

Item, may it please you that are lord bishops to show your brother Martin how you can escape the danger of a premunire, seeing you urge her Majesty's subjects to subscribe, clean contrary to the statute 13 Elizabeth?[107] What have you to show for yourselves, for I tell you, I heard some say that for urging subscription, you were all within the premunire, insomuch that you have been driven closely to buy your pardons, you have forfeited all that you have unto her Majesty, and your persons are void of her Majesty's protection: you [22] know the danger of a premunire I trow? Well, but tell me what you have to show for yourselves? Her Majesty's prerogative? Have you? Then I hope you have it under seal. No, I warrant you, her Majesty is too wise for that. For it shall never be said that she ever authorized such ungodly proceedings, to the dishonor of God, and the wounding of the consciences of her best subjects. Seeing you have nothing to show that it is her Majesty's will, why should any man subscribe contrary to statute? Forsooth, men must believe such honest creatures as you are on your words? Must they? As though you would not lie: yes, yes, bishops will lie like dogs. They were never yet well beaten for their lying.

May it please your honorable worships, to let worthy Martin understand why your Canterburiness and the rest of the lord bishops favor papists and recusants,[108] rather than puritans? For if a puritan preacher, having a recusant in his parish, and shall go about to deal with the recusant for not coming to church: sir, will the recusant say, you and I will answer the matter before his grace (or other the high commissioners, as lord bishops, seevillains (I mean) popish doctors of the bawdy courts).[109] And as soon as the matter is made known unto my lord, the preacher is sure to go by the worst, and the recusant to carry all the honesty: yea, the preacher shall be a busy envious fellow, one that doth not observe the book, and conform himself according unto order, and perhaps go home by beggar's bush, for any benefice he hath to live upon.[110] For it may be the bishops will be so good unto him, as to deprive him for not subscribing. As for the recusant, he is known to be a man that must have the liberty of his conscience. Is this good dealing, brethren? And is it good dealing, that poor men should be so troubled to the chancellor's court,[111] that they are even weary of their lives, for such horrible oppression as there reigns? I tell you Doctor Stanhope (for all you are so proud), a premunire will take you by the back one day, for oppressing and tyrannizing over her Majesty's subjects as you do. [23]

Doth your grace remember what the Jesuit at Newgate said of you, namely, that my Lord of Canterbury should surely be a cardinal, if ever popery did come again into England (yea and that a brave cardinal too)?[112] What a knave was this Jesuit! Believe me, I would not say thus much of my Lord of Canterbury for a thousand pound, lest a *scandalum magnatum* should be had against me.[113] But well fare him that said thought is free.

Pitifully complaining, is there any reason (my lord's grace) why knave Thackwell the printer, which printed popish and traitorous Welsh books in Wales,[114] should have more favour at your graceless hands, than poor Waldegrave, who never printed book against you, that containeth either treason or impiety? Thackwell is at liberty to walk where he will, and permitted to make the most he could of his press and letters: whereas Robert Waldegrave dares not show his face for the bloodthirsty desire you have for his life, only for printing of books which toucheth the bishops' mitres. You know that Waldegrave's printing press and letters were taken away: his press being timber, was sawn and hewed in pieces, the iron work battered and made unserviceable, his letters melted, with cases and other tools defaced (by John Wolfe, alias Machiavel, beadle of the Stationers, and most tormenting executioner of Waldegrave's goods),[115] and he himself utterly deprived for ever printing again, having a wife and six small children.[116] Will this monstrous cruelty never be revenged, think you? When Waldegrave's goods was to be spoiled and defaced, there were some printers, that rather than all the goods should be spoiled, offered money for it towards the relief of the man's wife and children, but this could not be obtained, and yet popish Thackwell, though he printed popish and traitorous books, may have the favor to make money of his press and letters. And reason too. For Waldegrave's profession overthro- [24] weth the popedom of Lambeth, but Thackwell's popery maintaineth the same. And now that Waldegrave hath neither press nor letters, his grace may dine and sup the quieter. But look to it brother Canterbury, certainly without your repentance, I fear me, you shall be Hildebrand indeed.[w][117] Waldegrave hath left house and home, by reason of your unnatural tyranny: having left behind him a poor wife and six orphans, without anything to relieve them. (For the husband, you have bereaved both of his trade and goods.) Be you assured that the cry of these will one day prevail against you, unless you desist from persecuting.

And good your grace,[x] I do now remember myself of another printer, that had press and letter in a place called Charterhouse in London (in anno 1587 near about the time of the Scottish Queen's death).[118] Intelligence was given unto your good grace of the same by some of the Stationers of London, it was made known unto you what work was in hand, what letter the book was on, what volume, vz. in 8° in half sheets,[119] what workmen wrought on the same: namely J. C., the earl of Arundel's man, and three of his servants, with their several names, what liberality was bestowed on those workmen, and by whom, etc.[120] Your grace gave the Stationers the hearing of this matter, but to this day the parties were never called *in coram* for it:[121] but yet by your leave my lord, upon this information unto your honorable worship, the Stationers had news that it was made known unto the printers what was done unto your good grace, and presently instead of the work which was in hand, there was other appointed, as they say, authorized by your lordship.[y] I will not say it was your own doing, but by your sleeve,[122] thought is free.[z] And my good lord (nay you shall be none of my lord but Master Whitgift, and you will), are you partial or no in all your actions tell

[25] me? Yes you are! I will stand to it! Did you get a decree in the high court of Star Chamber only for Waldegrave?[123] If it be in general (and you not partial) why fet you not that printing press and letters out of Charterhouse,[124] and destroy them as you did Waldegrave's? Why did you not apprehend the parties, why? Because it was popery, at the least, that was printed in Charterhouse: and that maintaineth the crown of Canterbury? And what is more tolerable than popery? Did not your grace of late erect a new printer contrary to the foresaid decree? One Thomas Orwin (who sometimes wrought popish books in corners: namely Jesus Psalter, Our Lady's Psalter, etc.) with condition he should print no such seditious books as Waldegrave

---

[w] [side note:] A firebrand indeed.   [x] [side note:] More knavery.
[y] [side note:] Is not he a very pope indeed that thus hideth popery and knavery.
[z] [side note:] It may be you hindered her Majesty of many thousands of pounds.

hath done?[125] Why, my lord?[a] Waldegrave never printed anything against the
state, but only against the usurped state of your paltripolitanship, and your
pope-holy brethren, the lord bishops and your antichristian swinish rabble,
being intolerable withstanders of reformation, enemies of the gospel, and
most covetous wretched and popish priests.

Now most pitifully complaining, Martin Marprelate: that the papists will
needs make us believe that our good John of Canterbury and they are at no
great jar in religion. For Rainolds the papist at Rheims, in his book against
Master Whitaker's, commendeth the works written by his grace, for the
defence of the corruption in our church, against Thomas Cartwright.[126] And
saith that the said John Cant. hath many things in him, which evidently
show a Catholic persuasion. Alas my masters, shall we lose our metropolitan
in this sort? Yet the note is a good note, that we may take heed the Spaniards
steal him not away, it were not amiss if her Majesty knew of it. We need not
fear (if we can keep him) the Spaniards and our other popish enemies,
because our metropolitan's religion and theirs differ not much. In the article
of Christ's descending into hell, they jump in one right pat: and in the
maintenance of the hierarchy of bishops, and ascribing the name of priest   [26]
unto them that are ministers of the gospel.[127]

I know not whether my next tale will be acceptable unto his grace or not.
But have it among you, my masters. Master Wigginton, the pastor of
Sidborough, is a man not altogether unknown unto you.[128] And I think his
worshipful grace got little or nothing by meddling with him, although he
hath deprived him. My tale is of his deprivation, which was after this sort.
The good quiet people of Sidborough, being troubled for certain years with
the said Wigginton, and many of them being infected by him with the true
knowledge of the gospel, by the word preached (which is an heresy that his
grace doth mortally abhor and persecute), at length grew in disliking with
their pastor, because the severe man did urge nothing but obedience unto
the gospel. Well, they came to his grace to find a remedy hereof: desiring
him that Wigginton might be deprived. His grace could find no law to
deprive him, no, although the pastor defied the archbishop to his face, and
would give him no better title than John Whitgift, such bug's words being
in these days accounted no less than high treason against a paltripolitan:[129]
though since that time, I think his grace hath been well inured to bear the
name of pope of Lambeth, John Cant., the prelate of Lambeth, with divers
other titles agreeable to his function. Well, Sidborough men proceeded
against their pastor, his grace would not deprive him, because he could find

---

[a] [side note:] This is no knavery, my lord.

no law to warrant him therein, and he will do little contrary to law, for fear
of a premunire, unless it be at a dead lift to deprive a puritan preacher.
Then indeed he will do against law, against God, and against his own
conscience, rather than that heresy of preaching should prevail. One man
of Sidborough, whose name is Atkinson, was very eager among the rest to
have his pastor deprived: and because his grace would not hear them but
departed away, this Atkinson desired his grace to resolve him and his
[27]   neighbours of one point which something troubled them: and that was,
whether his grace or Wigginton were of the devil. For, quoth he, you are so
contrary the one from the other, that both of you cannot possibly be of
God. If he be of God, it is certain you are of the devil, and so cannot long
stand: for he will be your overthrow. Amen. If you are of God, then he is of
the devil, as we think him to be, and so he being of the devil, will not you
deprive him? Why should you suffer such a one to trouble the church? Now
if he be of God, why is your course so contrary to his? And rather, why do
not you follow him, that we may do so to? Truly, if you do not deprive him,
we will think him to be of God, and go home with him, with gentler good
will towards him, than we came hither with hatred, and look you for a fall.
His grace, hearing this northern logic, was moved on the sudden you must
think, promised to deprive Wigginton, and so he did. This Atkinson this
winter 1587 came up to London, being as it seemed afflicted in conscience
for this fact, desired Wigginton to pardon him and offered to kneel before
her Majesty, that Wigginton might be restored again to his place, and to
stand to the truth hereof, to his grace's teeth. The man is yet alive, he may
be sent for, if you think that Master Martin hath reported an untruth.[130]
No, I warrant you, you shall not take me to have fraught my book with lies
and slanders, as John Whitgift and the dean of Sarum did theirs. I speak
not of things by hearsay as of reports, but I bring my witnesses to prove my
matters.

   May it please you to yield unto a suit that I have to your worships. I pray
you send Wigginton home unto his charge again, I can tell you it was a foul
oversight in his grace, to send for him out of the north to London, that he
might outface him at his own door. He would do his Canterburiness less
hurt if he were at his charge, than now he doth. Let the Templars have
[28]   Master Travers their preacher restored again unto them, he is now at leisure
to work your priesthood a woe I hope.[131] If such another book as the
Ecclesiastical Discipline was drop out of his budget, it were as good for the
bishops to lie a day and a night in Little Ease in the Counter.[132] He is an
odd fellow in following an argument, and you know he hath a smooth
tongue, either in Latin or English. And if my Lord of Winchester

understood either Greek or Hebrew, as they say he hath no great skill in neither, I would pray your priestdoms to tell me which is the better scholar, Walter Travers or Thomas Cooper. Will you not send Master Wiburn to Northampton, that he may see some fruits of the seed he sowed there 16 or 18 years ago?[133] That old man Wiburn hath more good learning in him, and more fit gifts for the ministry in his little toe, than many braces of our lord bishops. Restore him to preaching again for shame. Master Paget shall be welcome to Devonshire,[b] he is more fit to teach men than boys.[134] I marvel with what face a man that had done so much good in the church, as he did among a rude people, could be deprived.

Briefly, may it please you to let the gospel have a free course, and restore unto their former liberty in preaching all the preachers that you have put to silence: and this far is my first suit.

My second suit is a most earnest request unto you, that are the hinderers of the publishing of [it, that] the confutation of the Rhemish Testament by Master Cartwright may be published.[135] A reasonable request, the granting whereof, I dare assure you, would be most acceptable unto all that fear God, and news of woeful sequel unto the papists. For shall I tell you what I heard once, from the mouth of a man of great learning and deep judgement, who saw some part of Master Cartwright's answer to the said Rhemish and traitorous Raffodie?[136] His judgment was this. That Master Cartwright had dealt so soundly against the papists, that for the answering and confuting of the adversary, that one work would be sufficient alone. He farther added,   [29] that that adversary was confuted by strange and unknown reasons, that would set them at their wits' end when they see themselves assailed with such weapons, whereof they never once dreamt that they should be stroken at. And will your grace, or any else that are the hinderers of the publishing of this work, still bereave the church of so worthy a jewel: nay, so strong an armour against the enemy? If you deny me this request, I will not threaten you, but my brother Bridges' and John Whitgift's books shall smoke for this gear, I'll have my pennyworth's of them for it.

Now may it please you to examine my worthiness your brother Martin, and see whether I said not true in the story of Giles Wigginton, where I have set down that the preaching of the word is an heresy which his grace doth mortally abhor and persecute, I can prove it without doubt. And first, that he persecuteth the preaching of the word (whether it be an heresy or not) both in the preacher and the hearer: the articles of subscription, the silencing of so many learned and worthy preachers do evidently show,[137]

---

[b] [side note:] Except persecuting Greenfield.

and if you doubt hereof, let my worship understand thereof, and in my next treatise I shall prove the matter to be clear with a witness, and I hope to your small commendations that will deny such a clear point. On the other side, that he accounteth preaching to be an heresy, I am now to insist on the proof of that point. But first you must know, that he did not account simple preaching to be an heresy, but to hold that preaching is the only ordinary means to salvation, this he accounteth as an heresy, this he mortally condemned. The case thus stood. John Penry the Welshman (I think his grace and my brother London would be better acquainted with him, and they could tell how) about the beginning of Lent, 1587 offered a supplication and a book to the parliament, entreating that some order

[30] be taken for calling his country unto the knowledge of God.[138] For his bold attempt, he was called before his grace with others of the high commission, as Thomas of Winchester, John London, etc. After that his grace had eased his stomach in calling him boy, knave, varlet, slanderer, libeller, lewd boy, lewd slanderer, etc. (this is true, for I have seen the notes of their conference), at the length a point of his book began to be examined, where nonresidents are thought intolerable. Here the Lord of good London asked Master Penry what he could say against that kind of cattle, answer was made that they were odious in the sight of God and man, because as much as in them lie, they bereave the people over whom they thrust themselves of the ordinary means of salvation, which was the word preached. John London demanded, whether preaching was the only means to salvation? Penry answered, that it was the only ordinary means, although the Lord was not so tied unto it, but that he could extraordinarily use other means. That preaching was the only ordinary means, he confirmed it by those places of scripture, Rom. 10:14, 1 Cor. 1:21, Ephes. 1:13. This point being a long time canvassed, at the length his worship of Winchester rose up, and mildly after his manner, brast forth into these words: I assure you, my lords, it is an execrable heresy.[139] An heresy (quoth John Penry) I thank God that ever I knew that heresy: it is such an heresy, that I will by the grace of God sooner leave my life than I will leave it. What sir (quoth the archbishop) I tell thee it is an heresy, and thou shalt recant it as an heresy! Nay (quoth Penry) never so long as I live God willing. I will leave this story for shame, I am weary to hear your grace so absurd. What say you to this gear, my masters of the Confocation House? We shall have shortly a good religion in England among the bishops, if Paul be said of them to write an heresy!

[31] I have heard some say, that his grace will speak against his own conscience. It is true. The proof whereof shall be his dealing with another Welshman, one Master Evans. An honorable personage, Ambrose Dudley,

now earl of Warwick (and long may he be so, to the glory of God, the good of his church, and the comfort of all his), in the singular love he bare to the town of Warwick, would have placed Master Evans there.[140] To the end that Master Evans might be received with a favorable subscription, etc., he offered the subscription which the statute requireth (whereunto men may subscribe with a good conscience).[141] The earl sent him with his letter to his gracelessness of Cant., thinking to obtain so small a courtesy at his hands. And I am sure, if he be Ambrose Dudley, the noble earl of Warwick (whose famous exploits, both in peace and war, this whole land hath cause to remember with thankfulness), that he is able to requite your kindness, Master John Cant. O, said his grace to Master Evans, I know you to be worthy a better place than Warwick is, and I would very gladly gratify my lord,[c] but surely, there is a Lord in heaven whom I fear, and therefore I cannot admit you without subscription. Thus the man with his poor patron, the earl of Warwick, were rejected by your grace, and the poor earl to this day knoweth not how to find the favour at your hands, that the man may be placed there. I tell you true John Canter. If I were a noble man, and a councillor too, I should be sick of the spleen:[142] nay I could not bear this at your hands, to be used of a priest thus, contrary to the law of God and this land.

It is no marvel though his honor could not obtain this small suit at your graceless hands, for I have heard your own men say, that you will not be beholding to never a noble man in this land, for you were the second person, etc.[143] Nay your own self spake proudly, yea and that like a pope: when as a worthy knight was a suitor unto your holiness for one of God's dear children (whom you have kept and do keep in prison) for his liberty. You answered him he should lie there still, unless he would put in sureties upon such bonds as never the like were heard of: and said further, that you are the second person in the land, and never a noble man nor councillor in this land should release him. Only her Majesty may release him, and that, you were sure, she would not. Do you think this to be he (I pray you) that was sometime Doctor Perne's boy, and carried his cloakbag after him?[144] Believe me he hath leapt lustily! And do not you know that after it is full sea, there followeth an ebb?[d] Remember your brother Haman? Do you think there is never a Mordecai to step to our gracious Hester, for preserving the lives of her faithfullest and best subjects, whom you so mortally hate, and bitterly persecute?[145] I hope you have not long to reign. Amen.

[32]

c [side note:] O monstrous hypocrite.
d [side note:] Is not this ambitious wretch at the highest, think you?

And you, Master bishop of Worcester,[146] how dealt you with Master Evans in the same case? Do you think that I do not know your knavery? You could by law require no other subscription of Master Evans than he offered, and yet forsooth you would not receive it at his hands, unless he would also enter into a bond to observe the Book of Common Prayer in every point, will law permit you to play the tyrant in this sort, bishop? I shall see the premunire on the bones of you one day for these pranks. And the massmonger your neighbor, the bishop of Gloucester,[147] thinks to go free, because in his sermon at Paul's Cross, preached 1586 in the parliament time, he affirmed that beef and brewess had made him a papist.[148] But this will not serve his turn: would you know what he did? Why, he convented an honest draper of Gloucester, one Singleton, and urged him being a lay man to subscribe unto the book.[149] The man affirming that no such thing could be required of him by law, denied to subscribe: upon his denial the bishop sent him to prison. Is it even so, you old popish priest? Dare you imprison lay men for not subscribing? It were not good for your corner cap that her Majesty knew her subjects to be thus dealt with. And if this be ever made known unto her, I hope to see you in for a bird.[150]

[33]   But brother Winchester, you of all other men are most wretched, for you openly in the audience of many hundreds, at Sir Mary Overie's church the last Lent, 1587 pronounced that men might find fault, if they were disposed to quarrel, as well with the Scripture, as with the Book of Common Prayer.[151] Who could hear this comparison without trembling?[e] But lest you should think that he hath not as good a gift in speaking against his conscience, as my Lord of Cant. is endued with: you are to understand, that both in that sermon of his, and in another which he preached at the Court the same Lent, he protested before God, and the congregation where he stood,[f] that there was not in the world at this day, nay there had not been since the apostles' time, such a flourishing estate of a church, as we have now in England.[152] Is it any marvel that we have so many swine, dumb dogs, nonresidents with their journeymen the hedge priests, so many lewd livers, as thieves, murderers, adulterers, drunkards, cormorants, rascals, so many ignorant and atheistical dolts, so many covetous popish bishops in our ministry, and so many and so monstrous corruptions in our church, and yet likely to have no redress? Seeing our impudent, shameless, and wainscot-faced bishops, like beasts, contrary to the knowledge of all men, and against their own consciences, dare, in the ears of her Majesty, affirm all to be well, where there is nothing but sores and blisters, yea where the grief is even deadly at the heart. Nay says my Lord of

[e] [side note:] O blasphemous wretch.   [f] [side note:] A flattering hypocrite.

Winchester (like a monstrous hypocrite, for he is a very duns, not able to defend an argument, but till he come to the pinch, he will cog and face it out,[153] for his face is made of seasoned wainscot, and will lie as fast as a dog can trot), I have said it, I do say it, and I have said it. And say I, you shall one day answer it (without repentance) for abusing the church of God and her Majesty in this sort. I would wish you to leave this villainy, and the rest of your devilish practises against God his saints, lest you answer it where your peevish and choleric simplicity will not excuse you.   [34]

I am ashamed to think that the church of England should have these wretches for the eyes thereof, that would have the people content themselves with bare reading only, and hold that they may be saved thereby ordinarily.[154] But this is true of our bishops, and they are afraid that anything should be published abroad whereby the common people should learn that the only way to salvation is by the word preached. There was the last summer a little catechism made by Master Davidson and printed by Waldegrave: but before he could print it, it must be authorized by the bishops, either Cant. or London, he went to Cant. to have it licensed, his grace committed it to Doctor Neverbegood (Wood), he read it over in half a year, the book is a great one of two sheets of paper.[155] In one place of the book the means of salvation was attributed to the word preached: and what did he, think you? He blotted out the word (preached) and would not have that word printed, so ascribing the way to work men's salvation to the word read.[156] Thus they do to suppress the truth, and to keep men in ignorance. John Cant. was the first father of this horrible error in our church, for he hath defended it in print,[157] and now as you have heard, accounteth the contrary to he heresy. And popish Goodman, abbot of Westminster, preaching upon Rom. 12:1, said that so much preaching as in some places we have is an unreasonable service of God.[158] Scribes, pharisees and hypocrites, that will neither enter in [y]ourselves, nor suffer those that will, to enter into heaven.

May it please your priestdoms to understand, that Doctor Cottington, archdeacon of Surrey, being belike bankrupt in his own country, cometh to Kingston-upon-Thames of mere good will that he beareth to the town (I should say, to usurer Harvey's good cheer and money bags), being out at the heels with all other usurers, and knowing him to be a professed adversary to Master Udall (a notable preacher of the gospel, and vehement reprover of sin), taketh the advantage of their controversy, and hoping to   [35] borrow some of the usurer's money, setteth himself most vehemently against Master Udall, to do whatsoever Harvey the usurer will have him: and taketh the help of his journeyman, Doctor Hone, the veriest coxcomb that ever wore velvet cap, and an ancient foe to Master Udall, because (indeed) he is popish dolt, and (to make up a mess) Steven Chatfield, the vicar of Kingston, as very a bankrupt and duns as Doctor Cottington (although he have consumed all the money he gathered to build a College at Kingston), must come and be resident there, that Master Udall may have his mouth stopped, and why?[159] Forsooth because your friend Master Harvey would have it so: for, saith Harvey, he raileth in his sermons. Is that true? Doth he rail, when he reproveth thee (and such notorious varlets as thou art) for thy usury, for thy oppressing of the poor, for buying the houses over their heads that love the gospel, and the Lord his faithful minster (Master Udall)? And art not thou a monstrous atheist, a belly God, a carnal wicked wretch, and what not? Master Chatfield, you think I see not your knavery? Is us do I, you cannot dance so cunningly in a net but I can spy you out![160] Shall I tell you why you sew pillows under Harvey's elbows?[161] Why man, it is because you would borrow an £100 of him! Go to you ass, and take in Master Udall again (for Harvey, I can tell, is as crafty a knave as you, he will not lend his money to such bankrupts as Duns Cottington and you are), and you do not restore Master Udall again to preach, I will so lay open your vileness, that I will make the very stones in Kingston streets shall smell of your knaveries. Now if a man ask Master Cottington, why Master Udall is put to silence? Forsooth, saith he, for not favoring the church government present. Doctor Hone (Cottington's journeyman, a popish doctor of the bawdy court) saith by his troth, for making such variance in the town.[162] Master Chatfield

[36] seemeth to sorry for it, etc.[163] But what cause was alleged why Master Udall must preach no longer? Surely this only: that he had not my Lord of Winchester's licence under seal to show: and because this was thought not to be sufficient to satisfy the people, Hone, the bawdy doctor, charged him to be a sectary, a schismatic, yea he affirmed plainly, that the gospel out of his mouth was blasphemy. Popish Hone, do you say so? Do ye? You are a knave, I tell you! By the same token your friend Chatfield spent thirteen score pounds in distributing briefs for a gathering towards the erecting of a College at Kingston-upon-Thames.

Wohohow, brother London, do you remember Thomas Allen and Richard Alworth, merchants of London, being executors to George Allen sometimes your grocer, but now deceased: who came unto you on Easter Wednesday last, being at your masterdom's palace in London, having been often to speak with you before and could not, yet now they met with you: who told you they were executors unto one George Allen (sometimes) your grocer, and among other his debts, we find you indebted unto him in the sum of £19 and upward, desiring you to let them have the money, for that they were to dispose of it according to that trust he reposed in them. You answered them sweetly (after you had paused a while) in this manner: you are rascals, you are villains, you are arrant knaves, I owe you nought, I have a general quittance to show.[g] Sir (said they) show us your discharge, and we are satisfied. No (quoth he) I will show you none, go sue me, go sue me. Then said one of the merchants, do you thus use us for asking our due? We would you should know, we are no such vile persons. Don John of London (hearing their answer) cried out, saying: hence away, citizens! Nay, you are rascals, you are worse than wicked Mammon (so lifting up both his hands, and flinging them down again, said), you are thieves, you are cozeners: take that for a bishop's blessing, and so get you hence.[h] But when they would have answered, his men thrust them out of the doors. But shortly after, he [37] perceived they went about to bring the matter to farther trial: he sent a messenger unto them confessing the debt, but they cannot get their money to this day. What reason is it they should have their money? Hath he not bestowed his liberality already on them? Can they not be satisfied with the blessing of this brave bouncing priest? But brethren bishops, I pray you tell me, hath not your brother London a notable brazen face to use these men so for their own?[164] I told you, Martin will be proved no liar, in that he saith that bishops are cogging and cozening knaves. This priest went to buffets with his son-in-law, for a bloody nose, well fare all good tokens.[165] The last Lent there came a commandment from his grace into Paul's Churchyard, that no Bible should be bound without the Apocrypha.[166] Monstrous and ungodly wretches, that to maintain their own outrageous proceedings thus mingle heaven and earth together, and would make the spirit of God to be the author of profane books. I am hardly drawn to a merry vein from such weighty matters.

But you see, my worshipful priests of this crew to whom I write, what a perilous fellow M. Marprelate is: he understands of all your knavery, and it may be he keeps a register of them: unless you amend, they shall all come into the light one day. And you, brethren bishops, take this warning from me. If you do not leave your persecuting of godly Christians and good subjects, that seek to live uprightly in the fear of God, and the obedience of her Majesty, all your dealing shall be made known unto the world. And I'se be sure to make you an example to all posterities. You see I have taken some pains with you already, and I will owe you a better turn, and pay it you with advantage, at the least thirteen to the dozen, unless you observe these conditions of peace which I draw between me and you. For I assure you

[g] [side note:] Can bishops face, cog, lie and cozen or no, think you.
[h] [side note:] Dumb John of London's blessing.

[38] I make not your doings known for any malice that I bear unto you, but the hurt that you do unto God's church, leave you your wickedness, and I'll leave the revealing of your knaveries.

☞ Conditions of Peace to be inviolably kept for ever, between the reverend and worthy Master Martin Marprelate gentleman on the one party, and the reverend fathers his brethren, the lord bishops of this land.

1. *In primis*,[167] the said lord bishops must promise and observe, without fraud or collusion, and that as much as in them lieth, they labor to promote the preaching of the word in every part of this land.
2. That hereafter they admit none unto the ministry but such as shall be known, both for their godliness and learning, to be fit for the ministry, and not these neither without cure, unless they be College ministers of either of the Universities, and in no case they suffer any to be nonresidents: and that they suffer Master Cartwright's answer to the Rhemish Testament to be published.[168]
3. That neither they nor their servants, vz. their archdeacons, chancellors, nor any other of the high commission, which serve their vile affections, urge any to subscribe contrary to the statute 13 Eliza.,[169] and that they suspend or silence none but such as either for their false doctrine or evil life shall show themselves to be unworthy the places of ministers: so that none be suspended or silenced, either for speaking (when their text giveth them occasion) against the corruptions of the church, for refusing to wear the surplice, cap, tippet, etc., or omitting the corruptions of the Book of Common Prayers, as churching of women, the cross in baptism, the ring in marriage, etc.[170]
4. That none be molested by them or any their aforesaid servants, for this my book, for not kneeling at the communion, or for resorting on the Sabbath (if they have not preachers of their own) to hear the word
[39]   preached, and to receive the sacraments.
5. Lastly, that never hereafter they profane excommunication as they have done, by excommunicating alone in their chambers, and that for trifles: yea before men's causes be heard. That they never forbid public fasts, molest either preacher, or hearer, for being present at such assemblies. Briefly, that they never slander the cause of reformation, or the furtherers thereof, in terming the cause by the name of Anabaptistery, schism, etc., and the men puritans, and enemies to the state.[171]

These be the conditions which you, brethren bishops, shall be bound to keep inviolably on your behalf. And I your brother Martin, on the other side, do faithfully promise upon the performance of the premisses by you, never to make any more of your knavery known unto the world. And howbeit that I have before threatened my brother Bridges in the cause of his superior priest, and your antichristian callings: notwithstanding, I will write no more of your dealings, unless you violate the former conditions. The conditions you see are so reasonable, I might bind you to give over your places which are antichristian: but I do not, lest men should think me to quarrel, and seek occasions for the nonce to fall out with my brethren. Therefore I require no more but such things as all the world will think you unworthy to live, if you grant them not. And this I do the rather, because you should not, according to your old fashion, say that my worship doth for malice lay open your infirmities: nay I have published not one of your secret faults, what you have not blushed to commit in the face of the sun, and in the justifying whereof you yet stand, these things only have I published. The best servants of God, I know, have their infirmities. But none of them will stand in the maintenance of their corruptions as you do, and that to the dishonour of God and the ruin of his church. You must either amend, or shortly you will bring our church to ruin: therefore it is [40] time that your dealings were better looked unto.

You will go about, I know, to prove my book to be a libel,[172] but I have prevented you of that advantage in law, both in bringing in nothing but matters of fact, which may easily be proved, if you dare deny them: and also in setting my name to my book. Well, I offer you peace upon the former conditions, if you will keep them, but if you violate them either in whole or in part (for why should you break any one of them?) then your learned brother Martin doth proclaim open war against you, and intendeth to work your woe two manner of ways as followeth. First, I will watch you at every half turn, and whatsoever you do amiss, I will presently publish it: you shall not call one honest man before you, but I will get his examination (and you think I shall know nothing of the oppression of your tenants by your bribery, etc.) and publish it, if you deal not according to the former conditions. To this purpose I will place a young Martin in every diocese, which may take notice of your practises. Do you think that you shall be suffered any longer to break the law of God, and to tyrannize over his people her Majesty's subjects, and no man tell you of it? No, I warrant you. And rather than I will be disappointed of my purpose, I will place a Martin in every parish. In part of Suffolk and Essex, I think I were best to have two in a parish.[173] I hope in time they shall be as worthy Martins as their father is, every one of them able to mar a prelate. Mark what will be the issue of these things, if you still keep your old bias. I know you would not have your dealings so known unto the world, as I and my sons will blaze them. Secondly, all the books that I have in store already of your doings shall be published upon the breach of the former covenants, or any of them. Here I know some will demand what these books are, because, saith one, I warrant you there will be old sport, I hope old father Palinode Doctor Perne shall

[41] be in there by the weeks.[174] Why my masters of the clergy, did you never hear of my books indeed? Foh, then you never heard of good sport in your life. The catalogue of their names and the arguments of some are as followeth.[i] As for my book named *Epistomastix*, I make no mention thereof at this time. First my *Paradoxes*, 2. my *Dialogues*, 3. my *Miscellanea*, 4. my *Variae lectiones*,[175] 5. *Martin's Dream*, 6. *Of the Lives and Doings of English Popes*, 7. my *Itinerarium, or Visitations*, 8. my *Lambethisms*. In my *Paradoxes* shall be handled some points which the common sort have not greatly considered of: as, 1. That our prelates, if they professed popery, could not do so much hurt unto God's church as now they do. 2. That the devil is not better practised in bowling and swearing than John of London is, with other like points. What shall be handled in my 2nd, 3rd, 4th, 5th, and 6th books, you shall know when you read them.[176]

Mine *Itinerarium* shall be a book of no great profit, either to the church or commonwealth: and yet had need to be in folio, or else judge you by this that followeth.[177] I mean to make a survey into all the dioceses in this land, that I may keep a visitation among my clergy men.[178] I would wish them to keep good rule, and to amend their manners against I come. For I shall paint them in their colours, if I find anything amiss: in this book I will note all their memorable pranks. As for example, if I find any priest to have done as Sir Geoffrey Jones of Warwickshire did, that must be set down in my visitations, and I think I had need to have many scribes, and many reams of paper for this purpose.[179] The said Sir Geoffrey Jones committed a part very well beseeming his priesthood, which was after this manner. Sir Geoffrey once in an alehouse (I do desire the reader to bear with me, though according to Master Bridges his fashion, I write false English in this sentence), whereunto he resorted for his morning draught, either because his hostess would have him pay the old score before he should run any

[42] further, or the new, or else because the gamesters his companions won all his money at trey trip:[180] took such unkindness at the alehouse, that he sware he would never go again into it. Although this rash vow of the good priest was made to the great loss of the alewife, who by means of Sir Geoffrey was wont to have good utterance for her ale:[181] yet I think the tap

---

[i] [side note:] Mine *Epitome* is ready.

had great quietness and ease thereby, which could not be quiet so much as an hour in the day, as long as Sir Geoffrey resorted unto the house, how sweet it was, poor Sir Jones felt the discommodity of his rash vow. Then alas, he was in a woe case, as you know: for his stomach could not be at all strengthened with the drink he got abroad. But better were a man not to feel his discommodity, than not to be able to redress the same. Therefore at length Sir Geoffrey bethought him of a feat whereby he might both visit the alestond,[182] and also keep his oath. And so he hired a man to carry him upon his back to the alehouse, by this means he did not go, but was carried thither, whereunto he made a vow never to go.[183]

I doubt not in my visitation but to get a hundred of these stratagems, especially if I travel near where any of the vicars of hell are. As in Surrey, Northampton, and Oxford shires.[184] And I would wish the pursuivants and the Stationers, with the Wolfe their beadle, not to be so ready to molest honest men.[185] And Stationers, I would wish you not to be so frank with your bribes, as you were to Thomas Draper, I can tell you his grace had need to provide a bag full of *Items* for you, if you be so liberal.[186] Were you so foolish (or so malicious against Waldegrave) to give that knave Draper five pounds to betray him into your wretched hands? He brought you to Kingston-upon-Thames, with pursuivants to take him, where he should be a-printing books in a tinker's house (your selves being disguised so, that Waldegrave might not know you, for of citizens you were become ruffians). There you were to seek that [which] could not be found, and many such journeys may you make.[187] But when you came to London, you laid Thomas Draper in the Counter for [43] cozenage. O well bowled, when John of London throws his bowl he will run after it and cry rub, rub, rub, and say the devil go with thee.[188]

But what think you shall be handled in my *Lambethisms*? Truly this, I will there make a comparison of John Whitgift's Canterburiness, with John Bridges his Lambethisms. To speak in plain English, I will there set down the flowers of errors, popish and others, wherewith those two worthy men have stuffed the books which they have written against the cause of reformation, in the defence of the government of bishops. I have in this book, as you shall see, gathered some flowers out of John of London's book, but my *Lambethisms* shall be done otherwise I trow.

And now if it may please you of the Confocation House to hear of any of the former books, then break the league which I offer to make with you, but if you would have my friendship, as I seek yours, then let me see that you persecute no more, and especially that you trouble none for this book of mine. For this must be an especial article of our agreement, as you know. And Dean John, for your part, you must play the fool no more in the pulpit.

We will end this matter with a pretty story, of a certain mischance that befell a bishop's corner cap, as followeth. Old Doctor Turner (I mean not Doctor Perne the old turner) had a dog full of good qualities.[189] Doctor Turner having invited a bishop to his table, in dinner while called his dog,[190] and told him that the bishop did sweat (you must think he labored hard over his trencher). The dog flies at the bishop and took of his corner cap (he thought belike it had been a cheese cake) and so away goes the dog with it to his master. Truly my masters of the clergy, I would never wear corner cap again, seeing dogs run away with them: and here endeth the story.

[44] May it please you that are of this House to tell me the cause, when you have leisure, why so many opinions and errors are risen in our church concerning the ministry, and the joining with preaching and unpreaching ministers? To tell you my opinion in your ear, I think it to be want of preaching, and I think your worships to have been the cause of all this stir. Some puritans hold readers for no ministers, some hold you our worthy bishops for little better than fair parchment readers, and say that you have no learning. Now whether readers be ministers or no, and whether our bishops be learned or no, I would wish you brethren bishops, and you brethren puritans, to make no great controversy, but rather labor that all evil ministers may be turned out of the church, and so I hope there should be a speedy end of all those questions between you. For then I doubt not but that lord bishops, whereat the puritans so repine, should be in a fair reckoning within short space, even the next to the door save the dog: and I see that you bishops are well towards this promotion already.[191] And truly, though the puritans should never so much repine at the matter, yet I tell you true, I am glad that you are so esteemed among men. And for mine own part, I think my masters that many of you our lord bishops and clergy men are men very notorious for their learning and preaching. And hereof under *Bendicite* between you and me (the puritans may stand aside now) I will bring you some instances.[192] First his grace and my Lord of Winchester have been very notable clerks, ever since Master Doctor Sparke set them at a *non plus* (some of their honors being present) in the conference between him and Master Travers on the puritans' side, and the two archbishops and the bishop of Winchester on the other side.[193] Doctor Sparke's argument was drawn from the corruption of the translation of the 28th verse of the 105th Psalm, in the Book of Common Prayer, and the contrariety of the translations allowed by the bishops themselves. For in the Book of Common Prayer you shall read thus: *And they were not obedient* [45] *unto his word* (which is a plain corruption of the text). In other privileged English translations it is, *And they were not disobedient unto his word*, which is according to the verity of the original.[194] By the way, ere I go any further

I would know with what conscience either my brother Cant. or any else of our bishops can urge men to allow such palpable corruptions by subscribing unto things mere contrary to the word. Here also I would show by the way, and I would have all my sons to note, that their uncle Canterbury's drift in urging subscription is not the unity of the church (as he would pretend) but the maintenance of his own pride and corruption, which should soon come to the ground if the word had free passage: and therefore he proveth the same, by stopping the mouths of the sincere preachers thereof. For if the unity of the church had been his end, why hath not he amended this fault in all the books that have been printed since that time, which now is not so little as three years, in which time many thousand of Books of Common Prayer have been printed? If he had other business in hand than the amending of the Book of Common Prayer, why had he not, nay why doth he not leave urging of subscription until that be amended? Can he and his hirelings have time to imprison and deprive men, because they will not sin by approving lies upon the Holy Ghost (which things they cannot, nor could not chose but commit, whosoever will or have subscribed unto the book and articles)? And can he have no time in three or four years to correct most gross and ungodly faults in the print, whereof the putting out of one syllable, even three letters (*dis*) would have amended this place? But it lieth not in his grace to amend the corruptions of the Book. Belike it lieth in him to do nothing but sin, and to compel men against their consciences to sin, or else to bring extreme misery upon them. If it lay not in him, yet he might have acquainted the parliament (for there was a parliament since the time he knew this fault) with the corruptions of the   [46] Book.[195] And I will come nearer home to him than so, in the article concerning the government whereunto men are urged to subscribe. You must (say the articles) protest that there is nothing in the ministry of the church of England that is not according to the word, or to such like effect they speak. I say that I cannot subscribe unto this article, because contrary to the express commandment of our Saviour Christ, and the examples of his apostles, there be lords in the ministry, or such as would be accounted ministers, will also be called and accounted lords, and bear civil offices, the words of Christ are those: The kings of the gentiles reign over them, and they that bear rule over them, are called gracious lords, but you shall not be so, Luke 22:25–26.[196] I say that out of this place, it is manifest that it is utterly unlawful for a minister to be a lord: that is, for any lord bishop to be in the ministry: and therefore I cannot subscribe unto that article which would have me justify this to be lawful. Now I will cease this point, because I doubt not but the articles of subscription will be shortly so made out of fashion, that the bishops will be ashamed of them themselves: and if no other will take them in hand, I'll turn one of mine own breed unto them, either Martin Senior, or some of his brethren.

To go forward, his Lordship of Winchester is a great clerk, for he hath translated his dictionary, called *Cooper's Dictionary,* verbatim out of Robert Stephanus his *Thesaurus,* and ill-favored too they say.[197] But what do I speak of our bishops' learning, as long as Bishop Overton,[198] Bishop Bickley,[199] Bishop Middleton,[200] the dean of Westminster,[201] Doctor Cole,[202] Doctor Bell,[203] with many others, are living, I doubt me whether all the famous dunses be dead. And if you would have an ilsample of an excellent pulpit man indeed, go no further than the bishop of Gloucester now living: and in him you shall find a plain instance of such a one as I mean.[204] On a time he

[47]   preaching at Worcester before he was bishop, upon Sir John's day:[205] as he traversed his matter, and discoursed upon many points, he came at the length unto the very pith of his whole sermon, contained in the distinction of the name of John, which he then showing all his learning at once, full learnedly handled after this manner: John, John, the grace of God, the grace of God, the grace of God: gracious John, not graceless John, but gracious John. John, holy John, holy John, not John full of holes, but holy John. If he showed not himself learned in this sermon, then hath he been a duns all his life. In the same sermon, two several Johns, the father and the son, that had been both recusants, being brought publicly to confess their faults, this worthy doctor, by reason that the young man having been poisoned beyond the seas with popery, was more obstinate than his father, and by all likelihood he was the cause of his father's perverseness: with a vehement exclamation, able to pierce a cobweb, called on the father aloud in this pathetical and persuading sort. Old John, old John, be not led away by the siren sounds and enticements of young John, if young John will go to the devil, the devil go with him. The puritans it may be, will here object that this worthy man was endued with these famous gifts before he was bishop, whereas since that time, say they, he is not able to say boo to a goose. You weigh this man belike my masters, according to the rest of our bishops. But I assure you it is not so with him. For the last Lent, in a sermon he made in Gloucester town, he showed himself to be the man that he was before. For he did in open pulpit confirm the truth of his text to be authentical, being the prophecy of Isaiah, out of the Book of Common Prayer, which otherwise would (it is to be feared) have proved Apocrypha. His text was, a child is born unto us,[206] which after he sweetly repeated very often as before, to the great destruction and admiration of the hearers,[207] saying: A child is born, a child

[48]   is born, a child is born unto us. This (saith he) is proved you know, where in

that worthy verse of the Book of Common Prayer: Thy honorable true and only son. Afterward, repeating the same words again: A child is born unto us, a child is born unto us: here, saith he, I might take occasion to commend that worthy verse in our Latenie,²⁰⁸ where this is made very manifest, that the prophet here speaketh: By thy Nativity and circumcision. What, should I prosecute the condemnation of this man, as though other our bishops and pulpit men have not as commendable gifts as he?

And once again to you, brother Bridges, you have set down a flaunting reason, in the 75th page of your book, against the continuance of the government which the puritans labor for, and I find the same syllogism concluded in no mood: therefore what if I was ashamed to put it down?²⁰⁹ But seeing it is your will to lay on the puritans with it as it is, put your corner cap a little near a to side,²¹⁰ that we may see your parti-coloured beard, and with what a manly countenance you give your brethren this scouring. And I hope this will please you, my clergy masters, as well as if I told you how our brother Bridges played my Lord of Winchester's fool in Sir Mary's pulpit in Cambridge,²¹¹ but no word of that: now to my reason.

Some kind of ministry ordained by the Lord was temporary (saith he), as for example, the Mosaical priesthood, and the ministry of apostles, prophets, etc. But the ministry of pastors, doctors, elders and deacons was ordained by the Lord. Therefore it was temporary.²¹²

Alack, alack Dean John, what have you done now? The puritans will be O the bones of you too bad,²¹³ for this kind of arguing, and they will reason after this sort.

1. Some man in the land (say they) weareth a wooden dagger and a coxcomb,²¹⁴ as for example, his grace of Canterbury's fool, Doctor Perne's cousin and yours. You, presbyter John Catercap,²¹⁵ are some man in the land. Therefore by this reason, you wear a wooden dagger and a coxcomb. [49]

2. Some presbyter priest or elder in the English ministry, is called the vicar of hell. As for example one about Oxford, another near Northampton, and the parson of Mickleham in Surrey.²¹⁶ But the dean of Sarum, John Catercap, is some priest in the English ministry. Ergo he is the vicar of hell.

3. Some presbyter priest or elder, preaching at Paul's Cross 1587, told a tale of a leaden shoeing-horn, and spake of catekissing:²¹⁷ and preaching at the Court on another time, thrust his hand into his pocket, and drew out a piece of sarsenet, saying, behold a relic of Mary's smock: and thrusting his hand into the other pocket, drew out either a linen or a woolen rag, saying, behold a relic of Joseph's breeches. But, quoth he, there is no reason why Mary's smock should be of sarsenet, seeing Joseph's breeches

were not of silk. This priest being lately demanded whether he should be bishop of Ely, answered that he had now no great hope to B. of Ely:²¹⁸ and therefore, quoth he, I may say well enough, *Eli, Eli, lamma sabachthani*, Eli, Eli, why hast thou forsaken me. Alluding very blasphemously unto the words which our Saviour Christ spake, in his greatest agony upon the cross.²¹⁹ The same priest calling before him one Master Benison a preacher, and would have urged him to take his oath to answer to such articles as he would propound against him, who answered saying, brother bishop, I will not swear, except I know to what. With that the priest fell sick of the spleen, and began to swear by his faith: quoth Benison, a bishop should preach faith, and not swear by it. This priest being in his melancholic mood, sent him to the Clink, where he lay till her Majesty was made privy of his tyranny, and then released to the priest's woe.²²⁰ As for example, the bishop of London did all those things, and more too. For lying at his house at Haddam in Essex, upon the Sabbath day (wanting his bowling mates) took his servants and went a-haymaking,²²¹ the godly ministers round about being exercised (though against his commandment) in fasting and prayer. But you, John Catercap, are some presbyter priest or elder. Therefore you profaned the word and ministry in this sort.

[50]

4. Some presbyter priest or elder in the land is accused (and even now the matter is in trial before his grace and his brethren) to have two wives, and to marry his brother unto a woman upon her death bed, she being past recovery. As for example, the bishop of Sir David's in Wales is this priest, as they say.²²² But you, presbyter John, are some priest. Therefore you have committed all these unnatural parts.

5. Some priest preaching at the funerals of one who died, not only being condemned by the law of God and of the land for attempting matters against her Majesty's person and the state, but also died an obstinate and professed papist, and without any repentance for her enterprises against her Majesty and the state: prayed that his soul and the souls of all the rest there present might be with the soul of the unrepentant papist departed. As for example, the bishop of Lincoln did this at Peterborough, August 2, 1587.²²³ But you are some priest. Ergo you made such a prayer.

6. Some priest in the land lately made, or very shortly meaneth to make, as they say, an old acquaintance of his own, Richard Patrick, clothier of Worcester, of the reading ministry. As for example, his grace of Canter. is this priest. But you, brother Sarum, are some priest as well as he. Ergo you have thrust a bankrupt clothier in the ministry.²²⁴

7. Some priest having given a man (whose wife had played the harlot) leave to marry another, desiring the man long after he had been married to

another woman, to show him his letters of divorcement, with promise to deliver them again. But having received them, they are retained of him most injuriously unto this day, and he troubleth the man for having two wives. As for example, the bishop of Sir Asse is this priest.[225] But you, Dean Catercap, are some priest. Ergo you do men such open injury.

8. Some men that break the law of God are traitors to her Majesty, as for [51] example, the Jesuits. But all our bishops are some men that break the law of God, because they continue in unlawful callings. Ergo by your reason they are traitors to her Majesty, but I deny your argument, for there may be many breaches of the law of God whereof they may be guilty, and yet no traitors.

9. Some men that will not have their lordships and their callings examined by the word are limbs of Antichrist, as for example, the pope and his cardinals. But our lord bishops are some men which will not have their lordships and their callings tried by the word. Therefore they are limbs of Antichrist.

10. Some men would play the turncoats, with the bishop of Gloucester, Doctor Kenold, Doctor Perne (I will let Doctor Goodman, abbot of West., alone now).[226] But all the lord bishops, and you brother Catercap, are some men. Ergo you would become papists again.

11. Some men dare not dispute with their adversaries, lest their ungodly callings should be overthrown, and they compelled to walk more orderly. But our bishops are some men. Ergo they dare not dispute lest their ungodly callings and places should be overthrown.

12. Some men are thieves and soul murderers before God, as for example, all nonresidents. Every lord bishop is a nonresident. Ergo he is a thief and a soul murderer before God.[227]

13. Some men are become apostataes from their ministry,[228] sinners against their own consciences, persecutors of their brethren, sacrilegious church robbers, withstanders of the known truth for their own filthy lucre's sake, and are afraid lest the gospel and the holy discipline thereof should be received in every place. But our bishops are some men. Therefore (by your reason, Master Doctor) they are become apostataes from their ministry, sinners against their own consciences, persecutors of their brethren, sacrilegious church robbers, and withstanders of the known truth, etc.

14. Some priest is a pope, as for example, that priest which is bishop of [52] Rome is a pope. But his grace of Cant. is some priest. Therefore Master Bridges, by your manner of reasoning, he is a pope.

You may see what harm you have done by dealing so loosely. I know not what I shall say to these puritans' reasons! They must needs be good, if yours be sound. Admit their syllogisms offended in form as yours doth: yet the common people, and especially Dame Lawson, and the gentlewoman whose man demanded of her, when she sat at the bishop of London's fire: why mistress, will you sit by Caiaphas his fire? will find an unhappy truth in many of these conclusions, when as yours is most false.[229] And many of their propositions are tried truths, having many eye and ear witnesses living.

Men when commonly they dedicate books unto any, enter into commendations of those unto whom they write. But I care not an I owe you my clergy masters a commendations, and pay you when you better deserve it. Instead thereof, I will give you some good counsel and advice, which if you follow, I assure you it will be the better for you.

First I would advise you, as before I have said, to set at liberty all the preachers that you have restrained from preaching: otherwise it shall be the worse for you, my reason is this. The people are altogether discontented for want of teachers. Some of them already run into corners, and more are like, because you keep the means of knowledge from them. Running into corners will breed Anabaptistry, Anabaptistry will alienate the hearts of the subjects from their lawful governor. And you are the cause hereof. And will not her Majesty then, think you, require the hearts of her subjects at your hands, when she shall understand that they are alienated (as God forbid they should) from her by your means? Yes, I warrant you. And if they should put up a supplication unto her Highness, that their preachers might be restored unto them, I doubt not but they should be heard. I can [53] tell you she tendreth the estate of her people, and will not discourage their hearts, in casting off their suits, to maintain your pride and covetousness: you were then better to set the preachers at liberty, than to suffer your cruelty and evil dealing to be made known unto her. For so they shall be sure, I doubt not, to prevail in their suit, and you to go by the worse. And try if her Majesty be not shortly moved in this suit. To it my masters roundly, you that mean to deal herein, and on my life you set the prelates in such a quandary, as they shall not know where to stand.

Now master prelates I will give you some more counsel, follow it. Repent clergy men, and especially bishops, preach faith bishops, and swear no more by it, give over your lordly callings. Reform your families and your children: they are the pattern of looseness. Withstand not the known truth no longer. You have seduced her Majesty and her people. Pray her Majesty to forgive you, and the Lord first to put away your sins. Your government is antichristian, deceive the Lord no longer thereby: you will grow from evil to worse unless betimes you return. You are now worse than you were 29 years ago.[230] Write no more against the cause of reformation: your ungodliness is made more manifest by your writings. And because you cannot answer what hath been written against you, yield unto the truth. If you should write, deal syllogistically: for you shame yourselves when you use any continued speech, because your style is so rude and barbarous. Rail no more in the pulpit against good men, you do more hurt to yourselves, and your own desperate cause, in one of your railing sermons, than you could in speaking for reformation. For every man that hath any light of religion in him will examine your grounds, which being found ridiculous (as they are) will be decided, and your cause made odious. Abuse not the high commission as you do, against the best subjects. The commission itself was ordained for very good purposes, but it is most horribly abused by [54] you, and turned clean contrary to the end wherefore it was ordained.[231] Help the poor people to the means of their salvation, that perish in their ignorance: make restitution unto your tenants, and such as from whom you have wrongfully extorted any thing. Usurp no longer the authority of making of ministers and excommunication. Let poor men be no more molested in your ungodly courts. Study more than you do, and preach oftener. Favor nonresidents and papists no longer. Labor to cleanse the ministry of the swarms of ignorant guides, wherewith it hath been defiled. Make conscience of breaking the Sabbath, by bowling and tabling.[232] Be ringleaders of profaneness no longer unto the people. Take no more bribes. Leave your simony. Favor learning more than you do, and especially godly learning. Stretch your credit, if you have any, to the furtherance of the gospel. You have joined the profanation of the magistracy, to the corruption of the ministry: leave this sin. All in a word, become good Christians, and so you shall become good subjects, and leave your tyranny. And I would advise you, let me hear no more of your evil dealing.

Given at my Castle between two wales,[233] neither four days from penniless bench,[234] nor yet at the west end of Shrovetide: but the fourteenth year at the least of the age of Charing Cross,[235] within a year of Midsummer, between twelve and twelve of the clock. *Anno pontificatus vestri Quinto,* and I hope *ultimo,* of all English popes.[236]

By your learned and worthy brother,
MARTIN MARPRELATE

TRACT II
The *Epitome*

The *Epitome*
(November 1588)

Robert Waldegrave printed the *Epitome* in Fawsley Hall, Sir Richard Knightley's manor in Northamptonshire, on the same press, with the same type, and in the same quarto format as the *Epistle* (see Introduction, li–lii). At forty-six pages, the *Epitome* is shorter than the *Epistle*, requiring six rather than seven sheets per copy (collating 4°: A^2 B–F^4 G^2; 24 leaves, unnumbered; the final leaf is blank). For fifteen lines its title page is almost identical to that of the *Epistle*; the eighteenth line begins "In this Epitome," providing the title by which the second Marprelate tract has always been known.

As the *Epistle* had promised, the *Epitome* offers a sustained response to John Bridges' *Defence of the Government Established in the Church of Englande* (1587). At the heart of Martin's attack is a claim for ironic decorum. By repeatedly critiquing Bridges' style as well as his arguments, Martin implies that a bad cause could be defended only by poor writing and specious logic. Martin justifies his own approach to controversy with the same ironic reasoning: he jests, he claims, because he writes against a jester who performs foolishness on behalf of his episcopal masters. The other major target of the *Epitome* is John Aylmer, bishop of London. Throughout the tract, Martin gleefully turns the denunciations of episcopal magnificence a young Aylmer had offered in his *An Harborowe for Faithfull and Trewe Subjectes* (1559) against the wealthy and powerful bishop Aylmer had become thirty years later. The Martinist voice developed in the *Epistle* remains on display throughout the *Epitome*, confidently colloquial and irreverent. To some extent, the *Epitome* pushes Martinist play with the conventions of printed debate even further than the *Epistle* had: in addition to chatty marginalia, the *Epitome* offers playful running heads (reproduced in the Appendix, 209–10) and a mockingly self-referential errata list. But in other respects, the *Epitome* is more traditionally polemical than the first Marprelate tract. Martin here offers fewer anecdotes and focuses more systematically on the ecclesiological debates in which reformers had been engaged for almost two decades. Does scripture offer a divine blueprint for church organization? What church offices are valid? Is clerical hierarchy founded in scripture? Should ministers hold civil offices? Which aspects of church governance and practice are necessary to salvation, and which are things indifferent? What roles should women play in church practice? These discussions remind us that the jesting Martin defends in *Epitome* was not an end in itself, but served instead as a means to publicize the reform movement's answers to these controverted questions.

Oh read over D. John Bridges, for it is worthy work:

Or an Epitome of the first book of that right worshipful volume
written against the puritans, in the defence of the noble clergy,
by as worshipful a priest, John Bridges, Presbyter, Priest or
Elder, Doctor of Divility, and Dean of Sarum. Wherein
the arguments of the puritans are wisely prevented,
that when they come to answer Master Doctor,
they must needs say something that
hath been spoken.

Compiled for the behoof and overthrow of the unpreaching
Parsons, Fyckers, and Currats, that have learnt their
catechisms, and are past grace: by the reverend
and worthy Martin Marprelate gentleman,
and dedicated by a second Epistle to
the Terrible Priests.[1]

In this Epitome, the foresaid Fickers, etc., are very
insufficiently furnished, with notable inability
of most vincible reasons, to answer the
cavil of the puritans.

And lest Master Doctor should think that no man can write
without sense but his self, the senseless titles of the
several pages,[2] and the handling of the matter
throughout the Epitome, show plainly that
beetleheaded ignorance must not
live and die with him alone.

Printed on the other hand of some of the Priests.

Martin Marprelate gentleman, primate,
and Metropolitan of all the Martins in
England. To all the clergy masters wheresoever,
saith as followeth.

Why my clergy masters, is it even so with your terribleness? May not a poor gentleman signify his good will unto you by a letter, but presently you must put yourselves to the pains and charges of calling four bishops together, John Canterbury, John London, Thomas Winchester, William of Lincoln, and posting over city and country for poor Martin?³ Why, his meaning in writing unto you was not that you should take the pains to seek for him. Did you think that he did not know where he was himself? Or did you think him to have been clean lost, that you sought so diligently for him? I thank you brethren, I can be well though you do not send to know how I be. My mind towards you, you shall from time to time understand by my pistles.⁴ As now, where you must know, that I think not well of your dealing with my worship, and those that have had of my books in their custody. I'll make you rue that dealing of yours, unless you leave it. I may do it, for you have broken the conditions of peace between us.⁵ I can do it, for you see how I am favored of all estates (the puritans only excepted). I have been entertained at the Court: every man talks of my worship.⁶ Many would gladly receive my books, if they could tell where to find them. I hope these courtiers will one day see the cause tried between me and you. I have many sons abroad that will solicit my suit. My desire is, to have the matter tried, whether your places ought to be tolerated in any Christian commonwealth. I say they ought not: and I say, John Canterbury and all ought to be out of his place. Every archbishop is a petty pope, so is every lord bishop. You are all the pack of you, either hirelings or wolves.⁷ If you dare answer my reasons, let me see it done. Otherwise, I trow, my friends and sons will see you one day deposed.⁸

The puritans are angry with me, I mean the puritan preachers.⁹ And why? Because I am too open. Because I jest. I jested, because I deal against a worshipful jester, D. Bridges, whose writings and sermons tend to no other end than to make men laugh. I did think that Martin should not have been blamed of the puritans, for telling the truth openly. For may I not say that John of Canterbury is a petty pope, seeing he is so? You must then bear with my ingramness.¹⁰ I am plain, I must needs call a spade a spade, a pope a pope. I speak not against him as he is a councillor, but as he is an archbishop, and so pope of Lambeth. What, will the puritans seek to keep out the pope of Rome, and maintain the pope at Lambeth? Because you will do this, I will tell the bishops how they shall deal with you. Let them say that the hottest of you hath made Martin, and that the rest of you were consenting thereunto, and so go to our magistrates and say, lo, such and such of our puritans have under the name of Martin written against your laws: and so call you in, and put you to your oaths whether you made Martin or no. By this manner Master Wigginton, or such as will refuse to take an oath against the laws of the land, will presently be found to have made Martin by the bishops, because he cannot be gotten to swear that he made him not: and here is a device to find a hole in the coat of some of you puritans.[11] In like sort, to find the printer, put every man to his oath, and find means that Schilders of Middelburg shall be sworn to, so that if any refuse to swear, then he may be thought to be the printer.[12] But bishops, let your fatherhoods tell me one thing. May you put men to their oath against law? Is there any law to force men to accuse themselves? No. Therefore look what this dealing will procure at the length. Even a plain premunire upon your backs, for urging an oath contrary to statute and which is a piece of the foreign power banished by statute.[13]

[A2v]

For the rest that will needs have my books and cannot keep them close: I care not how the bishops deal with such open fellows. And bishops, I would I could make this year 1588 to be the wonderful year, by removing you all out of England.[14] Martin hath told the truth, you cannot deny it, that some of you do injuriously detain true men's goods, as John of London: and some have accounted the preaching of the word to be heresy, as John of Canterbury, etc.[15] All of you are in an unlawful calling, and no better than a brood of petty popes. It will be but folly for you to persecute the courtier Martin until you have cleared yourselves (which you can never do) of the crimes he hath laid to your charge. Alas poor bishops, you would fain be hidden in a net I perceive.[16] I will grow to a point with you. Have but a free disputation with the puritans for the unlawfulness of your place, and if you be not overthrown I will come in, and do unto you what you think good: for then I will say that you are no popes. There was the *Demonstration of Discipline*, published together with mine *Epistles*, which is a book wherein you are challenged by the puritans to adventure your bishoprics against their lives in disputation.[17] You have gotten a good excuse to be deaf at that challenge, under colour of seeking for Martin: your dealing therein is but to hold my dish, while I spill my pottage: you defend your legs against Martin's strokes, while the puritans by their *Demonstration* crush the very brain of your bishopdoms. Answer that book, and give the puritans the overthrow by disputation, or else I see that Martin hath undone you. Be packing bishops, and keep in the pursuivants, or if you will needs send them abroad to molest good men, then pay them their wages, and let them not pull it out of poor men's throats like greedy dogs as they do.[18] You strive in vain, you are laid open already. Friars and monks were not so bad: they lived in the dark, you shut your eyes, lest you should see the light. Archbishops Titus and Timothy will never maintain your popish callings.[19] I have pulled off your vizards, look to yourselves, for my sons will not see their father thus persecuted at your hands. I will work your woe and overthrow, I hope: and you are already clean spoiled, unless you will grant the puritans a free disputation, and leave your persecuting.

Either from country or Court,
M. Martin Marprelate, will do you hurt.
Rhyme doggerel,
Is good enough for bishops I can tell,
And I do much marvel,
If I have not given them such a spell,
As answer it how they cannot tell.
Doctor Bridges up and down,
Writeth after this fashion.

[B1r]   The Epitome of the first book of this worthy volume,
          written by my brother Sarum, Dean John. *Sic fœliciter incipit.*[20]

The whole volume of Master Dean's containeth in it sixteen books, besides a
large Preface, and an Epistle to the reader. The Epistle and the Preface are not
above eight sheets of paper, and very little under seven. You may see when
men have a gift in writing, how easy it is for them to daub paper.
The complete work (very briefly comprehended in a portable book, if your
horse be not too weak, of an hundred threescore and twelve sheets, of good
demy paper[21]) is a confutation of *The Learned Discourse of Ecclesiastical
Government.*[22] This *Learned Discourse* is a book allowed by all the puritan
preachers in the land, who would have all the remnants and relics of
Antichrist banished out of the church, and not so much as a lord bishop
(no, not his grace himself),[23] dumb minister (no, not dumb John of London
his self), nonresident, archdeacon, abbey lubber, or any such loiterer tolerated in our ministry. Insomuch, as if this stronghold of theirs be overthrown,
ho then all the fat is run to the fire with the puritans. And therefore hath
not the learned and prudent Master Dean dealt very valiantly (how wisely
let John Cant. cast his cards and consider[24]) in assaulting this fort of our
precise brethren, which he hath so shaken with good vincible reasons, very
notably out of reason, that it hath not one stean in the foundation mear than
it had.[25]

      Trust me truly, he hath given the cause sicken a wipe in his bricke, and so
lambskinned the same, that the cause will be the warmer a good while for
it.[26] The reasons that moved him to take this pains was, that at the first
[B1v]   coming out of the *Learned Discourse*, the dean in a sermon of his at Paul's
Cross did not only confute a great part of this book,[27] but by his said
learned sermon, made many of the puritans relent and distrust their own
cause: what cannot a smooth tongue and a scholar-like wit bring to pass?[a]
Some other of the puritans, indeed, being more untoward to learn than the
rest, stood stiff in their former opinions concerning the government of
bishops (notwithstanding this sermon of Master Doctor's) and challenged
him for his sermon, offered him the disputation (yea and the *non plus* too,
or else I am deceived). Here Master Dean promised them a large confutation of the *Learned Discourse*, which in this book he hath now performed: wherein he hath behaved himself very scholar-like. His style is as
smooth as a crabtree cudgel. The reader cannot choose but take as great

---

[a] [side note:] Ah brother dean that you are such a doer.

delight therein, as a jackanapes hath in a whip: he hath so thumped the
cause with cross blows, that the puritans are like to have a good and a sound
cause of it as long as they live. In this one thing I dare prefer him before any
that ever wrote: to wit, that there be not three whole periods, for every page
in the book, that is not graced with a very fair and visible solecism. O most
excellent and surpassing eloquence. He speaketh everything so fitly to the
purpose, that he never toucheth the matter in question. A rare gift in a
learned writer. He hath used such variety of learning, that very often he
hath translated out of one man's writing six or seven pages together, note
here a new-found manner of bookmaking. And which is more strange, he
bringeth those testimonies for his purpose, whose very words translated
and set down by him are as flat against the purpose whereto he bringeth
them, as fire in quality is contrary to water. Had not he a right use of his
wits think you, while they were thus bestowed? Not to stand long in this
place of those qualities in him, whereof before I have made some mention
to his praise in the former *Epistle*. Whatsoever might be for the ornament   [B2r]
and furthering of an honest cause, he hath in this book so defied them all,
that elsewhere you are to seek for them, for here they are not to be found.
Wherein he hath very wisely and prudently observed the *decorum* of the
cause in hand. Like lips, like lettuce, as it is in the proverb.[28] The goodness
and honesty of the matter he handled required such good and honest
proofs as he brought. Let those that handle honest and godly causes,
labor to bring good proofs and a clear style. Presbyter John defended our
church government which is full of corruptions, and therefore the style and
the proofs must be of the same nature that the cause is. The priest leaves not
so much as the title of the *Discourse* unexamined. The title forsooth is
A Learned Discourse, etc. A saucy title, but what saith the learned Bridges
unto it? O you know he is good at a stale jest, ever since he played my Lord
of Winchester's fool in his sermon at Sir Mary's Church in Cambridge, and
therefore he jesteth at the title.[29] Ay us, the puritans have nothing to do
with that sermon: why should they hit their brother in the teeth therewith?
He hath made their betters to laugh at him for his sermon since that time.
And why should he not? For his grace will allow him, because he is content
that bishops should be lords: he hath subscribed, weareth a corner cap and a
tippet,[30] and would gladly come to the honor, to wear that which might
make him a lord spiritual, and if it were a shaven crown, or a coxcomb,
which his grace his articles would enjoin him to wear,[31] what hurt could
that do unto him?

Now I wonder what our brethren will say to this, that their book is
scoffed at, at the first dash. I am sure their noses can abide no jest. What say

they man, do you make any question of that? I warrant you they will affirm
that the author of the *Learned Discourse*, and 500 green heads more that are
on their side,[32] within two syllogisms would set the Dean of Sarum at a flat
[B2v]　　*non plus*, and answer his whole work in a threepenny book.[33] Are they so
good at disputing and writing indeed? I hope his Canterburiness will look
to this gear, and suffer them to have liberty neither to write nor to dispute,
the black ox hath trodden on his foot,[34] he hath had some trial by woeful
experience, what small credit and less gain there is to be had, either in
writing or disputing with these fellows.

　　To the matter. The state of the whole controversy between my
brethren bishops and my brethren the puritans, and so between this
worthy doctor and these discoursers, is: whether the external government
of the church of Christ be a thing so prescribed by the Lord in the New
Testament, as it is not lawful for any man to alter the same, any more
than it was lawful to alter the form of regiment prescribed under the
law in the Old Testament. And see whether if there be any government
in the church (as necessarily there must be, or else all confusion will
ensue), the same must be by those offices and officers alone, and by no
other, which the Lord hath set down and limited in his word. Or else
whether man may alter these offices and officers at his will and pleasure,
and make new offices and officers, as he may in the civil governments.
The puritans say that these offices and officers, which our Saviour Christ
and his apostles did ordain, are unchangeable, and that it is not lawful
for any prince to alter them, no not though the circumstances of times,
places and persons should seem, in regard of convenience, to enforce
him thereunto. The doctor with all the lordly priests in the land, hold
the contrary. And swear it to be lawful for the magistrate to ordain
what government he will in the church: yea, that the church governors,
contrary to the flat commandment of our Saviour Christ, Luke 22:25–26,
may be lords. And that the church government prescribed by our Saviour
[B3r]　　Christ, and enjoined by the Apostle, was not immutable, as the regiment
under the law was. Insomuch as in the opinion of Master Bridges and
the rest of the clergy, Paul was deceived, Ephesians the 4:13, in saying
that pastors and doctors were to continue in the church until we all
meet together: that is, unto the end of the world. Here then is the
puritans' *aye* for the permanency of this government, and Master
Doctor's *no*. Our brethren (for so of his mere courtesy it pleaseth
Master Dean to call them, whom men commonly call puritans and
precisians) to make their party good,[35] propound the cause by a like
example after this sort.

The sacrifices of the old law (after the building of the temple) were to be offered only at Jerusalem,[b] by a Levite of the line of Aaron only:[c] unless a prophet extraordinarily ordained it otherwise, as Eliah did.[d] And the said sacrifices were to be consumed and burned, only by a fire proceeding from the Lord.[e] Briefly, none were to meddle with the tabernacle, or anything belonging to the service of God, but the sons of Levi, whom the Lord appointed for his own service.[f] So that if any sacrifice were offered out of Jerusalem by any other than a son of Aaron, consumed by any strange fire,[g] or any service about the tabernacle performed by a stranger, not appointed by the Lord:[h] then an horrible breach of God's ordinance was committed, and punished very memorable by the Lord in Uzza,[i] Corah, Dathan, Abiram, and the two hundred and fifty captains of the congregation, who, not being of the sons of Aaron, would needs offer incense before the Lord.[j]

In like sort, Christ Jesus ordained that when there should be any ministers in his church, they should be able to gather together the saints,[k] and that these in their proper and limited places should be either pastors or doctors. In like sort, he ordained that some should bear rule and oversee the flock with the minister, and they should be elders,[l] [and] that the oversight of the church treasury and the care for the maintenance of the   [B3v] poor should be committed unto deacons, under which also the widows and church servants are contained.[m] He farther ordained, that before these officers should be instituted, and as it were invested into their offices, there should be had due examination of their fitness to execute the same,[n] and their unreproveable life.[o] And that their ordination should be by imposition of hands, with fasting and prayer.[p] And by these four officers (say our brethren), pastors, doctors, elders and deacons, God hath appointed that all matters of the church should be decided and determined. For these officers only (and none else) must have to do with the preaching of the word, administering the sacraments, making of ministers,

---

[b] [side note:] Deut. 22:21 [for 12:11], 1 Kings 8:29, 2 Chron. 6:5.
[c] [side note:] Numb. 3:3 Levit. 8, 9 [not Leviticus, but the discussion of "Levites" in Numb. 3:8–9].
[d] [side note:] 1 Kings 28:32 [for 18:32].   [e] [side note:] Levit. 9:24.
[f] [side note:] Numb. 3:12, 35 [for 45].   [g] [side note:] Levit. 30:10 [for 10:1].
[h] [side note:] Ezek. 44:8.   [i] [side note:] 2 Sam 6:7.
[j] [side note:] Numb. 16:1–35.   [k] [side note:] Ephes. 4:12.
[l] [side note:] Acts 20:17, 28 and 14:23, 1 Tim. 5:17, Titus 1:5, Rom. 12:8.
[m] [side note:] Acts 6:6, Rom. 12:8, Phil. 1:1, 1 Tim. 3:8.
[n] [side note:] 1 Tim. 5:22 and 3:10.
[o] [side note:] Rom. 12:3, Titus 1:6–7, 1 Tim. 3:8 and 5:11 [for 6:11].
[p] [side note:] Acts 14:23 and 6:6, 2 Tim. 1:6.

excommunicating, and administering of all other church censures and punishments. But as for civil government, punishment and censures, they must not meddle with them. Because these things only belongeth to the civil magistrate, whose office is not to be usurped by any of the former. Thus our brethren set down the whole state of the controversy, and thus by scripture they confirm their *aye* and overthrow Master Doctor's *no*. Parlous fellows I assure you. For believe me, it would put a man to his trumps to answer these things soundly by scripture again.[36]

Well, Master Dean, on the other side, very stoutly proveth his *no*, page 54 of his,[q] by a connex axiom to begin withal,[37] in this manner. *If this church government, by pastors, doctors, elders and deacons, be necessary, then the church in some age and place, either had this government, or hath labored for it.*[r] A most true and tried truth, what then, brother Sarum, do you assume from this true government? Nay soft there, ka Mass Dean,[38] I trow the puritans will not drive me to make syllogisms in this book. That is no part of mine intent, for if I had thought they would drive me to such pinches, I would not have meddled with them. Nay by their leave, if the assumption or proposition be either more than I can prove, or be against myself, I will omit them. Pardon me I pray ye my masters, I will set down nothing against myself, I have brought in a true proposition, and that is enough for one man, I think.[s] Let me see what you can say to that. Mine assumption shall be brought forth at leisure. Is the wind at that door with you, brother Dean? I perceive you will be of the surer side, howsoever it goeth. But brethren, what then say you to Master Dean's reason? Your answer, I know, may be of three sorts. First, you may say that the reason is popish. Secondly, you may demand whether it be midsummer moon with him or no,[39] because he bringeth in a connex proposition, and assumeth nothing. Can you blame him in so doing? For the assumption must have been either affirmative, or negative. Now if he had assumed affirmatively, he had overthrown himself: if negatively, then you, brethren, would have denied the assumption, which Master Dean would never have been able to prove. So a man might put himself to a peck of troubles indeed. And this is a point for your learning, closely to pass by that wherewith a man shall have no honesty to deal. Thirdly, you may grant the proposition to be very true

[B4r]

---

q [side note:] Page 54.
r [side note:] A very fit reason to prove the mutability of the church government.
s [side note:] Now good doctor send me the measure of thy head, that I may provide thee a good nightcap.

(to what end then did Sarum bring it in?) because Geneva and other the Helvetian churches have this government, and you labor for it.

Silly fellows, can you say no more? Then upon them again Master Dean with your second reason thus concluded, page 55, with four good substantial terms.[t] *No government is an uniform prescript that cannot be altered, but that which God in his word prescribeth to be such. But the Lord hath not prescribed the church government to be such, as all things appertaining thereunto, is an uniform prescript that cannot be altered. Therefore the church government is not an uniform prescript which cannot be altered.*[40]

[B4v]

Thou knowest not how I love thee for thy wit and learning's sake, brother John (as for thy godliness, I might carry it in mine eye, and see never a whit the worse). Notwithstanding, methinks your syllogism should have four terms: 1. the church government, 2. all things belonging to church government, 3. an uniform prescript, etc., 4. a government prescribed in the word.

And ten to one brother, you never dreamt to have met with your brother Martin when you wrote this volume. Well, seeing we are now come together, let me about this point of church government fathermillerly spur a question unto you. Tell me then, bethout dissimblation,[41] what the bishops and you mean, when the question is concerning church government, to run by and by into the controversy of things appertaining to church government: which for the most part are indifferent, and not set down in the word, but left to the discretion of the church?[u] As though there were no difference between the questions. By what and how many offices and officers the church is to be governed? In what causes it is lawful for church governors to employ themselves: whether it be lawful for one of them to meddle with the office of another? Or for one to do that action wherein the whole church should be an agent? Whether they may be magistrates and church governors both at one time? As though (I say) there were no difference between these questions, which are grounded upon the certain prescript rule of the word that cannot be changed, and other questions, which, although they belong to the service of God and the outward government of the church, yet depend not upon anything prescribed and exactly set down in the word, but upon the grounds of what, in regard of the changeable circumstances of time and place, may be most comely, most decent, most orderly, and best belonging to edification. Of

---

[t] [side note:] Page 55.
[u] [side note:] The bishops' wonted manner in this controversy, to run from the consideration of those things that are moral unto things indifferent.

[C1r]   this latter sort are these points: whether it be most convenient that prayer
should begin at eight or nine of the clock: whether the sermon should
continue an hour or an hour and an half: whether the pulpit should be of
wood or of stone, etc. Concerning which, the word hath expressly set down
nothing, but commanded that all of them should be squared according
unto the rule, let all things be done honestly by order, and to edification.ᵛ

Now reason with one of our corrupt bishops, or any other that defend
their corruptions, and say that our church government is wicked and
unlawful, because it is not expressly set down in the word. They will by
and by demand, whether anything belonging to the service of God be
lawful, but that whereof there is express mention made in the word. And
whether anything belonging to church causes be changeable. As whether it
may be lawful for the minister to preach in his gown, whereas there is no
express mention that our Saviour Christ and his apostles did so? Or
whether it may not be lawful for the church of Geneva to begin his sermon
at eight of the clock, whereas it may be the church of Helvetia beginneth at
nine or at ten? So the worshipful dean of Lincoln (sometimes unlearned
John Whitgift), not being able to deny but that the ministers ought to be
chosen by voice, demandeth whether women forsooth were not to have a
voice in their election or no?⁴² And thus all the pack of them run from the
matter in controversy unto the question of things indifferent. By this
means thinking they may blear the eyes of men if they can bring any
cavil, though never so impertinent to the matter. As who say, all men were
so ignorant, unlearned, and blinded with the world, as nonresidents and
bishops are. I'll besire them to leave this order,⁴³ or else they are like to hear
of it. And I'll besire you, presbyter Bridges, not to bring four terms in your
syllogism again, for an you do, it shall cost me the setting on. My brethren
[C1v]   the puritans in this place, it may be, would grant your syllogism to have but
three terms in it, and so would say that the words *all things* in the
assumption may be taken ambiguous,⁴⁴ for if thereby your worship mean
all things appertaining to the circumstances of the outward service of God,
as the hours of prayers, the number of communicants in one congregation,
etc., as you set down your meaning to be, page 56, sect. 3, then they say your
assumption is nothing to the matter in question. The question my masters?
Why, what a question is that? Did not I warn you aforehand that Master
Dean had made a vow not to meddle with the question? But if, say they,
you mean the church officers and their subjects, concerning which the
controversy is instituted, then we deny the assumption.

ᵛ [side note:] 1 Cor. 14:40.

And I warrant you brethren, he proveth the assumption by two reasons, page 55: *First Christ is the owner and governor of his house which is the church, concerning the inward and spiritual government of the heart. Therefore he hath not prescribed the outward government thereof.*[w] Surely brother John, I marvel upon what topic place this reason is grounded,[45] for scripture is not the foundation (you know) of the established government you defend. As though (will Master Bridges say) you are ignorant brother Martin whence I drew this argument. You would make the world believe, that you know not that I reasoned as my brother London did,[x] in his *Harborowe of Faithful Subjects.*[46] I tell you, I drew mine argument from that place whence he drew his, which you shall find set down, page 42 of his book (for I am sure, Master Marprelate, your book hath the pages set down in it, although the printed book hath them not).[47] O I remember well indeed, brother Sarum, the place you mean, and I remember that John Elmar's reason is very like yours. For (saith Elmar), *The scripture meddleth with no civil policy, any farther than to teach obedience, therefore it teacheth not what persons should bear rule.* And again, page 44: *The minister's office is over the soul, therefore a minister must not reprehend disorders in the civil state.* Page 47: *Paul's commission is to teach obedience, therefore he hath nothing to do to call for a redress of matters in civil policy.* Yea in this 47th page, line 19, John of London hath these words, which to his commendation I will set down as followeth: *And this being a great matter of policy* (saith he) *as it is the greatest (for it containeth the whole) it cannot be within the compass of Paul's commission, and so it followeth, that Paul in this place meant no such matter as they gather, or if he did, he did it without the compass of his commission, etc.*

[C2r]

Now truly brother Bridges, I thank you heartily for putting me in mind of this point, I hope my brother London cannot be offended with us for quoting him for our authority. I see now it is no marvel though Paul be put to silence within the diocese of London, for I perceive there is an old grudge between my lord and him: yet I commend your fatherhood better than his lordship in this point. For in the 57th [=56th] page of your book you allow Paul a larger commission, where you say, *that the word of God is able to make the civil government perfect: yea, and that the perfection of the civil government, must be out of the word, and in the word inclusively.* But for all this, you must give me leave to doubt how this reason of yours followeth. Christ hath prescribed the inward government, therefore he hath not prescribed the outward. It may be your second reason will make the matter

[w] [side note:] Page 55.   [x] [side note:] The bishop of London's book.

more clear unto me, which is in the same page,^y and thus framed. *We are his*
church if we hold fast the confidence of our hope unto the end. Therefore there is

[C2v] *no external government of the church set down in the word.* This reason, to
omit what ground it hath in the word, is very plausible even in nature: is it
not, think you? A man is a man though he go naked. Therefore, by Master
Dean's reason, the Lord hath ordained no covering for his nakedness.
Again, a man is a man if he be once born, though he never eat meat:
therefore it is not the ordinance of God he should eat meat. Let our cavilling
brethren go see now what may be brought to reproach the credit of such
inforcible proofs. Master Doctor doubtless will stand to his tackle whatsoever they bring. If they should be so ignorant as to deny the consequence of
both these reasons, they must stay until Master Dean hath read over his
predicables and predicaments with Friar Titleman's rules *de inveniendis*
mediis, vz. until he hath gotten a bishopric, before he prove either of
them.⁴⁸ And it may be then, too, that he will prove what they deny, as
Master Canterbury hath proved that which Master Cartwright confuted.⁴⁹

In the mean time, mark how stoutly Master Dean goeth forward.^z And
although, page 56, he meet by the way with his known sweet friend
Bellarmine's,⁵⁰ a popish writer's, distinction of agreeable and not contrary
to the word (the papists affirming all their traditions to be agreeable, and
none of them contrary to the word), yet his answer, page 57,^a to the place of
Paul, 2 Tim. 3:7 [for 3:17], is as good and as canonical as any of the former
reasons, concluded thus. *The place of scripture which doth not deny but that*
the civil government, which must be inclusively according to the word,^b *may be*
elsewhere prescribed than in the word, that place also doth not forbid the
church government to be fetched from some other fountain than the prescription
of the word. But this place 2 Tim. 3:7 [for 3:17] *doth not deny but that civil*
government being a government not prescribed in the word, may be learned

[C3r] *elsewhere than out of the word, and yet be according to the word. Also it doth*
not deny but that the church government may be a church government
according to the word, which is not therein prescribed.

It is a hard matter, I tell you, to conceive all the wisdomness of this
syllogism. For if you mark the proposition very well, you shall therein find
the errors (as Master Doctor accounteth them) of Peter and Paul very
notably overthrown. The one of them calleth the civil government an
human ordinance:^c the other affirmeth our Saviour Christ to have ordained
every minister and church officer that were at any time to be in the church,

---

^y [side note:] Page 55.   ^z [side note:] Page 56.   ^a [side note:] Page 57.
^b [side note:] Your consequent is false, Master Dean.   ^c [side note:] 1 Peter 2:13.

and to have tied the ministry unto two ordinary functions, of pastors and doctors.[d] But his worship, lighting upon William Woodcock's divinity,[51] putteth in the propositions, both, that the church government is an ordinance of man, invented and ordained by man, and also that there may be as many sorts of ministers in the church (if the magistrate will have it so) as there be degrees of civil officers in a commonwealth. For the church government is no more prescribed in the word (saith the dean) than the civil government is.

You may see then, how heady and perverse these our brethren are, that had rather stick unto a poor fisherman and tentmaker, Peter and Paul, in a matter of truth, than embrace the manifest falsehood of so plain an untruth, with a fat dean and all the brave spiritual lords in the land. Well fare our clergymen yet, who (being like the priest whereof John of London maketh mention of in his foresaid book,[e] page 32, line 3, that sware by his priesthood, that if the Trinity were not in his portesse, he would not believe it)[52] will allow of nothing, but that which is in the bishop of Canterbury's articles, be it never so often read in Paul's writings.[53]

And I trow Master Doctor's reasons following will make the puritans [C3v] stoop unto his grace, and leave their peevishness, and running beyond their commission, after the example of Paul, in speaking against any established government: yea and a government established by act of parliament. I think my Lord of London gave Paul enough, as we heard before, for meddling with state matters. And his grace admonisheth the puritan preachers often enough, that howsoever they have truth of their side, yet they must not run beyond a law, and without law: if they do, though they have Peter and Paul to speak for them, yet by your leave he hath in his hand that which will tame them and all their fautors, if the abusing of the high commission and an whole popedom be able to do it.[54]

But all this while, we go not on forward with you, brother Sarum. Therefore in the next page[f] let us hear how you fetch your brethren over the coals with your next reason,[55] whereof, trust me, I know not almost, though it were to gain a bishopric, how I should make a good syllogism, but I do my best after this manner: *It sufficeth that such orders as are not prescribed in the word as things necessary to salvation, be they civil or ecclesiastical, be only folded up within those that are prescribed, and to make them as things expedient to edification, order and comeliness, for obedience sake, although they be none of those things that appertain to any necessity of our salvation, or to any absolute*

[d] [side note:] Ephes. 4:12, Rom. 12:8, 1 Cor. 12:28.
[e] [side note:] Another course at you, brother London.   [f] [side note:] Page 57.

necessity of our obedience. But such is the church government, as it is not prescribed in the word, as necessary to salvation, or of any absolute necessity of our obedience. Therefore it is sufficient that the church government be only folded up within the things prescribed in the word, and be of the nature of the things that only belong to edification, order and comeliness.

[C4r] I was never so afraid in my life, that I should not come to an end till I had been windless. Do you not see how I pant? Our brethren now are to come to their answer. Concerning *necessary to salvation* then, say they, we would know, brother Bridges, and thrice learned brother Bridges, we would know what you mean: whether such a necessity as without which men cannot be saved? I mean even the same (saith Master Dean), as it appeareth page 60, lines 21–22 of my book. Then we reply that nothing is of this necessity, but only justifying faith, and we deny the sacraments to be of this necessity. For the thief on the gallows was saved without them.^g And we think, moreover, that your impiety and ignorance (Master Dean) to be outrageous, and intolerable (say they) in that you go about to teach the Holy Ghost what he shall prescribe in the word: because by this proposition of yours, nothing should be prescribed therein concerning the sacraments: for they are not there prescribed as things necessary to salvation, in such sort as men cannot be saved without them.

But if you meant not this necessity, then we would know, if you can tell yourself, what you would have (forsooth brethren, a bishopric he would have, and all such troublesome fellows as you are banished the land). Ho, you mean such a necessity, as every church is not bound to observe the same order upon their obedience?^h For example, you mean that every church or several congregation in Europe professing the truth is not bound to have their church covered with lead, as the monastery of Sarum is,⁵⁶ for they may lawfully have it covered with slate or tile? You mean that they are not bound, every one of them, to have a sermon upon the Wednesday, for they may lawfully have it upon any other day in the week? That every church is not bound to have a pulpit four foot high, for they may without sin have one

[C4v] lower or higher, if expediency and edification require the same? That is even my meaning indeed, and so I would, page 59 (saith Master Dean), *That these things should be urged no otherwise, than Paul doth urge them: that is, not placing the perfection of religion in them, or making them orders necessary for the*

---

^g [side note:] Luke 23:43.
^h [side note:] Master Dean, my friend, is not so precise as he thinks it necessary for them to have a sermon upon the Sabbath.

building, but rather for the ornaments of the building, and so squaring them all according unto the rule: Let all be done honestly, and by good order. Is this your meaning (Master Doctor)? You have spun a fair thread. Can you tell your brother Marprelate, with all your learning, how to decline what is Latin for a goose?[57] Why, this every one of your brethren his self will grant to be true, and they never denied it at any time. But this is not the question. For it is neither concerning church officer, office, or any part of church government whereof the question is instituted: but it is concerning matter of circumstance. Yet (brother John) what do you mean by these contrarieties in this point? For you have heard, page 59, you mean by things necessary to salvation, matters of indifferency: and page 60, lines 21–22, you mean an absolute necessity, without which men cannot be saved. Do you think that you can answer men by saying that you indeed wrote page 59, but Doctor Perne wrote page 60, the which you had no leisure to oversee?[58] This is a pretty answer, is it not, think you? Let me take you again in such a prank, and I'll course you, as you were better to be seeking Gammer Gurton's needle, than come within my fingers.[59] And learned Master Doctor, say the puritans, we will give you leave to take either of these two necessities to be your meaning. If you mean, as page 59, be necessary to salvation, then they deny the assumption. And yet they will have one course more at the proposition before they go, because it came from Rome: and will bring forth a Jesuit, unless betimes it be had to the house of correction. They say then that you still join with Bellarmine. For in the state of the question concerning [D1r] tradition, he hath the same cavil, cap. 3, lib. 2, against Calvin, Luther and Kemnitius, which you have concerning comeliness and order in this place, against your brethren.[60] What a saucy fellow was that Bellarmine, that must needs publish his work for the pope one just year before you published yours for the archbishop. Could he not keep it in, until both your books might be published together? For now these puritans do shake you very shrewdly, for borrowing popish stuff from Bellarmine, and overthrowing her Majesty's supremacy: whereas I am persuaded, that although Bellarmine had never written, yet the master that taught him would in time have fully instructed you in all these points that are forged upon his anvil. And although (as I think) he saved you a great deal of study, yet I pray you let Doctor Perne write unto him, that he may know his fault, and you be certified when he writeth again, that both your books may come forth together.

Now if in your assumption (say our brethren), if you mean by necessity to salvation, that without which men cannot be saved, as before: it is true, that the church government is not of this necessity, for in that sense, as was said, the sacraments are not necessary to salvation, or of any absolute necessity unto our obedience. Nay, to be no traitor, no idolator, no whore-monger, is not of that absolute necessity to salvation, but that he may be saved which hath been (so that now he be none) sometimes an idolator, etc. If you mean that other necessity, whereby all they that will have any government in the church are bound to have that only, and none else, which God hath prescribed in the word, or else transgress the inviolable prescript ordinance of God concerning the government of his church: then they deny the assumption. Here is a pretty matter, that one poor syllogism

[Dɪv] must be thus handled, I would his worship knew who they were, that thus deal with him. I hope it should not be long ere Watson the pursuivant (as unnatural a sourfaced knave, as ever was in that office) should trudge for them.[61] They shall be met with one day, I doubt not.

Master Dean, page 58, showeth very wisely that men must warily take heed how they build (for the bishops have these thirty years so built, that they are almost come to dig at the foundation of the church), lest belike men should, by building after the manner of the apostles, overthrow the monastery of Sarum. And that were pity, seeing from thence these natural reasons following have issued.[i]

Everything that is prescribed in the word containeth in it the perfection of religion. But the church government doth not contain in it the perfection of religion. Therefore the church government is not prescribed in the word. No, brother John, nor baptism neither: for baptism doth not contain the perfection of religion in it, and therefore, as you may wisely conclude, it is not prescribed in the word. We may alter what we will now, so that the part which we alter contain not the perfection of religion in it, and be agreeable unto my Lord of Cant.'s articles. For they must be altered in no case. And what reason is it that the Lord's Supper should be received under both kinds, if the civil magistrate and the church will otherwise ordain? For no sacrament containeth in it the perfection of religion: and therefore by Master Dean's proposition, the celebration thereof is not prescribed in the word. A man might keep good stir in the pulpit, or in writing, having but this ground allowed him. And I think of such a preacher as this should be, John of London spake in his foresaid book, page 49, line 2, where he describeth his preacher after this manner: *that he should be no milksop, no white livered gentleman, that for the frowning and cloudy countenance of every man in authority, will leave his flock and cry* peccavi. And again, in this page,

[D2r] *When they come to handgrips, they must not only flourish, but they must know*

---

[i] [side note:] Page 58.

their quarter strokes, and the way how to defend their head, etc.[j] [62] Such a preacher I say as this would quickly with his quarter strokes overturn all religion, and with very good reason, if Dean John's proposition be true, That every thing which is prescribed in the word containeth in it the perfection of religion.

Will you have any more of these blows, brethren? Then touch them again, parson John, with the second reason in this page. *Everything that is prescribed in the word is of the substance of the building. The church government is not of the substance of the building. Therefore it is not prescribed in the word.* Nothing but paralogisms.[63] Sir Bridges, do you not know before whom you speak? You think now that you play my Lord of Winchester's fool, do you?[64] Or that you are in the monastery of Sarum among your roaring choristers? I would advise you, learn this of me: that the church government is a substantial point of religion. And therefore of the substance of the building. That it is a substantial point, it appeareth, because it is included within the commandment which our Saviour Christ gave unto his apostles when he sent them to build his church,[k] commanding them, not only to teach and baptize all nations (which are the things that you think only to be substantial unto the building, nay, wicked bishops, will not acknowledge preaching to be of the substance of the building), but also to teach them to observe whatsoever he commanded them. Now, he ordained, he commanded that the church should be governed by these four offices,[l] or else the apostles would never have observed them, and prescribed them unto the church.[m] Was there nothing wanting unto the building in Crete, while they wanted elders there? If there was not, why should Titus stay there to ordain elders in every city? If there was, what a dunce are thou to deny the church government to be of   [D2v] the substance of the building. Paul saith in that place, Tit. 1:5, that he appointed that Titus should ordain elders there. Paul belike in this place did appoint these things to be ordained, which were not of the substance of the building. You were best to say that Paul had nothing to do with church government, but to teach obedience, and therefore went beyond his commission, in meddling with these matters. Archbishop Titus, belike whereof you speak now, should be all the doer in church matters: yet I am glad of one thing, that Paul was so bold as to command Archbishop Titus, and to

[j]   [side note:] John Elmar, you must know, was very good with a two-hand sword in his youth.
[k]   [side note:] Math. 28:19–20.
[l]   [side note:] Rom. 12:6, 1 Cor. 12:8, 28, Acts 15:6, Ephes. 4:12.
[m]   [side note:] Acts 6:6 and 14:23, 1 Cor. 23 [for 12:28], 1 Tim. 5:17, Jam. 5:14, Titus 1:5.

enjoin him what he should do in his own diocese.[n] I say in his own diocese, for Master Doctor proveth anon that Titus was archbishop of Crete. Now if Titus, who I doubt not was as good an archbishop as his grace of Canterbury (if ever he was any, as he was not) and might every day in the week go cheek by jowl with his grace, did yet suffer himself in his own diocese to be commanded by Paul,[o] and presumed to do nothing but that which Paul commanded him to do, then I see no reason why Paul should not bear a little more sway in Canterbury diocese than he doth. And I see no reason why his grace should presume to do things so flat contrary to Paul's mind as he doth. Whereas he ought to do nothing but by Paul's commandment. His grace shall one day answer me this point or very narrowly escape me a scouring, and you Dean John go forward: I am content to let you pass my fingers at this time.

If any were saved (saith the Dean, page 60) *without this government, then it is not necessary to salvation. But many were saved without this government that our brethren would have: therefore it is not necessary to salvation.*[p] John of London with his two-hand sword could have quitted himself no better than this.[65] Our brethren grant all this, brother John, because you mean by
[D3r] necessity to salvation, such a necessity as without which men cannot be saved. The next reason is for the golden pen.[66] *Either necessary, or unnecessary. But not necessary to salvation. Ergo, unnecessary.* Thus Master Doctor carrieth away the matter very clearly. Only he straineth a little courtesy with the *Learned Discourse*, in putting *necessary to salvation* for *appertaining to salvation.*[67] You know he that can with a guilty conscience have a faculty for two livings, may as well be dispensed with for a lie or two. And I wis these fellows need not to be so precise of swearing by faith and troth,[68] and straining out a small lie for a benefit, they commit grosser sins many times. And thus Master Doctor hath overthrown their whole building in general. Now he cometh to the spoiling of every particular part thereof.

But before I come to these points, I care not, inasmuch as there hath been often mention made of my Lord of London's book between our brother Bridges and me, if I set down some part of my judgement concerning that book.

O but Master Martin, will my brother Bridges say, will you meddle with that book, which Master Elmar wrote in the defence of her Majesty's government?[q] So you will give me and the bishops just cause to say that

[n] [side note:] Paul commandeth Archbishop Titus in his own diocese.
[o] [side note:] A worthy note. [p] [side note:] Page 60.
[q] [side note:] Here is an indecorum personae in this speech I know, for the doctor should not give me this warning, but you know my purpose is to play the dunce afer his example.

you are a seditious fellow, and one that disliketh of her Majesty's government. And by this means you will incense many against you, that otherwise
could not but favor your worthiness and learning. I would they durst say,
even any bishop of them all, say that I dislike her Majesty's government.
I would make poor bishops of them or I had done with them, if they should
slander me in this sort. And they dare but raise up this slander against me,
I will persecute the whole generation of them, and make them weary of
slandering while they live. Shall they deal with me, as you do (brother
Bridges think you) with Danaeus in your book, whom you bring as an
enemy to her Majesty's government: whereas he by name, and in manifest   [D3v]
words, commendeth and praiseth very highly her Majesty's regiment above
all others?[69] Or will they deal with me, as they have done with Master
Beza?[70] Master Beza, cap. 44 of his *Confessions* written in Latin, saith that
he disliketh their judgements, who think it unlawful for women to bear
rule. This book is translated into English, but it hath all this point left
out in the English copy,[r] to the end they may (as it is reported) bear her
Majesty in hand,[71] that Master Beza is against her regiment, and so that
her Majesty may be brought in detestation of the church government
which Master Beza favoreth, as being a church government that cannot
stand with the civil government of women.[72] What say you to this gear,
bishops, have you dealt well with Master Beza? Deal thus with me an you
dare. If you will say that you had no such intent as to slander Master Beza,
in leaving out the said point, then I say that you are enemies unto her
Majesty's government, in that you will wipe out of a printed and a
translated book that which was written in her defence: especially suffering
the rest of the book to be printed.

To return to John of London's foresaid book, I say although he hath
therein spoken against bishops, even our bishops now living, and so against
himself as being now a bishop, yet that his book is a carnal and unlearned
book, smelling altogether of earth, without rhyme, and without reason.
And that his speaking against bishops therein was but a snare to catch a
bishopric, as it now appeareth. The particular sentences and marginal notes
shall be set down, and where I set any note upon your book there shall be an
(M) for difference sake added thereunto. We will begin with your own
words unto the bishops, that is, unto yourself and your brethren, page 23.[s]

Oh they may thank God (say you) *that they have this time to breathe them,
and bethink them of their naughty and hellish cruelty, and to call daily and*   [D4r]

---

[r] [side note:] A horrible part and an ungodly. Confer the English with the Latin copy.
[s] [side note:] Page 23. The prelates have time of repentance.

hourly for pardon and forgiveness, for let them think, that if they be not punished in this life nor repent: God accounteth their deeds so vile, and their faults so heinous, that no temporal pains be enough for such offences.^t *And therefore reserveth them to eternal damnation. Oh howl and wail you priests and prelates, not for the danger you stand in of losing your bishoprics and benefices, your pride and your pomp, your dignities and honors, your riches and wealth: but for that hell hath opened her mouth wide, and gapeth to swallow you, for the shedding of so much innocent blood, for murdering so many martyrs* (though this be true in our bishops, yet let me instead thereof say, for imprisoning so many innocents, and murdering the souls of so many in ignorance) *and spoiling Christ's church of so many glistering and glorious ornaments, commended of all for their learning, and discommended of none for their living.*^u [73] Now lest any man should think that he writeth these things to popish bishops, you are to know, that he wrote them unto such as were bishops in the reign of her Majesty, unto bishops professing the gospel in name, but indeed denying the power thereof.[74] And in the next page, line 10, he hath these words against those bishops, and now against himself.^v

But Christ, knowing the bounds of his office, would not meddle with extern policies, translating of realms, and depriving of true inheritors. No, when he was desired to be arbiter betwixt two brethren: he asked not how the plea stood, but who made him an officer?^w *Divines (methinks) should by this example not give themselves too much the bridle, and too large a scope, to meddle with matters of policy, as this is, whereupon dependeth either the welfare or illfare of the realm.*^x *If these two offices, I mean ecclesiastical and civil, be so jumbled together, as it may be lawful for both parties to meddle in both functions, here* [D4v] *can be no quiet, nor well ordered commonwealth.*^y [75]

Thus the reader may see what a pattern of hypocrisy this wicked bishop, since he wrote this book, hath showed himself to be: in taking upon him not only that calling, which in his own judgement is unlawful, but also in joining those two offices together: the coupling whereof he confesseth to be joined as well with the most vile disorder, as with the dangerous disquietness of the commonwealth. And yet he hath not here left off speaking against bishops. Therefore, as before in the *Epistle* hath been touched,[76] he dealeth more roundly with them, page 103, than before, in these words.^z
Come off you bishops, away with your superfluities, yield up your thousands, be

^t [side note:] Note you prelates.   ^u [side note:] The Queen deceived by her churchmen.
^v [side note:] Page 24.   ^w [side note:] Luke 12 [:13–14].
^x [side note:] Spiritual men should not meddle with policy.
^y [side note:] Mark this well you that are statesmen. (M)
^z [side note:] Advice to the bishops.

content with your hundreths, as they be in other reformed churches, where be as great learned men as you are. Let your portion be priestlike, and not princelike. Let the Queen have the rest of your temporalities and other lands,[a] *to maintain these wars which you procured, and your mistress left her, and with the rest to build and found schools throughout the realm:*[b] *that every parish church may have his preacher, every city his superintendent,*[c] *to live honestly, and not pompously, which will never be, unless your lands be dispersed and bestowed upon many, which now feedeth and fatteth but one. Remember that Abimelech, when David in his banishment would have dined with him, kept such hospitality that he had no bread in his house to give him but the shewbread.*[d] *Where was all his superfluity to keep your pretenced hospitality? For that is the cause you allege, why you must have thousands, as though you were commanded to keep hospitality, rather with a thousand, than with a hundred. I would our countryman Wickliffe's book which he wrote,* De Ecclesia, *were in print,*[e] *and there should you see, that your wrinches and cavillations be nothing worth.*[77]

Hitherto you see that this Balaam,[78] who hath, I fear me, received the [E1r] wages of unrighteousness, spoken in general, as well against the callings of bishops and their usurping of civil offices, as against their pride, pomp and superfluity. Must not he, think you, have either a most seared or a most guilty conscience, that can find of his heart to continue in that calling: yea, and in the abuse of that calling, which his own conscience, if he would but awake it, telleth him to be unlawful? The Lord give him repentance, if he belongeth unto him, or speedily rid his church of such a scourge. And may not all the former speeches be fitly applied unto him? Is, without doubt.[79] But the next he may be thought to have written to himself, which he hath set down, page 34.[f] *As if you should say, my lord Lubber of London is a tyrant, ergo he is no bishop. I warrant you though he granted you the antecedent, which he can hardly deny, yet he would deny the consequent, or else he would call for wily Watson to help him.*[g] [80] Here, brother London, you have crossed yourself over the costard once in your days.[81] I think you would have spent three of the best elms which you have cut down in Fulham,[82] and

---

[a] [side note:] Bishops' lands.
[b] [side note:] Will you be content, bishop, it shall be so now? (M)
[c] [side note:] In any case, let there be one minister above the rest of his brethren. (M)
[d] [side note:] 1 Sam. 21 [:6].
[e] [side note:] And I would mine *Epistomastix* were in print, there should you see that would not like you. (M)
[f] [side note:] Page 34, line 15.
[g] [side note:] Doth he mean Watson the pursuivant, trow you? (M)

threepence halfpenny besides, that I had never met with your book. But unless you, and John of Exeter, with Thomas Winchester, who have been in times past hypocrites as you have been, leave off to hinder the word, and vex godly men, I will make you to be noble and famous bishops for ever.[83] And might not a man well judge you three to be the desperate Dicks which you, brother London, page 29, affirm to be good bishops in England?[84] For to allude unto your own words, pages 28, 29:[85] Whereas other bishops in the land, for the most (only John Canterbury excepted), lest they should one day answer for their proceedings unto her Majesty, and gain the evil will of the noble men and gentlemen that favour the sincerity of the gospel, will not seem to be such dealers as you three are, though they serve at an [E1v] inch in their place to maintain his grace's pride and cruelty,[86] to stay the course of the gospel, and to fetch in men within the compass of subscription, yet are they those for the most part that will imprison none, and trouble very few, unless it be for fear that if they should tolerate too much, they should have a check of their worshipful Paltripolitan. But you three, like furious and senseless brute beasts, dread no peril, look no farther than your feet, spare none, but with tooth and nail cry out, down with that side that favoreth the gospel so. Fetch them up with pursuivants, to the Gatehouse, to the Fleet, to the Marshalsea, to the Clink, to Newgate, to the Counter with them.[87] It makes no matter with you (I follow your own words, brother London) so you may show yourselves (in show though not in truth) obedient subjects to the Queen, and disobedient traitors to God and the realm.

Thus far I have followed your words, howbeit I think you are not well pleased with me, because you mean not to stand to anything you have written. Nay, you hold it unlawful now for a preacher, as far as the two tables of the law do reach, to speak against bishops, much less any ungodly statute. And yet you say, page 49, line 7, *That preachers must not be afraid to rebuke the proudest, yea kings and queens, so far forth as the two tables of the law do reach. As we see in Samuel, Nathan, Elias, John Baptist, and many other. They may not stoop to every man's beck, and study to please man more than God.* Thus far are your words, and they are as far from your practice as you are from the imitation of these godly examples which you have brought. I see a bishopric hath cooled your courage, for in those days that you wrote this book you would have our parliament to overrule her Majesty, and not to yield an inch unto her of their privileges. Your words I will set down.[h]

---

[h] [side note:] Page 53, line 19.

In like manner (say you, page 53) *if the parliament use their privileges, the* [E2r]
king can ordain nothing without them: if he do, it is his fault in usurping it,
and their folly in permitting it: wherefore in my judgement, those that in King
Henry the 8's days would not grant him that his proclamations should have the
force of a statute,[i] *were good fathers of their country and worthy of commenda-*
tion in defending their liberty, etc.

I assure you, brother John, you have spoken many things worthy the
noting, and I would our parliament men would mark this action done in
King Henry the 8's days, and follow it in bringing in reformation, and
putting down lord bishops, with all other points of superstition: they may
in your judgment not only do anything against their king's or queen's mind
that is behooveful to the honor of God and the good of the commonwealth, but even withstand the proceedings of their sovereign.

But methinks you have a palpable error, in the 48th, 49th and 50th page
of your book, which is that women are uncapable of the ministry,[j] not in
regard of their sex, but of certain wants and imperfections in their sex, vz.
their want of learning and courage, so that if a woman should be brought
up in learning, and trained in disputations, and were not milder in nature
than men (of all which wants in women you speak, page 48), but knew their
quarter stroke (which knowledge you require in the minister, page 49),
then by your reason they might preach in your diocese: whosoever will read
your 50th and 51st pages shall find this to be your judgment.[88]

Besides all this, the reader shall find such earthly and carnal stuff in all
these pages, that you must needs give this judgment of the whole book:
surely flesh, even a lump of mere flesh, writ it. For there you shall see
the English man preferred before other people: only because he feedeth
upon (and hath in his possession plenty of) sheep, oxen, kie,[89] calves (I keep [E2v]
John Elmar's words),[k] conies, fish, and whereas other nations feed upon
roots, raw herbs, oil, grapes, etc. In the last place against the French king he
raileth and outrageth in this wise.[90] *That Turkish Valesius, that French*
tyrant. Is he a king or a devil, a Christian or a Lucifer, that by his cursed
confederacy with the Turk, [etc.].[l] Page 113, line 4: *O wicked caitiff and*
firebrand of hell. And line 8: *O foolish Germans, which conspire not together*

---

[i] [side note:] The parliament resisted King Henry the 8.
[j] [side note:] Women capable of the ministry in regard of their sex, by the bishop of
London's judgment.
[k] [side note:] Pages 110 and 111. Yea we have such plenty of calves in England that we have
calves to our bishops.
[l] [side note:] Page 112, line 27.

with the rest of Christian princes, to pull out such a traitor to God and his
kingdom by the ears out of France and hang him against the sun a-drying.

The discreet reader of that which hath been spoken, may apparently see
the undiscreet brutishness that was in you, even then, when you were best
worthy to be accounted of. And thereby may gather what you are now,
when you have bidden farewell not only unto the sincerity of religion,
which then you seemed to embrace, but even unto all humanity and civil
behaviour. And yet you do not thus leave the French king, but in this, page
113, line 13, you say that the devil hath none of his side now but him to
maintain both the spiritual and the temporal Antichrist: in the same page,
Wherefore seeing he hath forsaken God, like an apostata, and sold himself to the
devil, etc. And lines 27, 28: *Proud Holofernes. Oh blessed is that man that*
loseth his life against such a termagant. Again, page 114, line 2: *but this Julian*
the Apostata is named a devil's name, Christianissimus. Line 3: *And like a*
traitorous Saracen is Christ's enemy. Here he leaveth the French king, and
here I leave his book.

Now I entreat the reader to consider these things that I have set down
out of his book, and judge whether such things as he wrote could proceed
from a religious heart: and whether the book be not an offspring proceeding from a lump of earthly flesh. This book is almost all the tokens of
[E3r]   Christianity that ever he showed. Since the time he became bishop, he hath
been a continual oppressor of the church of God. His practices against God
and his saints was the only cause why I have taken this pains with his book,
and he shall be more beholding unto me, unless he leave his tyranny.

But now alas, alas brother Bridges, I had forgotten you all this while, my
brother London and I were so busy that we scarce thought of you. Why
could not you put me in mind that you stayed all the while? But it is no
matter, we will make the quicker dispatch of our business. You shall see
I will be the more favorable to you. And let me see how roundly you overturn
these puritans, for you are now to overthrow the several parts of their
discipline. Our brethren say, that our Saviour Christ ordained an holy
ministry of men for the building of his church, and prove the saying by the
place of Paul, Ephe. 4:11–12. Your mastership three manner of ways show
the place they allege, to make nothing for their purpose. First, say you, Paul
speaketh of divers functions, therefore nothing of ecclesiastical government. This reason, brethren, is a very sound one, if you should deny it, then
indeed I must think you not to be altogether so leadenheaded as your
brother Bridges. For do you think that a man entreating of the mayor of
London, the two sheriffs, and their offices, speaketh by and by of some part
of the order and government of the city of London? Or of some of the

governors of the city? As though my lord mayor and the two sheriffs were now become to be any of the governors of the city of London, or their offices any part of that government. Who seeth not by this example the folly of our precise brethren's reason evidently declared? The Apostle (say they) speaketh of apostles, prophets, evangelists, pastors, doctors and their functions (for this Master D. confesseth), therefore he speaketh of some ecclesiastical governors, and of some part of ecclesiastical government. Apostles, prophets, pastors and doctors are church governors with them,   [E3v] and their office a part of ecclesiastical government. Let them learn, let them learn simple siginnes as they are,[91] that the Apostle speaketh in this place of ecclesiastical functions, and not of any part of eccclesiastical government. For so Master D. in this 61st page (compare line 17 with line 22) teacheth us to speak English: making an ecclesiastical function to be a thing altogether differing in nature from every part of ecclesiastical government. A very proper and pleasant distinction.

In the second place, this testimony brought in by our brethren is proved to make nothing to their purpose, by two reasons. And what bommination umberty of reasons here be, to perceed forth one head,[92] and yet every one false, as it is true that my good brother Overton, the bishop of Lichfield and Coventry, sold his chancellorship at one time unto two several men:[m] to wit, to Doctor Becon and the good chancellor, Master Zachary Babington.[93] Well, parson Bridges his first reason is after this sort. That place which showeth gifts and functions to be ordained in the church to the building up of the body of Christ in the unity of the faith and knowledge: maketh nothing to prove that there is an ecclesiastical government prescribed in the word. Thou sayst even true, parson John. For what hath the functions of pastors, doctors, apostles, etc., to do with church government? A pretty matter, every beggarly apostle, pastor, doctor, or evangelist that cannot spend, no I am sure not 40 marks yearly,[94] by all the spiritual living he hath in his hand: must now be a church governor with our brethren, and their offices be a part of church government. Why brethren, what mean you by this place you have brought? Do you think that the Apostle by those functions and those persons spoken of, Ephes. 4:12, meaneth that any of them functions should be a lordlike function, or any of the persons, lord?   [E4r] You say he doth not. No, doth not? Then out of your own grant he speaketh nothing of ecclesiastical government and governors. Because every ecclesiastical governor must needs be a lord, and so ecclesiastical

---

[m] [side note:] You see that cosenage is likely within a while to be the steward of my brother Lichfield's house.

government, a lordly government. If this be not true, ask my brother Bridges. For should God ordain great men and great lords to be rulers in commonwealths, over whom he hath not so great care as he hath for his church, and ordain none but beggarly fellows (not able to spend 200 marks by the year, nay nor 20 neither) to bear rule in his church?

I grant indeed that you, brethren puritans, say the truth as it ought to be, that bishops or ministers ought not to be lords in any wise, either as ministers, or as civil magistrates. Thus indeed it ought to be, I and my brethren the bishops do grant unto you. And you know we would it were so. But you know also that our laws will have church governors to be lords, and what? should our bishops (good noble men) refuse that which the law would have them to take? Get you the law to be against their lordly callings, and see whether they will not give over their lord bishopdoms, whensoever law compelleth them. And whensoever they give over, they shall have no cause to thank such envious brethren as you are. Howsoever it be, you see the Apostle, speaking of all sorts of ministers, by your own confession speaketh nothing of any lord, or lordly government among them all, and therefore speaketh nothing of church government. Again, all those functions whereof the Apostle maketh any mention (as my brother Bridges hath well noted) are ordained to the building of the body of Christ, in the unity of faith and knowledge. Now, I would any puritan of you all durst say that our church governors, that is, our venerable and worshipful lord bishops,
[E4v]   are ordained of God for the building of his body, which I know you will say to be done by preaching? As though lord bishops, being civil governors, should preach. Were it meet (I pray you) to see Steven Gardiner, being then of the privy council, in the pulpit?[95] Councillors now must have something to do with pulpit matters, must they I pray you? Will you allow that civil governors should be ordinary preachers in your new platform of a reformed church? I know you will not. And what reason is it then, that you should require bishops to be ordinary preachers, seeing every bishop is a civil governor? I tell you true, I am so far from thinking that bishops ought to be ordinary preachers, seeing they are civil governors, that I hold it a sin for them to preach ordinarily. And brethren, you do not well, therefore, in urging civil governors to preach, especially seeing you yourselves, in your platforms, are against this point. And because it shall be seen that I deal uprightly between you and the P. P. prelates,[96] I will set down my reason, and answer it when you can: it shall be concluded I warrant you in mood and figure.[97] But indeed I have invented a new mood of mine own (for I have been a great schoolman in my days) which containeth in it a great mystery. The mystery I will expound, it may be, in a book for the purpose.

In the meantime, if you resort to my son Martin Senior, that worthy wight, he it may be shall be able to unfold the secrecy thereof. This is the syllogism, the mood answereth unto *Celarent*, elder daughter to *Barbara*, and I will have it called, *Perncanterburikenold.*⁹⁸

PERNE	No civil magistrate can be an ordinary preacher without sin	*Cel*
CANTERBURY	Every lord bishop is a civil magistrate. Therefore,	*la*
KENOLD	No lord bishop can be an ordinary preacher without sin.	*rent*

What say you now, brethren, would you have civil governors (such as [F1r] our bishops are) to preach? I hope not. For although I cannot deny but some of our bishops are very great break-pulpits, and have as marvelous raw gifts in preaching as any that ever came to Paul's wharf, yet surely I cannot see what warrant you have to urge civil officers to preach.⁹⁹ Wherefore also you do not well in crying out against civil governors, because they preach not, as though their function were an ecclesiastical function, or as though you would have any to preach who had not an ecclesiastical function. If you demand then whether bishops be ecclesiastical or civil governors, they themselves say beath, and ai say, brethren, that for the stopping of your meaths and other causes, I wad counsel them, if they wad be ruled bai me, to be neither nother.¹⁰⁰ Now if yaw demand again, whether bishops sin in being ministers, seeing they are civil officers, or in bearing civil offices, seeing they are ministers, I have already showed that civil officers must be no ministers. And my brother London hath long since affirmed it to be dangerous for the commonwealth, that ministers should be civil governors: and therefore, brethren, to answer this question of yours, you are to know that I am fully of your brother London's mind, who saith page 24, line 19 of his *Harborowe*: *These two offices, I mean the ecclesiastical and civil, be so jumbled together, as it may be lawful for both parties to meddle in both functions, there can be no quiet, nor any well ordered common wealth.* Now brethren you must not think the worse of this learned man's judgment, because he is a bishop himself. For even since he hath joined these two offices together he hath proved his own saying to be true for his part, in that his whole endeavor hath been, ever since he was bishop, that we should have no quiet nor any well ordered church or commonwealth. I hope by this time you see it plain that bishops sin, both because they are [F1v] civil governors, and being civil governors, because they are bishops.

Your second reason is page 61, line 39: *Paul speaketh of these gifts and of this building, and of the orders and ends thereof: therefore he speaketh nothing of ecclesiastical government.*[101] This is put home I trow, and overthroweth the puritans out of all cess.[102] It is altogether as good a reason, as an old man yielded sometimes to Sir Thomas More, concerning the cause of Goodwin Sands, and the stopping of Sandwich Haven: which was, that Tenterden's steeple was the cause of Goodwin Sands.[103] Master D.'s second reason to show that the place of Paul maketh nothing for ecclesiastical government, is after this sort: *Paul in reckoning up these gifts, referreth all to the unity in doctrine of faith, and to the holy conversation of life. Ergo he maketh no mention of ecclesiastical order of government.*[104]

That were a pitiful hearing indeed, sir, that the Apostle should speak of ecclesiastical government, and speak not a word of any lordlike government: that the Apostle should make any mention of ecclesiastical governors, and not name a lord among them all. Fie, fie, this were too bad, and my Lord of Canterbury would never abide such scripture.

But in good sadness (saith the puritans), presbyter John Bridges, will this place of Paul prove no part of this government which you oppugn? Will it not prove that God hath ordained pastors and doctors to continue in his church unto the world's end? No forsooth will it not, quoth the dean. And I am so far from thinking that God hath ordained your preaching pastors and doctors to continue always in his church, that I have made a prayer, page 655, line 28, of my book (as my brother Martin you know hath noted already),[n] *that we might never see that day in England, wherein preaching might be had in all places.*[105] His grace of Canterbury (I tell you) hath condemned the preaching of the word (as being the only ordinary means to salvation) to be an heresy. This scripture of Paul, that God hath appointed preaching pastors to continue in his church unto the world's end, is a chief ground of the former heresy. I will allow of no such scripture, I trow, as may impeach the opinion which my Lord Canterb. conceived of the preaching of the word.

[F2r]

You see therefore, my friends, that Master Dean in this point will have nothing to do with you, or Paul's testimony. And you are not ignorant, I am sure, how soon all lords would be out of the ministry, if we had none in England but the pastors spoken of by Paul, and therefore Master Doctor hath prayed against this order. Yea, and he hath brought such a reason against this your platform of government, as is just *secundum usum Sarum.*[106] For indeed it is popish, and therefore you might smell it afar off. *If the Lord* (saith he, page 62) *had thought this government needful for his church, then he would not have suffered his church to be without the same. But*

[n] [side note:] In the Epistle to the Terrible Priests.

he suffered his church of a long time to be without this government. Ergo he thought it not needful.

Ah craft, craft, craft and subtlety, that can in jest deceive his brethren with a popish reason in this sort. But my masters, you must not think that our brother Sarum bringeth this in good earnest, but only to try whether you be so simple, as you cannot know a popish reason when you see it. And to this purpose, I think that both his worship, and John Whitgift's grace,[107] have brought in their writings many things that are palpable popish, that they might try, whether of knowledge, or of peevish and choleric rashness, you speak against their government. Now, if so be that you could not discern their popish reasons (whereof indeed you shall find great store, every third reason I warrant you, in all their books) then they would have [F2v] this advantage against you, that you were not able to know truth from popery. For (might they say) we brought in popish reasons of purpose, but silly fellows, their skill is so small in all kind of learning, that they cannot know a popish reason, especially if we can face it out with a brag that we have old and new writers of our side. Now brethren, you must not then mislike your brother Bridges' purpose, in bringing in this popish syllogism. This I speak, to the end you should not cry out (as some of you have done) that our bishops have no better warrant for themselves than the pope hath, for their government. I grant indeed, that if you should take Master Dean at the worst, you might say that he might herein reason as well for the Mass, as he doth for the established government. As, for example, he might thus argue. If the Lord had thought the Mass to have been a false worship of him, then he would not have suffered it so long to have continued, where any weak one should be endangered of being enforced to be present thereat. But he suffered it to continue a long time, etc. Therefore he thought it not to be a false worship. I say you must not mistake Master Doctor in this sort, but know that he dealt after the manner of the schools, wherein it is lawful (as Thomas Cartwright, who hath been professor of divinity, both in Cambridge and in Geneva, knoweth well enough) for men to argue *pró* and *contrá*, as well with as against the truth: and all is to try out the truth, which is only the sole meaning that Master D. hath not at all thought of. But I pray you, let us pass from hence unto the 64th page, where you shall find the calling of an archbishop most notably proved out of our brethren's own words. *Our brethren* (ka the cloister master of Sarum) *affirm that Paul and Barnabas ordained presbyters, priests or elders* (for thus Master D., to his neverlasting fame, hath full often in his book translated the Greek word *presbyteros*) *at Derbe, Iconium and Lystra. Ergo, some of these* [F3r] *priests or elders were ordained over whole towns, some over regions.* And what

could be more aptly spoken to the purpose, or more fitly prove a archiepiscopal calling? But the reason following proveth it yet more evident, and
that is the ilsample of Archbishop Titus, whom the D. of Divility in this
65th page affirmeth to have been archbishop of Crete.° Nay, good Master D.,
not many archbishops in the person of Titus I pray you. Titus was an
evangelist, therefore no archbishop. Yea, saith he, Titus was a very archbishop, and there is plain scripture to prove it, which is the subscription of
the Epistle to Titus. Whoop papist, say the puritans, is that become
scripture with you?ᴾ Why Master Beza hath long since proved this to be
no scripture, but an uncertain and false guess, added by some scholiast.¹⁰⁸
You know also that your brother Turrian the Jesuit, bringing in this for
scripture, was soundly confuted by Master Sadeel, and dare you, Dean
John, bring this in for scripture?¹⁰⁹ Yes, that I dare (saith he), and prove
Titus to have been an archbishop, even by this reason: because Paul gave
him the authority to be the ordinary of all the bishops in Crete. And this
I prove, because Crete, where my Lord Archbishop Titus his grace was
Primate and Paltripolitan, had many famous cities in it. This is my very
reason, page 65, line 21, and I'll stand to it.

Now Master fickers, parsons, and curates, if ever I heard better proof in
my life, I would all dumb dogs were whipped out of the church. Now truly
this is sport alone. But brother parson Bridges, I pray you tell me, was there
canonical obedience sworn to Archbishop Titus? What else man? Did they
call him my lord's grace too? Do you doubt of it? Did his gentleman usher
go bareheaded before him? As though he could not be as popelike and
[F3v]   pontifical as my Lord of Canterbury. But I hope a poor hedge priest might
have his letters of orders of him,¹¹⁰ though he would give no bribes unto his
secretary, cook, butler, etc. Might he so, Goodman Noddy?¹¹¹ Then how
should his men I pray you be able to live? As though bishops should give
their men any wages! Their blessing I trow will serve their men instead of
wages.¹¹²

In page 66, Master Doctor demandeth a question, and that is, whether
one man might not have divers of these offices and gifts which were in the
apostles' time. Indeed, brother parson, we read of never an apostle that was
a nonresident, but of one Judas, one Simon Magus, and one Diotrephes, in
all that time.¹¹³ The reason belike was, that men wrought miracles in those
days, which gift the noble lords of our clergy have now bestowed upon their

---

° [side note:] But truly, I think brother Bridges that Titus was neither archbishop nor dean
of Sarum.
ᴾ [side note:] The reason of Archbishop Titus is no popish reason.

horses. For in the apostles' time, a horse usually carried not above one or
two men at the most: whereas you know that Master Doctor Humphrey
and Doctor Matthew had two horses between them that never carried
under fourteen men,^{q} whensoever their masters were on their backs.^{114} And
our bishops are so expert in adorning horses with those miraculous gifts,
that they are no sooner on their horsebacks, than presently the horse
whereon they ride is able to carry as many as either of the two former,
besides their boots, two or three pair of trulling square dice, and so many
pair of cards.^{115}

Parson Bridges, page 68, saith there are more gifts and callings than four
(pastors, doctors, elders and deacons) remaining, because, saith he, page
69, *the gifts of doing miracles, prophesy, the gifts of healing, divers among the*
papists have and do enjoy, and especially the gift of tongues, not attained unto
by study, had divers of them, as Anthony, etc. Anthony among the papists had
the gift of tongues without study: now what a goodyear was that
Anthony?^{116} The god of the pigs, trow ye?^{117} Indeed, Master D. quoteth
no author for his warrant, he is read you know in the Legend of Lies.^{r} ^{118} [F4r]
There it is: what have the puritans to do where he found it? Let them
answer to it. What if he found it in Hodge his breeches, seeking for
Gammer Gurton's needle?^{119} Is the reason worse than the rest of his
book, because it is without authority?

As for the matter contained in the 70th, 71st, 72nd pages, Master D.
confirmeth it by the authority of a puritan writer, which wrote (as he saith)
A Fruitful Sermon upon the 1 Cor. 12 printed by Robert Waldegrave, 1584.
A sermon upon the 1 Cor. 12 printed by Robert Waldegrave: say our
brethren, why, there was never any sermon upon that text printed by
Robert Waldegrave. Master D. belike meaneth the sermon upon Rom.
12.^{120} Tush brethren, what should you tell us of Master D.'s meaning, he
meaneth the sermon upon 1 Cor. 12. If you do not believe me, look the
225th page of his book, and there you shall see the sermon upon 1 Cor. 12
twice cited. Master D., if he were more beetleheaded than he is, could not
possibly miss so often in the naming of the sermon upon Rom. 12, which is
so commonly known. It may be indeed, you never saw any sermon extant
upon that text: but I warrant you Dean John knoweth the way to Salisbury,
so do not many thousands of you puritans. Why, you never saw the Syriac
Testament translated by Junius (for that which is abroad, was done by
Tremellius alone), but Master D. hath quoted Junius his Syriac Testament.

^{q} [side note:] Or so many simoniacal promotions.
^{r} [side note:] There is a book of this name, which Master Doctor made as they say.

Why then may he not as well find a sermon upon 1 Cor. 12 printed by Robert Waldegrave, as a Syriac Testament of Junius his translation? Now, say the puritans, what a notorious block is this dean, who inasmuch as he hath heard that Master Tremellius and Master Junius were joined together in the translation of the Bible, thinketh therefore that Junius translated the Syriac Testament, which was done by Tremellius only.[121]

[F4v]   For shame my masters, deal more charitably and bear with the infirmities of your brethren. I grant indeed it was Master D.'s oversight in naming Junius his Syriac Testament: and the sermon upon 1 Cor. 12 instead of Rom. 12. But what then, should you therefore take him up for it, as though he were the veriest ass in a country? Learned men may easily commit such oversights, especially quoting authors upon other men's reports, as Master D. hath done. But it is no marvel that you deal thus with Master Dean, when you dare abuse Antichrist, and say, as the author of the *Learned Discourse* hath done, that this government of yours continued in the church until Antichrist brought in all kind of false doctrine and confusion.[122] Nay, whoa there masters mine,[123] quoth Master Dean, for these be his own words, take my reason with you, you slander Antichrist.[s] For,

If your government had continued in the church until all kind of false doctrine came in, it had been exercised without interruption until this day (especially until the year 1587, wherein you made this book). *For I doubt me whether all kind of false doctrine hath been yet sown. But your government hath been interrupted long since.[t] Therefore you slander Antichrist.*[124]

They slander him indeed, John o' Sarum, if they say that he brought in all kind of false doctrine. And you have never proved proposition better in your life, than you have proved this. For any man that will read your book, or John Whitgift's, will say that Antichrist brought not in all kind of false doctrine, if he had, your book I am sure had not been sold for seven shillings as it is. In the 78th page, Master D. showeth that the office of archbishops, and lord bishops, are in nature pastoral, though in dignity they are of another office and ministry. And what say you to that, brethren? Even this, say they. In dignity they are popes, in office proud prelates, and

[G1r]   in ministry, plain dumb dogs for the most part. This is proved, hath been proved, and will be proved, to the proudest of the bishops' teeth, if they do dispute with us in these points. I would wish you, my puritan masters, to keep you well while you are well. It may be you shall answer this sauciness of yours, to offer disputation to my lord's grace before the high

---

[s] [side note:] For Antichrist, and against the government of Christ.
[t] [side note:] This is the D.'s reason in very deed.

commissioners. Master D. hath confuted all the pack of you. In the 82nd page, by a tale or two of a fox-tail,[125] and another of the ass loaden with sponges, page 83.[126] From the 90th page to the end of the book, he goeth so readily to work about the office of the civil magistrate, that I marvel that men will not say that he deserveth to be cased in a good motley cloakbag for his labor.[127] In the 93rd page, he proveth that no man ought to direct the magistrate in anything. For, saith he, brethren I go plainly and simply to work, he that directeth he governeth." Alas the day, brother (cloister master), do the puritans say indeed that the magistrate should be directed by any within his own dominions? Belike then if they should find a magistrate out of his way, they would go about to direct him, would they? And that in his own dominions too? Why, brother Bridges, can this stand with the duty of a good subject? Why? He that directeth he governeth. I perceive it is time that such fellows were looked unto. We should never have done with them I perceive, if we should still stand answering their absurd fancies. By this time, I hope, they see their folly. They have been sufficiently confuted, or else let Andrew *ambo* judge between you,ᵛ he is an indifferent man.[128] From the 99th page unto the 130th, just 31 pages, at which game o' the cards Doctor Redman archdeacon of Canterbury is very good, besides his rare skill in juggling,[129] and to the end of this book, they agree with you in anything that lawfully belongeth to the office of the civil magistrate.

How say you now, master country parsons and fickers? Are you not by this time able to withstand the cavils of the puritans? Do you not see upon what [Gɪᴠ] good ground our church government and my Lord of Canterbury's chair is built? I would you did else. And let the learned reader judge whether other men cannot play the ignorant sots as well as you, brother Bridges. Tush, tush, I would not have you claim all the skill in barbarisms and solecisms unto yourself. Other men can behave themselves with commendations that way as well as you, though indeed not so naturally I grant. Farewell sweet Doctor, and make much of the courtier Martin.

Errata, or faults escaped

1. Wheresoever the prelates are called my lords, either in the *Epistle* to the confocation house, or in this *Epitome*, take that for a fault. Because they are none of Master Martin's lords, neither shall any priest of them all be

---

ᵘ [side note:] Simply I'll be sworn thou goest simply to work.
ᵛ [side note:] Doctor Perne.

my lord. For I tell thee true, I think foul scorn they should be my lords, or the lords of any of my sons.

2. There is nothing spoken at all of that notable hypocrite Scambler, bishop of Norwich.[130] Take it for a great fault, but unless he leave his close dealing against the truth, I'll bestow a whole book of him. And let the rest of you hypocrites take heed of persecuting.

3. But the greatest fault of all is that I could say against our ungodly priests,[131] but unless they mend, I'll fully amend this fault, and I can do it with a small warning. And I would devise them not to persecute men for my worship's book as they do.[132]

Certain Mineral and Metaphysical Schoolpoints

Certain Mineral and Metaphysical Schoolpoints
(late January/early February 1589)

The broadsheet *Certain Mineral and Metaphysical Schoolpoints* was printed by Robert Waldegrave in White Friars, a manor in Coventry owned by John Hales, using the same press and type he had employed for the first two tracts. Waldegrave printed about 1,000 copies, and the wholesale price was one pence apiece (see Introduction, lii). Only two copies are extant, one in Lambeth Palace Library (see illustration no. 2) and the other, slightly imperfect, in the Bodleian Library; these are the only two institutions to own copies of all seven Marprelate tracts.

Why a broadsheet? One possibility is that Job Throkmorton and John Penry initially had no plans to extend the Marprelate project past the publication of the *Epitome*. Penry apparently wanted to use their press to print his own work about the condition of the church in Wales (see Introduction, xli, lii), and Throkmorton, having made his points about John Bridges' *Defence*, might very well have contemplated laying aside the Marprelate persona in favor of more traditional polemic. But the publication in January 1589 of Thomas Cooper's *Admonition to the People of England*, with its often self-implicating responses by John Aylmer, John Whitgift, and Cooper himself to the first two tracts, provided the Martinists with an irresistible new target. A short text that could be printed quickly, the *Schoolpoints* kept Martin's voice and arguments in the public sphere while the press was occupied with printing Penry's *A Viewe* (Coventry, 1589) and while the next Marprelate tract, the lengthy *Hay any Work for Cooper*, was being prepared. The broadsheet format furthermore encouraged readers to associate *Schoolpoints* with the reform tradition, initiated by Martin Luther's ninety-five theses (1517), of listing points of contention: English Presbyterian versions included works such as Anthony Gilby's "An hundred pointes of Poperie, yet remayning, which deforme the Englishe reformation," published in his *A Pleasaunt Dialogue* (1581), and the lists of syllogisms in Dudley Fenner's *Defence of the Godlie*

Ministers (Middelburg, 1587) and in the second edition of John Penry's *An Exhortation* (East Molesey, 1588).

Another possible model of a polemical text imagined as both public announcement and invitation to public challenge was provided by Cambridge University "act verses," versified theses published as broadsheets and "circulated by those taking part in public disputations" (see *STC* 4474.1 et seq.). Martin here offers an ironic version of this mode of academic debate. As its title indicates, *Schoolpoints* lists a series of theses or debating points to be defended by the church officials from whose speech, writing, or actions each schoolpoint has been derived. Some reflect personal scandals: Marmaduke Middleton, bishop of St David's, for example, is challenged to defend bigamy. But most of the schoolpoints, however sardonically presented, address the conventional issues that animated reform polemic: forms of church government, clerical hierarchy, a preaching ministry, pluralism, divorce, baptism, vestments, church music, episcopal revenues, long prayers, the *ex officio* oath, Christ's descent into hell, and the use of Apocryphal texts in the BCP. Several schoolpoints, and the concluding address to the reader, repeat the reformers' insistence that their challenge to the established church was not treasonous, as their opponents insisted, but a sign of their true loyalty to the Queen, whose authority was being undermined by the encroaching powers of the episcopacy.

In addition to its pervasive use of irony, the *Schoolpoints* is characteristically Martinist in its willingness to name names, and in the care it takes to maintain the appearance of legal fairness by providing sources for its claims. Of the thirty-seven schoolpoints, twenty-five derive from books published by Martin's opponents (seventeen from Thomas Cooper's *Admonition*, five from John Bridges' *Defence*, the remainder from printed works by John Aylmer, Robert Some, and Richard Cosin). Most of the rest originate in reports of sermons, investigations, and trials, and usually record the specific occasion. Many of these passages and incidents reappear in *Hay any Work*, where they form the basis for more extended narratives. As presented here, these debating points might reflect the manner in which the Martinists abstracted material from the texts to which they respond, thereby illuminating their methods in compiling their own publications.

Certain Mineral and Metaphysical Schoolpoints,[1] to be defended
by the reverend bishops and the rest of my clergy masters of the
Convocation House, against both the universities and all the
reformed churches in Christendom. Wherein is laid open
the very quintessence of all catercorner divinity.[2] And
withal, to the preventing of the cavils of these
wrangling puritans, the persons by whom,
and the places where these mysteries are
so worthily maintained, are for the
most part plainly set down to the
view of all men, and that to the
'ternal praise of the most
reverend Fathers.

1. That the puritans may as well deny the son of God to be *Homouseos*, that
   is, consubstantial with God the father, as they may deny the superiority
   of archbishops and bishops to be lawful. The defendant in this point is
   father John of Fulham, in his preface before Barnardeus de Loque's
   book *Of the Church*, published in English.[3]

2. That a lord bishop may safely have two wives *in esse* at once: the defendant
   in this point is father Marmaduke, bishop of St David's, who hath two
   now living: the one Elizabeth Gigge, the other Ales Pryme. Proved against
   him before the high commission.[4]

3. That our Saviour Christ in soul descended into hell: the defendant in this
   point is father John of Lambeth, T. C. page 44. But you must not take
   this T. C. of mine for Thomas Cartwright, this is profane T. C.[5]

4. That our Saviour Christ in his sermons usually sware by his faith. For
   he said Amen, Amen, which is as much to say, as by my faith: the
   defendant in this point is father Thomas of Winchester, alias profane
   T. C., page 62.[6]

5. That Moses in giving a bill of divorcement, Deut. 24, brake the moral
   law of God: the defendant in this point is Thomas of Winchester, alias
   profane T. C., page 111.[7]

6. That papistry is better than the sincere profession of the gospel, which
   falsely men call puritanism: the defendant in this point is father
   Edmund of Worcester.[8]

7. That the public fasts and the prayers of the puritans were the cause of
   the invasion of the Spaniards, and of all other troubles and turmoils
   within the land: the defendant in this point is father William of
   Lichfield and Coventry, alias Parson of Solihull.[9]

8. That the long prayers of the puritans before and after their sermons are nothing else but beeble babble, beeble babble: the defendant in this point is father John of Fulham, in Master Cawdrey's examination.[10]

9. That there is no other way of trial before the high commission but by appeaching and accusing a man's self, and that no state can stand without such answering and swearing: the defendants in this point are Thom. Cooper, John Cant., and some others, at the examination of Master Wigginton, at Lambeth, in December last, 1588.[11]

10. That it is as lawful for our lord bishops to make bad ministers, as it was for the disciples of our Saviour to pluck the ears of corn on the Sabbath to slake their hunger: the defendant in this point is father Thomas of Winchester, alias profane T. C.[12]

11. That reading is preaching: the defendant in this point is father John a Bridges, pages 564, 565.[13]

12. That the magistrate may lawfully maim and deform the body of Christ, to wit, the church: the defendants in this point are all the 24 orders of bishops and especially father Canterbury.[14]

13. That more good may be wrought by our ordinary service than by preaching, the defendant in this point is father John a Bridges, page 652.[15]

14. That the cross in baptism, and organs in cathedral churches, are as necessary as a preaching ministry: the defendant in this point is father Goodman of Westminster.[16]

15. That our lord bishops in England are the bishops of the devil: the defendant in this point (I thank him) is father John o' Sarum, pages 339, 340.[17]

16. That true baptism may be out of the church: the defendant in this point is father Robert Some, page 158 of his book against J. P.[18]

17. That it is no more unlawful for a minister to have many benefices than for a temporal man to have many lordships: the defendant in this point is father Richard Cosin.[19]

18. That one priest or elder may have a lawful superior authority over the universal body of the church: the defendant in this point is father John a Bridges, page 448, line 3.[20]

19. That S. Paul erred very grossly, 1 Cor. 1:21, Rom. 10:14, in holding the preaching of the word to be the only ordinary means of salvation. The defendants in this point are all the clergy masters of the Convocation House.[21]

20. That the people ought to have as much to do in matters of state as in the election of their ministers: the defendant in this point is father Thom. of Winchester, alias profane T. C., page 43.[22]

21. That our Common Book of Prayer is without all suspicion of error: the defendant is father John o' Sarum, in his preface and page 652.[23]

22. That the surplice is her Majesty's badge and cognisance: the defendant in this point is father John Mar-elm, in Master Cawdrey's examination.[24]

23. That the bishops gather up sums of money beforehand, against the time of the necessary service of their country: the defendant in this point is father Thomas of Winchester, profane T. C., page 148.[25]

24. That he may be a lawful and good minister of the gospel, which is not fit to teach: the defendant is father Thomas of Winchester, T. C., pages 109, 110.[26]

25. That the archbishop of Canter., etc., in holding baptism administered by women to be the seal of God's covenant, is an absurd heretic: the defendant in this point is father Robert Some, in his table of Master Penry's errors, page 3.[27]

26. That the archbishop of Cant. is a giddy head and to be bridled, because he allowed the defacing of the Apocrypha by Master Doctor Whitaker, in his readings against Bellarmine: the defendant is father Tho. of Winch., profane T. C., page 49.[28]

27. That without two benefices, a minister cannot well furnish himself of books: the defendant in this point is father Boleyn of Lichfield.[29]

28. That all reformed churches are to be condemned, and the popish church only to be embraced, in these three points, vz., first in the descending of Christ's soul into hell, secondly in the superiority of ministers over their fellow brethren, thirdly in attributing the name priest unto the ministers of the New Testament: the defendant in this point, against all men, is father John of Lambeth, *cum privilegio* profane T. C., pages 44, 45.[30]

29. That the state of England at this present is so disordered, that whatsoever an ecclesiastical officer may do by authority, the same a private subject thinketh he may do at his own will and pleasure: the defendant in this point is Mistress Cooper's husband, alias profane T. C., page 94.[31]

30. That it is the general disease of Englishmen to have in admiration the persons and states of other countries, and to loathe their own: the defendant in this point is father Thomas of Eastmeon, alias profane T. C., page 105.[32]

31. That her Majesty and our governors cannot take away bishops' livings from them, unless they be entrapped by the devil's sophistry to suffer him to work mischief in the church, and to trouble the commonwealth: the defendant is the Tub-trimmer of Winchester, profane T. C., page 155.[33]

32. That the doctrine of our Saviour Christ concerning the equality of ministers, Luke 22:25, and the doctrine of S. Paul concerning the

perpetuity of the church government by pastors, doctors, elders and deacons, Rom. 12:6, 7, 8, Ephes. 4:13, 1 Tim. 6:13, 14, is too great a bridle unto Christian liberty: the defendant in this point is father Thomas of Winchest., alias profane T. C., page 135, and all the Terrible Priests.[34]

33. That Christ Jesus the son of God was not so faithful in the government of his own house as Moses was, for Moses ordained a government that might not be changed by man, so did not Christ: the defendants in this point are all the 24 orders of bishops, and all the clergy masters.[35]

34. That the Creed of the Apostles and of Athanasius, the Nicene, etc., contain many palpable lies in them, for the Apocrypha (which hath many outrageous lies in it, as in 2 Esdras 14:21, Judith 11:5, 18, Tobit 5:12) is in authority next to the canonical scriptures: the defendant in this point is father Thomas of Winchester, profane T. C., page 49.[36]

35. That it is not lawful for her Majesty to bestow the bishops' livings upon lay men: the defendant in this point is father Tho. Winch., profane T. C., 252.[37]

36. That it may be accounted for one of our bishops' great faults that they have not hitherto by excommunication constrained our prince and magistrates to do, that which by persuasion they would not do: the defendant in this point is father Thomas of Winchester, profane T. C., page 137.[38]

37. That the state of England cannot possibly stand without lord bishops. And so, that the crown of England cannot stand without the crown of Canterbury. The defendant in this point is father Thomas of Winchester, profane T. C., page 78, and all the 24 orders of bishops.[39] Upon whom I bestow this odd point.

Good reader, if thou know of any that dare argue or dispute against any of the former points: that is, if thou know any that dare defend Christ Jesus and his prerogative, the truth of his word, the credit of S. Paul, the verity of the Apostles' Creed, her Majesty and her prerogative, and stand to the received truth in the reformed churches, and gainsay popish errors. Briefly, if thou know of any that dare defend the state of England not to be so disordered, as before is set down, Article 29, and dare withstand the public, general dishonour and slander of the whole English nation, Article 30, let him set up his name, and we will send a pursuivant for him. Whosoever he be, the matters shall be, according unto order, quietly tried out between him and the bare walls in the Gatehouse, or some other prison.

Hay any Work for Cooper

Hay any Work for Cooper
(March 1589)

Hay any Work for Cooper, like the broadsheet *Certain Mineral and Metaphysical Schoolpoints*, was printed by Robert Waldegrave in White Friars, John Hales's manor in Coventry, with the same "Dutch letters" as the first three Marprelate tracts and in the same quarto format as the *Epistle* and the *Epitome*. At fifty-eight pages, *Hay any Work* is the longest of the seven Marprelate tracts, just slightly longer than the *Epistle*: each copy required seven sheets plus a concluding single leaf (collating 4°: A^4 B–G^4 H^1; 29 leaves, [*10*] 1–48). Waldegrave needed about three weeks to complete the print run of at least 1,000 copies, and the wholesale price was sixpence apiece (see Introduction, lii–liii).

The tract's title announces Martin's new target, Thomas Cooper, bishop of Winchester, with a play on the street cry of itinerant coopers (see back cover illustration). A preliminary letter explains the title by thanking the bishops for publishing Cooper's anti-Martinist *Admonition to the People of England* (1589), a work that included responses by John Whitgift, John Aylmer, and other bishops to Martin's accusations in the *Epistle*. These responses, Martin notes, further publicized the deeds the bishops sought to excuse, and he slyly suggests that any charges not denied in the *Admonition* could now be taken by the public as true. The text proper begins as a traditional animadversion, printing quotations from the *Admonition* followed by Martin's responses. But *Hay any Work* soon drops the bantering mode of the earlier tracts for a sustained and finely honed exposition of the Presbyterian platform. In a key passage midway through this discussion, Martin justifies his use of satire in the earlier tracts. The Martinist approach to controversy, he explains, brought arguments for reform to the attention of a public bored by the conventions of traditional polemic. Martin also acknowledges, however, that many in the reform movement disapproved of his tactics (115–20). While less characteristically "Martinist" than the first two tracts, the first half of *Hay any Work* is nonetheless well-written polemic, its chains of reasoning anchored in scriptural exegesis and heavily reliant on syllogistic argument. If John Penry did provide copy for the extant Marprelate tracts, this section is a likely candidate (see Introduction, xli).

About two-thirds of the way through *Hay any Work*, the Martin of the *Epistle* leaps back onto center stage with a self-reflexive nod to readers who had noticed the relative absence so far of his voice: "Whau, whau, but where have I been all this while? Ten to one among some of these puritans. Why Martin? Why Martin I say, hast tow forgotten thyself?" (126). The text then returns to animadversion, countering Thomas Cooper's principled generalities with mockery and authority-puncturing specifics. *Hay any Work* concludes with detailed responses to the attempts by Aylmer, Whitgift, and Cooper to rebut the stories told in the *Epistle*: Martin marshals his witnesses, corroborates details, pounces when he sees weakness or prevarication, and, when he feels he has the facts in hand, gives his opponents the lie direct.

Two reprints of *Hay any Work* appeared during the renewed debates over episcopacy in the early 1640s. One bore a new title, *Reformation no Enemie. Or a True Discourse, Betweene the Bishops and the Desirers of Reformation* (1641) (Wing R741), but retained "Hay any worke for Cooper" as its running head. The title page of the other reprint (1642) (Wing H1205) reproduced that of the 1589 original.

Hay any Work for Cooper:[1]

Or a brief pistle directed by way of an hublication to the reverend bishops,[2] counselling them, if they will needs be barrelled up for fear of smelling in the nostrils of her Majesty and the state, that they would use the advice of reverend Martin for the providing of their Cooper. Because the reverend T. C. (by which mystical letters is understood either the bouncing Parson of Eastmeon, or Tom Coakes his chaplain[3]) hath showed himself in his late *Admonition to the People of England* to be an unskillful and a beceitful tubtrimmer.[4]

Wherein worthy Martin quits himself like a man I warrant you, in the modest defence of his self and his learned Pistles, and makes the Cooper's hoops to fly off, and the bishops' tubs to leak out of all cry.[5]

Penned and compiled by Martin the Metropolitan.

Printed in Europe,
not far from some of the Bouncing Priests.[6]

A man of worship, to the men of worship, that is, Martin
Marprelate gentleman, Primate and Metropolitan of
all the Martins wheresoever. To the John of all the
Sir Johns,⁸ and to the rest of the terrible
priests: saith, have among you once
again my clergy masters. For,

O brethren, there is such a deal of love grown of late I perceive between you
and me, that although I would be negligent in sending my Pistles unto you,
yet I see you cannot forget me. I thought you to be very kind when you sent
your pursuivants about the country to seek for me. But now that you
yourselves have taken the pains to write, this is out of all cry. Why, it passes
to think what loving and careful brethren I have, who, although I cannot be
gotten to tell them where I am, because I love not the air of the Clink or
Gatehouse in this cold time of winter,⁹ and by reason of my business in
pistle-making, will notwithstanding make it known unto the world that
they have a month's mind towards me.¹⁰ Now truly, brethren, I find you
kind, why ye do not know what a pleasure you have done me. My worship's
books were unknown to many before you allowed T. C. to admonish the
people of England to take heed, that if they loved you, they would make
much of their prelates, and the chief of the clergy. Now many seek after my
books, more than ever they did. Again, some knew not that our brother
John of Fulham was so good unto the porter of his gate, as to make the poor
blind honest soul to be a dumb minister.¹¹ Many did not know either that
Amen is as much as *by my faith*, and so that our Saviour Christ ever sware by
his faith:¹² or that bowling and eating of the Sabbath are of the same
nature:¹³ that bishops may as lawfully make blind guides, as David might
eat of the shewbread:¹⁴ or that father Thomas Tubtrimmer of Winchester,
good old student, is a Master of Arts of 45 years standing.¹⁵ Many, I say,
were ignorant of these things, and many other pretty toys, until you wrote   [A2v]
this pretty book. Besides whatsoever you overpass in my writings, and did
not gainsay, that I hope will be judged to be true. And so John a Bridges his
treason out of the 448th page of his book, you grant to be true.¹⁶ Yourselves
you deny not to be petty popes. The bishop of Sir David's in Wales, you
deny not to have two wives,¹⁷ with an hundred other things which you do
not gainsay: so that the reader may judge that I am true of my word, and
use not to lie like bishops. And this hath greatly commended my worship's
good dealing. But in your confutation of my book, you have showed
reverend Martin to be truepenny indeed: for you have confirmed, rather

than confuted him. So that, brethren, the pleasure which you have done unto me is out of all scotch and notch.[18] And should not I again be as ready to pleasure you? Nay, then I should be as ungrateful towards my good brethren, as John of Cant. is to Thomas Cartwright. The which John, although he hath been greatly favored by the said Thomas, in that Thomas hath now these many years let him alone and said nothing unto him for not answering his books, yet is not ashamed to make a secret comparison between himself and Thomas Cartwright. As who say, John of Lambeth were as learned as Thomas Cartwright. What say you old Dean John a Bridges, have not you showed yourself thankful unto her Majesty, in overthrowing her supremacy in the 448th page of your book? I will lay on load on your skin-coat for this gear anon.[19]

And I will have my pennyworth's of all of you brethren, ere I have done with you, for this pains which your T. C. hath taken with me. This is the puritans' craft, in procuring me to be confuted I know: I'll be even with them too. A crafty whoresons brethren bishops, did you think because the puritans' T. C. did set John of Cant. at a *non plus*, and gave him the overthrow, that therefore your T. C., alias Thomas Cooper bishop of Winchester, or Thomas Cooke his chaplain,[20] could set me at a *non plus*? Simple fellows, methinks he should not.

I guess your T. C. to be Thomas Cooper (but I do not peremptorily affirm it) because the modest old student of 52 years standing setteth Winchester after Lincoln and Rochester in the contents of his book, which blasphemy would not have been tolerated by them that saw and allowed the book, unless Mistress Cooper's husband had been the author of it.[21]

Secondly, because this T. C. the author of this book is a bishop, and therefore Thomas Cooper, he is a bishop, because he reckoneth himself charged, amongst others, with those crimes whereof none are accused but bishops alone, page 101, line 26. Ha old Martin yet I see thou hast it in thee, thou wilt enter into the bowels of the cause in hand I perceive. Nay, if you will commend me, I will give you more reasons yet. The style and the phrase is very like her husband's, that was sometimes wont to write unto Doctor Day of Wells.[22] You see I can do it indeed. Again, none would be so grosshead as to gather,[23] because my reverence telleth Dean John that he shall have twenty fists about his ears more than his own (whereby I meant indeed, that many would write against him, by reason of his bomination learning, which otherwise never meant to take pen [in] hand), that I threatened him with blows, and to deal by Stafford law.[24] Whereas that was far from my meaning, and could by no means be gathered out of my words, but only by him that pronounced *eulojin* for *eulogein* in the pulpit:[25]

[A3r]

and by him whom a papist made to believe, that the Greek word *eulogein*, that is, to give thanks, signifieth to make a cross in the forehead: py hy hy hy. I cannot but laugh, py hy hy hy. I cannot but laugh, to think that an old soaking student in this learned age is not ashamed to be so impudent as to presume to deal with a papist, when he hath no grue in his pocket.[26] But I promise you, sir, it is no shame to be a lord bishop if a man could, though he were as unlearned as John of Gloucester or William of Lichfield.[27] And I tell you true, our brother Westchester had as lief play twenty nobles in a night at primero on the cards, as trouble himself with any pulpit labor, and yet he thinks himself to be a sufficient bishop.[28] What, a bishop such a cardplayer? A bishop play 20 nobles in a night? Why, a round threepence serveth the turn to make good sport 3 or 4 nights amongst honest neighbours. And take heed of it brother Westchester: it is an unlawful game, if you will believe me. Foh, in winter it is no matter to take a little sport for an odd cast, braces of 20 nobles, when the weather is foul, that men cannot go abroad to bowls, or to shoot. What, would you have men take no recreation? Ye but it is an old said saw, enough is as good as a feast. And recreations must not be made a trade and an occupation, ka Master Martin Marprelate. I tell you true brother mine, though I have as good a gift in pistle-making as you have at primero, and far more delight than you can have at your cards, for the love I bear to my brethren, yet I dare not use this sport but as a recreation, not making any trade thereof. And cards, I tell you, though they be without horns, yet they are parlous beasts. Be they lawful or unlawful, take heed of them for all that. For you cannot use them but you must needs say your brother T. C. his Amen, that is, swear by your faith,[29] many a time in the night, well I will never stand argling the matter any more with you.[30] If you will leave your card playing, so it is, if you will not, trust to it, it will be the worse for you.

    I must go simply and plainly to work with my brethren that have published T. C. Whosoever have published that book, they have so hooped the bishops' tubs, that they have made them to smell far more odious than ever they did, even in the nostrils of all men. The book is of 252 pages.[31] The drift thereof is, to confute certain printed and published libels. You bestow not full 50 pages in the answer of anything that ever was published in print.[32] The rest are bestowed to maintain the belly, and to confute: what, think you? Even the slanderous inventions of your own brains for the most part. As, that it is not lawful for her Majesty to allot any lands unto the maintenance of the minister, or the minister to live upon lands for this purpose allotted unto him, but is to content himself with a small pension, and so small, as he have nothing to leave for his wife

[A3v]

[A4r]

and children after him (for whom he is not to be careful, but to rest on God's providence), and is to require no more but food and raiment, that in poverty he might be answerable unto our Saviour Christ and his apostles. In the confutation of these points, and the scriptures corruptly applied to prove them, there is bestowed above an 100 pages of this book, that is, from the 149th unto the end. Well T. C., whosoever thou art, and whosoever Martin is, neither thou nor any man or woman in England shall know while you live, suspect and trouble as many as you will, and therefore save your money in seeking for him, for it may be he is nearer you than you are ware of. But whosoever thou art, I say, thou showest thyself to be a most notorious wicked slanderer, in fathering these things upon those whom they call puritans, which never any enjoying common sense would affirm. And bring me him, or set down his name and his reasons, that holdeth any of the former points confuted in thy book, and I will prove him to be utterly bereaved of his wits, and his confuter to be either stark mad, or a stark enemy to all religion, yea to her Majesty and [A4v] the state of this kingdom. No no, T. C., puritans hold no such points. It were well for bishops, that their adversaries were thus sottish. They might then justly incense her Majesty and the state against them, if they were of this mind. These objections, in the confutation whereof thou hast bestowed so much time, are so far from having any puritan to be their author, as whosoever readeth the book, were he as blockheaded as Thomas of Winchester himself, he may easily know them to be objections only invented by the author of the book himself. For although he be an impudent wretch, yet dareth he not set them down as writings of any other: for then he would have described the author and the book by some adjent.[33]

The puritans indeed hold it unlawful for a minister to have such temporal revenues as whereby ten ministers might be well maintained, unless the said revenues come unto him by inheritance.

They hold it also unlawful for any state to bestow the livings of many ministers upon one alone, especially when there is such want of ministers' livings.

They hold it unlawful for any minister to be lord over his brethren. And they hold it unlawful for any state to tolerate such under their government. Because it is unlawful for states to tolerate men in those places whereinto the word hath forbidden them to enter.

They affirm that our Saviour Christ hath forbidden all ministers to be lords, Luke 22:25. And the Apostle Peter showeth them to be none of God's ministers which are lords over God's heritage, as you bishops are, and would be accounted. These things, T. C., you should have confuted, and not troubled yourself to execute the fruits of your own brains as an enemy to the state. And in these points, I do challenge you T. C., and you Dean John, and you John Whitgift, and you Doctor Cosin, and you Doctor Capcase (Copcot I think your name be) and as many else as have or dare write in the defence of the established church government.[34] If you cannot confute my former assertions, you do but in vain think to maintain yourselves by slanders, in fathering upon the puritans the offsprings of your own block-heads. And assure yourselves, I will besoop you if you cannot defend yourselves in these points,[35] as all the world shall cry shame upon you, you think prettily to escape the point of your antichristian callings by giving out that puritans hold it unlawful for her Majesty to leave any lands for the use of the minister's maintenance. I cannot but commend you, for I promise you, you can shift of an heinous accusation very prettily. [B1r]

A true man bringeth unanswerable witnesses against a robber by the highway side, and desireth the judge that the law may proceed against him. O no my Lord, saith the thief, in any case let not me be dealt with. For these mine accusers have given out that you are a drunkard, or they have committed treason against the state: therefore I pray you believe my slander against them, that they may be executed: so when I come to my trial, I shall be sure to have no accusers. A very pretty way to escape, if a man could tell how to bring the matter about. Now brethren bishops, your manner of dealing is even the very same. The puritans say truly, that all lord bishops are petty antichrists, and therefore that the magistrates ought to thrust you out of the commonwealth. Now of all loves, say the bishops, let not our places be called in question, but rather credit our slanders against the puritans, whereby, if men would believe us when we lie, we would bear the world in hand that these our accusers are malcontents and sottish men,[36] holding it unlawful for the magistrate to allot any lands for the minister's portion, and unlawful for the minister to provide for his family. And therefore you must not give ear to the accusations of any such men against us. And so we shall be sure to be acquitted. But brethren, do you think to be thus cleared? Why, the puritans hold no such points as you lay to their charge. Though they did, as they do not, yet that were no sufficient reason why you being petty popes should be maintained in a Christian commonwealth. Answer the reasons that I brought against you: otherwise, *Come off you bishops, leave your thousands, and content yourselves with your hundreds*, saith John of London.[37] So that you do plainly see, that your Cooper, T. C., is but a deceitful workman, and if you commit the hooping of your bishoprics unto him, they will so leak in a short space, as they shall [B1v] be able to keep never a lord bishop in them. And this may serve for an answer unto the latter part of your book, by way of an Interim, until *More Work for Cooper* be published.[38]

[1]   Hay any Work for Cooper

And now reverend T. C. I am come to your epistle to the reader, but first you and I must go out alone into the plain fields, and there we will try it out, even by plain syllogisms, and that, I know, bishops cannot abide to hear of.

The Reverend T. C. to the reader, page 1

I draw great danger upon myself, in defending our bishops and others the chief of the clergy of the church of England. Their adversaries are very eager: the saints in heaven have felt of their tongues, for when they speak of Paul, Peter, Mary, etc., whom others justly call saints: they in derision call them Sir Peter, Sir Paul, Sir Mary.

Reverend Martin

Alas poor reverend T. C. Be not afraid. Here be none but friends man. I hope thou art a good fellow, and a true subject, yea but I defend the bishops of the church of England saith he, then indeed I marvel not though thy conscience accuse thee, and thou art sure to be as well favoredly thwacked for thy labour as ever thou wast in thy life. Thy conscience, I say, must needs make thee fear in defending them. For they are petty popes and petty antichrists, as I have proved, because they are pastor of pastors, etc. Thou hast not answered my reasons, and therefore swaddled thou shalt be for thy pains, and yet if thou wilt yield I will spare thee. Thou canst not be a good and a sound subject and defend the hierarchy of lord bishops to be lawful, as I will show anon. Concerning Sir Paul, I have him not at all in my writings. And therefore the reader must know that there is a Canterbury trick, once to patch up an accusation with a lie or two.

[2]   Sir Peter was the oversight of the printer, who omitted this marginal note, vz., He was not Saint Peter which had a lawful superior authority over the universal body of the church. And therefore the priest whereof Dean John speaketh was Sir Peter.[39]

And good reverend T. C., I pray thee tell me, what kin was Saint Mary Overies to Mary the Virgin?[40] In my book learning, the one was some popish trull, and the other the blessed virgin. But will you have all those who are saints indeed, called saints? Why then, why do you not call Saint Abraham,

Saint Sarah, Saint Jeremy? If John of Canterbury should marry, tell me good T. C., dost thou not think that he would not make choice of a godly woman? I hope a would.[41] And T. C., though you are learned, yet you go beyond your books if you said the contrary: being a godly woman, then she were a saint. And so by your rule, her name being Mary, you would have her called Saint Mary Canterbury. But I promise thee, did his grace what he could, I would call her Sir Mary Canterbury as long as he professed himself to be a priest, and this I might do lawfully. For he being Sir John,[42] why should not his wife be Sir Mary? And why not Sir Mary Overies, as well as Sir Mary Canterbury? I hope John of Canterbury, whom I know (though I know no great good in him), to be as honest a man as Master Overies was, whom I did not know. Neither is there any reason why you, T. C., should hold Master Overies and his Mary, because they are within the diocese of Winchester, to be more honest than Master Canterbury and his wife. Nay, there is more reason why Master Canterbury and his wife, dwelling at Lambeth, should be thought the honester of the two, than Overies and his wife, because they dwell o' the Bankside.[43] But good Tom Tubtrimmer, tell me what you mean by the chief of the clergy in the church of England? John Canterbury I am sure. Why good T. C., this speech is either blasphemous or traitorous, or by your own confession an evident proof that John of Canterbury is lord over his brethren. He that is chief of the clergy is chief of God's heritage, and that is Jesus Christ only, and so to make the pope of Canterbury chief of God's heritage in this sense is blasphemous. If you mean by clergy, as Dean John doeth page 443 of his book,[44] both the people and ministers of the church of England: in this sense her Majesty is chief of the clergy in the church of England, and so your speech is traitorous. Lastly, if by clergy you mean the ministers of the church of England, none in this sense can be chief of the clergy but a petty pope. For our Saviour Christ flatly forbiddeth any to be chief of the clergy in this sense, Luke 22:26. And none ever claimed this unto himself but a petty pope. Therefore T. C., you are either by your own speech a blasphemer or a traitor, or else John of Cant. is a petty pope. Here is good spoonmeat for a Cooper.[45] Take heed of writing against Martin, if you love your ease.

[3]

Reverend T. C., page 2, Epistle

But I fear them not, while I go about to maintain the dignity of priests.

Reverend Martin

Well fare a good heart yet, stand to thy tackling, and get the high commission to send abroad the pursuivants, and I warrant thee thou wilt do something. Alas good priests, that their dignity is like to fall to the ground. It is pity it should be so, they are such notable pulpit men. There is a neighbour of ours, an honest priest, who was sometimes (simple as he now stands) a Vice in a play for want of a better, his name is Glibery of Halstead in Essex, he goes much to the pulpit.[46] On a time, I think it was the last May, he went up with a full resolution to do his business with great commendations. But see the fortune of it. A boy in the church, hearing either the Summer Lord with his May Game, or Robin Hood with his Morris dance, going by the church, out goes the boy.[47] Good Glibery, though he were in the pulpit, yet had a mind to his old companions abroad (a company of merry grigs you must think them to be,[48] as merry as a Vice on a stage), seeing the boy going out, finished his matter presently with John of London's Amen, saying, ha, ye faith boy, are they there, then ha' with thee, and so came down and among them he goes. Were it not then pity that the dignity of such a priest should decay? And I would, gentle T. C., that you would take the pains to write a treatise against the boy with the red cap, which put this Glibery out of his matter at another time. For Glibery being in the pulpit, so fastened his eyes upon a boy with a red cap that he was clean dashed out of countenance, insomuch that no note could be heard from him at that time, but this: Take away red cap there, take away red cap there: it had been better that he had never been born, he hath marred such a sermon this day, as it is wonderful to think. The Queen and the council might well have heard it for a good sermon, and so came down. An admonition to the people of England to take heed of boys with red caps, which make them set light by the dignity of their priests, would do good in this time, brother T. C., you know well.

[4]

Reverend T. C.

The cause why we are so spited,[w] is because we do endeavor to maintain the laws which her Majesty and the whole state of the realm have allowed, and do not admit a new platform of government, devised I know not by whom.

Reverend Martin

Why T. C., say *eulojin* for *eulogein* as often as you will, and I will never spite you, or the bishop of Winchester either for the matter.[49] But do you think our church government to be good and lawful, because her Majesty and the state, who maintain the reformed religion, alloweth the same? Why, the Lord doth not allow it, therefore it cannot be lawful. And it is the

[5]

---

[w] [side note:] You may hereby perceive that T. C. is a bishop.

fault of such wretches as you bishops are, that her Majesty and the state alloweth the same. For you should have otherwise instructed them. They know you not yet so thoroughly as I do. So that if I can prove that the Lord disliketh our church government, your endeavors to maintain the same show that thereby you cannot choose but be traitors to God and his word, whatsoever you are to her Majesty and the state. Now T. C., look to yourself, for I will presently make all the hoops of your bishoprics fly asunder. Therefore,

> *Our church government is an unlawful church government, and*
> *not allowed in the sight of God.*
> *Because,*

that church government is an unlawful church government, the offices and officers whereof the civil magistrate may lawfully abolish out of the church, mark my craft in reasoning, brother T. C., I say the offices and officers, for I grant that the magistrate may thrust the officers of a lawful church government out of the church if they be Diotrepheses, Mar-elms, Whitgifts, Simon Maguses, Coopers, Pernes, Kenolds, or any such like Judases (though the most of these must be packing, offices and all), but their offices must stand, that the same may be supplied by honester men.[50] But the offices of archbishops and bishops, and therefore the officers much more, may be lawfully abolished out of the church by her Majesty and our state. And truly this were brave weather to turn them out: it is pity to keep them in any longer.[51] And that would do me good at the heart, to see John of London and the rest of his brethren so discharged of his business, as he might freely run in his cassock and hose after his bowl, or flourish with his two-hand sword. O, 'tis a sweet trunch-fiddle.[52]   [6]

But the offices of archbishops and bishops may be lawfully abolished out of the church by her Majesty and the state. As I hope one day they shall be. Therefore (mark now, T. C., and carry me this conclusion to John o' Lambeth for his breakfast) our church government by archbishops and bishops is an unlawful church government. You see, brother Cooper, that I am very courteous in my minor, for I desire therein no more offices to be thrust out of the church at one time, but archbishops and bishops. As for deans, archdeacons and chancellors, I hope they will be so kind unto my lord's grace as not to stay, if his worship and the rest of the noble clergy lords were turned out to grass. I will presently prove both major and minor of this syllogism. And hold my cloak there somebody, that I may go roundly to work. For I'se so bumfeg the Cooper,[53] as he had been better to have hooped half the tubs in Winchester than write against my worship's pistles.

No civil magistrate may lawfully either maim or deform the body of Christ, which is the church, but whosoever doth abolish any lawful church officer out of the church government, he doth either maim or deform the church. Therefore, T. C., no civil magistrate, no prince, no state, may without sin abolish any lawful officer, together with his office, out of the government of the church, and *per consequence*, the offices of archbishops and lord bishops, which her Majesty may without sin lawfully abolish out of the church, are no lawful church officers, and therefore also, the church government practised by John Whitgift, John Mar-elm, Richard Peterborough, William of Lincoln, Edmund of Worcester, yea and by that old steal-counter mass priest, John o' Gloucester, with the rest of his brethren, is to be presently thrust out of the church.[54] And methinks this

[7] gear cottons indeed my masters. And I told you, T. C., that you should be thumped for defending bishops. Take heed of me while you live. The minor of my last syllogism, that whosoever doth abolish the office of any lawful church officer out of the church, he either maimeth or deformeth the church, I can prove with a wet finger.[55] Because every lawful church officer, even by reason of his office, is a member of the body of Christ Jesus, which is the church, and being a member of the body, if the magistrate doth displace him by abolishing his office, and leaveth the place thereof void, then the magistrate maimeth the body. If he put another office unto an officer instead thereof, he deformeth the same. Because the magistrate hath neither the skill nor the commission to make the members of the body of Christ. Because he cannot tell to what use the members of his making may serve in the church. Do you think, T. C., that the magistrate may make an eye for the visible body of the church? (For you must understand, that we all this while speak of the visible body). Can he make a foot or a hand for that body? I pray you, in what place of the body would you have them placed? If our Saviour Christ hath left behind him a perfect body, surely he hath left therein no place or no use for members of the magistrate's making and invention: if an unperfect and maimed body, I am well assured that the magistrate is not able to perfect that which he left unfinished. But I hope, T. C., that thou wilt not be so mad and wicked as to say that our Saviour Christ left behind him here on earth an unperfect and maimed body. If not, then where shall these offices, namely these members invented by the magistrate, be placed therein?

Would you have the natural eyes put out (as your brethren the bishops have done in the church of England, ever since John of Canterbury urged

[8] his wretched subscription[56]) and unnatural squint-goggled eyes put in their stead: when the body cannot see with any eyes but with the natural eyes

thereof? Displace them, howsoever you may seem to help the matter by putting others in their stead, yet the body shall be still blind and maimed. What say you, T. C., may the magistrate cut off the true and natural legs and hands of the body of Christ, under a pretense to put wooden in their stead? I hope you will not say that he may. How then commeth it to pass, T. C., that you hold John of Canterbury his office, and John Mar-elm's, to be true and natural members of the body, that is, true officers of the church, and yet hold it lawful for her Majesty to displace them out of the church? I cannot tell brother what you hold in this point. Methink I have disturbed your senses. Do you think that the magistrate may displace the true members of the body of Christ, and place wooden in their stead? Why, this is to hold it lawful for the magistrate to massacre the body. Do you think he may not? Then may not her Majesty displace John of Canterbury's office out of our church? If she may not displace his office, then either he by virtue of his office is a lawful pope above all civil magistrates, or else the church government is so prescribed in the word, as it is not lawful for the magistrate to alter the same. But John of Canterbury, as the puritans their selves confess, is no pope.[x] Then either the church government is so prescribed in the word as it may not be altered, or else the magistrate may abolish a lawful church government and place another instead thereof. If the church government be so prescribed in the word as it cannot be altered, then either our government is the same which was therein prescribed, or our church government is a false church government. If ours be the same which is mentioned in the word: then Paul and Peter were either no true church governors, or else Paul and Peter and the rest of church governors in their time were lords, for all our church governors are lords. But Paul and Peter, [9] etc., were no lords, and yet true church governors. Therefore our church government is not that which is prescribed in the word: and therefore a false and unlawful church government. If you think that the magistrate may displace the lawful offices of the body, then, as I said before, you hold it lawful for the magistrate to maim or deform the body. Because whatsoever he putteth in the room of the true and right members,[57] must needs be a deformity, and what place soever he leaveth unfurnished of a member, must needs be a maim. And this is the only and sole office of Christ only, to place and displace the members of his body: to wit, the officers of his church, he may lawfully do it, so cannot man. And therefore the sots (of which number you T. C., and you John Whitgift, and you Dean John, and you Doctor Cosin, and you Doctor Copcot,[58] with the rest of the ignorant and wretched

[x] [side note:] Puritans confess John Cant. to be no pope.

defenders of our corrupt church government, are to be accounted) which think that the offices of pastors, doctors, elders and deacons, or the most of them, may be as well now wanting in the church, as the offices of apostles, prophets and evangelists: do notably bewray their vile ignorance, but the cause they do not hurt. For the beasts do not consider that the offices of apostles, evangelists and prophets were removed out of the church not by man but by the Lord, because he in his wisdom did not see any use of such members in his body, after the time of the first planting of the church.^{y} I say they were removed by the Lord himself and not by man: because, partly the gifts wherewith they were endued, partly the largeness of their commission, with certain other essential properties to them belonging, were by him abrogated and taken away, which no man could do. Again, the apostolical,

[10] evangelical and prophetical callings were either lawfully or unlawfully abolished out of the church. If lawfully, then they were abolished by the Lord: and therefore they are neither to be called back until he showeth it to be his pleasure that it should be so, neither can the church be truly said to be maimed for want of them: because he which could best tell what members were fit for his church did abolish them. If unlawfully, then those callings may be lawfully called back again into the church, and the church without them is maimed, that is, wanteth some members. For if their callings were injuriously abrogated, they are as injuriously kept out of the church: and being members of the church, the church is maimed without, unless the Lord hath showed that the time of their service in the body is expired. But they are not injuriously kept out (for so her Majesty should be said to injury the church,^{59} unless she would see apostles, prophets and evangelists planted therein), neither can the church be said to be maimed for want of them, because the Lord by taking them away hath declared that now there can be no use of them in the body: therefore the Lord abrogated them. Therefore also they may be wanting, and the church neither maimed nor deformed thereby. Whereas the keeping out of either of the former offices of pastors, doctors, elders and deacons is a maiming of the church, the placing of others in their stead, a deforming. Now reverend T. C., I beseech you entreat Mistress Cooper to write to Master Doctor Day, sometimes of Magdalen's,^{60} that he may procure Doctor Cooper to know of him that was the last Thomas of Lincoln whether the now bishop of Winchester be not persuaded that reverend Martin hath sufficiently proved it to be unlawful for the civil

^{y} [side note:] The apostles chose none in stead of James, being beheaded, as they did in stead of Judas, Acts 1, which they would have done if the apostolical calling had been permanent.

magistrate to abolish any lawful church officer out of the church.⁶¹ Because it is unlawful for him to maim or deform the body of Christ, by displacing the members thereof. But it may be your Cooper's noddle, profane T. C., doubteth (for I know you to be as ignorant in these points, as John Whitgift or Dean John their selves), [11]

Whether a lawful church officer, in regard of his office, be a member of the body of Christ, which is the church.

Therefore look Rom. 12, verses 4, 5, etc., and there you shall see, that whosoever hath an office in the body is a member of the body. There also you shall see, that he that teacheth, which is the doctor: he that exhorteth, which is the pastor: he that ruleth, which is the elder: he that distributeth, which is the deacon (as for him that showeth mercy that is there spoken of, he is but a church servant, and no church officer), there, I say, you shall also see that these four offices of pastors, doctors, elders and deacons are members of the body: and 1 Cor. 12:8 and 28, you shall see that God hath ordained them. Out of all which hitherto I have spoken, T. C., I come upon you and your bishoprics with four or five (yea half a dozen and need be) such dry soops,⁶² as John of London with his two-hand sword never gave the like. For they answer your whole profane book. First, that the platform of government by pastors, doctors, elders and deacons, which you say was devised you know not by whom, is the invention of our Saviour Christ. For God ordained them, saith the Apostle, 1 Cor. 12:8, 28. And therefore unless you will show yourself either to be a blasphemer, by terming Jesus Christ to be you cannot tell whom, or else to be ignorant who is Jesus Christ: you must needs acknowledge the platform of government, which you say was invented by you know not whom, to have Christ Jesus for the author thereof.

Secondly, that the word of God teacheth that of necessity the government by pastors, doctors, elders, etc., ought to be in every church which is neither maimed nor deformed.ᶻ Because that church must needs be maimed which wanteth those members which the Lord hath appointed [12] to be therein: unless the Lord himself hath, by taking those members away, showed that now his body is to have no use of them. But as hath been said, God hath ordained pastors, doctors, elders and deacons to be in his church, proved out of Rom. 12:6, 7, 8, 1 Cor. 12:8, 28, Ephe. 4:12. And he hath not taken these officers away out of his church, because the church hath

ᶻ [side note:] This T. Cooper gainsaieth page 2 of his Epistle.

continual need of them. As of pastors to feed with the word of wisdom: of the doctors to feed with the word of knowledge, and both to build up his body in the unity of faith: of elders, to watch and oversee men's manners: of deacons to look unto the poor, and church treasury. Therefore, where these four officers are wanting, there the church is imperfect in her regiment.

Thirdly, that this government cannot be inconvenient for any state or kingdom.[a] For is it inconvenient for a state or kingdom to have the body of Christ perfect therein?

Fourthly, that every Christian magistrate is bound to receive this government by pastors, doctors, elders and deacons into the church within his dominions, whatsoever inconvenience may be likely to follow the receiving of it. Because no likelihood of inconvenience ought to induce the magistrate willingly to permit the church under his government to be maimed or deformed.

Fifthly, that the government of the church by lord archbishops and bishops is a government of deformed and unshapen members, serving for no good use in the church of God. Because it is not the government by pastors, doctors, elders and deacons, which, as I have showed, are now the only true members, that is, the only true officers of the visible body.

[13] Sixthly and lastly. That they who defend this false and bastardly government of archbishops and bishops, and withstand this true and natural government of the church by pastors, doctors, elders and deacons, are likely in awhile to become Mar-prince, Mar-state, Mar-law, Mar-magistrate, Mar-commonwealth.[63] As for Mar-church and Mar-religion, they have long since proved themselves to be.

These six points do necessarily follow of that which before I have set down, namely, that it is not lawful for any to abolish or alter the true and lawful government of the church, because it is not lawful for them to maim or deform the body of the church.

And I challenge you T. C., and you Dean John, and you John Whitgift, and you Doctor Cosin, and you Doctor Copcot, and all the rest that will or dare defend our established church government, to be tried with me in a judgement of life and death, at any bar in England in this point. Namely,

That you must needs be, not only traitors to God and his word, but also enemies unto her Majesty and the land, in defending the established church government to be lawful.

[a] [side note:] T. Cooper saith it is, page second, Epistle.

You see the accusation which I lay to your charge, and here followeth the proof of it. They who defend that the prince and state may bid God to battle against them, they are not only traitors against God and his word, but also enemies to the prince and state. I think John of Gloucester himself will not be so senseless as to deny this.[64]

But our archbishops and bishops, which hold it lawful for her Majesty and the state to retain this established form of government, and to keep out the government by pastors, doctors, elders and deacons which was appointed by Christ, whom you, profane T. C., call you know not whom, hold it lawful for her Majesty and the state to bid God to battle against them. Because they bid the Lord to battle against them which maim and deform the body of Christ, vz. the church. And they, as was declared, [14] maim and deform the body of the church, which keep out the lawful offices appointed by the Lord to be members thereof, and in their stead place other wooden members of the invention of man. Therefore you T. C., and you Dean John, and you John Whitgift, and you the rest of the beastly defenders of the corrupt church government, are not only traitors to God and his word, but enemies to her Majesty and the state. Like you any of these nuts, John Canterbury? I am not disposed to jest in this serious matter. I am called Martin Marprelate. There be many that greatly dislike of my doings. I may have my wants, I know. For I am a man. But my course I know to be ordinary and lawful. I saw the cause of Christ's government, and of the bishops' antichristian dealing, to be hidden. The most part of men could not be gotten to read anything written in the defence of the one and against the other. I bethought me therefore of a way whereby men might be drawn to do both, perceiving the humors of men in these times (especially of those that are in any place) to be given to mirth. I took that course. I might lawfully do it. Aye, for jesting is lawful by circumstances, even in the greatest matters. The circumstances of time, place and persons urged me there-unto.[65] I never profaned the word in any jest. Other mirth I used as a covert, wherein I would bring the truth into light. The Lord being the author both of mirth and gravity, is it not lawful in itself for the truth to use either of these ways, when the circumstances do make it lawful?

My purpose was and is to do good. I know I have done no harm, howsoever some may judge Martin to mar all. They are very weak ones that so think. In that which I have written, I know undoubtedly that I have done the Lord and the state of this kingdom great service. Because I have in some sort discovered the greatest enemies thereof. And by so much the most pestilent enemies, [15] because they wound God's religion, and corrupt the state with atheism and looseness, and so call for God's vengeance upon us all, even under the colour of religion. I affirm them to be the greatest enemies that now our state hath, for if it were not for them, the truth should have more free passage herein, than now it hath. All states thereby would be amended: and so we should not be subject unto God's displeasure, as now we are by reason of them.

Now let me deal with these that are in authority. I do make it known unto them, that our bishops are the greatest enemies which we have. For they do not only go about, but they have long since, fully persuaded our state that they may lawfully procure the Lord to take the sword in hand against the state: if this be true, have I not said truly, that they are the greatest enemies which our state hath? The papists work no such effect, for they are not trusted. The atheists have not infected our whole state, these have. The attempts of our foreign enemies may be pernicious. But they are men as we are. But that God, which when our bishops have and do make our prince and our governors to wage war, who is able to stand against him?

Well, to the point: many have put her Majesty, the parliament and council in mind that the church officers now among us are not such as the Lord alloweth of: because they are not of his own ordaining. They have showed that this fault is to be amended, or the Lord's hand to be looked for. The bishops, on the other side, have cried out upon them that have thus dutifully moved the state. They with a loud voice gave out, that the magistrate may lawfully maintain that church government which best fitteth our estate, as living in the time of peace. What do they else herein, but say that the [16]   magistrate, in time of peace, may maim and deform the body of Christ his church? That Christ hath left the government of his own house unperfect, and left the same to the discretion of the magistrate, whereas Moses, before whom in this point of government the Lord Christ is justly preferred, Heb. 3:6, made the government of the legal polity so perfect, as he left not any part thereof to the discretion of the magistrate? Can they deny church officers to be members of the church? They are refuted by the express text, 1 Cor. 12. Will they affirm Christ to have left behind him an unperfect body of his church, wanting members, at the leastwise having such members as were only permanent at the magistrate's pleasure? Why, Moses, the servant, otherwise governed the house in his time. And the Son is commended in this point for wisdom and faithfulness before him, Heb. 3:6. Either, then, that commendation of the Son before the servant is a false testimony, or the Son ordained a permanent government in his church. If permanent, not to be changed. What then do they, that hold it may be changed at the magistrate's pleasure, but advise the magistrate, by his positive laws, to proclaim that it is his will that if there shall be a church within his dominions, he will maim and deform the same? He will ordain therein what members he thinketh good. He will make it known, that Christ under his government shall be made less faithful than Moses was. That he hath left the placing of members in his body unto the magistrate. O cursed beasts, that bring this guilt upon our estate. Repent, caitiffs, while you have time. You shall not have it, I fear, when you will. And look, you that are in authority, unto the equity of the controversy between our wicked bishops and those who would have the disorders of our church amended. Take heed you be not carried away with slanders. Christ's government is neither Mar-prince, Mar-state, Mar-law, nor Mar-magistrate. The living God whose cause is pleaded for [17] will be revenged of you, if you give ear unto this slander, contrary to so many testimonies as are brought out of his word, to prove the contrary. He denounceth his wrath against all you that think it lawful for you to maim or deform his church: he accounteth his church maimed, when those offices are therein placed which he hath not appointed to be members thereof: he also testifieth that there be no members of his appointment in the church, but such as he himself hath named in his word, and those that he hath named, man must not displace, for so he should put the body out of joint. Now, our bishops holding the contrary, and bearing you in hand that you may practise the contrary, do they not drive you to provoke the Lord to anger against your own souls? And are they not your enemies? They hold the contrary I say, for they say that her Majesty may alter this government now established, and thereby they show either this government to be unlawful, or that the magistrate may presume to place those members in God's church which the Lord never mentioned in his word. And I beseech you mark how the case standeth between these wretches, and those whom they call puritans.

1. The puritans (falsely so called) show it to be unlawful for the magistrate to go about to make any members for the body of Christ.
2. They hold all officers of the church to be members of the body, Rom. 12:6, 1 Cor. 12:8, 28.
3. And therefore they hold the altering or the abolishing of the offices of church government to be the altering and abolishing of the members of the church.
4. The altering and abolishing of which members they hold to be unlawful, because it must needs be a maim unto the body.
5. They hold Christ Jesus to have set down as exact and as unchangeable a [18] church government as ever Moses did, Heb. 3:6.

These and such like are the points they hold, let their cause be tried, and if they hold any other points in effect but these, let them be hanged every man of them.

Now I demand, whether they that hold the contrary in these points, and cause the state to practice the contrary, be not outrageous wicked men and dangerous enemies of the state, it cannot be denied but they are. Because the contrary practise of any the former points, is a way to work the ruin of the state.

Now our bishops hold the contrary unto them all, save the 3rd and 2nd points, whereunto it may be they will yield, and cause our estate to practise the contrary: whence at the length, our destruction is like to proceed. For,

1. They deny Christ Jesus to have set down as exact and as unchangeable a form of church government as Moses did. For they say that the magistrate may change the church government established by Christ, so could he not do that prescribed by Moses.

2. In holding all offices of the church to be members of the body (for if they be not members, what should they do in the body?), they hold it lawful for the magistrate to attempt the making of new members for that body.

3. The altering or abolishing of these members by the magistrates, they hold to be lawful. And therefore the maiming or deforming.

Now you wretches (archbishops and lord bishops I mean), you Mar-state, Mar-law, Mar-prince, Mar-magistrate, Mar-commonwealth, Mar-church, and Mar-religion. Are you able for your lives to answer any part of the former syllogism, whereby you are concluded to be the greatest enemies unto her Majesty and the state? You dare not attempt it, I know. For you [19] cannot deny, but they who hold it and defend it lawful (yea enforce the magistrate) to maim or deform the body of Christ, are utter enemies unto that magistrate and that state wherein this disorder is practised. You cannot deny yourselves to do this, unto our magistrate and state: because you bear them in hand, that a lawful church government may consist of those offices which the magistrate may abolish out of the church without sin: and so, that the magistrate may lawfully cut off the members of Christ from his body, and so may lawfully massacre the body. You are then the men by whom our estate is most likely to be overthrown, you are those that shall answer for our blood which the Spaniard or any other enemies are like to spill,[66] without the Lord's great mercy: you are the persecutors of your brethren (if you may be accounted brethren), you and your hirelings are not only the wound, but the very plague and pestilence of our church. You are those who maim, deform, vex, persecute, grieve, and wound the church. Which keep the same in captivity and darkness, defend the blind leaders of the blind, slander, revile and deform Christ's holy government, that such broken and wooden members as you are may be still maintained to have the rooms of the true and natural members of the body. Tell me, I pray, whether the true and natural members of the body may be lawfully cut off by the magistrate? If you should say they may, I know no man would abide the speech. What? May the magistrate cut off the true and natural members of the body of Christ? O impudency, not to be tolerated. But our magistrate, that is, her Majesty and our state, may lawfully by your own confession cut you off, that is, displace you and your offices out of our church. Deny this if you dare. Then indeed it shall appear, that John of Canterbury meaneth to be a pope indeed, and to have the sovereignty over the civil magistrate. Then will you show yourself indeed to be Mar-prince, Mar-law and Mar-state. Now, if the magistrate may displace you as he [20] may, then you are not the true members. Then you are (as indeed you ought) to be thrust out, unless the magistrate would incur the wrath of God for maiming and deforming the body of the church, by joining unnatural members thereunto.

Answer but this reason of mine, and then hang those that seek reformation if ever again they speak of it, if you do not, I will give you little quiet. I fear you not. If the magistrate will be so overseen as to believe,[67] that because you which are the maim of the church are spoken against, therefore they, namely our prince and state, which are God's lieutenants, shall be in like sort dealt with, this credulity will be the magistrates' sin. But I know their wisdom to be such as they will not. For what reason is this which you, profane T. C., have used, page 103?[68]

The sinful, the unlawful, the broken, unnatural, false and bastardly governors of the church, to wit archbishops and bishops, which abuse even their false offices, are spoken against. Therefore the true, natural, and lawful, and just governors of the commonwealth shall be likewise shortly misliked. Ah senseless and undutiful beasts, that dare compare yourselves with our true magistrates, which are the ordinances of God, with yourselves, that is, with archbishops and bishops, which as you yourselves confess (I will by and by prove this) are the ordinances of the devil.

I know I am disliked of many which are your enemies, that is, of many which you call puritans.[69] It is their weakness I am threatened to be hanged by you. What though I were hanged, do you think your cause shall be the better? For the day that you hang Martin, assure yourselves, there will twenty Martins spring in my place. I mean not now, you gross beasts, of any commotion as profane T. C., like a senseless wretch not able to understand an English phrase, hath given out upon that which he calleth [21] the threatening of fists.[70] Assure yourselves, I will prove Marprelate ere

I have done with you. I am alone. No man under heaven is privy, or hath been privy unto my writings against you, I used the advice of none therein. You have and do suspect divers, as Master Paget, Master Wigginton, Master Udall, and Master Penry, etc., to make Martin.[71] If they cannot clear their selves their silliness is pitiful, and they are worthy to bear Martin's punishment. Well, once again, answer my reasons, both of your antichristian places in my first Epistle unto you, and these now used against you. Otherwise the wisdom of the magistrate must needs smell what you are. And call you to a reckoning, for deceiving them so long, making them to suffer the church of Christ under their government to be maimed and deformed.

Your reasons for the defence of your hierarchy, and the keeping out of Christ's government, used by this profane T. C. are already answered. They show what profane beasts you are. I will here repeat them. But here first the reader is to know what answer this T. C. maketh unto the syllogisms, whereby I prove all lord bishops to be petty popes and petty antichrists. I assure you, no other than this: he flatly denieth the conclusion, whereas he might (if he had any learning in him, or had read anything) know, that every dunstical logician giveth this for an inviolable precept, that the conclusion is not to be denied. For that must needs be true, if the major and minor be true, he in omitting the major and minor, because he was not able to answer thereby, granteth the conclusion to be true. His answer unto the conclusion is, that all lord bishops were not petty popes. Because, page 74, Cranmer, Ridley, Hooper were not petty popes.[72] They were not petty popes, because they were not reprobates. As though, you block you, every petty pope and petty Antichrist were a reprobate. Why, no man can deny Gregory the Great to be a petty pope, and a petty and petty Antichrist.[73] For he was the next immediate pope before Boniface the first, that known Antichrist: and yet this Gregory left behind him undoubted testimonies of a chosen child of God: so might they, and yet be petty popes, in respect of their office.[74] Profane T. C. his 1st and 2nd reason, for the lawfulness of our church government. And what though good men gave their consent unto our church government, or, writing unto bishops, gave them their lordly titles? Are their offices therefore lawful? Then so is the pope's office. For Erasmus was a good man, you cannot deny, and yet he both allowed of the pope's office since his calling, and writing unto him, gave him his titles.[75] So did Luther, since his calling also, for he dedicated his book of Christian liberty unto Pope Leo the Tenth. The book and his Epistle unto the pope are both in English.[76] Here I would wish the magistrate to mark what good reasons you are able to afford for your hierarchy.

[22]

Thirdly, saith profane T. C., page 75, all churches have not the government of pastors and doctors: but Saxony and Denmark have lord bishops.[77] You are a great statesman undoubtedly, T. C., that understand the state of other churches so well. But herein the impudency of a proud fool appeareth egregiously. As though the testimony of a silly schoolmaster,[78] being also as unlearned as a man of that trade and profession can be, with any honesty, would be believed against known experience. Yea, but Saxony and Denmark have superintendents, what then? Ergo lord archbishops and bishops? I deny it. Though other churches had lord archbishops and bishops, this proved nothing else, but that other churches are maimed and have their imperfections. Your reason is this, other good churches are deformed, therefore ours must needs be so too. The king's son is lame, therefore the children of no subjects must go upright. And these be all the [23] good reasons which you can bring for the government of archbishops and bishops, against the government of Christ. You reason thus. It must not be admitted into this kingdom, because then civilians shall not be able to live in that estimation and wealth wherein they now do.[79] Carnal and senseless beasts, who are not ashamed to prefer the outward estate of men before the glory of Christ's kingdom. Here again, let the magistrate and other readers consider whether it be not time that such brutish men should be looked unto. Which reason thus. The body of Christ, which is the church, must needs be maimed and deformed in this commonwealth, because otherwise civilians should not be able to live. Why, you enemies to the state, you traitors to God and his word, you Mar-prince, Mar-law, Mar-magistrate, Mar-church, and Mar-commonwealth: do you not know that the world should rather go a-begging, than that the glory of God by maiming his church should be defaced? Who can abide this indignity? The prince and state must procure God to wrath against them, by continuing the deformity of his church, and it may not be otherwise, because the civilians else must fall to decay. I will tell you what, you monstrous and ungodly bishops, though I had no fear of God before mine eyes, and had no hope of a better life, yet the love that I owe, as a natural man, unto her Majesty and the state would enforce me to write against you: her Majesty and this kingdom (whom the Lord bless with his mighty hand, I unfeignedly beseech) must endanger themselves under the peril of God's heavy wrath, rather than the maim of our church government must be healed, for we had rather it should be so, say our bishops, than we should be thrust out, for if we should be thrust out, the study of the civil law must needs go to wrack.[80] Well, if I had lived sometimes a citizen in that old and ancient (though [24] heathenish) Rome, and had heard King Deiotarus, Caesar, yea or Pompey himself give out this speech, namely: that the city and empire of Rome must needs be brought subject unto some danger, because otherwise Catiline, Lentulus, Cethegus, with other of the nobility, could not tell how to live, but must needs go a-begging.[81] I would surely, in the love I owed to the safety of that state, have called him that had used such a speech in *judicium capitis*,[82] whosoever he had been: and I would not have doubted to have given him the overthrow. And shall I, being a Christian English subject, abide to hear a wicked crew of ungodly bishops, with their hang-ons and parasites,[83] affirm that our Queen and our state must needs be subject unto the greatest danger that may be, vz. the wrath of God, for deforming his church, and that God's church must needs be maimed and deformed among us, because otherwise a few civilians shall not be able to live? Shall I hear and see these things professed and published, and in the love I owe unto God's religion and her Majesty, say nothing? I cannot, I will not, I may not be silent at this speech: come what will come of it. The love of a Christian church, prince and state shall, I trust, work more in me than the love of a heathen empire and state should do. Now judge, good reader, who is more tolerable in a commonwealth: Martin that would have the enemies of her Majesty removed thence, or our bishops which would have her life and the whole kingdom's prosperity hazarded, rather than a few civilians should want maintenance. But I pray thee tell me, T. C., why should the government of Christ impoverish civilians? Because, saith he, page 77, the canon law by which they live must be altered if that were admitted.[84] Yea, but civilians live by the court of admiralty and other courts as well, as by the arches, vz., also the probates of testaments, the [25]   controversies of tithes, matrimony, and many other causes, which you bishops Mar-state do usurpingly take from the civil magistrate, would be a means of civilians' maintenance.[85] But are not you ashamed to profess your whole government to be a government ruled by the pope's canon laws, which are banished by statute out of this kingdom?[86] This notably showeth that you are Mar-prince and Mar-state. For how dare you retain these laws, unless by virtue of them you mean ether to enforce the supremacy of the prince to go again to Rome, or to come to Lambeth. It is treason by statute for any subject in this land to proceed Doctor of the Canon law, and dare you profess your church government to be ruled by that law?[87] As though one statute might not refer all matters of the canon law unto the temporal and common law of this realm: and is this all you can say, T. C.?

2.[88] Yes, saith he, the government of Christ would bring in the judicial law of Moses. As much as is moral of that law, or of the equity of it, would be brought in.[89] And do you gainsay it? But you sodden-headed ass you, the most part of that law is abrogated. Some part thereof is in force among us, as the punishment of a murderer by death, and presumptuous obstinate theft by death, etc.

3. Her Majesty's prerogative in ecclesiastical causes should not be a whit diminished, but rather greatly strengthened by Christ's government. And no law should be altered, but such as were contrary to the law of God, and against the profit of the commonwealth: and therefore there can be no danger in altering these.

4. The minister's maintenance by tithe, no puritan denieth to be unlawful. For Martin (good Master Parson), you must understand, doth account no Brownist to be a puritan,[90] nor yet a sottish Cooperist.

5. The inconvenience which you show of the government, which is, that men would not be ruled by it, is answered afore. And I pray you, why should they not be better obedient unto God's law, if the same also were established by the law of the land, than to the pope's law and his canons? You think that all men are like yourselves: that is, like bishops, such as cannot choose but break the laws and good orders of God and her Majesty. [26]

7. [=6] The laws of England have been made when there was never a bishop in the parliament, as in the first year of her Majesty. And this reason, as all the rest, may serve to maintain popery, as well as the hierarchy of bishops.

8. [=7] The government of the church of Christ is no popular government, but it is monarchical in regard of our head Christ, aristocratical in the eldership, and democratical in the people. Such is the civil government of our kingdom: monarchical in her Majesty's person: aristocratical in the higher house of parliament, or rather at the council table: democratical in the body of the commons of the lower house of parliament. Therefore, profane T. C., this government seeketh no popularity to be brought into the church: much less intendeth the alteration of the civil state, that is but your slander, of which you make an occupation. And I will surely pay you for it.

I must be brief now, but *More Work for Cooper* shall examine your slanders. They are nothing else but proofs that as by your own confessions you are bishops of the devil, so you are enemies unto the state. For by these slanders, you go about to blind our state that they may never see a perfect regiment of the church in our days. I say, that by your own confession you are bishops of the devil. I will prove it thus. You confess that your lordly government were not lawful and tolerable in this commonwealth, if her Majesty and the state of the land did disclaim the same. Tell me, do you not confess this? Deny it if you dare. For will you say that you ought lawfully to be here in our commonwealth whether her Majesty and the council will or

[27]   no? Is this the thanks that her Majesty shall have for tolerating you in her kingdom all this while, that now you will say, that you and your places stand not in this kingdom by her courtesy, but you have as good right unto your places as she hath unto her kingdom? And by this means your offices stand not by her good liking, and the good liking of the state, as do the offices of our lord high chancellor, high treasurer, and high steward of England. But your offices ought to stand and to be in force, in spite of her Majesty, the parliament, council, and every man else, unless they would do you injury. So that I know, aye, you dare not deny but that your offices were unlawful in our commonwealth, if her Majesty, the parliament, and the council would have them abolished. If you grant this, then you do not hold your offices as from God, but as from man. Her Majesty she holdeth her office, and her kingdom, as from God, and is beholding for the same unto no prince nor state under Heaven. Your case is otherwise, for you hold your offices as from her Majesty, and not from God. For otherwise, you needed not to be any more beholding unto her Majesty for the same in regard of right, than she is bound to be beholding unto other states in regard of her right: and so you, in regard of your lordly superiority, are not the bishops of God, but, as Jerome saith, the bishops of man.[91] And this the most of you confess to be true, and you see how dangerous it would be for you to affirm the contrary: namely, that you hold your offices as from God. Well sir, if you say that you are the bishops of man, then tell me whether you like of Dean John his book. O yes, saith T. C. For his grace did peruse that book, and we know the sufficiency of it to be such, as the puritans are not able to answer it.[b] Well then, whatsoever is in this book is authentical. It is so, saith T. C., otherwise his grace would not have allowed it. What say

[28]   you then to the 140th [=340th] page of that book, where he saith (answering the treatise of the bishop of God, the bishop of man, and the bishop of the devil), that there is no bishop of man at all, but every bishop must be either the bishop of God, or the bishop of the devil.[92] He also affirmeth none to be the bishop of God, but he which hath warrant, both inclusively and also expressly in God's word.[c] Now you bishops of the devil, what say you now, are you spited of the puritans because you, like good subjects, defend the laws of her Majesty, or else because like incarnate devils, you are bishops of the devil's, as you yourselves confess?[93]

---

[b] [side note:] T. C., page 38.   [c] [side note:] Dean John, lib. 4, page 340, line 7.

Here again, let the magistrate once more consider what pestilent and dangerous beasts these wretches are unto the civil state. For either by their own confession they are the bishops of the devil (and so by that means will be the undoing of the state, if they be continued therein), or else their places ought to be in this commonwealth whether her Majesty and our state will or no: because they are not (as they say) the bishops of man, that is, they have not their superiority and their lordly callings over their brethren by human constitution, as my lords chancellor, treasurer, and other honorable personages have, but by divine ordinance. Yea, and their callings they hold (as you have heard) not only to be inclusively but also expressly in the word. What shift will they use to avoid this point? Are they the bishops of men, that is, hold they their jurisdiction as from men? No, saith Dean Bridges, no, saith John of Canterbury and the rest of them (for all of them allow this book of John Bridges), for then we are the bishops of the devil, we cannot avoid it. Are they then the bishops of God, that is, have they such a calling as the apostles, evangelists, etc., had: that is, such a calling as ought lawfully to be in a Christian commonwealth (unless the magistrate would injury the church, yea, maim, deform, and make a monster of the church) whether the magistrate will or no? We have, say   [29] they. For our callings are not only inclusively but also expressly in the word. So that by Dean Bridges his confession, and the approbation of John Canterbury, either our bishops are bishops of the devil, or their callings cannot be defended lawful, without flat and plain treason, in overthrowing her Majesty's supremacy. And so Dean Bridges hath written, and John Whitgift hath approved and allowed, flat treason to be published.

Is Martin to be blamed for finding out and discovering traitors? Is he to be blamed for crying out against the bishops of the devil? If he be, then indeed have I offended in writing against bishops. If not, whether is the better subject, Martin or our bishops? Whether I be favored or no, I will not cease, in the love I owe to her Majesty, to write against traitors, to write against the devil's bishops. Our bishops are such by their own confession. For they protest themselves to be bishops of the devil. If they should hold the pre-eminence to be from man, if they hold it otherwise than from man, they are traitors. And until this beast Doctor Bridges wrote this book, they never as yet durst presume to claim their lordships any otherwise lawful than from her Majesty, yea and D. Bridges about the 60th page saith the same.[94] But they care not what contrariety they have in their writings, what treason they hold, as long as they are persuaded that no man shall be tolerated to write against them. I have once already showed treason to be in this book of the Dean of Sarum, page 448.[95] I show the like now to be, page 340. Because Dean

Bridges durst not answer me. They have turned unto me, in his stead, a beast whom by the length of his ears I guess to be his brother, that is, an ass of the same kind. But I will be answered of the Dean himself in this and the former point of treason, or else his cloister shall smoke for it. And thus, profane T. C., [30] you perceive what a good subject you are, in defending the established government. Thus also I have answered all your book in the matters of the lawfulness of the government by pastors, doctors, elders and deacons, and the unlawfulness of our bastardly church government by archbishops and bishops, where also the reader may see, that if ever there was a church rightly governed, that is, a church without maim or deformity, the same was governed by pastors, doctors, elders and deacons.

Whau, whau, but where have I been all this while? Ten to one among some of these puritans. Why Martin? Why Martin I say, hast tow forgotten thyself? Where hast ti been, why man, cha bin a-seeking for a salmon's nest, and cha vound a whole crew,⁹⁶ either of ecclesiastical traitors, or of bishops of the devil, of broken and maimed members of the church: never wink on me good fellow, for I will speak the truth, let the puritans do what they can. I say then that they are broken members, and I say John of Canterbury, if he be a member of the church, I say he is a broken member, and that Thomas of Winchester is a choleric member. Yea and cha vound that profane T. C. is afraid lest her Majesty should give bishops' livings away from them. And therefore shutteth his book with this position, vz. That it is not lawful to bestow such livings upon lay men, as are appointed by God's law upon ministers. But hereof *More Work for Cooper* shall learnedly dispute.

Reverend T. C., Admonition, pages 1, 2, 3

We use the ministers most vile nowadays. God will punish us for it, as he did those which abused his prophets.

Reverend Martin

Look to it T. C. then. For out of thine own mouth shalt thou be judged, thou unrighteous servant. Our bishops are they which abuse the ministers. [31] Our bishops were never good ministers as yet, and therefore they are not to be compared with the prophets.

Reverend T. C., page 4

Some men will say, that I do great injury to the prophets and apostles, in comparing our bishops unto them. But we may be happy if we may have tolerable ministers in this perilous age.

Reverend Martin

I hope T. C. that thou dost not mean to serve the church with worse than we have: what, worse than John of Canterbury? Worse than Tom Tubtrimmer of Winchester? Worse than the vicars of hell, Sir Geoffrey Jones,[97] the parson of Mickleham, etc.?[98] I pray thee, rather than we should have a change from evil to worse, let us have the evil still. But I care not if I abide the venture of the change. Therefore get John with his Canterburiness removed, etc. (whom thou acknowledgest to be evil) and I do not doubt, if worse come in their stead, but the devil will soon fetch them away, and so we shall be quickly rid both of evil and worse. But good T. C., is it possible to find worse than we have? I do not marvel though thou callest me libeller, when thou darest abuse the prophets far worse than in calling them libellers: for I tell thee true, thou couldest not have any way so stained their good names, as thou hast done, in comparing them to our bishops. Call me libeller as often as thou wilt, I do not greatly care: but and thou lovest me, never liken me to our bishops of the devil. For I cannot abide to be compared unto those. For by thine own comparison, in the 9th page, they are just Balaams up and down.[99]

Reverend T. C., pages 8, 9, 10

Though our bishops be as evil as Judas, the false apostles, and Balaam, yet because they have sometimes brought unto us God's message, we must think no otherwise of them, than of God's messengers. For God will not suffer devilish and antichristian persons to be the chief restorers of his gospel. [32]

Reverend Martin

First, T. C., I have truly gathered thine argument, though thou namest neither Judas nor the false apostles. Prove it otherwise. Then hast thou, reverend Martin, proved thyself a liar. Now secondly then, seeing it is so, I pray thee good honest T. C. desire our Judases (who was also one of the first apostles) not to sell their master for money, desire our false apostles (who preached no false doctrine for the most part) not to insult over poor Paul, and desire our good Balaams not to follow the wages of unrighteousness. The counsel is good. For Judas, though one of the first publishers of the gospel (so were not our bishops in our time), yet hung himself. The false apostles had their reward, I doubt not. And Balaam, as soon as ever the Israelites took him, was justly executed for his wickedness. The forced blessing wherewith he blessed them saved him not.

Reverend T. C., pages 10, 11, 12, 13

Many conjectural speeches fly abroad of bishops, as that they are covetous, give not to the poor, hinder reformation, simoniacs, etc., but the chief governors ought to take heed, that they give no credit to any such things. I trust never any of them committed idolatry as Aaron did.

Reverend Martin

Yea, I beseech you that are in authority in any case, not to believe any truth against our bishops. For these puritans (although the bishops grant themselves to be as evil as Balaam) could never yet prove the good fathers to have committed idolatry as Aaron did. And as long as they be no worse than Balaam was, there is no reason why they should be disliked. You know [33] this is a troublesome world, men cannot come unto any mere living without friends. And it is no reason why a man should trouble his friend and give him nothing, a hundred pounds and a gelding is yet better than nothing.[100] To bowl but seven days in a week is a very tolerable recreation.[101] You must know that John of London hath sometimes preached (as this profane T. C. hath given out to his no small commendations) thrice in a year at Paul's Cross. A sore labor, it is reason that he should bestow the rest of the year in maintaining his health by recreation, and providing for his family: give him leave but to keep out the government of the church, to swear like a swag,[102] to persecute, and to take some small ten in the hundred:[103] and truly he will be loath ever to commit idolatry as Aaron did. I hope, though Judas sold his master, yet that it cannot be proved since his calling that ever he committed idolatry.

Reverend T. C., pages 16, 17

Though bishops should offend as Noah did in drunkenness, yet good children should cover their father's faults. For natural children, though they suffer injuries at their father's hands, yet they take their griefs very mildly.

Reverend Martin

Bishop Westfaling? But what then?[104] Parson Gravat, parson of Sir John Pulchres in London (one of dumb John's bousing mates), will be drunk but once a week.[105] But what then? Good children should take links in a cold morning,[106] and light them at his nose, to see if by that means some part of the fire that hath so flashed his sweet face might be taken away: this were their duty, saith T. C., and not to cry red nose, red nose. But T. C., what if a man should find him lying in the kennel? Whether should he take him up (all to be mired like a swine) in the sight of the people and carry him home on his back, or fling a coverlet on him, and let him there take his rest until his legs would be advised by him to carry him home? But methinks, brother [34] T. C., you defend the bishops but evil-favoredly in these points. For you do, as though a thief should say to a true man, I must needs have thy purse, thou must bear with me, it is my nature, I must needs play the thief. But yet thou dealest uncharitably with me if thou blazest it abroad: for though I make an occupation of theft, yet charity would cover it. So say you, though our bishops make a trade of persecuting and depriving God's ministers, though they make a trade of continuing in antichristian callings, yet charity would have their faults covered, and have them mildly dealt with. As though, T. C., there were no difference betwixt those that fall by infirmity into some one sin, not making it their trade, and not defending the same to be lawful, and our bishops, which continue in an antichristian calling and occupation, and defend they may do so. But will they leave think you, if they be mildly and gently dealt with? Then good John of Canterbury, I pray thee leave thy persecuting: good John of Canterbury, leave thy popedom: good father John of London, be no more a bishop of the devil: be no more a traitor to God and his word. And good sweet boys, all of you, become honest men: maim and deform the church no longer: sweet fathers now, make not a trade of persecuting: gentle fathers, keep the people in ignorance no longer: good fathers now, maintain the dumb ministry no longer. Be the destruction of the church no longer, good sweet babes now: leave your nonresidency, and your other sins, sweet popes now: and suffer the truth to have free passage. Lo T. C., now I have mildly dealt with the good fathers, I will now expect a while to see whether they will amend by fair means, if not, let them not say but they have been warned.

Reverend T. C., from the 20th to the 30th [pages]

Though the bishops be faulty, yet they are not to be excused that find fault with them for sinister ends. And the prince and magistrates is to take heed that by their suggestions, they be not brought to put down lord [35] bishops, to take away their livings, and put them to their pensions. For the putting of them to their pensions would discourage young students from the study of divinity.

Reverend Martin

I thought you were afraid to lose your livings by the courtier Martin's means. But brethren fear it not. I would not have any true minister in the land want a sufficient living. But good souls, I commend you yet, that are not so bashful but you will show your griefs. Is it the treading under foot of the glory of God that you fear, good men? No no say they, we could reasonably well bear that loss. But we die if you diminish the allowance of our kitchen. Let us be assured of that, and our lordly callings, and we do not greatly care how other matters go. I will, when *More Work* is published, help those good young students unto a means to live, though they have none of your bishopdoms, if they will be ruled by me.

Reverend T. C., pages 35, 36

There have been within these few weeks three or four pamphlets published in print against bishops. The author of them calleth himself Martin, etc.

Reverend Martin

But good Tom Tubtrimmer, if there have been three or four published, why doth Bishop Cooper name one only, why doth he not confute all? Why doth he invent objections of his own, seeing he had three books more to confute, or two at least, than he hath touched, nay, why doth he not confute one of them thoroughly, seeing therein his bishopdom was reasonably caperclawed?[107] I have only published a Pistle and a Pitome, wherein also I grant that I did reasonably pistle them. Therefore, T. C., you begin with a lie, in that you say that I have published either three or four books.

[36]   *Reverend T. C., page 38*

His grace never felt blow as yet, etc. What, is he past feeling? Wilt thou tell me that, T. C., he sleepeth belike in the top of the roost? I would not be so well thwacked for the popedom of Canter. as he hath borne, poor man. He was never able to make good syllogism since, I am sure. He allowed D. Bridges his book, quoth T. C. I pray thee, what got he by that, but a testimony against himself that either he hath allowed treason, or confessed himself to be the bishop of the devil?

T. C., page 38: He that readeth his grace his answer, and Master Cartwright's reply, shall see which is the better learned of the two.[108] So he shall indeed T. C., and he were very simple which would not discern that. And there is so much answered already, as thou sayest, that his grace dare answer no more for shame. And, T. C., you yourselves grant T. Cartwright to be learned, so did I never think John Whitgift to be, what comparison can you make between them? But Thomas Cartwright, shall I say that thou madest this book against me, because *T. C.* is set to it, well take heed of it, if I find it to be thy doing, I will so besoop thee, as thou never bangedst John Whitgift better in thy life.¹⁰⁹ I see here that they have quarreled with thee Walter Travers, John Penry, Thomas Sparke, Giles Wigginton, Master Davidson, etc.¹¹⁰ Nay, it is no matter, you are e'en well served, this will teach you, I trow, to become my chaplains. For if you were my chaplains once, I trow John Whitgift, nor any of his, durst not once say black to your eyes.¹¹¹ And if I had thy learning, Thomas Cartwright, I would make them all to smoke.¹¹² But though I were as very an asshead as John Catercap is, yet I could deal well enough with clergy then: yea with old Winken de Word, Doctor Prime his self.¹¹³ And I'll bepistle you Doctor Prime, when I am at more leisure, though indeed I tell you true, that as yet I do disdain to deal with a contemptible trencher chaplain, such as you, [37] Doctor Bancroft, and Chaplain Duport are.¹¹⁴ But I'se be with you all three to bring one day,¹¹⁵ you shall never scape my fingers, if I take you but once in hand. You see how I have dealt with Dean John, your entertainment shall be alike. But Thomas Cartwright, thou art T. C., so is Tom Cooper too. The distinction then between you both shall be this: he shall be profane T. C., because he calleth Christ Jesus, by whom the government by pastors, doctors, elders and deacons was commanded, to be he knows not whom: and thou shalt be simple T. C.

Concerning Mistress Lawson, profane T. C., is it not lawful for her to go to Lambeth by water, to accompany a preacher's wife, going also (as commonly godly matrons in London do) with her man?¹¹⁶ No, saith T. C., I do not like this in women. Tush man, Thomas Lawson is not Thomas Cooper, he has no such cause to doubt of Dame Lawson's going without her husband, as the bishop of Winchester hath had of Dame Cooper's gadding.ᵈ ¹¹⁷ But *More Work for Cooper* will say more for Mistress Lawson.

From whomsoever Chard had his protection, his face is glad of it, for otherwise he knoweth not how to get a printer for the established government, because the books will not sell.¹¹⁸

Touching the premunire,¹¹⁹ let the libeller and his do what he dare.ᵉ Why brethren, what wisdom is this in you to dare your betters? Do you not know that I can send you my mind by a Pistle, and then prove you to be petty popes, and enemies to the state? And how can you mend yourselves? It is certain you are in a premunire. If her Majesty will give me leave to have the law, I will be bound to bring 10,000 pounds into her coffers upon that bargain. And therefore foolish men, dare your betters no more. And here [38]

ᵈ [side note:] *Qui pergit quod vult dicere quæ non vult audiet.*
ᵉ [side note:] T. C., page 40.

I pray thee mark how I have made the bishops to pull in their horns. For, whereas in this place they had printed the word *dare*, they bethought themselves that they had to deal with my worship, which am favored at the Court, and being afraid of me, they pasted the word *can* upon the word *dare*,[120] and so, where before they had me and mine do what we durst: now they bid us do what we can, hoping thereby to have a friend in a corner, who would not suffer us to do what we ought and durst: and so our ability should not be according unto their demerit. Mark now, ye bishops of the devil, whether you be not afraid of me: I will see you jolled with the premunire one day.[121]

 The like thing you shall find in the 135th page. For there, having said that they will not deny the discipline to have been in the apostles' time, they have now pasted there upon that, *That is not yet proved*.[122] So that although their consciences do tell them that the discipline was then, yet they will bear the world in hand, that that is not yet proved. Here you see that if this patch T. C. had not used two patches to cover his patchery, the bishops would have accounted him to be as very a patch as Dean John.[123]

 Ah, but these knave puritans are more unmannerly before his grace than the recusants are, and therefore the recusants have more favor. I cannot blame them, for we ought to have no popes. The papists liketh the archiepiscopal pall, and therefore reverenceth a petty pope therein.[124] And though the recusant come not to hear the sermons, yet he is an informer very often, upon other men's information.

 His grace denieth that ever he heard of any such matter,[f] as that the Jesuit should say he would become a brave cardinal, if popery should come again.[125] I know, T. C., that long since he is past shame, and a notorious [39] liar, otherwise how durst he deny this, seeing Cliff, an honest and a godly cobbler dwelling at Battle Bridge, did justify this before his grace his teeth, yea and will justify the same again if he be called?[126] So will Atkinson too.[127] Send for them if he dare. Ministers of the gospel ought to be called priests, saith his grace,[g] what say you by that?[128] Then good Sir John o' Cant., when wilt thou say Mass at our house? His grace is also persuaded, that there ought to be a lordly superiority among ministers.[h] So was Judas persuaded to sell his master. If you would have these things proved, profane T. C. referreth you to his grace his answer unto simple T. C., and to Doctor Bridges. That is, if you would learn any honesty, you must go to the stews, or if you would have a good savour, you must go to the sink for it.[129] Why thou unsavourly snuff, dost tow think that men know not D. Bridges and John Whitgift? Yea

---

[f] [side note:] Page 41. [g] [side note:] Page 46 [=45]. [h] [side note:] Page 44.

but his grace also firmly believeth that Christ in soul descended into hell. This is the 3rd point of his Catholic persuasion: but tell him from me, that he shall never be saved by this belief, and my finger in his mouth. Let him tell what our Saviour Christ should do, if he did not harrow hell.[130] Where thou sayest Master Young had only the dealing with Thackwell the popish printer, without his grace's privity, thou liest in thy throat: Master Young himself brought him to his grace, who ordered the matter as it is set down in my Pistle.[131] But did not I say truly of thee, that thou canst cog, face and lie as fast as a dog can trot,[132] and that thou hast a right seasoned wainscot face of ti nown, chwarnt tee, ti vorehead zaze hard as horn.[133]

Concerning Waldegrave,[134] it's no matter how you deal with him, he's a foolish fellow to suffer you to spoil his press and letters: an a had been my worship's printer, I'd a kept him from your clouches.[135] And yet it is pity to belie the devil: and therefore you shall not belie him and go scotfree. As for the press that Waldegrave sold, he did it by order, vz. he sold it to an allowed printer, J. C., one of his own Company,[136] with the knowledge of   [40] his warden, Henry Denham, etc. And call you this favor, in releasing him after long imprisonment? But I will give you a precedent of great favour indeed, wherein you may see what an ungrateful fellow Waldegrave is to his grace, who hath been so good unto him from time [to] time. There being a controversy between another printer and Waldegrave (all matters of print-ing being committed by the lords of the council to his grace), Waldegrave made one of his Company his friend (who could do much with his grace) to deal for him, who brake the matter to his worship, being at Croydon in his orchard: so soon as the party named Waldegrave, he sweetly answered him, saying: if it had been any of the Company save him, he would have granted the suit, but in no case to Waldegrave. Well, Waldegrave obtained the right honourable lord treasurer's letter in his behalf to his grace,[137] who when he had read it, said, I will answer my lord treasurer: with that Waldegrave entreated for his favorable letter to the wardens of his Company, which in the end through Doctor Cosin he obtained (though late),[138] yet went home at night, thinking to deliver it in the morning: but before he was ready, the wardens were with him, and rested him with a pursuivant upon his grace's commandment,[139] Waldegrave telling them there was a letter from his grace, which he received late the last night at Croydon: who answered, they knew it well enough, but this is his pleasure now: so they carried Waldegrave to prison, and in this his grace was so good unto him, as to help him with an hundred marks over the shoulders.[i] If this

---

[i] [side note:] A new revenge for an old grudge.

be your favour, God keep me from you, ka M. Marprelate. Bishops have justly received according to their deserts, having found greater favour at my worship's hands than ever they deserved, being notorious, disobedient and godless persons, unthrifty spenders and consumers of the fruits, not of their own labors (as you say Waldegrave was), but of the possessions of the church, persons that have violated their faith to God, his church, her Majesty, and this whole kingdom, and wittingly bring us all without the great mercy of God to our undoing: so that our wives, children and servants have cause to curse all lord bishops.[140] Lo T. C., you see that I have a good gift in imitation, and methinks I have brought your words into a marvelous good sense, whereas before in the cause of Waldegrave, they were ill-favoredly wrested: and as for his wife and children, they have just cause to curse John of London, and John of Canterbury, for their tyrannizing over him: by imprisoning and spoiling his goods, and vexing his poor wife and children with continual rifling his house with their pursuivants: who in November last, violently rushed into his house, breaking through the main wall thereof after midnight, taking away his goods, for some of the pursuivants sold his books up and down the streets, to watchmen and others. Ah, you antichristian prelates, when will you make an end of defending your tyranny, by the blood and rapine of her Majesty's subjects? You have been the consumers of the fruits of Waldegrave's labors: for have you not sent him so often to prison, that it seemed you made a common occupation thereof? For as soon as any book is printed in the defence of Christ's holy discipline, or for the detecting of your antichristian dealings, but your ravening pursuivants fly city and country to seek for Waldegrave, as though he were bound by statute unto you, either to make known who printed seditious books against my L. Face,[141] or to go to prison himself and threatened with the rack.[j] And are you not ashamed to say that he ever violated his faith? You know well enough that he is neither archbishop nor lord bishop. The case thus stood: after he had remained a long time in prison, not that time when Hartwell, his grace's secretary, wished that his grace might never eat bit of bread after he released him.[142] Nor at that time when you, profane T. C., told him that all puritans had traitorous hearts. Nor at that time Waldegrave told his grace that he was worse than Bonner in regard of the time.[143] Nor that time when he was strangely released by one of the Lord of good London's Swans.[144] Neither was it at that time when his grace (good conscionable noble man) violated his promise, in that he told the wardens of the Stationers' that if Waldegrave would come quietly to him, and cease

[41]

[42]

---

[j] [side note:] O, the greatness of his grace's favor.

printing of seditious books, he would pardon what was past, and the wardens promised his wife that if he were committed, they would lie at his grace's gate till he were released, and for all this, yet he was committed to the White Lion, where he lay six weeks.[145] Nor it was not at that time, when his grace allowed Watson the pursuivant to take of Waldegrave 13s. 4 pence for carrying of him to the White Lion.[146] But it was that time, when his grace kept him twenty weeks together in the White Lion for printing the *Complaint of the Commonalty*, the *Practise of Prelates*, *A Learned Man's Judgment*, etc.[147] Means being used for his liberty, his friend who was bound for him told him his liberty was obtained in manner following. You must be bound, saith he, in a 100 pounds, to print no more books hereafter, but such as shall be authorized by her Majesty or his grace, or such as were before lawfully authorized: whereunto he answered, that it was not possible for him to contain himself within the compass of that bond, neither should his consent ever go to the same[k] (the same will Doctor Cosin witness, that maidenly doctor who sits cheek by jowl with you, if he will speak a truth, which words Waldegrave uttered to him, going in the old palace at Westminster with his keeper before he was released), yet he would gladly have his liberty if he might lawfully. For, said he, I being a poor workman to my Company, cannot possibly observe it. For many books heretofore printed had *cum privilegio*, and yet were never authorized: and again, that it were but a folly for him to sue to her Majesty, the office were very base and unfit for her. And he might be well assured that Caiaphas of Cant. would never authorize anything for his behoof, and so it fell out. And thus Martin hath proved you in this, as in all other things, to be liars. And what is it that you bishops and your hang-ons will not say by Waldegrave, whom you would hang if you could. I will be brief in the rest, but so, as [the] reader may perceive that T. C. was hired to lie by commission. [43]

I will stand to it, that his grace accounteth the preaching of the word, being the only ordinary means of salvation, to be an heresy,[l] and doth mortally persecute the same: his appellation to the obedient clergy shall stand him in no stead,[m] when *More Work for Cooper* is published.[148] And there I will pay thee for abusing Master Wigginton and Master Davidson, whose good names can take no stain from a bishop's chops. If his grace rejected Master Evans for want of conformity,[n] why is the *quare impedit* gotten against the bishop of Worcester by the noble earl of Warwick his patron?[149] I hope he will see both the *quare impedit*, and the premunire too,

[k] [side note:] Whereby it may appear he swore not to his friend.
[l] [side note:] Page 46.   [m] [side note:] Page 47.   [n] [side note:] Page 47.

brought upon the bones of father Edmund of Worcester. It is a common brag with his grace his parasites, and with himself, that he is the second person in the land.[o] [150] *More Work* shall pay his grace for commending the Apocrypha, a profane and a lying story in many places,[p] to be unseparably joined with the holy word of God. You grant Doctor Sparke to have set his grace and yourself, T. C., at a *non plus*,[q] for the *septuaginta* is contrary to the Hebrew, and therefore you maintain contrary translations, and require men to approve both.[151] Martin hath marred Richard Patrick's market, for otherwise he was in good hope to have a benefice at his grace his hand, and to be made a minstrel.[152] Shameless and impudent wretches that dare deny
[44] John of Cant. to have been at any time under Doctor Perne, but as a fellow of the house where he was master, whereas all the world knoweth him to have been a poor scholar in that house,[153] yea, and his grace hath often confessed that he being there a poor scholar, was so poor as he had not a napkin to wipe his mouth, but when he had gotten some fat meat off o' the fellows' table, would go to the screen,[154] and first wipe his mouth on the one side and then o' the other, because he wanted a napkin, judge you whether this be not a meaner state than to carry a cloakbag, which is not spoken to upbraid any man's poverty, but to pull the pride of God's enemy an ace lower.[155] Although we cannot believe Doctor Perne in the pulpit, yet in this point we will not refuse his testimony. I am glad John of London you will not deny but you have the dyers' cloth, make restitution then.[156] Thou madest the porter of thy gate a minister, John, and thou mightest do it lawfully?[r] Why so, I pray thee? Why man, because he was almost blind, and, at Paddington, being a small people, he could not starve as many souls as his master doth, which hath a great charge?[157] I hope Master Madox will think scorn, to ask John of London forgiveness.[s] The substance of the tale is true.[158] I told you that I had it at the second hand. Are you not ashamed to deny the elms to be cut down at Fulham?[159] Why, her Majesty's taker took them from John of London. And, simple fellow, are you not able to discern between a pleasant frump given you by a councillor, and a speech used in good earnest?[160] Alas poor John o' London, doest thou think that Master vice-chamberlain spake as he thought? Then it is time to beg thee for a swag.[161] And so it is, if thou thinkest we will believe the turncoat Doctor Perne speaking unto us in his own name, who like an *apostatae* hath out of the pulpit told so many untruths.[t] And, as it is as lawful to bowl o' the

[o] [side note:] Pages 48, 49. [p] [side note:] 2 Esdras 14, 21, 37, etc.
[q] [side note:] Page 50. [r] [side note:] Pages 51, 52, 53, 54.
[s] [side note:] Pages 55, 56. [t] [side note:] Pages 57, 58.

Sabbath as it is to eat, and for you to make dumb ministers as it was for   [45]
David to eat of the shewbread, page 110, or for the Maccabees to fight on
the Sabbath, or for Moses to grant a bill of divorcement?[162] I perceive these
men will have the good divinity, if it be to be gotten for money. Yea, and
our Saviour Christ sware by his faith very often?[u] How so, good John.
I never heard that before. Why, saith T. C., he said *Amen, Amen* very often,
and *Amen* is as much as, *by my faith*, page 62. Horrible and blasphemous
beasts, whither will your madness grow in a while, if you be not restrained?
Master Allen the grocer is paid all save 10 pound?[v] For the use of that, the
executors have John o' London's blessing.[163] And I think they are reasonably well served. If the tale of Benison be not true,[a] why was John of
London allotted by the council to pay him (I think) 40 pounds for his false
imprisonment?[164] John of London is not dumb, because he preacheth
sometimes thrice a year at Paul's Cross?[b] Then we shall never make our
money of it I see.[165] But I pray thee, T. C., how canst thou excuse his
blasphemy of *Eli, Eli, lamma sabachthani*? There have been two outrageous
facts amongst others committed in the world by those that profess true
religion, the one was the betraying of our Saviour by Judas an apostle, the
other was the horrible mocking of his agony and bitter passion by John
Elmar, a bishop, in this speech.[166] If he had been in some reformed
churches, the blasphemer would have hardly escaped with his life. And it
is true sweet boy indeed? Hath Leicestershire so embraced the gospel
without contention, and that by Dumb John's means?[167] Little doest
thou know what thou hast done now, how if Martin be a Leicestershire
man, hast not thou then set out the praise of thine own bane? For Martin,
I am sure, hath wrought your Caiaphas Chair more wrack and misery than
all the whole land beside.[168] And therefore thou seest a man may be so mad
sometimes that he may praise he cannot tell what. The bishop of Rochester   [46]
in presenting himself to a parsonage did no more than law allowed him?[c]
And do so again good John of Rochester, and it will be for thy credit.[169]
Foh, these puritans would find fault I think with John of Cant., if he
(believing that Christ in soul went to hell) should hold it unlawful for a
man to pray unto Christ being in hell.[170] And sweet John of Cant., if ever
thou prayedst in thy life for any bodies' souls, now pray for thy brother
Doctor Squire and Tarleton's souls.[171] They were honest fellows, though
I think Dean John's ears be longer. For why, good sweet John, may not your

[u] [side note:] Page 62.   [v] [side note:] Page 58.   [a] [side note:] Page 59.
[b] [side note:] Pages 6, 61, 62.   [c] [side note:] Page 63.

worship do this, as well as William of Lincoln might pray that our souls should be with the souls of professed traitorous papists?[d][172]

The good bishop of Winchester did not protest that at Sir Mary Overies which was laid to his charge, but he spake some things that way?[e] Well, brother Winchester, you confess the most part, and we will believe the rest for your sake without witness.[173] The bishop of Winchester never said that it was an heresy to hold that the preaching of the word was the only ordinary means to salvation, but inasmuch as Penry held that the effect of salvation could not be wrought by the word read, he said that was not far from heresy?[f] Why, brother Cooper, what is this else but open confession?[174] For John Penry, as appeareth in his writings, holdeth the word read to be no ordinary means of salvation at all. This I know you will account an heresy, otherwise your case is damnable, that cause the people to content themselves with reading, and hold that they may ordinarily be saved thereby.[g] Yea, but Thomas of Winchester disputed a Master of Art 45 years ago in divinity? Here is an old lad once. I hope that disputation was very cholericly performed. And he did once as pretty a thing as that came to. For once, preaching at Canter., he was disposed to note out T. C., I mean simple T. C.,[175] in his sermon, his part [47] he played after this sort. He noted four great hydras of the gospel in his sermon: 1. carnal security, 2. heathenish gentility, 3. obstinate papistry, 4. saith he, when I look in his forehead, I find *T. C.* written therein, which I cannot otherwise interpret than thankless curiosity, thankless for the benefits already received, and more curious than needs in vain and needless questions. The old student did not know himself to be T. C. when he thus spake, and this is that thankless curiosity that hath answered Martin. Yea, and he saw Martin's picture drawn when he was a young man?[176] I perceive then he was not blind, as the old porter of Paddington whom John of London bedeaconed and beminstrelled.[177] Lucian of Winchester himself was the painter.[178] Midas of Cant. the judge.[179] The one of the two women called Ignorance was the goodwife of Bath, Doctor Culpable, warden of New College,[180] that other called Jealous Suspicion was that fox, John of Exeter.[181] Then came in Winkendeword, alias Doctor Prime, calumniator.[182] This Winken and his Lord of Winchester drew Innocency, to wit, Martin Marprelate gentleman, by the hair of the head. Then followed *Dolus, Fraus, Insidiæ.*[183] To wit, Doctor Perne, Doctor Kenold and Doctor Cosin.[184] The treader was Cankered Malice, his eyes were fiery, his face thin and withered, pined away with melancholy, and this was Doctor Copcot.[185] Then followed

[d] [side note:] Pages 63, 64.   [e] [side note:] Pages 14 [=64], 65, 66, etc.
[f] [side note:] Page 71.   [g] [side note:] Pages 72, 75 [=73].

Doleful Repentance, that is, Dean John, repenting that ever he had written in the bishops' behalf, because his grace is not as good as his word.[186] T. C., consider this picture until we meet again. Now my business calleth me away, I am travelling towards Banbury, for I hear say that there hath been old ado.[187] For bakers' daughters would have knights, whether they would or no.[188] I will learn the truth hereof, and so I will post to Solihull,[189] and visiting some parts of Stafford, Warwick, and Northampton shires, I will make a journey back again to Norfolk and Suffolk: I have a register at Bury, and by that time my visitors will be come out of Cornwall, Devon and Hampshire.[190] And now fare thee well, good profane T. C. I cannot now [48] meddle with the long period which thou hast in the 33rd [and] 34th pages of thy book, it is but 38 lines: thou art longer winded than Dean John is I see, though he hath longer periods than that which I set down.[191] Whereas thou dost complain that the livings of our bishops are so small, that some of their children are like to go a-begging.[192] There is a present remedy for that. For to what end else is John of Cant. unmarried, but to provide for the bishops' children who shall be poorly left? Though indeed, I never said in my life that there was ever any great familiarity (though I know there was some acquaintance) between Mistress Toye and John Whitgift.[193] And I'll befy 'em, I'll befy 'em that will say so of me.[194] And wherefore is Richard of Peterborough unmarried, but to provide for other men's children? O now I remember me, he has also a charge to provide for his hostess and cousin of Sibson. The petticoat which he bestowed upon her within this six months was not the best in England, the token was not unmeet for her state.[195] Farewell, farewell, farewell old Martin, and keep thee out of their hands for all that. For thou art a shrewd fellow, thou wilt one day overthrow them. Amen. And then thou swearest by thy faith, quoth John of London.

Martin Metropolitan to John the Metropolitan sayth,
Nemo confidat nimium secundis.[196]

Martin to his troubled sons sayth,
Nemo desperet meliora lapsus.[197]

Anglia Martinis disce favere tuis.[198]

Faults escaped[199]
Title, line ten, read, Chaplain hath showed himself in his late *Admonition to the People of England* to be, etc.
Epistle, page third, read *eulogein* for *enlogeni*.

Bear with the rest of the faults.

Oh read ouer D. John Bridges/ for it is a worthy worke:

Or an epitome of the
fyrste Booke/ of that right worshipfull vo-
lume/ written against the Puritanes/ in the defence of
the noble cleargie/ by as worshipfull a prieste/ John Bridges/
Presbyter/ Priest or elder/ doctor of Diuillitie/ and Deane of
Sarum. Wherein the arguments of the puritans are
wisely prevented/ that when they come to answere M. Doctor/ they must needes
say something that hath
bene spoken.

Compiled for the behoofe and overthrow of
the Parsous/ Fyckers/ and Currats/ that haue lernt
their Catechismes/ and are past grace: By the reverend
and worthie Martin Marprelate gentleman/ and
dedicated to the Confocationhouse.

The Epitome is not yet published/ but it shall be when
the Bishops are at convenient leysure to view the same.
In the meane time/ let them be content with
this learned Epistle.

Printed oversea/ in Europe/ within two furlongs of a Bounsing Priest/ at the cost and charges
of M. Marprelate/ gentleman.

1. The first Marprelate tract, the *Epistle*, printed in October 1588 by Robert Waldegrave
in the house of Elizabeth Crane in East Molesey. Houghton Library, Harvard University,
STC 17453.

2. The only surviving undamaged copy of the Marprelate project's one broadsheet, printed in early 1589 by Robert Waldegrave in White Friars, the house of John Hales in Coventry. Lambeth Palace Library, broadside 1588.22 no. 7.

THESES MARTINIANAE:

That is,

CERTAINE DEMONSTRATIVE
Conclusions, sette downe and collected (as it
should seeme) by that famous and renowmed
Clarke, the reuerend Martin Marprelate the
great: seruing as a manifest and sufficient confutation of al that euer the Colledge of Catercaps with their whole band of Clergie-priests,
haue, or can bring for the defence of their ambitious and Antichristian Prelacie.

PVBLISHED AND SET FOORTH
*as an after-birth of the noble Gentleman himselfe, by a
prety striplling of his,* MARTIN IVNIOR, *and
dedicated by him to his good neame and nuncka, Maister* Iohn Kankerbury : *Howv the yongm in came by
them, the Reader shall vnderstande sufficiently in the
Epilogue . In the meane time, vvhosoeuer can bring
mee acquainted vvith my father, Ile bee bonnde hee
shall not loose his labour.*

Printed by the assignes of
Martin Iunior, without any pri-
*uiledge of the Cater-
caps.*

3. The first appearance by one of Martin's sons: *Theses Martinianae*, printed in July 1589
by John Hodgkins in the house of Roger Wigston in Wolston. Beinecke Library,
Yale University, Zd 720.

THE PROTESTATYON.
OF MARTIN MARPRELAT

Wherin not wih standing the sur-
prizing of the printer, he maketh it
known vnto the world that he fear
eth, neither proud priest, Antichti
stian pope, tiranous prellate, nor
godlesse catercap: but desiethe all
the race of them by these presents
and offereth conditionally, as is
farthere expressed hearein by open
disputation to apear in the defence
of his cause against them and
theirs

Which chaleng if they dare not
maintaine aginst him : then doth he al-
foe publishe that he never meaneth by
the assitaunce of god to leaue the a stayl-
ing of them and theire generation vn-
till they be vterly extinguifed
out of our church
Published
by the worthie gentleman D martin mar
prelat D. in all the faculties primat and
metropolitan

4. The final Marprelate tract, printed in September 1589 in Wolston.
The first gathering was apparently printed by amateurs. Beinecke Library,
Yale University, Zd 719.

MARTINS
Months minde,

THAT IS,

A certaine report, and true description of the
Death, and Funeralls, of olde *Martin Marre-*
prelate, the great makebate of *England,*
and father of the Factious.

Contayning the cause of his death, the manner
of his buriall, and the right copies both of his
Will, and of such Epitaphs, as by sundrie
his dearest friends, and other of his
well willers, were framed
for him.

Martin the Ape, the dronke, and the madde,
The three Martins are, whose workes we haue had.
If Martin the fourth come, after Martins so euill,
Nor man, nor beast comes, but Martin the deuill.

1589.

5. *Martins Months Minde*, by Marphoreus (London, 1589). One of the better pieces of
anti-Martinist polemic, this pamphlet reports on the dying Martin's final days,
providing his speeches of repentance, the results of the autopsy, his funeral, and last
will. Houghton Library, Harvard University, STC 17452.

A DIALOGVE,

WHERIN
IS PLAINLY LAYD
OPEN THE TYRAN:

NICALL DEALING OF LORD *BISHOPS*
AGAINT GODS CHILDREN,

WITH

CERTAINE POINTS OF DOCTRINE,
WHEREIN THEY APPROVE THEM-
felves (according to Dr. *Bridges* his judgement)
to be truely the Biſhops of the *Diuell.*

Publiſhed, by the worthy Gentleman Dr. MARTIN MAR-PRELAT,
Doctor in all the Faculties, Primat and Metropolitan.

MALLACH. 2.7,8,9.

The Prieſts lippes ſhould preſerve knowledge, and they ſhould ſeek the Law at his mouth : for he is the meſſenger of the Lord of hoſts. But ye are gone out of the way : ye have cauſed many to fall by the Law, ye have broken the covenant of Levi. Therefore have I alſo made you to be deſpiſed, and vile before all the peo-ple, becauſe ye keep not my wayes, but have been partiall in the Law.

publiſhd in Qveen Eliz.' time

Reprinted in the time of *Parliament, Anno Dom.* 1640.

6. Martin resurrected: *A Dialogue* (Amsterdam: Cloppenburg Press? 1640) is a para-Martinist text attributed to Job Throkmorton and originally published, as the contemporary inscription notes, in "Queen Elizabeth's time" (La Rochelle, 1589). Reprinted as part of the renewed campaign against episcopacy that preceded the civil wars of the 1640s. Houghton Library, Harvard University, STC 6805.3 (A).

TRACT V

Theses Martinianae

Theses Martinianae
(July 1589)

Theses Martinianae was printed by John Hodgkins, Valentine Simmes, and Arthur Thomlin in The Priory, the house of Roger Wigston in Wolston, a few miles southeast of Coventry. They worked the same press on which the first four tracts were printed but used a roman rather than black letter type and set the tract in octavo rather than the quarto format employed for *Epistle*, *Epitome*, and *Hay any Work*. At thirty-two pages, each copy required only two sheets (collating 8° in 4s: A–D⁴; 16 leaves, unnumbered); the wholesale price was threepence. The printers completed a run of 1,500 copies shortly after July 22, 1589, the date with which the tract closes (see Introduction, liii–liv).

From its first appearance, *Theses Martinianae* has also been known as "Martin Junior," the name of the persona it deploys. The tract consists of several elements. A short preface by Martin Junior introduces a list of 110 theses by Martin Marprelate that argue the Presbyterian case in a chain of "demonstrative conclusions" or arguments. This list breaks off in mid-sentence, and the text continues with an epilogue in which Martin Junior defends his decision to publish his father's incomplete manuscript and then banters with the family's episcopal opponents in a manner indistinguishable from his father's style. Some scholars have taken the tract's fictive frame at face value and assert that Martin Junior and Martin Marprelate represent different writers. But while the arguments in the 110 theses might very well be the product of collaboration, Martin Junior's colloquial mockery is clearly the work of the same pen that produced the voice of Martin himself.

Martin *père* prefaces his theses with a note of explanation. Because church officials and puritans alike disapproved of his polemical manner in the previous tracts, he had decided to present his case in the form of logical extrapolations: no attacks on persons, no inveighing against causes. Martin holds to this promise for the initial forty-two theses, which more or less systematically argue the first principles of Presbyterianism. As Martin Junior acknowledges, many of these points were already argued at length in

Hay any Work, "whence they seem to have been collected" (159). After this initial group, however, the theses become increasingly polemical and focus on the argument that anti-episcopal attack was not a new cause but a continuation of a centuries-long battle. Many of these remaining theses rest on the claim that the anti-prelatical writings of William Tyndale, Robert Barnes, and John Frith – heroes of the English Reformation – constituted official church doctrine because their *Whole Workes,* edited by John Foxe in 1573, was published "*Cum gratia & Priuilegio Regiae Maiestatis*" (according to its title page). The idea that approval to print meant official sanction of all content was a dubious argument, even by the standards of Renaissance polemic: as Matthew Sutcliffe wrote in reply to this claim in his *Answere* (1595), "the words *Seene & allowed,* which are prefixed before divers pamphlets have no other force, then to signifie that they are allowed to bee printed, not allowed for law or trueth" (66v). Martin Junior acknowledges that the claim was one "which the most have not considered of" (159), a signal that the point might not have been made entirely in earnest. But reformers did take seriously the argument that Reformation attacks on Catholic prelates applied equally well to a Protestant episcopate. Whether or not they reflected "official" church doctrine, Tyndale's denunciations of clerical hierarchy, non-residency, pluralism, church courts, abuses of excommunication, the use of "priest" rather than minister, and the lack of separation between the ministry and the civil magistracy lay at the heart of the reform agenda. The large group of theses that Martin derives from the *Whole Workes* of Tyndale, Frith, and Barnes functions primarily to align the Presbyterian cause with earlier, more reputable reform polemic.

Martin Junior concludes the tract by abandoning his father's pretense of dispassionate logic and reverting to the Martinist weapons of irreverence, mockery, and the *ad hominem* thrust. One new element he adds is an engagement with the broader anti-Martinist campaign: Martin Junior takes up polemical arms against the verse of "Mar-Martin" and theatrical anti-Martinism. While the first few tracts had painted John Bridges as a clownish spokesman for episcopacy, the latest "marvelous fit upholders of Lambeth Palace, and the crown of Canterbury," Martin Junior notes, were the rhymers and stage-players, "poor silly hunger-starved wretches" who "have not so much as an honest calling to live in the commonwealth" (161–62).

Theses Martinianae:

That is,
Certain demonstrative conclusions,
set down and collected (as it should
seem) by that famous and renowned clerk, the reverend
Martin Marprelate the Great: serving as a manifest and sufficient
confutation of all that ever the
College of Catercaps,[1] with their whole band of clergy-priests,
have, or can bring for the defence
of their ambitious and antichristian prelacy.

Published and set forth
as an after-birth of the noble gentleman himself, by a pretty stripling
of his, MARTIN JUNIOR, and
dedicated by him to his good neame and nuncka, Master John
Kankerbury.[2] How the young man
came by them, the reader shall understand sufficiently in
the Epilogue. In the meantime,
whosoever can bring me acquainted with my father,
I'll be bound he shall not lose his labour.

Printed by the assigns of
Martin Junior, without any privilege
of the Catercaps.[3]

Martin Junior,
son unto the renowned and worthy Martin Marprelate the Great,
to the Reader

Thou shalt receive (good reader) before I set down unto thee anything of mine own, certain of those things of my father's doings which I found among his unperfect papers. I have not changed anything in them, detracted anything from them, nor added unto them aught of mine own, but as I found them, so I have delivered them unto thee. Mine own meaning thou shalt understand at the latter end, in my Epilogue to my nunckle Canterbury. This small thing that followeth before his Theses is also his own. I have set down the speech as I found it, though unperfect. One thing I am sorry for, that the speech pretendeth the old man to be something discouraged in his courses.[4]

[Martin Marprelate to the Reader]

I see my doings and my course misliked of many, both the good and the [A2r] bad, though also I have favourers of both sorts. The bishops and their train, though they stumble at the cause, yet especially mislike my manner of writing. Those whom foolishly men call puritans, like of the matter I have handled, but the form they cannot brook. So that herein I have them both for mine adversaries. But now what if I should take the course in certain Theses or Conclusions,[5] without inveighing against either person or cause? Might I not then hope my doings would be altogether approved of the one, and not so greatly scorned at by the other? Surely, otherwise they should do me great injury, and show that they are those who delight neither in heat nor cold, and so make me as weary in seeking how to fit them, as the bishops are in labouring how to find me. The bishops I fear are past my cure,[6] and it may be I was unwise in taking that charge upon me: if that which I have already done can do them any good, or any wise further the cause which I love, I shall be glad, if not, what hope is there of amending them this way? The best is, I know how to mend myself. For good leave have I to give over my desperate cure, and with this my farewell unto them, I wish them a better surgeon. Yet ere I leave them, I do here offer unto the view of the world some part of their monstrous corruptions; in defence whereof, for their lives dare not they in any learned meeting or assembly dispute with me, or attempt to overthrow mine assertions by modest writings handled anything scholar-like, that is, by good and sound syllogisms, which [A2v] have both their major and minor confirmed by the word.[7] I would once see them enter into either of these courses, for as yet they have been far from

147

both. Fire and faggot, bands and blows, railing and reviling, are and have been hitherto their common weapons, as for slandering and lying, it is the greatest piece of their holy profession. And these, with their bare assertions and their wretched cleaving to popish absurdities, are in a manner the only proofs and tried maxims they offer unto the church in this age.

And so if a man would be confuted, I must needs say, my Lord of Winchester hath long ago sufficiently and dexterely performed it.[8] I am not of opinion (saith he) that *una semper debet esse œconomia Ecclesiae*, That the government of the church should always, and in all places, be one and the same, especially by a company of elders.[9] Lo sir, what say you to this? Here is enough, I trow, for any man's satisfaction, that bishop Cooper *is not of opinion*. Yea but our Saviour Christ, his apostles, and holy martyrs are of opinion that the government of the church should always, and in all places, be one, especially by a company of elders. As for my Lord of Winchester's *opinion*, we have little or nothing to do with that: nor no great matter which side it lean to, whether with or against the truth. For if his bishopric and unruly jurisdiction were no more noisome and hurtful to the church of God, than his learning and opinion is hurtful to the cause of Discipline,[10] he might sit long enough undistempered in his chair for us: the good old [A3r]   man might cough his fill, and be quiet, having his faithful promise and book-oath (as we have also John a Bridges' and Bancroft's) that by arguments he will never hurt us.[11] For they must think that it is not such dry blows as this,[12] *I am not of opinion, etc.*, that will satisfy the learned, and answer the demonstrations that are brought on the contrary side. If then they have indeed any purpose at all to quiet the contentions of our church, let them bring unto us, not these bables of their own,[13] *We are not of opinion, etc.*, but some sound warrant from the word, that Christ and his apostles were not of opinion with us in the points wherein we truly charge them to have erred, otherwise their 812, their 1401.[14]

THESES MARTINIANAE:

That is,
The unanswerable conclusions of MARTIN,
wherein are plainly set down many strange and unknown things
(if hereafter they may be proved) against the bishops.

Compiled by Martin the Great:
found and published by Martin Junior, for the benefit of posterity,
if his father should be slain.

1. That all the officers of a true and lawful church government, in regard of their offices, are members of the visible body of Christ, which is the church. Rom. 12:4, 5, etc.; 1 Cor. 12:8, 28.

2. That none but Christ alone is to ordain the members of his body, to wit, of the church: because,   [A3v]

3. That the Lord in his word hath left the church perfect in all her members, which he should not have done if he had not ordained all the officers, namely, the members thereof, and so he should leave the building of his church unperfect, and so it must continue, for who will presume to finish that which he hath left undone in the building of his church?

4. That to ordain a perfect and an unchangeable government of the church is a part of Christ's prerogative royal, and therefore cannot, without the great derogation of the Son of God, be claimed by any church or man.

5. That if Christ did not ordain a church government, which at the pleasure of man cannot be changed, then he is inferior unto Moses, for the government placed by him might no man to alter, and thereto might no man add any thing. Heb. 3:2, 3.

6. That the Lord in the New Testament did appoint as perfect and unchangeable a form of church government in the offices and officers thereof, as Moses did in the Old.

7. That the Lord never placed any offices in the New Testament, but the offices of apostles, prophets, evangelists, pastors, doctors, elders, and deacons.

8. That unto the end of the world there were no other offices to be placed in the church, but only these.

9. That none of these were, and so no offices of a lawful church government are to be removed out of the church by any but by the Lord Christ himself, who placed them, because they are the members of his   [A4r] body, in the placing or displacing whereof man hath no skill, nor yet commission to deal.

10. That the Lord for the causes seeming good to his own wisdom (whereof any further than he hath set down in his word man is not to enquire) hath removed out of the church the offices of apostles, prophets, and evangelists.

11. That the want of these can be no maim unto the church, seeing the Lord by removing them thence showeth that the body can have no use of them.

12. That the church is now unto the world's end to have none other offices in it, but of pastors, doctors, elders, and deacons.

13. That the displacing or the want of these, is a maim unto the church: and therefore,

14. That the churches of God in Denmark, Saxony, Tygurium,[15] etc., wanting this government by these offices, are to be accounted maimed and unperfect.

15. That it is as good a reason, yea, and a far better, to say that learned men and valiant captains must have their eyes put out, because Homer and Zisca were blind,[16] as to avouch that the church of England may not be governed by pastors, doctors, elders, and deacons, because other good churches want this regiment.

16. That to place others in the stead of these, is both a maiming and a deforming of the church.

17. That no magistrate may lawfully maim or deform the body of Christ, which is the church: and therefore,

[A4v]   18. That no lawful church government is changeable at the pleasure of the magistrate.

19. That the platform of government by pastors, doctors, elders, and deacons was not devised by man, but by our Saviour Christ himself, the only head and alone universal bishop of his church, as it is set down Rom. 12:4, 5, Ephes. 4:12, and 1 Cor. 12:8, 28. God hath ordained, saith the Apostle.

20. That no inconvenience can possibly come unto any state by receiving this government.

21. That the true stability of all Christian states and commonwealths consisteth in the sound execution of this church government by pastors, doctors, elders, and deacons.

22. That of necessity all Christian magistrates are bound to receive this government by pastors, doctors, elders, and deacons, and to abolish all other church governments.

23. That a church government being the ordinance of the magistrate or of the church, is an unlawful church government.

24. That it is merely and utterly unlawful for any man, church, or state to ordain any church government or any church officer, save that government and those officers before named: because,

25. That a church government consisting of any other officers but pastors, doctors, elders, and deacons is a government of maimed and mis-shapen members: therefore,

26. That our church government in England by lord archbishops and bishops is a government of maimed, unnatural, and deformed mem-

[B1r]   bers, serving for no use in the church of God: therefore also,

27. That no lord bishop is to be maintained in any Christian commonwealth.

28. That those kingdoms and states who defend any church government, save this of pastors, doctors, elders, and deacons, are in danger of utter

destruction, inasmuch as they defend the maim and deformity of the church: and therefore,

29. That our lord archbishops and bishops, in defending this their ungodly government, are not only traitors to God and his church, but utter enemies unto her Majesty and the state, inasmuch as they enforce the Lord by these their sins to draw the sword against us to our utter ruin.

30. That our lord archbishops and bishops hold it lawful for our magistrates to maim or deform the church.

31. That they hold Jesus Christ to have left behind him an unperfect and a maimed church, wanting some of her members.

32. That they hold it lawful for the magistrate to abolish the true and natural members of the body, and to attempt the making of new by his own invention.

33. That they, to wit, archbishops and bishops, are the maim of our church, and like to be the destruction of our commonwealth.

34. That the warrant that the archbishops and bishops have for their places, can be no better than the warrant which the maintenance of the open and most monstrous whoredom in the stews had in times past amongst us.[17] For by the word they are condemned to be the maim or deformity of the church, or both. And as for the laws that maintain them, being the wound and sore of the church, they are no more to be accounted of than the laws maintaining the stews. [Biv]

35. That the places of lord bishops are neither warranted by the word of God, nor by any lawful human constitutions.

36. That the government of the church of England by lord archbishops and bishops is not a church government set down in the word, or which can be defended to be God's ordinance.

37. That the government of lord archbishops and bishops is unlawful, notwithstanding it be maintained and in force by human laws and ordinances.

38. That the human laws maintaining them are wicked and ungodly, and to be abrogated of all Christian magistrates.

39. That to be a lord bishop then is simply unlawful in itself, that is, in respect of the office, though the man sustaining the same should not abuse it as our prelates do.

40. To be a lord bishop in itself, simply, besides the abuse, consisteth of two monstrous parts, whereof neither ought to be in him that professeth himself a minister.

41. The first is, to bear an inequal and a lordly superiority over his brethren in the ministry, and the rest of the church of God under his jurisdiction.

42. The second is, the joining of the civil magistracy unto the ministry.
    That both these parts are condemned by the written word of God: Luke 22:25, 1 Pet. 5:1–2, Matt. 20:25, Mark 10:42, 1 Cor. 8:10, Luke 12:14, 2 Tim. 2:4, and John 18:36, compared with Matt. 10:25, Luke 16:13.

43. That the hierarchy of bishops, in their superiority over their brethren, and their civil offices, hath been gainsaid and withstood by the visible church of God successively and without intermission for these almost 500 years last past.[18]

44. That this cause of overthrowing the state of lord bishops, and bringing in the equality of ministers, is no new cause, but that which hath been many years ago held and maintained, even in the fire, by the holy martyrs of Christ Jesus.

45. That this wicked government of bishops was an especial point gainsaid by the servants of God in the time of King Henry the eight, and Queen Mary; and in the withstanding whereof they died, the holy martyrs of Christ Jesus.

46. That none ever defended this hierarchy of bishops to be lawful, but papists, or such as were infected with popish errors.

47. That we have not expelled and banished every part of popery, as long as we maintain lord bishops and their seats.

48. That the offices of lord archbishops and bishops, together with other their corruptions, are condemned by the doctrine of the church of England.

49. That the doctrine of the church of England condemning the places of lord bishops is approved by the statutes of this kingdom, and her Majesty's royal prerogative.

50. That to be a lord bishop is directly against the statute 13 Eliz. rightly understood, and flatly condemned by her Majesty's royal privilege.[19]

51. That all her Majesty's loving subjects, ministers especially, are bound by statute (and have the allowance of the doctrine of the church of England, published with her Majesty's prerogative) not to acknowledge, yea, to disavow and withstand the places and callings of lord bishops.[20]

52. That the doctrine of the church of England in the days of Henry the eight was the doctrine which the blessed martyrs of Christ Jesus Master Tyndale, Master Doctor Barnes, and Master Frith taught them and delivered unto us.[21]

53. That this doctrine of theirs is now to be accounted the doctrine of the church of England, inasmuch as (being the doctrine of Christ and his

apostles) it is published in print by Master Foxe, and that by her Majesty's privilege.[22]

54. That this their doctrine is maintained by statute, under the name of the doctrine of the faith and sacraments.[23]

55. That the doctrine which according to the word is published by Master Foxe in the *Book of Martyrs*, seeing it is *cum privilegio*, is also to be accounted the doctrine of faith and sacraments in the church of England, and so is approved by statute.[24]

56. That upon these former grounds we may safely hold these conclusions following, and are thereby allowed by statute, and her Majesty's prerogative.[25]

57. That by the doctrine of the church of England, it is not possible that naturally there can be any good lord bishop: Master Tyndale's *Practise for Prelates*, page 374.[26]   [B3r]

58. That by the doctrine of the church of England, a bishopric is a superfluous honour and a lewd liberty, *ibid.*[27]

59. That by the doctrine of the church of England, our bishops are none of the Lord's anointing, but servants of the Beast.[28]

60. That by the doctrine of the church of England, our lord bishops are none of Christ's bishops, but the ministers of Antichrist.[29]

61. That by the doctrine of the church of England, our bishops and their government are no part of Christ's kingdom, but are of the kingdom of this world.[30]

62. That by the doctrine of the church of England, lord bishops are a part of that body whereof Antichrist is the head.

63. That by the doctrine of the church of England, the places of archbishops and bishops are the seats of Antichrist.

64. That by the doctrine of the church of England, a bishop can have no other lawful authority, but only to preach the word.[31]

65. That by the doctrine of the church of England, the desire of a bishopric, or any other honour, in a minister, is a note of a false prophet.[32]

66. That according to the doctrine of the church of England, all our bishops and their chaplains are false prophets.

67. That the doctrine of the church of England concerning the civil offices of our prelates is, That all civil rule and dominion is by the word of God flatly forbidden unto the clergy.[33]

68. That according to the doctrine of the church of England, the ministry   [B3v]
and the magistracy cannot by the ordinance of God be both in one person.

69. That by the doctrine of the church of England, the joining together of the ministry [and the magistracy] in one person doeth put every kingdom out of order.[34]

70. That for a lord bishop to be of the privy council in a kingdom, according to the doctrine of the church of England, is as profitable unto the realm as the wolf is to the lambs.

71. That bishops ought to have no prisons wherein to punish transgressors.[35]

72. That according to the church of England, all ministers be of equal authority.[a]

73. That according to the doctrine of the church of England, those doctors (who are daily alleged by our bishops in the defence of their superiority over their brethren) to wit, Cyprian, Jerome, Augustine, Chrysostom, knew of no authority that one bishop should have above another, neither thought, or once dreamed, that ever any such thing should be.[36]

74. That according to the doctrine of the church of England, a bishop and an elder or a minister note out in the word of God the one and the self same person and church officer, the contrary whereof is popery.[37]

75. That by the doctrine of the church of England, it is popery to translate the word *presbyteros* into priest, and so to call the ministers of the gospel, priests.[38]

76. That according to the doctrine of the church of England, Doctor Bancroft in his sermon at Paul's the 28th of January 1588 [=1589] maintained a popish error, in avouching that in the days of Cyprian there was a difference between a bishop and a priest or minister.[39]

77. That according to the doctrine of the church of England, John Cant. is a maintainer of a popish error, in terming the ministers of the gospel by the name of priests.

78. That according to the doctrine of the church of England, our prelates have no authority to make ministers, or to proceed to any ecclesiastical censure.[40]

79. That by the doctrine of the church of England, to have a bishop's licence to preach is the very mark of the beast Antichrist.[41]

80. That by the doctrine of the church of England, the godly ministers ought to ordain those that would enter into that function without any leave of the prelates, and not so much as once to suffer them to take any approbation of the prelates.

81. That according to the doctrine of the church of England, there ought to be no other manner of ecclesiastical censure but that which is noted,

[B4r]

---

[a] [side note:] Mark this (good reader).

Matt. 18:15, 17, which is, to proceed from a private admonition, to one or two witnesses, and thence to the church, that is, not to one, but unto the governors of the church, together with the whole congregation.

82. That according to the doctrine of our church, the citations, processes, excommunications, etc., of the prelates are neither to be obeyed nor regarded.

83. That according unto the doctrine of the church of England, men ought not to appear in their courts, seeing their proceedings are so directly [B4v] against the truth, as now they are manifested to be, seeing the doctrine of the church warranteth them no such calling.

84. That according to the doctrine of the church of England, that a man being excommunicated by them ought not to seek any absolution at their hands.

85. That according unto the doctrine of the church of England, every minister is bound to preach the gospel, notwithstanding the inhibition of the bishops.[42]

86. That according unto the doctrine of the church of England, a man, being once made a minister, is not to be kept back from preaching by the inhibition of any creature.

87. That according unto the doctrine of our church, our prelates notably profane the censure of the church by sending them out against those who are not offenders against God, for money matters and other trifles, etc.

88. That according unto the doctrine of the church of England, it is great tyranny in them to summon and cite poor men, as they do, to come before them for hearing the word, or speaking against their hierarchy.

89. That it is tyranny by the doctrine of the church of England, and the badge of Antichrist's disciples, for our prelates to break up into men's consciences, to compel them by oaths to testify against themselves.

90. That by the doctrine of the church of England, our prelates learned this abomination of Pilate, Matt. 26:93 [=63].[43]

91. That according unto the doctrine of the church of England, none [C1r] ought to be in the ministry, but such as are able to preach.

92. That according unto the doctrine of the church of England, non-residents and pluralities of benefices are most intolerable in the sight of God and man.[44]

93. That all true subjects have better warrant to deny the superiority of bishops, than the bishops have to impose themselves upon the church.

94. That her Majesty's true subjects in oppugning the state of lord bishops have the warrant of the word of God, the warrant of our laws and

statutes, the doctrine of the church of England, the consent of the church of God for the space of above 400 years, and her Majesty's privilege.[45]

95. That the bishops have nothing for their defence but the corruption received into our church contrary unto the word, contrary unto our statutes, contrary unto her Majesty's privilege, contrary unto the doctrine of our church.

96. That our bishops in this controversy for their hierarchy have not me, poor man, for their only adversary, but our Saviour Christ, his apostles and holy martyrs, our laws and statutes, her Majesty's privileges, and the doctrine of our church hath long ago condemned them for traitors unto God, unto his word, his church, and unto our laws and privileges.

97. That Master Thomas Cartwright, together with all those learned men, and myself also, that have written against the state of the clergy, could do no less than we have done, except we would betray the truth

[C1v]   of God, the laws of this land, and the doctrine of our church.

98. That our magistrates in maintaining both the doctrine of our church, and also the hierarchy of our bishops, maintain two contrary factions under their government, which their wisdoms know to be dangerous.[46]

99. That this faction is likely to continue until either of the parties give over.

100. That those who defend the doctrine of our church in oppugning of our bishops neither can nor will give over the cause, inasmuch as it is confirmed by the word professed in our church, allowed by our statutes, and maintained by her Majesty's privilege.

101. That the bishops will not give over, in any likelihood to die for it, as long as the state will maintain them.

102. That the continuance of these contrary factions is likely in a while to become very dangerous unto our state, as their wisdoms who are magistrates do well know and perceive.

103. That their wisdoms then are bound, even for the quieting of our outward state, to put down either the doctrine of our church, or the corruption, vz. our bishops, and their proceedings.

104. That they cannot, without the endangering of themselves, under the wrath of God, and the odious and most monstrous sin of inevitable apostasy from the truth, put down and abolish the doctrine of our church.

105. That they cannot any longer maintain the corruptions of our church,

[C2r]   namely, archbishops and bishops, without the shameful contradiction of our doctrine, and the discontentedness of their subjects.

106. That all ministers are bound by subscription, by virtue of the statute that requireth their subscription unto the doctrine of faith and sacraments in the church of England, to disavow the hierarchy of bishops.[47]

107. That it were well that all these ministers who are urged to subscribe would require a resolution in this point, before they yield their subscription.

108. That Doctor Bancroft in affirming her Majesty to be a petty pope[b] in his sermon preached at Paul's the ninth of February 1588 [=1589] preached treason against her Majesty's royal crown and dignity.[48]

109. That the said Bancroft is a traitor, in affirming her Majesty to usurp that authority within her dominions in causes ecclesiastical, which the pope usurped in times past.[49]

110. That our bishops in suffering the said sermon to be published in print, containing the former points of treason, are accessary unto Bancroft's treason.

That our prelates. Here the father left his writings unperfect, and thus perfectly begins the son.

Martin Junior's Epilogue   [C2v]

To the worshipful his very good neame,
Master John Canterbury

After my hearty commendations unto your worship (good nunckle Canterbury), trusting that you, with the rest of the catercaps, are as near your overthrow, as I your poor nephew am from wishing the prosperity of your antichristian callings. The cause of my writing unto you at this instant is to let you understand, first, that I was somewhat merry at the making hereof, being indeed sorry, together with others of my brethren, that we cannot hear from our good father, Master Martin Marprelate, that good and learned discoursing brother of yours, but especially grieved that we see not the utter subversion of that unhappy and pestilent government of lord bishops, at the helm whereof ye sit like a Pilate, or a Caiaphas rather. Moreover, I do you to weet,[50] that you shall receive by this bearer certain unperfect writings of my father's, praying your prelacy, if you can send me, or any of my brethren, any word of him, that you would return us an answer with speed.

---

[b] [side note:] Page 68, line 19.

Many flim flam tales go abroad of him, but of certainty nothing can be
heard, inasmuch as he keepeth himself secret from all his sons. Some think
that he is even now employed in your business;[51] and I think so too, my
reason is, quoth Robert Some, because it was for your sakes and good that
he first fell a-studying the art of pistle-making.[52] Others give out that in the
service of his country, and her Majesty's, he died, or was in great danger at
the Groine.[53] And those others (ka mine uncka Bridges) have seen motives
inducing them to be of this mind.[54] Some there are also, who fear that you
have him in your hands. Howsoever it be, somewhat is not well, that he is
silent all this while. We his sons must needs be disquieted, seeing we can
neither know where our father is, nor yet hear from him. If we could but
hear by some pistle, though it were but of twenty sheets of paper,[55] that he
is well, we would not then be so inquisitive of him. But now that he hath
been so long time tongue-tied these four or five months, we must needs
enquire of the matter.[56] Speak then, good nuncles, have you closely murdered the gentleman in some of your prisons? Have you strangled him?
Have you given him an Italian fig?[57] Or, what have you done unto him?
Have you choked him with a fat prebend or two? What? I trow my father
will swallow down no such pills. And he do, I can tell he will soon purge
away all the conscience he hath, and prove a mad hind ere he die.[58] But tell
me, I pray you, what you mean to do unto him if you have him in hold? Do
you mean to have the keeping of him, lest he should not be otherwise well
[C3v]   looked unto? Why, what need tat?[59] I am sure he hath 500 sons in the land,
of good credit and ability, with whom he might have othergates wel-
come,[60] than with any catercap o' them all. And I pray you, nunckles,
never trouble yourselves with the keeping of him, I trust he shall do well,
though he never come near any of you all. And I think in reason it were
more meet his sons than his brethren should be charged with him, if it so
came to pass that he were forced to lean unto others. This I know full well,
that my father would be sorry from his heart to put you to any such cost, as
you intend to be at with him. A meaner house, and of less strength than the
Tower, the Fleet, Newgate, or the Gatehouse is, would serve him well
enough: he is not of that ambitious vein that many of his brethren the
bishops are, in seeking for more costly houses than ever his father built for
him. And therefore, good sweet neames now, if you have him, let him be
dispatched out of your hands, with honesty and credit. My father is of a
kingly nature, I perceive by him he would do good unto you, but he would
not be recompensed for it again. He will none of your courtesies, unless it

be for your own sakes, that you will give over your bishopdoms, that is the greatest benefit he accounts of from you, other recompense he seeks none.

If you demand of me where I found this, the truth is, it was taken up (together with certain other papers) besides a bush, where it had dropped from somebody passing by that way.[61] I hope my father's worship will not be offended with me for publishing of it, being not so perfect as question-   [C4r] less he would have had it. He, and you, cannot but commend my good dealing in setting it out; for I chose rather to leave the sentences unperfect than to add anything more than I found legible. The arithmetical numbers in the end of his preamble show that when he had written so far, he had something more in his head than all men do conceive, which made him leave in the middest of a period. I myself do perceive some tautologies in the Conclusions as being the first draft, but I would not presume to mend them, that I refer to himself, if he be yet living, if dead, yet posterities may have his after-birth to be altogether his own. And let them take this as his *cygneam cantionem*, vz. his farewell to book-making.[62] But that would I be sorry of. For who can be able to prove the points which he hath set down here, concerning the doctrine of our church, maintained by statute, and her Majesty's privilege, so soundly, and so worthily, as he himself would perform it? A thirty or forty of the first Conclusions are already showed in *Hay any Work for the Cooper*, and therefore they need no further proof than the reading over that worthy treatise, whence they seem to have been collected. The rest I hope shall be showed in *More Work for the Cooper*.[63]

And, vather,[64] if you can prove these things out of the doctrine of our church, then certainly you deserve to be chronicled for ever. Then John Canterbury, come down with thy popery,[65] ka Master Martin Junior: for now art thou let out in thy colours to be an adversary, not only of Christ and his apostles, which all men might know, but even also an utter enemy   [C4v] unto the doctrine of the church of England sowed here by the holy martyrs, and sealed with their blood, yea, allowed by statute, and published with her Majesty's royal privilege, which is a point which the most have not considered of. And who is he now that dares persuade Martin to give over his course, unless the same also will show himself an enemy to the doctrine of the church of England? For Martin in his writings is not so much an enemy unto the bishops, as a defender of the doctrine of our church. And therefore you puritans that mislike of him, take heed that you be not found amongst posterities to be the betrayers of this doctrine (for your ease and quietness' sake) which you are bound to deliver unto your children, without corruption or mangling, though it cost you your lives a thousand times. For to tell you the truth, if you do but read over the writings of Master Tyndale, Master Frith, Master Barnes, Master Hooper, Master Knox, Master Lambert,[66] etc., which were the first planters of the gospel amongst us, you shall find yourselves in faithfulness, courage and zeal, yea, even the best of you, far behind them; which I speak not but to your great shame, with a desire of your amendment. And therefore I tell you true, I think it a great blessing of God that hath raised up this Martin, whom you can hardly brook, to hold tackling with the bishops, that you may have some time of breathing, or rather a time to gather courage and zeal, joined with knowledge, to set upon these enemies of the doctrine of our church, even the doctrine of God, I mean, maintained in our church.

[D1r]   For that as hitherto ye have done, you be so loth (for the disturbing of our state forsooth, and the offending of her Majesty) not only to speak against, but even utterly to reject this hierarchy of our bishops, even to have no more to do with it than with the seat of the Beast, you shall declare unto our children, that God raised up but a company of white-livered soldiers, to teach the gospel in sincerity under her Majesty, and take heed lest our forenamed fathers rise up in judgement against you. As for her Majesty, or the state, I think she hath little cause to thank you for your wisdom, in seeking the quietness of this commonwealth by winking at the sin of the pompous ministry. And methinks you are bound unto her, and her people, to make so much at the least known, as she maintaineth publicly in books, by her statutes and privileges, to be the doctrine of this our church under her government. Therefore, look unto these things, for certainly, if ever the Lord shall make the proceedings of our wicked bishops known unto her Majesty, to be so contrary to word of God, the profession of holy martyrs, and the doctrine of our church maintained both by our statutes and privileges, as in these Theses they are set down, assure yourself, that she will then enquire whether she had not any faithful preachers in her kingdom, that would stand to the defence of the truth, until she saw further into it.

[D1v]   As for the bishops, they may herein see, to their woe, what wicked caitiffs they are, in maintaining themselves and their thrice cursed popedom against such clear light. But the beasts, I fear, were born to no other end than to be the Lord's scourge, to chastise his church, and then to be burnt in hell. And out upon them, they are as unlike Christ, his apostles, and holy martyrs, which were the planters of our church, as the wretches are like unto themselves. A man would have thought, if they had not been desperate in their wickedness, that by the warning which Martin gave them, they would have been restrained from their villainy in some sort. But, as though their very reason had been clean gone, the more they are threatened to have their proceedings displayed, the more wicked do they manifest themselves. As if they would declare unto the world, that they will not be made known unto posterity, but upon the condition that they may be the most wicked that ever were in the church of God. They will be so many Judases, so many Diotrepheses, so many Simon Maguses, as now they are wicked bishops of England, or else they think not themselves well dealt with.[67] Wherefore, reverend father, if you be as yet on your feet, and have escaped out of the danger of gun shot, begin again to play the man. Fear none of these beasts, these pursuivants, these Mar-Martins, these stage-players,[68] these prelates, these popes, these devils, and all they can do. Quit your self but as like a man as you have done in *Hay any Work*, and I doubt not but you will make these roguish priests lie in the kennel. The report abroad goeth that you are drawn dry, and can say no more. They are fools that so think, I say. Let [D2r] these Conclusions be judge, whereby I tell you true, I hope you shall be able to empty every bishopric in England, if weight of truth can do it. There be that affirm, the rimers and stage-players to have clean put you out of countenance,[69] that you dare not again show your face. Alas poor hagglers, their fathers are too young to outface the least of your sons. And I do think that, lay aside their tyranny, all the bishops of England are too weak to deal with a scare-crow that hath but the name of reverend Martin written upon it. And therefore, I persuade myself that they their selves are thoroughly so persuaded, ka my nuncka Bridges,[70] that you contemn such kennel rakers and scullions, as to their shame, in the time of your silence, have sold themselves for pence a piece, to be derided of come who so will, to see a company of disguised asses.

Concerning Mar-Martin, if he be a Londoner, or an university man, ten to one but you shall see him, one of these odd days, carted out of the town for his honesty of life.[71] Why, that rime of his showeth that he had no other bringing up than in a brothel-house. And herein I would crave pardon of the universities, and the famous city of London, if I should be thought to give out that such a ribalder as this is were there maintained. To speak what I do think of the youth, I cannot be induced to think that he hath had his bringing up at any other trade, than in carrying Long Meg of Westminster's hand-basket, and in attending upon some other of his aunts at her appoint-ment while she lived.[72] After her death, it may be he hath been promoted [D2v] unto the service of some laundress in a bishop's house, where, in hope to be preferred by his good lords, he hath undertaken to mar-rimes, in publishing bawdry and filthiness for the defence of these honest bishops.

The stage-players, poor silly hunger-starved wretches, they have not so much as an honest calling to live in the commonwealth: and they, poor varlets, are so base minded, as at the pleasure of the veriest rogue in England, for one poor penny, they will be glad on open stage to play the ignominious fools for an hour or two together. And therefore, poor rogues, they are not so much to be blamed if, being stage-players, that is, plain rogues (save only for their liveries),[73] they in the action of dealing against Master Martin, have gotten them many thousand eye witnesses of their witless and pitiful conceits. And indeed they are marvelous fit upholders of Lambeth Palace, and the crown of Canterbury. And therefore, men should not think, of all other things, that they should any ways make Master Martin, or his sons, to alter their course. And hereof, good Master Canterbury, assure yourself.

Well, to grow to a point with you, if you have any of your side, either in the universities, or in your cathedral churches, or anywhere within the compass of all the bishopdoms you have, that dare write or dispute against any of these points set down by my father, here I do by these my writings,
[D3r] cast you down the glove in my father's name, and the names of the rest of his sons. If my father be gone, and none else of my brethren will uphold the controversy against you, I myself will do it. And take my challenge if you dare. By writing you may do it, and be sure to be answered. By disputations, if you will appoint the place, with promise that you will not deal *vi et armis*, you shall be taken also by me, if I think I may trust you.[74] Otherwise, the puritans will, I doubt not, maintain the challenge against you.

But here by the way, John Canterbury, take an odd advice of your poor nephew, and that is this. First, in regard of yourself, play not the tyrant as you do, in God's church; if you go on forward in this course, the end will be a woeful reckoning. Thou hast been raised up out of the dust, and even from the very dunghill, to be president of her Majesty's council, being of thyself a man altogether unmeet for any such pre-eminence, as neither endued with any excellent natural wit, nor yet with any great portion of learning. The Lord hath passed by many thousands in this land far meeter for the place than is poor John Whitgift. Well then, what if thou, having received so great blessings at the Lord's hand (being of all others in no comparison anything near the fittest for it, or the likeliest to obtain it), shalt now show thyself ungrateful unto thy merciful Lord God, or become a cruel persecutor, and a tyrant in his church, a cruel oppressor of his children, shall not all that thou hast received be turned unto a curse unto thee, even into
[D3v] thine own bosom? Yea verily. For the Lord in one day is able to bring more shame upon thee, and that in this life, than he hath heaped blessings upon thee now for the space of thirty years and upward. But when I do consider thy pre-eminence and promotion, I do sensibly acknowledge it to be joined with a rare curse of God, even such a curse as very few (I will not say none) in

God's church do sustain. And that is thy wicked and antichristian prelacy. The consideration of which popedom of thine maketh me think, that thy other place in the civil magistracy, being in itself a godly and a lawful calling, is so become infectious, that it will be thy bane, both in this life, and in the life to come. And I am almost fully persuaded that that archbishopric of thine, together with thy practises therein, show verily that the Lord hath no part nor portion in that miserable and desperate caitiff wicked John Whitgift, the pope of Lambeth. Leave therefore both thy popedom and thy ungodly proceedings, or look for a fearful end.

My second and last advise is this in a word. Suffer no more of these haggling and profane pamphlets to be published against Martin, and in defence of thy hierarchy. Otherwise thou shalt but commend thy folly and ignorance unto the world to be notorious. Mar-Martin, Leonard Wright,[75] Frégeville,[76] Dick Bancroft,[77] Tom Blan. o' Bedford,[78] Kemp,[79] Underhill,[80] serve thee for no other use, but to work thy ruin and to bewray their own shame and miserable ignorance. Thus far of these matters.

And methinks you see, nunckle Canterbury, that though I be but young, yet I begin prettily well to follow my father's steps; for I promise you, I am   [D4r] deceived, unless I have a pretty smattering gift in this pistle-making, and I fear in a while I shall take pride in it. I pray you, if you can, now I have showed you my mind, that you would be a means that my vather, or my brethren, be not offended with me for my presuming this of mine own head. I did all of a good meaning, to save my father's papers: and it would have pitied your heart to see how the poor papers were rain- and weather-beaten, even truly in such a sort as they could scant be read to be printed. There was never a dry thread in them. These sea-journeys are pitiful I perceive.[81] One thing methinks my father should like in me, and that is, my modesty, for I have not presumed to publish mine in as large a print or volume as my father doth his.[82] Nay I think it well, if I can dribble out a pistle in octavo now and then. Farewell, good nunckle, and pay this bearer for the carriage.[83] July 22, 1589. With as great speed as I might.

Your worship's nephew,
MARTIN JUNIOR

TRACT VI

The Just Censure and Reproof
of Martin Junior

The Just Censure and Reproof of Martin Junior
(July 1589)

The *Just Censure*, like *Theses Martinianae*, was printed by John Hodgkins, Valentine Simmes, and Arthur Thomlin in Roger Wigston's manor in Wolston, near Coventry. Both tracts are thirty-two page octavo pamphlets with identical collations (8° in 4s: A–D⁴; 16 leaves, unnumbered), requiring two sheets per copy. Both took a week, or a little less, to print, with *Just Censure* completed before the end of July (see Introduction, liv). As its full title indicates, *Just Censure* purports to be the response of Martin Senior, Martin Marprelate's eldest son, to his younger brother, Martin Junior, for publishing their father's incomplete work in *Theses Martinianae*. Despite the change in pseudonym, there is no reason to believe that "Martin Senior" and "Martin Junior" (as these two tracts are often known) are the work of different writers: the two manuscripts were written in the same hand, the hand that Matthew Sutcliffe identified as Job Throkmorton's (see Introduction, xliv–xlv).

Just Censure is the most archly self-reflexive of the Marprelate tracts. Martin Senior begins by chiding his brother for provoking the church into renewing its hunt for their father. While the anti-Martinist campaign had degenerated into a jesting matter of rhymesters and stage-players that posed the family no real threat, he argues, the publication of their father's syllogistic theses would scare the church into a return to more serious anti-Martinist strategies. Martin Senior then describes the form this revitalized campaign might take in a remarkable oration he scripts for the villain of his drama, John Whitgift. The imagined occasion has the archbishop instructing his band of pursuivants in their search for Martin and his press. The speech is a bold piece of self-advertising for the Marprelate project, playing with public awareness of the identities of those involved with the tracts and, more generally, of the people and places associated with the cause of reform. In addition, Martin Senior uses this oration to dramatize the hunt that had chased the Marprelate press from one safe house to another over the previous nine months. "Whitgift" discusses the use of spies and *agents provocateurs*, outlines strategies for infiltrating networks and for luring booksellers into admitting that they had copies of the tracts, suggests that his searchers track down the project's suppliers of printing material, and explains the usefulness of the *ex officio* oath, blank commissions, and other procedures of dubious legality. While the speech is fiction, the legal strategies "Whitgift" deploys are similar to those outlined in the letter of instruction sent by high commission to local church officials (see Introduction, lviii). In addition to this speech and Martin Senior's bantering addresses to his brother, *Just Censure* features a brief oration in the voice of John Aylmer, an allegorical dream vision of the investiture of John Bridges as John Whitgift's court fool, and some concluding verses against Mar-Martin.

Throughout *Just Censure*, Martin Senior displays an interest in the uses and abuses of language. The speeches he gives his opponents characterize them as men interested in language and argument as tools not for discovering truth but for condemning their enemies and consolidating their power. A list of accusations against the bishops emphasizes this point by imitating the legal forms deployed in the interrogatories Whitgift wrote for the use of high commission when administering the *ex officio* oath. As an alternative to this use of language as weapon, Martin Senior offers a supplication to the Queen and privy council that advocates instead a "quiet and orderly taking up of these controversies" (182). A concluding lesson on the rules of "bishops' English" summarizes Martin Senior's view of the arguments with which the church defended itself. To speak and write the language of the bishops, Martin Senior informs his younger brother, is "to wrest our language in such sort, as they will draw a meaning out of our English words, which the nature of the tongue can by no means bear" (183). As intended, the examples he proceeds to offer appear self-evidently absurd and tendentious. At the same time, however, they exemplify the mutual incomprehension that polarized the Martinist call for reform on one side and the official response on the other. While reformers believed they were simply making common-sense objections to Catholic holdovers in liturgical language, their opponents read their calls for change as posing fundamental challenges to religious and civil authority.

The Just Censure and Reproof
of Martin Junior.

Wherein the rash and undiscreet headiness of the foolish youth is sharply
met with, and the boy hath his lesson taught him, I warrant you, by
his reverend and elder brother, Martin Senior, son and heir unto the
renowned Martin Marprelate the Great.

Where also, lest the springal should
be utterly discouraged in his good
meaning, you shall find that he
is not bereaved of his due
commendations.[1]

Whoa then!² And boys will now be a pistle-making, either without their father's leave, or their elder brother's advice, we shall have our father's Art brought to a pretty pass within a while, I could a told 'tis long ago, that my father would get him so many sons, as John Canterbury would have no cause to sit quiet at dinner or supper, for looking to his young nephews. I thought boys would be a-doing. But, foolish stripling, canst thou tell what thou hast done? I ween not: if my father should be hurt, either at the Groine, or at the suburbs of Lisbon, is this the way either to cure him or to comfort him, to publish his scrabbled and weather-beaten papers in this sort?³ What if he had in purpose to write no more, seeing the danger and trouble that comes of it? Will this be any means to work the old man's quietness, for a foolish and a heady springal to go set abroad his papers? Thou sawest well enough, that Martin's doings were now almost forgot and huisht.⁴ And the men of sin themselves,ᶜ I mean the Canterbury Caiaphas, with the rest of his antichristian beasts, who bear his abominable mark, were content in a manner to turn his purposes from a serious matter to a point of jesting, wherewith they would have only rimers and stage-players (that is, plain rogues, as thou hast well noted) to deal.⁵ So that had   [A2v] not thy untimely folly bewrayed itself, it may be that the syllogisms whereby our father hath cracked the crown of Canterbury should have had no other answer, or he himself none other punishment but this. I' faith let him go, Martin is a mad knave. Whereas now upon this scrabbling and paltering of thine, mark whether John Canterbury will not send for all the knave pursuivants that belongs unto his popedom, and set them a-work with the confutation of Martin, using some such speech as this is, in the direction of them, for the choice of their arguments against him.

        An Oration of John Canterbury to the pursuivants,
    when he directeth his warrants unto them to post after Martin⁶

Now sirs, is not her Majesty's high commission, and myself also, being the chief thereof and one of her Majesty's privy council, well set up with a company of messengers, as long as we have you to go of our business? What think you? Have you been careful of us and our places, to find us out the press and letters wherewith these seditious Martins are printed? Or, have you diligently sought me out Waldegrave the printer, Newman the cobbler,

---

ᶜ [side note:] Bear witness, reader, that I give my lords their right titles.

Sharpe the bookbinder of Northampton, and that seditious Welshman
Penry, who you shall see will prove the author of all these libels?⁷ I thank
you Master Munday, you are a good gentleman of your word.⁸ Ah thou
Judas, thou that hast already betrayed the papists, I think meanest to betray
us also. Diddest thou not assure me, without all doubt, that thou wouldest
bring me in Penry, Newman, Waldegrave, press, letters, and all, before
Saint Andrew's Day last?⁹ And now thou seest we are as far to seek for
them, as ever we were. Nay, unless we have them now, they are like to
trouble our church more than ever they did.ᵈ For here is a young Martin
hatched out of some poisoned egg of that seditious libeller, old Martin.
Why truly it grieves me, at the heart, that I, by her Majesty's favor, having
more authority in mine hand to repress these puritans than any bishop else
hath had in England these thirty years, yet should be more troubled and
molested by them these six years, than all my predecessors have been these
six and twenty years. And all this cometh by reason of your unfaithfulness
and negligence, whom we send for them. Well, I give you warning, look
better unto your offices, or else let me be damned body and soul,ᵉ if I turn
you not all out of your places. Therefore look to it: for now every one
of you shall have warrants, both for himself, and as many as you will
substitute under you besides. Bring us whomsoever you suspect, your
warrants shall serve you to do it. And if you can find us either young or
old Martin, Penry, or Waldegrave, so that you bring the press and letters,
he shall have forty pounds for his labour, whosoever will bring them, his
charges and all borne clear. But if you bring us neither Martin, the press,
nor those aforenamed, never look us in the face more. And methinks for
your own good, you should be careful to get in these seditious men: for if
we that are lords of the clergy go down once, then shall you be sure to fall:
for, poor men, you have nothing but what you get in our service that are
your lords and masters.ᶠ And methinks, if these wayward men had any
conscience in them, they would not seek our overthrow with tooth and
nail, as they do, seeing so many honest poor men, yea, and many a good
gentleman too by my troth, live only by us and our places.

Well, if ever you mean to do any good in this matter, take me this course,
which we here in commission have thought meetest.¹⁰ Let a six or seven

ᵈ [side note:] But not the church of Christ, good uncle: you do not so greatly care though
they did.
ᵉ [side note:] Never condition for the matter man, for except thou repent, thou art sure of
that already.
ᶠ [side note:] And you have nothing neither yourselves, but what you get in the service of
your lord and master the devil.

of you, or your substitutes that stay here in London, watch me Paul's Churchyard, especially have an eye to Boyle's shop at the Rose.[11] And let some one or two of you that are unknown go in thither, and if there be any strangers in the shop, fall in talk with them of Martin, commend him, and especially his son's last libel (and here, he that will take that course, take me this, that if need be you may show it), showing, that by great friendship you got one of them, saying also, that you understood a man might there help his friend to some, if he were acquainted with Master Boyle, and offer largely for it. Now sir, if any shall either enter with you unto any speeches against the state, and in defence of these libels: or else, if any can procure you to the sight of the books, be sure to bring them before us. Though you learn not their names, yet your warrants shall serve your terms, inasmuch as you do suspect them. And thus I would have some of you bestowed.

Let three or four more of you or your substitutes be every day at the Blackfriars, Lincoln's Inn, Whitechapel, Paul's Chain, as often as Charke,[12] Gardiner,[13] Egerton,[14] or Cooper[15] do preach (and truly, my Lord of London, I marvel you suffer these men all this while to trouble the state by their preachings: by the Mass, I had not thought they should have stood half this time),[g] and there see if you can draw by speech anything from any Martinist, and let us talk with them. Especially mark if you see any, before the sermon begins, setting their heads together, and whispering under their cloaks, if you do, be sure they are reading Martin, and have them forthwith to the prison until we send for them, or cause them to put in sufficient sureties to appear the next court day.

[A4r]

You that stay here in London must also be sure, if possibly you can, to have a watch at all common inns, to see what carriage of paper and other stuff either goes from, or comes to London. Thereby you may haply learn something. And mark if any puritan receiveth any thing, open his pack, that you may be sure he hath no Martins sent him. We will direct our warrants so, that you may search all packs at your discretion.[h] We will take order also that the Court may be watched, who disperse, or read these libels there. And in faith I think they do my Lord of Essex great wrong, that say he favours Martin: I do not think he will be so unwise as to favour these, who are enemies unto the state.[16] For if he do, her Majesty, I can tell him, will withdraw her gracious favour from him; but take you no care for the

---

[g] [side note:] Surely nuncle I dare swear for him he is not in the fault: for they stand against his will.

[h] [side note:] I hope the pursuivants in time shall be able to make a good living, in taking toll of those packs which they do not open.

Court. Watch you London, and learn me where Newman and Waldegrave's haunt is, and there be sure to watch early and late. Have an eye also unto all the puritans' houses in London, especially my Lord Mayor Alderman Martin's,[17] and the preachers' houses. Let none that you suspect be uncited.

[A4v]   As for you that go into the country, I would have ye especially go into Northampton and Warwick shires, and command the mayor and constables of Northampton to keep watch and ward for Sharpe and Penry,[18] and if they can take them, let them bring them up, and we will be sure to content them well for their pains. Others must go into Essex, Suffolk, and Norfolk. And if you can bring us no Martinists from thence (at the least, that by that means your charges may be borne),[19] I would ye might starve for me. There is More,[20] there is Allen,[21] there is Knewstub,[22] there is Wright,[23] with many others, all very seditious men, that is pity, by my troth, that so many worshipful and good nurtured knights and gentlemen are carried away with them and their waywardness, as in those parts are seduced. But I hope her Majesty will have an uniformity. To be brief, I have said enough unto you already, but my meaning is, that you should go all the ground her Majesty hath, or find out Martin.[24] Go me to Devonshire, and to the North parts, where my Lord's grace of York also will direct his warrants by you, to seek this traitor Martin.[25] For I will have him, or else I will no longer be archbishop of Canterbury. He die at the Groine, as they say? Nay, he'll be hanged ere he'll die there. He is in some corner of England, lurking and doing mischief. I tell you true,[i] I do think him and his brood to be worse than the Jesuits. These Martinists are all of them traitors and enemies unto her Majesty,[j] they will overthrow the state, they are most rebellious and disobedient unto all good proceedings. No warning will serve them, they grow worse and worse. I persuaded myself, that none ever durst attempt to write besides this desperate wretch

[B1r]   Martin himself, if he still enjoy his liberty, his brood will become as desperate as himself, his impunity will make them presume to speak against the state. And therefore, either get him, or we shall never stay their course. And I think I shall grow stark mad with you,[k] unless you bring him. Therefore, my Masters, as you have any care for the pacifying of the state, and your own preferment, some way or other compass me to find the first Martin himself wheresoever he be. Spare no charges. Get him, and see what we'll do for you. For if we were not in hope to come by him

---

[i] [side note:] I'll believe you o' your word.

[j] [side note:] Saving your reverence uncle Canter., you lie in your throat.

[k] [side note:] Amen, good John, if thou doest not belong to the Lord, ka M. Martin Senior.

through your means, we would cast about another way to suppress his libelling. For we would make friends to have him proclaimed traitor, and have it felony, if we could, for any man to read his writings. And here an end with you.

Lo, sir boy, have you not spun a fair thread, for our father's ease and quietness, and for the quietness of your brethren? If our uncle Canterbury should take this course, where shall the old man stay then? You see England will be made too hot for him, if he be living. Why thou simple and unexperienced lad thou, my father, my father I tell thee, had been better, it may be, that thou haddest never, I tell thee truth, learned a word of Irish in thy life, than to have in this heat of the year published his unperfect questions.[26] Doest thou not see thy uncle Canterbury abroad in his visitation? Doest thou not see with how many men Esau rides, that if he meet with his poor brother Jacob, he may be sure to suck his blood?[27] Is seven score horse nothing, thinkest thou, to be in the train of an English priest? Whereof also there are thirty gold chains?[28] Doest thou think, that [B1v] the kingdom of Christ which thy father seeketh to build shall be able to stand, seeing John Canterbury, with so many men, rideth about the country, to proclaim nothing else but fire and sword, unto as many as profess themselves to be the true subjects thereof? Why, thou seest he goes a-visiting purposely for no other end, but to make it known what an enmity and hatred he beareth to the gospel and kingdom of Christ Jesus, and to show how careful he is, that that heresy of preaching may not prevail. Doest thou then persuade thyself, silly stripling, that there is any good to be done in sending a Pistle unto him, seeing he hath so many men in his train who will swear for him, that he loves none of these hot preachers? Methinks my father himself should be afraid of him, being so well horsed as he is. And therefore folly for one of his young sons, to think his strength sufficient to bear the encounter.

It may be thou wilt say, that thy father is every day in the week able to make as many men of his own charges; I would he were else: if he be, it is more than I know, I promise thee, and I think more than thou canst prove. But howsoever it goes, thou seest what a credit it is for an English priest to have so many men following of him, as in the day of judgement there may be enough of those that wear his livery to witness against him, that in this life he was a monstrous antichristian pope, and a most bloody oppressor of God's saints.

Be it my father were dead, as you seem to give out, and, for mine own part, I will not gainsay you, because I for my part may truly say, that his [B2r] eldest child never knew him, and therefore is ignorant whether he be living or dead: yet brother Martin, I do see in the publishing of these things by you, two great slips committed; the one of inconsideracy, the other of undutifulness. Your rashness and want of wisdom, other men, I see, are like to feel, your undutifulness is only towards myself, which I cannot well put up, and because of thy rashness, mark whether those poor men before-named,[29] to wit, Penry, Sharpe, Waldegrave, Newman, etc., with many other good men, who, I dare swear for them, did never meddle nor make at any time with the metropolitical writings of our renowned father, shall not be now as hotly pursued after, as ever they were. And all this comes of thy foolish and paltry meddling in matters too high for thy capacity. And thus other men are like to smart by thy folly.

As for myself, to omit the honourable mention that my father (my father, I say, *Quem honoris causa nomino, quoties nomino, nomino autem saepissime*) made of me in his writings, whereas he did not once vouchsafe to speak a word of such a dilling as thou art,[30] I should have thought that the very name of an elder brother should have taught thee that there had been one in the world to whom, by right of inheritance, the pistling of bishops had belonged, after the decease of reverend Martin himself. Why, who should set out my father's writings but I, Martin Senior, his son? At the least, who should publish them without my leave? So that herein thy undutifulness is no less than thy heady and rash inconsideracy.

[B2v]

To return again unto our reverend father. Of all other things, I would wish thee not to come within his reach, if he be living, for an thou doest, I can tell thee he'll give thee such a lesson for thy sauciness, as I think thou shalt never be lord bishop while thou livest. For it may be, that the expectation which men have conceived of the proof of such points as thou hast laid down, will force him to alter his purpose in *More Work for the Cooper*, and fall a-proving of these things, lest men should hold themselves deluded by thee.[1] And will this be no pain think you, sir boy? Will it be no labour for a man, having finished a book, to alter his course, and make it wholly new? And this thou knowest he must do, unless his wisdom hath beforehand prevented the inconvenience. I deny not indeed, but it is easier for him to alter his course, than for any one writer that I know of, because he hath chosen him such a method as no man else besides hath done. Nay, his syllogisms, axioms, method, and all are of his own making, he will borrow none of these common school rules, no not so much as the common grammar, as it appeareth by that excellent point of poetry, written in Latin by him against Doctor Wingken de Werd.[m][31] There thou shalt see such

---

[1] [side note:] My father, I tell you, saving his worship, stands upon the credit of his children.
[m] [side note:] Doctor Prime.

grammar, such art, such wit and conveyance of matter, as for the variety of the learning, and the pleasantness of the style, the like is not elsewhere to be found.

But lest I should utterly discourage thee, poor knave, I will, before I touch the rest of thine oversights, attribute unto thee thy deserved commendations. I confess then, that thou canst do prettily well; thou canst [B3r] enter reasonably into the sinews of thine uncle Canterbury's popedom, and make a tolerable Anatomy thereof. I must needs also say for thee, Jack, that thou fearest none of these popes.[32] And I promise thee, I think thou hast a pretty mother wit of thine own; but, poor boy, thou wantest wisdom withal to govern thy wit. Thou wantest that which thine uncka Bridges hath not, that is, wisdom to direct thee in the carriage of those pretty crotchets that thou hast in thy head. And the poor old Drone o' Sarum lacks that altogether, wherewith thou art prettily furnished, vz. a natural wit. Neither do I deny, boy, but that thou art Tom Tell-troth,[33] even like thy father, and that thou canst not abide to speak unto thine uncle Canter. by circumlocutions and paraphrases, but simply and plainly thou breakest thy mind unto him, and tellest him unto his face, without all these frivolous circumstances of, What is your name? and, Who gave you that name? of, An't please your worship, etc. Thou tellest him plainly to his face, I say, that he is a very antichristian beast, and an intolerable oppressor of God's church. And methought, when I read that point in thy Epilogue: then thought I, it will prove a vengeable boy in time.[34] For methinks that already, *patrizat sat bene certe*.[35] And trust me, Jack, I commend thee for thy plainness. And do so still, boy, for truth never shames the Master, I warrant thee, and take it o' my word. For indeed thine uncle Canter. is no less than a most vile and cursed tyrant in the church. And a plain Antichrist he is even by the doctrine of the Church of England, and so by the doctrine [B3v] of our church are the rest of our cursed bishops, in the proof of which point by and by I will a little insist. And because many take snuff that my father should account them,[36] yea, and prove them petty antichrists, I will manifestly prove them to be so, even by the doctrine of the church of England, maintained by statute and her Majesty's royal privilege. For my father now hath taught us such a way to reason against these Caiaphases, in the Theses set down by thee, as will anger all the veins in John Canterbury's heart. And that is, to show that they are enemies unto the doctrine of our church. Unto the point I will come anon. But first, brother Martin, I will school you in a point or two for your learning, in these things wherein I find your Epilogue to be unperfect. First then, I trow, I would have had some other manner of accusations against our puritans for their slackness, than wherewith you have charged them, as presently I will declare. Secondly, I would have propounded some things of mine own against our bishops, or else it should have cost me a fall.[37] And that should have been after this, or the like sort:

> I, Martin Senior, gentleman, son and heir to the reverend and worthy
> Metropolitan Martin Marprelate the Great, do protest, affirm,
> say, propound, and object against John Canterbury and
> his brethren, in manner and form following:[38]

[B4r]
First, I protest and affirm that the foresaid John Whitgift, *alias* Canterbury, which nameth himself archbishop of Canterbury, is no minister at all in the church of God, but hath and doeth wrongfully usurp and invade the name and seat of the ministry, unto the great detriment of the church of God, the utter spoil of the souls of men, and the likely ruin of this commonwealth, together with the great dishonour of her Majesty and the state. And in this case do I affirm all the lord bishops in England to be.

2. Item, I do protest that the entering in of this cursed man John Whitgift, and of all others our bishops in England, is not an entering into the church of God by the door Christ Jesus. Wherefore I affirm all of them to be thieves, robbers, wolves, and worriers of the flock, and therefore no true shepherds.

3. Item, I do proclaim the said John Canterbury, with the rest of our prelates, to be common simoniarchs,[39] such as make merchandize of church livings and benefices, by faculties, dispensations, etc., and make as common a gain of church censures, by absolutions and commutations of penance, etc., as any men in the land do of their lawful trades and occupations.

4. Item, I do propound and affirm that the said John Canterbury and his brethren do hinder and let with all their might the true knowledge of God amongst her Majesty's loving subjects, the inhabitants of this kingdom, and thereby, besides their own fore-provided damnation, are guilty of the blood of infinite thousands.

5. Item, I do proclaim that the said John Whitgift, with the rest of his brethren, doth spend and waste the patrimony of the church (which
[B4v]
ought to be employed in the maintenance of true faithful ministers, and other church uses) in the persecuting the true members of Christ, her Majesty's most trusty and loving subjects, and also upon their own pomp and ambitious pride, in maintaining a rude ungodly train of vile men, and a company of lewd and graceless children.

6. Item, I do propound that the said John Whitgift and his brethren do, as much as in them lieth, sow sedition and discontentedness between her Majesty and her true loyal subjects, by pretending that their practises in urging subscription, and in depriving men contrary to law, as for the surplice, denying to subscribe, etc., is at her Majesty's commandment.[40] As though her Highness would command that which were contrary unto the true doctrine of our church, and contrary unto her lawful statutes and privileges: or, as though she would so delude her loving subjects, as publicly to maintain that true doctrine, and these godly statutes, which privately she would have violated and trodden under feet.

7. Item, I, the said Martin Senior, do protest and affirm the said John Whitgift, with the rest of his brethren, to have incurred the statute of *premunire facies*, for depriving of ministers for not subscribing, not wearing the surplice, and for other their manifold proceedings against law and equity.[41]

8. Item, I do propound all our bishops for their said practises to be *ipso facto* depriveable, and that her Majesty, if she will do them but right, may by law deprive them all tonight before tomorrow.

9. I do also propound and avouch the said John Whitgift, and the rest of his wicked fraternity, though by outward profession they are in the church, yet to be none of the church, but to have, until they repent and desire to be received into the church, cut themselves (by the persecuting of the truth, and other their heinous sins) from the church, and so, without their repentance, from the interest and inheritance of the kingdom of heaven.

[C1r]

Item, I do protest and affirm that the true church of God ought to have no more to do with Jo. Canterbury his brothers and their synagogue, namely, with their antichristian courts of faculties,[42] etc., with their officers of commissaries, archdeacons, chancellors, officials, dumb ministers, etc., than with the synagogue of Satan. And that he their head and pope, together with his foresaid rabble, are not to be accounted for that church, whose censures we are to reverence and obey, and in the unity whereof we are to remain.

Item, particularly, concerning John Canterbury himself, I do affirm, but yet no further than *quatenus probabile*, that is, by great likelihoods,[43] that he is so finally hardened in his heinous sins against God and his church, that as he cannot be reclaimed: for his mouth is full of cursing against God and his saints, his feet are swift to shed the blood of the holy ones, he teareth in pieces the churches which he ought to foster, wilfully pulling the shepherds from their sheep, and so scattering them in a most lamentable sort, making much of wicked men that maintain his popedom, and smiting

the righteous for gainsaying his ways, bringing in daily into the church,
either by himself or his hang-ons, new errors not heard of before.[44]
Blaspheming the way of truth. And being rooted in malice against that
truth of Christ Jesus (who is blessed for ever) which he may see, if he did
not hoodwink himself, he with all his power contrarieth and striveth
against the going forward of the gospel, lest by the light thereof his sins
should be reproved. Finally, he hath in him too too many likely testimonies
of an heir of the kingdom of darkness, where, without his true turning unto
the Lord, he shall live in hell for ever.

[CIv]

And wicked man! if thou meanest to be elsewhere received, that is, into
Christ's kingdom, turn thee from thy wickedness, and let men and angels be
witnesses of thy conversion. Thy high place cannot save thee from his wrath
whose truth thou suppressest, and whose members thou doest persecute and
imprison. And I would not wish thee to defer thy repentance, lest thou callest
with the foolish virgins when there is no opening.[45] Thou seest even here upon
earth manifest tokens of God's anger towards thee. For thou seekest for
honour; but alas, I know none more contemptible than thyself, the poorest
faithful minister in the Lord hath more true reverence in one day than thou
hast had since the first time of thy popedom. There are almost none of God's
children but had as lief see a serpent as meet thee, not because they fear thy
face, but inasmuch as it grieveth them that their eyes are forced to look upon so
wicked an enemy of God and his church. Thine own creatures themselves
honour thee, but as tyrants are commonly honoured of their parasites and
sycophants. Thy brother the pope hath the like honor unto thine, that is, an
honor whose end will be shame and confusion of face for ever. The fearful and
contemptible end that have been brought upon many of them, ought to terrify
thee. Nay, the message of death which the Lord sent lately, even into thine own
house, ought to move thee, and face thee to confess that thy years also, yea, and
days are numbered. Doctor Perne, thou knowest, was thy joy, and thou his
darling. He was the dragon from whose serpentine breasts thou diddest first
draw this poison, wherewith now thou infectest the church of God, and
feedest thyself unto damnation. He lived a persecutor, an atheist, an hypocrite,
and a dissembler, whom the world pointed at, and he died, thou knowest, the
death due unto such a life as he led; thou knowest he died suddenly, even at
thine own palace of Lambeth, when, in thine own judgement, he was likely, in
regard of bodily strength, though not of age, to out-live thee.[46] And take thou
his death for a forewarning of thy destruction, except thou repent.

[C2r]

And these, brother Martin, with such like points, or some of those
positions, wherewith I could have thwacked my uncles about the shoulders

I ween, an I had been in thy place. There is one question more which I would have propounded for mine uncka Bridges his sake; O, I love him, thou knowest. And therefore thus would I have set down my proper-sition on his behalf.[47]

I, Martin Senior, Gentleman, do here protest, affirm, propound, and defend, that if John Canterbury will needs have a fool in his house, wearing a wooden dagger and a cockscomb, that none is so fit for that place as his brother John a Bridges, dean of Sarum. And that he, vz. John Bridges, is by right to displace the other with whom Lambeth now plays the ass, and is himself to be after a solemn manner, according to the book of ordaining bishops and priests, invested unto that room. Having for his officers and daily attendants these gentlemen following.[48] First and foremost Doctor Robert Some for his confessor, who also, when his master John Sarum hath no use of his service, may be at my lord grace's commandment to read the *starve-us* book in his chapel at Lambeth.[49] Secondly, if he were not something touched with the coinquination of the flesh, I would appoint none but Doctor Underhill to be his almoner.[50] Thirdly, Bancroft and drunken Gravat should be the yeomen of his cellar.[51] Anderson, parson of Stepney,[n] should make room before him with his two-hand staff, as he did once before the Morris dance at a market town in the edge of Buckingham or Bedford shires, where he bare the Potter's part.[52] His two supporters always to lead him by the arms must be Sir Leonard Wright and Sir Tom Blan. o' Bedford, the one whereof also must carry his bauble, and the other a looking glass for their Master, to see whether his catercap doth every way reach over his ears, and so stand according to his calling.[53] As for Mar-Martin and John Frégeville, they, *alterius vicibus*, shall be the grooms of his stool.[54] The rest of his officers I refer to the discretion of my father, unto whose censure also I do humbly submit this conceit of mine. And it may be I am bold to appoint these men their offices, who haply are at my father's direction, to give their attendance where he hath appointed them their places. But this I'll bide by, though my father say nay, that John Bridges deserves to have his place that wears the wooden dagger, the cockscomb, and the copper chain at Lambeth.[55] I'se abide by it, come what will of the matter.

The next thing that we are to consider, brother Martin, is a more just reprehension of the puritans, than that wherewith thou blamest them. For

[C2v]

[C3r]

---

[n] [side note:] This chaplain robbed the poor men's box at Northampton, played the Potter's part in the Morris dance, and begot his maid with child in Leicestershire: and these things he did since he was first priest.

thou findest fault with the preachers only, and that justly, I confess, because they are no more forward in casting off these our popes. But I say, that with more equity thou mightest have blamed both the gentlemen and people together with the ministers, than the ministers alone. For the ministers, although they be faulty, yet notwithstanding thou canst not deny but the gentlemen and people are as deep in fault as they are. And I would wish them both the one and the other to take this, or some such course as I here set down, which also for a great part of it, though not all, I saw in a puritan's hand, and so came by a copy of it, thinking if I could have heard of my father, to let him have the use of my copy: but now you see I publish it myself. I would then have all the puritans in the land, both lords, knights, gentlemen, ministers, and people, to become joint suitors in one supplication unto her Majesty and the lords of her honorable privy council in these petitions:

1. First, that there may be a redress of the great ignorance wherewith our whole land is overgrown, by placing able and faithful teachers over every congregation as near as may be.

2. Secondly, that all unlawful and sinful callings may be removed out of our ministry and church.

3. Thirdly, that the church within her Majesty's dominions may be governed by these offices and officers only, which the Lord Christ Jesus hath set down in his word.

4. Fourthly, that for the quiet and orderly taking up of these controversies which are risen in our church, concerning the government and ceremonies thereof, between our prelates, and those learned men which are contrary minded unto them, there might be had a quiet meeting of both the parties, and the controversies determined on their side, who shall be found to deal for (and not against) the truth. Or, if this fourth petition cannot take place, I would have this in the stead thereof, vz.:

   That it may please her Majesty, and the lords of her Majesty's honourable privy council, to see that the true subjects of this crown may not be troubled, as now they are, for defending such points as, being according unto the word of God, are also according to the privileged doctrine of the church of England, which is maintained by the statutes of this land; and that in case the prelates do molest any man, as now they do, for maintaining the doctrine of our church, or otherwise contrary unto the laws of our land, it may be lawful for him or them thus injuried to have his remedy at the King's Bench, against the said prelates.[56]

Now Jack, what sayest thou? I am sure thou canst not deny but these petitions, in thy judgement, would be an easy suit. I trow so too, and

I think that now thou findest greater fault, or at the least as great, with the   [C4r]
puritan noblemen, gentlemen, and people, as with the ministers, because
this or the like course goeth not on forward. And I can tell thee there would
be gotten an hundred thousand hands to this supplication, of known men
in the land, all her Majesty's most loyal and trusty loving subjects.⁵⁷ Thou
mayest then well think what a stroke so many would strike together,
especially in so reasonable and just a suit. And hereby our bishops should
be proved to be lord bishops indeed, that is, ungodly and slanderous liars,°
when her Majesty saw that the puritans seek not any intolerable course (for
if the foresaid petitions be not to be borne, I know not what is sufferable),
as the bishops would pretend. And further, it should appear that they are
not a few, and of small reputation, but in a manner the strength of our
land, and the sinew of her Majesty's royal government, which our bishops
do falsely note with the names of puritans. The consideration whereof, I
tell thee, even in policy, would make that this their suit should not be
hastily rejected, especially in such a time as wherewith we now live, in
danger of our enemies abroad, and therefore had need of no causes of
discouragement at home. Why man, this were also such a course as it would
descry our bishops' English to be plain slander and treachery against the
truth and the maintainers thereof, as indeed it is.

The bishops' English, wilt thou say?ᴾ Now I pray you, reverend brother,
what is that? Why, Jack, doest thou not understand what our bishops' English
meaneth? I do not greatly marvel, because I myself came but lately unto the   [C4v]
knowledge of it aright. But now that I have bestowed a little study that way, I
do think there are but a few in England that see into it as far as I do, *semper
excipio Platonem* you know, I always give place to my father,⁵⁸ for he made the
first Grammar and Lexicon in our time for the understanding hereof. Thy
small experience then considered, I wonder not of thine ignorance in this
point. But to satisfy thy demand, the bishops' English is to wrest our language
in such sort, as they will draw a meaning out of our English words, which the
nature of the tongue can by no means bear. As for example, *Receive the Holy
Ghost*, in good bishops' English is as much as, *I pray God thou mayest receive
the Holy Ghost*.�q ⁵⁹ And again, *My desire is, that I may be baptized in this faith*,
to their understanding, and in their dialect, is after this sort, *My desire is, not
that I myself, but that this child whereunto I am a witness, may be baptized in this*

° [side note:] A pretty brief definition of a lord bishop.   ᴾ [side note:] Bishops' English.
q [side note:] I am sure, that they would not for forty pence, that *receive a bishopric*, should
be expounded unto *I wish thou mayest receive a bishopric*, when they receive the Holy
Ghost.

faith.[60] Further, to entreat her Majesty and the parliament that the miseries of the church may be redressed, in the prelates' language is, to seek the overthrow of the state and the disquietness of her subjects. And if a man should go and ask thine uncle Canterbury (but stay boy, I mean not that thou shouldest go and demand the question of him) what it were in the tongue, which he and his brethren do commonly use, to put up such a dutiful supplication as before I have set down, why his answer would be presently, that to deal in such a suit were to rebel against her Majesty, to pull the crown off of her head, to make a faction to wrest the scepter out of her hand, and to shake off all authority. A

[Dɪr] wonderful thing in thy conceit I know it will be, to think that *humbly and dutifully to entreat*, should in the English tongue signify *by unbridled force undutifully to compel*, and that to seek the removing of unlawful callings out of the church, should be to threaten that the lawful magistrate should be thrust out of the commonwealth: but, simple boy, such English must thou study to understand, or else thou shalt never be able to pistle thine uncle Canterbury so learnedly as my father and I can do. And therefore I would wish, that of the first money which thou meanest to bestow in books, thou wouldest buy thee thy father's Grammar and his Lexicon, with a brief thing called his *Capita concordantiarum*,[r] and study these well but one month, and out o' doubt thou shalt, with the pretty skill which thou hast already, be able to overturn any catercap of them all.[61] I would thou knewest what great light to the understanding of all the bishops' treacheries a little time bestowed in these volumes have afforded unto me.

Well, by this time I think thou perceivest what a brave way this supplication which I speak of were, to prove our bishops to be treacherous and vile slanderers. For hereby her Majesty should perceive, that the rumors which the bishops raise falsely, concerning the great danger that would ensue unto her crown by the reformation which the puritans seek and labor for, are nothing else, but in a cunning and mystical kind of unnatural English to translate, *The puritans by the establishing of the kingdom of Christ, seek the sure upholding of the*

[Dɪv] *crown and dignity of their dread sovereign Lady Elizabeth*, into this handsome bishoplike miter:[62] *The puritans by their platform of reformation seek the utter ruin and subversion of Lady Elizabeth, her crown and dignity.* I am sure her Majesty would well-favouredly laugh at such a translation as this is, and yet behold, such she must be content with, if she will vouchsafe to yield her ears unto a bishop's persuasion. Yet thus much must I say of them, namely, that although they be not the best expounders of words that ever I read, yet do they never translate anything *e verbo ad verbum*, which by learned men is

[r] [side note:] These books are not yet printed.

commended as an especial virtue in a translator.[63] But O that I, as simple as I am, might read a lecture or two concerning this bishoplike translation, if not before her Majesty, yet at the least before some of her nobles, I would not doubt but to unfold such a deal of strange English (and yet the very *vernacula*, vz., the natural mother tongue of our unnatural prelates) as was never heard of in this land since the Saxons' time.

Here, I know, that thou art ready to enquire two points of me for thine instruction: the one, how our prelates can be proved antichrists by the church of England, the other, how thou mayest come by those books of my father before quoted. Well, thus I will briefly answer thee in both.

For the first, Master Tyndale in the Preface of his book called *The Obedience of a Christian Man*, page 102, proveth them to be Antichrists, inasmuch as in their doctrine and their doings concerning non-residency, they are directly against Christ and his word. I charge thee read the place, because at this time I am not at leisure to set it down; I can tell thee the reading of it will be double worth thy pains.[64]   [D2r]

My father's books afore spoken of are not in print, I confess, I would they were. Yet it may be I could direct thee where to go, to have mine.[65] But because I mean yet further to punish thee for thy slips in thy Pistle, I will not do thee that pleasure. For now indeed it cometh into my mind, that thou hast dealt foolishly in two points, besides all other thy fore-reckoned oversights.

First thou hast hereby exasperated against thy father and other poor men his well-willers, not only thy uncle Caiaphas, but hast set on the most of thine neames, to give their advice how to entrap him and his favourers.[66] For ten to one, but that Beelzebub of London will discharge the pursuivants to go to their business, with this or the like madmonition:[67]

My masters, you must not sleep in this matter. The maintenance of the peace of our church standeth now in your faithfulness and care. They are desperately set to overthrow all. And by the Mass I will be a pursuivant myself, rather than abide this tumult. And if I were, I trow I would watch about Travers his house in Milk Street,[68] who go in and out there, and I would know what they carried under their cloaks too, even any of them all. There is Paget at Hounslow,[69] I beshrew my heart if I would show him any such favour as my lord's grace here doeth: They are naught, they are naught, all the pack of them, I'll trust none of them all.[70] There is Cartwright too at Warwick, he hath got him such a company of disciples, both of the worshipful and other of the poorer sort, as we have no cause to thank him.[71] Never tell me that he is   [D2v]
too grave to trouble himself with Martin's conceits.[72] Tush, they will do anything to overthrow us, that they might have our livings any o' them all. I know what a good living is able to do with the best of us all. Cartwright seeks

the peace of our church no otherwise than his platform may stand. And you know, my lord, that there is no biting to the old snake.[73] And I do not see, o' my troth, but that Martin's abetters may be worse than himself, and do more mischief. Therefore go me to all their houses, spare me none of them, knights, gentlemen, and all. For I trust the high commission may go to any knight, yea, or nobleman's house in England. Therefore, my lords, I would wish that some continual spy may be in all those places which are most suspected. And let him learn to be wise, to creep into acquaintance with some of the preciser sort, and look smoothly for a time, until he can execute his commission.

Lo, young man, do not you deserve stripes, for fleshing on these blood-hounds in this sort? Let men look to keep them in as good temper as possibly they can, yet will they have a black tooth in their heads,[s] do what we may. But yet I would have borne with all this, if thou haddest taken a little pains in rhyming with Mar-Martin, that the catercaps may know how the meanest of my father's sons is able to answer them, both at blunt and sharp. And for thy further instruction against another time, here is a sample for thee of that, which in such like cases thou art to perform, if I or my father should set thee a work.

[D3r]   ¶ The first rising, generation, and original of *Mar-Martin*

> From Sarum came a goose's egg,
>   with specks and spots bepatched,
> A priest of Lambeth couched thereon:
>   thus was Mar-Martin hatched.[t]
> Whence hath Mar-Martin all his wit,
>   but from that egg of Sarum?
> The rest comes all from great Sir John,
>   who rings us all this 'larum.
> What can the cockatrice hatch up,
>   but serpent like himself?
> What sees the ape within the glass,
>   but a deformed elf?
> Then must Mar-Martin have some smell
>   of forge or else of fire,
> A sot in wit, a beast in mind:
>   for so was dam and sire.

---

[s] [side note:] The manifest token of a mad dog.
[t] [side note:] Mar-Martin engendered of Canterbury and Sarum.

Or else thou mightest have requited him in this Epitaph thus:[74]

If that Mar-Martin die the death, that to the dog is due,
Upon his tomb engrave this verse, and you shall find it true:

He lies enditched here that from the ladder top
Did once bebless the people thus, but first he kissed the rope.

Come near, quoth he, take heed by me,[u]
   I loved to lie by rhyming,
'Tis just you see, and doth agree,
   that now I die by climbing:
What wretch but I, that vowed to lie,
   all falsehood still defending?
Who may say fie? No beast but I,
   lo here you see my ending.
I lived a wretch, I die the stretch,   [D3v]
   my days and death agree:
Whose life is blameful, his death is shameful,
   be warned ye rogues by me.
The justest I hated, the godliest I rated,
   and thus I railed my fill:
The good I detested, the best things I wrested,
   to serve mine own beastly will.
Religion I loathed, myself I betrothed,
   to all the lewd snares of sin.
'Tis shame to say more, take heed of a whore,
   her marks stick yet in my skin.[v]
Ask you the cause? I spurned at God's laws,
   and hence comes all my wrack,
Where should he dwell, that fears not hell,
   but with the furies black?
A beast that braves, a tongue that raves,
   will God revenge in ire.
Then vengeance must (for God is just)
   fall to Mar-Martin's hire.

[u] [side note:] Mar-Martin's auricular confession from the top of a gibbet.
[v] [side note:] Believe him then, but drink not with him.

My tongue in ribaldry,^w
My heart in villainy,
My life in treachery,
Hath wrought me my fall.
I strove for the prelacy,
And so shook off honesty,
O vile indignity!
Yet would this were all.

Lo, youth: though I were loth to file my fingers with such a brothel beast as this Mar-Martin is,[75] yet because thou diddest let him go by thee (methought) half unbranded, I was the willinger, as thou seest, to give him a wipe or two, which I believe he will never claw off with honesty while he lives. And I would wish him, with the rest of the rimers, if they be wise, to take heed of my next Pistle. Indeed, I deny not but thou hast said prettily to him, neither would I have thee discouraged in thy good and honorable course against these prelates. Nevertheless, I muse thou diddest let him go clear away with his popery of Sir Nicholas priests.[76] Also, where like a good Catholic he counsels us (we thank him) to say a round *Pater noster* for Queen Elizabeth,[77] I muse thou saidst nothing to that, considering how much her Majesty is beholden to him in that regard. And much more had she been, if he had added an *Ave Marie* to it: those both together, with a piece of S. John's Gospel about one's loins,[78] would have been a principal receipt for the colic. But sure, now I think on it, he brought it in only but to make up his rhyme. And if you scan it well, 'tis a pretty one, mark it well:

O England now full often must thou Pater noster say.

How sayst thou, hast thou any skill in music? If thou have, then I am sure thou wilt confess with me, that this bastard pentamenter verse hath a fine sweet loose at the latter end, with a draught of Darby ale.[79] But what sayest thou to it? Whether likest thou better of these Nicholas priests that can so amble away with the *Pater noster*, or of that little priest of Surrey, who bade his maid in her extremity of sickness, say *Magnificat*, say *Magnificat*?[80]

Well boy, to draw to an end, notwithstanding thy small defects, persuade thyself that I love thee: doubt not of that. And here before we part, take this one grave lesson of thine elder brother: Be silent and close, hear

[D4r]

[D4v]

---

^w [side note] Take example then, my clergy chaplains, by this lamentable fall of your Mar-Martin.

many, confer with few. And in this point do as I do; know not thy father though thou mayest. For I tell thee, if I should meet him in the street, I would never ask him blessing: walk smoothly and circumspectly, and if any offer to talk with thee of Martin, talk thou straight of the voyage into Portugal, or of the happy death of the Duke of Guise, or some such accident; but meddle not with thy father.[81] Only, if thou have gathered anything in visitation for thy father, and hast a longing to acquaint him therewith, do no more but entreat him to signify in some secret printed Pistle where a will have it left,[82] and that'll serve thy turn as good as the best. The reason why we must not know our father is, that I fear lest some of us should fall into John Canterbury his hand, and then he'll threaten us with the rack unless we bewray all we know. And what get we then by our knowledge? For I had rather be ignorant of *That'll* do me no good, than know *That'll* hurt me, ka Master Martin Senior.[83] Farewell boy, and learn to reverence thy elder brother.

[Errata][84]
Page 6, line 18: for, give all the good, read, go all the ground
Page 14, line 12: for, avoiding, read, urging

The Protestation of Martin Marprelate

The Protestation of Martin Marprelate
(September 1589)

The final Marprelate tract, the *Protestation*, was printed in Roger Wigston's house in Wolston, near Coventry, a month after officials seized John Hodgkins, Valentine Simmes, Arthur Thomlin, and the second Marprelate press. The first gathering (of four leaves) was set by amateurs, probably Job Throkmorton and John Penry themselves, on the original Marprelate press that had been left behind in Wolston once Hodgkins had finished printing *Theses Martinianae* and *Just Censure*. The quality of the printing improves markedly with the second gathering, when Robert Waldegrave stopped by on his way to Scotland and lent a needed hand (see Introduction, lv). Like *Theses Martinianae* and *Just Censure*, the *Protestation* is an octavo of thirty-two pages, requiring two sheets per copy (collating 8° in 4s: A^4 B–D^4; 16 leaves, *1–2* 3–32 (32 misprinted as "23"). But this pamphlet is substantially shorter than the two that had preceded it, because the new roman type Penry acquired for the purpose was a larger font than the one Hodgkins had used.

The *Protestation* opens with the capture of Hodgkins and his press. With three men now in custody and in danger of torture, was the work of publicizing reform ultimately worth the risks they had undertaken? Martin's answer is yes, and he proceeds to justify the Marprelate project, encouraging readers not to interpret this recent turn of events providentially: "*Reason not from the success of things unto the goodness of the cause*" (198). Despite this setback, Martinism – "the descrying and displaying" (198) of church authorities – will continue long after he has been silenced, because the cause of reform rested on truth. The point of Martinism, he argues, was not simply to entertain but to promote public discussion of the controverted issues that reformers believed the church was working actively to suppress. This confidence in the power of debate to reveal the truth of the Presbyterian platform underlies the "protestation" that gives the tract its title, a characteristically self-dramatizing offer by Martin to take on the entire episcopate in open disputation; equally characteristic is the formal proclamation of victory that pre-emptively follows. Martin then summarizes *More Work for Cooper*, the sheets of which had been destroyed along with the press on which they had been printed. From this description, the lost tract appears to have deployed a full range of fictive and satirical strategies against many of Martin's favorite targets, from his clerical opponents to the "puritans" unsympathetic to his efforts. These passages of *ad hominem* banter balance the earnest defense of the Marprelate enterprise with which the tract opens, giving the *Protestation* as a whole a typically Martinist tone of serious jesting. Martin then ends the *Protestation*, and the entire Marprelate project, with a playful invitation to the "good reader" he has been addressing throughout the tracts: "if thou canst but learn the day of my marriage . . . thou shalt be better welcome unto me, than the best lord catercap of them all" (206–07).

The Protestation of
Martin Marprelate

Wherein notwithstanding the surprising of the printer, he maketh
it known unto the world that he feareth neither proud priest,
antichristian pope, tyrannous prelate, nor godless catercap:
but defieth all the race of them by these presents, and
offereth conditionally, as is farther expressed herein,
by open disputation to appear in the defence
of his cause against them and theirs.

Which challenge if they dare not maintain against him: then doth
he also publish that he never meaneth by the assistance of God
to leave the assailing of them and their generation until
they be utterly extinguished out of our church.

Published
by the worthy gentleman Doctor Martin Marprelate,
Doctor in all the Faculties, Primate and Metropolitan.

Thou canst not lightly be ignorant, good reader, of that which hath lately fallen unto some things of mine, which were to be printed, or in printing: the press, letters, workmen and all, apprehended and carried as malefactors before the magistrate, whose authority I reverence, and whose sword I would fear were I as wicked as our bishops are. These events I confess do strike me, and give me just cause to enter more narrowly into myself, to see whether I be at peace with God or no: but utterly to discourage me from mine enterprise, a greater matter than that comes to, I hope shall never be able. The state of the poor men that are taken I do bewail, not because they can hurt me, for I assure thee they know not who I am, but inasmuch as I fear the tyranny of our wicked priests will do that against them which neither the word of God doth warrant, nor law of the land doth permit. *For* [4] *as their hatred unto the cause is without ground, so their cruelty to those that profess the same is without measure.*[1] Therefore, good reader, if thou hear of any mean or compassionable punishment inflicted upon them (who to say the truth have deserved none at all, I mean the printers), I would never have thee stand to expostulate with our bishops for this untimely lenity of theirs, for whom I dare take mine oath (for I know them so well) that if there fall out any good to those poor men through the providence of God, and the gracious clemency of her Majesty, they for their parts are no more guilty or accessory unto it than the Spanish inquisitors themselves.[2] For indeed in this one point they are of my mind, vz. *That reformation cannot well come to our church without blood.* And that no blood can handsomely be spilt in that cause, unless they themselves be the butchers and horse-leeches to draw it out. Thou seest evidently they claim that as a piece and portion of [5] their inheritance.[3]

But tell them from me: that we fear not men who can but kill the body: because we fear that God who can cast both body and soul into unquenchable fire.[4] And tell them also this. *That the more blood the church loseth the more life and blood it gets.* When the fearful sentence pronounced against the persecutors of the truth is executed upon them, I would then gladly know, whether they who go about thus to shed our blood, or we whose blood cryeth for vengeance against them, shall have the worst end of the staff. We are sure to possess our souls in everlasting peace, whensoever we leave this earthly tabernacle: and in the meantime we know that an hair of our head cannot fall to the ground without the will of our heavenly father:[5] who of his great mercy loveth us in and for our Saviour Christ Jesus, and that with a love as far passing the love of a natural father toward his children, as he who

[6]   so loveth us excelleth all earthly parents. This persuasion being steadfastly
        engrafted in their hearts, who either now or hereafter shall be troubled for
        this cause, will be a comfort to them in the midst of all their distresses.

            And, good reader, whosoever thou art I would not have thee discouraged
        at this that is lately fallen out. *Reason not from the success of things unto the
        goodness of the cause.* For that savoureth too much of the flesh. If in beholding
        the state of the Low Countries and of France thou wouldest have so reasoned
        with thyself, thou mightest easily have given the holy religion of God the slip
        twenty years ago.[6] Thou must think that in these successes, though they be
        many times lamentable to the children of God, yet the Lord himself hath a
        special hand to try it may be who they are that with a double face, and who
        with a single heart, do affect the cause.[7] As to the present action, howsoever,
        there may escape me some corruption in the handling. Let them be well
[7]   assured it was not undertaken to be intermitted at every blast of evil success.
        Nay, let them know that by the grace of God the last year of *Martinism*, that
        is, of the descrying and displaying of lord bishops, shall not be till full two
        years after the last year of *Lambethism*,[8] that is, of joining most godless
        proceedings unto the maintenance of an antichristian and unlawful calling in
        God's church against the known truth: for that indeed is rightly called
        Lambethism or *Cooperism*, choose you whether.[9]

            And be it known unto them that *Martinism* stands upon another manner
        of foundation than their prelacy doth or can stand. Therefore if they will
        needs overthrow me, let them go in hand with the exploit,[10] rather by
        proving the lawfulness of their places, than by exercising the force of their
        unlawful tyranny. For once again I fear not their tyranny. And one sound
        syllogism (which I tell you is dainty ware in a bishop's breast) brought in for
        the proof of their unlawful callings shall more dismay and sooner induce me
        to give over my course than a thousand warrants, a thousand pursuivants, a
[8]   thousand threats, and a thousand racks. Which course, because they take not,
        therefore all their other drifts and devices are to none other end, than to show
        the great care and skill they have to carry away all the blows. But what get
        they by their tyranny: seeing it is truth and not violence that most uphold
        their places?[11] Do they not know that the more violence they use, the more
        breath they spend? And what wisdom were this trow ye, for a man that had
        coursed himself windless, to attempt the recovery of his breath by running
        up and down to find air? So you know he might soon have as much life in his
        members, as lord bishops have religion and conscience in their proceedings.

            The whole issue of their force and bloodthirsty attempts,[12] doth nothing
        else but witness against them that they are the children of those fathers,
        who never as yet durst abide to have their proceedings examined by the

word, and methinks they should be ashamed to have it recorded unto ages to come that they have ever shunned to maintain their cause, either by open disputation, or by any other sound conference or writing. Let me be [9] overthrown by any of these ways, and I do here by these my writings publicly protest, that I will never molest lord bishop again while I live, but will with very great vehemency, to the uttermost of my endeavour, maintain them and their cause, as ever I did oppugn the same; otherwise I do with the like constancy and resolution protest, that by the aid and assistance of God, I will never leave the displaying of them and their proceedings until they be made as odious in our church and commonwealth, as that they be thought of all sorts, unworthy to be harboured therein.

And this offer of mine, so reasonable and in every respect so easy to be yielded unto, if they refuse: who seeth not therein a secret implying, and a close granting of the desperateness and misery of their cause? Which shaketh and quivereth, and shrinketh as it were in the sinews, to think that there should be any buckling towards;[13] and therefore doth wisely shift of all honest and lawful means of trial, as having nothing to uphold it, but [10] tyranny and blood.

Now, because they would gladly know Martin, I will here set them down a way whereby they may not only know him, but (that which is more delightful unto them) they may quench their thirst with his blood if they will: provided that they be able to make their cause good against him by the word of God.

I do therefore by this my protestation make it known to the whole church of England, especially unto our magistrates, more especially unto our gracious sovereign, and unto all posterities to come, that I who do now go under the name of Martin Marprelate, do offer personally to appear, and there to make my self known in open disputation, upon the danger not only of my liberty but also of my life, to maintain against all our bishops, or any else whosoever that [11] *shall dare in any scholastical manner to take their parts, the cause of the church government, which is now in controversy betwixt me and our prelates: so that I may have this condition following inviolably kept and observed, vz. That for appearing, or for anything that I have either published or caused to be published in this cause, I be not dealt with, or molested, except they overthrow me by the word of God, which if they do, confusion be upon me if I do not yield. But if in this encounter I overthrow them (as I make no question of it, if they dare abide the push), then they to truss up and be packing to ROME, and to trouble our church no longer. Provided also, that if any of the puritans will join with me, and venture their lives in the cause, it may be lawful for them to come in freely against these dragons in disputation.* [12]

I call thee here again (good reader) to witness the indifferency of my challenge and offer, and to judge what account thou oughtest to make of our present church government by lord archbishops and bishops, upon the refusal of the former condition by them; and whether thereupon I may not justly and lawfully proclaim the victory over them in manner following.

Be it known unto all states, churches, and universities under heaven; and unto all men, either present or to come, of what estate or condition soever: that inasmuch as Master Fenner's and Master Penry's syllogisms, whereby Doctor Bridges his book is confuted, and the cause of reformation unanswerably proved;[14] Master Travers',[15] Master Cartwright's,[16] and Master Gilby's,[17] the *Demonstration of Discipline*,[18] the *Abstract*, the *Counter-Poyson*,[19] Master Tyndale, Master Frith, Master Barnes,[20] Master Hooper,[21] Master Pilkington,[22] Master Foxe,[23] and Master Martin Marprelate's writ-
[13]   ings, together with other learned discourses mo;[24] whereby the corruption and the unlawfulness of the places and proceedings of lord bishops are shamefully laid open unto the world, are as yet unanswered; and likely to be no otherwise confuted, than with slanders, ribaldry, scurrility, reviling, imprisonment, and torture; and inasmuch as they dare not maintain their cause against me by open and public disputation; that therefore they do manifestly confess their cause and proceedings to be clean foiled, overthrown, and made even with the ground, in such sort, as beside whorish impudency, halter, axe, bonds, scourging and racking, with such other weapons as were bequeathed unto them by their forefathers, the ancient enemies and persecutors of the church, they have not left any instrument to defend themselves.

And let them be sure, seeing they dare come to no lawful way of trial with me, that there shall not be a post in any great street or place of concourse, almost in the land, but I will make an affix, and set up this my
[14]   foresaid declaration of the victory had over them, to their shame: and I will also make foreign nations ring of their villainies and ungodliness, if the publishing of their doings in Latin can do it.[25]

And as for myself, my life, and whatsoever else I possess, I have long agone set up my rest,[26] making that account of it, as in standing against the enemies of God and for the liberty of his church, it is of no value in my sight. My life in this cause shall be a gain to the church, and no loss to my self, I know right well: and this is all the reckoning which by the assistance of the Lord I will make as long as I live, of all the torments they have devised for me. I am blamed of many in this mine attempt, not only for throwing myself into great danger, but also for the utter undoing of my wife and children. I do thank them with all my heart for their care over those poor souls, and commend them for their secrecy and wisdom, that in knowing my wife and my children, they have not, by showing their unmeasurable love towards them, discovered me. You see what it is when wise men have the handling of a matter. I perceive if these men were not very provident and wary, that Martin could not be long unknown. For I tell you, if a man's wife and children be once known, it is not possible that he can be secret any long time; and yet methinks that all their wisdom and all their care over my wife and children, when the matter is well weighed, is scant worth three straws. For what if Martin had neither wife nor child in all his life, are they not then something too much overweened in their own conceit, who give out that he hath both? Will you believe me then if I tell you the truth? To put you therefore out of all doubt, I may safely protest unto you with a good conscience, that howsoever the speech may seem strange unto many, yet the very truth is, that hitherto I never had wife nor child in all my life: not that I never mean to have any; for it may be, notwithstanding all the rage and barking of the Lambethetical whelps, I may be married, and that ere it be long.[27]

[15]

[16]

For methinks this should be enough that two only of the Metropolitans of the land should continue maiden (though I fear scarce virgin) priests.[28] But whensoever I am married, it would do me good at the heart to see a dozen of good and honest lord bishops dance at my wedding, saving that as Master Tyndale has very well noted, *Practise of Prelates*, page 374, it is not possible naturally, there should be any good and honest lord bishop.[29] Well, howsoever it goes with me, you see how little cause as yet my wife and children have to fear that Antichrist of Lambeth and his instruments.

To omit these matters, will they know indeed why I fear them not, and wherefore they ought not to terrify thee (good reader, if the Lord hath bestowed upon thee the same mind that he hath vouchsafed me)? Why surely it is, because they against whom I deal, have so provoked the anger of God, and the prayers of his church against them, as stand long they cannot, if either the Lord be true of his promise, or the prayers of the church made in faith, can be heard. Of both which I make no question. Hereunto you may add, that I fear them not, inasmuch as the end wherefore I have taken this work in hand was only the glory of God, by delivering his church from the great tyranny and bondage wherewith these tyrants do oppress the same. I dealt not herein, as the Lord knoweth, because I would please myself, or my reader, in a pleasant vein of writing. If that be the thing I sought or seek after, then let my writings be buried in the grave of all proud prelates; that is, never mentioned in the church of God without detestation. Even so was it as far from me, that by sharpening my pen against them, I should thereby (as some foolishly give out) make a way for

[17]

myself, or other great men, unto their livings and promotion.[30] For if the possession and enjoying of a good conscience, but for one day alone, be not

[18] more dear to me than all their ungodly pomp and ambitious preeminence; then let mine adversaries prey upon me, and let my reward be nothing else, but the very bitterness of their malicious hearts. I have, I thank God, of mine own, wherewith I am better content than they are with all their spoil and robbery.[31] And if I wanted, I could tell how to live in an honest calling, with better credit in the church of God, than all the lord bishops of England do: and I may safely say, it is so far from me to bring the church livings into the hands of any but the ministers and officers thereof, that I can no more abide church-robbery in a temporal man, than I can brook sacrilege in a presumptuous priest: as I hate the one, so I abhor the other.[32]

But as concerning the laying open of their bishoprics to the spoil of such cormorants as gape for their downfalls, thereby only to enrich themselves, I greatly muse that our prelates will be so overseen as to charge me therewith.[33] For it is well known that none of them all, no not the proudest priest

[19] in the land, doth so cumber himself in caring how he should live that comes after him: but that now all of them begin prettily, either of their wonted love to themselves, or of their natural spite to their successors, to take such charitable order, as that if they may have their wills, I hope there shall not be much left in a while to allure any covetous courtier to the spoil.[34] Wherein, no dispraise to any, I must needs commend for their forecast in this point a couple of as arrant bishops (for it were pity to bereave the devil of his due commendation) as any the land yieldeth. The men, or rather beasts that I mean, are John London and Thomas Winchester: whereof the one at Fulham, the other by Whitney in Oxfordshire, have so contended in throwing down elms, as if the wager had been whether of them should most have impoverished their bishoprics.[35] And yet I blame not Mar-elm so much as Cooper for this fact: because it is no less given him by his name to

[20] spoil elms, than it is allotted him by the secret judgement of God to mar the church. Whereas a man of Master Cooper's age and occupation, so well seen in that trade, might easily know that tubs made of green timber must needs leak out of all cry. And yet now I consider with myself, I do not so greatly marvel at the matter: for he that makes no conscience to be a deceiver, and a false prophet in the building of the church, will not stick for his gain to be a deceitful workman in making of tubs.

Well, concerning the care that our prelates have in leaving of things behooveful for their successors, I may truly say, that were it not more for fear of law than for any conscience of the maintenance of the ministry, the whole bishopric, even today before tomorrow, would not yield a lord bishop so much as might purchase him an handsome halter to hang himself with, as the poet sayth.[36] Therefore let them never talk more for shame (as their T. C. doth) of the care they have that the church's maintenance should not decay.[37]

And as herein their spoil and robbery is apparent, so on the other side   [21] their tyranny and bloodthirsty proceedings [against good men] is unexcusable:[38] and yet is the manner of their proceedings more intolerable and dangerous to the state, than their very practises themselves.

First, you see they may examine of what they will. For who can let them, when they be both sole judges and sole witness themselves, and none other by, but the poor examinate? To which effect, what is the seat of justice they commonly use in these cases, but only some close chamber at Lambeth, or some obscure gallery in London palace? Where, according to the true nature of an evil conscience, that flyeth and feareth the light, they may juggle and foist in what they list without controlment; and so attempt (if they will) to induce the party examined to be of a conspiracy with them, to pull the crown off her Majesty's head.[39] And I put case they should do so   [22] (as here you see is a way laid open for them, to broach any conspiracy in the world): what remedy should the party that stands there alone have, by appeaching or complaining?[40] Any other trow you than this: he lies like a puritan knave; I'll have the *scandalum magnatum* against him: for he hath slandered the high commission, and the president of her Majesty's council, namely, my Lord of Canterbury's worship?[41] And here behold the poor man's reward.

Secondly, you must lay your hand on the book, and not know whereunto you must be sworn: yea, they be so honest, that they will compel you to accuse yourself, or else you shall lie by it; which ungodly practise of theirs, savoreth so rankly of the Spanish inquisition, that it is flat contrary to all humanity, the express laws of the land, and the doctrine of our church.[42] For the law is so far from compelling any to appeach himself in a cause wherein either life, goods, or good name is called into question, that   [23] it altogether condemneth those for oppressors of the common liberty of her Majesty's subjects, and for unreasonable violators and wresters of all good order of justice, that will urge or require any such thing at their hands, as may more at large appear in a plain statute of the 25 of Henry 8, in the title of heresy.[43] And therefore men may see what account they ought to make of those shameless speeches of that worthy grayhead, Mistress Cooper's husband: who as he hath been long since too old to blush, so did he not let, openly to avouch, that before God, there was no other way of trial, nor no state could stand and continue without it.[44]

To conclude this point. It is too manifest, that 1. by these their private whispering examinations in corners, 2. by the oath thus administered at random, 3. by the enforcing of men to accuse themselves, our bishops with their wretched favourers may in time (as it is not unlikely but they will) bring one of these mischievous inconveniences upon her Majesty's best subjects: vz. either perpetual imprisonment, loss of ears or some other limb, or else (as I said before) an enforcement to conspire the overthrow of her Majesty's crown and dignity. Whether these matters be not worthy the consideration of the gravest councillors in the land, I leave it to the judgement of every true Englishman that loveth his Prince and the liberty of his country. But Martin is an intolerable busy fellow, for molesting the state of the clergy in this sort.

Now I hasten to other matters, where it may be, good reader, thou wilt ask what was in that Pistle of mine?[45] To tell thee true, I sigh to remember the loss of it, it was so pretty, and so witty. And I know if thou hadst it, thou wouldest lay it up among other thy honest recreations for thy delight.

First then, there was set down for thy learning, the true, proper, and natural definition, or rather description, of Martinism, to this effect: that to be a right Martinist indeed, is to be neither Brownist,[46] Cooperist, Lambethist, schismatic, papist, atheist, traitor, nor yet lord bishop; but one that is at defiance with all men, whether he be French, Dutch, Spanish, catercap, pope, or popeling, so far forth as he is an enemy to God and her Majesty. Whereupon, I remember, I did then ask the reader whether it were not good being a Martinist: and as I did then, so do I still heartily rejoice to think that all the honestest and best affected subjects her Majesty hath, will one day become Martinists.

Then among all the rimers and stage-players, which my lords of the clergy had suborned against me. I remember Mar-Martin, John a Cant his hobby-horse, was to his reproach newly put out of the Morris, take it how he will, with a flat discharge for ever shaking his shins about a May-pole again while he lived.[47] Hereabouts I placed Doctor Underhill and Doctor Wood of All Souls College,[48] to be chaplains unto a certain chaste ficker of Hell, called Sir James King, of Hertfordshire;[49] and somewhere it was, that I so slived Dick Bancroft over the shoulder, as his chaplainship is never able to recover his credit, if that Pistle of mine be once published.[50] Next to this (as I take it) followed a preamble to an epitaph upon the death of old Andrew Turn-coat, to be sung antiphonically in his grace's chapel,[51] on Wednesdays and Fridays, to the lamentable tune of Orawhynemeg.[52]

Then was there a certain vulneral[53] sermon of old Lockwood of Sarum,[54] upon the sudden and untimely death of his said brother Perne, wherein he did undertake for him, that he was never a puritan in his life, but always an orderly man, and a maintainer of the state of the clergy. And if his grace did appoint any other to preach at his old good master's funerals,[55] but only this quick-witted Bridges, he was certainly foully overseen. For there would have been such a mess and such a match, such a pair of saints, the one living and the other dead, as I believe the *Legenda aurea* would not yield the like:[56] both old standards, both proculstants,[57] both catercaps, both priests, both deans, both hypocrites, both asses: why sans mercy said I, etc. But alas, chave haulf forgotten the rest.[58] [27]

After this, I had a fling at these puritans, concerning whom, my desire is, that wherein I am faulty, ye puritans would set me down the particulars. It is odds, I shall some way or other hear of it. For albeit there have been some jars of unkindness betwixt us, yet I would have you know, that I take the worst of you, in regard of his calling, to be an honester man than the best lord bishop in Christendom. The report goeth, that some of you have preached against me, and I believe it in part; well look to it, for I may happen be even with you in this manner: I will not rest till I have learned what it is that ye have said of me; and if I find it to be a just reproof, I will mend my fault, be as angry as ye will: if unjust, trust unto it, I will hold on my course, and there is one rap more than ye looked for.[59]

The next pretty thing to this was, to my remembrance, Chaplain Some confuted with the bald sheath of his own dagger, wherein all his short cuts, Latin apothegs, and childish pen-and-inkhorn proverbs were wholly inverted upon himself.[60] I then said, and so say I still, that if it were not for those whom our bishops hate and persecute, it is known they would make a mad piece of confuting of the Brownists and other sectaries amongst them: as may appear by that which they suffer to come out so nakedly and patchedly against them, by this father Robert of theirs.[61] And this is he that hath crazed his brain at Lambeth, and his conscience at Girton;[62] whose bald writings, without sap or edge, unworthy of a boy of twelve year old, have (I am persuaded) made and will make (if it be not looked unto) more Brownists in our church, than all that ever they have hitherto published themselves. [28]

This (if you know him not) is the very same doctor, that in publishing three pretty treatises, hath so handled the matter, by a geometrical dimension, that the last (if it be well scanned) is the same with the first, and the middlemost, all one with them both:[63] the man in all likelihood never goeth without a little saunce-bell in his pocket, and that doth nothing else but *Ting, Ting, Ting*; and what doth it *Ting*?[64] If you give good ear, nothing else, I warrant you, but My sermons, My writings, My reasons, [29]

My arguments, and all is My, My, My, as if the depth of all learning were included in the channel of his brain.[65] This is even he, that let him write as many books as he will (though he should never so much disguise himself, and conceal his name), yet we should be sure to know him by one of these rapping figures: either by hitting the white, or by missing the butt, or by resting on his reason, or by thirty-two dozen of full points, or by some such broken wooden dish or other.[66]

[30]   Then was there recorded a brave agreement which Martin of his courtesy is contented to make with the bishops, which agreement was taught once in the pulpit by a certain lame ficker of Warwick, a chaplain of their own stamp.[67] His text was out of Matthew, *agree with thine adversary quickly*. We have an adversary, said he, who is that? The devil. How shall we agree with the devil? Even thus, said he, and if you mark, it is a good lesson: shake him off, never come nigh him, nor have nothing to do with him. Even so, I'll be bound that myself, and all the puritans, shall agree with the bishops while the world stands: on this condition, that we shake them off, never come nigh them, nor have nothing to do with them.

    'Twere pity to forget Martin's *Tolbooth*,[68] in the midst whereof were many rare conceits: as a great ashen chair, wherein John a Bridges was placed by patent during his life; and Leonard Wright appointed to keep it clean, by scraping and rubbing the feet of it.[69] Round about this Tolbooth were placed a foul rank of catercaps, conferring and disputing hotly about the third declension, the churching of women, or such like matters of life [31]   and death.[70] On the first form sat in rank John, John, and William; on the second, Richard, Richard, and Thomas; on a third, John, William, and Marmaduke, etc.[71]

    After this followed something, a large confutation of Friar Frégeville,[72] and of wringlefaced Wright;[73] within which compass were contained, 1. a manifest proof that reformation importeth the overthrow of the state of the clergy, and that according unto the doctrine of our church; 2. an antithesis between our Saviour Christ, and that cursed pope of Lambeth, John Whitgift; 3. a proof of many of those theses which that unhappy boy of mine published so untimely: but as for him and his elder brother, together with that blind ass Pasquill, I will have them talked with elsewhere.[74] With these and such like points, with an honourable mention of all noble soldiers, a complaint of the loss of my papers, and the misery of sea journeys, I ended my Pistle, being the first tome of *More Work for the Cooper*. And here also I end this my protestation. Desiring thee (good [32]   reader), according unto thy place, to be careful of the relief and deliverance of the distressed printers. In requital whereof, if thou canst but learn the day of my marriage (for as I protested unto thee without all fraud and ambiguity, I was never as yet married in my life), thou shalt be better welcome unto me, than the best lord catercap of them all, and so tell them from me when thou wilt.

[Errata]

Page 6, line 23, read single for siuule. Page 21, there is something twice set down, mend that thyself if thou wilt, for I promise thee I cannot. Yet hear me a word afore thou goest, an thou be a goodfellow, commend me to George Boleyn, dean of Lichfield, by these four tokens: 1. the wind is south, the wind is south, 2. that he lately taught in Coventry, that men may fall from grace, 3. that taking himself with a fault in the same sermon, he said, there I lied, there I lied, 4. being at another time in the pulpit, hearing his dog cry, he out with this text: why how now, ho, can you not let my dog alone there? Come *Spring*, come *Spring*.[75]

Appendix. Running heads in the Marprelate tracts

Spelling is modernized by the same conventions as the remainder of the edition, except that abbreviations are not expanded and original capitalization is retained. Apostrophes are added to possessives with a final "s," but the final "s" has not been added to possessive abbreviations (e.g., "M. D. prudency"). There are no running heads in the broadsheet *Schoolpoints* or in the final tract, the *Protestation*.

THE *EPISTLE*

A2v–4v   An Epistle to the terrible Priests of the Confocation house.
B1r–4v   The Epistle to the terrible Priests of the Confocation house.
C1r–G4r   An Epistle to the terrible Priests of the Confocation house.

THE *EPITOME*

A2v   The second Epistle to the terrible Priests.
B1r   A very portable book, a horse may carry it if he be not too weak.
B1v   Challenged for his sermon.   A smooth style.
B2r   How M. D. played my L. of Winchester's fool in his sermon.
B2v   Black Ox hath trodden on his grace's foot.   State of the question.
B3r   Ministers of the old Testament.   Ministers of the new Testament.
B3v   What offices and officers the Church is to be governed by.
B4r   M. D. prudency, in omitting that which he cannot prove.
B4v   What offices and officers the Church is to be governed by.
C1r   Dean o Lincoln (sometimes unlearned John Whitgift) his question.
C1v   John Elmar, the B. of London his book.
C2r   Paul hath gone beyond his commission, saith John of London.
C2v   Bellarmine's opinion, and the M. D. all one in this point.
C3r   William Woodcock's divinity.   Peter and Paul confuted.
C3v   His grace is able now to make the puritans to stoop, I warrant you.
C4r   William Woodcock's divinity.
C4v   A proposition fet from Rome and like to breed a Jesuit.

HAY ANY WORK FOR COOPER

THESES MARTINIANAE

THE JUST CENSURE

Notes

1 THE *EPISTLE*

1. *Oh read over* responding to an epigraph on the title page of John Bridges' *Defence*, "Take it up and Read" (from Augustine, *Confessions*, 8.12.29).
2. *Presbyter, Priest or Elder* three etymologically related words: "priest" is a contraction of "presbyter," which derives from the Greek word for "elder." Disagreements over their precise scriptural meanings underlay much ecclesiological debate in the period. *Doctor of Divility* punning on "Divinity." *Sarum* Salisbury (the ecclesiastical name, derived from the Latin Sarisburia).
3. *prevented* anticipated.
4. *Fyckers* sometimes "fickers": vicars, imitating the Welsh or West Country dialect substitution of "f" for "v" (cf. the characteristic f/v substitutions by Captain Fluellen in Shakespeare's *Henry V*). In this case, the substitution might play on "fuckers": the earliest *OED* citation of "fucker" is from 1598, but the spelling used in the disapproving reference in *Martins Months Minde* (1589) to Martin's use of *"Parsons, Fukars, and Currats"* (F1v) suggests earlier uses: "fuk" was a common period spelling of "fuck" (*OED*). *Currats* curates: commonly spelled in the period without the "e," but here with a possible pun on "cur" combined with "rats."
5. *past grace* in university language, having fulfilled the requirements for a degree; here, punning on the idea that these officials were "beyond" grace or redemption.
6. *Confocation House* Convocation (with the dialect f/v substitution), the traditional legislative assembly of the clergy of the Church of England.
7. *Bouncing* blustering, boastful, swaggering (*OED*).
8. *Fickers General* vicars general (with the dialect f/v substitution): officials deputed to represent bishops or archbishops in certain ecclesiastical functions. *Paltripolitan* Martinist coinage that combines "paltry" with metropolitan, the title a bishop assumes when exercising extra-diocesan powers. *Holy League of Subscription* Martinist conflation that associates John Whitgift's efforts to have clergy "subscribe" to his 1584 articles (see Introduction, xxi) with the activities of France's militantly Catholic Holy League.
9. *poisoned* pun on "puissant" (used above in the address to the bishops).
10. *Duns* capitalized here in the original, and spelled "duns" throughout this tract, possibly to emphasize the derivation of "dunce" from the scholastic theologian

Johannes Duns Scotus (*c.* 1265–1308), whose writing was associated with hair-splitting quibbles: Martin condemns Bridges for the same fault.

11. *Cambridge* John Bridges had been a student at Pembroke Hall, Cambridge, graduating BA (1556), when he was made a fellow of the College, and MA (1560). A "patch" is a fool or clown: Martin characterizes Bridges as a performer of nonsense on behalf of the episcopate and might have expected readers to remember that Cardinal Thomas Wolsey's domestic jester was nicknamed Patch.

12. *Cartwright* Thomas Cartwright (1535–1603), one of the most prominent Presbyterian divines; see *ODNB*. His 1570 Cambridge lectures offered the first systematic exposition in England of Presbyterianism, the platform of which he honed in books published in polemical battle with John Whitgift: *A Replye* (Hemel Hempstead? 1573), *The Second Replie* (Heidelberg, 1575), and *The Rest of the Second Replie* (Basle, 1577). In the next paragraph Martin taunts Whitgift for giving Cartwright the last word in this exchange; see note 23 below.

13. *Cant.* abbreviation for Canterbury, but punning on "cant" as the language of vagabonds and thieves (*OED v³*).

14. *Mass Dean* referring to John Bridges, dean of Salisbury; ostensibly an abbreviation for "Master," but playing on the Catholic implication of "Mass."

15. *twenty fists about your ears* Martin claimed in a later tract that he here meant only that others would take pen in hand to write on behalf of the Presbyterian cause (*Hay any Work*, 102). But his opponents justifiably read this passage as suggesting physical violence: Richard Bancroft, e.g., complained that "*Martin* in his first booke threateneth *Fists*" (*Sermon*, 83), a charge repeated in Cooper's *Admonition*, 40, 51, 61.

16. *in the title* on the title page. The 1586 Star Chamber decree for order in printing had attempted to regularize book licensing. Martin banteringly suggests that Bridges had failed to get his book approved for publication, though two sentences later he takes the opposite tack and mocks Whitgift for his poor judgment in "overseeing" the *Defence*.

17. *Cosin* Dr Richard Cosin (1548?–97), diocesan chancellor to John Whitgift, high commissioner, and one of the period's most prominent ecclesiastical lawyers. His *Answer to ... a Certeine Factious Libell* (1584) defended the lawfulness of pluralism and a non-preaching ministry, and his *Apologie for Sundrie Proceedings* (1593) responded to attacks on the *ex officio* oath and became the standard defense of high commission and the church courts (*ODNB*).

18. *had their grace ... in Flanders* Martin suggests that the bishops had allowed Bridges, Cosin, and other opponents of reform to graduate only after they had passed the "practical" test of skill in slander: in university language, a "grace" was a dispensation required to take a degree. Martin's gibe plays with the typographical similarity of "Flanders" (if spelled with a long "s") and "slanders." Flanders, the location of the English College founded by William Allen in 1568 and the University of Louvain, was a primary center for exiled English Catholics and for the training of English seminary priests. This association of

Flanders with "slanderous" Catholic writing is repeated in the para-Martinist tract attributed to Throkmorton, *M. Some Laid Open in his Coulers* (La Rochelle, 1589), 89.

19. *my Lord of Winchester* Thomas Cooper (*c.* 1517–94), bishop of Winchester from 1584. Cooper's anti-Martinist *Admonition to the People of England* (1589) won the bishop a role as major target in the final five Marprelate tracts. *Lambeth* Lambeth Palace, the residence of the archbishops of Canterbury.

20. *Abstract ... Counter-Poyson* referring to texts published in the "Abstract" controversy: *An Abstract, of Certain Acts of Parliament* (1583), attributed to William Stoughton, sought to publicize the legal basis of Presbyterian objections to John Whitgift's articles of subscription (see Introduction, xxi). Richard Cosin defended the church with *An Answer* (1584), and was met in turn by *A Counter-Poyson* (1584), usually attributed to Dudley Fenner. Cosin then left further defense to John Copcot (see note 22 below).

21. *public fasts* public fasts played important social, cultural, and organizational roles in the Presbyterian movement in addition to their devotional functions; church authorities consequently began to suppress unauthorized fasts in the later 1580s. See Collinson, *Movement*, 208–21, and Collinson, "Elizabethan and Jacobean Puritanism," esp. 50–56. These letters of instruction from John Aylmer (1520/21–94), bishop of London from 1577, to William Tabor, Aylmer's chaplain and archdeacon of Essex from 1585, appear not to be extant.

22. *Copcot* Dr John Copcot (d. 1590), master of Corpus Christi College, Cambridge. He responded to the Presbyterian *Counter-Poyson* (see note 20 above) in a 1584 sermon at Paul's Cross. This sermon prompted the anonymous *A Defence of the Reasons of the Counter-Poyson* (Middelburg, 1586), and Martin suggests that Copcot's subsequent silence was an admission of defeat. Copcot's sermon was not published, but *A Defence of the Reasons* prints extracts from notes taken when the sermon was delivered (A3–A4).

23. *Cartwright's books have been ... unanswered* John Whitgift replied to the Presbyterian manifesto by John Field and Thomas Wilcox, *An Admonition to the Parliament* (Hemel Hempstead? 1572) with *An Answere to a Certen Libel* (1572). When challenged by Cartwright's 1573 *A Replye*, Whitgift responded with *The Defense of the Aunswere* (1574); Cartwright returned with the two parts of *The Second Replie* in 1575 and 1577 (see note 12 above). Presbyterian polemicists frequently taunted Whitgift for allowing Cartwright the last word. In reply to Martin, Whitgift argued that further reply had been unnecessary because Cartwright's last two publications had brought nothing new to the debate (Cooper, *Admonition*, 38). For the *Admonition* controversy, see Milward, *Religious Controversies of the Elizabethan Age*, 29–33; Lake, *Anglicans and Puritans?*, ch. 1.

24. *quoth John Elmar* quoting from John Aylmer's *An Harborowe for Faithfull and Trewe Subjectes* (1559), a book written before Aylmer himself had been made bishop: "Come of you bishoppes, away with your superfluities, yeld up your thousands, be content with hundreds as they be in other reformed Churches, where be as greate learned men as you are. Let your portion be priestlike and

not princelike" (O4r–v). Martin cites Aylmer's self-implicating denunciations of episcopal luxury again in *Epitome*, 71–76, and *Hay any Work*, 105.

25. *swag* "blustering fellow" (*OED*, earliest citation); Martin uses the word again in *Hay any Work* (128, 136) to emphasize Aylmer's swearing. The word was new to Aylmer: Martin, he responded, "termeth him a Swag. What hee meaneth by that, I will not divine: but as all the rest is lewde, so surely herein hee hath a lewde meaning" (*Admonition*, 62).

26. *ilsample* play on "ensample" or "example" to suggest "ill-example" (*OED*, only citation).

27. Martin lists, respectively, John Whitgift; John Aylmer; John Woolton (*c.* 1537–94), bishop of Exeter from 1579; John Young (*c.* 1532–1605), bishop of Rochester from 1578; Thomas Cooper; William Wickham (1539–95), bishop of Lincoln from 1584 and subsequently bishop of Winchester; Edmund Freake (*c.* 1516–91), bishop of Worcester from 1584; and Richard Howland (1540–1600), bishop of Peterborough from 1584.

28. *minor* second term or premiss in a syllogism; here, that all bishops "are petty popes, and petty antichrists."

29. Martin imitates Bridges' scoffing style throughout this passage. The marginal note sends readers to the semi-quoted passages from the *Defence*: "What do they (brethren)? Saye me that againe: doo they deale thus with everie *matter whatsoever?*" (107); "yea (my *learned* masters) are ye good at that?" (113).

30. *suresby* one who is "sure" or dependable (cf. *OED* rudesby).

31. *bowls* lawn bowling. Martin repeatedly denounces Aylmer's bowling, particularly his habit of bowling on Sundays; see also below, 21, 36, 37, 42, 45.

32. *prelate of Lichfield* William Overton (1524/25?–1609), bishop of Lichfield and Coventry from 1580; he is mentioned again in *Epitome*, 77, *Schoolpoints*, 91, and *Hay any Work*, 103. A 1586 manuscript calendared in *SPR* charges Overton with "misdemeanours, corruptions, and misgovernments, notorious and infamous to the whole countrie," by means of which the bishop obtained "infinite summes of money" that "vanish in ignominie and discredit through an unknowne bottomles purse" (II, 16–17). While reports of his extravagance and venality "seem well founded," Overton, whose patron was the earl of Leicester, also had a "known preference for radical preachers of whom Marprelate must have approved" (*ODNB*).

33. *Bridewell* former royal palace used by the City of London to accommodate homeless children and to incarcerate disorderly women and petty offenders.

34. *Cato . . . margent* Dionysius Cato's *Disticha de moribus*, a late classical collection of versified moral counsel and standard Renaissance school text: Martin's talkative "standers-by" have studied Cato's rules of behavior and learned that the proper place for commentary was in a book's margent (margin).

35. *horned* referring to the bishop's mitre, cleft at the top; probably also referring to the horns of the devil and/or cuckold.

36. *bishop of Hereford* Herbert Westfaling (1531/32?–1602), bishop from 1586. Westfaling was of somewhat advanced Protestant views and had a reputation for being incorruptible: Martin appears to acknowledge his integrity but

implies that even Westfaling was corrupt by nature of the office he held (*ODNB*; Harington, *Briefe View*, II, 184).

37. *Harmony of the Confessions* citing *An Harmony of the Confessions of the Faith of the Christian and Reformed Churches*, comp. J. F. Salvart (Cambridge, 1586). Each section of the *Harmony* reprints the doctrinal statements of various European Reformed churches on a given subject; the eleventh section is "Of the ministers of the church, and of their calling and office" (337–76). Martin lists the First (1536) and Second (1566) Helvetic Confessions; the Gallican ("French") Confession (1559, modified 1571); the Bohemian Hussite or "Waldensian" Confession (1532); the Belgic ("Low Countries") Confession (1561); the Saxon Confession (1551); the Tetrapolitan ("Swevia" or Swabian) Confession (1530); and the first Scottish Confession (1560). A preliminary "Catalogue" of the confessions printed in the *Harmony* notes that the Second Helvetic Confession was "approved and subscribed unto" by the Church of Poland; Martin lists that church separately. Neither the Danish Confessio Hafnica (1530) nor the Heidelberg Confession (1563), compiled at the behest of Frederick III, Elector Palatine, are cited in this section of the *Harmony*, though Martin adds them to his list of authorities.

38. *Thomas Thomas* (1553–88), printer to Cambridge University from 1583. Thomas printed several works of Calvinist theology, including texts by such leading English Presbyterians as William Fulke and Walter Travers, justifying Martin's description of him as "puritan." *STC* does not list Thomas as the translator of the *Harmony*, but the attribution is plausible: a scholar and lexicographer, Thomas compiled a Latin–English dictionary and edited Ovid (McKerrow, *Dictionary*, 264–65; McKitterick, *History*, 73–108; *ODNB*).

39. *the bishops have called them in* Whitgift prevented the London publication of the *Harmony* and then suppressed the edition Thomas printed in Cambridge (Arber, *Transcript*, I, 543; McKitterick, *History*, 101; Strype, *Annals*, III, pt 1, 650).

40. For Robert Waldegrave, printer to the Marprelate project, see Introduction, xlix–l. Waldegrave's shop was raided in April 1588 after he had printed *The State of the Church of Englande* (1588), popularly known as the *Dialogue*; Diotrephes, an interlocutor in the dialogue, is a bishop. In May, the court of the Stationers' Company ordered Waldegrave's press, type, and tools "defaced and made unserviceable" (Arber, *Transcript*, I, 528; Greg and Boswell, eds., *Records*, 28). Martin elaborates on Waldegrave's fate below, 23–25, and returns to the incident in *Hay any Work*, 133–35.

41. *We believe . . . any other* quoting from the Calvinist Gallican Confession (1559, modified 1571), as printed in *Harmony of the Confessions* (1586), 359; see also note 37 above.

42. *at a dead lift* (side note): as a last resort, in extremity (*OED*).

43. *our own English Confession* referring to part two of *Apologia ecclesiae anglicanae* (1562), by John Jewel, bishop of Salisbury, selections from which were printed in *Harmony of the Confessions* (1586); see note 37 above. Jewel cites Gregory the Great, *Epistolae*, lib. 5, epist. 18, in which Gregory protests the title of

"Ecumenical" or "Universal" bishop assumed by the Patriarch of Constantinople.

44. *dumb ministers* or "dumb dogs" (from Isaiah 56:10), phrases used by reformers to describe ministers who read the liturgy and homilies, but who did not preach sermons.

45. *sent home by Weeping Cross* suffer grievous disappointment or failure (proverbial; *OED*).

46. *corner caps* four-cornered caps worn by clergy; Martin often also uses "catercap." For an illustration, see the woodcut on the front cover. *tippets* now a band worn over the surplice, at the time the tippet resembled a scarf, stole, or graduate's hood (*ODCC*). Reformers objected to these components of clerical dress because of their link to Catholic practice.

47. *all is fish that comes to the net* proverbial.

48. Aylmer in reply defended himself, but in so doing revealed that Martin's story was substantially accurate: since the stolen cloth was found on his lands at Fulham Manor, Aylmer argued, ownership "was altered and transferred" to the lord of the manor, himself (*Admonition*, 52). Martin responds in *Hay any Work*: "I am glad John of London you will not deny but you have the dyers' cloth, make restitution then" (136).

49. *Bonner* Edmund Bonner (d. 1569), Marian bishop of London notorious among Protestants for his enforcement of laws against (Protestant) heresy.

50. *Old Swan* public house off Upper Thames Street just to the west of London Bridge, next door to Dyers' Hall.

51. *Mistress Lawson* Margaret Lawson was evidently well known for her public challenges of church officials; scattered references to her are found in texts connected with the Marprelate and Coppinger–Hacket controversies. Martin respected her sharp wit (see below, 44, and *Hay any Work*, 131). Aylmer in reply denied this incident, claiming that if he had heard such "impudent and unwomanly speech" from Lawson, he was "not so soft, but shee shoulde have felt of discipline, and of the Queenes authoritie" (*Admonition*, 56). *Paul's Gate* located in the northeast corner of the Cathedral wall, this gate was the most direct exit from Paul's Cross and so a good site for public harangues. *unsavory salt* see Matthew 5:13.

52. *Bridewell* prison where "disorderly" women were punished. Whitgift in reply acknowledged making the threat to incarcerate Lawson, though he denied that the cause was the story Martin tells: "This is a notorious untrueth. For neither did he, nor *D. Perne* ever heare (but of this Libeller) that shee spake any such wordes of him. But in trueth, aswell for the immodestie of her tongue, wherein she excelleth beyond the seemelinesse of an honest woman, as also for her unwomanly and skittish gadding up & down to Lambehith, & from thence in companie unfit for her, without her owne husband, he threatned to send her to Bridewel, if she reformed not the same: which he meaneth to performe if she continue her lightnesse" (*Admonition*, 39). A document calendared in *SPR* records Whitgift's threat to send Lawson to Bridewell (II, 35–36). Martin defends Lawson from the charge of "lightnesse" in *Hay any Work*, 131.

53. *Perne* Dr Andrew Perne (1519?–89), dean of Ely, master of Peterhouse, Cambridge, and John Whitgift's close friend; see also notes 70, 84, 144, and 174 below. Perne was known for his temporizing shifts from Protestantism to Catholicism then back to Protestantism during the reigns of Edward VI, Mary, and Elizabeth; he appears under such names as Doctor Turncoat, Andrew ambo, Father Palinode, and the old turner throughout the tracts (the names play on the Latin *pernere*, to turn). See *ODNB*; for Perne's Elizabethan reputation, see Collinson, "Perne the Turncoat." Margaret Lawson's gibe refers to Perne's prominent role in the 1557 Marian council that posthumously condemned as a heretic the Reformed theologian Martin Bucer (1491–1551), Regius professor of divinity at Cambridge; in consequence, Bucer's remains were exhumed and publicly burned. In a passage that appeared in all Elizabethan editions of *Acts and Monuments*, John Foxe described the "slanderous" and "railing" sermon Perne preached at the sentencing of Bucer's body.

54. Margaret Lawson's husband was Thomas Lawson (*Hay any Work*, 131). Whitgift's uncle, named Shaller (here, "Shorie"), was a verger at St Paul's Cathedral.

55. *Stanhope* Sir Edward Stanhope (*c.* 1546–1608), civil lawyer and high commissioner with a reputation as an "implacable opponent of puritans" (*ODNB*). Lucius Tarquinius Superbus, the last Roman king (534–510 BCE), was commonly invoked to represent arrogant, insolent pride. *Mistress Blackwell* unidentified.

56. *book entitled an* Answer referring to Dudley Fenner, *Defence of the Godlie Ministers, against the Slaunders of D. Bridges* (Middelburg, 1587); see Introduction, xxiv. *Sohow* variation of "so-ho" and imitating John Bridges' colloquial sentence beginnings, e.g., "Nay who there," "Well, well," "A ha," "And how now" (*Defence*, 76, 85, 99, 119).

57. *Chard* Thomas Chard, the bookseller who published Bridges' *Defence*, had been awarded legal protection against action for debt. Martin implies that Chard was in trouble because nobody wanted to buy Bridges' book. Whitgift claimed in response that the protection had nothing to do with debts incurred to produce Bridges' 1,400-page tome but refused to supply an alternative explanation: "That which he calleth a Protection, *Chard* had from the Lords of her Majesties privy Counsell, upon charitable and good causes mooving their Lordships" (*Admonition*, 40). Chard had also published Richard Cosin's *Answer* (1584) to the Presbyterian *Abstract* (see above, notes 17 and 20), a book Martin claims had no market other than as paper for kitchen use. Martin returns to Chard in *Hay any Work*, 131.

58. *Gammer Gurton's Needle* comic play, printed in 1575 and probably written in the 1550s by William Stevenson, but (implausibly) rumored in the period to have been written by Bridges. The play is mentioned again in *Epitome*, 67, 83.

59. Martin cites two works by John Bridges. *The Supremacie of Christian Princes, over all Persons throughout their Dominions* (1573) responded to arguments by

Catholic theologians Thomas Stapleton and Nicholas Sanders. The versification "of all the names attributed unto the Lord in the Bible" was published in his *Sacro-sanctum novum testamentum* ... *in hexametros versus translatum* (1604), A3r–5v, though the reference here indicates that the poem was written, and known about, much earlier. Bridges' *Sacro-sanctum* was printed by Valentine Simmes, who fifteen years earlier had helped print *Theses Martinianae* and *Just Censure*.

60. *O is* "O yes" or "Oyez" (*OED*). *this great volume* Bridges' *Defence*.

61. ob *and* sol abbreviations for "objection" and "solution," often used in theological and metaphysical controversy; the phrase was shorthand for subtle disputation.

62. *Father Bricot* French theologian Thomas Bricot (d. 1516) published scholastic commentaries on Aristotle's *Logic*, *Physics*, and *Posterior Analytics*. In 1535, royal injunctions mandating curriculum changes at Cambridge listed Bricot among the writers whose "frivolous questions and obscure glosses" were no longer to be read by arts students: see Leader, *History of the University of Cambridge*, I, 332. *Doctor Terence* possibly an ironic reference to Bricot, whom Martin (mistakenly) might have thought connected with Oxford. To call somebody a "Doctor Terence" was to compliment their prose: the Roman playwright Terence (Publius Terentius, *fl.* 166–60 BCE) was considered one of the most elegant Latin stylists.

63. *yet afterward* Martin conflates "although ... afterward" and "yet ... appeareth" from the passage he cites from Bridges.

64. *I, John of Rochester, present John Young* Martin accuses John Young (*c.* 1532–1605), bishop of Rochester, of presenting himself with a benefice. Thomas Cooper in reply acknowledged that such self-presentations were illegal but noted that if Young "hath procured a benefice in way of *Commendam* (as they call it) it is by lawe allowed, and hath bene done by other" (*Admonition*, 63). To hold a benefice *in commendam* was to receive its revenues during a vacancy, theoretically temporary but often in practice permanent; Young was allowed to hold a number of benefices in this way because his was not a rich see (*ODNB*).

65. *Learned Discourse* title by which William Fulke's Presbyterian manifesto *A Briefe and Plaine Declaration* (1584) was commonly known; see Introduction, xxii.

66. Bridges' "contrary" prayer implies that to have "preaching in all places" would be a divine punishment.

67. *Yea some ... salvation* the quotation (*Defence*, 69) is accurate, apart from a few dropped words. Bridges was trying to argue that possessing miraculous gifts, such as speaking in tongues or prophesying, was neither necessary to salvation nor proof of election. Martin returns to this sentence in *Epitome*, 83, where he addresses Bridges' argument rather than his style.

68. *treason* the idea that a priest could enjoy "superior authority over the universal body of the church" was treasonous because it undermined royal supremacy; Martin elaborates in the following paragraph. Martin returns to this passage in *Schoolpoints*, 92.

69. See note 40 above for the *Dialogue*, the popular title of *The State of the Church of Englande* (1588), attributed to John Udall and seized by authorities in April 1588. Among the dialogue's interlocutors, Tertullus speaks for Catholicism. Diotrephes, a bishop, asks, "Howe can I tell her [Elizabeth] that all is well, when I have beene constrained to tell divers preachers, that have so sore urged me with the text, that I could wish things were amended: but the Q. wil not at any hand?" Tertullus responds, "Surely, you are a very simple man, my Lord, (as though) the Queene heares what you saye to them, or they, what you saye to the Queene" (G1v).

70. *the fox Doctor Perne ... author* here and elsewhere in the tracts, Martin suggests that Perne had contributed to Bridges' *Defence*, with Bridges acting as proxy; see, e.g., *Epitome*, 67. *fox* traditional emblem in Protestant polemic for a covert Catholic: see Collinson, "Perne the Turncoat," 213–14.

71. The side note cites statute 13 Eliz. c. 1 (1571), "An act whereby certeine offences be made treason"; offences included affirming the Queen to be "an heretike, schismatike, tyrant, infidell."

72. *Sir Peter* (in text and side note): clerics were accorded the honorific title "Sir" (*OED* sir *n* 4). But the usage could also be pejorative: a "Sir John" was a simple or inferior sort of priest. As a result, Martin's "Sir Peter" scandalized Thomas Cooper: "when they speake of *Peter, Paul*, or the *Blessed Virgine Mary*, etc. whome other justlie call Saintes, their phrase in derision is, *Sir Peter, Sir Paule, Sir Marie*" (*Admonition*, A2r). Martin jokingly explains his use here of "Sir" for "St" in *Hay any Work*: since St Peter gave no allowance for a "superior priest" to wield authority over the whole church, Bridges' authority must be somebody else, and "therefore the priest whereof Dean John speaketh was Sir Peter" (106). From this moment forward, Martin repeatedly substitutes "Sir" for "St" in the names of people and churches.

73. *articles* John Whitgift's 1584 articles of belief, to which ministers were required to subscribe; for the debates over subscription, see Introduction, xxi.

74. Referring to statute 5 Eliz. c. 1 (1563), reaffirmed 13 Eliz. c. 2 (1571), which abolished "the usurped power and jurisdiction of the bishop of Rome" and prohibited any attempt to "set forth, mainteine, defend, or extoll the same usurped power: or attribute anie maner jurisdiction, authoritie, or prehemi-nence to the same."

75. *triple crown* the three-tiered papal tiara.

76. *Lateinos* misprinted "*Latenios*" in the original. The identification of the beast of Revelation 13:18 with the pope was a standard Protestant reading, codified in the marginal gloss in the Geneva Bible that Martin cites: the number 666 "signifieth Lateinus, or Latin, which noteth the Pope or Antichrist who useth in all things the Latin tongue ... and because Italie in olde time was called Latinum."

77. *I trow* I trust, I suppose. *ka* quoth (dialect or colloquial).

78. *I con thee thank* I thank you (*OED* con *v*[1] 4).

79. *Hippo* St Augustine (354–430) was bishop of Hippo, in North Africa.

80. *accidents* accompaniments, accessories, or attributes (*OED* 6a, 7).

81. *Pope Joan . . . Urban the 5* John Bale explains the rumored Englishness of both figures in his *Pageant of Popes* (1574): Bale claims that Joan, the legendary female pope, had been raised by an English monk and was therefore "called John Englishe" (56r, misnumbered "55"), and that Pope Urban V (1309–70), born Guillaume de Grimoard in Languedoc, was the son of an English physician named William (139r). *woon* acquired or seized.

82. *Clement the 5, John 22, Benedict 12* the first three Avignon popes. Martin's incorrect dates are the same as those provided in Bale's *Pageant of Popes* (130r, misnumbered "133"): Clement V fixed his residence in Avignon in 1309, and the papacy returned to Rome in 1377.

83. *ingram* ignorant (dialect).

84. *Doctor Turncoat's – Perne, I should say – scholar* Andrew Perne, dean of Ely; for his shifts between Protestantism and Catholicism, see note 53 above. An interlocutor in the para-Martinist *A Dialogue. Wherin is Plainly Laide Open* (La Rochelle, 1589) exclaims: "Doctor *Pearne*? why he is the notablest turne-coate in al this land, there is none comparable to him? Why every boy hath him in his mouth, for it is made a proverbe . . . that if one have a coate or cloake that is turned, they saye it is *Pearnd*" (D2v). Perne's "scholar" is John Whitgift: Martin refers to a period in the 1550s when Whitgift was a fellow of Peterhouse, Cambridge, while Perne was college master. Martin returns to this relationship: see below note 144.

85. *Hildebrand* Gregory VII (*c.* 1021–85), elected pope in 1073. Contemporary Protestants considered Hildebrand an ambitious tyrant: John Foxe argued that his pontificate marked the moment when the true church and true doctrine "began first to decay" (*Actes and Monumentes* (1570), ☞3r); John Bale described him as a crafty, violent servant of the devil who treasonously usurped the authority of temporal princes (*Pageant of Popes*, 82r–86r).

86. *grease* pun, for "grace."

87. *caudle of hempseed . . . plaster of neckweed* sardonic figures for the hangman's rope, which, like a caudle (a warm spiced gruel for invalids) and a medical plaster, offers a cure for life's ills.

88. *course* to hunt game with hounds; cf. the comparison of bishops with foxes later in the paragraph.

89. For Thomas Cartwright's polemical "victory" over John Whitgift, see above, 8.

90. *kneeling at the communion* Thomas Cooper in reply summarized the church's position on this issue: kneeling was "an externall gesture" (*Admonition*, 120), of no signification in itself. But to reformers, genuflexion was associated with Catholic worship, and standing or sitting to receive the communion, as advocated by Martin Bucer ("Aretius"), was the opposite of kneeling, not evidence for its acceptability. *SPR* calendars many texts that include objections to kneeling.

91. *pastor and a doctor* the scriptural authority for both offices, and the division of their responsibility within a parish, was clear to Presbyterians: "he that teacheth, which is the doctor: he that exhorteth, which is the pastor" (*Hay*

any Work, 113). But in the section of the *Defence* Martin cites, Bridges questioned the proof texts Presbyterians offered for this separation of duties (226ff.). Martin replies here that the Presbyterian ideal of two spiritual guides for each congregation remedied, rather than supported, the church's tolerance of non-residency.

92. *is us have I* the same apparently idiomatic phrase appears below, 32: "you think I see not your knavery? Is us do I." Possibly, "Is us do, aye" ("I" was a common spelling of "aye"); "is" might be a colloquial or dialect elision (e.g., "bless"), or variant spelling (e.g., "yes").

93. *the Papa* the pope.

94. *Sir Edward Horsey* (d. 1583), soldier, diplomat, and captain of the Isle of Wight. John Bridges was nominated dean of Salisbury in late 1577. No evidence has been discovered to support (or challenge) the charge of simony made here.

95. *Tarleton* Richard Tarleton (d. 1588), comic actor famous for his jigs and extemporized routines; he is mentioned again in *Hay any Work*, 137. Anti-Martinist writers invoked Tarleton to paint Martin as a scoffing fool (see Introduction, lxiii). The cellars of Fulham Palace, the residence of the bishops of London, were occasionally used as a prison, notoriously so by the Marian bishop of London, Edmund Bonner.

96. *made the porter of his gate a dumb minister* John Aylmer did allow his unlearned and (literally) purblind porter to serve a congregation in Paddington, and in reply justified the appointment on the grounds that "no Preacher coulde be had" for the impoverished living (*Admonition*, 54). Martin responds in *Hay any Work*, 136. The appointment would also be mentioned in "Certain motions for a conference on religion," a reform document prepared for the 1589 parliament (Hartley, ed., *Proceedings*, II, 454–55). Martin's phrasing probably also suggests the devil-porter of hell gate from theatrical tradition.

97. *Stanhope* for the high commissioner Edward Stanhope, see above, note 55. The court of high commission was England's highest ecclesiastical court; it was particularly unpopular among reformers for its use of the oath *ex officio* (see Introduction, xxii).

98. *cut down the elms at Fulham* Martin accuses Aylmer of plundering his episcopal estate by selling its trees. Aylmer in reply claimed that the trees were still standing (*Admonition*, 55–56). But the bishop had in fact been reprimanded by the privy council in 1579 for clearing more than 120 acres of woods on the estate; the council renewed the charges in 1586. When Richard Bancroft became bishop of London in 1597, he sued Aylmer's heirs, alleging that his predecessor had made £6,000 from the woods, leaving him "scarce enough" for fuel (Strype, *Life of Aylmer*, 46–48, 66–67, 128).

99. *fasts* for Aylmer's efforts to discourage puritan fasts, see above, 8.

100. *bowls* Aylmer defended his bowling on Sundays by invoking Mark 2:27: "the Sabboth was made for man, and not man for the Sabboth" (*Admonition*, 57).

101. *figure* rhetorical figure, in this case anthypophora or rogatio (asking questions and immediately answering them). Martin does not cease to attack the

"figure" of John Aylmer but instead shifts to a different rhetorical figure to use against him: the anecdote.

102. *court of requests* court of equity that heard the causes of poor men.

103. *Dale* Valentine Dale (*c.* 1520–89), administrator, civil lawyer, and diplomat with wide international experience and a reputation for ready wit (*DNB*, *ODNB*).

104. *wasp . . . nose* popular idiom for being provoked to anger.

105. *but a Jack . . . be a Jack* playing on senses of "Jack" as knave, as familiar form of John, and in idioms meaning to strike (as in "Jack of the clock") or lay on blows (*OED n*¹ 1a, 2a, 6; *n*² 1c).

106. This incident was only one in a long-running dispute between John Aylmer and John Madox (Maddocks) of Fulham. Madox at one point complained to the privy council that he had been beaten by the bishop's servants while walking with his pregnant wife. Lord Burghley asked Aylmer to order his men to do Madox no injury; Aylmer blamed Madox for the affray (Strype, *Life of Aylmer*, 97–100). Aylmer in reply claimed that Whitgift had declared him the injured party in this dispute (*Admonition*, 55). But the court of requests had in fact refused the bishop's request that his man, the estate's executor, be protected from legal action. Martin responds briefly in *Hay any Work*, 136.

107. *premunire* or *praemunire facias*, a statute that covered a broad range of offences classified as challenging royal supremacy. Here and subsequently, Martin cites statute 13 Eliz. c. 12 (1571), "An act to reforme certeine disorders touching ministers of the church," which required ministers to subscribe only to the 1562 articles of religion.

108. *recusants* Catholics who refused to attend the parish church. Whitgift responded, "He saith we favour Recusants rather then Puritans, etc. Herein he doeth notoriously abuse us: though the Recusant for the most part, behaveth himself more civilly before the Magistrate then doth the *Puritane*: who is commonly most insolent, and thereby deserveth more sharpe wordes and reproofes then the other" (*Admonition*, 40).

109. *seevillains* punning on the high commission civilians (authorities on civil law) as "see-villains" (with "see" referring to episcopal see or seat).

110. *the book* Book of Common Prayer. *beggar's bush* any tree under which a beggar might find shelter (proverbial).

111. *chancellor's court* court of chancery, a court of equity intended to redress the harshness of the common law.

112. *Jesuit at Newgate* unidentified. Variations on this charge were commonplace. The Catholic priest John Ballard (d. 1586), imprisoned in 1586 in connection with the Babington plot, e.g., "obstinately affirmed, he would require no better books to prove his doctrine of Popery by, than the Archbishop's writings against Cartwright, and his Injunctions set forth in her majesty's name" (report from Sir Francis Knollys to Whitgift, in Strype, *Life of Whitgift*, I, 506). Martin later cites the Catholic William Rainolds as making similar claims in print (see below, 25).

113. *scandalum magnatum* the charge of slandering any great personage or state officer.

114. *Thackwell the printer* little is known of Roger Thackwell and the secret Catholic press he operated in a seaside cave near Rhiwledyn in North Wales. Whitgift claimed in reply that he knew nothing of the project (*Admonition*, 41), but Martin challenged this account in *Hay any Work* (133); Whitgift had in fact been informed about the press in April 1587 (PRO SP Dom. 12/200/31). For Thackwell, see Jones, *History of Printing and Printers in Wales*, 16–27, and Rogers, "'Popishe Thackwell' and Early Catholic Printing in Wales"; Gruffydd, "Gwasg Ddirgel yr Ogof yn Rhiwledyn"; Gruffydd, *Argraffwyr cyntaf Cymru*.

115. *Wolfe* the stationer John Wolfe (d. 1601) began his career by challenging the legal and economic foundations of the print trade but eventually gave up the role of renegade and became an established member of the Stationers' Company (*ODNB*). In 1587 he was made Company beadle, with the job of tracking down surreptitious printing of the kind he himself had formerly produced. To Martin, Wolfe was not only "Machiavellian" in his politic strategies, he was also "alias Machiavel" by virtue of having published, under false imprints, several titles by Machiavelli (*STC* 17158 et seq.).

116. For Robert Waldegrave, see above, 11, and Introduction, xlix–l. Whitgift in reply blamed Waldegrave for any misfortunes the printer and his family had suffered: "*Waldegrave* received justly according to his deserts, having founde before that time, greater favour then hee deserved, being a notorious disobedient & godlesse person, an unthriftie spender, & consumer of the fruits of his owne labours, one that hath violated his faith to his best and dearest friends, & wittingly brought them into danger, to their undoing. His wife & children have cause to curse all wicked and ungodly Libellers" (*Admonition*, 41). Martin rewrites this passage, with bishops as its subject, in *Hay any Work*, 134.

117. For Whitgift as a Hildebrand, see above, 18–19.

118. *another printer . . . Scottish Queen's death* Mary Queen of Scots was executed on February 8, 1587. Charterhouse was owned by the Howard family. Whitgift in reply acknowledged the existence of this secret Catholic press but denied having any responsibility for the case (*Admonition*, 42). Martin and Whitgift both probably refer to a press now thought to have operated in Arundel House, also owned by the Howards (see below, note 120).

119. *8° in half sheets* octavo volume with gatherings of four leaves (half the normal number), the result of printing both sides of the sheet from one forme on which both sides of four leaves were set, rather than from two formes, one with the "inner" side of eight leaves, the other with the "outer." The imposition was unusual, but for secret printing had the advantages of requiring fewer pages in type at one time and possibly of producing finished pages more quickly. Among the Marprelate tracts, *Theses Martinianae, Just Censure*, and *Protestation* are all octavos in half sheets.

120. *J. C., the earl of Arundel's man* John Charlewood (d. 1593), London bookseller and printer since the late 1550s; in the early 1580s he styled himself in imprints

the "servant" or "printer" to Philip Howard, thirteenth earl of Arundel (1557–95), a Catholic convert imprisoned since 1585. Two extant books are thought to have been printed by Charlewood in Arundel House in 1587–88, *STC* 1032 and 22946; both are indeed octavo editions. Charlewood apparently bought his press from Robert Waldegrave (*Hay any Work*, 133; *Admonition*, 42).

121. *called* in coram here, called to account (*OED*).

122. *by your sleeve* referring to the distinctive wide sleeves of the linen surplice.

123. *decree . . . for Waldegrave* referring to the 1586 Star Chamber decree for order in printing, the period's major attempt to control the print trade. Whitgift acknowledged in reply that the decree "had his furtherance in deede, & should have, if it were to doe againe," and described its purpose as "the maintenance of good orders among the printers" and "the suppression of inordinate persons, such as *Waldegrave* is" (*Admonition*, 42).

124. *fet* fetched.

125. *new printer . . . Orwin* the printer Thomas Orwin (d. 1593) ran into trouble with the court of Star Chamber in March 1588, and the Stationers' Company ordered him to cease printing. But in May the Stationers' Company received a letter signed by John Whitgift and John Aylmer, among others, in consequence of which Orwin was named Master Printer (Greg and Boswell, eds., *Records*, 27–28; McKerrow, *Dictionary*, 108). The reasons for Orwin's difficulties are not known, and there is no other evidence for his involvement in the secret printing of Catholic psalters, though some were indeed printed in England in the late 1570s and early 1580s (e.g., *STC* 14563.7, 17278.4 et seq.). Whitgift claimed in reply that "Hee erected no newe Printer, contrary to that decree: but used meanes by way of perswasion for that party" (*Admonition*, 42).

126. *Rainolds* William Rainolds' *A Refutation of Sundry Reprehensions* (Paris, 1583) defended the translation of the New Testament produced by the English Jesuit College in Rheims against remarks made by William Whitaker in his *Ad Nicolai Sanderi demonstrationes quadraginta* (1583); the Catholic Rainolds approvingly cited Whitgift's *Defense* (1574) for its attacks on Cartwright and the "puritan" party (e.g., 22, 24, 28, 33–34, 87). Whitgift replied, "It is no disparagement to receive testimonie of a mans adversarie" (*Admonition*, 43).

127. *Christ's descending into hell . . . hierarchy of bishops . . . name of priest* three controverted issues on which reformers argued that the church's position remained overly Catholic: the maintenance of a clerical hierarchy; the use of "priest" instead of "minister"; and the belief that Christ's descent into hell (from the Apostles' Creed) was more than a symbolic statement of his suffering on the cross. Whitgift in reply defended "superioritie among the Ministers" and the use of "priest" and sought to differentiate his interpretation of the descent from the literal "Harrowing" of Catholic teaching (*Admonition*, 44–45).

128. *Wigginton* Giles Wigginton (*fl.* 1564–97), vicar of Sedbergh, Yorkshire, until he was deprived in 1586 (*ODNB*). The argument between Whitgift and

Wigginton extended back to the late 1560s. Wigginton was among those suspected of being Martin, and he was questioned by high commission in December 1588. Proving a defiant witness, he was imprisoned for refusing the oath *ex officio*, a fate Martin duly noted in *Epitome*, 54, and *Schoolpoints*, 92. Records of Wigginton's lengthy history of troubles and examinations are calendared in *SPR*, II, 238–58.

129. *bug's words* words meant to frighten or terrify.

130. Whitgift dismissed the "tale of *Atkinson*" as a "lowde, notorious, and knowen lie" (*Admonition*, 46).

131. *Templars ... Travers* Walter Travers (1548?–1635), a leading figure of the Presbyterian movement, was appointed deputy of Temple Church in 1581. The appointment of Richard Hooker as Master in 1585 led to the contrast famously described by Thomas Fuller in *The History of the Worthies of England* (1662): "the Pulpit spake pure *Canterbury* in the *Morning*, and *Geneva* in the *Afternoon*, until *Travers* was silenced" (I, 264). Whitgift banned Travers from lecturing in 1586.

132. *Counter* or Compter, a name used for several prisons in London. The "Little Ease" was a cell designed so that a prisoner was compelled to squat the entire period of confinement, being unable to stand, sit, or lie at length.

133. *Wiburn* Percival Wiburn (1533/34–1606) ran a Genevan-model ministry in Northampton in 1570–72, backed by the earl of Leicester and probably by such local puritan notables as George Carleton, Sir Richard Knightley, Roger Wigston, Antony Cope, and Peter Wentworth (*ODNB*; Collinson, *Movement*, 79–83, 141–44, 439).

134. *Paget* Eusebius Paget (1546/47–1617), Presbyterian divine with a long history of suspension, deprivation, arrest, and imprisonment; see *ODNB*; *SPR*, I, 286–89; Collinson, *Movement*, 143, 151, 193, 405; Collinson, "Ecclesiastical Vitriol," 162–63. As Martin indicates, Paget, deprived in 1585 of ministerial employment in Kilkhampton, Cornwall, had taken work as a teacher. Paget injured his arm when young, and afterward signed himself "Lame" Paget; anti-Martinist writers repeatedly refer to his lameness, though they assume a lameness of the leg. He is mentioned again in *Hay any Work*, 120 (as suspected of being Martin), and *Just Censure*, 185. *Greenfield* (side note): Sir Richard Grenville (1542–91), naval commander (*ODNB*). Grenville, head of the most prominent family in Kilkhampton, was accused of using "unlawful violence" in evicting Paget's wife from the parsonage after her husband had been deprived. See PRO SP Dom. 12/176/58 (Grenville's response to the charge), Ritchie, "Sir Richard Grenville and the Puritans," and Sir Francis Hastings, *Letters*, no. 20, 25–27.

135. *Rhemish Testament* English translation of the Vulgate with Catholicizing textual apparatus, primarily by Gregory Martin, published in 1582 at the English College at Rheims. Sir Francis Walsingham, the earl of Leicester and others encouraged Thomas Cartwright to undertake a refutation, but Cartwright later wrote that "he had received commandement" from Whitgift in 1586 "to deale no further in it": see Cartwright, *A Confutation of the Rhemists*

Translation (Leiden, 1618), A2v. For the history of Cartwright's project, see Pearson, *Thomas Cartwright*, 198–210; Collinson, *Movement*, 235; and Lake, *Moderate Puritans*, 69–75.

136. *Raffodie* not in *OED*. Possibly a compound formed from raff (worthless jumble, trash; cf. riff-raff) and rhapsody (in the contemporary sense of confused medley), or a version of the French *raffarder* (to rail or scoff at). Capitalized in the original.

137. For the controversy over John Whitgift's 1584 articles, see Introduction, xxi.

138. For John Penry (1559–93), manager of the Marprelate project, see Introduction, xxxviff. His *A Treatise Containing the Aequity of an Humble Supplication* (Oxford, 1587) urged the need for ministers in his native Wales. The pamphlet was printed openly by a licensed printer, and was received by parliament without censure. John Whitgift, however, had Penry arrested and ordered the Stationers' Company to confiscate the edition. Penry was brought before high commission and sentenced to twelve days in prison. He discusses these events in *Th'Appellation of John Penri* (La Rochelle, 1589), 3–5, 39–43.

139. *Winchester ... execrable heresy* Thomas Cooper replied that he did not remember Penry's precise words, but that for his part he had remained seated, had not raised his voice, and had "quietly sayd, My Lord, this is not farre from Heresie" (*Admonition*, 72r).

140. *Ambrose Dudley, now earl of Warwick* (c. 1530–90), patron of the reform movement and the elder brother of Robert Dudley, earl of Leicester. The vicarage in question appears to be St Mary's, Warwick, which became vacant in August 1586. "Master Evans" has not been identified with certainty; one possibility is William Evans of Newington (mentioned in Strype, *Life of Whitgift*, I, 245; *SPR*, I, 230, 240). John Whitgift in reply noted that he had rejected Evans "for lacke of conformitie to the orders of the Church" (*Admonition*, 47).

141. *subscription which the statute requireth* statute 13 Eliz. c. 12 (1571) required subscription only to the 1562 articles of religion; reformers objected to Whitgift's insistence on subscription to his 1584 articles as well (see Introduction, xxi).

142. *sick of the spleen* here, sick to the heart (*OED* 2c).

143. *the second person* Martin accuses the archbishop of claiming to be the most powerful person in the country after the Queen; Whitgift in reply denied the charge and noted in addition that he did not "use that familiaritie with his men" (*Admonition*, 48).

144. *Perne's boy, and carried his cloakbag* for Andrew Perne, see notes 53 and 84 above. In the late 1550s, Whitgift was a fellow of Peterhouse, Cambridge, while Perne was college master; their close friendship lasted until Perne's death. According to Sir George Paule, the friendship began when Perne helped see Whitgift through an illness and then "winked" at Whitgift's Protestant views, allowing the future archbishop to remain at Cambridge rather than joining other Marian exiles abroad: see Paule, *Life of Whitgift* (1612), 3–4. The friendship attracted unfavorable contemporary comment, as

Whitgift acknowledged in a 1572 letter: "howsoever the world uncharitably judgeth of him, and of me, for using his familiarity, (being by sundry means bound unto him, and knowing him very well,) yet the day will come, when both they and we shall be known, as we are" (Strype, *Life of Whitgift*, I, 63). Martin's remark in the next sentence that Whitgift had "leapt lustily" when he was Perne's "boy" might be a sexual innuendo: cf. *Just Censure*, where Martin Senior describes Whitgift as Perne's "darling" (180). In reply, Whitgift bypassed the question of the friendship to focus on the literal charge: "He was never D. *Perns* boy, nor under him at any time, but as fellow of the house where hee was master. Neither did he ever cary his, or any other mans cloakebagge: Although if he had so done, it had bin no disgrace to him. Better mens sonnes then the Libeller is, have caried cloakebags" (*Admonition*, 48–49).

145. *Haman ... Mordecai ... Hester* referring to the biblical story in Esther 3–7: the Persian courtier Haman schemed to destroy the Jews (here, the reformers), but, exposed by the loyal Mordecai (= Martin) to his kinswomen Queen Esther (= Queen Elizabeth), was hanged on gallows he himself had built. Thomas Cooper in reply invoked the same story, only in his reading Haman represents Martin, telling lies about the people (= church officials) chosen by God to lead the population into truth (*Admonition*, 24).

146. *Worcester* Edmund Freake (*c.* 1516–91), bishop of Worcester from 1584.

147. *Gloucester* John Bullingham (d. 1598), Catholic exile in the reign of Edward VI and chaplain to Bishop Gardiner under Mary; he refused to take the oath of supremacy upon Elizabeth's accession but conformed in the 1560s and was made bishop of Gloucester in 1581 (*ODNB*). Even fellow bishops thought him intellectually unfit for episcopal office: Matthew Parker and John Aylmer both offered disparaging comments (mentioned in *ODNB*, quoted in White, *Lives*, 278–79). Bullingham appears to have been a popular target for ridicule: in December 1589, thirteen reformers in Gloucester were examined for being "privy to" manuscript libels written against the bishop (PRO SP Dom. 12/229/46).

148. *beef and brewess* brewess (brewis) is meat broth, with "beef and brewess" a traditional combination (*OED*). This sermon was not published, but Martin implies that Bullingham blamed his former Catholicism on eating too much beef, a habit sometimes thought to dull the mind: Thomas Nashe refers to a "slowe ice-braind beefe-witted gull" (*Works*, I, 370); cf. also *Twelfth Night* (1.3.84–85) and *Troilus and Cressida* (2.1.13).

149. *convented* summoned for examination. *book* Book of Common Prayer.

150. *in for a bird* confined, imprisoned.

151. *Winchester ... Book of Common Prayer* Thomas Cooper in reply acknowledged making the argument that reformers who found fault with the BCP might as well do so with scripture but explained that he did not "compare the booke of *Common prayer* with the holy Scriptures in dignitie, trueth, or majestie" (*Admonition*, 70v–71r); Martin responds in *Hay any Work*, 138. Reformers argued that the Apocrypha were human writings, not divinely

inspired ones, and that some Apocryphal texts included in the BCP contradicted scripture. These beliefs underlay many reformers' unwillingness to
subscribe to Whitgift's article affirming that the BCP "containeth nothing in
it contrary to the word of God." *SPR* calendars many documents that detail
reform objections to the church's use of Apocryphal texts (e.g., I, 125, 197, 199,
211, 277–81, 299–300). *Sir Mary Overie* St Mary Overie, now Southwark
Cathedral, in Cooper's diocese of Winchester. For Martin's use of "Sir" for
"St," see note 72 above.

152. *that sermon . . . and in another* neither of these sermons was published. But a
marginal note by an anonymous contemporary next to these lines in the
Harvard University copy (Houghton Library, STC 17453) reads "this he
[Cooper] also affirmede the 17 day of November 1588 at pals crose: I my
selfe hard it." Cooper in reply reiterated the point he had apparently
preached, that with respect to doctrine and order of worship "there was
never Church upon the face of the earth, so nigh the sinceritie of Gods
trueth, as the Church of England is at this day" (*Admonition*, 65r).

153. *cog* cheat, deceive, employ fraud. *face* show a false face.

154. *eyes* referring to the etymological root of "bishop" as overseer or watcher.
reading only as opposed to preaching.

155. *Davidson* John Davidson (*c.* 1549–1604), Scottish minister who preached in
London. His *Short Christian Instruction* was printed by Robert Waldegrave in
1588. *Wood* a "Dr Wood" is listed as a senior licenser of the press in 1586; he is
usually identified as Dr Richard Wood, prebendary of Westminster from
1587, though John Wood, Whitgift's chaplain, is also named as a licenser in
one book (Greg, *Licensers*, 99–100). *great one* ironic: the book is a forty-page
octavo.

156. *would not have that word printed* Martin omits to mention that Davidson
and/or Waldegrave ignored the licenser's correction: the catechism's answer
to the question "By what meanes attaine we to this faith wherby onely we are
saved?" remains "Faith commeth by hearing, and hearing by the word of God
preached" (B3r).

157. John Whitgift addressed the issue of preaching versus reading in *Defense*
(1574), 568ff. But he defended the reading of scripture as a complement to
preaching, not as a substitute for it (as Martin implies): "I denie not but that
preaching is the most ordinary and usuall meanes, that God useth to worke
by in the heartes of the hearers . . .: but this doth nothing derogate from the
might and power of the woord of God being read of them" (570).

158. *Goodman* Gabriel Goodman (1528–1601), dean of Westminster from 1561 and
high commissioner. Martin repeatedly calls him "popish," probably because
he had conformed under Mary (*ODNB*). He is mentioned again below, 40,
43, and in *Schoolpoints*, 92.

159. For John Udall, Presbyterian minister and polemicist, see Introduction, xlviii.
In June 1588, James Cottington (d. 1609), archdeacon of Surrey, deprived
Udall of his position as lecturer in Kingston-upon-Thames, Surrey, where
Stephen Chatfield (d. 1598) was the absentee vicar. Udall's deprivation was

the culmination of a long-standing dispute with Dr John Hone, Cottington's local official. In a 1586 letter, Hone described the "contemptuous disorders in church matters" caused by Udall's encouragement of "new ceremonies, new forme of prayer, new feasts and fasting dayes, private meetinges, singeinge of psalmes, and lectures or readinges, and interspersing [interpretings?] of scriptures in private houses, contrary to the lawes and customes of this church of England" (*SPR*, II, 39–40; printed in full in Waddington, *Surrey Congregational History*, 6–7). Nothing further is known of Master Harvey the usurer; Martin here and Udall in his 1590 trial (*State Trials*, I, 1274) accuse him of pressuring Hone to silence Udall. Nor is there any extant evidence concerning the charge that Chatfield fraudulently retained funds raised to endow a grammar school in town; the project itself is mentioned in Collinson, *Movement*, 184. *mess* group of four persons: here, Cottington, Harvey, Hone, and Chatfield.

160. *Is us do I* see note 92 above. *dance . . . in a net* hide in plain sight (proverbial; cf. Tilley N130).

161. *sew pillows* use flattery. From Ezekiel 13:18, a passage that targets prophetesses; the significance of their "pillows" (translated in the Revised Standard Version as "magic bands") remains unclear.

162. *bawdy court* Hone was a judge in the archdeacon's court, a venue known as the "bawdy court" because, among other kinds of cases, it handled accusations of sexual immorality.

163. *to sorry* to sorrow.

164. John Aylmer began his reply to this story as if in full possession of the moral high ground: "*Martin* with his bitter stile of malicious *Momus* dipt in the gall of ungodlinesse, proceedeth in a shamelesse untrueth touching the bishops answere to the executors of *Allein* the Grocer, as though hee shoulde flatly deny the payment of a certaine debt." But he soon admits using "some sharpe wordes" when the executors approached him, acknowledges the debt, and concludes by noting that he still owed his creditors £10 (more than half the original amount), all the while maintaining that Martin's story was "a lye" (*Admonition*, 58). *brazen face* "unabashed or hardened countenance" (*OED*, this place cited).

165. *went to buffets with his son-in-law* Aylmer's son-in-law was Dr Adam Squire (d. 1588), master of Balliol College, Oxford, and archdeacon of Middlesex. According to John Harington, Squire sought to cover his own infidelity by forging a letter that implicated his wife in an intrigue; Aylmer discovered the ploy and "with a good waster he so mortified this old Adam . . . that he needed no other pennance" (*Briefe View*, II, 39; Strype, *Life of Aylmer*, 123). Squire is mentioned again in *Hay any Work*, 137. In Aylmer's conflicts with John Madox (see note 106 above), the bishop warned his opponent that "he was a man of metal, and could use his hands well" (Strype, *Life of Aylmer*, 99). At the time of both incidents, Aylmer was in his late 60s.

166. *Paul's Churchyard* center of London's book trade. Whitgift in reply defended these instructions, arguing that the Apocrypha had not been separated from

the Bible "from the beginning of Christianity to this day" (*Admonition*, 49). For reformist objections to the church's use of Apocryphal texts in the BCP, see above, note 151.

167. *In primis* "in the first place."

168. *Cartwright's answer to the Rhemish Testament* see note 135 above.

169. *statute 13 Eliza.* see note 74 above.

170. *corruptions of the church ... ring in marriage* reformers opposed all these components of church service as remnants of Catholic practice. "Churching" is the rite of thanksgiving that marked a woman's re-entry into the community after childbirth; reformers objected to the ceremony as "superstitious" (see, e.g., *SPR*, I, 53, 127–28, 259).

171. See Introduction, lxviff., for attempts to link reform with Anabaptism and treason.

172. *libel* Martin would indeed be referred to as "the Libeller" throughout Thomas Cooper's *Admonition*.

173. *Suffolk and Essex* the 1586 "Survey of the Ministry" claimed that of 335 parishes examined in Essex, 173 contained "ignorant and unpreaching ministers," of whom 61 were double beneficed, 10 were non-resident, and 12 were of notably "scandalous life" (*SPR*, II, 97). Suffolk was not covered by the "Survey"; presumably reformers considered the state of the ministry there similarly inadequate.

174. *father Palinode* Andrew Perne, dean of Ely; the nickname refers to his "backward and forward" shifts between Protestantism and Catholicism; see note 53 above. The gibe implies that contemporaries recognized Perne in the Catholicizing "Palinode" in the May eclogue of Edmund Spenser's *The Shepheardes Calender* (1579). *by the weeks* ensnared, caught.

175. *Variae lectiones* "various readings"; emended from "*leiciones*" in the original.

176. The books jokingly listed here did not exist per se. But their names suggest the kinds of manuscript materials that underlay the tracts, as the ensuing descriptions indicate.

177. *Itinerarium* emended from "*Iterarium*" in accordance with the more conventional spelling employed in the previous paragraph. *in folio* the largest book format (required to contain all the "pranks" Martin discovers).

178. *visitation* formal visit, usually by a bishop or archdeacon, to examine the state of a parish, county, or diocese; Martin in effect threatens to complete and publish the 1586 "Survey of the Ministry."

179. *Geoffrey Jones* the "Sir" is a mocking honorific. Probably the Jefferie Jones listed in the 1586 "Survey of the Ministry" as the parson of Corley, Warwickshire and described as "dumbe, drunkard, gamster, quareller, swearer, pilferer, adulterer" (*SPR*, II, 171).

180. *trey trip* game with dice "in which success probably depended on the casting of a trey or three" (*OED*).

181. *have good utterance for* have good sales of.

182. *alestond* ale barrel.

183. *go ... go* using "go" in the literal sense of "walk."

184. *Surrey, Northampton, and Oxford shires* the 1586 "Survey of the Ministry" categorized 98 of 123 Oxford and Oxfordshire incumbents as non-preaching; Surrey fared even worse, with only 24 ministers for 140 parishes, 125 of which were "alltogether destitute of sufficient teachers." Northamptonshire is listed as one of the counties for which "we have not the Surveie, but it is verie likelie to be as badde as others" (*SPR*, II, 93–94). "Vicar of hell" appears to have been a phrase in popular use: the "Survey" notes that Matthew Pickering, vicar of Harbery, Warwickshire, was "surnamed the vicar of hell for his ruffianly life" (*SPR*, II, 173). Martin names a specific "ficker of Hell," James King of Hertfordshire, in *Protestation*, 204.

185. *pursuivants* officers with power to execute warrants; Martin mentions several by name in subsequent tracts, the best known being the writer Anthony Munday (see *Just Censure*, 172). *Wolfe* John Wolfe, beadle of the Stationers' Company; see note 115 above.

186. *his grace* John Whitgift, the authority behind the raid Martin proceeds to describe. *Items* articles in an enumeration or account.

187. *brought you to Kingston-upon-Thames* this raid took place in June 1588, in hopes of catching Robert Waldegrave with an unauthorized press. Arber prints the list of expenses charged to the Stationers' Company for the unsuccessful trip, misdating the expedition to 1589 (*Transcript*, I, 528).

188. *cry rub* call for the ball "to encounter some impediment which retards or diverts its course" (*OED v¹* 14b, earliest citation).

189. *Turner* William Turner (1509/10–1568), dean of Wells, physician, and botanist; suspended for nonconformity in the 1560s, Turner was known for his opposition to vestments and church ceremonial (*ODNB*). For Andrew Perne as a "turner" or (Catholicizing) turncoat, see notes 53 and 84 above.

190. *dinner while* dinner time.

191. *next to the door* idiom for being farthest from the protection of the fire and therefore closest to the "weather" of the world's assaults; here also with the sense of being on their way out.

192. *under* Benedicite in confidence; *benedicite* (bless me) was the penitent's first word upon entering the confessional.

193. *the conference* the Lambeth Conference (December 1584) was the only formal disputation John Whitgift allowed the Presbyterians. In the presence of Lord Burghley, Sir Francis Walsingham, the earl of Leicester and others, Presbyterian divines Thomas Sparke and Walter Travers discussed "things needfull to be reformed in the booke of Common prayer" with Whitgift, Thomas Cooper, and Edwin Sandys, archbishop of York. *SPR* calendars Travers' report of the discussion (I, 275).

194. *corruption of the translation ... 105th Psalm* Psalm readings in the BCP were based on the translation by Miles Coverdale included in the Great Bible (1539); they would remain unchanged until the twentieth century. Whitgift in reply argued that "they were not obedient" and "they were not disobedient" were not contradictory readings because the word "they" was ambiguous (*Admonition*, 50). For a discussion of this passage, see Lander, *Inventing Polemic*, 85–88.

195. *there was a parliament* the 1586 parliament, in which Job Throkmorton sat as MP.

196. *gracious lords* citing the Geneva translation, though not Laurence Tomson's revision of the New Testament, first printed in 1587, which replaced "gracious lords" with "bountifull."

197. *Winchester ... his dictionary* Thomas Cooper's *Thesaurus linguae Romanae et Britannicae* (1565) combines a revision of Sir Thomas Elyot's *Dictionary* (1538) and a thesaurus based on works by the French scholar-printer Robert Estienne (Robertus Stephanus). Cooper acknowledged his reliance on these sources. For a discussion of the plagiarism charge, see Starnes, *Renaissance Dictionaries*, 86–98.

198. *Overton* William Overton, bishop of Lichfield and Coventry; see note 32 above, *Epitome*, 77, *Schoolpoints*, 91, and *Hay any Work*, 103. Overton had enjoyed a distinguished university career, but Martin likely thought the bishop's reputation for extravagance and corruption a better indication of his "learning" than his academic credentials.

199. *Bickley* Thomas Bickley (*c.* 1518–96), warden of Merton College, Oxford, and from 1586 bishop of Chichester. Bickley was possibly the oldest man to be made bishop under Elizabeth (*ODNB*), but unless his age is the issue, there is no strong evidence either to support or challenge his appearance in this list.

200. *Middleton* Marmaduke Middleton (d. 1593), bishop of St David's from 1582, was the subject of scandal throughout his career. He would be tried in 1592 before both high commission and Star Chamber, and found guilty of dilapidation, embezzlement of church property, and forging a will; he was deprived of office, one of the few Anglican bishops ever to be dismissed. Later in this tract Martin charges Middleton with bigamy and with marrying his brother to a woman on her deathbed (42), repeating the charge of bigamy in *Schoolpoints*, 91, and *Hay any Work*, 101.

201. *dean of Westminster* Gabriel Goodman; see note 158 above. He is mentioned again below, 43, and in *Schoolpoints*, 92.

202. *Cole* probably Dr William Cole (*c.* 1530–1600), president of Corpus Christi College, Oxford, and subsequently dean of Lincoln. An important figure in early Elizabethan Protestantism, Cole had over time reconciled himself to the Elizabethan Settlement and become a modest pluralist with little sympathy for further reform (*ODNB*).

203. *Bell* Dr John Bell (*c.* 1531–91), master of Jesus College, Cambridge, from 1579 and subsequently dean of Ely. In October 1583 he was granted a shared commission to exercise episcopal jurisdiction in Ely (Strype, *Life of Whitgift*, I, 260). His name appears alongside that of Andrew Perne in documents connected with attempts to enforce conformity (e.g., Strype, *Annals*, III, pt 1, 218, 496; III, pt 2, 121).

204. *bishop of Gloucester* John Bullingham; see note 147 above.

205. *Sir John's day* the feast day of St John (December 27). The use of "Sir" for "St" plays on the bishop's name (John) and "Sir John" as a term for an unlearned priest; see note 72 above.

206. *a child is born* Isaiah 9:6. Martin objects to Bullingham's use of passages from the BCP to "prove" the authenticity of scripture, as if the text of the BCP were equally authoritative.

207. *destruction* satirical malapropism for "instruction."

208. *Latenie* litany, punning on the Latin (Catholic) origins of the service.

209. *mood* one of the classes into which valid syllogisms could be divided. Several moods had mnemonic names, an idea Martin plays with in *Epitome*, 79.

210. *near a to side* "near a toe side" in the original. Pierce and Arber suggest an error for "near at one side" (*Marprelate Tracts*, 92; *Epistle*, ed. Arber, 43), but the phrase probably reproduces a more colloquial idiom.

211. *Bridges played . . . fool in Sir Mary's pulpit* the place is Great St Mary's, the University Church of Cambridge (for the use of "Sir" for "St," see note 72 above); the occasion is unidentifed. A repeat mention in *Epitome*, 57, indicates that the reference is to a sermon Bridges had preached. Probably referring to a performance arranged by Thomas Cooper, the bishop of Winchester named repeatedly in the tracts; possibly referring to an occasion in the 1560s or 1570s, when John Bridges was associated with Cambridge and his career was being advanced by Robert Horne, bishop of Winchester until 1580.

212. *Some kind of ministry . . . therefore it was temporary* John Bridges challenged the scriptural warrant for the Presbyterian "tetrarchy" of pastors, doctors, elders, and deacons, arguing that while these offices may once have existed, they were not decreed in perpetuity. He also noted that reformers conceded that some offices mentioned in scripture, such as prophets, apostles, and evangelists, had ceased (*Defence*, 75–76). Martin rewords this argument as a faulty syllogism that he then uses as a model for a series of insults.

213. *O the bones of you* an exclamation (*OED*, this place cited).

214. *wooden dagger and a coxcomb* the jester's customary props; a coxcomb, used earlier in its general sense to mean a knave, was the traditional jester's cap.

215. *Catercap* the four-cornered cap worn by clergy; Martin uses "catercap" and "cornercap" as metonymies for cleric throughout the tracts.

216. *parson of Mickleham* Richard Ellis (d. 1613), vicar of Mickleham, Surrey, from 1562. He is mentioned again in *Hay any Work*, 127. The other two "vicars of hell" are not identifiable from the 1586 "Survey of the Ministry."

217. *catekissing* catechizing. This is the only extant reference to a 1587 sermon by John Aylmer at Paul's Cross; Aylmer published none of his sermons. Martin objects to the bishop's use of jokes and puns: apparently, the sermon included a joke about a leather shoehorn, and a play on catechizing and kissing "cates" (delicacies, or women named Kate).

218. *to B. of Ely* perhaps an error for "no great hope to *be* B. of Ely"; or perhaps suggesting that Aylmer punned on "B." (an abbreviation for "bishop") as an homonym for "be" (he has "no great hope to 'be' of Ely").

219. *the words which . . . Christ spake* in Matthew 27:46; the version in Mark 15:34 ("Eloi" rather than "Eli") mars the pun. This charge might derive from a passage in Aylmer's *Harborowe* (1559) in which he tells the story of a vicar who

misread the line as meaning that the bishop of Ely owned the book in which the words were written (G3v).

220. *Benison* John Aylmer in reply described the London clergyman Barnaby Benison as "comming from *Geneva*, ful fraught with studie of *Innovations*, and utterly emptie of obedience," and acknowledged imprisoning Benison for refusing to subscribe (*Admonition*, 59). Benison was kept in one prison or another from 1579 to 1584 and spent at least thirty weeks in close confinement; the Clink was a prison in Southwark on the palace grounds of the bishops of Winchester. A 1584 letter signed by eleven privy councillors reprimanded Aylmer for "hard dealinge" in the case and advised him to offer Benison compensation "to repaye that wronge you have done unto him." Aylmer claimed that his "poor estate" prevented him from making any payment and suggested the offer of a small clerical benefice (*SPR*, I, 246–48; Strype, *Life of Aylmer*, 137–39; Hartley, ed., *Proceedings*, II, 442–43).

221. *a-haymaking* attending the merriment associated with making hay.

222. *bishop of Sir David's in Wales* Marmaduke Middleton; see note 200 above. Martin repeats the (apparently accurate) charge of bigamy in *Schoolpoints*, 91, and *Hay any Work*, 101.

223. *bishop of Lincoln* William Wickham (1539–95), bishop of Lincoln from 1584 and subsequently bishop of Winchester. The "one who died" was Mary Queen of Scots, whose funeral sermon Wickham preached in Peterborough Cathedral on August 1 (not 2), 1587.

224. *Richard Patrick, clothier of Worcester* John Whitgift in reply denied any intent of making Patrick a minister (*Admonition*, 50); Martin glibly responded that he had "marred Richard Patrick's market" (*Hay any Work*, 136).

225. *bishop of Sir Asse* William Hughes (*c.* 1535–1600), bishop of St Asaph from 1573. A 1587 investigation charged Hughes with misgovernment, extortion, and leasing out his bishopric (Strype, *Annals*, II, pt 1, 435–36; II, pt 2, 524–28; III, pt 2, 471–75); he was also accused of holding more than twenty benefices, making him one of the period's most extensive pluralists (*ODNB*).

226. *Gloucester ... Kenold ... Perne ... Goodman* John Bullingham, bishop of Gloucester (see note 147 above); John Kenold or Kennall (d. 1592), archdeacon of Oxford from 1561; Andrew Perne, dean of Ely (see note 53 above); Gabriel Goodman, dean of Westminster (see note 158 above). Martin suggests that all four harbored Catholic tendencies.

227. *nonresident ... thief and a soul murderer* to reformers, non-residents robbed their parish not only of the income it provided but also of the word preached, and therefore "murdered" their flock by depriving them of the "ordinary means" to salvation.

228. *apostataes* apostates. Martin uses the Latin form throughout the tracts.

229. *Dame Lawson* Margaret Lawson; see note 51 above. *Caiaphas* high priest before whom Christ was tried and condemned, and a traditional figure in Protestant polemic for a bad bishop; Martin refers to Whitgift as the Caiaphas of Canterbury throughout the tracts. Simon Peter denied Christ while warming himself beside a fire at the door of Caiaphas' court (John 18:18).

230. *29 years ago* 1559, the year Elizabeth ascended the throne; Martin suggests that his opponents hindered religion even more than their Catholic predecessors did.
231. *commission . . . wherefore it was ordained* statute 1 Eliz. c. 1 (1559), "An act restoring to the crowne the ancient jurisdiction over the state ecclesiasticall and spirituall," restored royal jurisdiction in ecclesiastical causes and outlined the purposes for which high commission was established: "to visit, reforme, redresse, order, correct, and amend all such errors, heresies, schismes, abuses, offenses, contempts, and inormities whatsoever" connected with the church.
232. *tabling* playing "tables" (backgammon).
233. *wales* Pierce emends to "whales," without explanation, and mistakenly indicates that the word is capitalized in the original (*Marprelate Tracts*, 101). Wilson reads as "Wales" and asserts "a clear reference to Monmouth" as evidence for his argument (clever, but utterly without foundation) that Martin was to be identified as Sir Roger Williams (*Martin Marprelate and Shakespeare's Fluellen*, 28). The word might also be read as "walls," for which "wales" was an alternative spelling. But the particular reading seems less important than the overall effect, which as the remainder of the subscription makes clear is one of teasingly nonsensical specificity about where Martin may be found.
234. *penniless bench* covered bench provided outside of churches, probably for the benefit of destitute wayfarers.
235. *fourteenth year at the least of the age of Charing Cross* Charing Cross was a site where proclamations were read and offenders pilloried; this "age" dates from the beginning of the official crackdown on the Presbyterian movement. Proclamations in June and October 1573 "enjoined conformity to the ecclesiastical laws," suppressed the *Admonition to the Parliament* and Thomas Cartwright's *Replye* to Whitgift, and mandated imprisonment for "anyone who defamed the Prayer Book" (Collinson, *Movement*, 149–52). These proclamations were followed by a warrant for Cartwright's arrest and the deprivation of Presbyterian ringleaders.
236. *Anno pontificatus vestri Quinto . . . ultimo* the fifth (and, Martin hopes, the last) year of the "pontificate" of John Whitgift, consecrated in October 1583.

2 THE *EPITOME*

1. The title pages of the *Epistle* and the *Epitome* are nearly identical for their first fifteen lines: see *Epistle*, 211 nn.2–5, for comments on "Presbyter, Priest or Elder"; "Doctor of Divility" (Divinity); "Sarum" (Salisbury); prevented (anticipated); "Fyckers" and "Fickers" (vicars, with possible suggestion of "fuckers"); "Currats" (curates); and "past grace."
2. *senseless titles* the tract's playful running heads; they are listed in the Appendix, 209–10.
3. *four bishops* John Whitgift, archbishop of Canterbury; John Aylmer, bishop of London; Thomas Cooper, bishop of Winchester; William Wickham, bishop of Lincoln. All four contributed to Cooper's *Admonition*.

4. *pistle*s variant spelling of "epistles," but also punning on "pistols" and "piz-zles": a dried bull's-pizzle was a "much-used instrument of flagellation" in the period (*OED*).

5. *conditions of peace* drawn up by Martin; they included the condition "That none be molested by them or any their aforesaid servants, for this my book" (*Epistle*, 34).

6. *I have been entertained at the Court* the most famous anecdote about Martin's presence at Court concerns a copy owned by the earl of Essex: see *Just Censure*, 275 n.16. During his December 1588 appearance before high commission, Giles Wigginton was asked if he had read Marprelate; he responded: "I understand by hearesay, (that which I suppose yow know well enough) that many lords and ladies, and other great and wealthy personages of all estates have had and read it, and so they will joyne with me in mine having and reading of it, if I have done eyther of both" (*SPR*, II, 254).

7. *wolves* for bad pastors as hireling wolves, see John 10:1–13.

8. *I trow* I trust, I suppose; a conversational usage, but not necessarily dialect.

9. Martin discusses puritan opposition to his tactics in *Epitome*, 53–54, *Hay any Work*, 119, and *Theses Martinianae*, 147; see also Introduction, xxx–xxxi.

10. *ingramness* ignorance (*OED* ingram).

11. *Wigginton* Giles Wigginton, the vicar of Sedburgh, Yorskshire, whom author-ities suspected of being Martin; see *Epistle*, 25–26. He was imprisoned in December 1588 for refusing to answer potentially self-incriminating questions about the tracts (*SPR*, II, 257).

12. *Schilders* Richard Schilders, the most prominent continental printer of books by English reformers. A native of the Low Countries, Schilders trained in London, printed there from 1568 to 1579, then moved to Middelburg, where he worked from 1580 to 1618. More than one hundred books have been attributed to his press, including many important Presbyterian publications.

13. *premunire . . . for urging an oath contrary to statute* Martin argues that the oath *ex officio* constituted a challenge to royal supremacy, and was therefore an offence classified under the statute of praemunire; see *Epistle*, 22, and Introduction, xxii.

14. *wonderful year* soothsayers across Europe predicted that 1588 would be the *annus mirabilis* or climacterial year, and in England these prophecies appeared to be confirmed by the defeat of the Armada. William Camden cites the prophecies in *Annales* (1615), 476.

15. For John Aylmer's refusal to return stolen goods found on his land, see *Epistle*, 13. For John Whitgift and the debate over reading versus preaching, see *Epistle*, 31.

16. *hidden in a net* hidden in plain sight (proverbial); cf. Tilley N130.

17. John Udall's *A Demonstration of the Trueth of that Discipline* was printed by Robert Waldegrave on the Marprelate press in East Molesey in October 1588, a few weeks before the *Epistle*. The passage Martin cites epitomizes the reformers' confidence in the power of disputation to reveal the truth: "Let us bee disputed with before indifferent judges, let the holy word of God bee the touch-stone to

trye our disputations by, and then shall it easily appeare, who hath the Lord on his side, and who not . . . Venture your byshopprickes upon a disputation, and wee will venture our lives, take the challenge if you dare" (B1v).

18. The costs of arrest, including the wages and expenses of the pursuivants, were usually borne by the person arrested. The custom was a source of corruption and much complaint.

19. *Titus and Timothy* invoked by John Bridges in the *Defence* as having exercised archiepiscopal functions; see below, 69–70 and 82, for Martin's response to the claim.

20. *Sic fæliciter incipit* "thus happily he begins."

21. Book length in the handpress period was often calculated by sheets rather than pages. Martin's estimate of the number required to print each copy of Bridges' 1,400-page *Defence* is accurate: the *Defence* is a quarto, a format that produced four leaves (eight pages) per sheet. Demy was a medium-sized sheet approximately 50 by 35–40 cm (20 by 14–16 inches).

22. William Fulke's Presbyterian manifesto *A Briefe and Plaine Declaration* (1584) was popularly known as *The Learned Discourse of Ecclesiastical Government*, its running head.

23. *his grace* here and subsequently, John Whitgift.

24. *cast his cards* count, or take stock of, the "hand" Bridges had dealt the church's defenders.

25. *stean . . . mear* "stone" and "more," in imitation of northern dialect; see the spellings listed under *OED* "more" and *DSL* "stan" (stone).

26. *sicken a wipe in his bricke* "such a blow in his breeches," in imitation of northern dialect (*OED* wipe *v* 7a; see also the spellings listed under "such" and "breek," and in *DSL* under "sikken" and "brekis, breikis"). *lambskinned* beaten, thrashed (*OED*).

27. This sermon was not published but appears to have been delivered *c.* 1584–85: in the preface to his *Defence* (1587), Bridges writes that he had delivered this sermon "about two yeares past," when Fulke's *Briefe and Plaine Declaration* (1584) was "lately set forth."

28. *Like lips, like lettuce* proverb meaning "like has met its like," or more particularly that similarly bad things suit one another.

29. *played my Lord of Winchester's fool in his sermon* the occasion is mentioned in *Epistle*, 41. For the use of "Sir" for "St," see *Epistle*, 219 n.72.

30. *corner cap and a tippet* clerical vestments to which reformers objected; see *Epistle*, 216 n.46.

31. *his grace his articles* referring to Whitgift's 1584 articles that prompted the subscription controversy; see Introduction, xxi.

32. *green heads* usually youthful or immature people, but here with an implication of simpletons (*OED*, this place cited).

33. *threepenny book* the least expensive book: Martin argues that a pamphlet of only one or two gatherings could refute Bridges' 1,400-page *Defence*, a book that cost seven shillings, because only one or two syllogisms were needed to baffle ("set at a *non plus*") its author.

34. *the black ox hath trodden on his foot* proverbial phrase meaning to suffer adversity or decay (*OED* ox 4b).
35. *party* part, side.
36. *put a man to his trumps* put to the last expedient, nonplus (*OED*).
37. *connex axiom* an axiom or proposition that includes a conditional "if."
38. *ka* dialect or colloquial variant of "quoth" (*OED*).
39. *midsummer moon* lunacy was thought to be particularly prevalent during the midsummer full moon.
40. Martin summarizes, in the form of a syllogism, Bridges' argument in *Defence*, 54–56.
41. *fathermillerly … bethout dissimblation* "familiarly" and "without dissimulation" (in imitation of rustic malapropisms).
42. John Whitgift was elected dean of Lincoln in 1571, just before he began to make his name in polemical battle with Thomas Cartwright in *An Answere to a Certen Libel* (1572) and *The Defense of the Aunswere* (1574). While Whitgift acknowledged the popular election of ministers in the early church (e.g., *An Answere*, 44ff.), he argued at length for its inconveniences (e.g., *Defense*, 211ff.). The point about the possible involvement of women appears in a section that prints Cartwright's voicing of his opponents' objections (*Defense*, 210).
43. *besire* "desire," with the dialect b/d substitution.
44. *all things* referring to the second of the four terms in Martin's preceding syllogistic summary of Bridges' *Defence*, 55–56.
45. *topic place* commonplace or general maxim (*OED*, this place cited).
46. For John Aylmer's *An Harborowe for Faithfull and Trewe Subjectes* (1559), see *Epistle*, 213 n.24.
47. Martin begins his page numbering of Aylmer's unpaginated *Harborowe* with signature B1, skipping the title page and other prefatory material. As in his quotations from Bridges' *Defence*, Martin offers paraphrases rather than word-for-word quotations. In the passage following he cites from *Harborowe*, G1v, G2r–v, and G4r. The use of "Elmar" for "Aylmer" is a reminder of the "Mar-elm" pun (see *Epistle*, 22).
48. *Friar Titleman* Franciscus Tittelmans (1502–37); the name is variously spelled. His *De consideratione dialectica* (many editions, under varying titles, from *c.* 1534), based on Aristotle's *Organon*, was a standard guide to traditional logic. It includes discussions of *predicables* (the five classes of predicates, or kinds of things said, about any subject), *predicaments* (the different classes of predicates or assertions about subjects), and the rules *de inveniendis mediis* or "of inventing the mean" (generating the middle term of a syllogism). Possibly also with a play on Tittelmans' name: Bridges can win the "title" of bishop by reading his "Title-man."
49. That is, once Bridges became a bishop he might "prove" that the scriptures contained no blueprint for church government, an argument "proved" by John Whitgift but denied by the puritans and already "refuted" by Thomas Cartwright. For the polemical battle between Whitgift and Cartwright, see *Epistle*, 212 n.12, 213 n.23.

50. Cardinal Robert Bellarmine (Roberto Bellarmino) (1542–1621), one of the most formidable Catholic controversialists of the period. Martin frequently argues that the church's ecclesiological arguments resembled the strategies used in Catholic apologetic. Bellarmine is mentioned again in *Schoolpoints*, 93. John Penry makes a similar argument in *A Viewe* (Coventry, 1589), claiming that Bridges (*Defence*, 448) defended episcopacy with the same arguments Bellarmine used (cap. 10, lib. 5, cont. 3) to argue for papal supremacy (20).

51. *William Woodcock's divinity* probably a generic name for a "bird-brained" argument: Martin claims in *Epistle* that Bridges' *Defence* displayed the "brains of a woodcock" (14).

52. Citing a story Aylmer tells in *Harborowe*, E4v. *portesse* breviary (variously spelled).

53. *articles* John Whitgift's 1584 articles; see Introduction, xxi.

54. *fautors* favourers, aiders, encouragers (*OED*).

55. *fetch ... over the coals* to call to account and convict; the phrase derives from the burning of heretics (*OED* coal *n* 12, this place cited).

56. *monastery of Sarum* Salisbury Cathedral: throughout the tracts, Martin reminds readers of the Catholic roots of the church practices the reformers opposed.

57. *Latin for a goose* goose in Latin is "anser": despite his word-spinning, Bridges "declines" to "anser" the question.

58. For Andrew Perne, see *Epistle*, 217 n.53 and 220 n.84. Here and elsewhere, Martin suggests that Perne contributed to Bridges' *Defence*: see, e.g., *Epistle*, 16, and 219 n.70. This particular argument, Martin implies, is a Catholic one, and Perne is often mentioned in contexts that remind readers of his return to Catholicism under Mary and his rumored adherence to Catholic beliefs well into Elizabeth's reign.

59. *Gammer Gurton's needle* comic play rumored to have been written by Bridges (see *Epistle*, 14); it is mentioned again below, 83. Gammer Gurton spends much of the play searching for her sewing needle; it is eventually found in the breeches of her servant Hodge.

60. Martin cites Bellarmine, *Disputationes de controversiis christianae fidei*, vol. I (Ingolstadt, 1586), first controversy, "De verbo Dei scripto et non scripta," lib. 4 ("2" is an error), cap. 3. Bellarmine here summarizes the "state of the question" concerning traditions: does scripture contain all doctrine necessary to salvation, or do church traditions contain the "non-scriptural" word of God? His authorities for Protestant arguments on the sufficiency of scripture include Luther, Calvin, and Martin Chemnitz or Kemnitius (1522–86), an eminent Lutheran theologian.

61. *Watson the pursuivant* Watson led a group of officers from the Stationers' Company to search a house in which Waldegrave was supposed to be operating a secret press; see *Epistle*, 37. He is mentioned again in *Hay any Work*, 135.

62. Quoting Aylmer, *Harborowe*, H1r. For Aylmer's bellicosity, see *Epistle*, 33, and 229 n.65.

63. *paralogisms* faulty or illogical syllogisms.
64. *play ... Winchester's fool* referring to a sermon by Bridges mentioned in *Epistle*, 41, and above, 57, and probably referring to Thomas Cooper, bishop of Winchester.
65. For Aylmer and his two-hand sword, see above, 69 (side note).
66. *golden pen* pen inspired by a higher power to produce suitably elevated writing. Martin is being ironic: the next stage in Bridges' argument is particularly "inspired."
67. William Fulke opens his discussion of the church offices sanctioned by scripture with the statement Martin accuses Bridges of misrepresenting: "wee ought diligently and reverently to search the holie scriptures, that wee may finde what order our saviour Christe our onely housholder hath set foorth in them, by which he woulde have his house or church to be directed in al things, appertaining to the eternall salvation of us men" (*Briefe and Plaine Declaration*, 2). Bridges, however, did quote Fulke's "appertaining" five times in these pages (*Defence*, 59–60) and specifically argued against the slippery distinction Fulke had attempted to make: if the reformers' fourfold system of church government "*necessarilie be apperteining to the salvation of us men*: then cannot we men without it be partakers of *salvation*" (60).
68. *I wis* "I wisse" in the original, for "iwis" (truly, certainly, assuredly). Often treated in the period as two words, with the "I" capitalized (*OED* iwis B).
69. *Danaeus* Bridges argued that the distinguished Calvinist theologian Lambert Daneau (*c.* 1530–95?) had shown himself an enemy to Elizabeth by condemning the "*publik government of women*, in the civil and politicall *state*" (*Defence*, 701–702), citing Daneau's gloss on 1 Tim. 2:12 in his *In D. Pauli priorem epistolam ad Timotheum commentarius* (Geneva, 1577).
70. *Master Beza* Theodore Beza (Théodore de Bèze) (1519–1605), distinguished Calvinist theologian whose writings played a central role in English Presbyterian ecclesiology; see Introduction, xxiii.
71. *bear ... in hand* persuade through deception (*OED* bear *v*¹ 3e).
72. Theodore Beza's *Confessio christianae fidei* (Geneva, 1560) was translated by Robert Filles as *A Briefe and Piththie Summe of the Christian Faith* (1563). Filles' translation does omit ch. 5, arts. 44 and 45, a discussion that treats the office of the Christian magistrate. Martin implies that church officials had a hand in the omission, allowing Bridges, e.g., to discuss Beza's "invectives against Womens government" (*Defence*, 788).
73. Quoting Aylmer, *Harborowe*, D4r. Martin makes hell feminine (Aylmer has "hys mouth").
74. Aylmer was writing against the Marian (Catholic) episcopacy, not the Elizabethan, as Martin implicitly acknowledges when he suggests the substitution of "imprisoning so many innocents, and murdering the souls of so many" for Aylmer's "murdering so many martyrs." But the accession of Elizabeth did not deprive the episcopacy of the civil powers to which Presbyterians objected, the central point Martin uses Aylmer's words to make.

75. Quoting Aylmer, *Harborowe*, D4v. Martin substitutes "meddle with matters of policy" for "meddle too far with matters of policy," overstating Aylmer's objections to bishops' civil roles.

76. *as before . . . touched* see *Epistle*, 8; the passage is from *Harborowe*, O4r–v.

77. *Wickliffe's book* John Wyclif (variously spelled), theologian and reformer (d. 1384). While several works by or attributed to Wyclif had been published by the time Aylmer was writing, *De ecclesia* (*c.* 1377–78) was not among them. But at least one manuscript copy of a Wyclif text with that title was circulating in the period: John Foxe writes in *Actes and Monumentes* (1570) that he had "found out certayne" of Wyclif's treatises, including *De ecclesia*, "which I entend hereafter, the Lord so graunting, to publishe abroad" (547). *wrinches* wrenched or forced interpretations (*OED* wrench n^2 4). *cavillations* false, deceitful, or specious arguments.

78. *Balaam* one who follows religion for gain, from the prophet in Numbers 22–24.

79. *Is* variant spelling of "yes" (*OED*).

80. *lord Lubber of London . . . wily Watson* Aylmer was referring to Edmund Bonner, the Marian bishop of London (see *Epistle*, 216 n.49), and Thomas Watson (1513–84), bishop of Lincoln from 1557–59; both were involved in the prosecution of (Protestant) heresy. Martin suggests in his marginal note that Aylmer, himself now bishop of London, also enjoyed the assistance of a Watson, in this case a pursuivant, to help him suppress reform.

81. *crossed yourself over the costard* hit yourself over the head.

82. For the charge that Aylmer had plundered his episcopal estate by cutting down and selling its trees, see *Epistle*, 21 and 221 n.98.

83. *John of Exeter . . . Thomas Winchester* John Woolton, bishop of Exeter (mentioned in *Epistle*, 9); Thomas Cooper, bishop of Winchester (see *Epistle*, 213 n.19).

84. Martin cites a marginal note in Aylmer's *Harborowe*, "Desperate dickes, good Bishops in England" (E3r); Aylmer was referring ironically to the "good" bishops who persecuted Protestants under Mary.

85. *your own words* Martin proceeds to rewrite a passage from Aylmer's *Harborowe* (E3r–v), casting Whitgift in the role of Edmund Bonner and Aylmer, John Woolton, and Thomas Cooper as the persecuting Marian bishops who imprisoned their opponents.

86. *at an inch* at hand, in readiness (*OED* inch n^1 3).

87. The Gatehouse, Fleet, Marshalsea, Clink, Newgate, and Counter were all prisons in or near London.

88. *women . . . might preach* an accurate summary of Aylmer's argument in *Harborowe*, G4v, H1r–v. While women preachers would be associated with religious radicalism throughout the seventeenth century, Elizabethan reformers consistently condemned the idea of female ministry and attacked the willingness of the church to countenance the possibility that women could play a role in church practice; the church's flexibility on this issue would begin to disappear in the early seventeenth century. John Whitgift's *Defense* (1574)

summarizes the debate by reprinting his exchange on the subject with Thomas Cartwright (506–507). See *Schoolpoints*, 93 and 250 n.27, for the related issue of women's ability to baptize infants.

89. *kie* variant of "kye" or cows, a form later associated with Scottish or northern dialect, but not necessarily so in this period (*OED*).

90. *French king* Henri II (1519–59), of the Valois dynasty, hence "Valesius."

91. *siginnes* as such in the original. Possibly a variant of, or error for, sigging(s), syggin(s), segging(s), all older forms of "saying(s)" (*OED* saying *vbl n*¹): Martin could be suggesting that Paul's "sayings" (the things he repeatedly "speaketh") are "simple." Possibly "simple siginnes" is a jokingly colloquial reference to "they" (the "precise brethren"): Pierce argues that "siginnes" means simpletons (*Marprelate Tracts*, 155). If so, the word appears to be unrecorded.

92. Martin affects a rustic persona with *bommination*, an aphetic form of abomination, used as an intensive for prodigious (*OED* 5), *umberty* for abundance (*OED*, this place cited), and *perceed* for proceed.

93. *Overton … sold his chancellorship* William Overton, bishop of Coventry and Lichfield from 1580; see also *Epistle*, 10, 40, *Schoolpoints*, 91, and *Hay any Work*, 103. Overton appointed John Becon, a reform-minded ecclesiastical lawyer, as his first chancellor and vicar general, possibly in return for Becon's support in getting Overton made bishop. But the two soon quarreled, and in 1583 Overton appointed Zachary Babington as Becon's coadjutor, initiating a dispute brought before Star Chamber and the privy council and which ended only with Becon's death in 1587. See *ODNB* (Becon, Overton), and White, *Lives*, 271–76.

94. *40 marks* a mark was equivalent to two-thirds of a pound: 40 marks was about £26.

95. Throughout this passage, Martin sarcastically voices his opponents' response to "puritan" objections to bishops in civil roles. Stephen Gardiner (*c.* 1495 × 8–1555), bishop of Winchester and the dominant figure in the Marian privy council, spent most of his career in the political rather than pastoral realm; to reformers, he was "a man hated of God and all good men" (Foxe, *Actes and Monumentes* (1570), 1951). Read either straight or ironically, the answer to Martin's question is "no": to the bishops Martin voices, it was not meet for a bishop busy in civil affairs to preach; to the puritans, it was not meet to see *that* bishop in the pulpit.

96. *P. P. prelates* "PP" is the Latin abbreviation for pope ("papa"). In English, the appropriation here suggests "PaPistical" or "PoPish"; cf. the repeated "p"s of "proud, popish, presumptuous, profane, paltry, pestilent and pernicious prelates" (*Epistle*, 10). A 1587 document calendared in *SPR* refers similarly to "the shameles faces of all P. P. Prelates and wicked reviling sclaunderers" (II, 231); and in Thomas Dekker's *The Double PP* (1606), "PP" stands for Catholicism, as opposed to the single "P" of Protestantism (A2r, D4r).

97. *mood* in scholastic logic, "any of the valid forms into which each of the four figures of categorical syllogism is subdivided" (*OED*).

98. *Celarent . . . Barbara* traditional mnemonics for two of the "moods" (see previous note) in formal syllogistic reasoning: Martin's new figure "answereth unto *Celarent*" because syllables with "e" represented propositions in the form of a universal negative, and those with "a," a universal affirmative. Martin's new mnemonic is based on the names (Andrew) Perne, (John Whitgift, archbishop of) Canterbury, and (John Kennall or) Kenold, archdeacon of Oxford. For a discussion of this syllogism, with illustrations of contemporary printed examples, see Lander, *Inventing Polemic*, 98–99.

99. *break-pulpits* boisterous preachers (*OED*). *Paul's wharf* the landing place on the Thames nearest St Paul's Cathedral.

100. Martin here affects a rural dialect, using variant or older forms for "both" (*beath*), "ay" (*ai*), "mouths" (*meaths*), "by" (*bai*), and, in the following sentence, "you" (*yaw*); the idiom *neither nother* for "neither the one nor the other" might also have been archaic or dialectical by this time (*OED*, this place cited).

101. Quoting Bridges's *Defence*, 61 (not Aylmer's *Harborowe*).

102. *out of all cess* beyond estimation, utterly (*OED*, this place cited).

103. According to a story told by Hugh Latimer, Sir Thomas More was sent on a commission to investigate the Goodwin Sands, a notorious hazard to navigation off the coast of Kent near Sandwich. An elderly local man informed More that the sands were caused by the great tower or steeple at Tenterden church, because he could not remember the sands being there before the steeple was built: see Latimer, *27 Sermons* (1562), 115v. "Tenterden's steeple was the cause of Goodwin sands" became proverbial for giving a ridiculous reason for something.

104. *Paul . . . government* conclusion of the sentence by Bridges with which the paragraph began (*Defence*, 611).

105. *hath noted already* see *Epistle*, 15.

106. *secundum usum Sarum* "according to the use of Salisbury": referring to the modified Catholic liturgy developed at the cathedral church of Salisbury. A translation of the Sarum ritual provided the foundation of the Anglican liturgy. As the next sentence indicates, Martin implies that the arguments offered by Bridges, dean of Salisbury, were similarly Catholic in origin.

107. *John Whitgift's grace* that is, John Whitgift, his grace.

108. The subscriptions to the New Testament Epistles printed in the Vulgate and in the Geneva and Authorized Version translations are considered later interpolations, and were first recognized as such by sixteenth-century editors. The subscription to Titus reads: "To Titus, elect the first bishope of the Church of the Cretians, written from Nicopolis in Macedonia" (Geneva translation). Theodore Beza labeled this subscription supposititious in his influential annotations, first published with his Latin translation of the New Testament (1556) and subsequently with his critical edition of the Greek text (1565).

109. *Turrian . . . Sadeel* French Calvinist theologian Antoine de La Roche de Chandieu (Antonius Sadeel or Sadeelius) (1534–91) published several responses

to the work of Spanish Jesuit Francisco Turrianus (Torres) (*c.* 1509–84) between 1577 and 1581; all were reprinted in his *De rebus grauissimis controversis disputationes* (Cambridge, 1584), 280–718, the most likely source for English readers.

110. *letters of orders* certificate of ordination.

111. *Goodman Noddy* fool, simpleton (*OED* noddy *n*[1]).

112. *Their blessing* referring to the story Martin had told of John Aylmer "blessing" with insults the executors of an estate to which he owed money, rather than paying them (*Epistle*, 33).

113. *Simon Magus ... Diotrephes* by offering to pay the apostles, the sorcerer Simon Magus gave his name to the practice (simony) of buying spiritual powers (Acts 8:9–24). Diotrephes, a church official who "loveth to have the preeminence" (3 John 8), was often glossed as representing clerical ambition and covetousness. Reformers read both as figures for episcopacy; they appear again in *Hay any Work*, 109, and *Theses Martinianae*, 161.

114. *Humphrey ... Matthew* probably Dr Laurence Humphrey (1525 × 7–89), regius professor of divinity and president of Magdalen College, Oxford, and Dr Tobie Matthew (1544?–1628), at the time dean of Durham and later bishop of Durham and archbishop of York. While Humphrey had solid reformist credentials, he was also accused of nepotism and corruption; Matthew had a reputation for ambition and promotion-seeking (*ODNB*). Both were pluralists, though Martin likely exaggerates when he accuses the two of holding fourteen preferments between them.

115. *trulling square dice* "throwing" dice (*OED* troll *v* 2). Martin accuses his opponents of dicing or cardplaying below, 85, *Epistle*, 16, 36, and *Hay any Work*, 103.

116. *goodyear* "meaningless expletive" (*OED*, this place cited).

117. *god of the pigs* the pig is one of the traditional emblems of St Anthony of Egypt (251?–356), an association usually interpreted as signifying the temptations of gluttony and sensuality Anthony successfully resisted; he is consequently the patron saint of swineherds and butchers. Pigs were also associated with the Order of Hospitallers named after Anthony.

118. *Legend of Lies* Protestant nickname for the *Golden Legend* (*Legenda aurea*), the standard medieval collection of saints' lives, compiled by Jacob de Voragine in the thirteenth century. Martin here applies the name to Bridges' *Defence*.

119. For the rumor that Bridges wrote the comedy *Gammer Gurton's Needle*, see *Epistle*, 14; the play is mentioned above, 67.

120. *sermon upon Rom. 12* referring to *A Fruitfull Sermon, upon the 3. 4. 5. 6. 7. and 8. verses, of the 12. chapter of the Epistle of S. Paul to the Romanes* (London: Robert Waldegrave, 1584), attributed to Laurence Chadderton or Edward Dering. Thomas Rogers, responding to this sermon in 1590, cited the Marprelate tracts to illustrate his opponent's ecclesiology: see *A Sermon upon the 6. 7. and 8. verses of the 12. chapter of Romanes* (1590), 6, 13–14, 21.

121. Franciscus Junius (François Du Jon) (1545–1602) and Joannes Immanuel Tremellius (1510–80) collaborated on a Latin translation of the Bible widely

regarded as the Protestant answer to the Vulgate. Tremellius' translation of the Syriac New Testament was included in *STC* 2056 et seq.

122. *you deal ... you dare ... yours* Martin is addressing the "puritans" and proceeds to cite Bridges' response to the claim in Fulke's *Briefe and Plaine Declaration* that Presbyterianism operated in the primitive church until Antichrist brought in false doctrine, such as episcopacy (*Defence*, 76).

123. *whoa* modernized from "who" in the original (*OED* who *int*). As Martin proceeds to note, he is quoting Bridges (*Defence*, 76), who often used such colloquialisms to begin sentences.

124. A close paraphrase of Bridges' argument, until Martin's concluding extrapolation. Bridges, implicitly targeting the reform platform, had argued that "*Sathan* hath alwayes beene sowing newe *kindes of false doctrine*, and I doubt whether *all* his *kindes of false doctrine* be yet *brought in*, or no" (*Defence*, 76).

125. *tale ... of a fox-tail* Bridges had offered this fable in response to his opponents' comparison of bishops to foxes: "I reade a tale of a *Foxe* that had lost his taile, and because other had tayles, and hee had none: he went about to perswade all his brethren, to *leave* their tailes, for they were but an unnecessary clogge and hinderance unto them, trayling in the myre: which if it were away, O how light and nimble should they bee. And for example to *perswade* them the better, he shewed them the *experience* (not in his neighbour) but in him-selfe. But one that knewe before on what necessity he had lost it: cried out unto him, Brother *Foxe*, brother *Foxe*; leave your faire *perswasion*. You have lost your owne, and therefore you would have us to *leave ours* to beare you company. But, what do ye tel vs heere (will our brethren say) a foolish flim flam tale of a *foxe taile*, to dallie out so waighty and so holie a matter ...? But ... why may not a fained fable applyed to truth, aunswere a feyned *perswasion*, grounded on falsehoode?" (*Defence*, 82–83).

126. In this story, an ass loaded with sponges watches a fellow ass rid itself of a burden of salt by sitting in a river and having the salt melt away. The ass with sponges tries the same trick, only, of course, to have its burden increase. Bridges draws the moral "*Experience* is not alwayes good uppon examples" (*Defence*, 86; "83" is an error).

127. *cloakbag* probably alluding to the earlier claim that Whitgift as a student had carried Andrew Perne's cloakbag, a figure for his having "served under" Perne (see *Epistle*, 29).

128. *Andrew* ambo Andrew Perne, dean of Ely: "*ambo*" for ambidextrous, referring to Perne's shifts between Catholicism and Protestantism (see *Epistle*, 217 n.53).

129. *Redman* William Redman (*c.* 1541–1602), archdeacon of Canterbury from 1576 and later bishop of Norwich. Martin refers to the card game "thirty-one," in which a player tries to amass high-ranking cards: the reference is probably an implicit accusation of court toadying. He also claims that Redman is skilled in "juggling," meaning trickery and deception. Redman does not appear to have had a reputation for corruption (beyond the usual pluralism), though he did maintain a "large and costly household" and died in debt (*ODNB*).

130. *Scambler* Edmund Scambler (*c.* 1520–94), bishop of Peterborough from 1561–84 and of Norwich from 1584. In 1570 Scambler had supported the Presbyterian movement in Northampton, and he was to show the movement some sympathy at moments throughout his career. But his reputation suffered among reformers as a result of his later actions: on his promotion to Norwich he agreed to the alienation of more than sixty manors and rectors belonging to the church, leading to the accusation that he was a despoiler of church property; and in October 1588, shortly before the *Epitome* was written, he brought charges against the religious radical Francis Kett, who would be burned in January 1589 (*ODNB*). Martin also plays here with the implications of "scamble": "to struggle in an indecorous and rapacious manner in order to obtain something" (*OED*).

131. That is, "that which I could say against our ungodly priests, but have not yet said."

132. *devise* order, direct (*OED v* 3).

3 *CERTAIN MINERAL AND METAPHYSICAL SCHOOLPOINTS*

1. *Schoolpoints* theses or debating points; they are described, with irony, as *mineral* (profound, deep, recondite; cf. *OED* I 4b) and *metaphysical* (preternatural, extraordinary, cf. *OED* II 4a, 4b); later in the title, they are *mysteries* (probably playing on the theological sense of doctrinal difficulties beyond human understanding; cf. *OED* I 2).

2. *catercorner* from "corner cap" or "catercap," the four-cornered cap worn by clergy. Possibly implying a divinity "diagonally" opposed to the (Presbyterian) truth: the *OED* cites no uses of "catercorner" in this sense before the nineteenth century, but it cites a sixteenth-century use of "cater," meaning to place diagonally.

3. That is, denying the legitimacy of clerical hierarchy was like denying orthodox doctrine on the Trinity: the Nicene Creed used *Homoousion* ("of one substance") to describe the relation between Father and Son, countering the Semi-Arian alternative, *Homoiousion* ("of like substance"). Bertrand de Loque's *Traité de l'église* (Geneva, 1577) was translated by the puritan minister Thomas Wilcox as *A Treatie of the Churche* (1581). The translation's prefatory "Admonition to the Reader," attributed here to John Aylmer, is unsigned; the analogy that provides this schoolpoint appears on 3*4r–v. The attribution to Aylmer and a condemnation of the analogy also appear in the para-Martinist *A Dialogue* (La Rochelle, 1589), B2v.

4. *two wives* the defendant is Marmaduke Middleton (d. 1593), bishop of St David's from 1582. For the many scandals with which he was associated, see *Epistle*, 232 n.200. Martin mentions the (apparently accurate) charge of bigamy again in *Hay any Work*, 101. *in esse* in actual existence.

5. *Christ . . . hell* John Whitgift "firmely beleeveth that Christ in soule descended into hell" (*Admonition*, 44). For the debate on this issue, see *Epistle*, 224 n.127; it is

mentioned again in schoolpoint no. 28 below. For Thomas Cooper as "profane" T. C., versus Thomas Cartwright as "simple" T. C., see *Hay any Work*, 131.

6. *our Saviour . . . sware by his faith* the defendant here should be John Aylmer, not Thomas Cooper. Responding to the accusation that he was prone to swearing (see *Epistle*, 8–9), Aylmer claimed that "in the phrase of our speech, *by my faith* signifieth no more, but, *in very trueth, bona fide, in trueth, assuredly, id est, Amen*" (*Admonition*, 62).

7. *Moses . . . brake the moral law* arguing that "God sometime beareth with breach of his commaundement," Thomas Cooper listed scriptural examples, concluding with the approval of divorce in Deuteronomy 24:1–4: "Yea, in a moral commandement of God, touching mariage, we see God to use a maner of dispensation, in respect of the frailty of mans nature" (*Admonition*, 110–11). Martin probably objects to the implication that marriage was a moral commandment, which he would have read as a return to the Catholic view of marriage as sacrament. For the reform movement's (limited) approval of divorce, and its opposition to attempts by the church to resanctify the marriage bond, see Knappen, *Tudor Puritanism*, 456–61, and Stone, *Road to Divorce*, 301–308.

8. *papistry is better than . . . puritanism* the defendant is Edmund Freake (1516–91), bishop of Norwich from 1575 and of Worcester from 1584; see also *Epistle*, 9, 30. Reformers accused Freake of crypto-Catholicism throughout his years in Norwich and Worcester. The privy council investigated his purges of reformist ministers and the repeated accusations that he tolerated recusancy (*ODNB*); the charge cited here was likely aired at one of the public inquiries that accompanied these investigations.

9. *public fasts . . . invasion of the Spaniards* the defendant is William Overton, bishop of Lichfield and Coventry from 1580; see also *Epistle*, 9, 40, *Epitome*, 77, and *Hay any Work*, 103. Solihull is a rectory in Warwickshire, near Birmingham, in Overton's diocese: Job Throkmorton might have had a personal interest in the state of the church in Solihull because the benefice had been in the patronage of the Throckmorton family before the accession of Elizabeth. According to the 1586 "Survey of the Ministry," the incumbent, Henry Smyth, was "dombe and unlearned, a tainted parson of life and suspected of drunkennes" (*SPR*, II, 169). This particular claim about the Spanish invasion being a punishment for puritan fasts and prayers is untraced, and probably was not made in print. *SPR* calendars an extended reformist denunciation of Overton's character and behavior (II, 16ff.).

10. *long prayers . . . beeble babble* the defendant is John Aylmer, the witness Robert Cawdrey, rector of South Luffenham in Rutland, examined by high commission in 1586 for denying the scriptural basis of clerical hierarchy, condemning non-residency, and speaking against the BCP; for Cawdrey, see Introduction, xxxiii. Several documents connected with Cawdrey's case are included in *SPR*, including Cawdrey's own narrative of "the greifes and hard-dealinges" offered him over the years by Aylmer. During his examination, Cawdrey writes, Aylmer made the "blasphemous" complaint that "You use such longe prayers before the sermons, which is nothing els but bible bable, bible bable" (*SPR*, II, 205).

11. *trial ... by appeaching and accusing a man's self* referring to the use of the oath *ex officio*; the defendants are the high commissioners and the witness Giles Wigginton, the minister they examined in December 1588 about his knowledge of the Marprelate project (see *Epistle*, 25–26). Wigginton's account of his examination is in *SPR*: he refused to take the oath *ex officio* and claimed that the commissioners defended "such answering and swearing" as a necessary means for defending the state (*SPR*, II, 253–58).

12. *as lawful ... to make bad ministers, as ... to pluck the ears of corn* Thomas Cooper had asked reformers to temper their criticism of church officials by acknowledging human imperfection, citing the story of the ears of corn in Mark 2:23–28, with its lesson that "The Sabboth was ordeined for man, and not man for the Sabboth" (*Admonition*, 111), as evidence that Christ himself acknowledged human inability always to live up to ideals.

13. *reading is preaching* Bridges had argued that preaching was not necessary for the efficacy of a sacrament because the liturgy so clearly expressed "all the pointes conteyned in that mysterie" that "the best *preacher* in the worlde cannot in effect say more" (*Defence*, 565).

14. *24 orders of bishops* sarcastic exaggeration of the levels of offices within the church hierarchy, none of which reformers found sanctioned in scripture. *Hay any Work*, 109ff., elaborates on this point.

15. *more good ... by our ordinary service than by preaching* Bridges had argued that the ordinary service "is so little to be opposed unto *preaching*: that it may better bee called a fruitefull kynde of preaching" (*Defence*, 652).

16. *cross in baptism, and organs ... necessary* the defendant is Gabriel Goodman, dean of Westminster and a member of high commission; see *Epistle*, 31, 40. Reformers had long objected to the use of the cross in baptism and to organ music during service as remnants of Catholic practice. The reformist "Six Articles" of 1562 had included proposals to make the use of the cross optional and to remove all organs from churches; Goodman resisted the proposals at the time and throughout his subsequent career on high commission. Objections to the use of the cross and organs appear repeatedly during the debates on subscription in the 1580s and in the documents collected in *SPR*. Goodman likely made this comment during one of the many examinations of non-subscribers in which he participated.

17. *bishops of the devil* the immediate source of the phrase was Theodore Beza, *The Judgement of a Most Reverend and Learned Man* (*c.* 1585), to which Bridges was responding; see Introduction, xxiii. A marginal note in Bridges' *Defence* summarized his position on Beza's "threefold" order of bishops: "There is no B. of man, but either he is the B. of God, or of the devil" (339). Martin draws the conclusion here. On the page following, Bridges asked, rhetorically, "doe ye thinke that a *power limited with orders or rules provided against tyrannie*, is not a good and lawefull power? Or is such *a power of the Divell*?" (340); Martin, of course, answers yes. The polemical point Bridges inadvertently provided was too good not to reuse: see *Hay any Work*, 119, 123–25.

18. *true baptism . . . out of the church* the defendant is Robert Some (1542–1609), chaplain of Peterhouse, Cambridge, until May 1589, when he was made College master; he is mentioned again in schoolpoint no. 25 below, *Theses Martinianae*, 158, *Just Censure*, 181, and *Protestation*, 205–06, and was the target of the para-Martinist *M. Some Laid Open in His Coulers* (La Rochelle, 1589). The second, enlarged edition of Some's *A Godly Treatise* (1588) responded to John Penry's discussions of baptism in *An Exhortation* (East Molesey, 1588) and *A Defence of that which hath bin Written* (East Molesey, 1588). Penry questioned whether baptism administered in the Catholic church were "true" baptism; Some invoked Augustine to argue that "There hath bene and may be true Baptisme out of the Church," though he added that "heretikes have lawfull baptisme, but they have it not lawfully" (158–59).

19. *no more unlawful . . . many benefices . . . many lordships* the defendant is Richard Cosin, high commissioner and dean of the court of arches; see *Epistle*, 212 n.17. His *An Answer* (1584) defended pluralism at some length (225–350) while responding to an attack on the practice in *An Abstract, of Certain Acts of Parliament* (1583), attributed to William Stoughton. Martin refers to a passage in which Cosin suggested that his opponent "will not denie (I hope) but that manie laie fees and temporall lordships may be possessed by some one, which yet he denieth to ecclesiasticall men, though perhaps their desert and contribution to the publike charges of the realme be as great as theirs, who enjoy in true value ten times as much revenue" (286).

20. *one priest . . . lawful superior authority* "Doth *S. Peter* then forbid, *that any one Elder should have & exercise any superior government over the cleargy. . .*? If he doth not, but alloweth it, & his self practised it; then . . . the matter is cleare, that *one Priest or Elder*, among the residue, may have a lawfull *superior auth. & government over the cleargy*; (that is) *over all the universal body of the Church, in every particular or several congregation*" (*Defence*, 448). Bridges' argument could be read as supporting papal supremacy, an implication Martin fore-grounds by quoting the phrase "universal body."

21. *preaching . . . only ordinary means of salvation* see *Epistle*, 28, which dramatizes the exchange on this question between John Penry and the high commissioners.

22. *matters of state . . . election of their ministers* Thomas Cooper concluded his discussion of "common election of Ministers" with the warning against popular rule that Martin cites: "It is greatly to bee feared, that they [the people] will very easily transferre the same to the governement of the common weale" (*Admonition*, 83; "43" is an error).

23. *Book of Prayer . . . error* Bridges defended the text and doctrine of the BCP throughout the *Defence*, though only implicitly in the pages cited here. But elsewhere he explicitly claimed that "there is no *error*, nor any suspicion *of error*" in texts in the BCP (1311; see also, e.g., 646, 804, 807, 1302–309).

24. *surplice* for John Aylmer as a tree-cutting "Mar-elm," see *Epistle*, 22; for the reformist minister Robert Cawdrey, see schoolpoint no. 8 above. The surplice, condemned by many reformers as a Catholic holdover, had been the subject of

debate since the "Vestments" or "Vestiarian" controversy (1566). Aylmer made wearing the surplice one of the conditions Cawdrey had to meet to avoid suspension (*SPR*, II, 205).

25. *sums of money . . . necessary service* "He that shal charitably consider the state of Bishops . . . wil not thinke it impietie in them, against the time of necessarie service of their countrey, to have some reasonable summe of money before hand, gathered in honestie, and just using of their owne" (*Admonition*, 148). Cooper was reminding readers that bishops were expected to support the crown financially through periodic subsidies.

26. *good minister . . . not fit to teach* another attack on the passage from Cooper's *Admonition* cited in note 12 above (to schoolpoint no. 10).

27. *archbishop . . . holding baptism administered by women . . . an absurd heretic* referring to Robert Some's response to Penry's challenge (*An Exhortation*, 31) of the validity of baptism by unpreaching ministers; for Some, see note 18 above. If Penry's arguments were true, Some claimed, then "the outwarde and bare element delivered by him, which in M. Penryes judgement, is no minister, is the seale of Gods covenant: Which is a most absurd heresie" (*A Godly Treatise*, G3r). Martin here uses Some's words to attack John Whitgift for allowing baptism by women: since women were not ministers, Whitgift should be guilty of the same "absurd heresy." The Elizabethan church did not endorse baptism by women, but neither did it forbid midwives from baptizing newborns who looked unlikely to survive. Reformers such as Thomas Cartwright insisted that baptism by women was a Catholic practice that needed to be abolished. In his polemical exchanges with Cartwright, Whitgift repeatedly evaded the question by arguing that the provision in the BCP for "private" baptism (that is, baptism in a private space such as a house) did not mean that the church supported baptism by women. Whitgift appears to have seen the practice as one the church could do little about: see *Defense* (1574), 29, 504, 509, 516, 793. The debate is summarized in Cressy, *Birth, Marriage, and Death*, 117–23.

28. *archbishop . . . Apocrypha . . . Whitaker . . . Bellarmine* the defendant should be John Whitgift, not Thomas Cooper. William Whitaker (1547/48–95), professor of Divinity at Cambridge, was a noted anti-Catholic polemicist. His *Disputatio ad sacra scriptura* (Cambridge, 1588), a response to the work of Cardinal Robert Bellarmine (see *Epitome*, 239 n.50), challenged the Catholic view of the Apocrypha and thereby implicitly supported the reform challenge to the use of Apocryphal texts in the BCP. Since the *Disputatio* would have been published with approval, Martin here turns against Whitgift the archbishop's own defense of the Apocrypha: "all learned men have from the beginning, given to the *Apocrypha* authoritie, next to the Canonicall Scriptures. And therfore such giddie heads, as seeke to deface them, are to be bridled" (*Admonition*, 49). Whitaker was a useful authority for reformers to invoke: long associated with Whitgift and an important voice in the established church, he had increasingly linked himself with members of the reform movement, and in 1591 would marry the widow of puritan stalwart Dudley Fenner (*ODNB*); he is mentioned in passing in *Epistle*, 25.

29. *without two benefices, a minister cannot furnish himself of books* the defendant is George Boleyn (d. 1603), dean of Lichfield from 1576. Martin also cites Boleyn in *Protestation*, 207, apparently drawing on notes made during one of Boleyn's sermons; this schoolpoint might be drawn from the same source. Boleyn had a reputation for protecting his own interests: a non-resident and pluralist, he was "clearly concerned about his own emoluments" (*ODNB*).

30. *descending of Christ's soul ... superiority of ministers ... the name priest* reformers repeatedly condemned the church's position on these three issues as Catholic; Whitgift defended them as Protestant doctrine, in detail in his replies to Thomas Cartwright and in brief in the pages of the *Admonition* cited here (44–45). *Epistle*, 224 n.127, provides some background for these debates. See also note 5 above (to schoolpoint no. 3).

31. *ecclesiastical officer ... private subject* "For such is nowe the state of this time, that whatsoever an Officer, specially Ecclesiasticall, may doe by lawfull authoritie, the private Subject thinketh hee may doe the same, at his owne will and pleasure" (*Admonition*, 94). The passage could be read as arguing that church officers enjoyed legal authority for behavior that Cooper himself would condemn in private subjects, a point Martin himself repeatedly makes. *Mistress Cooper's husband* referring to the widespread rumors that Amy Cooper had a lover (and that Cooper was therefore subordinate to his wife). See *ODNB*; Harington, *Briefe View*, II, 90; and Thomas Bulkeley, "Libel of Oxford" (*c.* 1564), the widely circulated manuscript libel discussed in the Introduction, xxviii. Martin repeats the insult in *Hay any Work*, 102, 112, where he names the suspected lover, Dr John Day, fellow and librarian of Magdalen College, Oxford.

32. *have in admiration ... other countries, and to loathe their own* "If men woulde cast so curious and captious eyes upon the Ministers of other countries, and note the blemishes and imperfections in them, as they doe in our owne: I am perswaded (under correction) they woulde not thinke so meanely of the state of the Ministerie of *Englande*, as they doe. But this is the generall disease of us Englishmen, to have in admiration the persons and states of other foreine countries, and loath their owne, be they never so commendable or good" (*Admonition*, 105). Martin presumably objects to the implication that reformers looked to foreign churches (and not to scripture) for their platform. *Eastmeon* parish in Hampshire in the possession of the bishops of Winchester: as bishop, Cooper was both patron of the vicarage and lord of the manor. Martin repeats the association of Cooper with this parish in *Hay any Work*, title page (99).

33. *bishops' livings* Cooper was responding to the reform argument that depriving bishops of their temporal offices and wealthy livings would render them "answerable to the Apostles" and free up money for the Queen's use: "But it behoveth all Christian Princes and Magistrates to take heede, that they be not intrapped with this sophistrie of Satans schoole. This is that Rhetorike that he useth, when he will work any mischief in the Church of God, or stirre up any trouble or alteration of a state in a common weale" (*Admonition*, 155). *Tub-trimmer* a play on Cooper's name that Martin uses throughout the next pamphlet, *Hay any Work*.

34. *doctrine of our Saviour . . . doctrine of S. Paul . . . too great a bridle* Cooper was "not of that opinion . . . that the externall government of the church, shoulde alwayes, and in all places be one, and specially by a College or companie of Elders." To the objection that "the Apostles afterward, and the Primitive Church did practise the same," Cooper responded with the argument Martin cites: reformers "shall never find a commandement in the scriptures, charging that it should for ever be so. It were too great a bridle of Christian liberty in things externall, to cast upon the Church of Christ" (*Admonition*, 134–35). In *Hay any Work*, 132, Martin notes the presence of a cancel slip with which Cooper modified his argument in this passage.

35. *Moses ordained a government . . . so did not Christ* Martin returns to this argument in more detail in *Hay any Work*, 116ff.

36. *Apocrypha . . . is in authority next to the canonical scriptures* the defendant should be Whitgift, who repeatedly defended the use of Apocryphal texts in the BCP; see note 28 above, and *Epistle*, 33 and 229 n.166.

37. *not lawful . . . to bestow the bishops' livings upon lay men* Cooper, implying that reformers attacked bishops because they hoped to gain financially from the redistribution of episcopal livings, writes that he "coulde with better reason and authoritie proove the contrary Proposition to that which they take upon them to maintaine: that is, *That it is not lawfull to bestowe such Livings upon Laye men, as are appoynted by godly lawes for Ministers and Preachers of the worde of God*" (*Admonition*, 252). Martin responds to this passage in *Hay any Work*, 126; in *Protestation*, 202, he notes that he did not approve of alienating church property into lay hands and objects to the charge that reformers were motivated by greed.

38. *one of our bishops' great faults that they have not . . . by excommunication constrained our prince and magistrats* an accurate quotation, but Cooper was employing some rather clumsy irony that Martin insists on reading straight. Cooper in fact credits bishops with reforming the abuse of excommunication, suggesting that it was reformers who were striving to establish excommunication "under the name of *Discipline*" (*Admonition*, 137).

39. *England cannot possibly stand without lord bishops* Cooper had argued that abolishing episcopacy would alter "the whole state of the lawes of this realme": canon law would disappear, and the validity of remaining laws would be called into question because the bishops, as lords spiritual, were one of the three estates on whose authority the laws stood. Among the laws that would be abrogated were those "maintaining the *Queenes supremacie in governing of the Church, and her prerogative in matters Ecclesiasticall*" (*Admonition*, 77r–v).

4 HAY ANY WORK FOR COOPER

1. *Hay any Work for Cooper* the title draws on the London street cry "Ha' ye any work for cooper?" For a seventeenth-century depiction of a cooper captioned with this cry, see the illustration on the back cover. For additional versions of this image, see Shesgreen, *Criers and Hawkers of London*, 17, 21, 23.

2. *pistle* epistle, but also punning on "pistol" and "pizzle"; see *Epitome*, 236 n.4. *hublication* rustic malapropism for "supplication," possibly conflating "humble supplication."

3. *Parson of Eastmeon* Thomas Cooper: as bishop of Winchester, he was patron of the Hampshire vicarage of Eastmeon; see also *Schoolpoints*, 251 n.32. Nothing further is known of Tom Coakes (spelled "Cooke" later in the tract), Cooper's chaplain. By feigning uncertainty over the identification, Martin suggests that the quality of argument in the *Admonition* was not that expected of a bishop.

4. The words "hath showed himself in his late *Admonition to the People of England*" are added, as directed by the concluding list of errata. *beceitful* deceitful, with the dialect b/d substitution.

5. *out of all cry* beyond measure, to excess.

6. *Bouncing* blustering, boastful, strapping, swaggering (*OED*).

7. The running head of the preliminary epistle is reproduced here as a section heading.

8. *Sir John* clerics were accorded the honorific "Sir," but a "Sir John" was a cleric of the simple or inferior sort (*OED* sir *n* 4). See *Epistle*, 219 n.72, for Martin's use of "Sir" for "St," and below, 106–07, for his defense of the usage.

9. *Clink or Gatehouse* two of London's prisons. *cold time of winter* Cooper's *Admonition* was published in January, this tract in March.

10. *month's mind* Catholic rite of commemoration held a month after a person's death; colloquially, as here, to have a person in remembrance. This passage likely inspired the anti-Martinist pamphlet *Martins Months Minde* (1589).

11. For Aylmer making his purblind porter a minister, see *Epistle*, 21. Martin repeats the charge below, 136.

12. For Aylmer's defense of his swearing, see *Schoolpoints*, 247 n.16. Martin repeats the charge below, 137.

13. Martin had mentioned Aylmer's Sunday bowling in *Epistle* (see 214 n.31). The bishop had defended himself in the *Admonition*: "And for your jesting at the bishop for bowling upon the Sabboth, you must understand that the best expositor of the Sabboth, which is Christ, hath saide, that the Sabboth was made for man, and not man for the Sabboth: and man may have his meate dressed for his health upon the Sabboth, & why may he not then have some convenient exercise of the body, for the health of the body?" (57). Martin repeats the charge below, 136–37.

14. See below, 137, for Martin's more detailed response to Cooper's argument concerning David and the shewbread.

15. Cooper had responded to the charge that he was unlearned: "It is knowen five and fourtie yeeres since, that he was Master of Arte, and student of Divinitie, & disputed in that faculty: since which time, he was never drawen from that exercise of good learning" (*Admonition*, 72v). Martin repeats this point below, 138.

16. Martin accuses Bridges of asserting clerical control over the church, thereby undermining royal supremacy. For more detailed versions of this argument,

see *Epistle*, 16–19, and *Schoolpoints*, 92. Martin clarifies his point at the end of this paragraph.

17. *bishop of Sir David's in Wales* the scandal-ridden Marmaduke Middleton; see *Epistle*, 232 n.200, and *Schoolpoints*, 246 n.4. For Martin's use of "Sir" for "St," see *Epistle*, 219 n.72.

18. *out of all scotch and notch* beyond all bounds or calculation (*OED* scotch n^1 3, earliest citation).

19. *lay on load* deal heavy blows (*OED* load *n* 7). *skin-coat* a person's skin (*OED* skin-coat 2, earliest citation), possibly also a play on "surplice," the etymological roots of which mean a coat worn over skin or fur (*OED*).

20. *Thomas Cooke* or "Coakes" (title page), apparently Cooper's chaplain.

21. The list of contents in the *Admonition* includes the entry "Against the Bishop of Rochester, Lincolne, and Winchester" (A4r). Bishops of Winchester rank fifth in the Anglican hierarchy, preceded only by the two archbishops and the bishops of London and Durham. Martin jokingly claims that Cooper must be the author, because nobody else would dare demote Winchester by listing him last among these three. For the gibe about Cooper's subordination to his wife ("Mistress Cooper's husband"), see next note.

22. *Doctor Day of Wells* Dr John Day, fellow and librarian of Magdalen College, Oxford, and from 1587 vicar general to Thomas Godwin, bishop of Bath and Wells. Day was named as Amy Cooper's lover in Thomas Bulkeley's "Libel of Oxford" (see Introduction, xxviii; *Schoolpoints*, 251 n.31; Harington, *Briefe View*, II, 90); he is mentioned again below, 112. In his edition of Wood's *Athenae Oxoniensis* (1813–20), Philip Bliss misidentified Bulkeley's Dr Day as Dr Thomas Day, canon of Christ Church and fellow of All Souls (I, 609–10); the misidentification is sometimes repeated in writing on Bulkeley and on Marprelate.

23. *grosshead* thick-headed, dull-witted (*OED*).

24. Martin's comment in *Epistle* that John Bridges would soon have "twenty fists" about his ears was widely read as a threat to physical violence; see *Epistle*, 212 n.15. Martin returns to the point below, 119. *Stafford law* "law" of clubs or blows, with a pun on "staff" (*OED*).

25. *eulojin ... eulogein* Martin's contempt for the mispronunciation was undermined by a typographical error in the original edition that left his "eulogein" spelled "enlogeni"; this mistake was noted in the errata list and is corrected here.

26. *soaking* drained, impoverished, exhausted (*OED* soaking *ppl a* 1b). *no grue* not a whit, nothing (*OED*). Possibly also a play on "no Greek."

27. *John of Gloucester or William of Lichfield* John Bullingham, bishop of Gloucester (see *Epistle*, 227 n.147); William Overton, bishop of Lichfield and Coventry (see *Epistle*, 214 n.32).

28. *Westchester* probably referring to William Chaderton (d. 1608), bishop of Chester from 1579 and later bishop of Lincoln; "Chester" was often called "Westchester" in the period. This is Martin's only explicit mention of Chaderton, who encouraged godly preachers and even protected

nonconforming ministers. But he was also a promotion-chasing pluralist with a reputation for avariciousness, though there is no other evidence for a habit of high-stakes card-playing (*ODNB*; Harington, *Briefe View*, II, 115–16). *primero* popular card game, the rules of which are now only imperfectly known. A noble was usually valued in the period at 6*s* 8*d*; 20 nobles would be more than £6.

29. *his Amen* for Aylmer's defense of swearing "by his faith" as a form of "Amen," see *Schoolpoints*, 247 n.6.

30. *argling* arguing, disputing (*OED*, the only citation before the 1820s).

31. Martin used the first of three 1589 editions of Cooper's *Admonition* (*STC* 5683a), the final page of which is numbered "252"; its actual total is 266 pages (65r–78v are numbered by leaves).

32. *You bestow not full 50 pages in the answer* the explicit response to Martin's *Epistle* occupies *Admonition*, 33–64, 65r–76v, 84–87.

33. *adjent* either "adjunct" or "agent": both words were recent, and they had overlapping meanings (*OED*). Martin claims that the "puritan" arguments Cooper rebuts were his own inventions: even if Cooper had named a source, that author would only "stand in" for Cooper himself, the real author of "the book" (the *Admonition*) in which these arguments appeared.

34. *Dean John* John Bridges. *Doctor Cosin* Richard Cosin, high commissioner (see *Epistle*, 212 n.17, and *Schoolpoints*, 249 n.19). *Copcot* Dr John Copcot, master of Christ's College, Cambridge (see *Epistle*, 213 n.22); "Capcase" puns on the clerical "corner" or "cater" cap.

35. *besoop* repeated below, 131; these are the only two instances recorded in *OED*, which suggests "to thrash, to lay about." Coined from "soop" (used below, 113), a variant of swoop, meaning a stroke or blow (*OED*), and probably also meant to suggest "bishop" used as a verb.

36. *bear the world in hand* to "bear in hand" is to persuade through deception (*OED* bear *v*¹ 3e). The phrase is used several times in this tract.

37. *Come off you bishops … hundreds* citing John Aylmer, *An Harborowe for Faithfull and Trewe Subjectes* (1559); Martin quotes the passage at length in *Epitome*, 72–73.

38. The printing of *More Work for Cooper* was in progress when authorities seized the Marprelate press; Martin describes the tract's contents in *Protestation*, 204–06.

39. *Sir Peter* referring to *Epistle*, 17; Martin here glibly explains the origin of his repeated substitution of "Sir" for "St."

40. Martin here continues to respond to Cooper's objection to the substitution of "Sir" for "St" (see *Epistle*, 219 n.72). Cooper had exclaimed at the use of "*Sir Marie*" for "the *Blessed Virgine Mary*" (*Admonition*, A2r). Martin banteringly denies any connection between the Mary of St Mary Overie and the "blessed virgin": since the parish of St Mary Overie included the chapel of St Mary Magdalene, Martin identifies its St Mary as this "popish trull."

41. *a* he; by this period chiefly used to create the effect of familiar speech (*OED* a *pron*).

42. *Sir John* familiar name given to clerics, usually of the simpler sort.

43. *Bankside* narrow street in Southwark alongside the Thames, an area traditionally associated with brothels.

44. For this passage from Bridges' *Defence*, and Martin's argument that it undermined royal supremacy, see *Epistle*, 16–19, and *Schoolpoints*, 92.

45. *spoonmeat* soft or liquid food prepared for infants or invalids.

46. *Glibery* William Glibery, vicar of St Andrews, Halstead, from 1560–90. The
1586 "Survey of the Ministry" lists Glibery among a selected group of
"Preachers of a scandalous life in Essex," describing him as "a verie ridiculous
preacher"(*SPR*, II, 163). PRO SP Dom. 12/159/27 is a 1583 list of Glibery's
"untrew, unreverent, scoffinge, prophane, and blasphemous" pulpit comments; it includes the story Martin tells later in the paragraph of the boy
with the red cap.

47. *Summer Lord* another name for the May King who presided over traditional
May Game pastimes, such as Morris dancing and Maypoles; some later
traditions identified him with Robin Hood, but other traditions kept the
two figures separate.

48. *merry grigs* "extravagantly lively" persons, "full of frolic and jest" (*OED*).

49. *eulojin . . . eulogein* see above, 102.

50. Reformers read Diotrephes (3 John 9) and Simon Magus (Acts 8:9–24) as
figures for episcopal pride, covetousness, and ambition (see *Epitome*, note 113);
Martin lists in their company John Aylmer, John Whitgift, Thomas Cooper,
Andrew Perne, and John Kenold (or Kennall), archdeacon of Oxford.

51. *brave weather Hay any Work* was written in February and March 1589.

52. *trunch-fiddle* the only citation in *OED*, which hazards no guess as to meaning.
Presumably a coinage relying on the adjective "trunch," meaning short and
thick (*OED*). Pierce suggests, "a short stumpy fiddle; Aylmer was a short,
stumpy man" (*Marprelate Tracts*, 229).

53. *bumfeg* apparently, to flog or thrash (*OED*, earliest citation; cf. bumbaste).
The author of *An Almond for a Parrat* (1590) tells an aspiring young anti-
Martinist, "Alas, you are but young, and never knewe what his [Martin's]
Bumfeging ment, for if you did, you woulde thinke five hundreth fistes about
your eares were more then Phisicke in a frosty morning" (Nashe, *Works*, III, 356).

54. Martin groups Richard Howland, bishop of Peterborough, William Wickham,
bishop of Lincoln, and Edmund Freake, bishop of Worcester, in a similar list in
Epistle, 9. For Howland, see also below, 139; for Wickham, see *Epistle*, 214 n.27;
for Freake, see *Epistle*, 214 n.27, and *Schoolpoints*, 247 n.8. John Bullingham,
bishop of Gloucester, was a Catholic exile in the reign of Edward VI and
chaplain to Bishop Gardiner under Mary; see *Epistle*, 227 n.147.

55. *with a wet finger* with utmost ease.

56. *subscription* referring to Whitgift's requirement that ministers subscribe to his
articles of belief or face deprivation (thereby, in the metaphor employed here,
depriving the church of ministers who were its true "eyes" or overseers); see
Introduction, xxi.

57. *putteth* emended from "pulleth."

58. Respectively, Dean John Bridges, Dr Richard Cosin (see *Epistle*, 212 n.17), and Dr John Copcot (see *Epistle*, 213 n.22).

59. *injury* used as a transitive verb in the period (*OED*).

60. *Day* Dr John Day, fellow (until 1586) of Magdalen College, Oxford, and widely rumored to be Amy Cooper's lover; see above, note 22, and *Schoolpoints*, 251 n.31.

61. *last Thomas of Lincoln* Thomas Cooper had been bishop of Lincoln before his translation to Winchester: Martin invites Amy Cooper to ask her lover to induce her husband to ask himself if he was persuaded by Martin's argument.

62. *dry soops* stiff or severe (*OED* dry *a* 12) strokes or blows (*OED* swoop *n*); see the uses of "besoop" above, 105, and below, 131.

63. Here and subsequently, Martin returns the names Cooper had applied to him: "I feare he wil prove himselfe to bee, not onely *Mar-prelate*, but *Mar-prince*, *Mar-state*, *Mar-lawe*, *Mar-magistrate*" (*Admonition*, 36).

64. *John of Gloucester* John Bullingham, bishop of Gloucester; see above, 110, and *Epistle*, 227 n.147.

65. *time, place and persons* Martin justifies the lawfulness of his satire by invoking the traditional terms used in classical discussions of decorum.

66. *you are those . . . like to spill* returning the argument Martin claims was made by William Overton, bishop of Lichfield and Coventry, that "the public fasts and the prayers of the puritans were the cause of the invasion of the Spaniards" (*Schoolpoints*, 91).

67. *overseen* deceived, deluded (*OED*).

68. *T. C. . . . page 103* citing Cooper's argument that challenges to church hierarchy were analogous to political treason, because church reformers and "rebellious subjects" both attributed their grievances unjustly to the authorities placed over them (*Admonition*, 103).

69. For disapproval of the Marprelate project among reformers, see Introduction, xxx.

70. *threatening of fists* see above, 102, and *Epistle*, 7 and 212 n.15.

71. Martin names four reformers suspected of having written the tracts: for Eusebius Paget, see *Epistle*, 225 n.134; for Giles Wigginton, see *Epistle*, 224 n.128; for John Udall, see Introduction, xlviii; and for John Penry, see Introduction, xxxviff. Presumably, official suspicion of all four was public knowledge by this point.

72. Cooper had defended episcopacy by noting that Protestant martyrs Thomas Cranmer (1489–1556), Nicholas Ridley (1500–55), and John Hooper (d. 1555), among others, had all accepted episcopal office (*Admonition*, 73v).

73. *and a petty and petty* as in the original; probably an error.

74. Martin argues that an attack on a church office was not necessarily an attack on its holder: he can praise Gregory I (*c.* 540–604), pope from 590, while deploring the office he held. Martin probably drew his accounts of the papacy from John Bale's *Pageant of Popes* (1574): Bale offers a largely positive account of Gregory (32v–33v). Martin confuses Boniface I, pope from 418 and about whom Bale has little to say, with Boniface II, pope from 530, whom Bale accuses of playing a key role in the development of episcopal power (30r).

75. That is, Desiderius Erasmus (*c.* 1436–1536), who wrote anti-papal satires, nonetheless acknowledged the office of the papacy even after he had received the "calling" of grace (implying, incorrectly, that Erasmus had become Protestant).

76. Citing Martin Luther, *A Treatise, Touching the Liberty of a Christian*, trans. James Bell (1579).

77. *Denmark* "Denmake" in some copies (e.g., Bodleian Library), "Denmark" in others (e.g., Houghton Library): a stop-press correction.

78. *schoolmaster* Cooper had been master of the school at Magdalen College, Oxford.

79. *civilians* civil lawyers.

80. Cooper had warned that since bishops were one of the three estates on which the authority of laws rested, their removal would require "the alteration of the state of all the lawes of this realme" (*Admonition*, 78r).

81. *Deiotarus* (d. 40 BCE), king of Galatia and supporter of Cicero and the Republican cause during the Roman civil wars. Cornelius Lentulus and Marcus Cethegus were members of the 62–63 BCE conspiracy of Roman patricians, headed by L. Sergius Catilina (Catiline), against Cicero and the senate; Cicero's speeches against the conspirators made these men classical exemplars of aristocratic extravagance, corruption, and debauchery.

82. *judicium capitis* usually *judicium capitale*, capital judgment or punishment.

83. *hang-ons* hangers-on.

84. Cooper had argued that a change in church government meant changes in the legal system that would deprive civil lawyers of their most lucrative business (*Admonition*, 77r).

85. Martin argues that even if canon law were abolished, legal venues would remain in which civil lawyers could make a living. The court of arches was the chief court of the archbishops of Canterbury; it handled cases that, as Martin points out, reformers believed should be tried under civil, not church, jurisdiction. Several documents calendared in *SPR* detail Presbyterian objections to canon law and offer the proposals Martin here sketches (see esp. II, 1–4).

86. *pope's canon laws ... banished by statute* statute 25 Hen. VIII c. 19 (1534), "An act concerning the submission of the clergie to the kings majestie," suspended canon laws as detrimental to royal prerogative, subject to their revision and royal approval.

87. *treason ... to proceed Doctor of the Canon Law* referring to statute 25 Hen. VIII c. 19 (see previous note). Study of canon law ceased at Oxford and Cambridge during the Henrician Reformation: see Leader, *History of the University of Cambridge*, I, 332–41; McConica, ed., *History of the University of Oxford*, III, 257–60.

88. The numbers that begin here list the consequences Cooper saw in a change of church government, with the impoverishment of civil lawyers being the unnumbered first. The numbering skips "6." In the original, these numbers are placed in the margin.

89. "Beside this, the Judiciall lawe of the Jewes, especially for such offences as are against the lawe of GOD, must bee brought into this common weale" (*Admonition*, 77v). Martin replies that reformers did not seek the full implementation of Mosaic codes, because much Old Testament law had been abrogated by the New Testament.

90. *Brownist* Separatist, from Robert Browne (*c.* 1550–1633), whose early 1580s writings helped establish the doctrine that each local church should be an autonomous, voluntary association not supported by public taxes such as tithes.

91. *as Jerome saith* the reference is probably borrowed from the book to which Bridges was responding in the passage Martin here discusses: Theodore Beza, *The Judgement of a Most Reverend and Learned Man* (*c.* 1585), which cites on this point Jerome's epistle to Evagrius (A6v–A7r). See also next note.

92. Bridges (*Defence*, 339–40) was responding to Beza's argument (see previous note) that the office of bishop was a human invention, a "bishop of man," that had over time degenerated into a "bishop of the devil": see Introduction, xxiii. This point is repeated from *Schoolpoints*, 92.

93. Martin in this passage returns an argument Bridges had made against Catholic doctrine: "But where their *doctrines and traditions* (which we refuse) are such, as are neither *expressed* nor included *in Gods word*: what are they but in effect against it? Proove this *Bishop* that ye call, *of man*, to be of that stampe, and then indeede: Out on him, yea and out with him. He is then *of man* (I graunt) but he is *of the Divill* also: and we will (God willing) with you renounce and defie him" (*Defence*, 340). The line 7 cited in the marginal note begins at "indeede: Out on him."

94. Martin discusses this passage from Bridge's *Defence* in *Epitome*, 65–70.

95. *I have once already showed* see *Epistle*, 16–19.

96. Martin imitates the dialect of western England, conventionally used for representing rustic speech: *tow* "thou," *ti* "ye," *cha vound* "I have found."

97. *Sir Geoffrey Jones* probably the Jefferie Jones listed in the 1586 "Survey of the Ministry" as the parson of Corley, Warwickshire, and described as "dumbe, drunkard, gamster, quareller, swearer, pilferer, adulterer" (*SPR*, II, 171); he is mentioned in *Epistle*, 36–37.

98. *parson of Mickleham* Richard Ellis (d. 1613), mentioned in *Epistle*, 41.

99. "*Balaam* was a covetous prophet, and yet by him God blessed his people. Nowe surely, if you have received at their handes the blessing of Gods trueth, and the light of his holy worde, as in deede you have: the cogitation of this benefite should move your minds more favourably to thinke of them, & more charitably to judge of their doings" (*Admonition*, 9). Martin summarizes Cooper's argument in the following paragraph. For the story of Balaam, the diviner hired by the Moabite king to curse Israel but who blessed them instead, see Numbers 22–24. As Martin proceeds to note, the Israelites eventually killed Balaam (Numbers 31:8).

100. *hundred pounds and a gelding* the gifts Martin had accused John Bridges of giving his patron in exchange for his deanery; see *Epistle*, 20.

101. *To bowl but seven days a week* Martin repeatedly condemns John Aylmer for bowling on Sundays, a practice Aylmer defended in the *Admonition*; see *Epistle*, 221 n.100.

102. *like a swag* like a swaggerer, or a blustering, quarrelsome fellow; see *Epistle*, 214 n.25. Martin condemns Aylmer's swearing throughout the tracts.

103. *to take some small ten in the hundred* to charge 10 percent interest on loans. While charging interest was slowly winning social and legal approval in the later sixteenth century, 10 percent was a customary threshold at which interest became usury.

104. *Westfaling* Herbert Westfaling, bishop of Hereford from 1586, was of somewhat advanced Protestant views and had a reputation for incorruptibility, as an earlier reference by Martin acknowledges; see *Epistle*, 214 n.36. The reference here probably implies that Martin sees Westfaling as a kind of Noah, a man whose probity was insufficient to save the remainder of his clerical brethren from the deluge brought on by their "faults."

105. *Gravat* William Gravat or Gravet (d. 1599), from 1566 vicar of St Sepulchre in London and of several other benefices, including Little Laver in Essex (*ODNB*). The 1586 "Survey of the Ministry" lists him among Essex ministers as "a drunkard and a glutton and a nonresident" (*SPR*, II, 161). He is mentioned again in *Just Censure*, 181. *bousing* boozing.

106. *links* torchlights.

107. *caperclawed* variant of "clapperclaw," to claw and scratch, or to thrash; figuratively, to revile or abuse (*OED*).

108. John Whitgift and Thomas Cartwright exchanged printed polemics from 1572 to 1577; see *Epistle*, 212 n.12, 213 n.23.

109. *besoop* beat or thrash; see above, notes 35 and 62.

110. Five reformers discussed, slightingly, in Cooper's *Admonition*: John Penry (71v–72r), Walter Travers (72v), Thomas Sparke (49–50, 72v–73r), Giles Wigginton (45–46), and John Davidson (49). For Penry, see Introduction, xxxviff.; for Travers and Sparke, see *Epistle*, 225 n.131, 231 n.193; for Wigginton, see *Epistle*, 224 n.128; for Davidson, see *Epistle*, 228 n.155.

111. *say black to your eyes* find fault with you, charge you with something (*OED* black *a* III 12, this place cited).

112. *to smoke* to smart, to suffer (*OED* smoke *v* 4).

113. *Winken de Word, Doctor Prime* Dr John Prime (1549/50–96), cleric and fellow of New College, Oxford. Prime defended Thomas Cooper from Martin Marprelate's "late most false, shameles, & unchristian libelling" in the dedication of his sermon *Consolations of David* (1588); the dedication is dated December 7, 1588, making this the earliest printed reference to the tracts. Wynkyn de Worde (d. 1534?), William Caxton's apprentice and successor, was one of the earliest printers in England. *ODNB* speculates that the association of Prime with de Worde "may refer to Prime as having been one of the signatories of the foreword to John Case's *Moral Questions* (1585), the first book from Oxford University's press." More plausibly, Martin had seen one of de Worde's editions of the *Golden Legend* (*STC* 24876ff.), the collection of

saints' lives Martin calls the "Legend of Lies" (*Epitome*, 000), and thereby associates Prime with lying books. A verbal play is another possibility: Martin might be implying that Prime is "winking at the word," or conniving with other church officials at the misuse of scripture. Martin repeats the association below, 138, and in *Just Censure*, 176.

114. *trencher chaplain* contemptuous term for a domestic chaplain, one who dines at his patron's table and presumably does the patron's bidding (*OED*, earliest citation). In addition to Prime (see previous note), Martin cites Richard Bancroft (1544–1610), at the time personal chaplain to Sir Christopher Hatton (see Introduction, lx–lxii), and John Duport (d. 1617/18), holder of several church livings and from 1590 master of Jesus College, Cambridge (*ODNB*).

115. *be with you all three to bring* that is, he will give them as good as he got; cf. Nashe, *Works*, IV, 63 for the idiom.

116. For Mistress Margaret Lawson, see *Epistle*, 216 n.51.

117. *Dame Cooper* Amy Cooper, Thomas Cooper's wife, was rumored to have kept a lover; see *Schoolpoints*, 251 n.31, and above, 102, 112. *Qui pergit quod vult dicere quæ non vult audiet* (side note): translated by a contemporary as "he which takes pleasure to speake what he please, he must now and then be content to heare what he would not": John Deacon, *Dialogicall Discourses of Spirits and Divels* (1601), a2r. Deacon attributes the expression to the Dutch scholar Johannes Drusius (1550–1616), who published numerous scriptural commentaries beginning in the 1580s.

118. For Thomas Chard, the bookseller who published John Bridges' *Defence*, see *Epistle*, 217 n.57.

119. *premunire* an offense classified as challenging royal supremacy; see *Epistle*, 222 n.107.

120. As Martin notes, the first edition of the *Admonition* featured a pasted cancel slip that replaced "let him and his doe what they dare" with the less aggressive "let him and his do what they can" (40, line 10).

121. *jolled* struck or beaten on the head with something (*OED*).

122. *they have now pasted there* responding to the argument that the apostles and the primitive church governed churches by a "companie of Elders," Cooper had initially printed "I will not deny it"; the cancel slip backtracked to "That is not yet proved" (*Admonition*, 134–35; the slip is on 135, line 20). This passage is cited at greater length in *Schoolpoints*, 252 n.34.

123. *patch* fool or clown; Martin had applied the term to John Bridges in *Epistle*, 7.

124. *pall* or pallium; a band of cloth with hanging strips worn by the pope, archbishops, and occasionally others as a sign that the wearer represents papal authority.

125. For the (unidentified) "Jesuit at Newgate," see *Epistle*, 23; as Martin's marginal reference notes, Whitgift in reply had denied hearing "any such matter" (*Admonition*, 41).

126. *Cliff* "profound Cliffe, the ecclesiasticall cobler" is mentioned in *An Almond for a Parrat* (Nashe, *Works*, III, 344, 351, 363); nothing further is known of him. Battle Bridge is probably the area in Southwark, just below

London Bridge; Battle Bridge Lane remains, though the bridge itself, which spanned a stream that fell into the Thames, no longer exists. Possibly the village of Battle Bridge, then outside London in the area of present-day King's Cross.

127. *Atkinson* the parishioner of Sedbergh, Yorkshire, who had sought the deprivation of his vicar Giles Wigginton, but later repented of his complaints; see *Epistle*, 26.

128. Some reformers objected to the use of "priest" on the grounds that it was a Catholic term without scriptural basis; see *Theses Martinianae*, 154, and, e.g., *SPR*, I, 198, 222. Whitgift had defended the usage on grounds of tradition, law, and etymology: "The ancient fathers so cal them. The church of *England* imbraceth that name, and that by the authority of the highest court in *England*. And why may not *Presbyter* be called *Priest*?" (*Admonition*, 45).

129. *sink* cesspool (*OED* n¹ I i a, this place cited).

130. For the three points of "Catholic persuasion" with which Martin accuses Whitgift, including Christ's descent into or "harrowing" of hell, see *Epistle*, 25.

131. For the underground Catholic printer Thackwell, see *Epistle*, 23 and 223 n.114. Richard Young, justice of the peace for Middlesex, was the official to whom Whitgift referred Thackwell's case.

132. *cog* cheat, deceive, employ fraud (*OED* v3 3, this place cited). *face* show a false face (*OED* I 1c, this place cited).

133. Imitating a rural or West England dialect: *chwarnt* an elision of "Ich (I) warrant."

134. For the printer Robert Waldegrave, see Introduction, xlix–l, and *Epistle*, 23–25.

135. *an a had* if he had. *clouches* variant spelling of "clutches"; not dialect.

136. *J. C.* probably John Charlewood; see *Epistle*, 223 n.120. Whitgift had tried to associate Waldegrave with the secret printing of Catholic texts in Arundel House (*Admonition*, 42). *Company* the Stationers' Company.

137. *lord treasurer* William Cecil, Lord Burghley (1520–98).

138. *Cosin* Richard Cosin, high commissioner; see *Epistle*, 212 n.17.

139. *rested* aphetic form of arrested (*OED*).

140. *Bishops have justly received . . . all lord bishops* Martin here rewrites Whitgift's remarks in the *Admonition* about Waldegrave; the original passage is quoted in *Epistle*, 223 n.116.

141. *L. Face* as in the original: punning on "my lord's grace," possibly with a suggestion of "my Lord Face" as a mock title.

142. *Hartwell* Abraham Hartwell, Whitgift's secretary; he often acted as notary at high commission hearings (see *SPR* index of persons). *ODNB* offers a brief life within the article on the Society of Antiquaries.

143. *Bonner* Edmund Bonner (c. 1500–69), the Marian bishop of London notorious among Protestants for his enforcement of laws against heresy.

144. *Lord of good London's Swans* apparently referring to John Aylmer, bishop of London (the same phrase appears in *Epistle*, 13), and to Waldegrave's

release from one of the two imprisonments Martin proceeds to mention. Possibly referring to a person named Swan (the word is capitalized in the original); one of the dyers who lodged a complaint against Aylmer was named Swan (*Epistle*, 13), but there is no evidence of a connection between that case and Waldegrave. Possibly an opaque allusion involving Waldegrave's own device, a swan in an oval medallion. Possibly a play on cygnet/signet to suggest some arbitrary exercise of authority.

145. *White Lion* one of several prisons in Southwark.

146. See *Epitome*, 54, for the practice of charging prisoners for expenses incurred while transporting them to prison.

147. Martin cites three Presbyterian manifestos printed by Robert Waldegrave: *A Lamentable Complaint of the Commonalty* (1585); *The Unlawfull Practises of Prelates against Godly Ministers* (*c.* 1584); and Theodore Beza, *The Judgement of a Most Reverend and Learned Man* (*c.* 1585).

148. Whitgift had concluded his discussion of the "heathenish untruth" that he "should accompt preaching of the word of God to be heresie" with an "appeale unto the whole State of the learned and obedient Clergie for his innocencie therein" (*Admonition*, 46–47). For Martin's original accusation, see *Epistle*, 27–28, 31.

149. For the story of Whitgift, Evans, and the earl of Warwick, see *Epistle*, 28–30. *quare impedit* legal action by which the right of presentation to a benefice is tried. Here, an action brought by Warwick against Edmund Freake, bishop of Worcester, for refusing to institute his nominee.

150. *second person in the land* for the accusation that Whitgift claimed to be second in authority after the Queen, see *Epistle*, 29.

151. *Doctor Sparke* Presbyterian divine Thomas Sparke; for the story of Sparke's debate with Whitgift about conflicting translations of scripture in the Bible and the BCP, see *Epistle*, 38–39.

152. *Richard Patrick* Worcester clothier Martin had accused Whitgift of planning to appoint to the ministry; see *Epistle*, 42.

153. For Whitgift's close friendship with Andrew Perne, see *Epistle*, 217 n.53, 220 n.84, 226 n.144.

154. *screen* partition dividing a room (*OED* *n*¹ 2a, this place cited).

155. *an ace lower* a particle, jot, or little bit lower (*OED* ace *n* 3).

156. For Aylmer and the dyers' cloth, see *Epistle*, 13.

157. For Aylmer appointing his purblind porter minister at Paddington, see *Epistle*, 21.

158. For the dispute between Aylmer and John Madox, see *Epistle*, 21–22.

159. For Aylmer cutting down the elms at Fulham, see *Epistle*, 21 and 221 n.98, and *Epitome*, 73.

160. *councillor* Sir Christopher Hatton (1540–91), the vice-chamberlain of Martin's following sentence. *frump* gibe, jest, mocking speech. In the course of denying that he had cut down the elms at Fulham, Aylmer had written: "And master *Vicehamberlaine* at her Majesties being at *Fulham,* tolde the Bishop that her Majestie misliked nothing, but that her Highnesse lodging

was kept from all good prospects by the thicknesse of the trees" (*Admonition*,
56). Since Aylmer had in fact removed many trees, Martin accuses the bishop
of misinterpreting (or misrepresenting) an ironic joke.

161. *swag* blustering, swaggering fellow; earlier uses, all related to Aylmer, also
noted swearing as a defining characteristic (see *Epistle*, 8, and above, 128). The
emphasis here appears to be on credulity or thick-headedness (see the
sentence that follows).

162. Martin cites the analogy Aylmer had invoked to defend his bowling on
the Sabbath (see *Epistle*, 221 n.100), and Thomas Cooper's argument
(*Admonition*, 110–11) that reformers should temper their critique of ministerial imperfections because even "God sometime beareth with breach of his
commaundement," listing as examples David eating the forbidden shewbread (1 Sam. 21:1–6), the Maccabees deciding to fight on the Sabbath (1
Macc. 2:40–41), and the Mosaic approval of divorce (Deut. 24:1–4).

163. For Aylmer's refusal to pay a debt to his grocer's estate, see *Epistle*, 32–33.

164. For Aylmer's dispute with the clergyman Barnaby Benison, see *Epistle*, 42.

165. The marginal note cites Aylmer's self-defense against the charge of "dumb-
ness" or non-preaching (*Admonition*, 61–62), and Cooper's argument that
"base persons" would not dare criticize the clergy "if they did not see
themselves backed by men of great authoritie, & receive reward for so
dealing. Such untrueths woulde soone vanish and bee forgotten, unlesse
they were nourished by them for whose pleasure they were devised"
(*Admonition*, 5–6). Martin mockingly claims that English reformers will
never get their money, because a bishop now claimed that three sermons a
year sufficed to deny the charge of non-preaching.

166. For the story of Aylmer quoting "*Eli, Eli, lamma sabachthani*" in loss of hope
for the bishopric of Ely, see *Epistle*, 42. The "Elmar" spelling reminds readers
of the charge that Aylmer had sold the trees on his episcopal estate; see
Epistle, 21 and 221 n.98.

167. Aylmer had written: "Is he dumbe because he was the only preacher in
Leicestershire for a space, as the noble Earle of *Huntington* can witnesse?
and by their two meanes, that shire, GOD be blessed, was converted and
brought to that state that it is nowe in? (*Admonition*, 61).

168. *Caiaphas Chair* Whitgift's "seat" as Caiaphas of Canterbury, a figure used
throughout the tracts to represent untrammeled clerical power; *Epistle*, 44.

169. For the charge that John Young, bishop of Rochester, presented himself with
a benefice, see *Epistle*, 15 and 218 n.64.

170. For Whitgift and the disputed issue of Christ's descent into hell, see
Epistle, 25 and 224 n.127.

171. *Doctor Squire and Tarleton* two recently deceased men whom Martin unflat-
teringly associates with Whitgift. For Richard Tarleton (d. 1588), the comic
actor, see *Epistle*, 221 n.95. Adam Squire (d. 1588) was John Aylmer's son-in-
law, master of Balliol College (resigned 1580), and archdeacon of Middlesex.
In addition to his attempt to cover up his own infidelity by falsely implicating
his wife (see *Epistle*, 229 n.165), Squire embezzled a legacy left to Balliol, and

took money to look the other way when the Catholic layman George Gilbert established a secret Catholic organization (*ODNB*, under Gilbert).

172. *William of Lincoln . . . traitorous papists* William Wickham, bishop of Lincoln, had preached the funeral sermon for Mary Queen of Scots; see *Epistle*, 42.

173. For this sermon by Thomas Cooper, see *Epistle*, 30; for the use of "Sir" for "St," see *Epistle*, 219 n.72.

174. For this exchange between Cooper and Penry on reading versus preaching, see *Epistle*, 28.

175. *simple T. C.* Thomas Cartwright, as opposed to "profane" T. C., Thomas Cooper.

176. *he saw Martin's picture drawn* the passage that follows mockingly rewrites an extended allegorical vision of reform by Thomas Cooper in *Admonition*, 84–85; Martin replaces Cooper's allegorical figures with various contemporary church officials.

177. *old porter of Paddington* see *Epistle*, 21, and above, 101 and 136.

178. *Lucian* Roman satirist (d. 180) whose works were a byword for venomous railing, hence Cooper's claim that Lucian was Martin's kin (*Admonition*, 84); Martin here returns the favor.

179. *Midas of Cant.* John Whitgift.

180. *Doctor Culpable* Martin Culpeper (1540–1605), warden of New College from 1573 and dean of Chichester from 1577; the Chaucerian gibe about the Wife of Bath remains opaque.

181. *John of Exeter* John Woolton (*c.* 1537–94), bishop of Exeter from 1578; he is mentioned in *Epistle*, 9, and *Epitome*, 74.

182. *Winkendeword, alias Doctor Prime* for the association of Dr John Prime with the early printer Wynkyn de Worde, see note 113 above.

183. *Dolus, Fraus, Insidiæ* Deceit, Fraud, Treachery.

184. For Andrew Perne, John Kenold (or Kennall), and Richard Cosin, see *Epistle*, 217 n.53, 234 n.226, and 212 n.17 respectively.

185. *Copcot* Dr John Copcot, master of Corpus Christi College, Cambridge; he was mentioned in *Epistle*, 8. *treader* an usher or servant who preceded his master.

186. *Dean John* John Bridges; Martin implies that Bridges was promised something, such as a bishopric, for writing the *Defence*, but that Whitgift had not yet honored the promise.

187. *Banbury* in Oxfordshire, a stronghold of the reform movement. In 1586 Banbury returned as its MP Sir Anthony Cope, sponsor of the Presbyterian "Bill and Book" (see Introduction, xxxvi). While the nature of any "ado" in Banbury remains unidentified, Martin might have been telling the truth about his travels there: the Marprelate project had a connection in Banbury. In September 1589, as the pursuivants were closing in, Throkmorton and Penry sent all the books remaining at Throkmorton's manor "to widdow Adams howse in Banburye" for safekeeping (HL Ellesmere MS 2148, 88r).

188. *bakers' daughters would have knights* the connection between this proverbial-sounding comment to any "ado" in Banbury remains obscure. The

expression might involve a pun (early rising bakers' daughters want nights, as well as knights).

189. *Solihull* Warwickshire rectory under the control of William Overton, bishop of Lichfield and Coventry, and the target of earlier Martinist gibes; see *Epitome*, 77, and *Schoolpoints*, 91.

190. *register* here, a collection of anti-episcopal documents such as that collected for the *Seconde Parte of a Register*; see Introduction, xlix, and *Epistle*, 33. *Bury* Bury St Edmunds, Suffolk, a center of reform activity throughout the 1570s and 1580s. Martin also awaits reports from his *visitors*, implying that he, like a bishop sent on an official visitation, employs people to observe church practices in various parishes; the Presbyterian version of such visitation reports underlay the 1586 "Survey of the Ministry."

191. *38 lines* Martin refers to the lengthy sentence with which Cooper had opened his discussion of Martin's *Epistle*. While the sentence featured a capitalized "That" after a quotation ending with "etc." in its 27th line, Martin reads the lines that follow as a rhetorical continuation, a legitimate interpretation of "period" in his time (*Admonition*, 33–34).

192. Responding to the objection that "Bishops ought not to make their wives Ladies," Cooper had argued that bishops need "moderately to provide for their wives & children": "For we may see the wives & children of divers honest & godly Preachers, yea, and of some Bishops also, that have given their blood for the confirmation of the Gospel, hardly to scape the state of begging" (*Admonition*, 149).

193. *Mistress Toye* Martin suggests that the unmarried archbishop could leave money to support the children whose lives, Cooper had suggested, were distressed by clerical poverty (see previous note). But Martin also implies that a man who supports another man's children would do so only because of a relationship with the other man's wife; the implication is spelled out in the succeeding gibe against Richard Howland. With mock fairness, Martin notes that he had not heard of any "great familiarity" between Whitgift and "Mistress Toye" that would justify such financial support. He might be referring to the wife of the printer Humphrey Toy or Toye (*c.* 1537–77), the publisher of all six editions of Whitgift's three works published in the 1570s. Martin might also be playing with the name "Toy" as an appropriate one for a "mistress" who was another man's wife. If so, and since "Mistress Toye" is implicitly married to a cleric, the reference is possibly an oblique one to Amy Cooper, the wife of Thomas Cooper; see *Schoolpoints*, 251 n.31, and above, 102, 112.

194. *befy* defy, with the dialect b/d substitution.

195. *Richard of Peterborough* Richard Howland (1540–1600), bishop of Peterborough from 1585. Howland was instituted to the rectory of Sibson in Huntingdonshire in 1573 and held it until his death (*ODNB*). He was indeed unmarried, though there are no other extant references to a local indiscretion. Howland is mentioned briefly in *Epistle*, 9, and above, 110.

196. *Nemo confidat nimium secundis* "no one should trust too much in success" (quoting Seneca, *Thyestes*, l. 615).

197. *Nemo desperet meliora lapsus* "no one should despair of misfortune improving" (quoting Seneca, *Thyestes*, l. 616).
198. *Anglia Martinis disce favere tuis* "Martin of England requests the pleasure of your favor." This device appears on the title page of the Leveller Richard Overton's *The Araignement of Mr. Persecution* (1645), and, rewritten as "Anglia Martinis parce favere malis," in the anti-Martinist tract *Mar-Martine* (1589), A1v, A3v.
199. *Faults escaped* both are corrected in this edition.

5 THESES MARTINIANAE

1. *Catercaps* metonymy for clerics, from their four-cornered hats.
2. *after-birth* apparently translating the Latin *agnatio*, a term from Roman law for a birth after the father's death or last will. *neame . . . nuncka* with "nunckle" on the page following, colloquial forms for "uncle" (*OED*). *Kankerbury* playing on Canterbury as "canker."
3. *assigns* assignees: in printing, the stationers to whom the right to publish certain texts had been legally transferred. *without any privilege* without pre-publication approval by an (episcopal) licenser of the press.
4. *pretendeth* signifies, indicates (*OED*).
5. Nearly one line's length of type, split over two lines of text, was set but then removed after "course" and before "in certain."
6. *past my cure* possibly playing on "cure" as spiritual charge or curacy, as well as medical cure.
7. *major and minor* major and minor premisses, the first two parts of a syllogistic proof.
8. *dexterely* dextrously; not recorded in this form by the *OED*.
9. *I am not of opinion . . . elders* an accurate paraphrase (*Admonition*, 134–35); the original passage is quoted in *Schoolpoints*, 252 n.34.
10. *Discipline* church government, often with particular reference to Presbyterian ecclesiology.
11. *promise and book-oath . . . never hurt us* mockingly asserting the harmlessness of the anti-reform arguments offered in Cooper's *Admonition* (1589), John Bridges' *Defence* (1587), and Richard Bancroft's *Sermon* (1589).
12. *dry blows* originally, and apparently here, blows that failed to draw blood; often used in the period to signify severe blows (*OED* dry *a* 12).
13. *bables* either "babbles" (foolish talk) or "baubles" (trifles, or the emblems of court fools): the senses of the two words often blurred together in the period (*OED* bauble, babble). *Just Censure* uses "bable" in a context where the meaning is clearly the court fool's "bauble" (181).
14. *their 812, their 1401* references to the two major books written by Martin's opponents: "812" is the final numbered page of John Whitgift's *Defense* (1574); "1401" is the final page of John Bridges' *Defence* (1587). Martin implies that these books, despite their length, offered only their authors' opinions, and not

(scripturally based) evidence for the positions they take. Martin Junior refers to these "arithmetical numbers" below, 159.

15. *Tygurium* Zurich (one of many variants of the Latin name). Protestant churches in Denmark and Saxony (both Lutheran) and Zurich (Zwinglian) did not employ the full Presbyterian system of church government. See *Epistle*, 11, for Martin's discussion of *An Harmony of the Confessions of the Faith* (1588), an anthology that contained the Danish Confessio Hafnica (1530), the Saxon Confession (1551), and the First (1536) and Second (1566) Helvetic Confessions that governed the church in Zurich.

16. *Zisca* the general John Trocznowski, "the one-eyed" (d. 1424); for fifteen years he successfully defended the Bohemian (Moravian) Brethren against Imperial and papal forces sent to quash their reform movement.

17. *stews* brothels: until they were closed in the 1540s, the Southwark stews were under the jurisdiction of the bishops of Winchester, who derived a large income from licensing the prostitutes (popularly known as "Winchester geese") and collecting rents from the brothels.

18. *these almost 500 years* Martin derives the number from John Foxe, who argued that popes Gregory VII (Hildebrand), elected in 1080 (actually 1073), and Innocent III, elected in 1215 (actually 1198), initiated a tradition of clerical authoritarianism that a persecuted "remnant" had resisted ever since: *Actes and Monumentes* (1570), *3r. Martin refers to this passage again in thesis no. 94 below. For Hildebrand, see also *Epistle*, 220 n.85.

19. *statute 13 Eliz.* statute 5 Eliz. c. 1 (1563), reaffirmed 13 Eliz. c. 2 (1571), abolished papal authority and prohibited any attempt to "maintain defend or extol the same usurped power." Martin reads the statute as applying to episcopal power in general, rather than to papal supremacy in particular. His note that the statute needed to be "rightly understood" acknowledges that his was not the standard interpretation.

20. *doctrine ... published with her Majesty's prerogative* explained in thesis no. 53 below.

21. *Tyndale ... Barnes ... Frith* leading figures of the English Reformation, all executed for heresy during the reign of Henry VIII. William Tyndale (*c.* 1494–1536) was the theologian and translator whose work provided the foundation for both the Geneva and Authorized versions of the Bible. Robert Barnes (1495–1540) promoted the use of Tyndale's translation and played an important role in the spread of Lutheran ideas in England. John Frith (*c.* 1503–33) assisted Tyndale while both were in exile and translated Luther; his writings eventually helped shape the Anglican understanding of the Eucharist. John Foxe collected their writings in *The Whole Workes of W. Tyndall, John Frith, and Doct. Barnes* (1573), a key text for reform polemicists.

22. *this doctrine of theirs is now ... doctrine* the argument here presumes that approval to print produced a "privileged" text. Since the *Whole Workes* (1573) of Tyndale, Frith, and Barnes was published "*Cum gratia & Priuilegio Regiae Maiestatis*" (title page), Martin claims its text had also received royal sanction, and therefore constituted official doctrine. He might not have meant this argument to be taken entirely seriously (see headnote).

23. The statute 13 Eliz. required subscription to the 1562 articles governing church doctrine; the argument here is that if the texts contained in *Whole Workes* of Tyndale, Barnes, and Frith also constituted doctrine (see the previous thesis), then they too were maintained by statute.

24. The conclusion of the argument presented in the previous two theses (see the previous two notes).

25. The remaining theses in Martin's list are drawn primarily from two works by Tyndale, *Obedience of a Christian Man* and *Practise of Prelates*, as published in the *Whole Workes* of Tyndale, Barnes, and Frith. Some specific references are noted in these annotations, but many theses are summaries of or extrapolations from arguments in these texts rather than direct quotations.

26. *not possible ... good lord bishop* quoting Tyndale, *Practise of Prelates*: Tyndale claimed that Cuthbert Tunstall's motives for becoming bishop were "covet-ousnes and ambition," and argued that it was not "possible naturally that there should be any good Bishop, so long as the bishoprickes be nothing save worldlye pompe and honour, superfluous abundance of all maner riches and libertie to do what a man listeth unpunished: thinges which onely the evill desire, and all good men abhore" (*Whole Workes*, 374a). Martin cites this passage again in *Protestation*, 201.

27. *a bishopric is a superfluous honour* quoting the marginal comment next to the passage from Tyndale cited in the previous note.

28. *bishops ... servants of the Beast* cf. Tyndale, *Obedience*: "Bishops and priestes that preach not, or that preach, ought save Gods word, are none of Christes, nor of hys annoyntyng: but servauntes of the beast whose marke they beare" (*Whole Workes*, 135b).

29. *bishops ... ministers of Antichrist* the identification of episcopacy with the pope and with Antichrist is made throughout the texts collected in *Whole Workes*; see, e.g., Tyndale, *Obedience*, 102 (cited again in *Just Censure*, 185), and 134ff. Martin extrapolates here and in theses nos. 62–63 to include the Protestant episcopate in these attacks on Catholic prelates.

30. *bishops ... are of the kingdom of this world* cf. Tyndale, *Practise of Prelates*: "the Popes kingdome is of the world" (*Whole Workes*, 343b).

31. *bishop ... no other lawful authority, but only to preach* see note 28 above, and cf. also Tyndale, *Obedience*: "The popes authoritie: is to preach gods word onely" (*Whole Workes*, 123b). Tyndale repeatedly argues this point.

32. *desire of a bishopric ... false prophet* cf. Tyndale, *Obedience*: "covetousnes and ambicion that is to say, lucre and desire of honor is the finall end of all false Prophetes and of all false teachers" (*Whole Workes*, 172a). The next thesis extrapolates from this point.

33. *civil offices of our prelates* theses nos. 67 to 70 draw on arguments and phrases (including an assertion that the pope was a wolf in lamb's skin) in a section of Tyndale's *Practise of Prelates* headed "Prelates appointed to preach Christ, may not leave Gods worde, and minister temporall offices" (*Whole Workes*, 342–43). Cf. also Tyndale, *Obedience*, in *Whole Workes*, 124ff.

34. The words "and the magistracy" appear to have been dropped after "the ministry."

35. *prisons* cf. Tyndale, *Obedience*: "But now say our Bishops, because the truth is come to farre abroad, and the lay people begyn to smell our wiles, it is best to oppresses them with craft secretly, & to tame them in prison" (*Whole Workes*, 134b). The cellars of Fulham Palace, the residence of the bishops of London, were occasionally used as a prison; see *Epistle*, 21 and 221 n.95.

36. *those doctors* cf. Tyndale, *Obedience*: "He [John Fisher, bishop of Rochester] alleageth for the Popes authoritie, Saint Ciprian, Saint Augustine, Ambrose, Hierome, and Origine: of which never one knew of any authoritie, that one Bishop should have above an other" (*Whole Workes*, 128a).

37. *bishop and . . . minister . . . the self same person* cf. Tyndale, *Practise of Prelates*, in *Whole Workes*, 345ff., and *Obedience*, in *Whole Workes*, 133ff. *note out* indicate, denote.

38. *popery . . . to call the ministers . . . priests* cf. Tyndale, *Obedience*, in *Whole Workes*, 144ff. For reform objections to the use of "priest" for minister, see *Hay any Work*, 262 n.128.

39. *Bancroft in his sermon at Paul's the 28th of January 1588* probably an error for the sermon Bancroft delivered at Paul's on February 9, 1589, cited below, 157: there is no other record of a sermon at Paul's on January 28, and Bancroft argued in his February sermon that the equality of bishop and priest was "within lesse then an hundredth yeeres after *Cyprian* . . . condemned as an heresie" (*Sermon*, 98). The writings of Cyprian, bishop of Carthage (d. 258), particularly his *De Catholicae Ecclesiae unitate*, played an important role in debates about the episcopate. Catholic commentators and defenders of episcopacy invoked his authority for the distinction between bishops and elders in the early church; Protestant reformers either questioned these interpretations of Cyprian's texts, or charged Cyprian with introducing the distinction.

40. *no authority . . . censure* for theses nos. 78–80, 85, and 91, cf. Tyndale, *Obedience*, in *Whole Workes*, 156a. The remaining theses appear to extrapolate from this and other discussions in *Obedience* of the censure process (e.g., 134ff.); they also draw on complaints rehearsed in the previous Marprelate tracts about the legal procedures used by church courts.

41. *bishop's license to preach* referring generally to the argument in the previous thesis that bishops have no power to make ministers, but also more specifically to John Whitgift's 1584 articles, which suspended licenses to preach and required ministers to subscribe before their licenses were granted; to have a license was therefore to have the "mark" of Whitgift's "antichristian" prelacy.

42. *inhibition* in ecclesiastical law, a bishop's command that a cleric cease exercising ministerial duties.

43. *break up into men's consciences* theses nos. 89 and 90 refer to the use in church courts of the oath *ex officio* (see Introduction, xxii). Martin cites Tyndale, *Obedience*, though mistakenly naming Pilate rather than Caiaphas and making the typographical error of "93" for "63" in the scriptural citation: let judges "not breake up into the consciences of men, after the

example of Antichristes disciples, and compell them either to forsweare them selves . . . or to testifie against them selves. Which abhomination our Prelates learned of Cayphas Math. xxvi" (*Whole Workes*, 122b).

44. *nonresidents and pluralities* cf. Tyndale, *Practise of Prelates*, in *Whole Workes*, 373b.

45. *above 400 years* from John Foxe's *Actes and Monumentes* (1570); see note 18 above.

46. *their wisdoms* the magistrates.

47. *statute* referring to the statute 13 Eliz., which required subscription to the 1562 articles; see note 19 above.

48. *Bancroft in affirming her Majesty to be a petty pope* Bancroft had extrapolated from the syllogistic argument Martin offered in *Epistle*, 9: upon Martin's principles, "a man may frame this rebellious argument; No pettie Pope is to be tollerated in a Christian common-wealth: But hir Majestie is a pettie Pope: Therefore hir Majestie is not to be tollerated in a Christian common-wealth" (*Sermon*, 68).

49. *Bancroft . . . affirming her Majesty to usurp that authority* Bancroft, continuing from the passage cited in the previous note, had constructed another syllogism to show the logic of Martin's "minor," the secondary assertion of the syllogism in *Epistle*, 9: "Whosoever doe take upon them, or usurpe the same authoritie in causes ecclesiastical within their dominions, which the Pope had, they are pettie Popes: But hir Majestie doth so: Therefore hir Majestie is a pettie Pope: and so consequently not to be tollerated in a Christian common-wealth" (*Sermon*, 68).

50. *weet* know: "I do you to weet" means "I cause you to know" or "I make known to you" (*OED* do *v* 22c).

51. *your business* that is, some think Martin was employed in writing another tract about the bishops; possibly also implying that Martin was doing the bishop's work (presumably, spiritual work they were not doing), or even that he had displaced the bishops from their offices.

52. *my reason is, quoth Robert Some* the sarcastic emphasis is on "my." In the *Protestation*, Martin notes Robert Some's repeated self-references: "My sermons, My writings, My reasons, My arguments, and all is My, My, My, as if the depth of all learning were included in the channel of his brain" (205–06). The same charge is treated at length in the para-Martinist *M. Some Laid Open in His Coulers* (La Rochelle, 1589), 15, 42–49. For Some, master of Peterhouse, Cambridge, see *Schoolpoints*, 249 n.18, 250 n.27; he is mentioned again in *Just Censure*, 181.

53. *Groine* Corunna (the Groyne), in Spain, attacked by Sir Francis Drake and Sir John Norris in April 1589; the bawdy pun is intentional. Martin Senior would continue the joke: "if my father should be hurt, either at the Groine, or at the suburbs of Lisbon, is this the way either to cure him or to comfort him . . .?" (*Just Censure*, 171).

54. *And those others (ka mine uncka Bridges)* the sarcastic emphasis is on "those others." Apparently referring to a passage in which Bridges quoted a line from

William Fulke's *Briefe and Plaine Declaration* (1584), "Others there be . . . that referre only indifferent matters to the disposition of Princes," and then for several pages repeatedly and scornfully invoked those words: "*Others* (they say) *there be*," "Who those *others* are," "the opinion of those *others*," "What? are these others then, judges also," "if you mean those *others*," etc. (*Defence*, 102ff.).

55. *were but of 20 sheets* comic understatement: twenty sheets of paper, folded in quarto (the format of *Epistle*, *Epitome*, and *Hay any Work*), would make a "pistle" of 160 pages; in octavo (the format of *Theses Martinianae*, *Just Censure*, and *Protestation*), one of 320 pages.

56. *four or five months* Martin's silence had lasted almost exactly four months: *Hay any Work* was published in late March, *Theses Martinianae* in late July.

57. *Italian fig* poisoned fig. Probably also with the sense of giving somebody the fig, that is, making a contemptuous, obscene gesture.

58. *hind* boy, lad, fellow (*OED*).

59. *tat* "that": imitating dialect, and not a typographical error, because the word is also spelled "tat" in its position as a catchword on the previous page.

60. *othergates* another kind of, a different (*OED*); also punning on the welcome the bishops offered in the prisons of Newgate or Gatehouse, mentioned two sentences later.

61. *it was taken up . . . besides a bush* the manuscript copy for the first part of this pamphlet had indeed been "dropped" on the side of the road near Throkmorton's house, where it was found by John Penry and the printer John Hodgkins (see Introduction, liv).

62. *cygneam cantionem* "swan song."

63. *More Work for the Cooper* the tract seized during printing; see Introduction, lv. Martin offers a summary of its contents in *Protestation*, 204–06.

64. *vather* father, with the dialect f/v substitution.

65. *come down with thy popery* borrowing a phrase from John Aylmer, as quoted in *Epistle*: "come down you bishops from your thousands, and content you with your hundreds" (8).

66. *Tyndale . . . Lambert* Martin Junior compares the bishops unfavorably with various leading figures of the British Reformations. For Tyndale, Frith, and Barnes, see note 21 above. *Hooper* John Hooper (d. 1555), bishop of Gloucester and Worcester, a chief English exponent of Zwinglian Protestantism and Marian martyr; he is mentioned in *Hay any Work*, 120, and *Protestation*, 200. *Knox* John Knox (*c.* 1514–72), the central figure of the (Presbyterian) Reformation in Scotland. *Lambert* John Lambert (d. 1538), born John Nicholson; burned at the stake for heresy after a case heard in person by Henry VIII.

67. Reformers read Diotrephes (from 3 John 9) and Simon Magus (from Acts 8:9–24) as figures for episcopal pride, covetousness, and ambition; see *Epitome*, 244 n.113.

68. *these Mar-Martins, these stage-players* referring to the anti-Martinist campaign, active throughout the summer of 1589; see Introduction, lxiiff., and below, 161–62.

69. *rimers* rhymers: makers of rimes, usually inferior verses (*OED*).
70. *thoroughly so persuaded, ka my nuncka Bridges* referring to a passage in which Bridges cited Fulke's *Briefe and Plaine Declaration* (1584) as claiming that the form of church government "that they have set forth *is (as they are throughly perswaded) agreeable to the word of God*." Bridges began his response, "I aunswer, this is not materiall, what they are or are not *throughly perswaded to bee agreeable to the word of God*," then played at length with the phrasing, e.g., "they can never *throughly perswade* other, to be *perswaded* as they bee, if they their selves be indeed (as they say they are) *throughly perswaded*. And although I may be somewhat easily *perswaded*, that they are somewhat *perswaded* . . .: yet as yet, I can neither be *throughly perswaded*, that they their selves are *throughly so perswaded* of this *forme* . . ." (*Defence*, 1369).
71. *Mar-Martin* the anti-Martinist verse collection *Mar-Martine* (1589); see Introduction, lxii–lxiii. Mar-Martin is mentioned again in *Just Censure*, 181.
72. *Long Meg of Westminster* famous figure from the reign of Henry VIII. Known for her strength and unruliness, Long Meg was credited with various folkloric exploits, mainly beating up men foolish enough to challenge her. She was the heroine of a 1594 play (not extant), and *The Life of Long Meg of Westminster: Containing the Mad Merry Prankes Shee Played in Her Life Time* (1635). In one of the stories collected in this *Life*, Meg works as a laundress; Martin proceeds to argue that his opponent was following Meg in this profession. *aunts* probably in the sense of "bawds."
73. *liveries* officially, stage-players were servants or retainers of noblemen, a form of social legitimation that saved them from being the "plain rogues" that Martin implies their profession otherwise revealed them to be.
74. *vi et armis* "with force and arms" or (the usual translation in law) "by main force."
75. *Leonard Wright* probably a clergyman, Wright (d. in or after 1591) wrote *A Summons for Sleepers* (1589), to which Martin Junior here responds; *The Hunting of Antichrist* (1589); and *A Friendly Admonition to Martine Marprelate, and His Mates* (1590). Wright's three books were among the milder anti-Martinist texts; his primary target was Catholicism. He is mentioned again in *Just Censure*, 181, and *Protestation*, 206.
76. *Frégeville* Jean de Frégeville, French author of *The Reformed Politicke. That is, An Apologie for the Generall Cause of Reformation* (1589). Frégeville was not an anti-Martinist writer, but Martin adds him to the list for recommending to Henri III the retention of bishops and clerical hierarchy, and for pointing to England as a model for a Protestant church that preserved the status of the clergy through episcopal magnificence (63–70). He is mentioned again in *Just Censure*, 181, and *Protestation*, 206.
77. *Dick Bancroft* Richard Bancroft; see Introduction, lx–lxii.
78. *Tom Blan. o' Bedford* Tobias Bland (*c.* 1563–1605), chaplain to Lord St John of Bletsoe. His sermon *A Baite for Momus* (1589) criticized factious reformers who "spit spight and venome, strife and rebellion against the higher powers" (35); the Marprelate tracts were Bland's clear, if unnamed, target. Bland is mentioned again in *Just Censure*, 181.

79. *Kemp* probably William Kemp (*fl.* 1585–1602), the comic actor, who as a member of Lord Strange's Company would have participated in anti-Martinist stage performances. *An Almond for a Parrat* (1589) was dedicated to "Monsieur du Kempe, Jestmonger and Vice-gerent generall to the Ghost of Dicke Tarlton," perhaps because Kemp was associated with this component of the anti-Martinist campaign.

80. *Underhill* Dr John Underhill (1544/45–92), rector of Lincoln College, Oxford, and later in 1589 made bishop of Oxford; he had a reputation for living beyond his means (*ODNB*) but does not appear to have published any anti-Martinist texts. He is mentioned again in *Just Censure*, 181, and *Protestation*, 204.

81. *sea-journeys* implying that the papers had been carried on ship, in reference to the joking rumor that Martin had accompanied Drake's expedition to Portugal (see note 53 above).

82. *I have not presumed to publish mine in as large a print or volume* this tract was published in octavo format rather than quarto, and in a roman font substantially smaller than the black letter font Robert Waldegrave had used for the first four tracts.

83. *pay this bearer for the carriage* playing on the idea that these tracts were indeed letters to the bishops: in the early modern postal system, the cost of mail was paid by the recipient.

6 *THE JUST CENSURE AND REPROOF OF MARTIN JUNIOR*

1. *springal* youth.

2. *Whoa* modernized from "Who" (*OED* who *int*). As Martin notes in *Epistle*, 000, the usage imitates Bridges' habitual colloquialisms, e.g., "Nay who there" (*Defence*, 76).

3. *Groine . . . Lisbon* referring to a pun (groin/Groyne) in *Theses Martinianae*, 158. Sir Francis Drake and Sir John Norris burned the shipping in the Spanish port of The Groyne (Corunna) in April 1589; in May, they led a disastrous attack on Lisbon. *scrabbled and weather-beaten* from being carried on this sea voyage (see *Theses Martinianae*, 163).

4. *huisht* quiet, silent (*OED*).

5. *as thou hast well noted* see *Theses Martinianae*, 161–62.

6. *An Oration . . . Martin* this heading is a side note in the original.

7. *Waldegrave . . . Newman . . . Sharpe . . . Penry* speaking in the voice of the archbishop, Martin Senior names four men suspected of involvement in the Marprelate project. While audacious, the naming of names was not a betrayal: their roles were sufficiently well known by July 1589 to make anonymity unnecessary. Martin himself had already acknowledged Waldegrave and Penry as suspects, Waldegrave implicitly (throughout the *Epistle*) and Penry explicitly (*Epistle*, 28, and *Hay any Work*, 120). While the "binder" (that is, stitcher) Henry Sharpe and the distributor Humphrey Newman had not been

mentioned previously, both were known to officials investigating the tracts. In addition, Sharpe and Newman helped produce and distribute this pamphlet, which suggests they did not think it revealed new information about their involvement.

8. *Munday* writer and pursuivant Anthony Munday (1560–1633); he had arrested Marprelate suspect Giles Wigginton in December 1588 (*SPR*, II, 253, 255). The "thank you" is ironic, as the following sentences make clear. In the late 1570s Munday had stayed in the English College in Rome, possibly as a spy. He published an account of the seminary in *The English Romayne Lyfe* (1582), and subsequently helped track down priests and other recusants. Martin Senior's "Whitgift" worries that Munday's failure to discover Martin suggests that he might betray the bishops as he had betrayed the Catholics.

9. *Saint Andrew's Day last* November 30, 1588, five weeks after the appearance of the *Epistle* and about the time the *Epitome* was published.

10. *commission* the court of high commission.

11. *Paul's Churchyard ... Boyle's shop at the Rose* St Paul's Churchyard was the center of the London book trade, and the obvious place to begin a search for illegal publications. The London bookseller Richard Boyle set up shop at the sign of the Rose in 1587. No other extant evidence indicates that he was known for under-the-counter sales of radical texts.

12. *Charke (of Lincoln's Inn)* William Charke (d. 1617), Presbyterian controversialist, lecturer at Lincoln's Inn from 1581 until he was suspended by Whitgift in 1593 (*ODNB*).

13. *Gardiner (of Whitechapel)* Richard Gardiner, reformist rector of St Mary Whitechapel from 1570 to 1617 (*SPR*, II, 184; Greenwood, *Writings*, 118, 192, 194, 321; Collinson, *Movement*, 320, 411–12).

14. *Egerton (of Blackfriars)* Stephen Egerton (*c.* 1555–1602), member of John Field's secret Presbyterian conference and from 1586 parish lecturer at St Anne Blackfriars (*ODNB*). In his *Defence* (1594), the one text he published under his own name, Job Throkmorton mentions attending the afternoon lecture at Blackfriars (A2v).

15. *Cooper (of Paul's Chain)* either Martin or Robert Cooper; both were appointed minor canons of St Paul's in 1590, and one was minister of St Gregory by Paul's, located in the southwest corner of Paul's Churchyard almost across from Paul's Chain, the street that runs south from the Churchyard. According to the Separatist John Greenwood, Margaret Lawson (see *Epistle*, 216 n.51) helped this Cooper get his license to preach (Greenwood, *Writings*, 117, 248; Collinson, *Movement*, 336, 341).

16. *Lord of Essex* Robert Devereux, second earl of Essex (1565–1601). Between the death of the earl of Leicester in 1588 and the judicial crackdown on Presbyterianism in 1590–91, Essex "flirted with the idea of setting himself up as the new political champion of puritanism" (*ODNB*; see also Collinson, *Movement*, 444–47). An anecdote first recorded in the seventeenth century dramatized Essex in the act of "favouring" Marprelate: in his *Life and Death, of the Illustrious Robert Earle of Essex* (1646), Robert Codrington writes that, as

Elizabeth was speaking of her proclamation that threatened punishment for anyone caught with one of the tracts, Essex pulled a copy from his pocket and exclaimed, "Why then . . . what will become of me"? (6).

17. *Lord Mayor Alderman Martin* Sir Richard Martin (1533/34–1617), city alderman from 1578, was elected Lord Mayor in May 1589 (*ODNB*). Martin Senior's "Whitgift" likely voices suspicion not so much of the mayor as of his wife: Dorcas Martin (née Eccleston) (1536/37–99), a translator and bookseller active in reform circles, had been involved in the distribution of Thomas Cartwright's 1573 *A Replye* to Whitgift, and would have been a person of interest to the real archbishop in his search for an underground distribution network. See *ODNB*, and White, "Biographical Sketch of Dorcas Martin."

18. *keep watch and ward* here, a "rhetorical and more emphatic" form of "keep watch" (*OED* watch *n* 7a). The association of Penry and Sharpe with Northampton was public knowledge: in his *Appellation* (1589), Penry mentions an official search of his study in Northampton and official orders for the arrest of Sharpe, "bookbinder of Northampton" (6–7, 46–47).

19. *that . . . your charges may be borne* costs of arrest were charged to the person arrested: "Whitgift" implies that his officials should make sure to cover their expenses by arresting somebody.

20. *More* John More, the "Apostle of Norwich" (*c.* 1542–92), one of the era's preeminent godly pastors; for "twenty years he unofficially supervised church affairs throughout much of Norfolk" (*ODNB*; see also Collinson, *Movement*, 186).

21. *Allen* Walter Allen, rector of Rushbrooke, Suffolk, the home of Sir Robert Jermyn, "the leading puritan gentleman of the county" (Collinson, *Movement*, 219, and Collinson, Craig, and Usher, eds., *Dedham Conference*, 184 and passim). With John Knewstub, Allen was a leading figure among Suffolk puritans and played an active role in the broader Presbyterian movement.

22. *Knewstub* John Knewstub (1544–1624), minister of Cockfield, Suffolk, and a leading figure of the reform movement; the earl of Leicester had appointed Knewstub his personal chaplain on his expedition to the Low Countries (*ODNB*; Collinson, Craig, and Usher, eds., *Dedham Conference*, 220–23).

23. *Wright* Robert Wright (*c.* 1550–1624), a leading figure in the Presbyterian conference movement, personal chaplain to Robert Rich, second Baron Rich, and from 1585 town preacher of Ipswich, Suffolk (*ODNB*; Collinson, Craig, and Usher, eds., *Dedham Conference*, 269–72).

24. *go all the ground* emended from "give all the good" (as noted in the original's errata list).

25. *my Lord's grace of York* John Piers (1522/23–94), bishop of Salisbury from 1577, archbishop of York from early 1589, and one of the few bishops to escape unscathed by a Martinist pen: this is the only reference to him in the tracts. Piers was not sympathetic to the cause of reform, but he did continue to preach throughout his career and he pursued Catholics at least as vigorously as he did reformers (*ODNB*; Collinson, *Movement*, 201, 249, 406–407).

26. *never . . . learned a word of Irish in thy life* apparently, "better if you had not been so practiced in doing pointless things as to publish" their father's

incomplete and therefore unimpressive text, an act that was probably pointless given the impressive estate of the man the text addresses (as the paragraph proceeds to explain).

27. Esau was accompanied by 400 men (Genesis 33:1); Martin Senior associates him with Whitgift and proceeds to remark on the magnificence of his archiepiscopal retinue (see next note).

28. *seven score horse . . . thirty gold chains* according to his biographer Sir George Paule, Whitgift traveled with a retinue "consisting of two hundred persons"; when joined by gentlemen of the country, "he did sometimes ride into the Citie of Canterburie, and into other Townes with eight hundred or a thousand horse." Martin Senior appears to refer here to a specific and quite recent "visitation": Paule describes Whitgift's "first journey into Kent" in July 1589, shortly before *Theses Martinianae* was published. Heading into Dover, the archbishop was "attended with an hundred of his owne servants, at least, in liverie, whereof there were fortie Gentlemen in chaines of gold. The traine of Cleargie, and Gentlemen in the Country, and their followers, was above five hundred horse": Paule, *Life of Whitgift* (1612), 78–79.

29. *because of thy rashness, mark whether those poor men* emended from the original, which ends the sentence with "rashness" and starts a new paragraph with "mark whether."

30. *mention that my father . . . made* Martin mentions "my son Martin Senior" in *Epitome*, 79. *Quem . . . saepissime* "whom I mention with honour, whenever and however often I mention him" (quoting, in part, Cicero, *Pro Sexto Roscio Amerino*, II.6). *dilling* here, the youngest of a family (*OED*).

31. For the association of Dr John Prime with the early English printer Wynkyn de Worde, see *Hay any Work*, 260 n.113. Martin's Latin poetry against Prime likely never existed.

32. *Jack* fellow, lad; a traditional generic name of address (*OED*).

33. *Tom Tell-troth* or Tell-truth, the traditional name for a truth-teller (*OED*).

34. *that point in thy Epilogue* see *Theses Martinianae*, 162–63.

35. *patrizat sat bene certe* "you certainly follow your father's example well enough" (cf. *OED* patrizate).

36. *take snuff* take offence.

37. *cost me a fall* lost him a round or bout (from wrestling), presumably in his fight against the bishops, but possibly in polemical competition with his "brother."

38. The legal language and form of the articles that follow are modeled on the articles Whitgift formulated for use by high commission in *ex officio* examinations.

39. *simoniarchs* not recorded in the *OED*, except in the adjectival form simoniacre (= simoniacal).

40. For the debates over subscription and the wearing of the surplice, see Introduction, xxi, and *Schoolpoints*, 249 n.24. *urging* emended from "avoiding" (as noted in the original's errata list).

41. *premunire facies* more properly, *praemunire facias*, a statute that covered offences classified as challenging royal supremacy; see *Epistle*, 222 n.107.

42. *courts of faculties* tribunal of the archbishop of Canterbury: "faculties" are the church-related licenses, dispensations, and permissions the court distributed. *Jo. Canterbury his brothers* emended from "brother": the remainder of the sentence indicates that the reference is to the archbishop's collective clerical "brethren."

43. *quaetenus probabile* "to the extent probable."

44. *hang-ons* hangers-on.

45. *the foolish virgins* see Matthew 25:1–12.

46. Dr Andrew Perne, Whitgift's longtime mentor and close friend, died unexpectedly on April 26, 1589, after a dinner in Lambeth Palace. The reference to Perne here as Whitgift's "joy" and to Whitgift as Perne's "darling" might suggest homoerotic intimacy (cf. *OED* darling n^1 b); see *Epistle*, 220 n.84 and 226 n.144.

47. *proper-sition* hyphenated in the original, to signal wordplay: probably a "proposition" that he "protests" and "propounds"; possibly a dialect or rustic pronunciation of "proposition."

48. *these gentlemen following* the ensuing passage, which mockingly assigns various church officials to positions in the household of John Bridges, the archbishop's new "fool," recalls the similar list in *Hay any Work*, 138–39, which was responding to Thomas Cooper's allegorical vision of Martin and his companions in *Admonition*, 84–85.

49. *Robert Some* master of Peterhouse, Cambridge (upon the death of Andrew Perne); see *Schoolpoints*, 249 n.18. *starve-us* punning on "service" (pronounced "sarvice") book: to reformers, the read liturgy "starved" the congregation of the sermons central to salvation.

50. *Doctor Underhill* John Underhill, rector of Lincoln College, Oxford, and subsequently bishop of Oxford; see *Theses Martinianae*, 163, where Martin associates him with the anti-Martinist campaign. He is mentioned again in *Protestation*, 204. *coinquination* pollution, defilement.

51. *Bancroft and drunken Gravat* for earlier references to Richard Bancroft as a "contemptible trencher chaplain" and to the drunkenness of William Gravat, vicar of St Sepulchre in London, see *Hay any Work*, 128, 131.

52. *Anderson* Anthony Anderson (*d.* 1593), vicar of Stepney, Middlesex, from 1587; he also held the livings of Medbourne, Leicestershire, from 1573 and Dengy, Essex, from 1587 (*ODNB*). *Potter's part* the Potter was a recurring character in Robin Hood stories; his characteristics were quarrelsome pride and skill with a quarter staff. See "Robin Hood and the Potter" (a manuscript ballad *c.* 1500) and "Robin Hood and the Potter," a play fragment printed in *A Mery Geste of Robyn Hoode* (1560), in Dobson and Taylor, eds., *Rymes of Robyn Hood*, 123–32, 215–19.

53. *Sir Leonard Wright* author of the anti-Martinist text *A Summons for Sleepers* (1589); see *Theses Martinianae*, 273 n.75. The "Sir" is an honorific (here ironic) accorded clerics. *Sir Tom Blan. o' Bedford* Tobias Bland, author of the anti-Martinist sermon *A Baite for Momus* (1589); see *Theses Martinianae*, 273 n.78. *bauble* the court fool's mock emblem of office, a baton topped with a carving of a head sporting the ears of an ass (*OED*).

54. *Mar-Martin* author of the anti-Martinist verse collection *Mar-Martine* (1589); see *Theses Martinianae*, 161, and Introduction, lxii–lxiii. *John Frégeville* Jean de Frégeville, author of *The Reformed Politicke* (1589); see *Theses Martinianae*, 273 n.76. *alterius vicibus* "either of the two by turns." *grooms of his stool* the groom of the stool (or stole) was a high-ranking officer in a royal household. Martin Senior probably intends readers to hear the title's (etymological) link to the excremental "stool" of stool chamber.

55. *the wooden dagger, the cockscomb, and the copper chain* the wooden dagger and cockscomb were traditional components of the fool's outfit; the copper chain presumably contrasts with the golden chains worn by Whitgift's other servants (see above, 175 and 277 n.28).

56. *King's Bench* the supreme court of common law in the kingdom.

57. *an hundred thousand hands* a government brief for the 1590–91 Star Chamber proceedings against the Presbyterian leadership cited this passage as proof that the threat of mass violence underlay reform agitation: "One of our late libellers braggeth of an hundreth thousand handes: & wisheth the Parlement to bring in this Refourmation, though it bee by with-standing her Queenes majestie" (BL Lansdowne MS 120/3, 75v). Sir George Paule likewise mentions the threat posed by "an hundred thousand seditious mutiners" (*Life of Whitgift*, 45).

58. *semper excipio Platonem* "always with the exception of Plato" (quoting Cicero, *Tusculan Disputations*, I.22).

59. *Receive the Holy Ghost* reformers objected to the use of this formula in the service for ordaining bishops, ministers, and deacons, arguing that it blasphemously suggested that one man could give another the inward gift of the spirit. Some bishops agreed "that it was impossible for any man to give the Holy Ghost" (*SPR*, I, 217) but defended the words with the interpretation Martin Senior here attacks. For reform objections to the ordinal, see *SPR*, I, 79, 122, 125, 127, 142, 151, 217, 259; II, 45, 70.

60. *I may be baptized* some reformers objected to the "catechising of infants" (*SPR*, I, 242), that is, the use in the BCP rite of baptism of questions to which witnesses or godparents would answer in the name of the child being baptized (see, e.g., *SPR*, I, 126, 142, 147, 200, 218, 242, 281; II, 38, 203, 214).

61. *thy father's Grammar and his Lexicon* cf. the list of Martin's other alleged books in *Epistle*, 36. *Capita concordantiarum* "heads of the agreement": presumably "brief" because he and the bishops agreed on so little.

62. *miter* variant spelling of "meter" (*OED*), the primary meaning here, but probably with a pun on the episcopal mitre.

63. *e verbo ad verbum* like good translators, the bishops never offer "word for word" translations.

64. *Tyndale . . . page 102* citing from the *Whole Workes of W. Tyndall, John Frith, and Doct. Barnes* (1573). Tyndale compared a non-resident minister with a schoolmaster who has been hired by a parish but who cannot teach because he dwells elsewhere: "And thus are we never taught, and are yet nevertheles compelled: ye compelde to hyre many costly scholemasters. These deedes are verely agaynst Christ. Shall we therefore judge you by your dedes, as Christ

commaundeth? So are you false Prophetes, and the Disciples of Antechrist, or agaynst Christ" (102b). For a similar argument, see *Theses Martinianae*, 153.

65. *to have mine* that is, to see my manuscript copies.

66. *neames* uncles (colloquial).

67. *Beelzebub of London* John Aylmer, bishop of London. *madmonition* conflation of "mad" and "admonition."

68. *Travers* Walter Travers, leading English Presbyterian; see *Epistle*, 225 n.131. Milk Street runs north from Cheapside, in Cripplegate Ward; it was an important residential quarter, with "many fayre houses for wealthy Marchantes and other" (Stow, *Survey*, I, 295). The house in question might be the Milk Street residence of Lord Mayor Richard Martin (see note 17 above), who, with his wife Dorcas, was actively involved in reform circles.

69. *Paget* Eusebius Paget, Presbyterian divine; see *Epistle*, 225 n.134.

70. *They are naught ... of them all* "Aylmer" implies that he is quoting words spoken by John Whitgift at one of Paget's examinations; the "favour" is ironic.

71. *Cartwright* Thomas Cartwright, one of the most prominent Presbyterian divines (see *Epistle*, 212 n.12). Since 1586 he had been master of the earl of Leicester's new hospital at Warwick and had played an active role there in the parochial ministry.

72. *Never tell me ... Martin's conceits* Thomas Cartwright in fact denied any involvement with the Marprelate tracts and expressed his disapproval of the project in a letter to Burghley; see Introduction, xxxi.

73. *my lord* probably an error for "my lords" (cf. "my masters" and "my lords" elsewhere in the speech). But Pierce suggests that this sentence and the one following are to be read as a parenthetical remark to Whitgift, imagined as present (*Marprelate Tracts*, 377).

74. This epitaph replies to one in *Mar-Martine* (1589) that began, "*If Martin* dy by hangmans hands, as he deserves no lesse, / This Epitaph must be engravde, his maners to expresse" (A4v).

75. *file* defile.

76. *his popery of Sir Nicholas priests* Mar-Martin had asked readers to say a prayer for Queen Elizabeth (see next note), "And for those mighty Potentatis, thou kenst what they bin hight, / The tout-puissant *Chevaliers* that fend S. Nichols right, / Els clarkis will soon all be Sir Johns, the preistis craft will empaire, / And Dickin, Jackin, Tom and Hob, mon sit in Rabbies chaire. / Let Georg and Nichlas cheek by jol bathe still on cockehorse yode, / That dignitie of pristis with thee may han a lang abode" (A3r–v). St Nicholas is the patron saint of priests (see *Epistle*, 219 n.72, for the Martinist substitution of "Sir" for "St"); Martin Senior objects here to the Catholic implications of both the invocation of the saint and the use of word "priest" for the clergy (see *Hay any Work*, 262 n.128).

77. *he counsels us ... for Queen Elizabeth* "For Soveraigne Dame *Elizabeth*, that Lord it lang she maie, / (O England) now full eften must thou *Pater Noster* say" (*Mar-Martine*, A3r).

78. *S. John's Gospel* probably referring to "Sir" John Bridges' *Defence*.
79. *pentamenter* possibly an error for "pentameter," possibly an intentional mala-propism appropriate to the "bastard" verse; the line, of course, is a fourteener, not pentameter. Possibly also with a play on the Latin *mentior, mentiri* (to lie). *loose* end, close, conclusion. *Darby ale* renowned for its quality: Mar-Martin's verse is sweet only if accompanied by a draught of the best ale available.
80. *Magnificat* Mary's song of praise from Luke 1:46–55, included in the evening service of the BCP. The story is untraced: Martin in effect accuses the "little priest of Surrey" of continuing to follow Catholic practices, possibly because he encourages his servant to recite the text in Latin, possibly because the recital in that context constitutes an invocation of a saint.
81. *the voyage into Portugal* by Drake and Norris; see *Theses Martinianae*, 271 n.53, and above, note 3. *Duke of Guise* Henri de Lorraine, 3rd duc de Guise (1550–88), a Catholic leader in the French wars of religion: he helped plan the St Bartholomew's Day Massacre in 1572 and founded the Catholic League in 1576. He was assassinated on December 23, 1588.
82. *a* he; by this period chiefly used to create the effect of familiar speech (*OED* a *pron*).
83. *That'll ... That'll* both uses are capitalized and italicized in the original.
84. *Errata* these changes have been made in this text.

7 *THE PROTESTATION OF MARTIN MARPRELATE*

1. The italicized passages in this tract, including Martin's "protestation" (199), reproduce an emphasis created in the original by the use of a larger type.
2. *mean or compassionable ... themselves* ironically asking the reader not to "expostulate" with the bishops if the captured printers were treated with moderation and compassion, since the "inquisitorial" church would not be responsible for any clemency shown the men.
3. *inheritance* implying that the bishops inherited their bloodthirstiness from their Catholic "fathers"; see also below, 203–04.
4. *we fear that God ... unquenchable fire* referring to Matthew 10:28.
5. *we know ... heavenly father* referring to Luke 21:18 and Acts 27:34.
6. *the state of the Low Countries and of France ... twenty years ago* twenty years earlier, Catholicism had been ascendant over Protestantism in both countries: the Low Countries were controlled by Catholic Spain, and France in the 1560s and early 1570s saw five wars of religion and the massacre of Protestants on St Bartholomew's Eve in 1572. But the Dutch Revolt, beginning in 1568, had by the late 1580s brought the northern provinces of the Netherlands de facto independence and placed them under Protestant rule. In France, the Catholic Henri III was assassinated on August 1, 1589, shortly before the *Protestation* was published, and the Protestant Henri IIII was now king. Henri would convert to Catholicism in 1593, but for the moment English Protestants would have been encouraged by events on the Continent.

7. *single* "siuule" in the original, corrected in accordance with the errata. Echoing "singleness of heart(s)" in the Geneva translation of Acts 2:46, Ephesians 6:5, and Colossians 3:22.

8. *last year of* Martinism … *shall not be till full two years after the last year of* Lambethism an accurate prophecy, in a sense: Richard Overton started publishing his seven "Martin Marpriest" tracts (1645–46) two years after the Long Parliament abolished episcopacy, though the target of his "Martinism" was now the triumphant Presbyterian party. See Introduction, lxxxix–xc.

9. *Cooperism* from Thomas Cooper, whose *Admonition* (1589) presented the self-defenses of several bishops against Martin's accusations.

10. *go in hand with* go forward with, begin.

11. *most uphold* apparently an error for "must uphold" or for wording such as "should most uphold."

12. *attempts* attacks, assaults (*OED n* 3); cf. "their tyranny and bloodthirsty proceedings" (below, 203).

13. *any buckling towards* any preparation for battle.

14. *Master Fenner's and Master Penry's syllogisms* referring to the syllogisms in Dudley Fenner's *Defence of the Godlie Ministers* (Middelburg, 1587), 86ff., and in the second edition of John Penry's *Exhortation* (East Molesey, 1588), 52–65.

15. *Travers* referring to Walter Travers, *Ecclesiasticae disciplinae* (Heidelberg, 1574), translated by Thomas Cartwright as *A Full and Plaine Declaration of Ecclesiasticall Discipline* (Heidelberg, 1574).

16. *Cartwright* referring to the works Thomas Cartwright published in polemical battle with John Whitgift in the 1570s; see *Epistle*, 212 n.12, 213 n.23.

17. *Gilby* Anthony Gilby (*c.* 1510–85), pastor of the English congregation at Geneva while a Marian exile, and from 1560 lecturer at Ashby-de-la-Zouch, Leicestershire. Gilby assisted with the Geneva translation of the Bible and published several important translations, commentaries, and polemical texts. Martin probably refers to the best known, *A Pleasaunt Dialogue, Betweene a Souldior of Barwicke, and an English Chaplaine* (Middelburg? 1581), which includes a list of "An hundred pointes of Poperie, yet remayning, which deforme the Englishe reformation."

18. *Demonstration* referring to John Udall, *A Demonstration of the Trueth of that Discipline* (East Molesey, 1588).

19. *Abstract … Counter-Poyson An Abstract, of Certain Acts of Parliament* (1584) publicized Presbyterian objections to Whitgift's 1584 articles; Richard Cosin defended the church with *An Answer* (1584), and was met in turn by *A Counter-Poyson* (1584), usually attributed to Dudley Fenner.

20. *Tyndale … Frith … Barnes* referring to *The Whole Workes of W. Tyndall, John Frith, and Doct. Barnes*, ed. John Foxe (1573), cited throughout *Theses Martinianae.*

21. *Hooper* John Hooper, bishop of Gloucester and Worcester and Marian martyr; he is mentioned in *Hay any Work*, 120, and *Theses Martinianae*, 160. Several of his many books, first published from the late 1540s to the early 1560s, were reprinted in the 1580s, two by Robert Waldegrave: *Certaine*

Godly, and Most Necessarie Annotations upon the Thirteenth Chapter to the Romanes (1583), and *A Declaration of the X. Holie Commaundements* (1588).

22. *Pilkington* James Pilkington (1520–76), Marian exile and the first Protestant bishop of Durham; he contributed to the 1559 Prayer Book, the Book of Homilies, and the Thirty-Nine Articles. Martin probably refers to Pilkington's most polemical work, *The Confutation of an Addition* (1563), an "uncompromising onslaught" on Catholic practices and beliefs (*ODNB*).

23. *Foxe* probably referring to the arguments in *Acts and Monuments* that could be read in an anti-episcopal light. But John Foxe also published numerous sermons and polemical texts.

24. *mo* more in number; not a dialect abbreviation (*OED*).

25. *the publishing of their doings in Latin* no Latin translations were made of any of the Marprelate tracts, though an English Jesuit claimed in 1592 that one had been translated into Spanish and presented to King Philip II (PRO SP Dom. 12/243/11). No Spanish version has been found, however, and the claim was likely made for propaganda purposes.

26. *set up my rest* stake everything, from the card game primero (*OED* rest n^2 6).

27. *I never had wife nor child* Job Throkmorton and John Penry were both married, Throkmorton in *c.* 1580, and Penry in September 1588. Martin Marprelate, however, was a fictive character, and so did not have a (real) wife and children. Martin's claim to have neither wife nor children "may seem strange" because two of his "sons" had published pamphlets.

28. *two only ... maiden ... priests* Martin had noted in earlier tracts that John Whitgift and Richard Howland, bishop of Peterborough, were both unmarried, and had suggested that Howland kept a mistress (*Hay any Work*, 139).

29. *Tyndale ... page 374* citing from *Whole Workes* (1573); see *Theses Martinianae*, 153 and 269 n.26.

30. *make a way for myself ... livings and promotion* reformers were frequently accused of mercenary motives in seeking to overthrow the bishops: see, e.g., Bancroft, *Sermon*, 23ff., and Cooper, *Admonition*, 155.

31. *of mine own* that is, he had an independent income.

32. *church-robbery in a temporal man* referring to lay impropriations, in which the income generated by a parish was controlled by a lay owner who might pass on only a percentage of the "living" to the minister who worked there. Reform groups periodically attempted to purchase impropriate livings to give ministers and local church officers control over a parish. Richard Bancroft warned his London audience, "especially to you of the richest," about the economic implications of reform hostility to lay impropriation (*Sermon*, 26).

33. *overseen* deluded, mistaken (*OED*).

34. Newly appointed bishops often sued the estates of their predecessors for dilapidations of the episcopal estate: Richard Bancroft, e.g., sued Aylmer's heirs when he succeeded as bishop of London (see *Epistle*, 221 n.98). For the economics of the Tudor episcopate, see Heal, *Of Prelates and Princes*, esp. (for dilapidations) 290, 292, 299–303.

35. For the charges against John Aylmer ("Mar-elm") of tree-cutting, see *Epistle*, 221 n.98. Thomas Cooper's finances are discussed in *ODNB* and Heal, *Of Prelates and Princes*, 276, 292, 300, 313. Neither discusses these specific charges, but both note that Cooper, despite making frequent claims of financial distress, was one of the richer bishops.

36. *an handsome halter to hang himself with* proverbial (Tilley H58): "as the poet says" is probably a joking colloquialism, not an implied attribution.

37. *care . . . that the church's maintenance should not decay* referring to one line of argument Cooper had offered in his extended defense of episcopal revenues (*Admonition*, 144ff.).

38. As the errata list notes (207), the sentence "And as herein . . . themselves" is printed twice in the original. The first version is attached to the end of the previous paragraph and reads "And as herein their spoile & robbery is apparent; on the other side; So their tyrannie and blood thirstie proceedinges against good men, is unexcusable." A new paragraph then begins with the second version, printed here, which offers clearer syntax and is better integrated into the text that follows. This second version, however, omits the phrase "against good men," here added editorially.

39. *pull the crown off her Majesty's head* reformers argued that the oath *ex officio* usurped the state's legal prerogatives by expanding the power of the church courts.

40. *appeaching* accusing, bringing a charge against.

41. *he lies . . . worship* Martin supplies comments by church officers in response to a putative victim's protests about the illegality of their proceedings. To have the *scandalum magnatum* against somebody was to charge that person with slandering a prominent figure.

42. *compel you to accuse yourself* referring to the oath *ex officio*, which enabled church courts to convict without the testimony of witnesses by demanding that the accused answer self-implicating questions. Lord Burghley likewise described these powers as "to much savouring of the Romish Inquisition" (see Introduction, xxii).

43. Statute 25 Hen. VIII c. 14, "An act for punishment of heresie" (1533–34), required "two lawfull witnesses" for an accusation of heresy and specified that the accused be allowed to answer accusations "in open court, and in an open place." The Act condemns *ex officio* proceedings, with their "captious interrogatories," as standing "not with the right order of justice nor good equitie." Repealed under Mary, these procedural requirements were reinstituted by statute 1 Eliz. c.1 (1559).

44. Cooper made this observation about the usefulness of the *ex officio* oath during the December 1588 examination of Giles Wigginton (*SPR*, II, 255); see *Schoolpoints*, 92. For the insulting reference to Cooper as "Mistress Cooper's husband," see *Schoolpoints*, 251 n.31, and *Hay any Work*, 102, 112.

45. *that Pistle of mine* that is, the pamphlet seized with the printers, *More Work for Cooper* (the usual title in the tracts, though in this tract Martin also uses *More Work for the Cooper*).

46. *Brownist* Separatist, from Robert Browne (*c.* 1550–1633), one of the founders of Separatism.
47. *Mar-Martin* author of the anti-Martinist verse collection *Mar-Martine* (1589); see Introduction, lxii, *Theses Martinianae*, 161, and *Just Censure*, 186–88. Morris dances, hobby-horses, and Maypoles were all elements of a traditional festive culture that was disappearing by the late sixteenth century. Martin and the anti-Martinists both associated one another's work with these pastimes in mutual accusations of a fundamental lack of seriousness.
48. *Underhill* John Underhill, later bishop of Oxford (see *Theses Martinianae*, 274 n.80, and *Just Censure*, 181); *Wood* William Wood, fellow of All Souls College, Oxford.
49. *Sir James King* vicar of Rushden, Hertfordshire (d. 1607). For "ficker" (vicar) and the honorific "Sir," see *Epistle*, 211 n.4, 219 n.72. Hertfordshire was not covered by the 1586 "Survey of the Ministry" but was described as "verie likelie to be as badde as others" (*SPR*, II, 94).
50. *Dick Bancroft* Richard Bancroft, at the time chaplain to Sir Christopher Hatton and author of an anti-Martinist sermon; see Introduction, lxff., and *Hay any Work*, 261 n.114. *slived* cut, sliced.
51. *Andrew Turn-coat* Andrew Perne; see *Epistle*, 217 n.53 and (for "Turn-coat" in particular) 220 n.84. He had died in April 1589 (see *Just Censure*, 278 n.46). His epitaph is to be sung antiphonically (that is, by two choirs singing alternate verses) to commemorate his "turns" or changes in religion. *epitaph* "Eblitaph" in the original; probably mis-set type, not dialect.
52. *Orawhynemeg* ballad (text not extant). John Lyly gives a different version of the title: "*Martin* tunes his pipe to the lamentable note of *Ora whine meg*" (*Works*, III, 411). Robert Langham (Laneham) provides the only other extant reference: in his description of the 1575 Kenilworth entertainment, he lists "over a whinny Meg" among the ballads owned by (the possibly fictitious) Captain Cox; a "whinny" is a furze thicket. See Langham, *Robert Laneham's Letter* (1907), ed. F. J. Furnivall, viii, xiii, cxxxi, 30, and Langham, *A Letter* (1983), ed. R. J. Kuin, 54, 142.
53. *vulneral* belonging to wounds, or to the healing of wounds (*OED*; this use precedes those cited), with wordplay on "funeral."
54. *Lockwood of Sarum* referring to John Bridges, dean of Salisbury (as the following sentence indicates). The same nickname is applied to Bridges in the para-Martinist *M. Some Laid Open in His Coulers* (La Rochelle, 1589), 81. "Lockwood" might be connected to other references that link Bridges with "wood" of various kinds: he displays the brains of a woodcock and borrows from "William Woodcock's" divinity (*Epistle*, 14, *Epitome*, 65); he wears a wooden dagger in his role as jester (*Just Censure*, 181); his style is "as smooth as a crabtree cudgel" (*Epitome*, 56). Possibly the name plays on the senses of "wood" as mad or irascible. Possibly also it involves a bawdy joke in which "Lockwood" suggests sexual readiness: the next paragraph associates Bridges with Perne as two "old standards" (a possible sexual pun) and "proculstants," a nonce word that incorporates the Latin word for buttocks (see below, n.57).

55. *his grace* Whitgift, who would appoint the person to preach at the funeral of
     Perne, his friend and one-time college master.
56. *Legenda aurea* "Legend-aure" in the original. Also known as *The Golden
     Legend*, the standard collection of saints' lives, by Jacobus de Voragine
     (1230–98).
57. *proculstants* nonce word. Possibly, not "protestants" but procul-stants ("procul"
     is Latin "afar"), men who stand at a distance, presumably from the true church
     (*OED*). But probably also with a play on "cul(e)" or buttocks (*OED*, from the
     Latin *culus*): earlier references to Perne appear to suggest an intimacy between
     Perne and Whitgift (see *Epistle*, 226 n.144, *Just Censure*, 278 n.46).
58. *chave haulf* "I have half," in imitation of southern English dialect (*OED* ch
     pron).
59. For reform opposition to the Marprelate project, see *Epitome*, 53–54, *Hay any
     Work*, 119, *Theses Martinianae*, 147, and Introduction, xxx–xxxi.
60. *Chaplain Some* Robert Some, master, and formerly chaplain, of Peterhouse,
     Cambridge; he is mentioned in *Schoolpoints*, 92, 93, *Theses Martinianae*, 158,
     and *Just Censure*, 181, and was also the target of the para-Martinist *M. Some
     Laid Open in His Coulers* (La Rochelle, 1589). *pen-and-inkhorn* writing that
     smelled of the study; ostentatiously learned.
61. Martin claims that the most effective opponents of the Separatists (Brownists)
     were the persecuted Presbyterian reformers, and points to Some's *A Godly
     Treatise* (1589) as exemplifying the inadequacy of the church's attempts to
     rebut Separatist doctrines.
62. Robert Some held the living at Girton, Cambridgeshire, as well as his College
     mastership.
63. *three pretty treatises* probably Robert Some's most recent publications: the two
     editions of *A Godly Treatise Containing and Deciding Certaine Questions* (1588)
     and *A Godly Treatise, Wherein are Examined and Confuted* (1589); all cover
     similar ground.
64. *saunce-bell* sacring, sanctus, or saint's bell, rung at certain points during Mass.
65. The para-Martinist *M. Some Laid Open in His Coulers*, attributed to Job
     Throkmorton, argues that "praising of him selfe" occupies Robert Some's
     writing "as if the ground of al good knowledge were graven in the very
     wrinkles of his forehead" (44), and provides examples (15, 42–49).
66. That is, Some's writings were identifiable by his *rapping* (striking) *figures*
     (characteristic modes of argument): *hitting the white* and *missing the butt*
     (from archery, hitting or missing the target); *resting on his reason* (relying,
     presumably overconfidently, on his argument); and *thirty-two dozen of full
     points* (employing numerous full rhetorical or syntactic stops). Each of these
     qualities was a *broken wooden dish* (presumably, worthless). Similar comments
     about Some's "short-winded" style appear in *M. Some Laid Open in His
     Coulers*, which complains that Some employs "above 1500 full points" in
     only forty leaves (121).
67. *lame ficker of Warwick* not identifiable from the list of Warwickshire ministers
     in the 1586 "Survey of the Ministry" (*SPR*, II, 165–74). Throkmorton would

have been familiar with the ministers in Warwick, his home county; he may well have helped compile their unusually detailed entries in the "Survey" (*ODNB*). The vicar's text is Matthew 5:25. For "ficker" (vicar), see *Epistle*, 211 n.4.

68. *Tolbooth* in addition to a building where tolls or customs are levied, a tolbooth in the period could also be a prison (as in Cambridge or Edinburgh), a town or guild hall, or a booth at a fair where fines were collected. The conceit here appears to be of a town or guild council meeting, with John Bridges occupying the chair of honor.

69. *Leonard Wright* author of anti-Martinist texts; see *Theses Martinianae*, 273 n.75.

70. That is, arguing about grammar (the third declension of Latin nouns) and church ceremony (in this case, the form of thanksgiving for women after childbirth). Presumably Martin thinks neither was really a life or death matter, though he earlier lists "churching of women" among other "corruptions of the church" (*Epistle*, 34).

71. Martin lists his major clerical opponents: John Whitgift, John Aylmer, and either William Wickham (bishop of Lincoln) or William Overton (bishop Lichfield); Richard Howland (bishop of Peterborough), Richard Bancroft, and Thomas Cooper; and probably John Bullingham (bishop of Gloucester), William Wickham or William Overton, and Marmaduke Middleton (bishop of St David's). Other possibilities for the third row are John Young (bishop of Rochester), John Woolton (bishop of Exeter), or William Chaderton (bishop of Chester).

72. *Friar Frégeville* Jean de Frégeville, author of *The Reformed Politicke* (1589); see *Theses Martinianae*, 273 n.76.

73. *wringlefaced* twist-faced; "to wringle" is to twist or writhe (*OED*, which does not record this usage and lists only one earlier use, as a verb).

74. *theses* those published in *Theses Martinianae* by Martin Junior. *elder brother* Martin Senior, "author" of *Just Censure*. *Pasquill* the pseudonymous author, sometimes identified as Thomas Nashe, of *A Countercuffe given to Martin Junior* (1589) and two additional anti-Martinist pamphlets that appeared after the *Protestation* was published (see Introduction, lxiii).

75. *Boleyn* George Boleyn (d. 1603), dean of Lichfield from 1576. Presumably Martin cites from notes made during recent sermons; these notes are not among the documents collected in *SPR*. The immediate point of these "four tokens" is not clear, other than to warn church officials that their remarks were being recorded. Boleyn is also a target in *Schoolpoints*, 93. Boleyn's affection for his dog appears to have been a source of popular anecdote: in 1602, John Manningham recorded in his diary that he had heard how "one Dr Bullein, the Queenes kinsman, had a dog which he doted one, soe much that the Queene understanding of it requested he would grant hir one desyre, and he should have what soever he would aske. Shee demaunded his dogge; he gave it, and 'Nowe, Madame,' quoth he, 'you promised to give me my desyre.' 'I will,' quothe she. 'Then I pray you give me my dog againe'" (Manningham, *Diary*, ed. J. Bruce, 148–49).

Works cited

MANUSCRIPTS

This section includes only those manuscripts cited directly in this edition: it does not list manuscripts printed in (and cited in this edition from) Edward Arber's *Introductory Sketch* and William Pierce's *Historical Introduction*, and it omits many unprinted manuscripts that were consulted but not quoted. For more comprehensive lists of manuscripts connected with the Marprelate controversy, see Carlson, *Martin Marprelate*, 408–10, and Black, "Pamphlet Wars," 314–19.

BODLEIAN LIBRARY

Tanner Papers, vol. 78, 192r–93v, extracts from the Marprelate tracts (*c.* 1590).
MS Rawlinson C. 849, 396r–v, "Martin the mery" (*c.* 1589).

BRITISH LIBRARY

Cotton MS Julius F vi, fol. 76 (old fol. 71), notes on the Marprelate press.
Lansdowne MS 53/71, Job Throkmorton to William Cecil, Lord Burghley (*c.* 1589).
Lansdowne MS 57/68, John Aylmer to William Cecil, Lord Burghley re John Madox (Apr. 14, 1588).
Lansdowne MS 57/69, John Madox to William Cecil, Lord Burghley re John Aylmer (Apr. 13, 1588).
Lansdowne MS 57/77, Richard Howland to William Cecil, Lord Burghley (Dec. 19, 1588).
Lansdowne MS 61/27, John Rainolds to Francis Knollys (Sept. 19, 1589).
Lansdowne MS 101/51, extracts from the Marprelate tracts (*c.* 1590).
Lansdowne MS 119/7, "The doctrines, and some practises of sundry troublesome Ministers in England" (*c.* 1590).
Lansdowne MS 120/3, "Proceedinges of certeyne undutifull [mi]nisters tending to innovation" (*c.* 1590).
Sloane MS 885, 102r–05v, "Observations of some Bookes writ against the Cleargey but more espesialley Marten Marprelate" (*c.* 1700).

CANTERBURY CATHEDRAL ARCHIVES

MS Dcb/PRC 44/3, high commission to Cathedral chapter officials, re the Marprelate tracts (Jan. 3, 1589).

HUNTINGTON LIBRARY

HL Ellesmere MS 2148, summary of evidence concerning the Marprelate project (1593).

INNER TEMPLE LIBRARY

Petyt MS 538, vol. 38, no. 68, John Whitgift re Richard Bancroft (1597).

LAMBETH PALACE LIBRARY

Library Record F1, catalogue of the library of Richard Bancroft (1612).
MS 2686, 29r–30v, Job Throkmorton to Christopher Hatton (Oct. 1590).
MS 3470, 105r–06v, "A breiffe of the depositions allredy taken, touching the printing and publishing of Martins Libelles, and of the supposed Author thereof" (late 1589/early 1590).

PIERPONT MORGAN LIBRARY

MS MA 276, speeches by Job Throkmorton from the 1586 parliament.

PUBLIC RECORD OFFICE

SP Dom. 12/159/27, notes on sermons by William Glibery (1583).
SP Dom. 12/167/21, Job Throkmorton to Ralph Warcuppe (Jan. 13, 1584).
SP Dom. 12/172/1, William Cecil, Lord Burghley to John Whitgift (July 1, 1584).
SP Dom. 12/176/58, Richard Grenville re Eusebius Paget (1585).
SP Dom. 12/200/31, William Griffith to John Whitgift, re the Rhiwledyn press (Apr. 1587).
SP Dom. 12/218/23, Francis Thynne to William Cecil, Lord Burghley (Nov. 15, 1588).
SP Dom. 12/229/46, re libels vs John Bullingham, bishop of Gloucester (Dec. 1589).
SP Dom. 12/235/81, "An advertisement towching seditious wrytings" (c. 1590).
SP Dom. 12/238/135, declaration of Roger Walton (Apr. 30, 1591).
SP Dom. 12/243/11, examination of George Dingley (Sept. 14, 1592).
SP Dom. 12/244/64, John Udall to William Cecil, Lord Burghley (Mar. 3, 1593).
SP Dom. 12/245/30, William Sterrel to Charles Paget (June 12, 1593).
SP Dom. 12/284/4, Thomas Phelippes to Robert Cecil (May 4, 1602).
SP Dom. 16/142/47, Leonel Sharpe to Dudley Carleton (May 8, 1629).
SP Dom. 16/177/8, Samuel Brooke to William Laud (Dec. 15, 1630).

SP Dom. 16/362/96, Nicholas Darton to William Laud ([June,] 1637).
SP Dom. Addenda 13/31/32, Thomas Phelippes to Thomas Barnes (June 23, 1589).
SP Dom. Addenda 13/31/33, Thomas Phelippes to Thomas Barnes (June 1589).

SURREY HISTORY CENTRE

Loseley MS, LM/1036/20, depositions re William Boswell and John Fenne (May 27, 1591).

PRIMARY WORKS

This section includes books printed before 1700 and modern editions of books and manuscript materials printed or written before 1700.

Acts of the Privy Council of England, ed. John Roche Dasent. 46 vols. Norwich: HMSO, 1899–1964.
An Almond for a Parrat, or Cutbert Curry-Knaves Almes. London, 1590.
Arber, Edward, ed. *A Transcript of the Registers of the Company of Stationers.* 5 vols. 1875–94; repr. Gloucester, MA: Peter Smith, 1967.
Asinus Onustus: The Asse Overladen. London, 1642.
Atra bilis est causa potissima diuturnae vitae / Martinomania est reip. perniciosa. Cambridge, *c.* 1589.
Aylmer, John. *An Harborowe for Faithfull and Trewe Subjectes.* London, 1559.
Babington, Gervase. *A Sermon Preached at Paules Crosse.* London, 1591.
Bacon, Francis. *Francis Bacon: A Critical Edition of the Major Works,* ed. Brian Vickers. Oxford: Oxford University Press, 1996.
    A Wise and Moderate Discourse, Concerning Church-Affaires. London, 1641.
Bale, John. *The Pageant of Popes, Contayninge the Lyves of all the Bishops of Rome.* London, 1574.
Bancroft, Richard. *Daungerous Positions and Proceedings, Published and Practised within this Iland of Brytaine, under Pretence of Reformation, and for the Presbiteriall Discipline.* London, 1593.
    A Sermon Preached at Paules Crosse the 9 of Februarie. London, 1589.
    A Survay of the Pretended Holy Discipline. London, 1593.
    Tracts Ascribed to Richard Bancroft, ed. Albert Peel. Cambridge: Cambridge University Press, 1953.
Barlow, William. *The Summe and Substance of the Conference ... at Hampton Court.* London, 1604.
Barrow, Henry. *The Writings of Henry Barrow.* Elizabethan Nonconformist Texts, vol. 3, ed. Leland H. Carlson. London: George Allen and Unwin, 1962.
Bastwick, John. *The Letany of John Bastwick.* Leiden, 1637.
Bellarmine, Robert. *Disputationes de controversiis christianae fidei.* Vol. I. Ingolstadt, 1586.
Beza, Theodore. *A Briefe and Piththie Summe of the Christian Faith,* trans. R. Filles. London, 1563.
    Confessio christianae fidei. Geneva, 1560.

The Judgement of a Most Reverend and Learned Man from Beyond the Seas, Concerning a Threefold Order of Bishops, trans. J. Field. London, *c.* 1585.

Bland, Tobias. *A Baite for Momus*. London, 1589.

Bridges, John. *A Defence of the Government Established in the Church of Englande for Ecclesiasticall Matters*. London, 1587.

Sacro-sanctum novum testamentum . . . in hexametros versus translatum. London, 1604.

The Supremacie of Christian Princes, over all Persons throughout their Dominions. London, 1573.

Browne, Robert. *The Writings of Robert Harrison and Robert Browne*. Elizabethan Nonconformist Texts, vol. 2, ed. Albert Peel and Leland H. Carlson. London: George Allen and Unwin, 1953.

Burges, Cornelius. *The Fire of the Sanctuarie Newly Uncovered, or, A Compleat Tract of Zeale*. London, 1625.

Burton, Samuel. *A Sermon Preached at the Generall Assises in Warwicke*. London, 1620.

Camden, William. *Annales rerum Anglicarum et Hibernicarum regnante Elizabetha*. London, 1615.

Annales. The True and Royall History of the Famous Empresse Elizabeth. London, 1625.

Cartwright, Thomas. *A Brief Apologie of Thomas Cartwright*, ed. J. Throkmorton. Middelburg, 1596.

A Confutation of the Rhemists Translation, Glosses, and Annotations on the New Testament. Leiden, 1618.

A Replye to An Answere made of M. Doctor Whitgifte. Hemel Hempstead? 1573.

The Second Replie of Thomas Cartwright: Agaynst Maister Whitgiftes Second Answer. Heidelberg, 1575.

The Rest of the Second Replie. Basle, 1577.

Clarendon, Edward Hyde, earl of. *Animadversions upon a Book, Intituled, Fanaticism Fanatically Imputed to the Catholic Church, by Dr. Stillingfleet*. London, 1673.

The History of the Rebellion and Civil Wars in England, ed. W. Dunn Macray. 6 vols. Oxford: Clarendon Press, 1888.

Codrington, Robert. *Life and Death, of the Illustrious Robert Earle of Essex*. London, 1646.

Coke, Sir Edward. *Booke of Entries*. London, 1614.

Collinson, Patrick, John Craig and Brett Usher, eds. *Conferences and Combination Lectures in the Elizabethan Church: Dedham and Bury St Edmunds 1582–1590*. Church of England Record Society, vol. 10. London: Boydell Press, 2003.

Cooper, Thomas. *An Admonition to the People of England*. London, 1589.

Cosin, Richard. *An Answer to the Two First and Principall Treatises of a Certeine Factious Libell*. London, 1584.

An Apologie for Sundrie Proceedings. London, 1593.

Conspiracie, for Pretended Reformation: viz. Presbyteriall Discipline. London, 1592.

Covell, William. *A Modest and Reasonable Examination, of Some Things in Use in the Church of England, Sundrie Times Heretofore Misliked.* London, 1604.

Cranmer, George. *Concerning the New Church Discipline, An Excellent Letter.* Oxford, 1642.

Crompton, Richard. *Star-Chamber Cases.* London, 1630.

Daneau, Lambert. *In D. Pauli priorem epistolam ad Timotheum commentarius.* Geneva, 1577.

Davidson, John. *A Short Christian Instruction.* London, 1588.

Davies, John. *Sir Martin Mar-People, His Coller of Esses.* London, 1590.

Deacon, John. *Dialogicall Discourses of Spirits and Divels.* London, 1601.

A Defence of the Reasons of the Counter-Poyson. Middelburg, 1586.

Dekker, Thomas. *The Double PP.* London, 1606.

A Dialogue, Concerning the Strife of our Churche. London, 1584.

A Dialogue. Wherin is Plainly Laide Open, the Tyrannicall Dealing of L. Bishopps against Gods Children. La Rochelle, 1589.
  Repr. Amsterdam, 1640.
  Repr. as *The Character of a Puritan.* London, 1643.

Dryden, John. *The Poems of John Dryden,* ed. Paul Hammond and David Hopkins. 5 vols. London: Longman, 1995–2005.

Elizabeth I. *Elizabeth I: Collected Works,* ed. Leah S. Marcus, Janel Mueller, and Mary Beth Rose. Chicago: University of Chicago Press, 2000.

The Examinations of Henry Barrowe, John Grenewood and John Penrie. Dort? 1596?

Fellowes, E. H. *English Madrigal Verse 1558–1632.* 3rd edn, rev. and enlarged Frederick W. Sternfeld and David Greer. Oxford: Clarendon Press, 1967.

Fenner, Dudley (attrib.). *A Counter-Poyson, Modestly Written for the Time.* London, 1584.
  A Defence of the Godlie Ministers, against the Slaunders of D. Bridges. Middelburg, 1587.

Field, John and Thomas Wilcox. *An Admonition to the Parliament.* Hemel Hempstead? 1572.

Foxe, John. *The Ecclesiasticall History Contaynyng the Actes and Monumentes.* 2 vols. London, 1570.

Frégeville, Jean de. *The Reformed Politicke. That is, An Apologie for the Generall Cause of Reformation.* London, 1589.

A Fruitfull Sermon, upon the 3. 4. 5. 6. 7. and 8. verses, of the 12. chapter of the Epistle of S. Paul to the Romanes. London, 1584.

Fulke, William. *A Briefe and Plaine Declaration, Concerning the Desires of all those Faithfull Ministers, that have and do Seeke for the Discipline and Reformation of the Church of Englande.* London, 1584.

Fuller, Thomas. *The Church-History of Britain.* London, 1655.
  The History of the Worthies of England. London, 1662.

Gilby, Anthony. *A Pleasaunt Dialogue, Betweene a Souldior of Barwicke, and an English Chaplaine.* Middelburg? 1581.

Greenwood, John. *The Writings of John Greenwood 1587–1590.* Elizabethan Nonconformist Texts, vol. 4, ed. Leland H. Carlson. London: George Allen and Unwin, 1962.

Greg, W. W., and E. Boswell, eds. *Records of the Court of the Stationers' Company: 1576 to 1602, from Register B.* London: Bibliographical Society, 1930.

Harington, Sir John. *A Briefe View of the State of the Church of England.* In *Nugae Antiquae,* ed. Henry Harington. 2 vols. London, 1804.

An Harmony of the Confessions of the Faith of the Christian and Reformed Churches. Comp. J. F. Salvart. Cambridge, 1586.

Hartley, T. E., ed. *Proceedings in the Parliaments of Elizabeth I.* 3 vols. Leicester and London: Leicester University Press, 1981–95.

Harvey, Gabriel. *Pierces Supererogation or A New Prayse of the Old Asse.* London, 1593.

Harvey, Richard. *Plaine Percevall the Peace-Maker of England.* London, 1590.

A Theologicall Discourse of the Lamb of God and His Enemies . . . with a Detection of Old and New Barbarisme, now Commonly Called Martinisme. London, 1590.

Hastings, Sir Francis. *The Letters of Sir Francis Hastings 1574–1609,* ed. Claire Cross. Somerset Record Society, 69 (1969).

Heylyn, Peter. *Aerius Redivivus, or, The History of the Presbyterians.* London, 1670.

Antidotum Lincolniense. Or An Answer to a Book Entituled, The Holy Table, Name, & Thing. London, 1637.

A Briefe and Moderate Answer, to the Seditious and Scandalous Challenges of Henry Burton. London, 1637.

Examen historicum. London, 1659.

Hill, Adam. *The Crie of England. A Sermon Preached at Paules Crosse in September 1593.* London, 1595.

Hoby, Margaret. *The Private Life of an Elizabethan Lady: The Diary of Lady Margaret Hoby 1599–1605.* Ed. Joanna Moody. Stroud: Sutton, 1998.

Hooker, Richard. *The Dangers of New Discipline, to the State and Church Discovered.* Oxford, 1642.

The Folger Library Edition of the Works of Richard Hooker. Gen. ed. W. Speed Hill. 7 vols. in 8. Cambridge, MA: Harvard University Press, 1977–98.

Of the Lawes of Ecclesiasticall Politie. London, 1593.

Howell, Thomas Bayley, ed. *Cobbett's Complete Collection of State Trials.* 34 vols. London, 1809–28.

Hughes, Paul L., and James F. Larkin, eds. *Tudor Royal Proclamations.* 3 vols. New Haven: Yale University Press, 1969.

Hughey, Ruth, ed. *The Arundel Harington Manuscript of Tudor Poetry.* 2 vols. Columbus, OH: Ohio State University Press, 1960.

James, William. *A Sermon Preached at Paules Crosse.* London, 1590.

Kemp, Thomas, ed. *The Black Book of Warwick.* Warwick, 1898.

L., A. *Antimartinus, sive monitio cuiusdam Londinensis, ad adolescentes utriusque academiae contra personatum quendam rabulam qui se anglice, Martin Marprelat.* London, 1589.

A Lamentable Complaint of the Commonalty, by Way of Supplication to Parliament, for a Learned Ministry. London, 1585.

Langham, Robert. *A Letter*, ed. R. J. P. Kuin. Leiden: E. J. Brill, 1983.
  Robert Laneham's Letter, ed. F. J. Furnivall. London: Chatto and Windus, 1907.

La Roche de Chandieu, Antoine de (Antonius Sadeel or Sadeelius). *De rebus grauissimis controversis disputationes accuratae theologice et scholastice tractatae*. Cambridge, 1584.

Latimer, Hugh. *27 Sermons*. London, 1562.

Laud, William. *The History of the Troubles and Tryal of . . . William Laud*. London, 1695.

Leigh, Richard. *The Transproser Rehears'd: Or the Fifth Act of Mr. Bayes's Play*. London, 1673.

Leighton, Alexander. *An Appeal to the Parliament, or Sions Pleas against the Prelacie*. Amsterdam, 1629.

Leishman, J. B., ed. *The Three Parnassus Plays (1598–1601)*. London: Ivor Nicholson and Watson, 1949.

L'Estrange, Roger. *Interest Mistaken, or, The Holy Cheat*. London, 1661.

The Life of Long Meg of Westminster: Containing the Mad Merry Prankes Shee Played in Her Life Time. London, 1635.

Lodge, Thomas. *Wits Miserie, and the Worlds Madnesse*. London, 1596.

Loque, Bertrand de. *Traité de l'église contenant un discours pour cognoistre la vraiye église et la discerner d'avec l'église romaine et toutes autres fausses assemblées*. Geneva, 1577.
  A Treatie of the Churche, trans. T. Wilcox. London, 1581.

Luther, Martin. *A Treatise, Touching the Liberty of a Christian*, trans. J. Bell. London, 1579.

Lyly, John. *The Complete Works of John Lyly*, ed. R. Warwick Bond. 3 vols. Oxford: Clarendon Press, 1902.
  Pappe with an Hatchet. London, 1589.

M. Some Laid Open in his Coulers. La Rochelle, 1589.

Manningham, John. *Diary of John Manningham*, ed. John Bruce. Camden Society, 99 (1868).

Markham, Gervase. *The Complete Farriar*. London, 1639.

Marlowe, Christopher. *Doctor Faustus and Other Plays*, ed. David Bevington and Eric Rasmussen. Oxford: Clarendon Press, 1995.

Marphoreus (pseud.). *Martins Months Minde, that is, a Certaine Report, and True Description of the Death, and Funeralls, of Olde Martin Marreprelate*. London, 1589.

Marprelate, Martin (pseud.). *The Marprelate Tracts 1588, 1589*, ed. William Pierce. London: James Clark, 1911.
  The Marprelate Tracts [1588–1589]. Leeds: Scolar Press, 1967.
  Certaine Minerall, and Metaphisicall Schoolpoints. Coventry, 1589.
  Hay any Worke for Cooper. Coventry, 1589.
    Repr. London, 1642.

Repr. as *Reformation No Enemie. Or a True Discourse, Betweene the Bishops and the Desirers of Reformation*. London, 1641.

The Just Censure and Reproofe of Martin Junior. Wolston, 1589.

Oh Read Over D. John Bridges, for it is a Worthy Worke: Or an Epitome . . . In the Meane Time, Let Them be Content with this Learned Epistle [the *Epistle*]. East Molesey, 1588.

Repr. as *The Epistle*, ed. Edward Arber. The English Scholar's Library, no. 11. London, 1880.

Repr. as *The Marprelate Tracts: Martin's Epistle*, ed. Maria Giannina Green. Kelowna, BC: Devere Press, 1990.

Oh Read Over D. John Bridges, for it is Worthy Worke: Or an Epitome . . . In this Epitome, the Foresaid Fickers, etc. are very Insufficiently Furnished . . . to Answere the Cavill of the Puritanes [the *Epitome*]. Fawsley, 1588.

The Protestatyon of Martin Marprelat. Wolston, 1589.

Theses Martinianae: That is, Certaine Demonstrative Conclusions, Sette Downe and Collected . . . by . . . Martin Marprelate the Great. Wolston, 1589.

Mar-Martine, I Know Not Why a Trueth in Rime Set Out. London, 1589.

Mar-Martin. I Knowe Not Why a Frutelesse Lye in Print. London, 1589?

[Another edn] *Marre Mar-Martin: or Marre-Martins Medling, in a Manner Misliked*. London, 1589?

Marten, Anthony. *A Reconciliation of all the Pastors and Cleargy of this Church of England*. London, 1590.

Marvell, Andrew. *The Rehearsal Transpros'd and The Rehearsal Transpros'd: The Second Part*, ed. D. I. B. Smith. Oxford: Clarendon Press, 1971.

Millman, Jill Seal and Gillian Wright, eds. *Early Modern Women's Manuscript Poetry*. Manchester: Manchester University Press, 2005.

Milton, John. *Complete Shorter Poems*, ed. John Carey. 2nd edn. London: Longman, 1997.

Morice, James. *A Briefe Treatise of Oathes Exacted by Ordinaries and Ecclesiasticall Judges*. Middelburg, 1590.

Nashe, Thomas. *The Unfortunate Traveller*. London, 1594.

The Works of Thomas Nashe, ed. Ronald B. McKerrow. 5 vols. London: A. H. Bullen, 1904–10.

Nichols, Josias. *The Plea of the Innocent*. London, 1602.

Ormerod, Oliver. *The Picture of a Puritane*. London, 1605.

Overton, Richard. *The Araignement of Mr. Persecution*. London, 1645.

Divine Observations. London, 1646.

Martin's Eccho: or A Remonstrance. London, 1645.

The Nativity of Sir John Presbyter. London, 1645.

The Ordinance for Tythes Dismounted. London, 1646.

A Sacred Decretall. London, 1645.

Vox Borealis, or The Northern Discoverie. Amsterdam, 1641 [i.e., 1640?].

Parker, Matthew. *Correspondence*, ed. J. Bruce and T. T. Perowne. Parker Society, 42. London: Parker Society, 1853.

Parker, Samuel. *A Defence and Continuation of the Ecclesiastical Politie*. London, 1671.

    A Discourse of Ecclesiastical Politie. London, 1670.

    A Reproof to the Rehearsal Transprosed, 1673.

Parsons, Robert (as Andreas Philopatrum). *Elizabethae Angliae Reginae haeresim Calvinianam propugnantis*. Antwerp, 1592.

    The Warn-Word to Sir Francis Hastinges Wast-Word. Antwerp, 1602.

A Parte of a Register. Middelburg, 1593?

Pasquill (pseud.). *A Countercuffe Given to Martin Junior*. London, 1589.

    The Firste Parte of Pasquils Apologie. London, 1590.

    The Returne of the Renowned Cavaliero Pasquill of England. London, 1589.

Paule, Sir George. *The Life of the Most Reverend and Religious Prelate John Whitgift*. London, 1612.

Peel, Albert, ed. *The Seconde Parte of a Register*. 2 vols. Cambridge: Cambridge University Press, 1915.

Penry, John. *Th' Appellation of John Penri, unto the Highe Court of Parliament*. La Rochelle, 1589.

    A Defence of that which hath bin Written in the Questions of the Ignorant Ministerie. East Molesey, 1588.

    An Exhortation unto the Governours and People of Her Majesties Countrie of Wales. London, 1588.

    Expanded edn. East Molesey, 1588.

    I John Penry doo Heare . . . Set Downe Sumarily the Whole Truth . . . in Regard of my Faith Towards my God and Dread Soveraigne Queene Elizabeth. Printed abroad? 1593?

    The Notebook of John Penry, 1593, ed. Albert Peel. Camden Society, vol. 67. London: Camden Society, 1944.

    Three Treatises Concerning Wales, ed. David Williams. Cardiff: University of Wales Press, 1960.

    A Treatise Containing the Aequity of an Humble Supplication . . . in the Behalfe of the Countrey of Wales. Oxford, 1587.

    A Treatise Wherein is Manifestlie Proved, that Reformation and Those that Sincerely Favor the Same, are Unjustly Charged to be Enemies, unto Hir Majestie, and the State. Edinburgh, 1590.

    A Viewe of Some Part of Such Publike Wants & Disorders as are in the Service of God, within Her Majesties Countrie of Wales. Coventry, 1589.

A Petition Directed to Her Most Excellent Majestie. Middelburg, 1592.

Piers Ploughman. *I Playne Piers which can not flatter*. London, 1550?

    Repr. as *O Read me, for I am of great antiquitie. I Plaine Piers which can not flatter*. London? 1588?

Prime, John. *The Consolations of David, Breefly Applied to Queene Elizabeth*. London, 1588.

A Proclamation against Certaine Seditious and Schismatical Bookes and Libels. London, 1588.

Queene Elizabeths Bishops. London, 1642.

Rainolds, John. *Dr. Reignolds His Letter to that Worthy Councellor, Sir Francis Knolles, Concerning some Passages in D. Bancroftes Sermon at Paules Crosse.* London, 1641.

The Judgement of Doctor Reignolds Concerning Episcopacy. London, 1641.

Rainolds, William. *A Refutation of Sundry Reprehensions.* Paris, 1583.

Recreation for Ingenious Head-peeces. London, 1650.

Repr. London, 1654.

Rid, Samuel. *Martin Mark-All, Beadle of Bridewell.* London, 1610.

Rogers, Thomas. *A Sermon upon the 6. 7. and 8. verses of the 12. chapter of Romanes.* London, 1590.

A Second Admonition to the Parliament. Hemel Hempstead? 1572.

Some, Robert. *A Godly Treatise Containing and Deciding Certaine Questions ... Touching the Ministerie, Sacraments, and Church.* London, 1588.

Enlarged edn. London. 1588.

A Godly Treatise, Wherein are Examined and Confuted Many Execrable Fancies, Given Out by H. Barrow and J. Greenewood. London, 1589.

The State of the Church of Englande, Laide Open in a Conference. London, 1588.

Stoughton, William (attrib.). *An Abstract, of Certain Acts of Parliament.* London, 1583.

Stow, John. *The Annales of England.* London, 1592.

A Survey of London, ed. Charles Lethbridge Kingsford. 2 vols. Oxford: Clarendon Press, 1908.

Sutcliffe, Matthew. *An Answere to a Certaine Libel Supplicatorie.* London, 1592.

An Answere unto a Certaine Calumnious Letter Published by M. J. Throkmorton. London, 1595.

The Examination of T. Cartwrights Late Apologie. London, 1596.

Sydenham, Humphrey. *Sermons upon Solemn Occasions.* London, 1637.

T., G. *Roger the Canterburian ... or The Character of a Prelaticall Man Affecting Great Heights.* London, 1642.

Taylor, John. *Crop-Eare Curried, or, Tom Nash His Ghost.* London, 1644.

Differing Worships, or, The Oddes, between Some Knights Service and God's. Or Tom Nash His Ghost (the Old Martin Queller) Newly Rous'd. London, 1640.

Tom Nash His Ghost. London, 1642.

Temple, Robert. *A Sermon Teaching Discretion in Matters of Religion.* London, 1592.

Throkmorton, Job. *The Defence of Job Throkmorton, against the Slaunders of Maister Sutcliffe.* Middelburg, 1594.

T., T. *A Myrror for Martinists, and all other Schismatiques.* London, 1590.

Tomkins, Thomas. *The Inconveniences of Toleration.* London, 1667.

Repr. London, 1683.

Tomkis, Thomas. *Lingua: or, The Combat of the Tongue.* London, 1607.

Travers, Walter. *A Defence of the Ecclesiastical Discipline Ordayned of God to be Used in His Church.* Middelburg, 1588.

Ecclesiasticae disciplinae. Heidelberg, 1574.

A Full and Plaine Declaration of Ecclesiasticall Discipline, trans. T. Cartwright. Heidelberg, 1574.

Tyndale, William. *The Whole Workes of W. Tyndall, John Frith, and Doct. Barnes*, ed. J. Foxe. London, 1573.

Udall, John. *A Demonstration of the Trueth of that Discipline which Christe hath Prescribed for the Governement of His Church*. East Molesey, 1588.

A New Discovery of Old Pontificall Practises for the Maintenance of the Prelates Authority and Hierarchy. London, 1643.

The Unlawfull Practises of Prelates against Godly Ministers. London, *c.* 1584.

Verstegan, Richard. *An Advertisement Written to a Secretarie of My L. Treasurers of Ingland* Antwerp? 1592.

Viret, Peter. *A Faithfull and Familiar Exposition Upon the Prayer of our Lorde*, trans. John Brooke. London, 1582.

Walton, Izaak. *The Life of Mr. Rich. Hooker*. London, 1665.

W., R. *Martine Mar-Sixtus*. London, 1591.

Wanley, Humphrey. *Letters of Humphrey Wanley*, ed. P. L. Heyworth. Oxford: Clarendon Press, 1989.

Watson, William. *A Decacordon of Ten Quodlibeticall Questions Concerning Religion and State*. London, 1602.

Weever, John. *Ancient Funerall Monuments*. London, 1631.

A Whip for an Ape: or Martin Displaied. London, 1589?

[Another edn] *Rythmes against Martin Marre-prelate*. London, 1589.

Whitaker, William. *Ad Nicolai Sanderi demonstrationes quadraginta*. London, 1583.

Disputatio ad sacra scriptura. Cambridge, 1588.

White, Thomas. *A Sermon Preached at Paules Crosse*. London, 1589.

Whitgift, John. *An Answere to a Certen Libel*. London, 1572.

The Defense of the Aunswere. London, 1574.

The Whole Volume of Statutes at Large. London, 1587.

Wood, Anthony. *Athenae Oxoniensis*. London, 1721.

Athenae Oxoniensis, ed. Philip Bliss. 4 vols. London, 1813–20.

Wright, Leonard. *A Friendly Admonition to Martine Marprelate, and His Mates*. London, 1590.

The Hunting of Antichrist. London, 1589.

A Summons for Sleepers. London, 1589.

SECONDARY WORKS

Adkins, Mary Grace Muse. "The Genesis of Dramatic Satire against the Puritan, as Illustrated in *A Knack to Know a Knave*." *Review of English Studies* 22 (1946), 81–95.

Ames, Joseph. *Typographical Antiquities: Being an Historical Account of Printing in England*. London, 1749.

Anselment, Raymond A. *"Betwixt Jest and Earnest": Marprelate, Milton, Marvell, Swift & the Decorum of Religious Ridicule*. Toronto: University of Toronto Press, 1979.

Appleton, Elizabeth. *An Anatomy of the Marprelate Controversy, 1588–1596*. Lewiston, NY: Edwin Mellen Press, 2001.

Arber, Edward. *An Introductory Sketch to the Martin Marprelate Controversy,* *1588–1590.* 1879; repr. London: Archibald Constable, 1895.

Babbage, Stuart Barton. *Puritanism and Richard Bancroft.* London: SPCK, 1962.

Baldwin, T. W. *"Errors* and Marprelate." In *Studies in Honor of DeWitt T. Starnes,* ed. Thomas P. Harrison *et al.* Austin: University of Texas Press, 1967. 9–23.

Bellany, Alastair. "A Poem on the Archbishop's Hearse: Puritanism, Libel, and Sedition after the Hampton Court Conference." *Journal of British Studies* 34 (1995), 137–64.

"'Raylinge Rymes and Vaunting Verse': Libellous Politics in Early Stuart England, 1603–1628." In *Culture and Politics in Early Stuart England,* ed. Kevin Sharpe and Peter Lake. London: Macmillan, 1994. 285–310.

Benger, John S. "The Authority of Writer and Text in Radical Protestant Literature 1540 to 1593 with Particular Reference to the Marprelate Tracts." PhD dissertation, University of Oxford, 1989.

Black, Joseph. "Pamphlet Wars: The Marprelate Tracts and 'Martinism,' 1588–1688." PhD dissertation, University of Toronto, 1996.

"The Rhetoric of Reaction: The Marprelate Tracts (1588–89), Anti-Martinism, and the Uses of Print in Early Modern England." *Sixteenth Century Journal* 28 (1997), 707–25.

Bonnard, Georges A. *La controverse de Martin Marprelate 1588–1590.* Geneva, 1916.

Brachlow, Stephen. *The Communion of Saints: Radical Puritan and Separatist Ecclesiology 1570–1625.* Oxford: Oxford University Press, 1988.

Brook, Benjamin. *Lives of the Puritans.* 3 vols. London, 1813.

Brown, Nancy Pollard. "Paperchase: The Dissemination of Catholic Texts in Elizabethan England." *English Manuscript Studies 1100–1700* I (1989), 120–43.

Bruster, Douglas. "The Structural Transformation of Print in Late Elizabethan England." In *Print, Manuscript, and Performance: The Changing Relations of the Media in Early Modern England,* ed. Arthur F. Marotti and Michael D. Bristol. Columbus: Ohio University Press, 2000. 49–89.

Burrage, Champlin. *John Penry: The So-Called Martyr of Congregationalism.* Oxford: Oxford University Press, 1913.

Cargill Thompson, W. D. J. "A Reconsideration of Richard Bancroft's Paul's Cross Sermon of 9 February 1588/89." *Journal of Ecclesiastical History* 20 (1969), 253–66.

"Sir Francis Knollys's Campaign against the *Jure Divino* Theory of Episcopacy." *Studies in the Reformation: Luther to Hooker,* ed. C. W. Dugmore. London: Athlone, 1980. 94–130.

Studies in the Reformation: Luther to Hooker, ed. C. W. Dugmore. London: Athlone, 1980.

Carlson, Leland H. *Martin Marprelate, Gentleman: Master Job Throkmorton Laid Open in His Colors.* San Marino, CA: Huntington Library, 1981.

Chadwick, Owen. "Richard Bancroft's Submission." *Journal of Ecclesiastical History* 3 (1952), 58–73.

Chambers, E. K. *The Elizabethan Stage.* 4 vols. 1923; repr. Oxford: Clarendon Press, 1967.

Clare, Janet. *"Art Made Tongue-Tied by Authority": Elizabethan and Jacobean Dramatic Censorship*. Manchester: Manchester University Press, 1990.

Clegg, Cyndia Susan. *Press Censorship in Elizabethan England*. Cambridge: Cambridge University Press, 1997.

  Press Censorship in Jacobean England. Cambridge: Cambridge University Press, 2001.

Cogswell, Thomas. "Underground Political Verse and the Transformation of English Political Culture." In *Political Culture and Cultural Politics in Early Modern Enland: Essays Presented to David Underdown*, ed. Susan D. Amussen and Mark A. Kishlansky. Manchester: Manchester University Press, 1995. 277–300.

Collinson, Patrick. "Ben Jonson's *Bartholomew Fair*: The Theatre Constructs Puritanism." In *The Theatrical City: Culture, Theatre and Politics in London, 1576–1649*, ed. David L. Smith, Richard Strier, and David Bevington. Cambridge: Cambridge University Press, 1995. 157–69.

  "Ecclesiastical Vitriol: Religious Satire in the 1590s and the Invention of Puritanism." In *The Reign of Elizabeth I: Court and Culture in the Last Decade*, ed. John Guy. Cambridge: Cambridge University Press, 1995. 150–70.

  "Elizabethan and Jacobean Puritanism as Forms of Popular Religious Culture." In *The Culture of English Puritanism, 1560–1700*, ed. Christopher Durston and Jacqueline Eales. New York: St Martin's Press, 1996. 32–57.

  The Elizabethan Puritan Movement. London: Jonathan Cape, 1967.

  "John Field and Elizabethan Puritanism." In *Elizabethan Government and Society: Essays Presented to Sir John Neale*, ed. S. T. Bindoff, J. Hurstfield, and C. H. Williams. London: Athlone, 1961. 127–62.

  "Perne the Turncoat: An Elizabethan Reputation." In *Elizabethan Essays*. London: Hambledon Press, 1994. 179–217.

  "Puritans, Men of Business and Elizabethan Parliaments." In *Elizabethan Essays*. London: Hambledon Press, 1994. 59–86.

Coolidge, John S. "Martin Marprelate, Marvell and *Decorum Personae* as a Satirical Theme." *PMLA* 74 (1959), 526–32.

Cox-Johnson, Ann. "Lambeth Palace Library 1610–1664." *Transactions of the Cambridge Bibliographical Society* 2 (1954–58), 105–26.

Cressy, David. *Birth, Marriage, and Death: Ritual, Religion, and the Life-Cycle in Tudor and Stuart England*. Oxford: Oxford University Press, 1997.

Crewe, Jonathan V. *Unredeemed Rhetoric: Thomas Nashe and the Scandal of Authorship*. Baltimore: Johns Hopkins University Press, 1982.

Croft, Pauline. "Libels, Popular Literacy, and Public Opinion in Early Modern England." *Historical Research* 68 (1995), 266–85.

  "The Reputation of Robert Cecil: Libels, Political Opinion and Popular Awareness in the Early Seventeenth Century." *Transactions of the Royal Historical Society*, 6:1 (1991), 43–69.

Crum, Margaret. *First-Line Index of English Poetry 1500–1800 in Manuscripts of the Bodleian Library Oxford*. 2 vols. Oxford: Clarendon Press, 1969.

Cushman, L. W. *The Devil and the Vice in the English Dramatic Literature Before Shakespeare*. Halle a/S, 1900.

Cust, Richard. "News and Politics in Early Seventeenth-Century England." *Past & Present* 112 (1986), 66–90.

Dexter, Henry Martyn. *The Congregationalism of the Last Three Hundred Years, as Seen in its Literature*. New York: Harper & Brothers, 1880.

Disraeli, Isaac. *Quarrels of Authors*. 3 vols. London, 1814.

Dobson, R. B. and J. Taylor, eds. *Rymes of Robyn Hood: An Introduction to the English Outlaw*. London: Heinemann, 1976.

Dusinberre, Juliet. "Topical Forest: Kemp and Mar-text in Arden." In *In Arden: Editing Shakespeare: Essays in Honour of Richard Proudfoot*, ed. Ann Thompson and Gordon McMullan. London: Arden Shakespeare, 2003. 239–51.

Dutton, Richard. *Mastering the Revels: The Regulation and Censorship of English Renaissance Drama*. Iowa City: University of Iowa Press, 1991.

"The Revels Office and the Boy Companies, 1600–1603: New Perspectives." *English Literary Renaissance* 32:2 (2002), 324–51.

Egan, James. "Andrew Marvell Refashions the Marprelate Tradition: An Aesthetic Reading of *The Rehearsal Transpros'd*." *Prose Studies* 18:2 (1995), 135–58.

"Milton and the Marprelate Tradition." *Milton Studies* 8 (1975), 103–21.

"Nathaniel Ward and the Marprelate Tradition." *Early American Literature* 15:1 (1980), 59–71.

Ferguson, W. Craig. *Valentine Simmes: Printer to Drayton, Shakespeare, Chapman, Greene, Dekker, Middleton, Daniel, Jonson, Marlowe, Marston, Heywood, and Other Elizabethans*. Charlottesville: Bibliographical Society of the University of Virginia, 1968.

Foster, Stephen. *Notes from the Caroline Underground: Alexander Leighton, the Puritan Triumvirate, and the Laudian Reaction to Nonconformity*. Hamden, CT: Archon Books, 1978.

Fox, Adam. *Oral and Literate Culture in England 1500–1700*. Oxford: Clarendon Press, 2000.

Gimelfarb-Brack, Marie. *Liberté, Égalité, Fraternité, Justice! La vie et l'oeuvre de Richard Overton, Niveleur*. Berne: Peter Lang, 1979.

Greene, Walter Kirkland. "The Martin Marprelate Controversy." 2 vols. PhD dissertation, Harvard University, 1923.

Greg, W. W. *Licensers for the Press*. Oxford: Oxford Bibliographical Society, 1962.

Gruffydd, Geraint. *Argraffwyr cyntaf Cymru*. Caerdydd: Gwasg Prifysgol Cymru, 1972.

"Gwasg Ddirgel yr Ogof yn Rhiwledyn." *Journal of the Welsh Bibliographical Society* 9:1 (1958), 1–23.

Gurr, Andrew. *The Shakespearean Company, 1594–1642*. Cambridge: Cambridge University Press, 2004.

The Shakespearean Stage 1574–1642. 3rd edn. Cambridge: Cambridge University Press, 1992.

Guy, John. "The Elizabethan Establishment and the Ecclesiastical Polity." In *The Reign of Elizabeth I: Court and Culture in the Last Decade*, ed. John Guy. Cambridge: Cambridge University Press, 1995. 126–49.

Halasz, Alexandra. *The Marketplace of Print: Pamphlets and the Public Sphere in Early Modern England.* Cambridge: Cambridge University Press, 1997.

Harline, Craig. *Pamphlets, Printing, and Political Culture in the Early Dutch Republic.* Dordrecht: M. Nijhoff, 1989.

Hasler, P. W., ed. *The History of Parliament: The House of Commons 1558–1603.* 3 vols. London: HMSO, 1981.

Heal, Felicity. *Of Prelates and Princes: A Study of the Economic and Social Position of the Tudor Episcopate.* Cambridge: Cambridge University Press, 1980.

Heinemann, Margot. *Puritanism and Theatre: Thomas Middleton and Opposition Drama under the Early Stuarts.* Cambridge: Cambridge University Press, 1980.

Hibbard, G. R. *Thomas Nashe: A Critical Introduction.* London: Routledge & Kegan Paul, 1962.

Hill, Christopher. "Radical Prose in Seventeenth-Century England: From Marprelate to the Levellers." *Essays in Criticism* 32 (1982), 95–118.

Hilliard, Stephen S. *The Singularity of Thomas Nashe.* Lincoln: University of Nebraska Press, 1986.

Hirst, Derek. *The Representative of the People? Voters and Voting in England under the Early Stuarts.* Cambridge: Cambridge University Press, 1975.

Holden, William Prescott. *Anti-Puritan Satire, 1572–1642.* New Haven: Yale University Press, 1954.

Honigman, E. A. J. "*John a Kent* and Marprelate." *Yearbook of English Studies* 13 (1983), 288–93.

Hughes, Ann. *Politics, Society, and Civil War in Warwickshire, 1620–1660.* Cambridge: Cambridge University Press, 1987.

Hunt, John. *Religious Thought in England, from the Reformation to the End of the Last Century.* 3 vols. London, 1870–73.

Hutson, Lorna. *Thomas Nashe in Context.* Oxford: Clarendon Press, 1989.

Johnson, A. F. "The 'Cloppenburg' Press." *The Library* 13 (1958), 280–82.

Jones, Ifano. *A History of Printing and Printers in Wales.* Cardiff: William Lewis, 1925.

Jones, J. Gwynfor. *Early Modern Wales, c. 1525–1640.* London: Macmillan, 1994.
  Wales and the Tudor State: Government, Religious Change and the Social Order 1534–1603. Cardiff: University of Wales Press, 1989.

Jones-Davies, M. T. *Un peintre de la vie Londienne: Thomas Dekker.* 2 vols. Paris: Marcel Didier, 1958.

Jorgensen, L. Caitlin. "'A Madman's Epistles Are No Gospels': Alienation in *Twelfth Night* and Anti-Martinist Discourse." *Renaissance Papers* (1999), 67–78.

Kaufman, Peter Iver. *Thinking of the Laity in Late Tudor England.* Notre Dame: University of Notre Dame Press, 2004.

Kendall, Ritchie. *The Drama of Dissent: The Radical Poetics of Nonconformity, 1380–1590.* Chapel Hill: University of North Carolina Press, 1986.

King, John N. *English Reformation Literature: The Tudor Origins of the Protestant Tradition.* Princeton: Princeton University Press, 1982.

Knapp, Jeffrey. "Preachers and Players in Shakespeare's England." *Representations* 44 (1993), 29–59.

Knappen, M. M. *Tudor Puritanism.* Chicago: University of Chicago Press, 1939.

Kumaran, Arul. "Robert Greene's Martinist Transformation in 1590." *Studies in Philology* 103 (2006), 243–63.

Lake, Peter. *Anglicans and Puritans? Presbyterianism and English Conformist Thought from Whitgift to Hooker.* London: Unwin Hyman, 1988.

"Defining Puritanism – Again?" In *Puritanism: Transatlantic Perspectives on a Seventeenth-Century Anglo-American Faith*, ed. Francis J. Bremer. Boston: Massachusetts Historical Society, 1993. 3–29.

Moderate Puritans and the Elizabethan Church. Cambridge: Cambridge University Press, 1982.

"Presbyterianism, The Idea of a National Church, and the Argument from Divine Right." In *Protestantism and the National Church in Sixteenth-Century England*, ed. Peter Lake and Maria Dowling. London: Croom Helm, 1987. 193–224.

Lake, Peter with Michael Questier. *The Antichrist's Lewd Hat: Protestants, Papists and Players in Post-Reformation England.* New Haven: Yale University Press, 2002.

Lander, Jesse. *Inventing Polemic: Religion, Print, and Literary Culture in Early Modern England.* Cambridge: Cambridge University Press, 2006.

Leader, D. R. *A History of the University of Cambridge, I: The University to 1546.* Cambridge: Cambridge University Press, 1988.

Lecocq, Louis. *La Satire en Angleterre de 1588 à 1603.* Paris: Didier, 1969.

Lewis, C. S. *English Literature in the Sixteenth Century Excluding Drama.* Oxford: Clarendon Press, 1954.

McConica, James, ed. *The History of the University of Oxford, III: The Collegiate University.* Oxford: Clarendon Press, 1986.

McCorkle, Julia Norton. "A Note Concerning 'Mistress Crane' and the Martin Marprelate Controversy." *The Library* 12 (1931), 276–83.

McGinn, Donald J. *John Penry and the Marprelate Controversy.* New Brunswick, NJ: Rutgers University Press, 1966.

"Nashe's Share in the Marprelate Controversy." *PMLA* 59 (1944), 952–84.

"The Real Martin Marprelate." *PMLA* 58 (1943), 84–107.

McKerrow, Ronald B. "The Marprelate Controversy." In *The Works of Thomas Nashe.* 5 vols. London: A. H. Bullen, 1904–10. V, 34–65.

Gen. ed. *A Dictionary of Printers and Booksellers in England, Scotland and Ireland, and of Foreign Printers of English Books, 1557–1640.* London: Bibliographical Society, 1910.

McKitterick, David. *A History of Cambridge University Press, I: Printing and the Book Trade in Cambridge, 1534–1698.* Cambridge: Cambridge University Press, 1998.

McRae, Andrew. "The Literary Culture of Early Stuart Libeling." *Modern Philology* 97:3 (2000), 364–92.

Literature, Satire, and the Early Stuart State. Cambridge: Cambridge University Press, 2004.

Mares, F. H. "The Origin of the Figure Called 'The Vice' in Tudor Drama." *Huntington Library Quarterly* 22 (1958), 11–29.

Maskell, William. *A History of the Martin Marprelate Controversy in the Reign of Queen Elizabeth*. London, 1845.

Martin, Julian. *Francis Bacon, the State, and the Reform of Natural Philosophy*. Cambridge: Cambridge University Press, 1992.

May, Steven W. and William A. Ringler Jr, eds. *Elizabethan Poetry: A Bibliography and First-Line Index of English Verse, 1559–1603*. 3 vols. London: Thoemmes, 2004.

Milward, Peter. *Religious Controversies of the Elizabethan Age: A Survey of Printed Sources*. London: Scolar Press, 1978.

Religious Controversies of the Jacobean Age: A Survey of Printed Sources. London: Scolar Press, 1978.

Morgan, John. *Godly Learning: Puritan Attitudes Towards Reason, Learning and Education, 1560–1640*. Cambridge: Cambridge University Press, 1986.

Moschovakis, Nicholas R. "Topicality and Conceptual Blending: *Titus Andronicus* and the Case of William Hacket." *College Literature* 33:1 (2006), 127–50.

Navitsky, Joseph. " 'Words with Words Revenged': Religious Conflict and the Rearticulation of Late Elizabethan Satire." PhD dissertation, Boston University, 2006.

Neale, J. E. *Elizabeth I and her Parliaments: 1584–1601*. London: Jonathan Cape, 1957.

The Elizabethan House of Commons. London: Jonathan Cape, 1949.

Nicholl, Charles. *A Cup of News: The Life of Thomas Nashe*. London: Routledge & Kegan Paul, 1984.

North, Marcy L. *The Anonymous Renaissance: Cultures of Discretion in Tudor-Stuart England*. Chicago: University of Chicago Press, 2003.

Pearson, A. F. Scott. *Thomas Cartwright and Elizabethan Puritanism 1535–1603*. Cambridge, 1925.

Perrott, M. E. C. "Richard Hooker and the Problem of Authority in the Elizabethan Church." *Journal of Ecclesiastical History* 49:1 (1998), 29–59.

Pierce, William. *An Historical Introduction to the Marprelate Tracts*. London: Archibald Constable, 1908.

John Penry: His Life, Times and Writings. London: Hodder and Stoughton, 1923.

Plomer, H. R. "Secret Printing During the Civil War." *The Library* 5 (1904), 374–403.

Poole, Kristen. *Radical Religion from Shakespeare to Milton: Figures of Nonconformity in Early Modern England*. Cambridge: Cambridge University Press, 2000.

Raymond, Joad. *Pamphlets and Pamphleteering in Early Modern Britain*. Cambridge: Cambridge University Press, 2003.

Rhodes, Neil. *Elizabethan Grotesque*. London: Routledge & Kegan Paul, 1980.

Ritchie, Carson I. A. "Sir Richard Grenville and the Puritans." *English Historical Review* 77 (1962), 518–23.

Rogers, D. M. "'Popishe Thackwell' and Early Catholic Printing in Wales." *Biographical Studies* 2:1 (1953), 37–54.

Sanderson, James L. "Thomas Bastard's Disclaimer of an Oxford Libel." *The Library* 17 (1962), 145–49.

Sanders, Vivienne. "John Whitgift: Primate, Privy Councillor and Propagandist." *Anglican and Episcopal History* 56 (1987), 385–403.

Sawyer, Jeffrey K. *Printed Poison: Pamphlet Propaganda, Faction Politics, and the Public Sphere in Early Modern France*. Berkeley: University of California Press, 1990.

Shesgreen, Sean. *The Criers and Hawkers of London*. Stanford: Stanford University Press, 1990.

Sheils, W. J. *The Puritans in the Diocese of Peterborough 1558–1610*. Northamptonshire Record Society, vol. 30. Northampton Record Society, 1979.

"Religion in Provincial Towns: Innovation and Tradition." In *Church and Society in England: Henry VIII to James I*, ed. Felicity Heal and Rosemary O'Day. London: Macmillan, 1977. 156–76.

Simmons, J. L. "A Source for Shakespeare's Malvolio: The Elizabethan Controversy with the Puritans." *Huntington Library Quarterly* 36 (1972–73), 181–201.

Simpson, Percy. *Proof-Reading in the Sixteenth Seventeenth and Eighteenth Centuries*. 1935; repr. Oxford: Oxford University Press, 1970.

Smith, Nigel. *Literature and Revolution in England 1640–1660*. New Haven: Yale University Press, 1994.

"Richard Overton's Marpriest Tracts: Towards a History of Leveller Style." *Prose Studies* 9 (1986), 39–66.

Sprunger, Keith. *Trumpets from the Tower: English Puritan Printing in the Netherlands 1600–1640*. Leiden: E. J. Brill, 1994.

Starnes, DeWitt T. *Renaissance Dictionaries*. Austin: University of Texas Press, 1954.

Steggle, Matthew. "A New Marprelate Allusion." *Notes and Queries* n.s. 44:1 (March 1997), 34–36.

Stern, Virginia F. *Gabriel Harvey: His Life, Marginalia and Library*. Oxford: Clarendon Press, 1979.

Stone, Laurence. *Road to Divorce: England 1530–1987*. Oxford: Oxford University Press, 1990.

Strype, John. *Annals of the Reformation*. New edn. 4 vols. in 7. Oxford, 1824.

Historical Collections of the Life and Acts of . . . John Aylmer. New edn. Oxford, 1821.

The Life and Acts of John Whitgift. 3 vols. Oxford, 1822.

Summersgill, Travis. "The Influence of the Marprelate Controversy upon the Style of Thomas Nashe." *Studies in Philology* 48 (1951), 145–60.

Thomas, Geoffrey. "John Penry and the Marprelate Controversy." In *The Trials of Puritanism*. London: Westminster Conference, 1993. 45–71.

Towers, S. Mutchow. *Control of Religious Printing in Early Stuart England*. Woodbridge: Boydell, 2003.

Tribble, Evelyn B. *Margins and Marginality: The Printed Page in Early Modern England*. Charlottesville: University Press of Virginia, 1993.

Van Eerde, Katherine S. "Robert Waldegrave: The Printer as Agent and Link between Sixteenth-Century England and Scotland." *Renaissance Quarterly* 1 (1981), 40–78.

Waddington, John. *Surrey Congregational History*. London, 1866.

Walsham, Alexandra. " 'Frantick Hacket': Prophecy, Sorcery, Insanity, and the Elizabethan Puritan Movement." *Historical Journal* 41 (1998), 27–66.

Wawn, Andrew N. "Chaucer, *The Plowman's Tale* and Reformation Propaganda: The Testimonies of Thomas Godfray and *I Playne Piers*." *Bulletin of the John Rylands University Library of Manchester* 56 (1973), 174–92.

White, Micheline. "A Biographical Sketch of Dorcas Martin: Elizabethan Translator, Stationer, and Godly Matron." *Sixteenth Century Journal* 30 (1999), 775–92.

White, Francis Overend. *Lives of the Elizabethan Bishops of the Anglican Church*. London: Skeffington, 1898.

Williams, Glanmor. "John Penry: Marprelate and Patriot?" *Welsh History Review* 3 (1966–67), 381–80.

Recovery, Reorientation, and Reformation: Wales c. 1415–1642. Oxford: Clarendon Press, and Cardiff: University of Wales Press, 1987.

Wilson, J. Dover. "Anthony Munday, Pamphleteer and Pursuivant." *Modern Language Review* 4 (1909), 484–90.

"The Marprelate Controversy." *The Cambridge History of English Literature, III: Renascence and Reformation*. Cambridge: Cambridge University Press, 1909. 425–52.

Martin Marprelate and Shakespeare's Fluellen. London: Alexander Moring, 1912.

Wolfe, Don. "Unsigned Pamphlets of Richard Overton: 1641–1649." *Huntington Library Quarterly* 21 (1958), 167–201.

Woodall, Joy. "Recusant Rowington." *Worcestershire Recusant: Journal of the Worcestershire Catholic Society* 31 (June 1978), 3–12.

Index